17th Conference on Computational Natural Language Learning

(CoNLL 2013)

Sofia, Bulgaria
8 – 9 August 2013

ISBN: 978-1-62993-007-7

Printed from e-media with permission by:

Curran Associates, Inc.
57 Morehouse Lane
Red Hook, NY 12571

Some format issues inherent in the e-media version may also appear in this print version.

Printed by Curran Associates, Inc. (2013)

For permission requests, please contact the Association for Computational Linguistics
at the address below.

Association for Computational Linguistics
209 N. Eighth Street
Stroudsburg, Pennsylvania 18360

Phone: 1-570-476-8006
Fax: 1-570-476-0860

acl@aclweb.org

Additional copies of this publication are available from:

Curran Associates, Inc.
57 Morehouse Lane
Red Hook, NY 12571 USA
Phone: 845-758-0400
Fax: 845-758-2634
Email: curran@proceedings.com
Web: www.proceedings.com

CoNLL-2013

Seventeenth Conference on Computational Natural Language Learning

Proceedings of the Conference

August 8-9, 2013
Sofia, Bulgaria

Preface

The 2013 Conference on Computational Natural Language Learning is the seventeenth in the series of annual meetings organized by SIGNLL, the ACL special interest group on natural language learning. CONLL-2013 will be held in Sofia, Bulgaria, Europe, August 8-9, 2013, in conjunction with ACL 2013.

For our special focus this year in the main session of CoNLL, we invited papers relating to compositional semantics. We received 107 submissions on this and other relevant topics, of which 7 were eventually withdrawn. Of the remaining 100 papers, 25 were selected to appear in the conference program as oral presentation. All accepted papers appear here in the proceedings. Each accepted paper was allowed eight content pages plus two pages containing only bibliographic references.

As in previous years, CoNLL-2013 has a shared task, Grammatical Error Correction. The Shared Task papers are collected in a companion volume of CoNLL-2013.

In contrast to previous conferences, we do not distinguish between long talks and posters. Instead, every CoNLL paper is allotted a 15 minute oral presentation slot as well as a poster. As a consequence, we have two poster sessions. Papers whose oral presentation is on Day 1 of the conference participate in the poster session on Day 1. The shared task posters and the CoNLL papers that are presented on Day 2 participate in the poster session on Day 2. This provides everybody with the opportunity to present their work in a plenary session, while also allowing more in-depth conversations during the two poster sessions.

We would like to thank all of the authors who submitted their work to CoNLL-2013, as well as the program committee for helping us select from among the many strong submissions. We are also grateful to our invited speakers, Ben Taskar and Roger Levy, who graciously agreed to give talks at CoNLL. Special thanks to the SIGNLL board members, Alexander Clark and Xavier Carreras, for their valuable advice and assistance in putting together this year's program, and to the SIGNLL information officer, Erik Tjong Kim Sang, for publicity and maintaining the CoNLL-2013 web page. We also appreciate the additional help we received from the ACL program chairs, workshop chairs, and publication chairs.

Finally, many thanks to Google for sponsoring the best paper award at CoNLL-2013.

We hope you enjoy the conference!

Julia Hockenmaier and Sebastian Riedel

CoNLL 2013 Conference Chairs

Conference Co-Chairs

Julia Hockenmaier (University of Illinois at Urbana-Champaign, USA)
Sebastian Riedel (University College London, United Kingdom)

Program Committee:

Timothy Baldwin (University of Melbourne, Australia), Kedar Bellare (University of Massachusetts Amherst, USA), Yonatan Bisk (University of Illinois, USA), John Blitzer (Google, USA), Thorsten Brants (Google, USA), Chris Brew (Nuance, USA), Sabine Buchholz (SynapseWork, United Kingdom), Chris Callison-Burch (Johns Hopkins University, USA), Claire Cardie (Cornell University, USA), Xavier Carreras (Universitat Politècnica de Catalunya, Spain), Ming-Wei Chang (Microsoft Research, USA), Colin Cherry (National Research Council, Canada), Yejin Choi (Stony Brook University, USA), Stephen Clark (University of Cambridge, United Kingdom), Alexander Clark (Royal Holloway University of London, United Kingdom), James Clarke (Basis Technology, USA), Shay Cohen (Columbia University, USA), Trevor Cohn (University of Sheffield, United Kingdom), Aron Culotta (Northeastern Illinois University, USA), Walter Daelemans (University of Antwerp, Belgium), Laura Dietz (University of Massachusetts Amherst, USA), Mark Dras (Macquarie University, Australia), Markus Dreyer (SDL Language Weaver, USA), Gregory Druck (Yummly, USA), Kevin Duh (Nara Institute of Science and Technology, Japan), Chris Dyer (Carnegie Mellon University, USA), Jacob Eisenstein (Georgia Institute of Technology, USA), Micha Elsner (The Ohio State University, USA), Radu Florian (IBM Research, USA), Bob Frank (Yale University, USA), Michel Galley (Microsoft Research, USA), Kevin Gimpel (Toyota Technological Institute at Chicago, USA), Yoav Goldberg (Bar Ilan University, Israel), Nizar Habash (Columbia University, USA), John Hale (Cornell University, USA), Keith Hall (Google, USA), David Hall (University of California at Berkeley, USA), Mark Hasegawa-Johnson (University of Illinois at Urbana-Champaign, USA) Rebecca Hwa (University of Pittsburgh, USA), Mark Johnson (Macquarie University, Australia), Philipp Koehn (University of Edinburgh, United Kingdom), Mamoru Komachi (Tokyo Metropolitan University, Japan), Shalom Lappin (King's College London, United Kingdom), Gideon Mann (Google, USA), Lluís Màrquez (Universitat Politècnica de Catalunya, Spain), André Martins (Priberam Labs, Portugal), Yuji Matsumoto (Nara Institute of Science and Technology, Japan), David McClosky (IBM Research, USA), Ryan McDonald (Google, USA), Haitao Mi (IBM Research, USA), Yusuke Miyao (National Institute of Informatics, Japan), Alessandro Moschitti (Trento University, Italy), Mark-Jan Nederhof (University of St Andrews, United Kingdom), Joakim Nivre (Uppsala University, Sweden), Miles Osborne (University of Edinburgh, United Kingdom), Alexandre Passos (University of Massachusetts Amherst, USA), Ari Rappoport (The Hebrew University of Jerusalem, Israel), Sujith Ravi (Google, USA), Roi Reichart (The Hebrew University of Jerusalem, Israel), Alan Ritter (University of Washington, USA), Dan Roth (University of Illinois at Urbana-Champaign, USA), Rajhans Samdani (University of Illinois at Urbana-Champaign, USA), Mark Sammons (University of Illinois at Urbana-Champaign, USA), Anoop Sarkar (Simon Fraser University, Canada), Nathan Schneider (Carnegie Mellon University, USA), Sameer Singh (University of Massachusetts Amherst, USA),

Lucia Specia (University of Sheffield, United Kingdom), Valentin Spitkovsky (Stanford University, USA), Mark Steedman (University of Edinburgh, United Kingdom), Mihai Surdeanu (University of Arizona, USA), Hiroya Takamura (Tokyo Institute of Technology, Japan), Partha Talukdar (Carnegie Mellon University, USA), Ivan Titov (Saarland University, Germany), Antal van den Bosch (Radboud University Nijmegen, Netherlands), Andreas Vlachos (University of Cambridge, United Kingdom), Peng Xu (Google, USA), Charles Yang (University of Pennsylvania, USA), Limin Yao (University of Massachusetts Amherst, USA), Dani Yogatama (Carnegie Mellon University, USA), Chen Yu (Indiana University Bloomington, USA), Luke Zettlemoyer (University of Washington, USA)

Invited Speakers:

Ben Taskar (University of Washington, USA)
Roger Levy (University of California at San Diego, USA)

Table of Contents

Conference Program

Thursday August 8 2013

	(8:30 AM - 10:30 AM) Session 1
8:30	Opening Remarks
8:45	*Online Active Learning for Cost Sensitive Domain Adaptation* Min Xiao and Yuhong Guo
9:00	*Analysis of Stopping Active Learning based on Stabilizing Predictions* Michael Bloodgood and John Grothendieck
9:15	*Improving Pointwise Mutual Information (PMI) by Incorporating Significant Co-occurrence* Om Damani
9:30	*Supervised Morphological Segmentation in a Low-Resource Learning Setting using Conditional Random Fields* Teemu Ruokolainen, Oskar Kohonen, Sami Virpioja and Mikko Kurimo
9:45	*Graph-Based Posterior Regularization for Semi-Supervised Structured Prediction* Luheng He, Jennifer Gillenwater and Ben Taskar
10:00	*A Boosted Semi-Markov Perceptron* Tomoya Iwakura
10:45	*Spectral Learning of Refinement HMMs* Karl Stratos, Alexander Rush, Shay B. Cohen and Michael Collins

Thursday August 8 2013 (continued)

(10:30 AM - 11:00 AM) Coffee break

(11:00 AM - 12:30 PM) Session 2

11:00 *Sentence Compression with Joint Structural Inference*
Kapil Thadani and Kathleen McKeown

11:15 *Learning Adaptable Patterns for Passage Reranking*
Aliaksei Severyn, Massimo Nicosia and Alessandro Moschitti

11:30 *Documents and Dependencies: an Exploration of Vector Space Models for Semantic Composition*
Alona Fyshe, Brian Murphy, Partha Talukdar and Tom Mitchell

11:45 *Hidden Markov tree models for semantic class induction*
Edouard Grave, Guillaume Obozinski and Francis Bach

12:00 *Better Word Representations with Recursive Neural Networks for Morphology*
Thang Luong, Richard Socher and Christopher Manning

12:15 *Separating Disambiguation from Composition in Distributional Semantics*
Dimitri Kartsaklis, Mehrnoosh Sadrzadeh and Stephen Pulman

(12:30 PM - 2:00 PM) Lunch break

(2:00 PM - 3:30 PM) Session 3

2:00 *Frame Semantics for Stance Classification*
Kazi Saidul Hasan and Vincent Ng

2:15 *Philosophers are Mortal: Inferring the Truth of Unseen Facts*
Gabor Angeli and Christopher Manning

2:30 *Towards Robust Linguistic Analysis using OntoNotes*
Sameer Pradhan, Alessandro Moschitti, Nianwen Xue, Hwee Tou Ng, Anders Björkelund, Olga Uryupina, Yuchen Zhang and Zhi Zhong

2:45 *Dynamic Knowledge-Base Alignment for Coreference Resolution*
Jiaping Zheng, Luke Vilnis, Sameer Singh, Jinho D. Choi and Andrew McCallum

Thursday August 8 2013 (continued)

3:00 *A Non-Monotonic Arc-Eager Transition System for Dependency Parsing*
Matthew Honnibal, Yoav Goldberg and Mark Johnson

3:15 *Collapsed Variational Bayesian Inference for PCFGs*
Pengyu Wang and Phil Blunsom

(3:30 PM - 5:00 PM) Poster session 1

(5:00 PM - 6 PM) Keynote 1

5:00 Invited Talk by Ben Taskar

Friday August 9 2013

(8:45 AM - 10:30 AM) Session 4

8:45 *Polyglot: Distributed Word Representations for Multilingual NLP*
Rami Al-Rfou, Bryan Perozzi and Steven Skiena

9:00 *Exploiting multiple hypotheses for Multilingual Spoken Language Understanding*
Marcos Calvo, Fernando García, Lluís-F. Hurtado, Santiago Jiménez and Emilio Sanchis

9:15 *Multilingual WSD-like Constraints for Paraphrase Extraction*
Wilker Aziz and Lucia Specia

9:30 *Topic Models + Word Alignment = A Flexible Framework for Extracting Bilingual Dictionary from Comparable Corpus*
Xiaodong Liu, Kevin Duh and Yuji Matsumoto

9:45 *Terminology Extraction Approaches for Product Aspect Detection in Customer Reviews*
Jürgen Broß and Heiko Ehrig

10:00 Shared Task Overview by Hwee Tou Ng

Friday August 9 2013 (continued)

(10:30 AM - 11:00 AM) Coffee break

(11:00 AM - 12:30 PM) Shared task orals

(12:30 PM - 2:00 PM) Lunch break

(2:00 PM - 3:00 PM) Keynote 2

2:00 Invited Talk by Roger Levy

(3:00 PM - 3:30 PM) Best Paper Award

3:00 *Acquisition of Desires before Beliefs: A Computional Investigation*
Libby Barak, Afsaneh Fazly and Suzanne Stevenson

(3:30 PM - 5:00 PM) Poster session 2 (incl. Shared Task)

Online Active Learning for Cost Sensitive Domain Adaptation

Min Xiao and **Yuhong Guo**
Department of Computer and Information Sciences
Temple University
Philadelphia, PA 19122, USA
{minxiao,yuhong}@temple.edu

Abstract

Active learning and domain adaptation are both important tools for reducing labeling effort to learn a good supervised model in a target domain. In this paper, we investigate the problem of online active learning within a new active domain adaptation setting: there are insufficient labeled data in both source and target domains, but it is cheaper to query labels in the source domain than in the target domain. Given a total budget, we develop two cost-sensitive online active learning methods, a multi-view uncertainty-based method and a multi-view disagreement-based method, to query the most informative instances from the two domains, aiming to learn a good prediction model in the target domain. Empirical studies on the tasks of cross-domain sentiment classification of Amazon product reviews demonstrate the efficacy of the proposed methods on reducing labeling cost.

1 Introduction

In many application domains, it is difficult or expensive to obtain labeled data to train supervised models. It is critical to develop effective learning methods to reduce labeling effort or cost. Active learning and domain adaptation are both important tools for reducing labeling cost on learning good supervised prediction models. Active learning reduces the cost of labeling by selecting the most informative instances to label, whereas domain adaptation obtains auxiliary label information by exploiting labeled data in related domains. Combining the efforts from both areas to further reduce the labeling cost is an important research direction to explore.

In this paper, we consider online active learning with domain adaptations. Online learning has been widely studied (Borodin and El-Yaniv, 1998) due to its advantages of low memory requirement and fast computation speed. Dredze and Crammer (2008) applied online learning on domain adaptation and proposed to combine multiple similar source domains to perform online learning for the target domain, which provides a new opportunity for conducting active learning with domain adaptation. Online active learning with domain adaptation, to our knowledge, has just gained attention recently and has been addressed in (Rai et al., 2010; Saha et al., 2011). The active online domain adaptation methods developed in (Rai et al., 2010; Saha et al., 2011) leverage information from the source domain by domain adaptation to intelligently query labels for instances only in the target domain in an online fashion with a given budget. They assumed a large amount of labeled data is readily available in the source domain.

In this work, we however tackle online active learning with domain adaptation in a different setting, where source domains with a large amount of free labeled data are not available. Instead we assume there are very few labeled instances in both the source and target domains and labels in both domains can be acquired with a cost. Moreover, we assume the annotation cost for acquiring labels in the source domain is much lower than the annotation cost in the target domain. This is a practical setting in many domain adaptation scenarios. For example, one aims to learn a good review classification model for high-end computers. It may be expensive to acquire labels for such product reviews. However, but it might be relatively much cheaper (but not free) to acquire labels for reviews on movies or restaurants. In such an active learning scenario, will a source domain with lower annotation cost still be helpful for reducing the labeling cost required to learn a good prediction model in the target domain? Our research result in this paper will answer this ques-

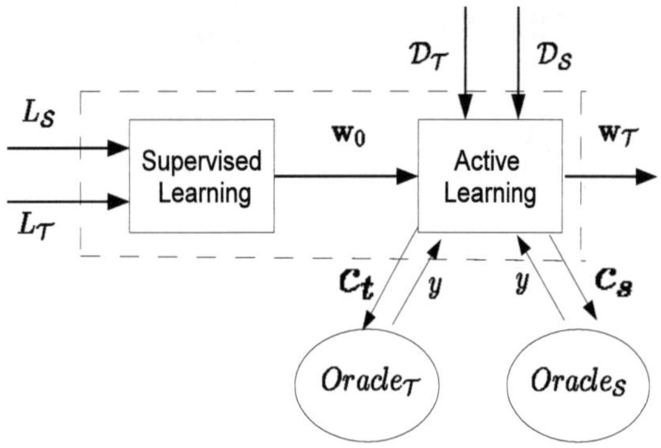

Figure 1: The framework of online active learning with domain adaptation.

tion. Specifically, we address this online active domain adaptation problem by extending the online active learning framework in (Cesa-Bianchi et al., 2006) to consider active label acquirement in both domains. We first initialize the prediction model based on the initial labeled data in both the source and target domains ($L_\mathcal{S}$ and $L_\mathcal{T}$). Then in each round of the online learning, we receive one unlabeled instance from each domain ($\mathcal{D}_\mathcal{S}$ and $\mathcal{D}_\mathcal{T}$), on which we need to decide whether to query labels. Whenever a label is acquired, we update the prediction model using the newly labeled instance if necessary. The framework of this online active learning setting is demonstrated in Figure 1. We exploit multi-view learning principles to measure the informativeness of instances and propose two cost-sensitive online active learning methods, a multi-view uncertainty-based method and a multi-view disagreement-based method, to acquire labels for the most informative instances. Our empirical studies on the tasks of cross-domain sentiment classification of Amazon product reviews show the proposed methods can effectively acquire the most informative labels given a budget, comparing to alternative methods.

2 Related Work

The proposed work in this paper involves research developments in multiple areas, including online active learning, active domain adaptation and multi-view active learning. In this section, we will cover the most related work in the literature.

Online active learning has been widely studied in the literature, including the perceptron-type methods in (Cesa-Bianchi et al., 2006; Monteleoni and Kääriäinen, 2007; Dasgupta et al., 2009). Cesa-Bianchi et al. (2006) proposed a selective sampling perceptron-like method (CBGZ), which serves as a general framework of online active learning. Monteleoni and Kääriäinen (2007) empirically studied online active learning algorithms, including the CBGZ, for optical character recognition applications. Dasgupta et al. (2009) analyzed the label complexity of the perceptron algorithm and presented a combination method of a modification of the perceptron update with an adaptive filtering rule. Our proposed online active learning methods are placed on an extended framework of (Cesa-Bianchi et al., 2006), by incorporating domain adaptation and multi-view learning techniques in an effective way.

Active domain adaptation has been studied in (Chan and Ng, 2007; Rai et al., 2010; Saha et al., 2011; Li et al., 2012). Chan and Ng (2007) presented an early study on active domain adaptation and empirically demonstrated that active learning can be successfully applied on out-of-domain word sense disambiguation systems. Li et al. (2012) proposed to first induce a shared subspace across domains and then actively label instances augmented with the induced latent features. Online active domain adaptation, however, has only been recently studied in (Rai et al., 2010; Saha et al., 2011). Nevertheless, the active online domain adaptation method (AODA) and its variant method, domain-separator based AODA (DS-AODA), proposed in these works assume a large amount of labeled data in the source domain and conduct online active learning only in the target domain, which is different from our problem setting in this paper.

Multi-view learning techniques have recently been employed in domain adaptation (Tur, 2009; Blitzer et al., 2011; Chen et al., 2011). In particular, instead of using data with conditional independent views assumed in standard multi-view learning (Blum and Mitchell, 1998), Blitzer et al. (2011) and Chen et al. (2011) randomly split original features into two disjoint subsets to produce two views, and demonstrate the usefulness of multi-view learning with synthetic two views. On the other hand, *multi-view active learning* has been studied in (Muslea et al., 2000, 2002; Wang and Zhou, 2008, 2010). These works all suggest to query labels for *contention points* (instances on which different views predict different labels). Our proposed methods will exploit this multi-view principle and apply it in our multi-view online active domain adaptation setting.

In addition, our proposed work is also related to *cost-sensitive active learning*. But different from the traditional cost-sensitive active learning, which assumes multiple oracles with different costs exist for the same set of instances (Donmez and Carbonell, 2008; Arora et al., 2009), we assume two oracles, one for the source domain and one for the target domain. Overall, the problem we study in this paper is novel, practical and important. Our research will demonstrate a combination of advances in multiple research areas.

3 Multi-View Online Active Learning with Domain Adaptation

Our online active learning is an extension of the online active perceptron learning framework of (Cesa-Bianchi et al., 2006; Rai et al., 2010) in the cost-sensitive online active domain adaption setting. We will present two multi-view online active methods in this section under the framework shown in Figure 1.

Assume we have a target domain ($\mathcal{D}_{\mathcal{T}}$) and a related source domain ($\mathcal{D}_{\mathcal{S}}$) with a few labeled instances, $L_{\mathcal{T}}$ and $L_{\mathcal{S}}$, in each of them respectively. The instances in the two domains are drawn from the same input space but with two different distributions specified by each domain. An initial prediction model ($\mathbf{w_0}$) can then be trained with the current labeled data from both domains. Many domain adaptation techniques (Sugiyama, 2007; Blitzer et al., 2011) can be used for training here. However, for simplicity of demonstrating the effectiveness of online active learning strategies, we use vanilla Perceptron to train the initial prediction model on all labeled instances, as the perceptron algorithm is widely used in various works (Saha et al., 2011) and can be combined seamlessly with the online perceptron updates. It can be viewed as a simple supervised domain adaptation training.

The very few initial labeled instances are far from being sufficient to train a good prediction model in the target domain. Additional labeled data needs to be acquired to reach a reasonable prediction model. However it takes time, money, and effort to acquire labels in all problem domains. For simplicity of demonstration, we use money to measure the cost and effort of labeling instances in each domain. Assume the cost of labeling one instance in the source domain is c_s and the cost of labeling one instance in the target domain is c_t, where $c_t > c_s$. Note the condition $c_t > c_s$ is one criterion to be guaranteed when selecting useful source domains. It does not make sense to select source domains with more expensive labeling cost. Given a budget $\mathbf{B}$, we need to make wise decisions about which instances to query in the online learning setting. We aim to learn the best prediction model in the target domain with the labels purchased under the given budget.

Then online active learning will be conducted in a sequence of rounds. In each round r, we will receive two randomly sampled unlabeled instances in parallel, $\mathbf{x}_{s,r}$ and $\mathbf{x}_{t,r}$, one from each domain, $\mathbf{x}_{s,r} \in \mathcal{D}_{\mathcal{S}}$ and $\mathbf{x}_{t,r} \in \mathcal{D}_{\mathcal{T}}$. Active learning strategies will be used to judge the informativeness of the two instances in a cost-sensitive manner and decide whether to query labels for any one of them to improve the prediction model in the target domain. After new labels being acquired, we use the newly labeled instances to make online perceptron updates if the true labels are different from the predicted labels.

In this work, we focus on binary prediction problems where the labels have binary values, $y \in \{+1, -1\}$. We adopt the online perceptron-style learning model of (Cesa-Bianchi et al., 2006) for the online updates of the supervised perceptron model. Moreover, we extend principles of multi-view active learning into our online active learning framework. As we introduced before, synthetic multi-views produced by splitting the original feature space into disjoint subsets have been demonstrated effective in a few previous work (Blitzer et al., 2011; Chen et al., 2011). We adopt this idea to generate two views of the instances in both domains by randomly splitting the common feature space into two disjoint feature subsets, such that $\mathbf{x}_{s,r} = \{\mathbf{x}_{s,r}^{(1)}, \mathbf{x}_{s,r}^{(2)}\}$ and $\mathbf{x}_{t,r} = \{\mathbf{x}_{t,r}^{(1)}, \mathbf{x}_{t,r}^{(2)}\}$. Thus the initial prediction model will include two predictors $(f^{(1)}, f^{(2)})$ with model parameters $(\mathbf{w}_0^{(1)}, \mathbf{w}_0^{(2)})$, each trained on one view of the labeled data using the perceptron algorithm. Correspondingly, the online updates will be made on the two predictors.

The *critical challenge* of this cost-sensitive online active learning problem nevertheless lies in how to select the most informative instances for labeling. Based on different measurements of instance informativeness, we propose two online active learning algorithms: a Multi-view

Uncertainty-based instance Selection (MUS) algorithm and a Multi-view Disagreement-based instance Selection (MDS) algorithm for cost-sensitive online active domain adaptation, which we will present below.

3.1 Multi-View Uncertainty-based Instance Selection Algorithm

We use the initial model $(f^{(1)}, f^{(2)})$, trained on the two views of the initial labeled data and represented by the model parameters $(\mathbf{w}_0^{(1)}, \mathbf{w}_0^{(2)})$, as the starting point of the online active learning.

In each round r of the online active learning, we receive two instances $\mathbf{x}_{s,r} = \{\mathbf{x}_{s,r}^{(1)}, \mathbf{x}_{s,r}^{(2)}\}$ and $\mathbf{x}_{t,r} = \{\mathbf{x}_{t,r}^{(1)}, \mathbf{x}_{t,r}^{(2)}\}$, one for each domain. For the received instances, we need to make two sequential decisions:

1. Between the instance $(\mathbf{x}_{s,r})$ from the source domain and the instance $(\mathbf{x}_{t,r})$ from the target domain, which one should we select for further consideration?
2. For the selected instance, do we really need to query its label?

We answer the first question based on the labeling cost ratio, c_t/c_s, from the two domains and define the following probability

$$P_c = e^{-\alpha(c_t/c_s - 1)} \tag{1}$$

where α is a domain preference weighting parameter. Then with a probability P_c we select the target instance $\mathbf{x}_{t,r}$ and with a probability $1 - P_c$ we select the source instance $\mathbf{x}_{s,r}$. Our intuition is that one should query the less expensive source domain more frequently. Thus more labeled instances can be collected within the fix budget. On the other hand, the more useful and relevant but expensive instances from the target domain should also be queried at a certain rate.

For the selected instance $\mathbf{x}_{*,r}$, we then use a multi-view uncertainty strategy to decide whether to query its label. We first calculate the prediction confidence and predicted labels of the selected instance based on the current predictors trained from each view

$$m_k = |\mathbf{w}^{(k)\top}\mathbf{x}_{*,r}^{(k)}|, \quad \widehat{y}^{(k)} = sign(\mathbf{w}^{(k)\top}\mathbf{x}_{*,r}^{(k)}) \tag{2}$$

where $k = 1$ or 2, standing for each of the two views. If the two predictors disagree over the prediction label, i.e., $\widehat{y}^{(1)} \neq \widehat{y}^{(2)}$, the selected instance is a contention point and contains useful information for at least one predictor, according to the principle of multi-view active learning. We then decide to pay a cost (c_s or c_t) to query its label. Otherwise, we make the query decision based on the two predictors' uncertainty (i.e., the inverse of the prediction confidence m_k) over the selected instance. Specifically, we sample two numbers, one for each view, according to

$$z_k = \text{Bernoulli}(b/(b + m_k)) \tag{3}$$

where b is a prior hyperparameter, specifying the tendency of querying labels. In our experiments, we use $b = 0.1$. If either $z_1 = 1$ or $z_2 = 1$, which means that at least one view is uncertain about the selected instance, we will query for the label y. The prediction model will be updated using the new labeled instances when the true labels are different from the predicted ones; i.e.,

$$\mathbf{w}^{(k)} = \mathbf{w}^{(k)} + (y\mathbf{x}_{*,r}^{(k)})I[y \neq \widehat{y}^{(k)}] \tag{4}$$

for $k = 1, 2$, where $I[\cdot]$ is an indicator function. This multi-view uncertainty-based instance selection algorithm (MUS) is given in Algorithm 1.

Algorithm 1 MUS Algorithm

Input: $\mathbf{B}, P_c, c_s, c_t, b,$
initial model $(\mathbf{w}_0^{(1)}, \mathbf{w}_0^{(2)})$
Output: prediction model $(\mathbf{w}^{(1)}, \mathbf{w}^{(2)})$
Initialize: $\mathbf{w}^{(1)} = \mathbf{w}_0^{(1)}, \mathbf{w}^{(2)} = \mathbf{w}_0^{(2)}$
for each round $r = 1, 2, \cdots$ **do**
  Receive two instances $\mathbf{x}_{s,r}, \ \mathbf{x}_{t,r}$
  Sample $d \sim U(0, 1)$
  if $\mathbf{B} < c_t$ **then** $d = 1$ **end if**
  if $d > P_c$ **then** $\mathbf{x}_{*,r} = \mathbf{x}_{s,r}, \ c = c_s$
   else $\mathbf{x}_{*,r} = \mathbf{x}_{t,r}, \ c = c_t$
  end if
  Compute $m_1, m_2, \widehat{y}^{(1)}, \widehat{y}^{(2)}$ by Eq.(2)
  Compute z_1, z_2 by Eq.(3)
  if $z_1 = 1$ or $z_2 = 1$ or $\widehat{y}^{(1)} \neq \widehat{y}^{(2)}$ **then**
   Query label y for $\mathbf{x}_{*,r}$, $\mathbf{B} = \mathbf{B} - c$
   Update $(\mathbf{w}^{(1)}, \mathbf{w}^{(2)})$ by Eq (4)
  end if
  if $\mathbf{B} < c_s$ **then** break **end if**
end for

3.2 Multi-View Disagreement-based Instance Selection Algorithm

MUS is restrained to query at most one instance at each round of the online active learning. In this section, we present an alternative multi-view disagreement-based instance selection algorithm (MDS) within the same framework.

In each round r of the online active learning, given the two instances $\mathbf{x}_{s,r}$ and $\mathbf{x}_{t,r}$ we received, the MDS algorithm evaluates both instances for potential label acquisition using the multi-view information provided by the two per-view predictors. Let $\widehat{y}_s^{(1)}$ and $\widehat{y}_s^{(2)}$ denote the predicted labels of instance $\mathbf{x}_{s,r}$ produced by the two predictors according to Eq (2). Similarly let $\widehat{y}_t^{(1)}$ and $\widehat{y}_t^{(2)}$ denote the predicted labels of instance $\mathbf{x}_{t,r}$. Follow the principle suggested in the multi-view active learning work (Muslea et al., 2000, 2002; Wang and Zhou, 2008, 2010) that querying labels for *contention points* (instances on which different views predict different labels) can lead to superior information gain than querying uncertain points, we identify the non-redundant contention points from the two domains for label acquisition.

Specifically, there are three cases: (1) If only one of the instances is a contention point, we query its label with probability P_c (Eq (1)) when the instance is from the target domain, and query its label with probability $1 - P_c$ when the instance is from the source domain. (2) If both instances are contention points, i.e., $\widehat{y}_s^{(1)} \neq \widehat{y}_s^{(2)}$ and $\widehat{y}_t^{(1)} \neq \widehat{y}_t^{(2)}$, but the predicted labels for the two instances are the same, i.e., $\widehat{y}_s^{(k)} = \widehat{y}_t^{(k)}$ for $k = 1, 2$, it suggests the two instances contain similar information with respect to the prediction model and we only need to query one of them. We then select the instance in a cost-sensitive manner stated in the MUS algorithm by querying the target instance with a probability P_c and querying the source instance with a probability $1 - P_c$. (3) If both instances are contention points but with different predicted labels, it suggests the two instances contain complementary information with respect to the prediction model, and we thus query labels for both of them.

For any new labeled instance from the target domain or the source domain, we update the prediction model of each review using Equation (4) when the acquired true label is different from the predicted label. The overall MDS algorithm is given in Algorithm 2.

3.3 Multi-View Prediction

After the training process, we use the two predictors to predict labels of the test instances from the target domain. Given a test instance $\mathbf{x}_t = (\mathbf{x}_t^{(1)}, \mathbf{x}_t^{(2)})$, we use the predictor that have larger prediction confidence to determine its label y^*. The prediction confidence of the kth view predictor on $\mathbf{x}_t$ is defined as the absolute prediction value $|\mathbf{w}^{(k)\top}\mathbf{x}_t^{(k)}|$. We then select the most confident predictor for this instance as

$$k^* = \arg\max_{k\in\{1,2\}} |\mathbf{w}^{(k)\top}\mathbf{x}_t^{(k)}| \quad (5)$$

The predicted label is final computed as

$$y^* = sign(\mathbf{w}^{(k^*)\top}\mathbf{x}_t^{(k^*)}) \quad (6)$$

With this multi-view prediction on the test data, the multi-view strengths can be exploited in the testing phase as well.

Algorithm 2 MDS Algorithm

Input: $\mathbf{B}, P_c, c_s, c_t, b$,
  initial model $(\mathbf{w}_0^{(1)}, \mathbf{w}_0^{(2)})$
Output: prediction model $(\mathbf{w}^{(1)}, \mathbf{w}^{(2)})$
Initialize: $\mathbf{w}^{(1)} = \mathbf{w}_0^{(1)}, \mathbf{w}^{(2)} = \mathbf{w}_0^{(2)}$
for each round $r = 1, 2, \cdots$ **do**
  Receive two instances $\mathbf{x}_{s,r}$, $\mathbf{x}_{t,r}$
  Compute $\widehat{y}_s^{(1)}, \widehat{y}_s^{(2)}, \widehat{y}_t^{(1)}, \widehat{y}_t^{(2)}$ by Eq (2)
  Let $d_s = I[\widehat{y}_s^{(1)} = \widehat{y}_s^{(2)}]$, $d_t = I[\widehat{y}_t^{(1)} = \widehat{y}_t^{(2)}]$
  Let $q_s = 0, q_t = 0$
  if $\mathbf{B} < c_t$ **then** $d_t = 0$ **end if**
  Sample $d \sim U(0, 1)$
  if $d_s = 1$ and $d_t = 0$ **then**
    if $d > P_c$ **then** $q_s = 1$ **end if**
  else if $d_s = 0$ and $d_t = 1$ **then**
    if $d \leq P_c$ **then** $q_t = 1$ **end if**
  else if $d_s = 1$ and $d_t = 1$
    if $\widehat{y}_s^{(1)} = \widehat{y}_t^{(1)}$ **then**
      if $d > P_c$ **then** $q_s = 1$ **else** $q_t = 1$ **end if**
    else $q_s = 1, q_t = 1$
    end if
  end if
  if $q_s = 1$ **then**
    Query label y_s for $\mathbf{x}_{s,r}$, $\mathbf{B} = \mathbf{B} - c_s$
    Update $(\mathbf{w}^{(1)}, \mathbf{w}^{(2)})$ by Eq (4)
  end if
  if $\mathbf{B} < c_t$ **then** $q_t = 0$ **end if**
  if $q_t = 1$ **then**
    Query label y_t for $\mathbf{x}_{t,r}$, $\mathbf{B} = \mathbf{B} - c_t$
    Update $(\mathbf{w}^{(1)}, \mathbf{w}^{(2)})$ by Eq (4)
  end if
  if $\mathbf{B} < c_s$ **then** break **end if**
end for

4 Experiments

In this section, we present the empirical evaluation of the proposed online active learning methods on the task of sentiment classification comparing to alternative baseline methods. We first describe the experimental setup, and then present the results and discussions.

4.1 Experimental Setup

Dataset For the sentiment classification task, we use the dataset provided in (Prettenhofer and Stein, 2010). The dataset contains reviews with four different language versions and in three domains, *Books (B)*, *DVD (D)* and *Music (M)*. Each domain contains 2000 positive reviews and 2000 negative reviews, with a term-frequency (TF) vector representation. We used the English version and constructed 6 source-target ordered domain pairs from the original 3 domains: *B2D, D2B, B2M, M2B, D2M, M2D*. For example, for the task of *B2D*, we use the Books reviews as the source domain and the DVD reviews as the target domain. For each pair of domains, we built a unigram vocabulary over the combined 4000 source reviews and 4000 target reviews. We further preprocessed the data by removing features that appear less than twice in either domain, replacing TF with TFIDF, and normalizing the attribute values into $[0, 1]$.

Approaches In the experiments, we mainly compared the proposed *MUS* and *MDS* algorithms with the following three baseline methods. (1) *MTS* (Multi-view Target instance Selection): It is a target-domain variant of the MUS algorithm, and selects the most uncertain instance received from the target domain to query according to the procedure introduced for MUS method. (2) *TCS* (Target Contention instance Selection): It is a target-domain variant of the MDS algorithm, and uses multi-view predictors to query contention instances received from the target domain. (3) *SUS* (Single-view Uncertainty instance Selection): It selects target vs source instances according to P_c (see Eq.(1)), and then uses uncertainty measure to make query decision. This is a single view variant of the MUS algorithm. In the experiments, we used $\alpha = 1$ for the P_c computation in Eq.(1).

4.2 Classification Accuracy

We first conducted experiments over the 6 domain adaptation tasks constructed from the sentiment classification data with a fixed cost ratio $c_t/c_s = 3$. We set $c_s = 1$ and $c_t = 3$. Given a budget $\mathbf{B} = 900$, we measure the classification performance of the prediction model learned by each online active learning method during the process of budget being used. We started with 50 labeled instances from the source domain and 10 labeled instances from the target domain. The classification performance is measured over 1000 test instances from the target domain. All other instances are used as inputs in the online process. We repeated the experiments 10 times using different random online instance input orders. The average results are reported in Figure 2.

The results indicate the proposed two algorithms, MUS and MDS, in general greatly outperform the other alternative methods. The SUS method, which is a single-view variant of MUS, presents very poor performance across all 6 tasks comparing to the other multi-view based methods, which demonstrates the efficacy of the multi-view instance selection mechanism. Among the multi-view based active learning methods, the MTS method and TCS method, which only query labels for more relevant but expensive instances from the target domain, demonstrated inferior performance, comparing to their cost-sensitive counterparts, MUS and MDS, respectively. This suggests that a cheaper source domain is in general helpful on reducing the labeling cost for learning a good prediction model in the target domain and our proposed active learning strategies are effective.

4.3 Domain Divergence

To further validate and understand our experimental results on the sentiment classification data, we evaluated the domain divergence over the three pairs of domains we used in the experiments above. Note, if the domain divergence is very small, it will be natural that a cheaper source domain should help on reducing the labeling cost in the target domain. If the domain divergence is very big, the space of exploring a cheaper source domain will be squeezed.

The divergence of two domains can be measured using the $\mathcal{A}$-distance (Ben-David et al., 2006). We adopted the method of (Rai et al., 2010) to proximate the $\mathcal{A}$-distance. We train a linear classifier over all 8000 instances, 4000 instances from each domain, to separate the two domains. The average per-instance hinge-loss for this separator subtracted from 1 was used as the estimate

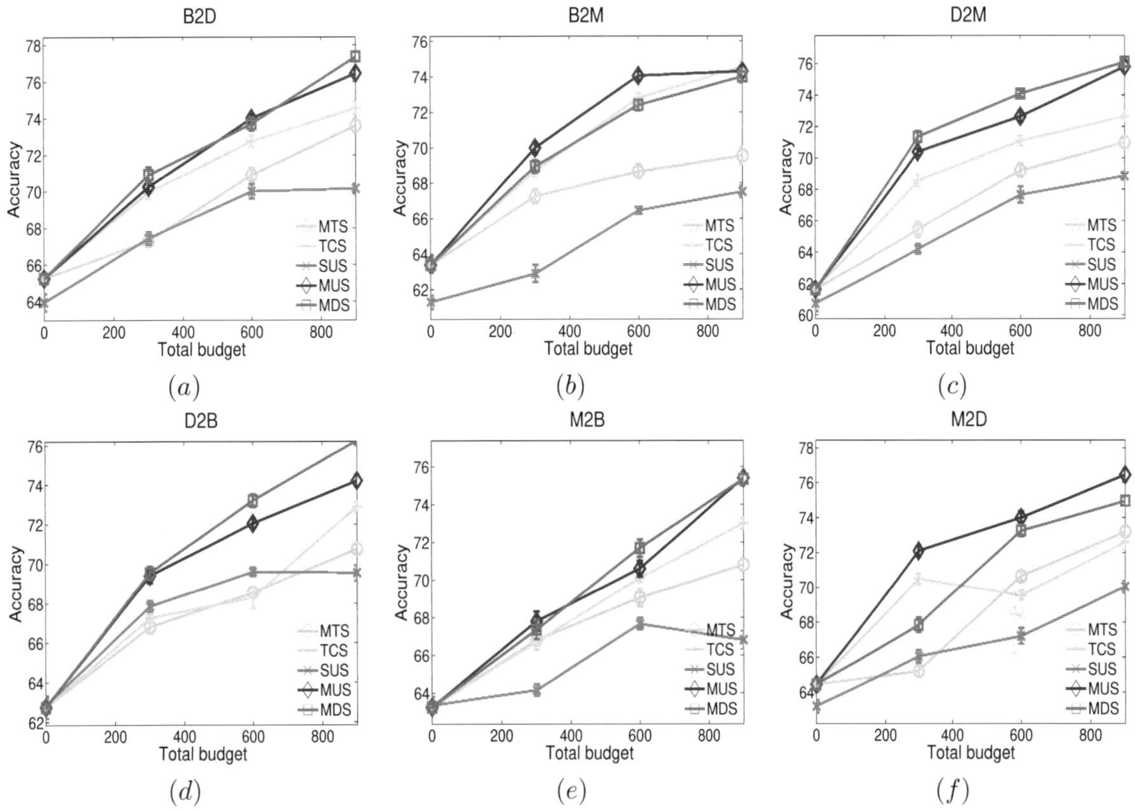

Figure 2: Online active learning results over the 6 domain adaptation tasks for sentiment classification, with a total budget B=900 and a fixed cost ratio $c_t/c_s = 3$.

of the proxy $\mathcal{A}$-distance. A score of 1 means perfectly separable distributions and 0 means the two distributions from the two domains are identical. In general, a higher score means a larger divergence between the two domains.

Table 1: Proxy $\mathcal{A}$-distance over domain pairs.

Domains	**$\mathcal{A}$-distance**
Books vs. DVD	0.7221
Books vs. Music	0.8562
DVD vs. Music	0.7831

The proxy $\mathcal{A}$-distances over the 3 domain pairs from the sentiment classification dataset are reported in Table 1. It shows that all the 3 pairs of domains are reasonably far apart. This justified the effectiveness of the online active domain adaptation methods we developed and the results we reported above. It suggests the applicability of the proposed active learning scheme is not bound to the existence of highly similar source domains. Moreover, the $\mathcal{A}$-distance between *Books* and *Music* is the largest among the three pairs. Thus it is most challenging to exploit the source domain in the adaptation tasks, B2M and M2B. This explains the good performance of the target-domain method TCS on these two tasks. Nevertheless, the proposed MUS and MDS maintained consistent good performance even on these two tasks.

4.4 Robustness to Cost Ratio

We then studied the empirical behavior of the proposed online active domain adaptation algorithms with different cost ratio values c_t/c_s.

Given a fixed budget $B = 900$, we set $c_s = 1$ and run a few sets of experiments on the sentiment classification data by setting c_t as different values from $\{1, 2, 3, 4\}$, under the same experimental setting described above. In addition to the five comparison methods used before, we also added a baseline marker, *SCS*, which is a source-domain variant of the *MDS* algorithm and queries contention instances from only the source domain. The final classification performance of the prediction model learned with each approach is recorded

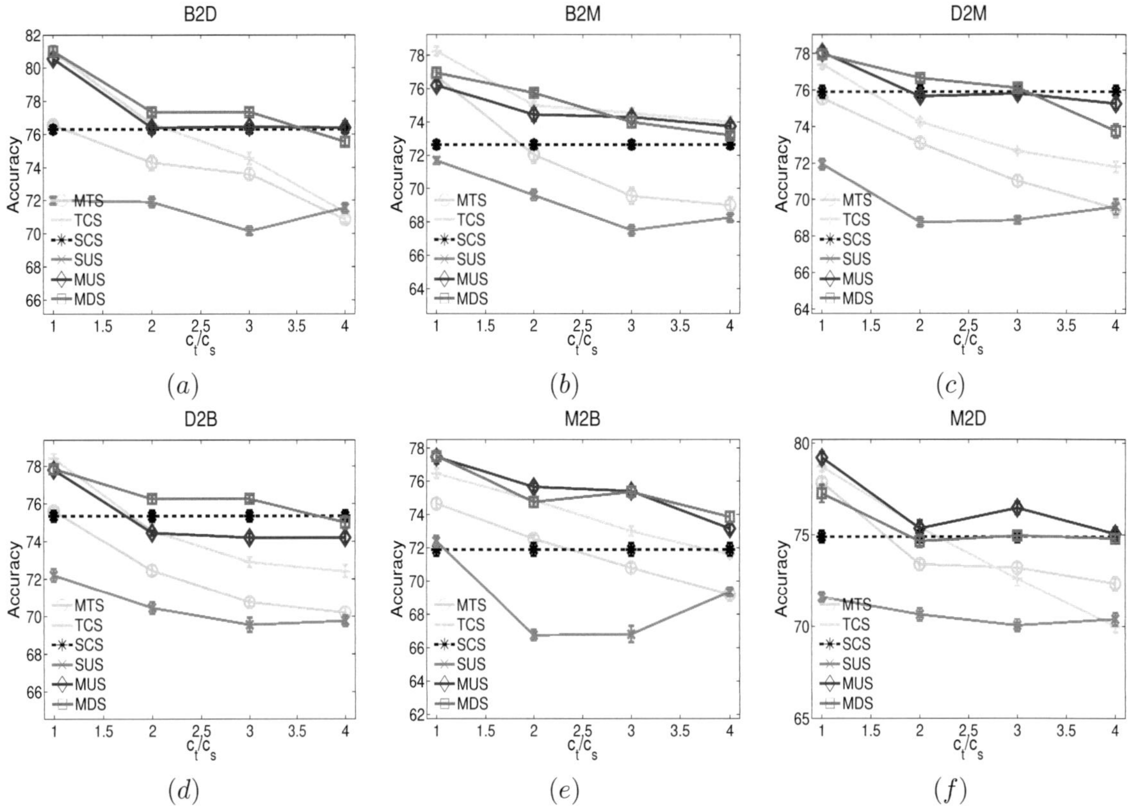

Figure 3: Online active learning results over the 6 domain adaptation tasks for sentiment classification, with different cost ratio values $c_t/c_s = \{1, 2, 3, 4\}$.

after the whole budget being used. The average results over 10 runs are reported in Figure 3.

We can see that: (1) With the increasing of the labeling cost in the target domain, the performance of all methods except *SCS* decreases since the same budget can purchase fewer labeled instances from the target domain. (2) The three cost-sensitive methods (SUS, MUS, and MDS), which consider the labeling cost when making query decisions, are less sensitive to the cost ratios than the MTS and TCS methods, whose performance degrades very quickly with the increasing of c_t/c_s. (3) It is reasonable that when c_t/c_s is very big, the SCS, which simply queries source instances, produces the best performance. But the proposed two cost-sensitive active learning methods, MUS and MDS, are quite robust to the cost ratios across a reasonable range of c_t/c_s values, and outperform both source-domain only and target-domain only methods. When $c_t = c_s$, the proposed cost-sensitive methods automatically favor target instances and thus achieve similar performance as TCS. When c_t becomes much larger than c_s, the proposed cost-sensitive methods automatically adjust to favor cheaper source instances and maintain their good performance.

5 Conclusion

In this paper, we investigated the online active domain adaptation problem in a novel but practical setting where we assume labels can be acquired with a lower cost in the source domain than in the target domain. We proposed two multi-view online active learning algorithms, MUS and MDS, to address the proposed problem. The proposed algorithms exploit multi-view active learning learning principles to measure the informativeness of instances and select instances in a cost-sensitive manner. Our empirical studies on the task of cross-domain sentiment classification demonstrate the efficacy of the proposed methods. This research shows that a cheaper source domain can help on reducing labeling cost for learning a good prediction model in the related target domain, with proper designed active learning algorithms.

References

S. Arora, E. Nyberg, and C. P. Rosé. Estimating annotation cost for active learning in a multi-annotator environment. In *Proceedings of the NAACL-HLT 2009 Workshop on Active Learning for Natural Language Processing*, 2009.

S. Ben-David, J. Blitzer, K. Crammer, and F. Pereira. Analysis of representations for domain adaptation. In *Advances in Neural Information Processing Systems (NIPS)*, 2006.

J. Blitzer, D. Foster, and S. Kakade. Domain adaptation with coupled subspaces. In *Proceedings of the Conference on Artificial Intelligence and Statistics (AISTATS)*, 2011.

A. Blum and T. Mitchell. Combining labeled and unlabeled data with co-training. In *Proceedings of the Conference on Computational Learning Theory (COLT)*, 1998.

A. Borodin and R. El-Yaniv. *Online computation and competitive analysis*. Cambridge University Press, 1998.

N. Cesa-Bianchi, C. Gentile, and L. Zaniboni. Worst-case analysis of selective sampling for linear classification. *Journal of Machine Learning Research (JMLR)*, 7:1205–1230, 2006.

Y. Chan and H. Ng. Domain adaptation with active learning for word sense disambiguation. In *Proceedings of the Annual Meeting of the Assoc. of Computational Linguistics (ACL)*, 2007.

M. Chen, K. Weinberger, and J. Blitzer. Co-training for domain adaptation. In *Advances in Neural Information Processing Systems (NIPS)*, 2011.

S. Dasgupta, A. T. Kalai, and C. Monteleoni. Analysis of perceptron-based active learning. *Journal of Machine Learning Research (JMLR)*, 10:281–299, 2009.

P. Donmez and J. G. Carbonell. Proactive learning: cost-sensitive active learning with multiple imperfect oracles. In *Proceedings of the ACM Conference on Information and knowledge management (CIKM)*, 2008.

M. Dredze and K. Crammer. Online methods for multi-domain learning and adaptation. In *Proceedings of the Conf. on Empirical Methods in Natural Language Processing (EMNLP)*, 2008.

L. Li, X. Jin, S. Pan, and J. Sun. Multi-domain active learning for text classification. In *Proceedings of the ACM SIGKDD International Conference on Knowledge Discovery and Data Mining (KDD)*, 2012.

C. Monteleoni and M. Kääriäinen. Practical online active learning for classification. In *Proceedings of the IEEE Conference on Computer Vision and Pattern Recognition, Online Learning for Classification Workshop*, 2007.

I. Muslea, S. Minton, and C. Knoblock. Selective sampling with redundant views. In *Proceedings of the National Conference on Artificial Intelligence (AAAI)*, 2000.

I. Muslea, S. Minton, and C. A. Knoblock. Active + semi-supervised learning = robust multi-view learning. In *Proceedings of the International Conference on Machine Learning (ICML)*, 2002.

P. Prettenhofer and B. Stein. Cross-language text classification using structural correspondence learning. In *Proceedings of the Annual Meeting for the Association of Computational Linguistics (ACL)*, 2010.

P. Rai, A. Saha, H. Daumé III, and S. Venkatasubramanian. Domain adaptation meets active learning. In *Proceedings of the North American Chapter of the Association for Computational Linguistics (NAACL)*, 2010.

A. Saha, P. Rai, H. Daumé III, S. Venkatasubramanian, and S. DuVall. Active supervised domain adaptation. In *Proceedings of the European Conference on Machine Learning (ECML)*, 2011.

M. Sugiyama. Direct importance estimation with model selection and its application to covariate shift adaptation. In *Advances in Neural Information Processing Systems (NIPS)*, 2007.

G. Tur. Co-adaptation: Adaptive co-training for semi-supervised learning. In *Proceedings of the IEEE Inter. Conference on Acoustics, Speech and Signal Processing (ICASSP)*, 2009.

W. Wang and Z. Zhou. On multi-view active learning and the combination with semi-supervised learning. In *Proceedings of the international conference on Machine learning (ICML)*, 2008.

W. Wang and Z. Zhou. Multi-view active learning in the non-realizable case. In *Advances in Neural Information Processing Systems (NIPS)*, 2010.

Analysis of Stopping Active Learning based on Stabilizing Predictions

Michael Bloodgood
Center for Advanced Study of Language
University of Maryland
College Park, MD 20740
meb@umd.edu

John Grothendieck
Raytheon BBN Technologies
9861 Broken Land Parkway, Suite 400
Columbia, MD 21046
jgrothen@bbn.com

Abstract

Within the natural language processing (NLP) community, active learning has been widely investigated and applied in order to alleviate the annotation bottleneck faced by developers of new NLP systems and technologies. This paper presents the first theoretical analysis of stopping active learning based on stabilizing predictions (SP). The analysis has revealed three elements that are central to the success of the SP method: (1) bounds on Cohen's Kappa agreement between successively trained models impose bounds on differences in F-measure performance of the models; (2) since the stop set does not have to be labeled, it can be made large in practice, helping to guarantee that the results transfer to previously unseen streams of examples at test/application time; and (3) good (low variance) sample estimates of Kappa between successive models can be obtained. Proofs of relationships between the level of Kappa agreement and the difference in performance between consecutive models are presented. Specifically, if the Kappa agreement between two models exceeds a threshold T (where $T > 0$), then the difference in F-measure performance between those models is bounded above by $\frac{4(1-T)}{T}$ in all cases. If precision of the positive conjunction of the models is assumed to be p, then the bound can be tightened to $\frac{4(1-T)}{(p+1)T}$.

1 Introduction

Active learning (AL), also called *query learning* and *selective sampling*, is an approach to reduce the costs of creating training data that has received considerable interest (e.g., (Argamon-Engelson and Dagan, 1999; Baldridge and Osborne, 2008; Bloodgood and Vijay-Shanker, 2009b; Bloodgood and Callison-Burch, 2010; Hachey et al., 2005; Haertel et al., 2008; Haffari and Sarkar, 2009; Hwa, 2000; Lewis and Gale, 1994; Sassano, 2002; Settles and Craven, 2008; Shen et al., 2004; Thompson et al., 1999; Tomanek et al., 2007; Zhu and Hovy, 2007)).

Within the NLP community, active learning has been widely investigated and applied in order to alleviate the annotation bottleneck faced by developers of new NLP systems and technologies. The main idea is that by judiciously selecting which examples to have labeled, annotation effort will be focused on the most helpful examples and less annotation effort will be required to achieve given levels of performance than if a passive learning policy had been used.

Historically, the problem of developing methods for detecting when to stop AL was tabled for future work and the research literature was focused on how to select which examples to have labeled and analyzing the selection methods (Cohn et al., 1996; Seung et al., 1992; Freund et al., 1997; Roy and McCallum, 2001). However, to realize the savings in annotation effort that AL enables, we must have a method for knowing when to stop the annotation process. The challenge is that if we stop too early while useful generalizations are still being made, then we can wind up with a model that performs poorly, but if we stop too late after all the useful generalizations are made, then human annotation effort is wasted and the benefits of using active learning are lost.

Recently research has begun to develop methods for stopping AL (Schohn and Cohn, 2000; Ertekin et al., 2007b; Ertekin et al., 2007a; Zhu and Hovy, 2007; Laws and Schütze, 2008; Zhu et al., 2008a; Zhu et al., 2008b; Vlachos, 2008; Bloodgood, 2009; Bloodgood and Vijay-Shanker, 2009a; Ghayoomi, 2010). The methods are all heuristics based on estimates of model confidence, error, or stability. Although these heuristic methods have appealing intuitions and have had experimental success on a small handful of tasks and datasets, the methods are not widely usable in practice yet because our community's understanding of the stopping methods remains too coarse and inexact. Pushing forward on understanding the mechanics of stopping at a more exact level is therefore crucial for achieving the design of widely usable effective stopping criteria.

Bloodgood and Vijay-Shanker (2009a) introduce the terminology *aggressive* and *conservative* to describe the behavior of stopping methods[1] and conduct an empirical evaluation of the different published stopping methods on several datasets. While most stopping methods tend to behave conservatively, stopping based on stabilizing predictions computed via inter-model Kappa agreement has been shown to be consistently aggressive without losing performance (in terms of F-Measure[2]) in several published empirical tests. This method stops when the Kappa agreement between consecutively learned models during AL exceeds a threshold for three consecutive iterations of AL. Although this is an intuitive heuristic that has performed well in published experimental results, there has not been any theoretical analysis of the method.

The current paper presents the first theoretical analysis of stopping based on stabilizing predictions. The analysis helps to explain at a deeper and more exact level *why* the method works as it does. The results of the analysis help to characterize classes of problems where the method can be expected to work well and where (unmodified) it will not be expected to work as well. The theory is suggestive of modifications to improve the robustness of the stopping method for certain classes of problems. And perhaps most important, the approach that we use in our analysis provides an enabling framework for more precise analysis of stopping criteria and possibly other parts of the active learning decision space.

In addition, the information presented in this paper is useful for works that consider switching between different active learning strategies and operating regions such as (Baram et al., 2004; Dönmez et al., 2007; Roth and Small, 2008). Knowing when to switch strategies, for example, is similar to the stopping problem and is another setting where detailed understanding of the variance of stabilization estimates and their link to performance ramifications is useful. More exact understanding of the mechanics of stopping is also useful for applications of co-training (Blum and Mitchell, 1998), and agreement-based co-training (Clark et al., 2003) in particular. Finally, the proofs of the Theorems regarding the relationships between Cohen's Kappa statistic and F-measure may be of broader use in works that consider inter-annotator agreement and its ramifications for performance appraisals, a topic that has been of long-standing interest in computational linguistics (Carletta, 1996; Artstein and Poesio, 2008).

In the next section we summarize the stabilizing predictions (SP) stopping method. Section 3 analyzes SP and Section 4 concludes.

2 Stopping Active Learning based on Stabilizing Predictions

The intuition behind the SP method is that the models learned during AL can be applied to a large representative set of unlabeled data called a *stop set* and when consecutively learned models have high agreement on their predictions for classifying the examples in the stop set, this indicates that it is time to stop (Bloodgood and Vijay-Shanker, 2009a; Bloodgood, 2009). The active learning stopping strategy explicitly examined in (Bloodgood and Vijay-Shanker, 2009a) (after the general form is discussed) is to calculate Cohen's Kappa agreement statistic between consecutive rounds of active learning and stop once it is above 0.99 for three consecutive calculations.

Since the Kappa statistic is an important aspect of this method, we now discuss some background regarding measuring agreement in general, and Cohen's Kappa in particular. Measurement of agreement between human annotators has received significant attention and in that context, the drawbacks of using percentage agreement have been recognized (Artstein and Poesio, 2008). Alternative metrics have been proposed that take chance agreement into account. Artstein and Poesio (2008) survey several agreement metrics. Most

[1]Aggressive methods stop sooner, aggressively trying to reduce unnecessary annotations while conservative methods are careful not to risk losing model performance, even if it means annotating many more examples than were necessary.

[2]For the rest of this paper, we will use F-measure to denote F1-measure, that is, the balanced harmonic mean of precision and recall, which is a standard metric used to evaluate NLP systems.

of the agreement metrics they discuss are of the form:

$$agreement = \frac{A_o - A_e}{1 - A_e}, \quad (1)$$

where A_o = observed agreement, and A_e = agreement expected by chance. The different metrics differ in how they compute A_e. All the instances of usage of an agreement metric in this article will have two categories and two coders. The two categories are "+1" and "-1" and the two coders are the two consecutive models for which agreement is being measured.

Cohen's Kappa statistic[3] (Cohen, 1960) measures agreement expected by chance by modeling each coder (in our case model) with a separate distribution governing their likelihood of assigning a particular category. Formally, Kappa is defined by Equation 1 with A_e computed as follows:

$$A_e = \sum_{k \in \{+1,-1\}} P(k|c_1) \cdot P(k|c_2), \quad (2)$$

where each c_i is one of the coders (in our case, models), and $P(k|c_i)$ is the probability that coder (model) c_i labels an instance as being in category k. Kappa estimates the $P(k|c_i)$ in Equation 2 based on the proportion of observed instances that coder (model) c_i labeled as being in category k.

3 Analysis

This section analyzes the SP stopping method. Section 3.1 analyzes the variance of the estimator of Kappa that SP uses and in particular the relationship of this variance to specific aspects of the operationalization of SP, such as the stop set size. Section 3.2 analyzes relationships between the Kappa agreement between two models and the difference in F-measure between those two models.

3.1 Variance of Kappa Estimator

SP bases its decision to stop on the information contained in the contingency tables between the classifications of models learned at consecutive iterations during AL. In determining whether to stop at iteration t, the classifications of the current model M_t are compared with the classifications of the previous model M_{t-1}. Table 1 shows the population parameters for these two models, where:

[3]We note that there are other agreement measures (beyond Cohen's Kappa) which could also be applicable to stopping based on stabilizing predictions, but an analysis of these is outside the scope of the current paper.

	M_t		
M_{t-1}	+	-	Total
+	π_{++}	π_{+-}	$\pi_{+.}$
-	π_{-+}	π_{--}	$\pi_{-.}$
Total	$\pi_{.+}$	$\pi_{.-}$	1

Table 1: Contingency table population probabilities for M_t (model learned at iteration t) and M_{t-1} (model learned at iteration t-1).

population probability π_{ij} for $i, j \in \{+, -\}$ is the probability of an example being placed in category i by model M_{t-1} and category j by model M_t; population probability $\pi_{.j}$ for $j \in \{+, -\}$ is the probability of an example being placed in category j by model M_t; and population probability $\pi_{i.}$ for $i \in \{+, -\}$ is the probability of an example being placed in category i by model M_{t-1}. The actual probability of agreement is $\pi_o = \pi_{++} + \pi_{--}$. As indicated in Equation 2, Kappa models the probability of agreement expected due to chance by assuming that classifications are made independently. Hence, the probability of agreement expected by chance in terms of the population probabilities is $\pi_e = \pi_{+.}\pi_{.+} + \pi_{-.}\pi_{.-}$. From the definition of Kappa (see Equation 1), we then have that the Kappa parameter K in terms of the population probabilities is given by

$$K = \frac{\pi_o - \pi_e}{1 - \pi_e}. \quad (3)$$

For practical applications we will not know the true population probabilities and we will have to resort to using sample estimates. The SP method uses a stop set of size n for deriving its estimates. Table 2 shows the contingency table counts for the classifications of models M_t and M_{t-1} on a sample of size n. The population probabilities π_{ij} can be estimated by the relative frequencies p_{ij} for $i, j \in \{+, -, .\}$, where: $p_{++} = a/n$; $p_{+-} = b/n$; $p_{-+} = c/n$; $p_{--} = d/n$; $p_{+.} = (a+b)/n$; $p_{-.} = (c+d)/n$; $p_{.+} = (a+c)/n$; and $p_{.-} = (c+d)/n$. Let $p_o = p_{++} + p_{--}$, the observed proportion of agreement and let $p_e = p_{+.}p_{.+} + p_{-.}p_{.-}$, the proportion of agreement expected by chance if we assume that M_t and M_{t-1} make their classifications independently. Then the Kappa measure of agreement K between M_t and M_{t-1} (see Equation 3) is estimated by

$$\hat{K} = \frac{p_o - p_e}{1 - p_e}. \quad (4)$$

	M_t		
M_{t-1}	+	-	Total
+	a	b	$a+b$
-	c	d	$c+d$
Total	$a+c$	$b+d$	n

Table 2: Contingency table counts for M_t (model learned at iteration t) and M_{t-1} (model learned at iteration t-1).

Using the delta method, as described in (Bishop et al., 1975), Fleiss et al. (1969) derived an estimator of the large-sample variance of $\hat{K}$. According to Hale and Fleiss (1993), the estimator simplifies to

$$Var(\hat{K}) = \frac{1}{n(1-p_e)^2}\times \left\{ \sum_{i\in\{+,-\}} p_{ii}[1-4\bar{p}_i(1-\hat{K})] - (\hat{K}-p_e(1-\hat{K}))^2 + (1-\hat{K})^2 \times \sum_{i,j\in\{+,-\}} p_{ij}[2(\bar{p}_i+\bar{p}_j)-(p_{i.}+p_{.j})]^2 \right\}, \quad (5)$$

where $\bar{p}_i = (p_{i.}+p_{.i})/2$. From Equation 5, we can see that the variance of our estimate of Kappa is inversely proportional to the size of the stop set we use.

Bloodgood and Vijay-Shanker (2009a) used a stop set of size 2000 for each of their datasets. Although this worked well in the results they reported, we do not believe that 2000 is a fixed size that will work well for all tasks and datasets where the SP method could be used. Table 3 shows the variances of $\hat{K}$ computed using Equation 5 at the points at which SP stopped AL for each of the datasets[4] from (Bloodgood and Vijay-Shanker, 2009a).

These variances indicate that the size of 2000 was typically sufficient to get tight estimates of Kappa, helping to illuminate the empirical success of the SP method on these datasets. More generally, the SP method can be augmented with a variance check: if the variance of estimated Kappa at a potential stopping point exceeds some desired threshold, then the stop set size can be increased as needed to reduce the variance.

Looking at Equation 5 again, one can note that when p_e is relatively close to 1, the variance of $\hat{K}$ can be expected to get quite large. In these situations, users of SP should expect to have to use larger stop set sizes and in extreme conditions, SP may not be an advisable method to use.

3.2 Relationship between Kappa agreement and change in performance between models

Heretofore, the published literature contained only informal explanations of why stabilizing predictions is expected to work well as a stopping method (along with empirical tests demonstrating successful operation on a handful of tasks and datasets). In the remainder of this section we describe the mathematical foundations for stopping methods based on stabilizing predictions. In particular, we will prove that even in the worst possible case, if the Kappa agreement between two subsequently learned models is greater than a threshold T, then it must be the case that the change in performance between these two models is bounded above by $\frac{4(1-T)}{T}$. We then go on to prove additional Theorems that tighten this bound when assumptions are made about model precision.

Lemma 3.1 *Suppose F-measure F and Kappa K are computed from the same contingency table of counts, such as the one given in Table 2. Suppose $ad - bc \geq 0$. Then $F \geq K$.*

Proof By definition, in terms of the contingency table counts,

$$K = \frac{2ad-2bc}{(a+b)(b+d)+(a+c)(c+d)} \quad (6)$$

and

$$F = \frac{2a}{2a+b+c}. \quad (7)$$

Rewriting F so that it will have the same numerator as K, we have:

$$F = F\left(\frac{d-\frac{bc}{a}}{d-\frac{bc}{a}}\right) \quad (8)$$

$$= \left(\frac{2a}{2a+b+c}\right)\left(\frac{d-\frac{bc}{a}}{d-\frac{bc}{a}}\right) \quad (9)$$

$$= \frac{2ad-2bc}{2ad+bd+cd-2bc-\frac{b^2c+bc^2}{a}}. \quad (10)$$

[4]We note that each of the datasets was set up as a binary classification task (or multiple binary classification tasks). Further details and descriptions of each of the datasets can be found in (Bloodgood and Vijay-Shanker, 2009a).

Task-Dataset	Variance of $\hat{K}$
NER-DNA (10-fold CV)	0.0000223
NER-cellType (10-fold CV)	0.0000211
NER-protein (10-fold CV)	0.0000074
Reuters (10 Categories)	0.0000298
20 Newsgroups (20 Categories)	0.0000739
WebKB Student (10-fold CV)	0.0000137
WebKB Project (10-fold CV)	0.0000190
WebKB Faculty (10-fold CV)	0.0000115
WebKB Course (10-fold CV)	0.0000179
TC-spamassassin (10-fold CV)	0.0000042
TC-TREC-SPAM (10-fold CV)	0.0000043
Average (macro-avg)	0.0000209

Table 3: Estimates of the variance of $\hat{K}$. For each dataset, the estimate of the variance of $\hat{K}$ is computed (using Equation 5) from the contingency table at the point at which SP stopped AL and the average of all the variances (across all folds of CV) is displayed. The last row contains the macro-average of the average variances for all the datasets.

We can see that the expression for F in Equation 10 has the same numerator as K in Equation 6 but the denominator of K in Equation 6 is $\geq$ the denominator of F in Equation 10. Therefore, $F \geq K$. ∎

Theorem 3.2 *Let M_t be the model learned at iteration t of active learning and M_{t-1} be the model learned at iteration $t-1$. Let K_t be the estimate of Kappa agreement between the classifications of M_t and M_{t-1} on the examples in the stop set. Let $\tilde{F}_t$ be the F-measure between the classifications of M_t and truth on the stop set. Let $\tilde{F}_{t-1}$ be the F-measure between the classifications of M_{t-1} and truth on the stop set. Let ΔF_t be $\tilde{F}_t - \tilde{F}_{t-1}$. Suppose $T > 0$. Then $K_t > T \Rightarrow |\Delta F_t| \leq \frac{4(1-T)}{T}$.*

Proof Suppose M_t, M_{t-1}, K_t, $\tilde{F}_t$, $\tilde{F}_{t-1}$, ΔF_t, and T are defined as stated in the statement of Theorem 3.2. Let F_t be the F-measure between the classifications of M_t and M_{t-1} on the examples in the stop set. Let Table 2 show the contingency table counts for M_t versus M_{t-1} on the examples in the stop set. Then, from their definitions, we have $K_t = \frac{2(ad-bc)}{(a+b)(b+d)+(a+c)(c+d)}$ and $F_t = \frac{2a}{2a+b+c}$. There exist true labels for the examples in the stop set, which we don't know since the stop set is unlabeled, but nonetheless must exist. We use the truth on the stop set to split Table 2 into two subtables of counts, one table for all the examples that are truly positive and one table for all the examples that are truly negative. Table 4 shows the contingency table for M_t versus M_{t-1} for all of the examples in the stop set that have true labels of +1 and Table 5 shows the contingency table for M_t versus M_{t-1} for all of the examples in the stop set that have true labels of -1.

	M_t		
M_{t-1}	+	-	Total
+	a_1	b_1	$a_1 + b_1$
-	c_1	d_1	$c_1 + d_1$
Total	$a_1 + c_1$	$b_1 + d_1$	n_1

Table 4: Contingency table counts for M_t (model learned at iteration t) versus M_{t-1} (model learned at iteration t-1) for only the examples in the stop set that have truth = +1.

	M_t		
M_{t-1}	+	-	Total
+	a_{-1}	b_{-1}	$a_{-1} + b_{-1}$
-	c_{-1}	d_{-1}	$c_{-1} + d_{-1}$
Total	$a_{-1} + c_{-1}$	$b_{-1} + d_{-1}$	n_{-1}

Table 5: Contingency table counts for M_t (model learned at iteration t) versus M_{t-1} (model learned at iteration t-1) for only the examples in the stop set that have truth = -1.

From Tables 2, 4, and 5 one can see that a is the number of examples in the stop set that both M_t and M_{t-1} classified as positive. Furthermore, out of these a examples, a_1 of them truly are pos-

Truth	M_t +	-	Total
+	$a_1 + c_1$	$b_1 + d_1$	n_1
-	$a_{-1} + c_{-1}$	$b_{-1} + d_{-1}$	n_{-1}
Total	$a + c$	$b + d$	n

Table 6: Contingency table counts for M_t (model learned at iteration t) versus truth. (Derived from Tables 4 and 5

Truth	M_{t-1} +	-	Total
+	$a_1 + b_1$	$c_1 + d_1$	n_1
-	$a_{-1} + b_{-1}$	$c_{-1} + d_{-1}$	n_{-1}
Total	$a + b$	$c + d$	n

Table 7: Contingency table counts for M_{t-1} (model learned at iteration t-1) versus truth. (Derived from Tables 4 and 5

itive and a_{-1} of them truly are negative. Similar explanations hold for the other counts. Also, from Tables 2, 4, and 5, one can see that the equalities $a = a_1 + a_{-1}$, $b = b_1 + b_{-1}$, $c = c_1 + c_{-1}$, and $d = d_1 + d_{-1}$ all hold. The contingency tables for M_t versus truth and M_{t-1} versus truth can be derived from Tables 4 and 5. For convenience, Table 6 shows the contingency table for M_t versus truth and Table 7 shows the contingency table for M_{t-1} versus truth. Suppose that $K_t > T$. This implies, by Lemma 3.1[5], that $F_t > T$. This implies that

$$\frac{2a}{2a+b+c} > T \tag{11}$$

$$\Rightarrow \quad 2a > (2a + b + c)T \tag{12}$$

$$\Rightarrow \quad 2a(1 - T) > (b + c)T \tag{13}$$

$$\Rightarrow \quad b + c < \frac{2a(1-T)}{T}. \tag{14}$$

Note that Equations 12 and 14 are justified since $2a + b + c > 0$ and $T > 0$, respectively.

From Table 6 we can see that $\tilde{F}_t = \frac{2(a_1+c_1)}{2(a_1+c_1)+b_1+d_1+a_{-1}+c_{-1}}$; from Table 7 we can see that $\tilde{F}_{t-1} = \frac{2(a_1+b_1)}{2(a_1+b_1)+c_1+d_1+a_{-1}+b_{-1}}$. For notational convenience, let: $g = 2(a_1 + c_1) + b_1 + d_1 + a_{-1} + c_{-1}$; and $h = 2(a_1 + b_1) + c_1 + d_1 + a_{-1} + b_{-1}$.

[5]Note that the condition $ad - bc \geq 0$ of Lemma 3.1 is met since $K_t > T$ and $T > 0$ imply $K_t > 0$, which in turn implies $ad - bc > 0$.

It follows that

$$\Delta F_t = \frac{2(a_1 + c_1)}{g} - \frac{2(a_1 + b_1)}{h} \tag{15}$$

$$= \frac{(2a_1 + 2c_1)h - (2a_1 + 2b_1)g}{gh} \tag{16}$$

For notational convenience, let: $x = 2(a_1c_1 + a_1b_{-1} + c_1^2 + c_1d_1 + c_1a_{-1} + c_1b_{-1})$; and $y = 2(a_1b_1 + a_1c_{-1} + b_1^2 + b_1d_1 + b_1a_{-1} + b_1c_{-1})$. Then picking up from Equation 16, it follows that

$$\Delta F_t = \frac{x - y}{gh} \tag{17}$$

$$= \frac{2[u_1 + c_1u_2 - b_1u_3]}{gh}, \tag{18}$$

where $u_1 = a_1c_1 - a_1b_1 + a_1b_{-1} - a_1c_{-1}$, $u_2 = c_1 + d_1 + a_{-1} + b_{-1}$, and $u_3 = b_1 + d_1 + a_{-1} + c_{-1}$.

For notational convenience, let: $d_A = c_1 - b_1$ and $d_B = c_{-1} - b_{-1}$. Then it follows that

$$\Delta F_t = \frac{2u_4}{gh}, \tag{19}$$

where: $u_4 = a_1(d_A - d_B) + d_A(d_1 + a_{-1} + b_1 + c_1) + c_1b_{-1} - b_1c_{-1}$.

Noting that $g = h + d_A + d_B$, we have

$$\Delta F_t = \frac{2u_4}{h(h + d_A + d_B)}. \tag{20}$$

Noting that $2u_4 = 2[d_A(a_1 + b_1 + c_1 + d_1 + a_{-1} + b_{-1}) - d_B(a_1 + b_1)]$ and letting $u_5 = a_1 + b_1 + c_1 + d_1 + a_{-1} + b_{-1}$, we have

$$\Delta F_t = \frac{2[d_Au_5 - d_B(a_1 + b_1)]}{h(h + d_A + d_B)}. \tag{21}$$

Therefore,

$$|\Delta F_t| \leq 2\left(\left|\frac{d_Au_5}{h(h + d_A + d_B)}\right| + \left|\frac{d_B(a_1 + b_1)}{h(h + d_A + d_B)}\right|\right) \tag{22}$$

Recall that $b + c = b_1 + b_{-1} + c_1 + c_{-1}$. Then observe that the following three inequalities hold: $b + c \geq d_A$; $b + c \geq d_B$; and $h(h + d_A + d_B) > 0$. Therefore,

$$|\Delta F_t| \leq \frac{2(b+c)[2a_1+2b_1+c_1+d_1+a_{-1}+b_{-1}]}{h(h+d_A+d_B)} \tag{23}$$

$$= \frac{2(b+c)h}{h(h+d_A+d_B)} \tag{24}$$

$$= \frac{2(b+c)}{h+d_A+d_B} \tag{25}$$

$$\leq \frac{2(2a)(1-T)}{T(h+d_A+d_B)} \tag{26}$$

$$= \left(\frac{4(1-T)}{T}\right)\left(\frac{a}{h+d_A+d_B}\right). \tag{27}$$

Observe that $h+d_A+d_B = 2a_1+b_1+2c_1+d_1+a_{-1}+c_{-1}$. Therefore, $\frac{a}{h+d_A+d_B} \leq 1$. Therefore, we have

$$|\Delta F_t| \leq \frac{4(1-T)}{T}. \quad \blacksquare \tag{28}$$

Note that in deriving Inequality 26, we used the previously derived Inequality 14. Also, the proof of Theorem 3.2 assumes a worst possible case in the sense that all examples where the classifications of M_t and M_{t-1} differ are assumed to have truth values that all serve to maximize one model's F-measure and minimize the other model's F-measure so as to maximize $|\Delta F_t|$ as much as possible. A resulting limitation is that the bound is loose in many cases. It may be possible to derive tighter bounds, perhaps by easing off to an expected case instead of a worst case and/or by making additional assumptions.[6]

Taking this possibility up, we now prove tighter bounds when assumptions about the precision of the models M_t and M_{t-1} are made. Consider that in the proof of Theorem 3.2 when transitioning from Equality 27 to Inequality 28, we used the fact that $\frac{a}{h+d_A+d_B} \leq 1$. Note that $\frac{a}{h+d_A+d_B} = \frac{a}{2a_1+b_1+2c_1+d_1+a_{-1}+c_{-1}}$, from which one sees that $\frac{a}{h+d_A+d_B} = 1$ only if all of a_1, b_1, c_1, d_1 and c_{-1} are all zero. This is a pathological case. In many practically important classes of cases to consider, $\frac{a}{h+d_A+d_B}$ will be strictly less than 1, and often substantially less than 1. The following two Theorems prove tighter bounds on $|\Delta F_t|$ than Theorem 3.2 by utilizing this insight.

Theorem 3.3 *Suppose M_t, M_{t-1}, K_t, $\tilde{F}_t$, $\tilde{F}_{t-1}$, ΔF_t, and T are defined as stated in the statement of Theorem 3.2. Let the contingency tables be defined as they were in the proof of Theorem 3.3. Let $M_{PositiveConjunction}$ be a model that only classifies an example as positive if both models M_t and M_{t-1} classify the example as positive. Suppose that $M_{PositiveConjunction}$ has perfect precision on the stop set, or in other words that every single example from the stop set that both M_t and M_{t-1} classify as positive is truthfully positive (i.e., $a_{-1} = 0$). Then $K_t > T \Rightarrow |\Delta F_t| \leq \frac{2(1-T)}{T}$.*

Proof The proof of Theorem 3.2 holds exactly as it is up until Equality 27. Now, using the additional assumption that $a_{-1} = 0$, we have $\frac{a}{h+d_A+d_B} \leq \frac{1}{2}$. Therefore, we have

$$|\Delta F_t| \leq \frac{2(1-T)}{T}. \quad \blacksquare \tag{29}$$

Theorem 3.3 is a special case (in the limit) of a more general Theorem. Before stating and proving the more general Theorem, we prove a Lemma that will be helpful in making the proof of the general Theorem clearer.

Lemma 3.4 *Let f, d_A, d_B and contingency table counts be defined as they were in the proof of Theorem 3.2. Suppose $a_1 = xa_{-1}$. Then $\frac{a}{h+d_A+d_B} \leq \frac{x+1}{2x+1}$.*

Proof $a_1 = xa_{-1}$ by hypothesis. $a = a_1 + a_{-1}$ by definition of contingency table counts. Hence, $a = (x+1)a_{-1}$. Therefore,

$$\begin{aligned} \frac{a}{h+d_A+d_B} &\leq \frac{(x+1)a_{-1}}{2xa_{-1}+a_{-1}} \quad (30) \\ &= \frac{(x+1)a_{-1}}{(2x+1)a_{-1}} \\ &= \frac{x+1}{2x+1}. \quad \blacksquare \end{aligned}$$

The following Theorem generalizes Theorem 3.3 to cases when $M_{PositiveConjunction}$ has precision p in $(0, 1)$.[7]

Theorem 3.5 *Suppose M_t, M_{t-1}, K_t, $\tilde{F}_t$, $\tilde{F}_{t-1}$, ΔF_t, and T are defined as stated in the statement of Theorem 3.2. Let the contingency tables be defined as they were in the proof of Theorem 3.2. Let $M_{PositiveConjunction}$ be a model that only classifies an example as positive if both models M_t and M_{t-1} classify the example as positive. Suppose that $M_{PositiveConjunction}$ has precision p on the stop set. Then $K_t > T \Rightarrow |\Delta F_t| \leq \frac{4(1-T)}{(p+1)T}$.*

Proof The proof of Theorem 3.2 holds exactly as it is up until Equality 27. $M_{PositiveConjunction}$ has precision p on the stop set $\Rightarrow p = \frac{a_1}{a_1+a_{-1}}$. Solving for a_1 in terms of a_{-1} we have $a_1 = \frac{p}{1-p}a_{-1}$. Therefore, applying Lemma 3.4 with $x = \frac{p}{1-p}$, we have $\frac{a}{h+d_A+d_B} \leq \frac{\frac{p}{1-p}+1}{\frac{2p}{1-p}+1}$. Therefore we have

$$\begin{aligned} |\Delta F_t| &\leq 4\left(\frac{\frac{p}{1-p}+1}{\frac{2p}{1-p}+1}\right)\frac{(1-T)}{T} \quad (31) \\ &= \frac{4(1-T)}{(p+1)T}. \quad \blacksquare \quad (32) \end{aligned}$$

[6] If one is planning to undertake this challenge, we would suggest further consideration of Inequalities 22, 23, 26, and 28 as a possible starting point.

[7] The case when $p = 0$ is handled by Theorem 3.2 and the case when $p = 1$ is handled by Theorem 3.3.

Precision	$\frac{1}{p+1}$ (to 3 decimal places)
50%	0.667
80%	0.556
90%	0.526
95%	0.513
98%	0.505
99%	0.503
99.9%	0.500

Table 8: Values of the scaling factor from Theorem 3.5 for different precision values.

The scaling factor $\frac{1}{p+1}$ in Theorem 3.5 shows how the precision of the conjunctive model affects the bound. Theorem 3.2 had the scaling factor implicitly set to 1 in order to handle the pathological case where the positive conjunctive model has precision = 0. In Theorem 3.3, where the positive conjunctive model has precision = 1 on the examples in the stop set, the scaling factor is set to 1/2. Theorem 3.5 generalizes the scaling factor so that it is a function of the precision of the positive conjunctive model. For convenience, Table 8 shows the scaling factor values for a few different precision values.

The bounds in Theorems 3.2, 3.3, and 3.5 all bound the difference in performance *on the stop set* of two consecutively learned models M_t and M_{t-1}. An issue to consider is how connected the difference in performance on the stop set is to the difference in performance on a stream of application examples generated according to the population probabilities. Taking up this issue, consider that the proof of Theorems 3.2, 3.3, and 3.5 would hold as it is if we had used sample proportions instead of sample counts (this can be seen by simply dividing every count by n, the size of the stop set). Since the stop set is unbiased (selected at random from the population), as n approaches infinity, the sample proportions will approach the population probabilities and the difference between the difference in performance between M_t and M_{t-1} on the stop set and on a stream of application examples generated according to the population probabilities will approach zero.

4 Conclusions

To date, the work on stopping criteria has been dominated by heuristics based on intuitions and experimental success on a small handful of tasks and datasets. But the methods are not widely usable in practice yet because our community's understanding of the stopping methods remains too inexact. Pushing forward on understanding the mechanics of stopping at a more exact level is therefore crucial for achieving the design of widely usable effective stopping criteria.

This paper presented the first theoretical analysis of stopping based on stabilizing predictions. The analysis revealed three elements that are central to the SP method's success: (1) the sample estimates of Kappa have low variance; (2) Kappa has tight connections with differences in F-measure; and (3) since the stop set doesn't have to be labeled, it can be arbitrarily large, helping to guarantee that the results transfer to previously unseen streams of examples at test/application time.

We presented proofs of relationships between the level of Kappa agreement and the difference in performance between consecutive models. Specifically, if the Kappa agreement between two models is at least T, then the difference in F-measure performance between those models is bounded above by $\frac{4(1-T)}{T}$. If precision of the positive conjunction of the models is assumed to be p, then the bound can be tightened to $\frac{4(1-T)}{(p+1)T}$.

The setup and methodology of the proofs can serve as a launching pad for many further investigations, including: analyses of stopping; works that consider switching between different active learning strategies and operating regions; and works that consider stopping co-training, and especially agreement-based co-training. Finally, the relationships that have been exposed between the Kappa statistic and F-measure may be of broader use in works that consider inter-annotator agreement and its interplay with system evaluation, a topic that has been of long-standing interest.

References

Shlomo Argamon-Engelson and Ido Dagan. 1999. Committee-based sample selection for probabilistic classifiers. *Journal of Artificial Intelligence Research (JAIR)*, 11:335–360.

Ron Artstein and Massimo Poesio. 2008. Inter-coder agreement for computational linguistics. *Computational Linguistics*, 34(4):555–596.

Jason Baldridge and Miles Osborne. 2008. Active learning and logarithmic opinion pools for hpsg parse selection. *Nat. Lang. Eng.*, 14(2):191–222.

Yoram Baram, Ran El-Yaniv, and Kobi Luz. 2004. Online choice of active learning algorithms. *Journal of Machine Learning Research*, 5:255–291, March.

Yvonne M. Bishop, Stephen E. Fienberg, and Paul W. Holland. 1975. *Discrete Multivariate Analysis: Theory and Practice*. MIT Press, Cambridge, MA.

Michael Bloodgood and Chris Callison-Burch. 2010. Bucking the trend: Large-scale cost-focused active learning for statistical machine translation. In *Proceedings of the 48th Annual Meeting of the Association for Computational Linguistics*, pages 854–864, Uppsala, Sweden, July. Association for Computational Linguistics.

Michael Bloodgood and K Vijay-Shanker. 2009a. A method for stopping active learning based on stabilizing predictions and the need for user-adjustable stopping. In *Proceedings of the Thirteenth Conference on Computational Natural Language Learning (CoNLL-2009)*, pages 39–47, Boulder, Colorado, June. Association for Computational Linguistics.

Michael Bloodgood and K Vijay-Shanker. 2009b. Taking into account the differences between actively and passively acquired data: The case of active learning with support vector machines for imbalanced datasets. In *Proceedings of Human Language Technologies: The 2009 Annual Conference of the North American Chapter of the Association for Computational Linguistics*, pages 137–140, Boulder, Colorado, June. Association for Computational Linguistics.

Michael Bloodgood. 2009. *Active learning with support vector machines for imbalanced datasets and a method for stopping active learning based on stabilizing predictions*. Ph.D. thesis, University of Delaware, Newark, DE, USA.

Avrim Blum and Tom Mitchell. 1998. Combining labeled and unlabeled data with co-training. In *COLT' 98: Proceedings of the eleventh annual conference on Computational learning theory*, pages 92–100, New York, NY, USA. ACM.

J. Carletta. 1996. Assessing agreement on classification tasks: The kappa statistic. *Computational linguistics*, 22(2):249–254.

Stephen Clark, James Curran, and Miles Osborne. 2003. Bootstrapping pos-taggers using unlabelled data. In Walter Daelemans and Miles Osborne, editors, *Proceedings of the Seventh Conference on Natural Language Learning at HLT-NAACL 2003*, pages 49–55.

J. Cohen. 1960. A coefficient of agreement for nominal scales. *Educational and Psychological Measurement*, 20:37–46.

David A. Cohn, Zoubin Ghahramani, and Michael I. Jordan. 1996. Active learning with statistical models. *Journal of Artificial Intelligence Research*, 4:129–145.

Meryem Pinar Dönmez, Jaime G. Carbonell, and Paul N. Bennett. 2007. Dual strategy active learning. In Joost N. Kok, Jacek Koronacki, Ramon López de Mántaras, Stan Matwin, Dunja Mladenic, and Andrzej Skowron, editors, *Machine Learning: ECML 2007, 18th European Conference on Machine Learning, Warsaw, Poland, September 17-21, 2007, Proceedings*, volume 4701 of *Lecture Notes in Computer Science*, pages 116–127. Springer.

Seyda Ertekin, Jian Huang, Léon Bottou, and C. Lee Giles. 2007a. Learning on the border: active learning in imbalanced data classification. In Mário J. Silva, Alberto H. F. Laender, Ricardo A. Baeza-Yates, Deborah L. McGuinness, Bjørn Olstad, Øystein Haug Olsen, and André O. Falcão, editors, *Proceedings of the Sixteenth ACM Conference on Information and Knowledge Management, CIKM 2007, Lisbon, Portugal, November 6-10, 2007*, pages 127–136. ACM.

Seyda Ertekin, Jian Huang, and C. Lee Giles. 2007b. Active learning for class imbalance problem. In Wessel Kraaij, Arjen P. de Vries, Charles L. A. Clarke, Norbert Fuhr, and Noriko Kando, editors, *SIGIR 2007: Proceedings of the 30th Annual International ACM SIGIR Conference on Research and Development in Information Retrieval, Amsterdam, The Netherlands, July 23-27, 2007*, pages 823–824. ACM.

Joseph L. Fleiss, Jacob Cohen, and B. S. Everitt. 1969. Large sample standard errors of kappa and weighted kappa. *Psychological Bulletin*, 72(5):323 - 327.

Yoav Freund, H. Sebastian Seung, Eli Shamir, and Naftali Tishby. 1997. Selective sampling using the query by committee algorithm. *Machine Learning*, 28:133–168.

Masood Ghayoomi. 2010. Using variance as a stopping criterion for active learning of frame assignment. In *Proceedings of the NAACL HLT 2010 Workshop on Active Learning for Natural Language Processing*, pages 1–9, Los Angeles, California, June. Association for Computational Linguistics.

Ben Hachey, Beatrice Alex, and Markus Becker. 2005. Investigating the effects of selective sampling on the annotation task. In *Proceedings of the Ninth Conference on Computational Natural Language Learning (CoNLL-2005)*, pages 144–151, Ann Arbor, Michigan, June. Association for Computational Linguistics.

Robbie Haertel, Eric Ringger, Kevin Seppi, James Carroll, and Peter McClanahan. 2008. Assessing the costs of sampling methods in active learning for annotation. In *Proceedings of ACL-08: HLT, Short Papers*, pages 65–68, Columbus, Ohio, June. Association for Computational Linguistics.

Gholamreza Haffari and Anoop Sarkar. 2009. Active learning for multilingual statistical machine translation. In *Proceedings of the Joint Conference of the 47th Annual Meeting of the ACL and the 4th International Joint Conference on Natural Language Processing of the AFNLP*, pages 181–189, Suntec, Singapore, August. Association for Computational Linguistics.

Cecilia A. Hale and Joseph L. Fleiss. 1993. Interval estimation under two study designs for kappa with binary classifications. *Biometrics*, 49(2):pp. 523–534.

Rebecca Hwa. 2000. Sample selection for statistical grammar induction. In Hinrich Schütze and Keh-Yih Su, editors, *Proceedings of the 2000 Joint SIGDAT Conference on Empirical Methods in Natural Language Processing*, pages 45–53. Association for Computational Linguistics, Somerset, New Jersey.

Florian Laws and Hinrich Schütze. 2008. Stopping criteria for active learning of named entity recognition. In *Proceedings of the 22nd International Conference on Computational Linguistics (Coling 2008)*, pages 465–472, Manchester, UK, August. Coling 2008 Organizing Committee.

David D. Lewis and William A. Gale. 1994. A sequential algorithm for training text classifiers. In *SIGIR '94: Proceedings of the 17th annual international ACM SIGIR conference on Research and development in information retrieval*, pages 3–12, New York, NY, USA. Springer-Verlag New York, Inc.

D. Roth and K. Small. 2008. Active learning for pipeline models. In *Proceedings of the National Conference on Artificial Intelligence (AAAI)*, pages 683–688.

Nicholas Roy and Andrew McCallum. 2001. Toward optimal active learning through sampling estimation of error reduction. In *In Proceedings of the 18th International Conference on Machine Learning*, pages 441–448. Morgan Kaufmann.

Manabu Sassano. 2002. An empirical study of active learning with support vector machines for japanese word segmentation. In *ACL '02: Proceedings of the 40th Annual Meeting on Association for Computational Linguistics*, pages 505–512, Morristown, NJ, USA. Association for Computational Linguistics.

Greg Schohn and David Cohn. 2000. Less is more: Active learning with support vector machines. In *Proc. 17th International Conf. on Machine Learning*, pages 839–846. Morgan Kaufmann, San Francisco, CA.

Burr Settles and Mark Craven. 2008. An analysis of active learning strategies for sequence labeling tasks. In *Proceedings of the 2008 Conference on Empirical Methods in Natural Language Processing*, pages 1070–1079, Honolulu, Hawaii, October. Association for Computational Linguistics.

H. S. Seung, M. Opper, and H. Sompolinsky. 1992. Query by committee. In *COLT '92: Proceedings of the fifth annual workshop on Computational learning theory*, pages 287–294, New York, NY, USA. ACM.

Dan Shen, Jie Zhang, Jian Su, Guodong Zhou, and Chew-Lim Tan. 2004. Multi-criteria-based active learning for named entity recognition. In *Proceedings of the 42nd Meeting of the Association for Computational Linguistics (ACL'04), Main Volume*, pages 589–596, Barcelona, Spain, July.

Cynthia A. Thompson, Mary Elaine Califf, and Raymond J. Mooney. 1999. Active learning for natural language parsing and information extraction. In *In Proceedings of the 16th International Conference on Machine Learning*, pages 406–414. Morgan Kaufmann, San Francisco, CA.

Katrin Tomanek, Joachim Wermter, and Udo Hahn. 2007. An approach to text corpus construction which cuts annotation costs and maintains reusability of annotated data. In *Proceedings of the 2007 Joint Conference on Empirical Methods in Natural Language Processing and Computational Natural Language Learning (EMNLP-CoNLL)*, pages 486–495.

Andreas Vlachos. 2008. A stopping criterion for active learning. *Computer Speech and Language*, 22(3):295–312.

Jingbo Zhu and Eduard Hovy. 2007. Active learning for word sense disambiguation with methods for addressing the class imbalance problem. In *Proceedings of the 2007 Joint Conference on Empirical Methods in Natural Language Processing and Computational Natural Language Learning (EMNLP-CoNLL)*, pages 783–790.

Jingbo Zhu, Huizhen Wang, and Eduard Hovy. 2008a. Learning a stopping criterion for active learning for word sense disambiguation and text classification. In *IJCNLP*.

Jingbo Zhu, Huizhen Wang, and Eduard Hovy. 2008b. Multi-criteria-based strategy to stop active learning for data annotation. In *Proceedings of the 22nd International Conference on Computational Linguistics (Coling 2008)*, pages 1129–1136, Manchester, UK, August. Coling 2008 Organizing Committee.

Improving Pointwise Mutual Information (PMI) by Incorporating Significant Co-occurrence

Om P. Damani
IIT Bombay
damani@cse.iitb.ac.in

Abstract

We design a new co-occurrence based word association measure by incorporating the concept of significant co-occurrence in the popular word association measure Pointwise Mutual Information (PMI). By extensive experiments with a large number of publicly available datasets we show that the newly introduced measure performs better than other co-occurrence based measures and despite being resource-light, compares well with the best known resource-heavy distributional similarity and knowledge based word association measures. We investigate the source of this performance improvement and find that of the two types of significant co-occurrence - corpus-level and document-level, the concept of corpus level significance combined with the use of document counts in place of word counts is responsible for all the performance gains observed. The concept of document level significance is not helpful for PMI adaptation.

1 Introduction

Co-occurrence based word association measures like PMI, LLR, and Dice are popular since they are easy to understand and computationally efficient. They measure the strength of association between two words by comparing the word pair's corpus-level bigram frequency to some function of the unigram frequencies of the individual words.

Recently a new measure called *Co-occurrence Significance Ratio (CSR)* was introduced in (Chaudhari et al., 2011) based on the notion of significant co-occurrence. Since CSR was found to perform better than other co-occurrence measures, in this work, our goal was to incorporate the concept of significant co-occurrence in traditional word-association measures to design new measures that may perform better than both CSR and the traditional measures.

Two different notions of significant co-occurrence are employed in CSR:

- *Corpus-level significant co-occurrence* determines whether the ratio of observed bigram occurrences to their expected occurrences across the corpus can be explained as a pure chance phenomenon, and,
- *Document-level significant co-occurrence* determines whether a large fraction of a word-pair's occurrences within a given document have smaller spans than that under a null model where the words in the document are permuted randomly.

While both these notions are employed in an integrated fashion in CSR, on analyzing CSR details, we realized that these two concepts are independent and can be applied separately to any word association measure which is a ratio of some variable's observed frequency to its expected frequency. We incorporate the concepts of corpus-level and document-level significant co-occurrence in PMI to design a new measure that performs better than both PMI and CSR, as well as other co-occurrence based word association measures. To incorporate document level significance, we need to use document level counts instead of word level counts (this distinction is explained in detail in Section 4.3). To investigate whether the performance gains observed are because of the concept of significant co-occurrence or simply because of the fact that we are using document counts instead of the word counts, we also design document count based baseline version of PMI called PMId, and several intermediate variants whose definitions are given in Table 1.

To our surprise, we discover that the concept of document level significant co-occurrence does

	without corpus level significance	with corpus level significance
word-based	PMI: $log\frac{f(x,y)}{f(x)*f(y)/W}$	cPMI: $log\frac{f(x,y)}{f(x)*f(y)/W+\sqrt{f(x)}*\sqrt{\ln\delta/(-2)}}$
document-based	PMId: $log\frac{d(x,y)}{d(x)*d(y)/D}$	cPMId: $log\frac{d(x,y)}{d(x)*d(y)/D+\sqrt{d(x)}*\sqrt{\ln\delta/(-2)}}$
with document level significance	PMIz: $log\frac{Z}{d(x)*d(y)/D}$	cPMIz: $log\frac{Z}{d(x)*d(y)/D+\sqrt{d(x)}*\sqrt{\ln\delta/(-2)}}$ CSR: $\frac{Z}{E(Z)+\sqrt{K}*\sqrt{\ln\delta/(-2)}}$

$f(x, y)$	Span-constrained (x, y) word pair frequency in the corpus
$f(x), f(y)$	unigram frequencies of x, y respectively in the corpus
W	Total number of words in the corpus
$d(x, y)$	Total number of documents in the corpus having at-least one span-constrained occurrence of the word pair (x, y)
$d(x), d(y)$	Total number of documents in the corpus containing at least one occurrence of x and y respectively
D	Total number of documents in the corpus
δ	a parameter varying between 0 and 1
Z	as per Definition 4.3
$E(Z)$	Expected value of Z as given in Section 2.2 of (Chaudhari et al., 2011)
K	Total number of documents in the corpus having at-least one occurrence of the word pair (x, y) regardless of the span

Table 1: Definitions[0] of PMI, CSR, and various measures developed in this work.

not contribute to the PMI performance improvement. Two newly designed, best-performing measures cPMId and cPMIz have almost identical performance. As the definitions in Table 1 show, cPMId incorporates corpus level significance in a document count based version of PMI but does not employ the concept of document level significance, whereas cPMIz employs both corpus and document level significance. This demonstrates that the concept of corpus level significance combined with document counts is responsible for all the performance gains observed.

To summarize, we make the following contributions in this work:

- We incorporate the notion of significant co-occurrence in PMI to design a new measure cPMId that performs better than PMI as well as other popular co-occurrence based word-association measures on both *free association* and *semantic relatedness* tasks. In addition, despite being resource-light, cPMId performs as well as the best known distributional similarity and knowledge based measures which are resource-intensive.

- We investigate the source of this performance improvement and find that of the two notions of significance - corpus-level and document-level significant co-occurrence, the concept of document level significant co-occurrence is not helpful for PMI adaptation. The concept of corpus level significance combined with document counts is responsible for all the performance gains observed.

2 Related Work

Word association measures can be divided into three broad categories: knowledge based, distributional similarity based, and co-occurrence based measures. Knowledge-based measures are based on thesauri, semantic networks, taxonomies, or other knowledge sources (Liberman and Markovitch, 2009; Yeh et al., 2009; Milne and Witten, 2008; Hughes and Ramage, 2007). Distributional similarity-based measures compare two words by comparing distributional similarity of other words around them (Agirre et al., 2009; Wandmacher et al., 2008; Bollegala et al., 2007). In this work, our focus is on Co-occurrence based measures and hence we do not discuss Knowledge-based and Distributional similarity-based measures further.

Co-occurrence based measures estimate association between two words by computing some function of the words unigram and bigram frequencies. Table 2 contains definitions of popular co-occurrence measures. The concept of document and corpus level significance can be applied to any word association measure which is defined as the ratio of a variable's observed frequency to its expected frequency. While Chi-Square (χ^2),

[0]We consider only those word-pair occurrences where inter-word distance between x and y is atmost s, the span threshold. For a particular occurrence of x, we get a window of size s on either side within which y can occur. Strictly speaking, there should be a factor $2s$ in the denominator of the formula for PMI. Since we are only interested in the relative rankings of word-pairs, we follow the standard practice of ignoring the $2s$ factor, as its removal affects only the absolute PMI values but not the relative rankings.

Measure	Definition
Chi-Square(χ^2)	$\sum_{x' \in \{x, \neg x\},\ y' \in \{y, \neg y\}} \frac{\left(f(x',y') - Ef(x',y')\right)^2}{Ef(x',y')}$
Dice (Dice, 1945)	$\frac{2f(x,y)}{f(x)+f(y)}$
Jaccard (Jaccard, 1912)	$\frac{f(x,y)}{f(x)+f(y)-f(x,y)}$
Log Likelihood Ratio(LLR) (Dunning, 1993)	$\sum_{x' \in \{x, \neg x\},\ y' \in \{y, \neg y\}} p(x',y') log \frac{p(x',y')}{p(x')p(y')}$
Pointwise Mutual Information(PMI) (Church and Hanks, 1989)	$log \frac{f(x,y)}{f(x)*f(y)/W}$
T-test	$\frac{f(x,y)-Ef(x,y)}{\sqrt{f(x,y)\left(1-\frac{f(x,y)}{W}\right)}}$

W	Total number of tokens in the corpus
$f(x), f(y)$	unigram frequencies of x, y in the corpus
$p(x), p(y)$	$f(x)/W, f(y)/W$
$f(x,y)$	Span-constrained (x, y) word pair frequency in corpus
$p(x,y)$	$f(x,y)/W$

Table 2: Definition of popular co-occurrence based word association measures.

LLR, and T-test already incorporate some notion of statistical significance, among Dice, Jaccard, and PMI, only the PMI meets this requirement. Hence our focus in this work is on designing new measures by incorporating the notion of significant co-occurrence in PMI.

3 Incorporating Corpus Level Significance

In (Chaudhari et al., 2011), the concept of corpus level significance was introduced by bounding the probability of observing a given corpus level phenomenon under a particular null model. In the formula for PMI, the observed frequency of a word pair's occurrences is compared with its expected frequency under a null model which assumes independent unigram occurrences. Near a given occurrence of the word x in the corpus, the word y can be observed with probability $f(y)/W$. Hence the expected value of $f(x,y)$ is $f(x) * f(y)/W$. Adapting from (Chaudhari et al., 2011) and using Hoeffding's Inequality, the probability of observing a given deviation between $f(x,y)$ and its expected value $f(x) * f(y)/W$ can be bounded. For any $t > 0$:

$$
\begin{aligned}
&P[f(x,y) \geq f(x) * f(y)/W + f(x) * t] \\
&\leq \exp(-2 * f(x) * t^2) \\
&= \delta
\end{aligned}
$$

The upper-bound δ ($= \exp(-2*f(x)*t^2)$) denotes the probability of observing more than $f(x) * f(y)/W + f(x) * t$ bigram occurrences in the corpus, just by chance, under the given independent unigram occurrence null model. With δ as a parameter ($0 < \delta < 1$) and $t = \sqrt{\ln \delta / (-2 * f(x))}$, we can define a new word association measure called *Corpus Level Significant PMI*(cPMI) as:

$$
\begin{aligned}
cPMI(x,y) &= log \frac{f(x,y)}{f(x) * f(y)/W + f(x) * t} \\
&= log \frac{f(x,y)}{f(x) * f(y)/W + \sqrt{f(x)} * \sqrt{\ln \delta / (-2)}}
\end{aligned}
$$

where $t = \sqrt{\ln \delta / (-2 * f(x))}$.

By taking the probability of observing a given deviation between $f(x,y)$ and its expected value $f(x) * f(y)/W$ in account, cPMI addresses one of the main weakness of PMI of working only with probabilities and completely ignoring the absolute amount of evidence. In two scenarios where all frequency ratios (that of $f(x)$, $f(y)$, $f(x,y)$, and W) are equal, PMI values will be same while cPMI value will be higher for the case where absolute number of occurrences are higher. This can be seen easily by multiplying all of $f(x)$, $f(y)$, $f(x,y)$, and W with some constant n:

$$
\begin{aligned}
&log \frac{n * f(x,y)}{n * f(x) * n * f(y)/n * W + \sqrt{n * f(x)} * \sqrt{\ln \delta/(-2)}} \\
&= log \frac{f(x,y)}{f(x) * f(y)/W + \sqrt{\mathbf{1/n}} * \sqrt{f(x)} * \sqrt{\ln \delta/(-2)}} \\
&> log \frac{f(x,y)}{f(x) * f(y)/W + \sqrt{f(x)} * \sqrt{\ln \delta/(-2)}} \\
&= cPMI(x,y)
\end{aligned}
$$

4 Incorporating Document Level Significant Co-occurrence

Traditional measures like PMI can be viewed as working with a null hypothesis where each word in a document is generated completely independently of the other words in that document. With each word, a global unigram generation probability is associated and all documents are assumed to be generated as per a multinomial distribution. Such a null model generates different expected span (inter-word gap) for high frequency words vs. low frequency words. In reality, if strongly associated words co-occur in a document then they do so with low span, i.e., they occur close to each-other regardless of the underlying unigram frequencies.

4.1 Determining Document Level Significance

To correct this span bias of traditional measures, a new null model is employed in (Chaudhari et al., 2011). A bag of word is associated with each document. The null model assumes that the observed document is a random permutation of the associated bag of words. Given the occurrences of a word-pair in the document, if the number of occurrences with span less than a given threshold can be explained by this null model then the word pair is assumed to be unassociated in the document. Else, some form of association is assumed. Following definitions are introduced in (Chaudhari et al., 2011) to formalize this concept.

Definition 1 (span-constrained frequency) *Let f be the maximum number of* non-overlapped occurrences *of a word-pair α in a document. Let $\widehat{f^s}(0 \leq \widehat{f^s} \leq f)$ be the maximum number of non-overlapped occurrences of α with span less than a given threshold s. We refer to $\widehat{f^s}$ as the* span-constrained frequency *of α in the document.*

For a given document of length ℓ and a word-pair with f occurrences in it, as we vary the span threshold s, the number of occurrences of the word-pair with span less than s, i.e. its span-constrained frequency $\widehat{f^s}$ varies. For a given s and the $\widehat{f^s}$ resulting from it, we can ask, what is the probability that $\widehat{f^s}$ out of f occurrences of a word-pair in a document of length ℓ will have span less than s, if the words in the document were to be permuted randomly. If this probability is less than some threshold ϵ, then we can assume that the words in the pair have some tendency of co-occurring in the document. Formally,

Definition 2 (ϵ-significant co-occurrence) *Let ℓ be the length of a document and let f be the frequency of a word-pair α in it. For a given a span threshold s, define $\pi_s(\widehat{f^s}, f, \ell)$ as the probability under the null that α will appear in the document with a span-constrained frequency of* at least $\widehat{f^s}$.

Given a probability threshold ϵ $(0 < \epsilon < 1)$ and a span threshold s, the document is said to support *the hypothesis "α is an ϵ-significant word-pair within the document" if we have $[\pi_s(\widehat{f^s}, f, \ell) < \epsilon]$.*

The key idea is that we should concentrate on those documents where a word pair has an ϵ-significant occurrence and ignore its occurrences in non ϵ-significant documents. This point is more subtle than it appears. Earlier, if the span of an occurrence was less than a threshold, it was counted, else it was ignored. In the new null model, instead of an individual occurrence, all occurrences of the word-pair in the document are considered as a single unit. Either all occurrences confirm to the null model or they do not. Of course, some occurrences will have span less than the threshold while others will have higher span, but when considering significance, all occurrences in the document are considered significant or insignificant as a unit. This point is discussed further in Section 4.3.

4.2 $\pi_s[]$ Computation Overhead

The detailed discussion of the computation of $\pi_s[]$ table can be found in (Chaudhari et al., 2011). For our work, it suffices to know that $\pi_s[]$ table needs to be computed only once and hence it can be done offline. We use the $\pi_s[]$ table made publicly available[1] by CSR researchers. The use of $\pi_s[]$ table simply entails a memory lookup and does not increase the computation cost of a measure.

4.3 Adapting PMI for Document Level Significance

Consider the cPMI definition given earlier. One way to adapt it for document significance is to alter the numerator such that only the span-constrained bigram occurrences in ϵ-significant documents are considered in computing $f(x, y)$.

However, this simple adaptation is problematic. Consider a document with f occurrences of a word-pair of which span of $\widehat{f^s}$ occurrences is at-most s, the given span threshold. In the definition of cPMI, the numerator takes in account only those occurrences whose span is less than s, i.e., only the $\widehat{f^s}$ occurrences from a document. As discussed earlier, the ϵ-significance of a document is determined by looking at all f occurrences as a whole. In the null model, whether a particular occurrence has span less than or greater than s is not so important, what matters is that span of $\widehat{f^s}$ occurrences out of f is at most s. The word-pair is considered an ϵ-significant pair within the document if the observed span of all f occurrences of the pair can be explained by the null model. Hence, when adapting for ϵ-significance, it is improper to count only $\widehat{f^s}$ occurrences out of f.

The way out of this difficulty is to count the documents and not the words. We do this adaptation

[1] http://www.cse.iitb.ac.in/ damani/papers/EMNLP11/resources.html

in two steps. First, we replace the word counts with document counts in the definition of cPMI, giving a new measure called *Corpus Level Significant PMI based on Document count* (cPMId):

$$cPMId(x, y) \quad = \quad log\frac{d(x, y)}{d(x) * d(y)/D + \sqrt{d(x)} * \sqrt{\ln \delta/(-2)}}$$

where $d(x, y)$ indicates the number of documents containing at least one span constrained occurrence of (x, y), and $d(x)$ and $d(y)$ indicate the number of document containing x and y, D indicates the total number of documents in the corpus, and as before, δ is a parameter varying between 0 and 1.

Having replaced the word counts with document counts, we now incorporate the concept of document level significant co-occurrence (as discussed in Section 4.1) in cPMId by replacing $d(x, y)$ in numerator with Z which is defined as:

Definition 3 (Z) *Let Z be the number of documents that support the hypothesis "the given word-pair is an ϵ-significant word-pair", i.e., Z is the number of documents for which $\pi_s(\widehat{f^s}, f, \ell) < \epsilon$.*

The new measure is called *Document and Corpus Level Significant PMI* (cPMIz) and is defined as:

$$cPMIz(x, y) \quad = \quad log\frac{Z}{d(x) * d(y)/D + \sqrt{d(x)} * \sqrt{\ln \delta/(-2)}}$$

Note that cPMIz has three parameters: span threshold s, the corpus level significant parameter δ $(0 < \delta < 1)$ and the document level significant parameter ϵ $(0 < \epsilon < 1)$. In comparison, cPMI/cPMId have s and δ as parameters while PMI has only s as the parameter. The three parameters of cPMId are similar to those of CSR.

cPMIz and cPMId differ in the fact that cPMId does not incorporate the document level significance. Similarly, we can design another measure that differs from cPMIz in that it does not incorporate corpus level significance. This measure is called *Document Level Significant PMI* (PMIz) and is defined as:

$$PMIz(x, y) \quad = \quad log\frac{Z}{d(x) * d(y)/D}$$

Baseline Measure: Suppose cPMIz were to do better than the PMI. One could ask whether the improvement achieved is due to the concept of significant co-occurrence or is it simply a result of the fact that we are counting documents instead of words. To answer this, we design a baseline version of PMI where we simply replace word counts with document counts. The new baseline measure is called *PMI based on Document count* (PMId) and is defined as:

$$PMId(x, y) \quad = \quad log\frac{d(x, y)}{d(x) * d(y)/D}$$

5 Performance Evaluation

Having introduced various measures, we wish to determine whether the incorporation of corpus and document level significance improves the performance of PMI. Also, if the adapted versions perform better than PMI, what are the sources of the improvements. Is it the concept of corpus level or document level significance or both, or is the performance gain simply a result of the fact that we are counting documents instead of words? Since the newly introduced measures have multiple parameters, how sensitive is their performance to the parameter values.

To answer these questions, we repeat the experiments performed in (Chaudhari et al., 2011), using the exact same dataset, resources, and methodology - the same 1.24 Gigawords Wikipedia corpus and the same eight publicly available datasets - Edinburgh (Kiss et al., 1973), Florida (Nelson et al., 1980), Kent (Kent and Rosanoff, 1910), Minnesota (Russell and Jenkins, 1954), White-Abrams (White and Abrams, 2004), Goldfarb-Halpern (Goldfarb and Halpern, 1984), Wordsim (Finkelstein et al., 2002), and Esslli (ESSLLI, 2008). Of these, Wordsim measures *semantic relatedness* which encompasses relations like synonymy, meronymy, antonymy, and functional association (Budanitsky and Hirst, 2006). All other datasets measure *free association* which refers to the first response given by a subject on being given a stimulus word (ESSLLI, 2008).

5.1 Evaluation Methodology

Each measure is evaluated by the correlation between the ranking of word-associations produced by the measure and the gold-standard human ranking for that dataset. Since all methods have at least one parameter, we perform five-fold cross validation. The span parameter s is varied between 5 and 50 words, and ϵ and δ are varied between 0 and 1. Each dataset is partitioned into five folds - four for

	Edinburgh (83,713)	Florida (59,852)	Kent (14,086)	Minnesota (9,649)	White-Abrams (652)	Goldfarb-Halpern (384)	Wordsim (351)	Esslli (272)
PMI	0.22	0.25	0.35	0.25	0.27	0.16	0.69	0.38
cPMI	0.23	0.28	0.40	0.29	0.29	0.17	0.70	0.46
PMId	0.22	0.26	0.37	0.26	0.28	0.17	0.71	0.42
cPMId	**0.27**	**0.32**	**0.44**	0.33	**0.36**	0.16	**0.72**	**0.54**
PMIz	0.24	0.26	0.38	0.26	0.28	**0.18**	0.71	0.39
cPMIz	**0.27**	**0.32**	**0.44**	**0.34**	0.35	**0.18**	0.71	0.53
CSR	0.25	0.30	0.42	0.31	0.34	0.10	0.63	0.43

Table 3: 5-fold cross validation comparison of rank coefficients for different measures. The number of word-pairs in each dataset is shown against its name. The best performing measures for each dataset are shown in bold.

	without corpus level significance	with corpus level significance
word-based	PMI: 0.075	cPMI: 0.044
document-based	PMId: 0.060	cPMId: 0.004
with document level significance	PMIz: 0.059	cPMIz: 0.004 CSR: 0.049

Table 4: Average deviation of various measures from the best performing measure for each dataset.

training and one for testing. For each association measure, the parameter values that perform best on four training folds is used for the remaining one testing fold. The performance of a measure on a dataset is its average Spearman rank correlation over 5 runs with 5 different test folds.

5.2 Experimental Results

Results of the 5-fold cross validation are shown in Table 3. From the results we conclude that the concept of significant co-occurrence improves the performance of PMI. The newly designed measures cPMId and cPMIz perform better than both PMI and CSR on all eight datasets.

5.3 Performance Improvement Analysis

We can infer from Table 3 that the concept of corpus level significant co-occurrence and not that of document level significant co-occurrence is responsible for the PMI performance improvement. The Spearman rank correlation for cPMIz and cPMId are almost identical. cPMId incorporates corpus level significance in a document count based version of PMI but unlike cPMIz, it does not employ the concept of document level significance.

To underscore this point, we also compute the difference between the correlation of each measure from the correlation of the best measure for each data set. For each measure we can then compute the average deviation of the measure from the best performing measure across datasets. In Table 4 we present these average deviations. We observe that:

- Average deviation reduces as we move horizontally across a row - from PMI to cPMI, from PMId to cPMId, and from PMIz to cPMIz. This shows that the incorporation of corpus level significance helps improve the performance.
- The average deviation reduces as we move vertically from the first row to the second - from PMI to PMId, and from cPMI to cPMId. This shows that the performance gain achieved is also due to the fact that we are counting documents instead of words.
- Finally, the average deviation remains practically unchanged as we move vertically from the second row to the third - from PMId to PMIz, from cPMId to cPMIz. This shows that the incorporation of document level significance does not help improve the performance.

5.4 Parameter Sensitivity Analysis

To find out the sensitivity of cPMId performance to the parameter values, we evaluate it for different parameter combinations and present the results in Table 5. To save space, we show some of the combinations only, though one can see the continuity of performance with gradually changing parameter values.

Parameters (s, δ)	Edinburgh (83,713)	Florida (59,852)	Kent (14,086)	Minnesota (9,649)	White-Abrams (652)	Goldfarb-Halpern (384)	Wordsim (351)	Esslli (272)
*, 0.1	**0.27**	**0.32**	0.43	**0.33**	0.35	0.12	0.65	**0.55**
*, 0.3	**0.27**	**0.32**	**0.44**	**0.33**	**0.36**	0.14	0.67	**0.55**
*, 0.5	**0.27**	**0.32**	0.43	**0.33**	**0.36**	0.15	0.68	0.54
*, 0.7	**0.27**	**0.32**	0.43	**0.33**	**0.36**	0.14	0.70	0.54
*, 0.9	**0.27**	0.31	0.43	0.32	0.35	0.16	**0.72**	0.53
5w, *	**0.27**	0.31	0.43	**0.33**	0.35	**0.18**	0.66	0.49
10w, *	**0.27**	**0.32**	0.43	**0.33**	**0.36**	**0.18**	0.70	0.52
20w, *	**0.27**	**0.32**	0.43	**0.33**	**0.36**	**0.18**	0.71	0.54
30w, *	**0.27**	**0.32**	0.42	0.32	**0.36**	**0.18**	0.71	0.54
40w, *	**0.27**	0.31	0.42	0.32	0.35	0.17	0.71	0.54
50w, *	**0.27**	0.31	0.42	0.31	**0.36**	0.17	**0.72**	0.53
*, *	**0.27**	**0.32**	**0.44**	**0.33**	**0.36**	0.16	**0.72**	0.54
20w,0.7	**0.27**	**0.32**	0.43	**0.33**	**0.36**	0.16	0.70	0.54
50w,0.9	**0.27**	0.31	0.41	0.31	0.35	0.17	**0.72**	0.53

Table 5: 5-fold cross validation performance of cPMId for various parameter combinations. * indicates a varying parameter.

	Edinburgh (83,713)	Florida (59,852)	Kent (14,086)	Minnesota (9,649)	White-Abrams (652)	Goldfarb-Halpern (384)	Wordsim (351)	Esslli (272)
PMI	0.22	0.25	0.35	0.25	0.27	0.16	0.69	0.38
PMId	0.22	0.26	0.37	0.26	0.28	**0.17**	0.71	0.42
PMI^2	0.24	0.30	**0.43**	0.31	0.29	0.08	0.62	0.44
PMI^{2}d	0.23	0.29	0.42	0.31	0.30	0.06	0.61	0.43
nPMI	0.25	0.30	0.41	0.30	0.31	0.13	**0.72**	0.47
nPMId	0.23	0.26	0.28	0.24	0.30	0.15	0.71	0.46
cPMId(δ : 0.9)	**0.27**	**0.31**	**0.43**	**0.32**	**0.35**	0.16	**0.72**	**0.53**

Table 6: 5-fold cross validation comparison of cPMId with other PMI variants.

From the results we conclude that the performance of cPMId is reasonably insensitive to the actual parameter values. For a large range of parameter combinations, cPMId's performance varies marginally and most of the parameter combinations perform close to the best. If one does not have a training corpus then one can chose the best performing $(20w, 0.7)$ as default parameter values.

As an aside, introducing extra tunable parameter occasionally reduces performance, as is the case for Goldfarb-Halpern and Esslli datasets where (*,*) is not the best performing cobination. This happens when the parameters combination that performs best on the four training fold turns out particularly bad for the testing fold.

5.5 Comparison with other measures

Before comparing cPMId with other measures, we note that while all co-occurrence measures being compared have span threshold s as a parameter, cPMId has an extra tunable parameter δ. While we would like to argue that part of power of cPMId comes from this extra tunable parameter, for an arguably fairer comparison, we would like to fix the δ value and then compare so that all methods have only one tunable parameter s. In Table 5 we find that $\delta = 0.9$ performs best on the fewest number of datasets and hence we select this fixed value for comparison. However most of the conclusions that follow do not change if we were to fix some other δ value, or keep it variable.

5.5.1 Comparison with other PMI variants

In Section 3 we pointed out the PMI only works with probabilities and ignores the absolute amount of evidence. Another side-effect of this phenomenon is that PMI over-values sparseness. All frequency ratios (that of $f(x)$, $f(y)$, and $f(x,y)$) being equal, bigrams composed of low frequency words get higher score than those composed of high frequency words. In particular, in case of perfect dependence, i.e. $f(x) = f(y) = f(x,y)$, $PMI(x,y) = log\frac{W}{f(x,y)}$. cPMId addresses this weakness by explicitly bounding the probability of observing a given deviation between $f(x,y)$ and its expected value $f(x) * f(y)/W$. Other re-

	Edinburgh (83,713)	Florida (59,852)	Kent (14,086)	Minnesota (9,649)	White-Abrams (652)	Goldfarb-Halpern (384)	Wordsim (351)	Esslli (272)
Dice	0.20	0.27	**0.43**	**0.32**	0.21	0.09	0.59	0.36
Jaccard	0.20	0.27	**0.43**	**0.32**	0.21	0.09	0.59	0.36
χ^2	0.24	0.30	**0.43**	0.31	0.29	0.08	0.62	0.44
LLR	0.20	0.26	0.40	0.29	0.18	0.03	0.51	0.38
TTest	0.17	0.23	0.37	0.26	0.17	-0.02	0.45	0.33
cPMId(δ : 0.9)	**0.27**	**0.31**	**0.43**	**0.32**	**0.35**	**0.16**	**0.72**	**0.53**

Table 7: 5-fold cross validation comparison of cPMId with other co-occurrence based measures.

Explicit Semantic Analysis (ESA) (Gabrilovich and Markovitch, 2007)	**0.74**
(reimplemented in (Yeh et al., 2009))	**0.71**
Compact Hierarchical ESA (Liberman and Markovitch, 2009)	0.71
Hyperlink Graph (Milne and Witten, 2008)	0.69
Graph Traversal (Agirre et al., 2009))	0.66
Distributional Similarity (Agirre et al., 2009))	0.65
Latent Semantic Analysis (Finkelstein et al., 2002)	0.56
Random Graph Walk (Hughes and Ramage, 2007)	0.55
Normalized Path-length (lch) (Strube and Ponzetto, 2006)	0.55
cPMId(δ : 0.9)	**0.72**

Table 8: Comparison of cPMId with knowledge-based and distributional similarity based measures for the Wordsim dataset.

searchers have addressed this issue by modifying PMI such that its upper value gets bounded.

Since the maximum value of $\frac{f(x,y)}{f(x)*f(y)/W}$ is $\frac{1}{f(x,y)/W}$, one way to bound the former is to divide it by later. (Daille, 1994) defined PMI^2 as:

$$PMI^2(x,y) = log\frac{\frac{f(x,y)}{f(x)*f(y)/W}}{\frac{1}{f(x,y)/W}} = log\frac{f(x,y)^2}{f(x)*f(y)}$$

In (Bouma, 2009), it was noted that max. and min. value of PMI^2 are 0,$-\infty$, whereas one can get 1,-1 as the bounds if one normalize PMI as nPMI:

$$nPMI(x,y) = \frac{log\frac{f(x,y)}{f(x)*f(y)/W}}{log\frac{1}{f(x,y)/W}}$$

In Table 6, we compare the performance of word and document count based variants of PMI^2 and nPMI with PMI and cPMId. We find that while both nPMI and PMI^2 perform better than PMI,cPMId performs better than both variants of nPMI and PMI^2 on almost all datasets.

5.5.2 Comparison with other co-occurrence based measures

In Table 7, we compare cPMId with other co-occurrence based measures defined in Table 2. We find that cPMId performs better than all other co-occurrence based measures. Note that performance of Jaccard and Dice measure is identical to the second decimal place. This is because for our datasets $f(x,y) \ll f(x)$ and $f(x,y) \ll f(y)$ for most word-pairs under consideration.

5.5.3 Comparison with non co-occurrence based measures

For completeness of comparison, we also compare the performance of cPMId with distributional similarity and knowledge based measures discussed in Section 2. Of the datasets discussed here, these measures have only been tested on the Wordsim dataset. In Table 8, we compare the performance of cPMId with these other measures on the Wordsim dataset. We can see that cPMId compares well with the best non co-occurrence based measures.

6 Conclusions and Future Work

By incorporating the concept of significant co-occurrence in PMI, we get a new measure which performs better than other co-occurrence based measures. We investigate the source of the performance improvement and find that of the two notions of significance: corpus-level and document-level significant co-occurrence, the concept of corpus level significance combined with use document counts in place of word counts is responsible for all the performance gains observed. We also find that the performance of the newly introduced measure cPMId is reasonably insensitive to the values of its tunable parameters.

Acknowledgements

We thank Dipak Chaudhari and Shweta Ghonghe for their help with the implementation.

References

Eneko Agirre, Enrique Alfonseca, Keith Hall, Jana Kravalova, Marius Pasca, and Aitor Soroa. 2009. A study on similarity and relatedness using distributional and wordnet-based approaches. In *NAACL-HLT*.

Danushka Bollegala, Yutaka Matsuo, and Mitsuru Ishizuka. 2007. Measuring semantic similarity between words using web search engines. In *WWW*, pages 757–766.

Gerlof Bouma. 2009. Normalized (pointwise) mutual information in collocation extraction, from form to meaning: Processing texts automatically. In *Proceedings of the Biennial GSCL Conference*.

Alexander Budanitsky and Graeme Hirst. 2006. Evaluating wordnet-based measures of lexical semantic relatedness. *Computational Linguists*, 32(1):13–47.

Dipak L. Chaudhari, Om P. Damani, and Srivatsan Laxman. 2011. Lexical co-occurrence, statistical significance, and word association. In *EMNLP*.

Kenneth Ward Church and Patrick Hanks. 1989. Word association norms, mutual information and lexicography. In *ACL*, pages 76–83.

B. Daille. 1994. *Approche mixte pour l'extraction automatique de terminologie: statistiques lexicales etl-tres linguistiques*. Ph.D. thesis, Universitie Paris 7.

L. R. Dice. 1945. Measures of the amount of ecological association between species. *Ecology*, 26:297–302.

Ted Dunning. 1993. Accurate methods for the statistics of surprise and coincidence. *Computational Linguistics*, 19(1):61–74.

ESSLLI. 2008. *Free association* task at lexical semantics workshop esslli 2008. `http://wordspace.collocations.de/doku.php/workshop:esslli:task`.

Lev Finkelstein, Evgeniy Gabrilovich, Yossi Matias, Ehud Rivlin, Zach Solan, Gadi Wolfman, and Eytan Ruppin. 2002. Placing search in context: the concept revisited. *ACM Trans. Inf. Syst.*, 20(1):116–131.

Evgeniy Gabrilovich and Shaul Markovitch. 2007. Computing semantic relatedness using wikipedia-based explicit semantic analysis. In *IJCAI*.

Robert Goldfarb and Harvey Halpern. 1984. Word association responses in normal adult subjects. *Journal of Psycholinguistic Research*, 13(1):37–55.

T Hughes and D Ramage. 2007. Lexical semantic relatedness with random graph walks. In *EMNLP*.

P. Jaccard. 1912. The distribution of the flora of the alpine zone. *New Phytologist*, 11:37–50.

G. Kent and A. Rosanoff. 1910. A study of association in insanity. *American Journal of Insanity*, pages 317–390.

G. Kiss, C. Armstrong, R. Milroy, and J. Piper. 1973. An associative thesaurus of english and its computer analysis. In *The Computer and Literary Studies*, pages 379–382. Edinburgh University Press.

Sonya Liberman and Shaul Markovitch. 2009. Compact hierarchical explicit semantic representation. In *Proceedings of the IJCAI 2009 Workshop on User-Contributed Knowledge and Artificial Intelligence: An Evolving Synergy (WikiAI09)*, Pasadena, CA, July.

David Milne and Ian H. Witten. 2008. An effective, low-cost measure of semantic relatedness obtained from wikipedia links. In *ACL*.

D. Nelson, C. McEvoy, J. Walling, and J. Wheeler. 1980. The university of south florida homograph norms. *Behaviour Research Methods and Instrumentation*, 12:16–37.

W.A. Russell and J.J. Jenkins. 1954. The complete minnesota norms for responses to 100 words from the kent-rosanoff word association test. Technical report, Office of Naval Research and University of Minnesota.

Michael Strube and Simone Paolo Ponzetto. 2006. Wikirelate! computing semantic relatedness using wikipedia. In *AAAI*, pages 1419–1424.

T. Wandmacher, E. Ovchinnikova, and T. Alexandrov. 2008. Does latent semantic analysis reflect human associations? In *European Summer School in Logic, Language and Information (ESSLLI'08)*.

Katherine K. White and Lise Abrams. 2004. Free associations and dominance ratings of homophones for young and older adults. *Behavior Research Methods, Instruments, & Computers*, 36(3):408–420.

Eric Yeh, Daniel Ramage, Chris Manning, Eneko Agirre, and Aitor Soroa. 2009. Wikiwalk: Random walks on wikipedia for semantic relatedness. In *ACL workshop "TextGraphs-4: Graph-based Methods for Natural Language Processing"*.

Supervised Morphological Segmentation in a Low-Resource Learning Setting using Conditional Random Fields

Teemu Ruokolainen[a] **Oskar Kohonen**[a] **Sami Virpioja**[a] **Mikko Kurimo**[b]
[a] Department of Information and Computer Science, Aalto University
[b] Department of Signal Processing and Acoustics, Aalto University
firstname.lastname@aalto.fi

Abstract

We discuss data-driven morphological segmentation, in which word forms are segmented into morphs, the surface forms of morphemes. Our focus is on a low-resource learning setting, in which only a small amount of annotated word forms are available for model training, while unannotated word forms are available in abundance. The current state-of-art methods 1) exploit both the annotated and unannotated data in a semi-supervised manner, and 2) learn morph lexicons and subsequently uncover segmentations by generating the most likely morph sequences. In contrast, we discuss 1) employing only the annotated data in a supervised manner, while entirely ignoring the unannotated data, and 2) directly learning to predict morph boundaries given their local sub-string contexts instead of learning the morph lexicons. Specifically, we employ conditional random fields, a popular discriminative log-linear model for segmentation. We present experiments on two data sets comprising five diverse languages. We show that the fully supervised boundary prediction approach outperforms the state-of-art semi-supervised morph lexicon approaches on all languages when using the same annotated data sets.

1 Introduction

Modern natural language processing (NLP) applications, such as speech recognition, information retrieval and machine translation, perform their tasks using statistical language models. For morphologically rich languages, estimation of the language models is problematic due to the high number of compound words and inflected word forms. A successful means of alleviating this data sparsity problem is to segment words into meaning-bearing sub-word units (Hirsimäki et al., 2006; Creutz et al., 2007; Turunen and Kurimo, 2011). In linguistics, the smallest meaning-bearing units of a language are called *morphemes* and their surface forms *morphs*. Thus, morphs are natural targets for the segmentation.

For most languages, existing resources contain large amounts of raw unannotated text data, only small amounts of manually prepared annotated training data, and no freely available rule-based morphological analyzers. The focus of our work is on performing morphological segmentation in this low-resource scenario. Given this setting, the current state-of-art methods approach the problem by learning *morph lexicons* from both annotated and unannotated data using *semi-supervised* machine learning techniques (Poon et al., 2009; Kohonen et al., 2010). Subsequent to model training, the methods uncover morph boundaries for new word forms by *generating* their most likely morph sequences according to the morph lexicons.

In contrast to learning morph lexicons (Poon et al., 2009; Kohonen et al., 2010), we study morphological segmentation by learning to directly predict *morph boundaries* based on their local substring contexts. Specifically, we apply the linear-chain conditional random field model, a popular *discriminative* log-linear model for segmentation presented originally by Lafferty et al. (2001). Importantly, we learn the segmentation model from solely the small annotated data in a *supervised* manner, while entirely ignoring the unannotated data. Despite not using the unannotated data, we show that by discriminatively learning to predict the morph boundaries, we are able to outperform the previous state-of-art.

We present experiments on Arabic and Hebrew using the data set presented originally by Snyder and Barzilay (2008), and on English, Finnish and

Turkish using the Morpho Challenge 2009/2010 data sets (Kurimo et al., 2009; Kurimo et al., 2010). The results are compared against two state-of-art techniques, namely the log-linear modeling approach presented by Poon et al. (2009) and the semi-supervised Morfessor algorithm (Kohonen et al., 2010). We show that when employing the same small amount of annotated training data, the CRF-based boundary prediction approach outperforms these reference methods on all languages. Additionally, since the CRF model learns from solely the small annotated data set, its training is computationally much less demanding compared to the semi-supervised methods, which utilize both the annotated and the unannotated data sets.

The rest of the paper is organized as follows. In Section 2, we discuss related work in morphological segmentation and methodology. In Section 3, we describe our segmentation method. Our experimental setup is described in Section 4, and the obtained results are presented in Section 5. In Section 6, we discuss the method and the results. Finally, we present conclusions on the work in Section 7.

2 Related work

The CRF model has been widely used in NLP segmentation tasks, such as shallow parsing (Sha and Pereira, 2003), named entity recognition (McCallum and Li, 2003), and word segmentation (Zhao et al., 2006). Recently, CRFs were also employed successfully in morphological segmentation for Arabic by Green and DeNero (2012) as a component of an English to Arabic machine translation system. While the segmentation method of Green and DeNero (2012) and ours is very similar, our focuses and contributions differ in several ways. First, while in our work we consider the low-resource learning setting, in which a small annotated data set is available (up to 3,130 word types), their model is trained on the Arabic Treebank (Maamouri et al., 2004) constituting several times larger training set (588,244 word tokens). Second, we present empirical comparison between the CRF approach and two state-of-art methods (Poon et al., 2009; Kohonen et al., 2010) on five diverse languages. Third, due to being a component of a larger system, their presentation on the method and experiments is rather underspeficied, while here we are able to provide a more thorough description.

In the experimental section, we compare the CRF-based segmentation approach with two state-of-art methods, the log-linear modeling approach presented by Poon et al. (2009) and the semi-supervised Morfessor algorithm (Kohonen et al., 2010). As stated previously, the CRF-based segmentation approach differs from these methods in that it learns to predict morph boundaries from a small amount of annotated data, in contrast to learning morph lexicons from both annotated and large amounts of unannotated data.

Lastly, there exists ample work on varying unsupervised (and semi-supervised) morphological segmentation methods. A useful review is given by Hammarström and Borin (2011). The fundamental difference between our approach and these techniques is that our method necessarily requires manually annotated training data.

3 Methods

In this section, we describe in detail the CRF-based approach for supervised morphological segmentation.

3.1 Morphological segmentation as a classification task

We represent the morphological segmentation task as a structured classification problem by assigning each character to one of four classes, namely {*beginning of a multi-character morph (B), middle of a multi-character morph (M), end of a multi-character morph (E), single character morph (S)*}. For example, consider the English word form

drivers

with a corresponding segmentation

driv + er + s .

Using the classification notation, this segmentation is represented as

START	B	M	M	E	B	E	S	STOP
<w>	d	r	i	v	e	r	s	</w>

where we have assumed additional word start and end markers *<w>* and *</w>* with respective classes *START* and *STOP*. As another example, consider the Finnish word form

autoilla (with cars)

with a corresponding segmentation

auto + i + lla .

Using the classification notation, this segmentation is represented as

START	B	M	M	E	S	B	M	E	STOP
<w>	a	u	t	o	i	l	l	a	</w>

Intuitively, instead of the four class set {B, M, E, S}, a segmentation could be accomplished using only a set of two classes {B, M} as in (Green and DeNero, 2012). However, similarly to Chinese word segmentation (Zhao et al., 2006), our preliminary experiments suggested that using the more fine-grained four class set {B, M, E, S} performed slightly better. This result indicates that morph segments of differerent lengths behave differently.

3.2 Linear-chain conditional random fields

We perform the above structured classification using linear-chain conditional random fields (CRFs), a discriminative log-linear model for tagging and segmentation (Lafferty et al., 2001). The central idea of the linear-chain CRF is to exploit the dependencies between the output variables using a chain structured undirected graph, also referred to as a Markov random field, while conditioning the output globally on the observation.

Formally, the model for input $\boldsymbol{x}$ (characters in a word) and output $\boldsymbol{y}$ (classes corresponding to characters) is written as

$$p\left(\boldsymbol{y} \,|\, \boldsymbol{x}; \boldsymbol{w}\right) \propto \prod_{t=2}^{T} \exp\left(\boldsymbol{w}^{\top} \boldsymbol{f}(y_{t-1}, y_t, \boldsymbol{x}, t)\right), \quad (1)$$

where t indexes the characters, T denotes word length, $\boldsymbol{w}$ the model parameter vector, and $\boldsymbol{f}$ the vector-valued feature extracting function.

The purpose of the feature extraction function $\boldsymbol{f}$ is to capture the co-occurrence behavior of the tag transitions (y_{t-1}, y_t) and a set of features describing character position t of word form $\boldsymbol{x}$. The strength of the CRF model lies in its capability to utilize arbitrary, non-independent features.

3.3 Feature extraction

The quality of the segmentation depends heavily on the choice of features defined by the feature extraction function $\boldsymbol{f}$. We will next describe and motivate the feature set used in the experiments.

Our feature set consists of binary indicator functions describing the position t of word $\mathbf{x}$ using all left and right substrings up to a maximum length δ. For example, consider the problem of deciding if the letter *e* in the word *drivers* is preceded by a morph boundary. This decision is now based on the overlapping substrings to the left and right of this potential boundary position, that is {*v*, *iv*, *riv*, *driv*, *<w>driv*} and {*e*, *er*, *ers*, *ers</w>*}, respectively. The substrings to the left and right are considered independently. Naturally, if the maximum allowed substring length δ is less than five, the longest substrings are discarded accordingly. In general, the optimum δ depends on both the amount of available training data and the language.

In addition to the substring functions, we use a bias function which returns value 1 independent of the input $\boldsymbol{x}$. The bias and substring features are combined with all the possible tag transitions.

To motivate this choice of feature set, consider formulating an intuitive segmentation rule for the English words *talked*, *played* and *speed* with the correct segmentations *talk* + *ed*, *play* + *ed* and *speed*, respectively. Now, as a right context *ed* is generally a strong indicator of a boundary, one could first formulate a rule

position t is a segment boundary
if its right context is *ed*.

This rule would indeed correctly segment the words *talked* and *played*, but would incorrectly segment *speed* as *spe* + *ed*. This error can be resolved if the left contexts are utilized as inhibitors by expanding the above rule as

position t is a segment boundary
if its right context is *ed*
and the left context is not *spe*.

Using the feature set defined above, the CRF model can learn to perform segmentation in this rule-like manner according to the training data. For example, using the above example words and segmentations for training, the CRFs could learn to assign a high score for a boundary given that the right context is *ed* and a high score for a non-boundary given the left context *spe*. Subsequent to training, making segmentation decisions for new word forms can then be interpreted as voting based on these scores.

3.4 Parameter estimation

The CRF model parameters $\boldsymbol{w}$ are estimated based on an annotated training data set. Common training criteria include the maximum likelihood (Lafferty et al., 2001; Peng et al., 2004; Zhao et al., 2006), averaged structured perceptron (Collins, 2002), and max-margin (Szummer et al., 2008). In this work, we estimate the parameters using the perceptron algorithm (Collins, 2002).

In perceptron training, the required graph inference can be efficiently performed using the standard Viterbi algorithm. Subsequent to training, the segmentations for test instances are acquired again using Viterbi search.

Compared to other training criteria, the structured perceptron has the advantage of employing only a single hyperparameter, namely the number of passes over training data, making model estimation fast and straightforward. We optimize the hyperparameter using a separate development set. Lastly, we consider the longest substring length δ a second hyperparameter optimized using the development set.

4 Experimental setup

This section describes the data sets, evaluation metrics, reference methods, and other details concerning the evaluation of the methods.

4.1 Data sets

We evaluate the methods on two different data sets comprising five languages in total.

S&B data. The first data set we use is the Hebrew Bible parallel corpus introduced by Snyder and Barzilay (2008). It contains 6,192 parallel phrases in Hebrew, Arabic, Aramaic, and English and their frequencies (ranging from 5 to 3517). The phrases have been extracted using automatic word alignment. The Hebrew and Arabic phrases have manually annotated morphological segmentations, and they are used in our experiments. The phrases are sorted according to frequency, and every fifth phrase starting from the first phrase is placed in the test set, every fifth starting from the second phrase in the development set (up to 500 phrases), and the rest of the phrases in the training set. [1] The total numbers of word types in the sets are shown in Table 1. Finally, the word forms in the training set are randomly permuted, and the first 25%, 50%, 75%, and 100% of them are selected as subsets to study the effect of training data size.

MC data. The second data set is based on the Morpho Challenge 2010 (Kurimo et al., 2010). It includes manually prepared morphological segmentations in English, Finnish and Turkish. The additional German corpus does not have segmentation annotation and is therefore excluded. The annotated data sets include training, development, and test sets for each language. Following Virpioja et al. (2011), the test set results are based on ten randomly selected 1,000 word sets. Moreover, we divide the annotated training sets into ten partitions with respective sizes of 100, 200, ..., 1000 words so that each partition is a subset of the all larger partitions. The data is divided so that the smallest set had every 10th word of the original set, the second set every 10th word and the following word, and so forth. For reference methods that require unannotated data, we use the English, Finnish and Turkish corpora from Competition 1 of Morpho Challenge 2009 (Kurimo et al., 2009). Table 2 shows the sizes of the MC data sets.

[1]We are grateful to Dr. Hoifung Poon for providing us instructions for dividing of the data set.

	Arabic	Hebrew
Training	3,130	2,770
Development	472	450
Test	1,107	1,040

Table 1: The numbers of word types in S&B data sets (Snyder and Barzilay, 2008).

	English	Finnish	Turkish
Unannot.	384,903	2,206,719	617,298
Training	1,000	1,000	1,000
Develop.	694	835	763
Test	10×1,000	10×1,000	10×1,000

Table 2: The numbers of word types in the MC data sets (Kurimo et al., 2009; Kurimo et al., 2010).

4.2 Evaluation measures

The word segmentations are evaluated by comparison with linguistic morphs using *precision*, *recall*, and *F-measure*. The F-measure equals the geometric mean of precision (the percentage of correctly assigned boundaries with respect to all assigned boundaries) and recall (the percentage of correctly assigned boundaries with respect to the reference boundaries). While using F-measure is a standard procedure, the prior work differ at least in three details: (1) whether precision and recall are calculated as *micro-average* over all segmentation points or as *macro-average* over all the word forms, (2) whether the evaluation is based on word *types* or word *tokens* in a corpus, and (3) if the reference segmentations have *alternative* correct choices for a single word type, and how to deal with them.

For the experiments with the S&B data sets, we follow Poon et al. (2009) and apply token-based micro-averages. For the experiments with the MC data sets, we follow Virpioja et al. (2011) and use type-based macro-averages. However, differing from their boundary measure, we take the best match over the alternative reference analyses (separately for precision and recall), since none of the methods considered here provide multiple segmentations per word type. For the models trained with the full training set, we also report the F-measures of the boundary evaluation method by Virpioja et al. (2011) in order to compare to the results reported in the Morpho Challenge website.

4.3 CRF feature extraction and training

The features included in the feature vector in the CRF model (1) are described in Section 3.3. We include all substring features which occur in the training data.

The CRF model is trained using the averaged perceptron algorithm as described in Section 3.4. The algorithm initializes the model parameters with zero vectors. The model performance, measured using F-measure, is evaluated on the development set after each pass over the training set, and the training is terminated when the performance has not improved during last 5 passes. The maximum length of substrings δ is optimized by considering $\delta = 1, 2, 3, \ldots$, and the search is terminated when the performance has not improved during last 5 values. Finally, the algorithm returns the parameters yielding the highest F-measure on the development set.

For some words, the MC training sets include several alternative segmentations. We resolve this ambiguity by using the first given alternative and discarding the rest. During evaluation, the alternative segmentations are taken into account as described in Section 4.2.

The experiments are run on a standard desktop computer using our own single-threaded Python-based implementation[2].

4.4 Reference methods

We compare our method's performance on Arabic and Hebrew data with semi-supervised Morfessor (Kohonen et al., 2010) and the results reported by Poon et al. (2009). On Finnish, English and Turkish data, we compare the method only with semi-supervised Morfessor as we have no implementation of the model by Poon et al. (2009).

We use a recently released Python implementation of semi-supervised Morfessor[3]. Semi-supervised Morfessor was trained separately for each training set size, always using the full unannotated data sets in addition to the annotated sets. The hyperparameters, the unannotated data weight α and the annotated data weight β, were optimized with a grid search on the development set. For the S&B data, there are no separate unannotated sets. When the annotated training set size is varied, the remaining parts are utilized as unannotated data.

The log-linear model described in (Poon et al., 2009) and the semi-supervised Morfessor algorithm are later referred to as POON-2009 and S-MORFESSOR for brevity.

5 Results

Method performances for Arabic and Hebrew on the S&B data are presented in Tables 3 and 4, respectively. The results for the POON-2009 model are extracted from (Poon et al., 2009). Performances for English, Finnish and Turkish on the MC data set are presented in Tables 5, 6 and 7, respectively.

On the Arabic and Hebrew data sets, the CRFs outperform POON-2009 and S-MORFESSOR substantially on all the considered data set sizes. On Finnish and Turkish data, the CRFs outperform S-MORFESSOR except for the smallest sets of 100 instances. On English data, the CRFs outperform S-MORFESSOR when the training set is 500 instances or larger.

Using our implementation of the CRF model, obtaining the results for Arabic, Hebrew, English, Finnish, and Turkish consumed 10, 11, 22, 32, and 28 minutes, respectively. These CPU times include model training and hyperparameter optimization. In comparison, S-MORFESSOR training is considerably slower. For Arabic and Hebrew, the S-MORFESSOR total training times were 24 and 22 minutes, respectively, and for English, Finnish, and Turkish 4, 22, and 10 days, respectively. The higher training times of S-MORFESSOR are partly because of the larger

[2]Available at http://users.ics.aalto.fi/tpruokol/

[3]Available at https://github.com/aalto-speech/morfessor

grids in hyperparameter optimization. Furthermore, the S-MORFESSOR training time for each grid point grows linearly with the size of the unannotated data set, resulting in particularly slow training on the MC data sets. All reported times are total CPU times for single-threaded runs, while in practice grid searches can be parallelized.

The perceptron algorithm typically converged after 10 passes over the training set, and never required more than 40 passes to terminate. Depending on the size of the training data, the optimized maximum lengths of substrings varied in ranges {3,5}, {2,7}, {3,9}, {3,6}, {3,7}, for Arabic, Hebrew, English, Finnish and Turkish, respectively.

Method	%Lbl.	Prec.	Rec.	F1
CRF	25	95.5	93.1	**94.3**
S-MORFESSOR	25	78.7	79.7	79.2
POON-2009	25	84.9	85.5	85.2
CRF	50	96.5	94.6	**95.5**
S-MORFESSOR	50	87.5	91.5	89.4
POON-2009	50	88.2	86.2	87.5
CRF	75	97.2	96.1	**96.6**
S-MORFESSOR	75	92.8	83.0	87.6
POON-2009	75	89.6	86.4	87.9
CRF	100	98.1	97.5	**97.8**
S-MORFESSOR	100	91.4	91.8	91.6
POON-2009	100	91.7	88.5	90.0

Table 3: Results for Arabic on the S&B data set (Snyder and Barzilay, 2008). The column titled *%Lbl.* denotes the percentage of the annotated data used for training. In addition to the given percentages of annotated data, POON-2009 and S-MORFESSOR utilized the remainder of the data as an unannotated set.

Finally, Table 8 shows the results of the CRF and S-MORFESSOR models trained with the full English, Finnish, and Turkish MC data sets and evaluated with the boundary evaluation method of Virpioja et al. (2011). That is, these numbers are directly comparable to the BPR-F column in the result tables presented at the Morpho Challenge website[4]. For each of the three languages, CRF clearly outperforms all the Morpho Challenge submissions that have provided morphological segmentations.

[4]`http://research.ics.aalto.fi/events/morphochallenge/`

Method	%Lbl.	Prec.	Rec.	F1
CRF	25	90.5	90.6	**90.6**
S-MORFESSOR	25	71.5	85.3	77.8
POON-2009	25	78.7	73.3	75.9
CRF	50	94.0	91.5	**92.7**
S-MORFESSOR	50	82.1	81.8	81.9
POON-2009	50	82.8	74.6	78.4
CRF	75	94.0	92.7	**93.4**
S-MORFESSOR	75	84.0	88.1	86.0
POON-2009	75	83.1	77.3	80.1
CRF	100	94.9	94.0	**94.5**
S-MORFESSOR	100	85.3	91.1	88.1
POON-2009	100	83.0	78.9	80.9

Table 4: Results for Hebrew on the S&B data set (Snyder and Barzilay, 2008). The column titled *%Lbl.* denotes the percentage of the annotated data used for training. In addition to the given percentages of annotated data, POON-2009 and S-MORFESSOR utilized the remainder of the data as an unannotated set.

6 Discussion

Intuitively, the CRF-based supervised learning approach should yield high segmentation accuracy when there are large amounts of annotated training data available. However, perhaps surprisingly, the CRF model yields state-of-art results already using very small amounts of training data. This result is meaningful since for most languages it is infeasible to acquire large amounts of annotated training data.

The strength of the discriminatively trained CRF model is that overlapping, non-independent features can be naturally employed. Importantly, we showed that simple, language-independent substring features are sufficient for high performance. However, adding new, task- and language-dependent features is also easy. One might, for example, explore features capturing vowel harmony in Finnish and Turkish.

The CRFs was estimated using the structured perceptron algorithm (Collins, 2002), which has the benefit of being computationally efficient and easy to implement. Other training criteria, such as maximum likelihood (Lafferty et al., 2001) or max-margin (Szummer et al., 2008), could also be employed. Similarly, other classifiers, such as the Maximum Entropy Markov Models (MEMMs) (McCallum et al., 2000), are applicable. However, as the amount of information in-

Method	Train.	Prec.	Rec.	F1
CRF	100	80.2	74.6	77.3
S-MORFESSOR	100	88.1	79.7	**83.7**
CRF	200	84.7	79.2	81.8
S-MORFESSOR	200	88.1	79.5	**83.6**
CRF	300	86.7	79.8	83.1
S-MORFESSOR	300	88.4	80.6	**84.3**
CRF	400	86.5	80.6	83.4
S-MORFESSOR	400	84.6	83.6	**84.1**
CRF	500	88.6	80.7	**84.5**
S-MORFESSOR	500	86.3	82.7	84.4
CRF	600	88.1	82.6	**85.3**
S-MORFESSOR	600	86.7	82.5	84.5
CRF	700	87.9	83.4	**85.6**
S-MORFESSOR	700	86.0	82.9	84.4
CRF	800	89.1	83.2	**86.1**
S-MORFESSOR	800	87.1	82.5	84.8
CRF	900	89.0	82.9	**85.8**
S-MORFESSOR	900	86.4	82.6	84.5
CRF	1000	89.8	83.5	**86.5**
S-MORFESSOR	1000	88.8	80.1	84.3

Table 5: Results for English on the Morpho Challenge 2009/2010 data set (Kurimo et al., 2009; Kurimo et al., 2010). The column titled *Train.* denotes the number of annotated training instances. In addition to the annotated data, S-MORFESSOR utilized an unannotated set of 384,903 word types.

Method	Train.	Prec.	Rec.	F1
CRF	100	71.4	66.0	68.6
S-MORFESSOR	100	69.8	71.0	**70.4**
CRF	200	76.4	71.3	**73.8**
S-MORFESSOR	200	75.5	68.6	71.9
CRF	300	80.4	73.9	**77.0**
S-MORFESSOR	300	73.1	71.8	72.5
CRF	400	81.0	76.6	**78.7**
S-MORFESSOR	400	73.3	74.3	73.8
CRF	500	82.9	77.9	**80.3**
S-MORFESSOR	500	73.5	75.1	74.3
CRF	600	82.6	80.6	**81.6**
S-MORFESSOR	600	76.1	73.7	74.9
CRF	700	84.3	81.4	**82.8**
S-MORFESSOR	700	75.0	76.6	75.8
CRF	800	85.1	83.4	**84.2**
S-MORFESSOR	800	74.1	78.2	76.1
CRF	900	85.2	83.8	**84.5**
S-MORFESSOR	900	74.2	78.5	76.3
CRF	1000	86.0	84.7	**85.3**
S-MORFESSOR	1000	74.2	78.8	76.4

Table 6: Results for Finnish on the Morpho Challenge 2009/2010 data set (Kurimo et al., 2009; Kurimo et al., 2010). The column titled *Train.* denotes the number of annotated training instances. In addition to the annotated data, S-MORFESSOR utilized an unannotated set of 2,206,719 word types.

corporated in the model would be unchanged, the choice of parameter estimation criterion and classifier is unlikely to have a dramatic effect on the method performance.

In CRF training, we focused on the supervised learning scenario, in which no unannotated data is exploited in addition to the annotated training sets. However, there does exist ample work on extending CRF training to the semi-supervised setting (for example, see Mann and McCallum (2008) and the references therein). Nevertheless, our results strongly suggest that it is crucial to use the few available annotated training instances as efficiently as possible before turning model training burdensome by incorporating large amounts of unannotated data.

Following previous work (Poon et al., 2009; Kohonen et al., 2010; Virpioja et al., 2011), we applied the boundary F-score evaluation measure, while Green and DeNero (2012) reported character accuracy. We consider the boundary F-score a better measure than accuracy, since the boundary-tag distribution is strongly skewed towards non-boundaries. Nevertheless, for completeness, we computed the character accuracy for our Arabic data set, obtaining the accuracy 99.1%, which is close to their reported accuracy of 98.6%. However, these values are not directly comparable due to our use of the Bible corpus by Snyder and Barzilay (2008) and their use of the Penn Arabic Treebank (Maamouri et al., 2004).

7 Conclusions

We have presented an empirical study in data-driven morphological segmentation employing supervised boundary prediction methodology. Specifically, we applied conditional random fields, a discriminative log-linear model for segmentation and tagging. From a methodological perspective, this approach differs from the previous state-of-art methods in two fundamental aspects. First, we utilize a discriminative model estimated using only annotated data. Second, we learn to predict morph

Method	Train.	Prec.	Rec.	F1
CRF	100	72.4	79.6	75.8
S-MORFESSOR	100	77.9	78.5	**78.2**
CRF	200	83.2	82.3	**82.8**
S-MORFESSOR	200	80.0	83.2	81.6
CRF	300	83.9	85.9	**84.9**
S-MORFESSOR	300	80.1	85.6	82.8
CRF	400	86.4	86.5	**86.4**
S-MORFESSOR	400	80.7	87.1	83.8
CRF	500	87.5	86.4	**87.0**
S-MORFESSOR	500	81.0	87.2	84.0
CRF	600	87.8	88.1	**87.9**
S-MORFESSOR	600	80.5	89.9	85.0
CRF	700	89.1	88.3	**88.7**
S-MORFESSOR	700	80.9	90.7	85.5
CRF	800	88.6	90.3	**89.4**
S-MORFESSOR	800	81.2	91.0	85.9
CRF	900	89.2	89.8	**89.5**
S-MORFESSOR	900	81.4	91.2	86.0
CRF	1000	89.9	90.4	**90.2**
S-MORFESSOR	1000	83.0	91.5	87.0

Table 7: Results for Turkish on the Morpho Challenge 2009/2010 data set (Kurimo et al., 2009; Kurimo et al., 2010). The column titled *Train.* denotes the number of annotated training instances. In addition to the annotated data, S-MORFESSOR utilized an unannotated set of 617,298 word types.

boundaries based on their local character substring contexts instead of learning a morph lexicon.

We showed that our supervised method yields improved results compared to previous state-of-art semi-supervised methods using the same small amount of annotated data, while not utilizing the unannotated data used by the reference methods. This result has two implications. First, supervised methods can provide excellent results in morphological segmentation already when there are only a few annotated training instances available. This is meaningful since for most languages it is infeasible to acquire large amounts of annotated training data. Second, performing morphological segmentation by directly modeling segment boundaries can be advantageous compared to modeling morph lexicons.

A potential direction for future work includes evaluating the morphs obtained by our method in real world applications, such as speech recognition and information retrieval. We are also interested in extending the method from fully supervised to semi-supervised learning.

Method	English	Finnish	Turkish
CRF	**82.0**	**81.9**	**71.5**
S-MORFESSOR	79.6	73.5	70.5

Table 8: F-measures of the Morpho Challenge boundary evaluation for CRF and S-MORFESSOR using the full annotated training data set.

Acknowledgements

This work was financially supported by Langnet (Finnish doctoral programme in language studies) and the Academy of Finland under the Finnish Centre of Excellence Program 2012–2017 (grant no. 251170), project *Multimodally grounded language technology* (no. 254104), and LASTU Programme (nos. 256887 and 259934).

References

M. Collins. 2002. Discriminative training methods for hidden markov models: Theory and experiments with perceptron algorithms. In *Proceedings of the 2002 Conference on Empirical Methods in Natural Language Processing (EMNLP 2002)*, volume 10, pages 1–8. Association for Computational Linguistics.

M. Creutz, T. Hirsimäki, M. Kurimo, A. Puurula, J. Pylkkönen, V. Siivola, M. Varjokallio, E. Arisoy, M. Saraçlar, and A Stolcke. 2007. Morph-based speech recognition and modeling of out-of-vocabulary words across languages. *ACM Transactions on Speech and Language Processing*, 5(1):3:1–3:29, December.

S. Green and J. DeNero. 2012. A class-based agreement model for generating accurately inflected translations. In *Proceedings of the 50th Annual Meeting of the Association for Computational Linguistics: Long Papers-Volume 1*, pages 146–155. Association for Computational Linguistics.

H. Hammarström and L. Borin. 2011. Unsupervised learning of morphology. *Computational Linguistics*, 37(2):309–350, June.

T. Hirsimäki, M. Creutz, V. Siivola, M. Kurimo, S. Virpioja, and J. Pylkkönen. 2006. Unlimited vocabulary speech recognition with morph language models applied to Finnish. *Computer Speech and Language*, 20(4):515–541, October.

O. Kohonen, S. Virpioja, and K. Lagus. 2010. Semi-supervised learning of concatenative morphology. In *Proceedings of the 11th Meeting of the ACL Special Interest Group on Computational Morphology and Phonology*, pages 78–86, Uppsala, Sweden, July. Association for Computational Linguistics.

M. Kurimo, S. Virpioja, V. Turunen, G. W. Blackwood, and W. Byrne. 2009. Overview and results of Morpho Challenge 2009. In *Working Notes for the CLEF 2009 Workshop*, Corfu, Greece, September.

M. Kurimo, S. Virpioja, and V. Turunen. 2010. Overview and results of Morpho Challenge 2010. In *Proceedings of the Morpho Challenge 2010 Workshop*, pages 7–24, Espoo, Finland, September. Aalto University School of Science and Technology, Department of Information and Computer Science. Technical Report TKK-ICS-R37.

J. Lafferty, A. McCallum, and F.C.N. Pereira. 2001. Conditional random fields: Probabilistic models for segmenting and labeling sequence data. In *Proceedings of the Eighteenth International Conference on Machine Learning*, pages 282–289.

M. Maamouri, A. Bies, T. Buckwalter, and W. Mekki. 2004. The penn arabic treebank: Building a large-scale annotated arabic corpus. In *NEMLAR Conference on Arabic Language Resources and Tools*, pages 102–109.

G. Mann and A. McCallum. 2008. Generalized expectation criteria for semi-supervised learning of conditional random fields. In *Proceedings of ACL-08: HLT*, pages 870–878. Association for Computational Linguistics.

A. McCallum and W. Li. 2003. Early results for named entity recognition with conditional random fields, feature induction and web-enhanced lexicons. In *Proceedings of the seventh conference on Natural language learning at HLT-NAACL 2003-Volume 4*, pages 188–191. Association for Computational Linguistics.

A. McCallum, D. Freitag, and F. Pereira. 2000. Maximum entropy Markov models for information extraction and segmentation. In Pat Langley, editor, *Proceedings of the Seventeenth International Conference on Machine Learning (ICML 2000)*, pages 591–598, Stanford, CA, USA. Morgan Kaufmann.

F. Peng, F. Feng, and A. McCallum. 2004. Chinese segmentation and new word detection using conditional random fields. In *Proceedings of the 20th International Conference on Computational Linguistics (COLING 2004)*, page 562. Association for Computational Linguistics.

H. Poon, C. Cherry, and K. Toutanova. 2009. Unsupervised morphological segmentation with log-linear models. In *Proceedings of Human Language Technologies: The 2009 Annual Conference of the North American Chapter of the Association for Computational Linguistics*, pages 209–217. Association for Computational Linguistics.

F. Sha and F. Pereira. 2003. Shallow parsing with conditional random fields. In *Proceedings of the 2003 Conference of the North American Chapter of the Association for Computational Linguistics on Human Language Technology-Volume 1*, pages 134–141. Association for Computational Linguistics.

B. Snyder and R. Barzilay. 2008. Crosslingual propagation for morphological analysis. In *Proceedings of the AAAI*, pages 848–854.

M. Szummer, P. Kohli, and D. Hoiem. 2008. Learning CRFs using graph cuts. *Computer Vision–ECCV 2008*, pages 582–595.

V. Turunen and M. Kurimo. 2011. Speech retrieval from unsegmented Finnish audio using statistical morpheme-like units for segmentation, recognition, and retrieval. *ACM Transactions on Speech and Language Processing*, 8(1):1:1–1:25, October.

S. Virpioja, V. Turunen, S. Spiegler, O. Kohonen, and M. Kurimo. 2011. Empirical comparison of evaluation methods for unsupervised learning of morphology. *Traitement Automatique des Langues*, 52(2):45–90.

H. Zhao, C.N. Huang, and M. Li. 2006. An improved chinese word segmentation system with conditional random field. In *Proceedings of the Fifth SIGHAN Workshop on Chinese Language Processing*, volume 1082117. Sydney: July.

Graph-Based Posterior Regularization for Semi-Supervised Structured Prediction

Luheng He **Jennifer Gillenwater**
Computer and Information Science
University of Pennsylvania
{luhe, jengi}@cis.upenn.edu

Ben Taskar
Computer Science and Engineering
University of Washington
taskar@cs.washington.edu

Abstract

We present a flexible formulation of semi-supervised learning for structured models, which seamlessly incorporates graph-based and more general supervision by extending the posterior regularization (PR) framework. Our extension allows for any regularizer that is a convex, differentiable function of the appropriate marginals. We show that surprisingly, non-linearity of such regularization does not increase the complexity of learning, provided we use multiplicative updates of the structured exponentiated gradient algorithm. We illustrate the extended framework by learning conditional random fields (CRFs) with quadratic penalties arising from a graph Laplacian. On sequential prediction tasks of handwriting recognition and part-of-speech (POS) tagging, our method makes significant gains over strong baselines.

1 Introduction

Recent success of graph-based semi-supervised learning builds on access to plentiful unsupervised data and accurate similarity measures between data examples (Zhu et al., 2003; Joachims, 2003; Belkin et al., 2005; Zhu and Lafferty, 2005; Altun et al., 2005; Zhu, 2005; Chapelle et al., 2006; Subramanya and Bilmes, 2009; Subramanya et al., 2010; Das and Petrov, 2011). Many approaches, such as Joachims (2003) and Subramanya and Bilmes (2009) use graph-based learning in the transductive setting, where unlabeled examples are classified without learning a parametric predictive model. While predicted labels can then be leveraged to learn such a model (e.g. a CRF), this pipelined approach misses out on the benefits of modeling sequential correlations *during* graph propagation. In this work we seek to better integrate graph propagation with estimation of a structured, parametric predictive model.

To do so, we build on the posterior regularization (PR) framework of Ganchev et al. (2010). PR is a principled means of providing weak supervision during structured model estimation. More concretely, PR introduces a penalty whenever the model's posteriors over latent variables contradict the specified weak supervision. Ganchev et al. (2010) show how to efficiently optimize a likelihood-plus-posterior-penalty type objective in the case where the penalty is linear in the model's marginals. Yet, there are many forms of supervision that cannot be expressed as a linear function of marginals. For example, graph Laplacian regularization. In this work, we extend PR to allow for penalties expressed as any convex, differentiable function of the marginals and derive an efficient optimization method for such penalties.

In our experiments, we explore graph Laplacian posterior regularizers for two applications: handwriting recognition and POS tagging. The methods of Altun et al. (2005), Subramanya et al. (2010), and Das and Petrov (2011) are the most closely related to this work. Altun et al. (2005) describes coupling a graph regularizer with a max-margin objective for pitch accent prediction and handwriting recognition tasks. Their method suffers from scalability issues though; it relies on optimization in the dual, which requires inversion of a matrix whose dimension grows with graph size.

The more recent work of Subramanya et al. (2010) tackles the POS tagging task and provides a more scalable method. Their method is a multi-step procedure that iterates two main steps, graph propagation and likelihood optimization, until convergence. Actually computing the optimum for the graph propagation step would require a matrix inversion similar to that used by Altun et al. (2005), but they skirt this issue by using an heuristic update rule. Unfortunately though, no guarantees for the quality of this update are established. Das and Petrov (2011) proceed very similarly, adapting the iterative procedure to include supervision from bi-text data, but applying the same heuristic update rule.

The work we present here similarly avoids the complexity of a large matrix inversion and iterates steps related to graph propagation and likelihood optimization. But in contrast to Subramanya et al. (2010) and Das and Petrov (2011) it comes with guarantees for the optimality of each step and convergence of the overall procedure. Further, our approach is based on optimizing a joint objective, which affords easier analysis and extensions using other constraints or optimization methods. The key enabling insight is a surprising factorization of the non-linear regularizer, which can be exploited using multiplicative updates.

2 Posterior regularization

We focus on the semi-supervised setting, showing how to extend the discriminative, penalty-based version of PR for a linear chain CRF. Our results apply more generally though to the unsupervised setting, the constraint-based versions of PR, and other graphical models.

In the standard semi-supervised setting we are given n data instances, $\{\boldsymbol{x}^1, \dots, \boldsymbol{x}^n\}$, and labels $\{\boldsymbol{y}^1, \dots, \boldsymbol{y}^l\}$ for the first $l \ll n$ instances. For simplicity of notation, we'll assume each $\boldsymbol{x}^i$ has T components. Modeling this data with a linear chain CRF, the standard conditional log-likelihood objective with a Gaussian prior (variance $\propto \sigma^2$) is:

$$\mathcal{L}(\theta) = \sum_{i=1}^{l} \log p_\theta(\boldsymbol{y}^i \mid \boldsymbol{x}^i) - \frac{||\boldsymbol{\theta}||_2^2}{2\sigma^2} . \quad (1)$$

Note that this discriminative objective does not attempt to leverage the unlabeled data. Since p_θ decomposes according to the independence assumptions of a linear chain CRF, it can be expressed as:

$$p_\theta(\boldsymbol{y} \mid \boldsymbol{x}) = \frac{\exp\left[\sum_{t=1}^{T} \boldsymbol{\theta}^\top \boldsymbol{f}(y_t, y_{t-1}, \boldsymbol{x})\right]}{Z_p(\boldsymbol{x})} \quad (2)$$

where the $Z_p(\boldsymbol{x})$ is a normalizer:

$$Z_p(\boldsymbol{x}) = \sum_{\boldsymbol{y}'} \exp\left[\sum_{t=1}^{T} \boldsymbol{\theta}^\top \boldsymbol{f}(y'_t, y'_{t-1}, \boldsymbol{x})\right] \quad (3)$$

and the $\boldsymbol{f}$ are arbitrary feature functions. We assume $\boldsymbol{f}(y_1, y_0, \boldsymbol{x})$ receives a special "start" marker for y_0. In what follows, we refer to functions over the $(y_t, y_{t-1}, \boldsymbol{x})$ as local factors, or *p-factors*; $p_\theta(\boldsymbol{y} \mid \boldsymbol{x})$ decomposes as a product of p-factors.

Given this decomposition, $\mathcal{L}$ and its gradient with respect to θ can be efficiently computed using the forward-backward algorithm for linear chains. This amounts to computing posterior marginals for each p-factor $(y_t, y_{t-1}, \boldsymbol{x})$. Following the gradient suffices to find the global optimum of $\mathcal{L}$, since likelihood is concave, and the Gaussian prior makes it strictly concave.

Penalty-based posterior regularization (PR) modifies the likelihood objective by adding a "penalty" term expressing prior knowledge about the posteriors (Ganchev et al., 2010). To allow for more efficient optimization, penalty terms are imposed on an auxiliary joint distribution q over the labels instead of directly on p_θ. Agreement between q and p_θ is encouraged by a KL term:

$$\mathbf{KL}(q \parallel p_\theta) = \sum_{i=1}^{n} \mathbf{KL}(q(\boldsymbol{Y} \mid \boldsymbol{x}^i) \parallel p_\theta(\boldsymbol{Y} \mid \boldsymbol{x}^i))$$

where $\boldsymbol{Y}$ is a random variable that can take on any possible labeling $\boldsymbol{y}$, and $q(\boldsymbol{Y}|\boldsymbol{x}^i)$ is a an arbitrary distribution over $\boldsymbol{Y}$ for each i[1]. The penalty term itself is restricted to be an essentially linear function of the p-factor marginals of $q(\boldsymbol{Y} \mid \boldsymbol{x}^i)$. To compactly express this, we first define some notation. Let $\boldsymbol{m}^i$ denote the p-factor marginals of $q(\boldsymbol{Y} \mid \boldsymbol{x}^i)$. For first-order linear chain models, if K is the total number of labels a y variable can take on, then $\boldsymbol{m}^i$ contains the marginals for $t \in \{1, \dots, T\}$ and all K^2 possible (y_t, y_{t-1}) label pairs. That is, $\boldsymbol{m}^i$ is a length $O(TK^2)$ vector with entries:

$$m^i_{t,k,j} = \sum_{\boldsymbol{y}} \mathbb{1}(y_t = k,\ y_{t-1} = j) q(\boldsymbol{y} \mid \boldsymbol{x}^i) . \quad (4)$$

Stacking all these $\boldsymbol{m}^i$, we let $\boldsymbol{m}$ represent the $O(nTK^2)$ vector $[\boldsymbol{m}^1, \dots, \boldsymbol{m}^n]$. We further define a matrix A of constraint features. The product $A\boldsymbol{m}$ is then the expectation of these features under q. Finally we have, with a vector $\boldsymbol{b}$ of limits, the following expression for the penalty term:

$$h_{lin}(\boldsymbol{m}) = ||\max(A\boldsymbol{m} - \boldsymbol{b}, \boldsymbol{0})||_\beta \quad (5)$$

where $||\cdot||_\beta$ denotes an arbitrary norm. This expression will be non-zero if the expected value of

[1] We use a notation that is slightly different than, but equivalent to, that of prior work, in order to facilitate our extensions later.

Am is larger than the limit b. The full posterior regularizer is then:

$$\mathcal{R}(\theta, q) = \mathbf{KL}(q \parallel p_\theta) + \lambda h_{lin}(\boldsymbol{m}) , \quad (6)$$

where λ is a hyperparameter that controls the strength of the second term.

> **Running example:** Consider the task of part-of-speech (POS) tagging, where the $\boldsymbol{y}$ are tags and the $\boldsymbol{x}$ are words. To encourage every sentence to contain at least one verb, we can penalize if the expected number of verbs under the q distribution is less than 1. Specifically, if "verb" is represented by tag number v, for sentence i we penalize unless:
>
> $$1 \leq \sum_{t=1}^{T} \sum_{y_{t-1}=1}^{K} m^i_{t,v,y_{t-1}} . \quad (7)$$
>
> In the notation of Equation (5), these penalties correspond to: an n-row A matrix, where row i has -1's to select exactly the portion of $\boldsymbol{m}$ from Equation (7), and a limit $\boldsymbol{b} = -\mathbf{1}$.

We briefly note here that generalized expectation (Mann and McCallum, 2007; Mann and McCallum, 2008) can be used to impose similar penalties, but without the auxiliary q distribution. Unfortunately though, this means the expectation of the A features is with respect to p_θ, so computing the gradient requires the covariance between the constraint features in A and the model features $\boldsymbol{f}$, under θ. For a linear chain CRF, this means the run time of forward-backward is squared, although some optimizations are possible. PR's use of the auxiliary q allows us to optimize more efficiently by splitting the problem into easier blocks.

The new objective that combines likelihood with the PR penalty is: $\mathcal{J}(\theta, q) = \mathcal{L}(\theta) - \mathcal{R}(\theta, q)$. While optimizing $\mathcal{L}(\theta)$ is easy, finding $\max_{\theta,q} \mathcal{J}(\theta, q)$ is NP-hard even for the simplest models. To optimize $\mathcal{J}$, Ganchev et al. (2010) employ an expectation maximization (EM) based method. At iteration $t+1$, the algorithm updates q and θ as follows:

$$\mathbf{E} : q^{t+1} = \arg\min_q \; \mathcal{R}(\theta^t, q) \quad (8)$$

$$\mathbf{M} : \theta^{t+1} = \arg\max_\theta \; \mathcal{L}(\theta) + \quad (9)$$

$$\delta \sum_{i=l+1}^{n} \sum_{\boldsymbol{y}} q^{t+1}(\boldsymbol{y} \mid \boldsymbol{x}^i) \log p_\theta(\boldsymbol{y} \mid \boldsymbol{x}^i)$$

where δ here is a hyperparameter that trades off between the labeled and unlabeled data. Though not stated above, note that in the E-step minimization over $q(\boldsymbol{Y} \mid \boldsymbol{x}^i)$ is constrained to the probability simplex. Ganchev et al. (2010) show that this E-step can be efficiently implemented, via projected gradient descent on the dual. The M-step is similar to optimizing the original $\mathcal{L}$, but with a contribution from the unlabeled data that further encourages q and p_θ to agree. Thus, the M-step can be implemented via the same gradient ascent methods as used for $\mathcal{L}$. As with standard EM, this method monotonically increases $\mathcal{J}$ and thus is guaranteed to converge to a local optimum.

In this work, we contemplate what other types of posterior penalty terms besides $h_{lin}(\boldsymbol{m})$ are possible. In the subsequent section, we show that it is possible to extend the class of efficiently-optimizable PR penalties to encompass all convex, differentiable functions of the marginals.

3 Non-linear PR

Let $h(\boldsymbol{m})$ denote an arbitrary convex, differentiable function of the marginals of q. Replacing $\mathcal{R}$'s penalty term with h, we have:

$$\tilde{R}(\theta, q) = \mathbf{KL}(q \parallel p_\theta) + \lambda h(\boldsymbol{m}) \quad (10)$$

Let $\tilde{\mathcal{J}}$ represent the full objective with $\tilde{R}$. We show that $\tilde{\mathcal{J}}$ can be efficiently optimized.

> **Running example:** Returning to our POS tagging example, let's consider one type of non-linear convex penalty that might be useful. Suppose our corpus has N unique trigrams, and we construct a graph $G = (V, E, W)$ where each vertex in V is a trigram and each edge $(a, b) \in E$ has a weight w_{ab} that indicates the similarity of trigrams a and b. To use the information from this graph to inform our CRF, we can use the graph Laplacian: $L = D - W$, where D is a diagonal degree matrix with $d_{aa} = \sum_{j=1}^{N} w_{aj}$. The form of L is such that for every vector $\boldsymbol{v} \in \mathbb{R}^N$:
>
> $$\boldsymbol{v}^\top L \boldsymbol{v} = \frac{1}{2} \sum_{a=1}^{N} \sum_{b=1}^{N} w_{ab}(v_a - v_b)^2 . \quad (11)$$
>
> The larger the disparity in $\boldsymbol{v}$ values of similar vertices, the larger the value of $\boldsymbol{v}^\top L \boldsymbol{v}$. The matrix L is positive semi-definite, so $\boldsymbol{v}^\top L \boldsymbol{v}$ is

convex in $\boldsymbol{v}$. If each entry v_a is a linear function of the vector of marginals $\boldsymbol{m}$ described above, then $\boldsymbol{v}(\boldsymbol{m})^\top L \boldsymbol{v}(\boldsymbol{m})$ is convex in $\boldsymbol{m}$. Thus, for any linear $\boldsymbol{v}(\boldsymbol{m})$, we can use this Laplacian expression as a PR penalty.

For example, we can define $\boldsymbol{v}(\boldsymbol{m})$ such that $h(\boldsymbol{m})$ applies a penalty if trigrams that are similar according to the graph have different expected taggings under the CRF model. To state this more formally, let's define a mapping $B : (\{1, \ldots, n\}, \{1, \ldots, T\}) \mapsto V$ from words in the corpus to vertices in the graph: $B(i, t) = a$ implies word x_t^i maps to vertex a. Then, for a given tag k, we have the following formula for the value of vertex a:

$$v_{a,k} = \tilde{m}_{a,k} = \frac{\sum\limits_{i=1}^{n} \sum\limits_{\substack{t=1 \\ B(i,t)=a}}^{T} \sum\limits_{y_{t-1}=1}^{K} m^i_{t,k,y_{t-1}}}{\sum_{i=1}^{n} \sum_{t=1}^{T} \mathbb{1}(B(i,t) = a)}$$

There are several issues to overcome in showing that EM with these more general $h(\boldsymbol{m})$ can still be run efficiently and will still reach a local optimum. First, we have to show that the optimal q for the E-step minimization can still be compactly representable as a product of p-factors.

3.1 Decomposition

Theorem 1. *If $h(\boldsymbol{m})$ is a convex, differentiable function of q's p-factor marginals, $q^* = \arg\min_q \tilde{\mathcal{R}}(\theta, q)$ decomposes as a product of p-factors.*

Proof. Consider the E-step gradient of $\tilde{R}(\theta, q)$ with respect to q. Using the shorthand $q^i_{\boldsymbol{y}}$ for $q(\boldsymbol{y} \mid \boldsymbol{x}^i)$, the gradient is:

$$\frac{\partial \tilde{\mathcal{R}}}{\partial q^i_{\boldsymbol{y}}} = \log q^i_{\boldsymbol{y}} + 1 - \log p_\theta(\boldsymbol{y} \mid \boldsymbol{x}^i) + \lambda \frac{\partial h(\boldsymbol{m})}{\partial \boldsymbol{m}}^\top \frac{\partial \boldsymbol{m}}{\partial q^i_{\boldsymbol{y}}} . \quad (12)$$

Here, $\frac{\partial \boldsymbol{m}}{\partial q^i_{\boldsymbol{y}}}$ is just a 0-1 vector indicating which of the marginals from $\boldsymbol{m}$ apply to $q^i_{\boldsymbol{y}}$. For example, for $y_t = k$ and $y_{t-1} = j$, the marginal $m^i_{t,k,j}$ is relevant. We can more simply write:

$$\frac{\partial h(\boldsymbol{m})}{\partial \boldsymbol{m}}^\top \frac{\partial \boldsymbol{m}}{\partial q^i_{\boldsymbol{y}}} = \sum_{t=1}^{T} \frac{\partial h(\boldsymbol{m})}{\partial m^i_{t,y_t,y_{t-1}}} . \quad (13)$$

Setting the gradient equal to zero and solving for $q^i_{\boldsymbol{y}}$, we see that it must take the following form:

$$q^i_{\boldsymbol{y}} = \frac{p_\theta(\boldsymbol{y} \mid \boldsymbol{x}^i) \exp\left[-\lambda \sum\limits_{t=1}^{T} \frac{\partial h(\boldsymbol{m})}{\partial m^i_{t,y_t,y_{t-1}}}\right]}{Z_q(\boldsymbol{x}^i)} . \quad (14)$$

From this expression, it is clear that $q^i_{\boldsymbol{y}}$ is proportional to a product of p-factors. □

Running example: Recall the graph Laplacian penalty, discussed above for a particular tag k. Summing over all tags, the penalty is:

$$h(\boldsymbol{m}) = \frac{1}{2} \sum_{k=1}^{K} \sum_{a=1}^{N} \sum_{b=1}^{N} w_{ab} (\tilde{m}_{a,k} - \tilde{m}_{b,k})^2 .$$

The derivative $\frac{\partial h(\boldsymbol{m})}{\partial m^i_{t,y_t,y_{t-1}}}$ is then:

$$2 \sum_{k=1}^{K} \sum_{a=1}^{N} w_{a,B(i,t)} (\tilde{m}_{B(i,t),k} - \tilde{m}_{a,k}) . \quad (15)$$

In words: for a given k, this gradient is positive if node $B(i, t)$ has larger probability of taking tag k than its close neighbors. Moving in the direction opposite the gradient encourages similar taggings for similar trigrams.

Theorem 1 confirms that the optimal q will decompose as desired, but does not address whether we can efficiently find this q. Previous PR work optimized the E-step in the dual. But while the dual is easy to compute in closed form for norms or linear functions, for arbitrary convex functions the dual is often non-trivial.

Running example: For the case of a graph Laplacian regularizer, in the primal the penalty takes the form of a quadratic program: $\boldsymbol{v}^\top L \boldsymbol{v}$. Unfortunately, the dual of a quadratic program contains a matrix inverse, L^{-1} (van de Panne and Whinston, 1964). Taking a matrix inverse is expensive, which makes optimization in the dual unattractive.

Since moving to the dual would be inefficient, optimizing $\tilde{R}$ will require some form of gradient descent on the $q^i_{\boldsymbol{y}}$. However, the standard gradient descent update:

$$q^i_{\boldsymbol{y}} \leftarrow q^i_{\boldsymbol{y}} - \eta \frac{\partial \tilde{\mathcal{R}}}{\partial q^i_{\boldsymbol{y}}} \quad (16)$$

where η is the step size, does not result in a feasible optimization scheme, for several reasons. First, it is possible for the updated q to be outside the probability simplex. To be sure it remains in the simplex would require a projection step on the full, exponential-size set of all $q^i_{\boldsymbol{y}}$, for each example $\boldsymbol{x}^i$. Second, the updated q may not be proportional to a product of p-factors. To be concrete, suppose the starting point is $q^i_{\boldsymbol{y}} = p_\theta(\boldsymbol{y} \mid \boldsymbol{x}^i)$, which does decompose as a product of p-factors. Then after the first gradient update, we have:

$$q^i_{\boldsymbol{y}} = p_\theta(\boldsymbol{y} \mid \boldsymbol{x}^i) - \eta \left(1 + \lambda \sum_{t=1}^{T} \frac{\partial h(\boldsymbol{m})}{\partial m^i_{t,y_t,y_{t-1}}} \right).$$

Unfortunately, while $p_\theta(\boldsymbol{y} \mid \boldsymbol{x}^i)$ decomposes as a product of p-factors, the other term decomposes as a sum. Naturally, as we discuss in the following section, multiplicative updates are more suitable.

3.2 Exponentiated Gradient

The exponentiated gradient descent (EGD) algorithm was proposed by Kivinen and Warmuth (1995), who illustrate its application to linear prediction. More recently, Collins et al. (2005) and Collins et al. (2008) extended EGD to exploit factorization in structured models. The most important aspect of EGD for us is that a variable's update formula takes a multiplicative rather than an additive form. Specifically, the update for $q^i_{\boldsymbol{y}}$ is:

$$q^i_{\boldsymbol{y}} \leftarrow q^i_{\boldsymbol{y}} \exp\left[-\eta \frac{\partial \tilde{\mathcal{R}}}{\partial q^i_{\boldsymbol{y}}} \right]. \quad (17)$$

Lemma 2. *EGD update Equation (17) preserves decomposition of q into p-factors.*

Proof. Applying the multiplicative EGD update formula to $q^i_{\boldsymbol{y}}$, we see that its new value equals the following product:

$$(q^i_{\boldsymbol{y}})^{1-\eta} p_\theta(\boldsymbol{y} \mid \boldsymbol{x}^i)^\eta \exp\left[-\eta\lambda \sum_{t=1}^{T} \frac{\partial h(\boldsymbol{m})}{\partial m^i_{t,y_t,y_{t-1}}} \right],$$

up to a normalization constant. Since $q^i_{\boldsymbol{y}}$ and $p_\theta(\boldsymbol{y} \mid \boldsymbol{x}^i)$ both decompose as a product of p-factors and since the update term is another product of p-factors, the updated expression is itself a product of p-factors (up to normalization). □

Note that normalization is not an issue with the EGD updates. Since q retains its decomposition, the normalization can be efficiently computed using forward-backward. Thus, Lemma 2 moves us much closer to the goal of running EM efficiently, though there remain several stumbling blocks. First and foremost, we cannot afford to actually apply EGD to each $q^i_{\boldsymbol{y}}$, as there are an exponential number of them. Thankfully, we can show these EGD updates are equivalent to following the gradient on a much smaller set of values. In particular, letting F represent the dimension of $\boldsymbol{m}$, which for example is $O(nTK^2)$ for linear chains, we have the following result.

Lemma 3. *Given the gradient vector $\frac{\partial h(\boldsymbol{m})}{\partial \boldsymbol{m}}$, one step of EGD on $\tilde{\mathcal{R}}(\theta, q)$ can be completed in time $O(F)$, where F is the dimension of $\boldsymbol{m}$.*

Proof. First, we re-express $q^i_{\boldsymbol{y}}$ in log-linear form. Applying Lemma 2, we know that $q^i_{\boldsymbol{y}}$ is proportional to a product of p-factors This means that there must exist some factors r such that $q^i_{\boldsymbol{y}}$ can be written:

$$q^i_{\boldsymbol{y}} = \frac{1}{Z_q(\boldsymbol{x}^i)} \exp\left[\sum_{t=1}^{T} r_{i,t}(y_t, y_{t-1}) \right]. \quad (18)$$

Re-expressing $\frac{\partial \tilde{\mathcal{R}}}{\partial q^i_{\boldsymbol{y}}}$ given these r, we have:

$$\frac{\partial \tilde{\mathcal{R}}}{\partial q^i_{\boldsymbol{y}}} = C + \sum_{t=1}^{T} \Bigg[r_{i,t}(y_t, y_{t-1}) - \quad (19)$$
$$\boldsymbol{\theta}^\top \boldsymbol{f}(y_t, y_{t-1}, \boldsymbol{x}^i) + \lambda \frac{\partial h(\boldsymbol{m})}{\partial m^i_{t,y_t,y_{t-1}}} \Bigg],$$

where $C = 1 - \log Z_q(\boldsymbol{x}^i) + \log Z_p(\boldsymbol{x}^i)$ is constant with respect to $\boldsymbol{y}$. This means that we can just update the individual r factors as follows:

$$r_{i,t}(y_t, y_{t-1}) \leftarrow (1-\eta) r_{i,t}(y_t, y_{t-1}) +$$
$$\eta \boldsymbol{\theta}^\top \boldsymbol{f}(y_t, y_{t-1}, \boldsymbol{x}^i) - \eta\lambda \frac{\partial h(\boldsymbol{m})}{\partial m^i_{t,y_t,y_{t-1}}}. \quad (20)$$

Note that if we start from $q^i_{\boldsymbol{y}} = p_\theta(\boldsymbol{y} \mid x^i)$, then the initial $r_{i,t}(y_t, y_{t-1})$ are just $\boldsymbol{\theta}^\top \boldsymbol{f}(y_t, y_{t-1}, \boldsymbol{x}^i)$. To conclude, since the number of r functions is equal to the dimension of $\boldsymbol{m}$, the overall update is linear in the number of marginals. □

At this point, just one small issue remains: how expensive is computing $\frac{\partial h(\boldsymbol{m})}{\partial \boldsymbol{m}}$? Work analyzing the reverse mode of automatic differentiation indicates that if computing a function h requires c operations, then computing its gradient vector requires no more than $O(c)$ operations (Griewank, 1988). Thus, as long as our penalty function is itself efficiently computable, the gradient vector will be too. We conclude by observing that our efficient algorithm converges to a local optimum.

Theorem 4. *The above EGD-based EM algorithm for optimizing $\tilde{\mathcal{J}}(\theta, q)$ converges to a local optimum of this objective.*

Proof. The M-step remains unchanged from standard PR EM, and as such is strictly convex in θ. The E-step is strictly convex in q, since KL-divergence is strictly convex and $h(\boldsymbol{m})$ is convex. Applying EGD, we know that we can efficiently find the E-step optimum. Therefore, the EGD-based EM algorithm efficiently implements coordinate ascent on $\tilde{\mathcal{J}}(\theta, q)$, with each step monotonically increasing $\tilde{\mathcal{J}}$:

$$\tilde{\mathcal{J}}(\theta^t, q^t) \leq \tilde{\mathcal{J}}(\theta^t, q^{t+1}) \leq \tilde{\mathcal{J}}(\theta^{t+1}, q^{t+1}) \,.$$

□

Hence, we have shown that it is possible to efficiently use an arbitrary convex, differentiable function of the marginals, $h(\boldsymbol{m})$, as a PR penalty function. In the following section, we apply one such function — the graph Laplacian quadratic from the running example — to several tasks.

4 Experiments

We evaluate the effect of a graph Laplacian PR penalty on two different sequence prediction tasks: part-of-speech (POS) tagging and handwriting recognition. Our experiments are conducted in a semi-supervised setting, where only a small number, l, of labeled sequences are available during training. Both the l labeled sequences and the remainder of the dataset (instances $l + 1$ through n) are used to construct a graph Laplacian[2]. We train a second-order CRF using the methods described in Section 3 and report results for a test set consisting of instances $l + 1$ through n.

4.1 Graph construction

For each task we define a symmetric similarity function on the task's vertices V, $\text{sim} : V \times V \mapsto \mathbb{R}$, and build the graph based on its values. Specifically, denoting the k nearest neighbors (NN) of node u by $\mathcal{N}_k(u)$, we use the following mutual k-NN criterion to decide which edges to include:

$$(u, v) \in E \iff u \in \mathcal{N}_k(v) \ \wedge \ v \in \mathcal{N}_k(u) \,.$$

[2]While these particular experiments are transductive, our method can easily be applied inductively as well.

Entries in the final edge weight matrix are: $w_{uv} = \mathbb{1}[(u, v) \in E]\text{sim}(u, v)$.

4.2 Part-of-speech tagging

We experiment on ten languages. Our English (EN) data is from the Penn Treebank (Marcus et al., 1993), Italian (IT) and Greek (EL) are from CoNLL-2007 (Nivre et al., 2007), and the remaining languages in Figure 1 (a): German (DE), Spanish (ES), Portuguese (PT), Danish (DA), Slovene (SL), Swedish (SV), and Dutch (NL) are from CoNLL-X (Buchholz and Marsi, 2006). We use a universal tag set (Das et al., 2012) throughout.

For each language, we first construct a mutual 60-NN graph[3] on trigram types, excluding trigrams whose center word is punctuation. Our smallest graph (Slovene) contains 25,198 nodes while the largest (English) has 611,730.

For the similarity function $\text{sim}(u, v)$, we follow the method used in (Subramanya et al., 2010) and (Das and Petrov, 2011), but with a somewhat modified feature set. For instance, while (Subramanya et al., 2010) uses suffixes of the trigram's center word, we find this type of feature is too easy for unrelated trigrams to match, leading to a noisy graph. Let a trigram and its left/right context be denoted by the 5-gram $(w_0, w_1, w_2, w_3, w_4)$. Then the features we use to build the graph are:

- Trigram features: w_{12}, w_{13}, w_{23}, w_2, $\text{suffix}(w_3)w_2$, $\text{suffix}(w_1)w_2$
- Context features: w_{0134}, w_{012}, w_{023}, w_{024}, w_{124}, w_{234}, w_{01}, w_{02}, w_{24}, w_{34}

where suffix indicates common suffixes collected from Wiktionary data. For a given feature f and trigram type t, the value of the feature is determined by pointwise mutual information (PMI): $\log \frac{\#(f \wedge t)}{\#(f)\#(t)}$. Then, for each pair of trigram types, $\text{sim}(u, v)$ is given by the cosine similarity of the trigrams' feature vectors.

For the second-order CRF, we use a fairly standard set of features:

- Emission features: $\mathbb{1}(y_t = k \ \wedge \ f(x_{t'}))$, where k can be any POS tag and $t' \in \{t, t - 1, t + 1\}$. The $f(x_{t'})$ takes the form of a function from the following set: one indicator for each word, lowercased word, and suf-

[3]In preliminary experiments we tested graphs with 20, 40, 60, 80, and 100 NNs and found that beyond 60 NNs additional performance gains are small.

fix, and also is-capitalized, is-punctuation, is-digit, contains-hyphen, and contains-period.

- Transition features: For any POS tags k_1, k_2, k_3, we have a feature $\mathbb{1}(y_t = k_1, y_{t-1} = k_2, y_{t+1} = k_3)$ and its backoffs (indicators for one or two matching tags).

4.3 Handwriting recognition

The handwriting dataset we use was collected by Kassel (1995) and filtered to 6,877 words (Taskar et al., 2003). For each word, the first letter is removed so that every remaining letter is one of the English language's 26 lowercase letters.

Again, we first build a mutual NN graph. In this case, we use 20-NN, since our graph has fewer nodes and a larger set of possible node identities (26 letters instead of 12 tags). Each node in this graph is one letter from the dataset, for a total of 52,152 nodes. As a first step, we compute cosine similarity on the pixels of each pair of nodes, and then consider only pairs with a similarity greater than 0.3. Next, we apply the Fast Earth Mover's distance $\widehat{\text{EMD}}(u, v)$ (Pele and Werman, 2009) with default parameters to compute the dissimilarity of each pair of images. We convert these into similarities via:

$$s(u, v) = \exp\left\{\frac{-\widehat{\text{EMD}}(u, v)}{\sigma^2_{EMD}}\right\} \tag{21}$$

where we set the variance $\sigma_{EMD} = 10$. The final similarity function $\text{sim}(u, v)$ is the weighted combination of the similarity of the nodes (u, v) and their left neighbors (u_l, v_l) and right neighbors (u_r, v_r) from their respective words:

$$\text{sim}(u, v) = \alpha s(u, v) + (1-\alpha)(s(u_l, v_l) + s(u_r, v_r))$$

where we fix $\alpha = 0.8$.

For the second-order CRF, the transition features are same as for POS tagging, but with tags replaced by the English alphabet. The emission features take a similar form, but with different meanings for the $f(x_{t'})$ indicator functions. Specifically, there is one indicator for each pixel location, with value 1 if the pixel is turned on. As there are many more emission than transition features, we count the number of fired emission and transition features, say f_e and f_t, then discount all emission features, multiplying them by $\frac{f_t}{f_e}$ to balance the amount of supervision.

4.4 Baselines

We compare our posterior regularization (PR) results with three baselines. We also include results for the first EM iteration of our PR method (PR_1), to show there is still significant optimization occurring after the first iteration.

The first baseline is graph propagation (GP). Specifically, we start from uniform posteriors for all the unlabeled nodes in the graph, then for each tag/letter k and each node v we apply the gradient update:

$$q_{k,v} \leftarrow q_{k,v} - \eta \sum_{u \in \mathcal{N}_k(v)} w^k_{uv}(q_{k,v} - q_{k,u}) \tag{22}$$

until convergence. We then select the tag/letter with the largest probability as the prediction for a node. If multiple tokens are mapped to a node, then all receive the same prediction.

The second baseline incorporates both graph propagation and sequence information. As a first step, we run the GP baseline, then use the decoding as additional labeled data to train a second-order CRF (see GP→CRF results). The third baseline is simply a second-order CRF, trained on the l labeled examples.

4.5 Training details

For optimizing the CRF, we use L-BFGS (Bertsekas, 2004) and a Gaussian prior with $\sigma = 100$ (chosen by cross-validation on the labeled training examples). The final predictions are obtained via posterior decoding. For PR, we run EM for at most 20 iterations, which is enough for convergence of the combined objective $\tilde{\mathcal{J}}(\theta, q)$. We cross-validate the constraint strength parameter λ over the following values: $\{0.1, 0.5, 1.0, 2.0\}$, ultimately selecting $\lambda = 1$ for the POS tagging task and $\lambda = 0.1$ for the handwriting recognition task.

4.6 Results and analysis

POS tagging. For each language, we randomly sample 1000 labeled examples and split them into 10 non-overlapping training sets of size $l = 100$. Figure 1 (a) shows the average error and its standard deviation for these training sets. If for each language we take the difference between the average error of PR and that of the best of the three baselines, the min, average, and max improvements are: 2.69%, 4.06%, and 5.35%. When analyzing the results, we observed that one region where PR makes substantial gains over the

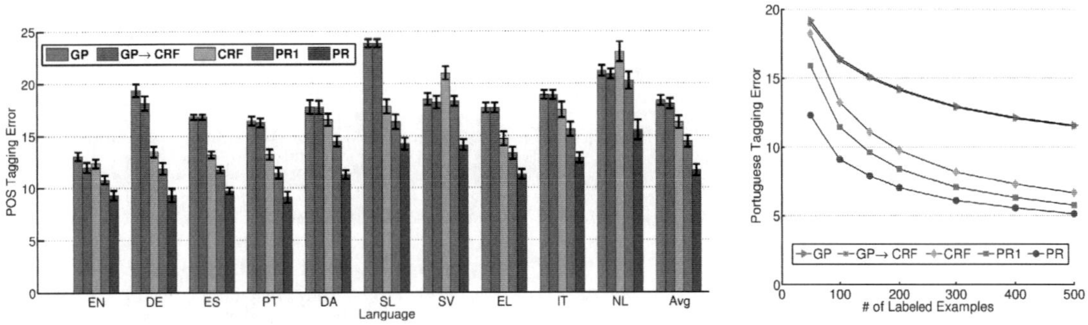

(a) (b)

Figure 1: (a): POS results for 10 languages. Each bar in each group corresponds to the average POS tagging error of one method; the left-to-right order of the methods is the same as in the legend. Whiskers indicate standard deviations. The final set of bars is an average across all languages. See supplement for a table with the exact numbers. (b): POS results on one language for a range of l.

CRF baseline is on unseen words (words that do not occur in the set of l labeled examples). If we measure performance only on such words, the gain of PR over CRF is 6.7%. We also test with $l = \{50, 100, 150, 200, 300, 400, 500\}$ on one language to illustrate how PR performs with different amounts of supervision. Figure 1 (b) shows that even when $l = 500$ our PR method is still able to provide improvement over the best baseline.

Handwriting recognition. For this task, the overall dataset contains 55 distinct word types. Thus, we set $l = 110$ and sample 10 training sets such that each contains 2 examples of each of word. Note that due to the well-balanced training sets, baselines are fairly high here compared to other similar work with this dataset. Table 1 shows there is an average improvement of 4.93% over the best of the three baselines.

	GP	GP→CRF	CRF	PR_1	PR
Mean	17.57	15.07	9.82	6.03	**4.89**
StdDev	0.30	0.35	0.48	0.20	0.42

Table 1: Handwriting recognition errors.

Even in a simpler setting closer to that of POS tagging, where we just draw $l = 100$ samples randomly, there are many cases where PR beats the baselines. Figure 2 shows predictions from such a setting and provides general intuition as to why PR does well on handwriting recognition. For the word 'Wobble' (with the first letter removed), the CRF predicts 'obble' as 'ovely', because of it relies heavily on sequential information; in our small training set, bigrams 'ov' (2 times) and 'ly' (12 times) are more frequent than 'ob' (1 time) and 'le' (7 times). GP correctly predicts these letters because the graph connects them to good neighbors. However, GP mislabels 'l' as 'i', since most of this letter's neighbors are i's. The coupling of GP and CRF via PR links the neighbor information with bigram information — 'bl' (5 times) is more frequent than 'bi' in the training set — to yield the correct labeling.

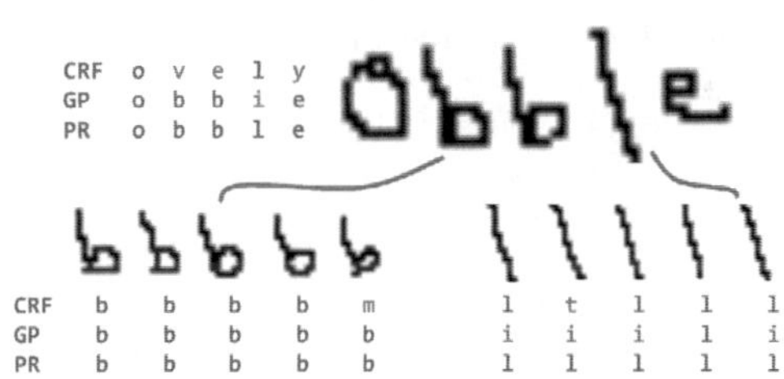

Figure 2: Predictions on the word 'Wobble' and the 5-NNs of its first 'b' and 'l'.

5 Conclusion

We have presented an efficient extension of the posterior regularization (PR) framework to a more general class of penalty functions. Encouraging results using a graph Laplacian penalty suggest potential applications to a much larger class of weakly supervised problems.

Acknowledgements

J. Gillenwater was supported by a National Science Foundation Graduate Research Fellowship. L. He and B. Taskar were partially supported by ONR Young Investigator Award N000141010746.

References

[Altun et al.2005] Y. Altun, D. McAllester, and M. Belkin. 2005. Maximum Margin Semi-Supervised Learning for Structured Variables. In *Proc. NIPS*.

[Belkin et al.2005] M. Belkin, P. Niyogi, and V. Sindhwani. 2005. On Manifold Regularization. In *Proc. AISTATS*.

[Bertsekas2004] D. Bertsekas. 2004. *Nonlinear Programming*.

[Buchholz and Marsi2006] S. Buchholz and E. Marsi. 2006. CoNLL-X Shared Task on Multilingual Dependency Parsing. In *Proc. CoNLL*.

[Chapelle et al.2006] O. Chapelle, B. Schölkopf, and A. Zien, editors. 2006. *Semi-Supervised Learning*.

[Collins et al.2005] M. Collins, P. Bartlett, D. McAllester, and B. Taskar. 2005. Exponentiated Gradient Algorithms for Large-Margin Structured Classification. In *Proc. NIPS*.

[Collins et al.2008] M. Collins, A. Globerson, T. Koo, and X. Carreras. 2008. Exponentiated Gradient Algorithms for Conditional Random Fields and Max-Margin Markov Networks. *JMLR*.

[Das and Petrov2011] D. Das and S. Petrov. 2011. Unsupervised Part-of-Speech Tagging with Bilingual Graph-Based Projections. In *Proc. ACL*.

[Das et al.2012] D. Das, S. Petrov, and R. McDonald. 2012. A Universal Part-of-Speech Tagset. In *Proc. LREC*.

[Ganchev et al.2010] K. Ganchev, J. Graça, J. Gillenwater, and B. Taskar. 2010. Posterior Regularization for Structured Latent Variable Models. *JMLR*.

[Griewank1988] A. Griewank. 1988. On Automatic Differentiation. Technical report, Argonne National Laboratory.

[Joachims2003] T. Joachims. 2003. Transductive Learning via Spectral Graph Partitioning. In *Proc. ICML*.

[Kassel1995] R. Kassel. 1995. *A Comparison of Approaches to On-line Handwritten Character Recognition*. Ph.D. thesis, Massachusetts Institute of Technology.

[Kivinen and Warmuth1995] J. Kivinen and M. Warmuth. 1995. Additive Versus Exponentiated Gradient Updates for Linear Prediction. In *Proc. STOC*.

[Mann and McCallum2007] G. Mann and A. McCallum. 2007. Simple, Robust, Scalable Semi-Supervised Learning via Expectation Regularization. In *Proc. ICML*.

[Mann and McCallum2008] G. Mann and A. McCallum. 2008. Generalized Expectation Criteria for Semi-Supervised Learning of Conditional Random Fields. In *Proc. ACL*.

[Marcus et al.1993] M. Marcus, M. Marcinkiewicz, and B. Santorini. 1993. Building a Large Annotated Corpus of English: Then Penn Treebank. *Computational Linguistics*.

[Nivre et al.2007] J. Nivre, J. Hall, S. Kübler, R. McDonald, J. Nilsson, S. Riedel, and D. Yuret. 2007. The CoNLL 2007 Shared Task on Dependency Parsing. In *Proc. CoNLL*.

[Pele and Werman2009] O. Pele and M. Werman. 2009. Fast and Robust Earth Mover's Distances. In *Proc. ICCV*.

[Subramanya and Bilmes2009] A. Subramanya and J. Bilmes. 2009. Entropic Graph Regularization in Non-Parametric Semi-Supervised Classification. In *Proc. NIPS*.

[Subramanya et al.2010] A. Subramanya, S. Petrov, and F. Pereira. 2010. Efficient Graph-Based Semi-Supervised Learning of Structured Tagging Models. In *Proc. EMNLP*.

[Taskar et al.2003] B. Taskar, C. Guestrin, and D. Koller. 2003. Max Margin Markov Networks. In *Proc. NIPS*.

[van de Panne and Whinston1964] C. van de Panne and A. Whinston. 1964. The Simplex and the Dual Method for Quadratic Programming. *Operational Research Quarterly*.

[Zhu and Lafferty2005] X. Zhu and J. Lafferty. 2005. Harmonic Mixtures: Combining Mixture Models and Graph-Based Methods for Inductive and Scalable Semi-Supervised Learning. In *Proc. ICML*.

[Zhu et al.2003] X. Zhu, Z. Ghahramani, and J. Lafferty. 2003. Semi-Supervised Learning Using Gaussian Fields and Harmonic Functions. In *Proc. ICML*.

[Zhu2005] X. Zhu. 2005. Semi-Supervised Learning Literature Survey. Technical report, University of Wisconsin-Madison.

A Boosted Semi-Markov Perceptron

Tomoya Iwakura
Fujitsu Laboratories Ltd.
1-1, Kamikodanaka 4-chome, Nakahara-ku, Kawasaki 211-8588, Japan
iwakura.tomoya@jp.fujitsu.com

Abstract

This paper proposes a boosting algorithm that uses a semi-Markov perceptron. The training algorithm repeats the training of a semi-Markov model and the update of the weights of training samples. In the boosting, training samples that are incorrectly segmented or labeled have large weights. Such training samples are aggressively learned in the training of the semi-Markov perceptron because the weights are used as the learning ratios. We evaluate our training method with Noun Phrase Chunking, Text Chunking and Extended Named Entity Recognition. The experimental results show that our method achieves better accuracy than a semi-Markov perceptron and a semi-Markov Conditional Random Fields.

1 Introduction

Natural Language Processing (NLP) basic tasks, such as Noun Phrase Chunking, Text Chunking, and Named Entity Recognition, are realized by segmenting words and labeling to the segmented words. To realize these tasks, supervised learning algorithms have been applied successfully. In the early stages, algorithms for training classifiers, including Maximum Entropy Models (Tsuruoka and Tsujii, 2005), AdaBoost-based learning algorithms (Carreras et al., 2002), and Support Vector Machines (SVMs) (Kudo and Matsumoto, 2001) were widely used. Recently, learning algorithms for structured prediction, such as linear-chain structured predictions, and semi-Markov model-based ones, have been widely used. The examples of linear-chain structured predictions include Conditional Random Fields (CRFs) (Lafferty et al., 2001) and structured perceptron (Collins, 2002). The examples of semi-Markov model-based ones include semi-Markov model perceptron (Cohen and Sarawagi, 2004), and semi-Markov CRFs (Sarawagi and Cohen, 2005). Among these methods, semi-Markov-based ones have shown good performance in terms of accuracy (Cohen and Sarawagi, 2004; Sarawagi and Cohen, 2005; Okanohara et al., 2006; Iwakura et al., 2011). One of the reasons is that a semi-Markov learner trains models that assign labels to hypothesized segments (i.e., word chunks) instead of labeling to individual words. This enables use of features that cannot be easily used in word level processing such as the beginning word of a segment, the end word of a segment, and so on.

To obtain higher accuracy, boosting methods have been applied to learning methods for training classifiers. Boosting is a method to create a final hypothesis by repeatedly generating a weak hypothesis and changing the weights of training samples in each training iteration with a given weak learner such as a decision stump learner (Schapire and Singer, 2000) and a decision tree learner (Carreras et al., 2002). However, to the best of our knowledge, there are no approaches that apply boosting to learning algorithms for structured prediction. In other words, if we can successful apply boosting to learning algorithms for structured prediction, we expect to obtain higher accuracy.

This paper proposes a boosting algorithm for a semi-Markov perceptron. Our learning method uses a semi-Markov perceptron as a weak learner, and AdaBoost is used as the boosting algorithm. To apply boosting to the semi-Markov perceptron, the following methods are proposed; 1) Use the weights of training samples decided by AdaBoost as the learning ratios of the semi-Markov perceptron, and 2) Training on AdaBoost with the loss between the correct output of a training sample and the incorrect output that has the highest score. By the first method, the semi-Markov perceptron can aggressively learn training samples that are incorrectly classified at previous iteration because such training samples have large weights. The second method is a technique to apply AdaBoost to learning algorithms for structured prediction that generate negative samples from N-best outputs (Cohen and Sarawagi, 2004), or consider all possible candidates (Sarawagi and Cohen, 2005). We also prove the convergence of our training method.

This paper is organized as follows: In Section 2, we describe AdaBoost and Semi-Markov perceptron is described in Section 3. Our proposed method is described in Section 4, and the experimental setting, the experimetal results and related work are described in Section 5, 6, and 7.

2 AdaBoost

Let $\mathcal{X}$ be a domain or sample space and $\mathcal{Y}$ be a set of labels $\{-1, +1\}$. The goal is to induce a mapping $F : \mathcal{X} \rightarrow \mathcal{Y}$. Let S be $\{(\mathbf{x}_1, y_1), ..., (\mathbf{x}_m, y_m)\}$, which is a set of training samples, where $\mathbf{x}_i$ is a sample in $\mathcal{X}$, and each y_i belongs to $\mathcal{Y}$. Each boosting learner learns T types of weak hypothesis with a given weak learner to produce a final hypothesis F:

$$F(\mathbf{x}) = sign(\sum_{t=1}^{T} \alpha_t h_t(\mathbf{x})).$$

where $sign(x)$ is 1 if x is positive, otherwise, it returns -1.

The h_t $(1 \leq t \leq T)$ is the t-th weak hypothesis learned by the weak learner. $h_t(\mathbf{x})$ is the prediction to $\mathbf{x} \in \mathcal{X}$ with h_t, and α_t is the confidence value of h_t that is calculated by the boosting learner.

The given weak learner learns a weak hypothesis h_t from training samples $S = \{(\mathbf{x}_i, y_i)\}_{i=1}^{m}$ and weights over samples $\{w_{t,1}, ..., w_{t,m}\}$ at round t. $w_{t,i}$ is the weight of sample number i at round t for $1 \leq i \leq m$. We set $w_{1,i}$ to $1/m$.

After obtaining t-th weak hypothesis h_t, the boosting learner calculates the confidence-value α_t for h_t. Then, the boosting learner updates the weight of each sample. We use the AdaBoost framework (Freund and Schapire, 1997; Schapire and Singer, 1999). The update of the sample weights in AdaBoost is defined as follows:

$$w_{t+1,i} = w_{t,i} \frac{e^{-y_i \alpha_t h_t(\mathbf{x}_i)}}{Z_t(\alpha_t)}, \quad (1)$$

where e is Napier's constant and

$$Z_t(\alpha_t) = \sum_{i=1}^{m} w_{t,i} e^{-y_i \alpha_t h_t(\mathbf{x}_i)} \quad (2)$$

Training data: $S = \{(\mathbf{X}_i, \mathbf{Y}_i)\}_{i=1}^{m}$
The learning rations of S: $\{\epsilon_i\}_{i=1}^{m}$
The maximum iteration of perceptron: P
SemiMarkovPerceptron(S, P, $\{\epsilon_i\}_{i=1}^{m}$)
$\mathbf{w} = \langle 0, ..., 0 \rangle$ # Weight vector
$\mathbf{a} = \langle 0, ..., 0 \rangle$ # For averaged perceptron
$c = 1$ # The total number of iteration
For $p = 1...P$
For $i = 1...m$
$\mathbf{Y}_i^* = \arg\max_{\mathbf{Y} \in \mathcal{Y}(\mathbf{X}_i)} \mathbf{w} \cdot \Phi(\mathbf{X}_i, \mathbf{Y})$
If $\mathbf{Y}_i^* \neq \mathbf{Y}_i$
$\mathbf{w} = \mathbf{w} + \epsilon_i(\Phi(\mathbf{X}_i, \mathbf{Y}_i) - \Phi(\mathbf{X}_i, \mathbf{Y}_i^*))$
$\mathbf{a} = \mathbf{w} + c\epsilon_i(\Phi(\mathbf{X}_i, \mathbf{Y}_i) - \Phi(\mathbf{X}_i, \mathbf{Y}_i^*))$
endIf
c++
endFor
endFor
return ($\mathbf{w}$ - $\mathbf{a}$ / c)

Figure 1: A pseudo code of a semi-Markov perceptron.

is the normalization factor for $\sum_{i=1}^{m} w_{t+1,i} = 1$.

Let π be any predicate and $[[\pi]]$ be 1 if π holds and 0 otherwise. The following upper bound holds for the training error of F consisting of T weak hypotheses (Schapire and Singer, 1999):

$$\frac{1}{m} \sum_{i=1}^{m} [[F(\mathbf{x}_i) \neq y_i]] \leq \prod_{t=1}^{T} Z_t(\alpha_t). \quad (3)$$

Eq. (1) and Eq. (3) suggest AdaBoost-based learning algorithms will converge by repeatedly selecting a confidence-value of α_t for h_t at each round, that satisfies the following Eq. (4) at each round:

$$Z_t(\alpha_t) < 1. \quad (4)$$

3 Semi-Markov Perceptron

In a semi-Markov learner, instead of labeling individual words, hypothesized segments are labeled. For example, if a training with an input 'I win' and a label set $\{NP, VP\}$ is conducted, considered segments with their labels are the following: "[I]$_{(NP)}$ [win]$_{(NP)}$", "[I]$_{(NP)}$ [win]$_{(VP)}$", "[I]$_{(VP)}$ [win]$_{(NP)}$", "[I]$_{(VP)}$ [win]$_{(VP)}$", "[I win]$_{(NP)}$", and "[I win]$_{(VP)}$".

Figure 1 shows a pseudo code of a semi-Markov perceptron (Semi-PER) (Cohen and Sarawagi, 2004). We used the averaged perceptron (Collins,

2002) based on the efficient implementation described in (Daumé III, 2006). Let $S = \{(\mathbf{X}_i, \mathbf{Y}_i)\}_{i=1}^m$ be a set of m training data, $\mathbf{X}_i$ be i-th training sample represented by a word sequence, and $\mathbf{Y}_i$ be the correct segments and the correct labeling of $\mathbf{X}_i$. $\mathbf{Y}_i$ consists of $|\mathbf{Y}_i|$ segments. $\mathbf{Y}_{i(j)}$ means the j-th segment of $\mathbf{Y}_i$, and $l(\mathbf{Y}_{i(j)})$ means the label of $\mathbf{Y}_{i(j)}$.

$\Phi(\mathbf{X}, \mathbf{Y})$ is a mapping to a D-dimensional feature vector defined as

$$\Phi(\mathbf{X}, \mathbf{Y}) = \sum_{d=1}^{D} \sum_{j=1}^{|\mathbf{Y}|} \phi_d(\mathbf{X}, \mathbf{Y}_{(j)}),$$

where ϕ_d is a feature represented by an indicator function that maps an input $\mathbf{X}$ and a segment with its label $\mathbf{Y}_{(j)}$ to a D-dimensional vector. For example, $\phi_{100}(\mathbf{X}, \mathbf{Y}_{(j)})$ might be the 100-th dimension's value is 1 if the beginning word of $\mathbf{Y}_{(j)}$ is "Mr." and the label $l(\mathbf{Y}_{(j)})$ is "NP".

$\mathbf{w}$ is a weight vector trained with a semi-Markov perceptron. $\mathbf{w} \cdot \Phi(\mathbf{X}, \mathbf{Y})$ is the score given to segments with their labels $\mathbf{Y}$ of $\mathbf{X}$, and $\mathcal{Y}(\mathbf{X})$ is the all possible segments with their labels for $\mathbf{X}$. The learning ratios of the training samples are $\{\epsilon_i\}_{i=1}^m$, and the ratios are set to 1 in a usual semi-Markov perceptron training.

In the training of the Semi-PER, for a given $\mathbf{X}_i$, the learner finds $\mathbf{Y}_i^*$ with the Viterbi decoding as described in (Cohen and Sarawagi, 2004):

$$\mathbf{Y}_i^* = \underset{\mathbf{Y} \in \mathcal{Y}(\mathbf{X}_i)}{\arg\max}\, \mathbf{w} \cdot \Phi(\mathbf{X}, \mathbf{Y}).$$

If $\mathbf{Y}_i^*$ is not equivalent to $\mathbf{Y}_i$ (i.e. $\mathbf{Y}_i^* \neq \mathbf{Y}_i$), the weight $\mathbf{w}$ is updated as follows:

$$\mathbf{w} = \mathbf{w} + \epsilon_i(\Phi(\mathbf{X}_i, \mathbf{Y}_i) - \Phi(\mathbf{X}_i, \mathbf{Y}_i^*)).$$

The algorithm takes P passes over the training samples.

4 A Boosted Semi-Markov Perceptron

This section describes how we apply AdaBoost to a semi-Markov perceptron training.

4.1 Applying Boosting

Figure 2 shows a pseudo code for our boosting-based Semi-PER. To train the Semi-PER within an AdaBoost framework, we used the weights of samples decided by AdaBoost as learning ratios. The initial weight value of i-th sample at boosting round 1 is $w_{1,i} = 1/m$. In the first iteration, Semi-PER is trained with the initial weights of samples.

Training data: $S = \{(\mathbf{X}_i, \mathbf{Y}_i)\}_{i=1}^m$
A weight vector at boosting round t: $\mathbf{W}_t$
The weights of S at round t: $\{w_{t,i}\}_{i=1}^m$
The iteration of perceptron training: P
The iteration of boosting training: T
SemiBoost(S, T, P)
$\mathbf{W_0} = \langle 0, ..., 0 \rangle$
Set initial value: $w_{1,i} = 1/m$ (for $1 \leq i \leq m$)
While $t \leq T$
  $\mathbf{w}_t$=**SemiMarkovPerceptron**(S,P,$\{w_{t,i}\}_{i=1}^m$)
  Find α_t that satisfies $\tilde{Z}_t(\alpha_t) < 1$.
  Update :$\mathbf{W}_t = \mathbf{W}_{t-1} + \alpha_t \mathbf{w}_t$
  For $i = 1...m$
   $w_{t+1,i} = w_{t,i} * e^{-\alpha_t d_t(\mathbf{X}_i)} / \tilde{Z}_t(\alpha_t)$
  t++
endWhile
return $\mathbf{W}_T$

Figure 2: A pseudo code of a boosting for a semi-Markov perceptron.

Then, we update the weights of training samples. Our boosting algorithm assigns larger weights to training samples incorrectly segmented or labeled. To realize this, we first define a loss for $\mathbf{X}_i$ at boosting round t as follows:

$$d_t(\mathbf{X}_i) = s_t(\mathbf{X}_i, \mathbf{Y}_i) - s_t(\mathbf{X}_i, \mathbf{Y}_i^t),$$

where,

$$\mathbf{Y}_i^t = \underset{\mathbf{Y} \in \mathcal{Y}(\mathbf{X}_i) \wedge \mathbf{Y} \neq \mathbf{Y}_i}{\arg\max}\, s_t(\mathbf{X}_i, \mathbf{Y}),$$

and

$$s_t(\mathbf{X}, \mathbf{Y}) = \mathbf{w}_t \cdot \Phi(\mathbf{X}, \mathbf{Y}).$$

$s_t(\mathbf{X}, \mathbf{Y})$ is a score of a word sequence $\mathbf{X}$ that is segmented and labeled as $\mathbf{Y}$, and $\mathbf{w}_t$ is a weight vector trained by Semi-PER at boosting round t. When a given input is correctly segmented and labeled, the second best output is generated with a forward-DP backward-A* N-best search algorithm (Nagata, 1994). Then we find a confidence-value α_t that satisfies $\tilde{Z}_t(\alpha_t) < 1$:

$$\tilde{Z}_t(\alpha_t) = \sum_{i=1}^{m} w_{t,i} e^{-\alpha_t d_t(\mathbf{X}_i)}. \quad (5)$$

After obtaining α_t, the weight of each sample is updated as follows:

$$w_{t+1,i} = w_{t,i} * e^{-\alpha_t d_t(\mathbf{X}_i)} / \tilde{Z}_t(\alpha_t). \quad (6)$$

If $s_t(\mathbf{X}_i, \mathbf{Y}_i)$ is greater than $s_t(\mathbf{X}_i, \mathbf{Y}_i^t)$ (i.e., $0 < d_t(\mathbf{X}_i)$), the weight of $\mathbf{X}_i$ is decreased because $\mathbf{X}_i$ is correctly segmented and labeled. Otherwise ($d_t(\mathbf{X}_i) < 0$), $\mathbf{X}_i$ has a larger weight value. The updated weights are used as the learning ratios in the training of Semi-PER at the next boosting round. Finally, we update the weight vector $\mathbf{W}_t$ trained with boosting as follows:

$$\mathbf{W}_t = \mathbf{W}_{t-1} + \alpha_t \mathbf{w}_t$$

This process is repeated T times, and a model $\mathbf{W}_T$, which consists of T types of Semi-PER-based models, is obtained.

In test phase, the segments and labels of a word sequence $\mathbf{X}$ is decided as follows:

$$\mathbf{Y}^* = \arg\max_{\mathbf{Y} \in \mathcal{Y}(\mathbf{X})} \mathbf{W}_T \cdot \Phi(\mathbf{X}, \mathbf{Y}).$$

4.2 Learning a Confidence Value

Since our algorithm handles real valued scores of samples given by Semi-PER on the exponential loss of AdaBoost, it's difficult to analytically determine a confidence-value α_t that satisfies $\tilde{Z}_t(\alpha_t) < 1$ at boosting round t.

Therefore, we use a bisection search to find a confidence-value. To detemin the range for the bisection search, we use a range between 0 and the confidence-value for a weak hypothesis h_t that returns its prediction as one of {-1,+1}. We define $h_t(\mathbf{X}_i)$ as $sign(d_t(\mathbf{X}_i))$. Schapire and Singer proposed an algorithm based on AdaBoost, called real AdaBoost (Schapire and Singer, 1999). The real AdaBoost analytically calculates the confidence-value that minimizes Eq. (2). The derivation of $Z_t(\alpha_t)$ with α_t is

$$Z_t'(\alpha_t) = \sum_{i=1}^{m} -h_t(\mathbf{X}_i) w_{t,i} e^{-\alpha_t h_t(\mathbf{X}_i)}.$$

By solving $Z_t'(\alpha_t) = 0$, we obtain

$$\tilde{\alpha_t} = \frac{1}{2}\log\left(\frac{\sum_{i=1}^{m} w_{t,i}[[h_t(\mathbf{X}_i) = 1]]}{\sum_{i=1}^{m} w_{t,i}[[h_t(\mathbf{X}_i) = -1]]}\right).$$

Finally, we select the value that minimizes Eq. (5) from the range between 0 and $2 \times \tilde{\alpha_t}$ with the bisection search as the confidence-value α_t. This is because we expect to find a better confidence-value from a wider range.

4.3 Convergence Analysis

If we repeatedly find a confidence-value ($0 < \alpha_t$) that satisfies $\tilde{Z}_t(\alpha_t) < 1$ at each boosting round, the training of the semi-Markov model will be converged as in the classification case described in Section 2.[1] The following bound on the training error can be proved:

$$\frac{1}{m}\sum_{i=1}^{m}[[\mathbf{Y}_i^* \neq \mathbf{Y}_i]] \leq \prod_{t=1}^{T} \tilde{Z}_t(\alpha_t)$$

where

$$\mathbf{Y}_i^* = \arg\max_{\mathbf{Y} \in \mathcal{Y}(\mathbf{X}_i)} \mathbf{W}_T \cdot \Phi(\mathbf{X}_i, \mathbf{Y}).$$

By unraveling Eq. (6), we have that

$$\begin{aligned} w_{T+1,i} &= w_{T,i} * e^{-\alpha_t d_t(\mathbf{X}_i)} / \tilde{Z}_t(\alpha_t) \\ &= \frac{e^{-\sum_{t=1}^{T} \alpha_t d_t(\mathbf{X}_i)}}{m\prod_{t=1}^{T} \tilde{Z}_t(\alpha_t)} \\ &= \frac{e^{-\sum_{t=1}^{T} \alpha_t \mathbf{w}_t \cdot (\Phi(\mathbf{X}_i, \mathbf{Y}_i) - \Phi(\mathbf{X}_i, \mathbf{Y}_i^t))}}{m\prod_{t=1}^{T} \tilde{Z}_t(\alpha_t)}. \end{aligned}$$

Therefore, if $\mathbf{Y}_i^* \neq \mathbf{Y}_i$,

$$\frac{e^{-\sum_{t=1}^{T} \alpha_t \mathbf{w}_t \cdot (\Phi(\mathbf{X}_i, \mathbf{Y}_i) - \Phi(\mathbf{X}_i, \mathbf{Y}_i^*))}}{m\prod_{t=1}^{T} \tilde{Z}_t(\alpha_t)} \leq w_{T+1,i},$$

since, for $1 \leq t \leq T$,

$$\mathbf{w}_t \cdot \Phi(\mathbf{X}_i, \mathbf{Y}_i^*) \leq \mathbf{w}_t \cdot \Phi(\mathbf{X}_i, \mathbf{Y}_i^t).$$

Moreover, when $\mathbf{Y}_i^* \neq \mathbf{Y}_i$, the following is satisfied.

$$\begin{aligned} 1 &\leq e^{-\sum_{t=1}^{T} \alpha_t \mathbf{w}_t \cdot (\Phi(\mathbf{X}_i, \mathbf{Y}_i) - \Phi(\mathbf{X}_i, \mathbf{Y}_i^*))} \\ &\leq e^{-\sum_{t=1}^{T} \alpha_t \mathbf{w}_t \cdot (\Phi(\mathbf{X}_i, \mathbf{Y}_i) - \Phi(\mathbf{X}_i, \mathbf{Y}_i^t))} \\ &= e^{-\sum_{t=1}^{T} \alpha_t d_t(\mathbf{X}_i)}. \end{aligned}$$

Therefore,

$$[[\mathbf{Y}_i^* \neq \mathbf{Y}_i]] \leq e^{-\sum_{t=1}^{T} \alpha_t d_t(\mathbf{X}_i)}.$$

These give the stated bound on training error;

$$\begin{aligned} \frac{1}{m}\sum_{i=1}^{m}[[\mathbf{Y}_i^* \neq \mathbf{Y}_i]] &\leq \frac{\sum_{i=1}^{m} e^{-\sum_{t=1}^{T} \alpha_t d_t(\mathbf{X}_i)}}{m} \\ &= \sum_{i=1}^{m}\left(\prod_{t=1}^{T} \tilde{Z}_t(\alpha_t)\right) w_{T+1,i} \\ &= \prod_{t=1}^{T} \tilde{Z}_t(\alpha_t). \end{aligned}$$

[1] $0 < \alpha_t$ means the weighted error of the current Semi-PER, $\sum_{i=1}^{m}[[\mathbf{Y}_i^t \neq \mathbf{Y}_i]] w_{i,t}$, is less than 0.5 on the training data. Fortunately, this condition was always satisfied with the training of Semi-PER in our experiments.

5 Experimental Settings

5.1 Noun Phrase Chunking

The Noun Phrase (NP) chunking task was chosen because it is a popular benchmark for testing a structured prediction. In this task, noun phrases called base NPs are identified. "[He] (NP) reckons [the current account deficit] (NP)..." is an example. The training set consists of 8,936 sentences, and the test set consists of 2,012 sentences.[2] To tune parameters for each algorithm, we used the 90% of the train data for the training of parameter tuning, and the 10% of the training data was used as a development data for measuring accuracy at parameter tuning. A final model was trained from all the training data with the parameters that showed the highest accuracy on the development data.

5.2 Text Chunking

We used a standard data set prepared for CoNLL-2000 shared task.[3] This task aims to identify 10 types of chunks, such as, NP, VP, PP, ADJP, ADVP, CONJP, INITJ, LST, PTR, and SBAR. "[He] (NP) [reckons] (VP) [the current account deficit] (NP)..." is an example of text chunking. The data consists of subsets of Penn Wall Street Journal treebank; training (sections 15-18) and test (section 20). To tune parameters for each algorithm, we used the same approach of the NP chunking one.

5.3 Japanese Extended NE Recognition

To evaluate our algorithm on tasks that include large number of classes, we used an extended NE recognition (ENER) task (Sekine et al., 2002). This Japanese corpus for ENER (Hashimoto et al., 2008) consists of about 8,500 articles from 2005 Mainichi newspaper. The corpus includes 240,337 tags for 191 types of NEs. To segment words from Japanese sentences, we used ChaSen.[4] Words may include partial NEs because words segmented with ChaSen do not always correspond with NE boundaries. If such problems occur when we segment the training data, we annotated a word chunk with the type of the NE included in the word chunk. The evaluations are performed based on the gold standard data for the test. We created the following sets for this experiment. Training data is news articles from January to October 2005 in the corpus, which includes 205,876 NEs. Development data is news articles in November 2005 in the corpus, which includes 15,405 NEs. Test data is news articles in December 2005 in the corpus, which includes 19,056 NEs.

Table 1: Features.

$[t_j, CL_j]$, $[t_j, WB_j]$, $[t_j, PB_j]$,
$[t_j, w_{bp}]$, $[t_j, p_{bp}]$,
$[t_j, w_{ep}]$, $[t_j, p_{ep}]$, $[t_j, w_{ip}]$,$[t_j, p_{ip}]$,
$[t_j, w_{bp}, w_{ep}]$, $[t_j, p_{bp}, p_{ep}]$,
$[t_j, w_{bp}, p_{ep}]$, $[t_j, p_{bp}, w_{ep}]$,
$[t_j, w_{bp-1}]$, $[t_j, p_{bp-1}]$, $[t_j, w_{bp-2}]$, $[t_j, p_{bp-2}]$,
$[t_j, w_{ep+1}]$, $[t_j, p_{ep+1}]$, $[t_j, w_{ep+2}]$, $[t_j, p_{ep+2}]$,
$[t_j, p_{bp-2}, p_{bp-1}]$, $[t_j, p_{ep+1}, p_{ep+2}]$,
$[t_j, p_{bp-2}, p_{bp-1}, p_{bp}]$, $[t_j, p_{ep}, p_{ep+1}, p_{ep+2}]$
% Features used for only Text Chunking and NP Chunking
$[t_j, w_{bp}, w_{ip}]$, $[t_j, w_{bp}, p_{ip}]$,
$[t_j, w_{bp}, p_{ip}]$, $[t_j, p_{bp}, p_{ip}]$,
$[t_j, w_{ep}, w_{ip}]$, $[t_j, w_{ep}, p_{ip}]$,
$[t_j, w_{ep}, p_{ip}]$, $[t_j, p_{ep}, p_{ip}]$,
$[t_j, w_{bp}, w_{ep}, w_{ip}]$, $[t_j, w_{bp}, w_{ep}, p_{ip}]$,
$[t_j, w_{bp}, w_{ep}, p_{ip}]$, $[t_j, w_{bp}, p_{ep}, p_{ip}]$

5.4 Evaluation Metrics

Our evaluation metrics are recall (RE), precision (PR), and F-measure (FM) defined as follows:

$$RE = C_{ok}/C_{all},\ PR = C_{ok}/C_{rec}$$

and

$$FM = 2 \times RE \times PR/(RE + PR),$$

where C_{ok} is the number of correctly recognized chunks with their correct labels, C_{all} is the number of all chunks in a gold standard data, and C_{rec} is the number of all recognized chunks.

5.5 Features

Table 1 lists features used in our experiments. For NP Chunking and Text Chunking, we added features derived from segments in addition to ENER features.[5]

w_k is the k-th word, and p_k is the Part-Of-Speech (POS) tag of k-th word. bp is the position of the first word of the current segment in a given

[2]We used the data obtained from ftp://ftp.cis.upenn.edu/pub/chunker/ .

[3]http://lcg-www.uia.ac.be/conll2000/chunking/

[4]We used ChaSen-2.4.2 with Ipadic-2.7.0. ChaSen's web page is http://chasen-legacy.sourceforge.jp/.

[5]We did not use the additional features for ENER because the features did not contribute to accuracy.

word sequence. ep indicates the position of the last word of the current segment. ip is the position of words inside the current segment ($bp < ip < ep$). If the length of the current segment is 2, we use features that indicate there is no inside word as the features of ip-th words. t_j is the NE class label of j-th segment. CL_j is the length of the current segment, whether it be 1, 2, 3, 4, or longer than 4. WB_j indicates word bigrams, and PB_j indicates POS bigrams inside the current segment.

5.6 Algorithms to be Compared

The following algorithms are compared with our method.

- **Semi-Markov perceptron (Semi-PER)** (Cohen and Sarawagi, 2004): We used one-best output for training. This Semi-PER is also used as the weak learner of our boosting algorithm.

- **Semi-Markov CRF (Semi-CRF)** (Sarawagi and Cohen, 2005): To train Semi-CRF, a stochastic gradient descent (SGD) training for L1-regularized with cumulative penalty (Tsuruoka et al., 2009) was used. The batch size of SGD was set to 1.

These algorithms are based on sequentially classifying segments of several adjacent words, rather than single words. Ideally, all the possible word segments of each input should be considered for this algorithm. However, the training of these algorithms requires a great deal of memory. Therefore, we limit the maximum size of the word-segments. We use word segments consisting of up to ten words due to the memory limitation.

We set the maximum iteration for Semi-PER to 100, and the iteration number for Semi-CRF trained with SGD to $100 \times m$, where m is the number of training samples. The regularization parameter C of Semi-CRF and the number of iteration for Semi-PER are tuned on development data.[6] For our boosting algorithm, the number of boosting iteration is tuned on development data with the number of iteration for Semi-PER tuned on development data. We set the maximum iteration number for boosting to 50.

[6] For C of Semi-CRF, $\{1, 10^{-1}, 10^{-2}, 10^{-3}, 10^{-4}, 10^{-5}, 10^{-6}, 10^{-7}, 10^{-8}, 10^{-9}\}$ were examined.

Table 2: Results of NP Chunking.

Learner	F-measure	Recall	Precision
Semi-PER	94.32	94.53	94.11
Semi-CRF	94.32	94.52	94.13
Semi-Boost	**94.60**	**94.85**	**94.35**

Table 3: Results of Text Chunking.

Learner	F-measure	Recall	Precision
Semi-PER	94.10	94.15	94.05
Semi-CRF	93.79	93.96	93.62
Semi-Boost	**94.15**	**94.27**	**94.03**

6 Experimental Results

We used a machine with Intel(R) Xeon(R) CPU X5680 @ 3.33GHz and 72 GB memory. In the following, our proposed method is referred as **Semi-Boost**.

6.1 NP Chunking

Table 2 shows the experimental results on NP Chunking. Semi-Boost showed the best accuracy. Semi-Boost showed 0.28 higher F-measure than Semi-PER and Semi-CRF. To compare the results, we employed a McNemar paired test on the labeling disagreements as was done in (Sha and Pereira, 2003). All the results indicate that there is a significant difference ($p < 0.01$). This result shows that Semi-Boost showed high accuracy.

6.2 Text Chunking

Table 3 shows the experimental results on Text Chunking. Semi-Boost showed 0.36 higher F-measure than Semi-CRF, and 0.05 higher F-measure than Semi-PER. The result of McNemar test indicates that there is a significant difference ($p < 0.01$) between Semi-Boost and Semi-CRF. However, there is no significant difference between Semi-Boost and Semi-PER.

6.3 Extended Named Entity Recognition

Table 4 shows the experimental results on ENER. We could not train Semi-CRF because of the lack of memory for this task. Semi-Boost showed 0.24 higher F-measure than that of Semi-PER. The results indicate there is a significant difference ($p <$

Table 4: Experimental results for ENER.

Learner	F-measure	Recall	Precision
Semi-PER	81.86	79.06	84.87
Semi-CRF	N/A		
Semi-Boost	**82.10**	**79.36**	**85.03**

Table 5: Training time of each learner (second) for NP Chunking (NP), Text Chunking (TC) and ENER. The number of Semi-Boost iteration is only one time. The +20 cores means training of Semi-Boost with 20 cores.

Learner	NP	TC	ENER
Semi-PER	475	559	13,559
Semi-CRF	2,120	8,228	N/A
Semi-Boost	499	619	32,370
+20 cores	487	650	19,598

0.01).[7]

6.4 Training Speed

We compared training speed under the following condition; The iteration for Semi-PER is 100, the iteration number for Semi-CRF trained with SGD is $100 \times m$, where m is the number of training samples, and the one time iteration of boosting with the perceptron iteration 100. Therefore, all training methods attempted $100 \times m$ times estimation.

Table 5 shows the training time of each learner. In NP Chunking, the training time of Semi-PER, Semi-CRF, and Semi-Boost were 475 seconds, 2,120 seconds, and 499 seconds. In Text Chunking, the training time of Semi-PER, Semi-CRF, and our method were 559 seconds, 8,228 seconds, and 619 seconds. Semi-Boost shows competitive training speed with Semi-PER and 4 to 13 times faster training speed in terms of the total number of parameter estimations The difference of time between Semi-PER and our method is the time for calculating confidence-value of boosting.

When Semi-Boost trained a model for ENER, the training speed was degraded. The training time of Semi-Boost was 32,370 and the training time of Semi-PER was 13,559. One of the reasons is the generation of an incorrect output of each training sample. In our observation, when the number of classes is increased, the generation speed of incorrect outputs with N-best search is degraded. To improve training speed, we used 20 cores for generating incorrect outputs. When the training with 20 cores was conducted, the training data was split to 20 portions, and each portion was processed with one of each core. The training time with the 20 cores was 19,598 for ENER. However, the training time of NP Chunking was marginally improved and that of Text Chunking was slightly increased. This result implies that multi-core processing is effective for the training of large classes like ENER in Semi-Boost.

[7]The results on the test data were compared by character units as in Japanese morphological analysis (Iwakura et al., 2011). This is because the ends or beginnings of Japanese NEs do not always correspond with word boundaries.

Table 6: The best results for NP Chunking (FM).

(Kudo and Matsumoto, 2001)	94.22
(Sun et al., 2009)	94.37
This paper	**94.60**

In fact, since Semi-Boost requires additional boosting iterations, the training time of Semi-Boost increases. However, the training time increases linearly by the number of boosting iteration. Therefore, Semi-Boost learned models from the large training data of ENER.

6.5 Memory Usage

Semi-Boost consumed more memory than Semi-PER. This is because our learning method maintains a weight vector for boosting in addition to the weight vector of Semi-PER. Compared with Semi-CRF, Semi-Boost showed lower memory consumption. On the training data for Text Chunking, the memory size of Semi-Boost, Semi-PER, and Semi-CRF are 4.4 GB, 4.1 GB, and 18.0 GB. When we trained models for ENER, Semi-PER consumed 32 GB and Semi-Boost consumed 33 GB. However, Semi-CRF could not train models because of the lack of memory. This is because Semi-CRF maintains a weight vector and a parameter vector for L1-norm regularization and Semi-CRF considers all possible patterns generated from given sequences in training. In contrast, Semi-PER and Semi-Boost only consider features that appeared in correct ones and incorrectly recognized ones. These results indicate that Semi-Boost can learn models from large training data.

Table 7: The best results for Text Chunking (FM).

Semi-supervised learning	
(Ando and Zhang, 2005)	94.39
(Iwakura and Okamoto, 2008)	94.32
(Suzuki and Isozaki, 2008)	95.15
With additional resources	
(Zhang et al., 2001)	94.17
(Daumé III and Marcu, 2005)	94.4
Without lexical resources	
(Kudo and Matsumoto, 2001)	93.91
(Kudo et al., 2005)	94.12
(Tsuruoka and Tsujii, 2005)	93.70
(Tsuruoka et al., 2009)	93.68
This paper	**94.15**

7 Related Work

7.1 NP Chunking

Table 6 shows the previous best results for NP Chunking. The F-measure of Semi-Boost is 94.60 that is 0.23 higher than that of (Sun et al., 2009) and 0.38 higher than that of (Kudo and Matsumoto, 2001).

7.2 Text Chunking

Table 7 shows the previous best results for Text Chunking. We see that our method attained a higher accuracy than the previous best results obtained without any additional lexical resources such as chunking methods based on SVM (Kudo and Matsumoto, 2001), CRF with reranking (Kudo et al., 2005), Maximum Entropy (Tsuruoka and Tsujii, 2005), and CRF (Tsuruoka et al., 2009). This result indicates that our method performs well in terms of accuracy.

The previous results with lexical resources or semi-supervised ones showed higher accuracy than that of our method. For example, lexical resources such as lists of names, locations, abbreviations and stop words were used (Daumé III and Marcu, 2005), and a full parser output was used in (Zhang et al., 2001). Semi-supervised ones used a generative model trained from automatically labeled data (Suzuki and Isozaki, 2008), the candidate tags of words collected from automatically labeled data (Iwakura and Okamoto, 2008), or automatically created classifiers by learning from thousands of automatically generated auxiliary classification problems from unlabeled data (Ando and Zhang, 2005). Our algorithm can also incorporate the lexical resources and the semi-supervised approaches. Future work should evaluate the effectiveness of the incorporation of them.

7.3 Extended Named Entity Recognition

For ENER, the best result was the Semi-PER one (Iwakura et al., 2011). The F-measure of Semi-PER was 81.95, and the result was higher than NE chunker based on structured perceptron (Collins, 2002), and NE chunkers based on shift-reduce-parsers (Iwakura et al., 2011). Our method showed 0.15 higher F-measure than that of the Semi-PER one. This result is also evidence that our method performs well in terms of accuracy.

7.4 Training Methods

There have been methods proposed to improve the training speed for semi-Markov-based learners. With regard to reducing the space of lattices built into the semi-Markov-based algorithms, a method was proposed to filter nodes in the lattices with a naive Bayes classifier (Okanohara et al., 2006). To improve training speed of Semi-CRF, a succinct representation of potentials common across overlapping segments of semi-Markov model was proposed (Sarawagi, 2006). These methods can also be applied to Semi-PER. Therefore, we can expect improved training speed with these methods.

Recent online learners update both parameters and the estimate of their confidence (Dredze and Crammer, 2008; Crammer et al., 2009; Mejer and Crammer, 2010; Wang et al., 2012). In these algorithms, less confident parameters are updated more aggressively than more confident ones. These algorithms maintain the confidences of features. In contrast, our boosting approach maintains the weights of training samples. In future work, we'd like to consider the use of these algorithms in boosting of semi-Markov learners.

8 Conclusion

This paper has proposed a boosting algorithm with a semi-Markov perceptron. The experimental results on Noun Phrase Chunking, Text Chunking and Japanese Extended Named Entity Recognition have shown that our method achieved better accuracy than a semi-Markov perceptron and a semi-Markov CRF. In future work, we'd like to evaluate the boosting algorithm with structured prediction tasks such as POS tagging and parsing.

References

Rie Ando and Tong Zhang. 2005. A high-performance semi-supervised learning method for text chunking. In *Proc. of ACL'05*, pages 1–9.

Xavier Carreras, Lluís Màrques, and Lluís Padró. 2002. Named entity extraction using adaboost. In *Proc. of CoNLL'02*, pages 167–170.

William W. Cohen and Sunita Sarawagi. 2004. Exploiting dictionaries in named entity extraction: combining semi-markov extraction processes and data integration methods. In *Proc. of KDD'04*, pages 89–98.

Michael Collins. 2002. Discriminative training methods for Hidden Markov Models: theory and experiments with perceptron algorithms. In *Proc. of EMNLP'02*, pages 1–8.

Koby Crammer, Alex Kulesza, and Mark Dredze. 2009. Adaptive regularization of weight vectors. In *Proc. of NIPS'09*, pages 414–422.

Hal Daumé III and Daniel Marcu. 2005. Learning as search optimization: Approximate large margin methods for structured prediction. In *Proc. of ICML'05*, pages 169–176.

Hal Daumé III. 2006. *Practical Structured Learning Techniques for Natural Language Processing*. Ph.D. thesis, University of Southern California.

Mark Dredze and Koby Crammer. 2008. Online methods for multi-domain learning and adaptation. In *Proc. of EMNLP'08*, pages 689–697.

Yoav Freund and Robert E. Schapire. 1997. A decision-theoretic generalization of on-line learning and an application to boosting. *J. Comput. Syst. Sci.*, 55(1):119–139.

Taiichi Hashimoto, Takashi Inui, and Koji Murakami. 2008. Constructing extended named entity annotated corpora. *IPSJ SIG Notes*, 2008(113):113–120.

Tomoya Iwakura and Seishi Okamoto. 2008. A fast boosting-based learner for feature-rich tagging and chunking. In *Proc. of CoNLL'08*, pages 17–24.

Tomoya Iwakura, Hiroya Takamura, and Manabu Okumura. 2011. A named entity recognition method based on decomposition and concatenation of word chunks. In *Proc. of IJCNLP'11*, pages 828–836.

Taku Kudo and Yuji Matsumoto. 2001. Chunking with Support Vector Machines. In *Proc. of NAACL'01*, pages 192–199.

Taku Kudo, Jun Suzuki, and Hideki Isozaki. 2005. Boosting-based parse reranking with subtree features. In *Proc. of ACL'05*, pages 189–196.

John D. Lafferty, Andrew McCallum, and Fernando C. N. Pereira. 2001. Conditional random fields: Probabilistic models for segmenting and labeling sequence data. In *Proc. of ICML'01*, pages 282–289.

Avihai Mejer and Koby Crammer. 2010. Confidence in structured-prediction using confidence-weighted models. In *Proc. of EMNLP'10*, pages 971–981.

Masaaki Nagata. 1994. A stochastic japanese morphological analyzer using a forward-dp backward-a* n-best search algorithm. In *Proc. of COLING'94*, pages 201–207.

Daisuke Okanohara, Yusuke Miyao, Yoshimasa Tsuruoka, and Jun'ichi Tsujii. 2006. Improving the scalability of semi-markov conditional random fields for named entity recognition. In *Proc. of ACL'06*, pages 465–472.

Sunita Sarawagi and William W. Cohen. 2005. Semi-markov conditional random fields for information extraction. In *Proc. of NIPS'04*, pages 1185–1192.

Sunita Sarawagi. 2006. Efficient inference on sequence segmentation models. In *Proc. of ICML'06*, pages 793–800.

Robert E. Schapire and Yoram Singer. 1999. Improved boosting algorithms using confidence-rated predictions. *Machine Learning*, 37(3):297–336.

Robert E. Schapire and Yoram Singer. 2000. Boostexter: A boosting-based system for text categorization. *Machine Learning*, 39(2/3):135–168.

Satoshi Sekine, Kiyoshi Sudo, and Chikashi Nobata. 2002. Extended named entity hierarchy. In *Proc. of LREC'02*.

Fei Sha and Fernando Pereira. 2003. Shallow parsing with conditional random fields. In *Proc. of NAACL HLT'03*, pages 134–141.

Xu Sun, Takuya Matsuzaki, Daisuke Okanohara, and Jun'ichi Tsujii. 2009. Latent variable perceptron algorithm for structured classification. In *Proc. of IJCAI'09*, pages 1236–1242.

Jun Suzuki and Hideki Isozaki. 2008. Semi-supervised sequential labeling and segmentation using giga-word scale unlabeled data. In *Proc. of ACL-08: HLT*, pages 665–673.

Yoshimasa Tsuruoka and Junichi Tsujii. 2005. Bidirectional inference with the easiest-first strategy for tagging sequence data. In *Proc. of HLT/EMNLP*, pages 467–474.

Yoshimasa Tsuruoka, Jun'ichi Tsujii, and Sophia Ananiadou. 2009. Stochastic gradient descent training for l1-regularized log-linear models with cumulative penalty. In *Proc. of ACL/IJCNLP*, pages 477–485.

Jialei Wang, Peilin Zhao, and Steven C.H. Hoi. 2012. Exact soft confidence-weighted learning. In *Proc. of ICML'12*, pages 121–128.

Tong Zhang, Fred Damerau, and David Johnson. 2001. Text chunking using regularized winnow. In *Proc. of ACL'01*, pages 539–546.

Spectral Learning of Refinement HMMs

Karl Stratos[1] **Alexander M. Rush**[2] **Shay B. Cohen**[1] **Michael Collins**[1]

[1]Department of Computer Science, Columbia University, New-York, NY 10027, USA
[2]MIT CSAIL, Cambridge, MA, 02139, USA
{stratos,scohen,mcollins}@cs.columbia.edu, srush@csail.mit.edu

Abstract

We derive a spectral algorithm for learning the parameters of a refinement HMM. This method is simple, efficient, and can be applied to a wide range of supervised sequence labeling tasks. Like other spectral methods, it avoids the problem of local optima and provides a consistent estimate of the parameters. Our experiments on a phoneme recognition task show that when equipped with informative feature functions, it performs significantly better than a supervised HMM and competitively with EM.

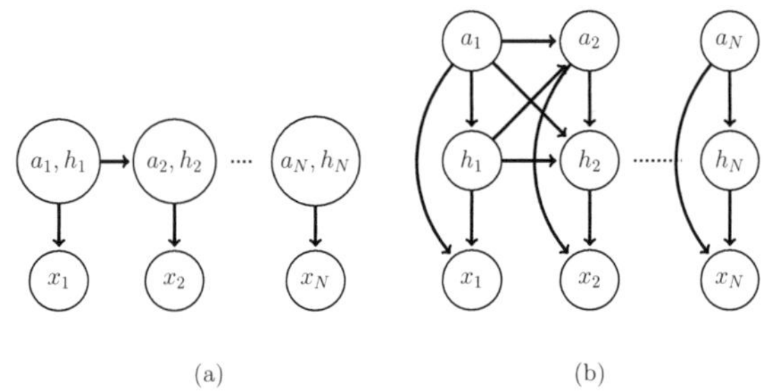

Figure 1: (a) An R-HMM chain. (b) An equivalent representation where labels and hidden states are intertwined.

1 Introduction

Consider the task of supervised sequence labeling. We are given a training set where the j'th training example consists of a sequence of observations $x_1^{(j)}...x_N^{(j)}$ paired with a sequence of labels $a_1^{(j)}...a_N^{(j)}$ and asked to predict the correct labels on a test set of observations. A common approach is to learn a joint distribution over sequences $p(a_1 \ldots a_N, x_1 \ldots x_N)$ as a hidden Markov model (HMM). The downside of HMMs is that they assume each label a_i is independent of labels before the previous label a_{i-1}. This independence assumption can be limiting, particularly when the label space is small. To relax this assumption we can refine each label a_i with a hidden state h_i, which is not observed in the training data, and model the joint distribution $p(a_1 \ldots a_N, x_1 \ldots x_N, h_1 \ldots h_N)$. This refinement HMM (R-HMM), illustrated in figure 1, is able to propagate information forward through the hidden state as well as the label.

Unfortunately, estimating the parameters of an R-HMM is complicated by the unobserved hidden variables. A standard approach is to use the expectation-maximization (EM) algorithm which has no guarantee of finding the global optimum of its objective function. The problem of local optima prevents EM from yielding statistically consistent parameter estimates: even with very large amounts of data, EM is not guaranteed to estimate parameters which are close to the "correct" model parameters.

In this paper, we derive a spectral algorithm for learning the parameters of R-HMMs. Unlike EM, this technique is guaranteed to find the true parameters of the underlying model under mild conditions on the singular values of the model. The algorithm we derive is simple and efficient, relying on singular value decomposition followed by standard matrix operations.

We also describe the connection of R-HMMs to L-PCFGs. Cohen et al. (2012) present a spectral algorithm for L-PCFG estimation, but the naïve transformation of the L-PCFG model and its spectral algorithm to R-HMMs is awkward and opaque. We therefore work through the non-trivial derivation the spectral algorithm for R-HMMs.

We note that much of the prior work on spectral algorithms for discrete structures in NLP has shown limited experimental success for this family of algorithms (see, for example, Luque et al., 2012). Our experiments demonstrate empirical success for the R-HMM spectral algorithm. The spectral algorithm performs competitively with EM on a phoneme recognition task, and is more stable with respect to the number of hidden states.

Cohen et al. (2013) present experiments with a parsing algorithm and also demonstrate it is competitive with EM. Our set of experiments comes as an additional piece of evidence that spectral algorithms can function as a viable, efficient and more principled alternative to the EM algorithm.

2 Related Work

Recently, there has been a surge of interest in spectral methods for learning HMMs (Hsu et al., 2012; Foster et al., 2012; Jaeger, 2000; Siddiqi et al., 2010; Song et al., 2010). Like these previous works, our method produces consistent parameter estimates; however, we estimate parameters for a supervised learning task. Balle et al. (2011) also consider a supervised problem, but our model is quite different since we estimate a joint distribution $p(a_1 \dots a_N, x_1 \dots x_N, h_1 \dots h_N)$ as opposed to a conditional distribution and use feature functions over both the labels and observations of the training data. These feature functions also go beyond those previously employed in other spectral work (Siddiqi et al., 2010; Song et al., 2010). Experiments show that features of this type are crucial for performance.

Spectral learning has been applied to related models beyond HMMs including: head automata for dependency parsing (Luque et al., 2012), tree-structured directed Bayes nets (Parikh et al., 2011), finite-state transducers (Balle et al., 2011), and mixture models (Anandkumar et al., 2012a; Anandkumar et al., 2012b).

Of special interest is Cohen et al. (2012), who describe a derivation for a spectral algorithm for L-PCFGs. This derivation is the main driving force behind the derivation of our R-HMM spectral algorithm. For work on L-PCFGs estimated with EM, see Petrov et al. (2006), Matsuzaki et al. (2005), and Pereira and Schabes (1992). Petrov et al. (2007) proposes a split-merge EM procedure for phoneme recognition analogous to that used in latent-variable parsing.

3 The R-HMM Model

We decribe in this section the notation used throughout the paper and the formal details of R-HMMs.

3.1 Notation

We distinguish row vectors from column vectors when such distinction is necessary. We use a superscript $\top$ to denote the transpose operation. We write $[n]$ to denote the set $\{1, 2, \dots, n\}$ for any integer $n \geq 1$. For any vector $v \in \mathbb{R}^m$, $\text{diag}(v) \in \mathbb{R}^{m \times m}$ is a diagonal matrix with entries $v_1 \dots v_m$. For any statement $\mathcal{S}$, we use $[[\mathcal{S}]]$ to refer to the indicator function that returns 1 if $\mathcal{S}$ is true and 0 otherwise. For a random variable X, we use $\mathbf{E}[X]$ to denote its expected value.

A tensor $C \in \mathbb{R}^{m \times m \times m}$ is a set of m^3 values $C_{i,j,k}$ for $i, j, k \in [m]$. Given a vector $v \in \mathbb{R}^m$, we define $C(v)$ to be the $m \times m$ matrix with $[C(v)]_{i,j} = \sum_{k \in [m]} C_{i,j,k} v_k$. Given vectors $x, y, z \in \mathbb{R}^m$, $C = xy^\top z^\top$ is an $m \times m \times m$ tensor with $[C]_{i,j,k} = x_i y_j z_k$.

3.2 Definition of an R-HMM

An R-HMM is a 7-tuple $\langle l, m, n, \pi, o, t, f \rangle$ for integers $l, m, n \geq 1$ and functions π, o, t, f where

- $[l]$ is a set of labels.
- $[m]$ is a set of hidden states.
- $[n]$ is a set of observations.
- $\pi(a, h)$ is the probability of generating $a \in [l]$ and $h \in [m]$ in the first position in the labeled sequence.
- $o(x|a, h)$ is the probability of generating $x \in [n]$, given $a \in [l]$ and $h \in [m]$.
- $t(b, h'|a, h)$ is the probability of generating $b \in [l]$ and $h' \in [m]$, given $a \in [l]$ and $h \in [m]$.
- $f(*|a, h)$ is the probability of generating the stop symbol $*$, given $a \in [l]$ and $h \in [m]$.

See figure 1(b) for an illustration. At any time step of a sequence, a label a is associated with a hidden state h. By convention, the end of an R-HMM sequence is signaled by the symbol $*$.

For the subsequent illustration, let N be the length of the sequence we consider. A *full sequence* consists of labels $a_1 \dots a_N$, observations $x_1 \dots x_N$, and hidden states $h_1 \dots h_N$. The model assumes

$$p(a_1 \dots a_N, x_1 \dots x_N, h_1 \dots h_N) = \pi(a_1, h_1) \times \prod_{i=1}^{N} o(x_i|a_i, h_i) \times \prod_{i=1}^{N-1} t(a_{i+1}, h_{i+1}|a_i, h_i) \times f(*|a_N, h_N)$$

Input: a sequence of observations $x_1 \dots x_N$; operators $\langle C^{b|a}, C^{*|a}, c^1_a, c^a_x \rangle$
Output: $\mu(a, i)$ for all $a \in [l]$ and $i \in [N]$

[Forward case]

- $\alpha^1_a \leftarrow c^1_a$ for all $a \in [l]$.
- For $i = 1 \dots N-1$

$$\alpha^{i+1}_b \leftarrow \sum_{a \in [l]} C^{b|a}(c^a_{x_i}) \times \alpha^i_a \text{ for all } b \in [l]$$

[Backward case]

- $\beta^{N+1}_a \leftarrow C^{*|a}(c^a_{x_N})$ for all $a \in [l]$
- For $i = N \dots 1$

$$\beta^i_a \leftarrow \sum_{b \in [l]} \beta^{i+1}_b \times C^{b|a}(c^a_{x_i}) \text{ for all } a \in [l]$$

[Marginals]

- $\mu(a, i) \leftarrow \beta^i_a \times \alpha^i_a$ for all $a \in [l], i \in [N]$

Figure 2: The forward-backward algorithm

A *skeletal sequence* consists of labels $a_1 \dots a_N$ and observations $x_1 \dots x_N$ without hidden states. Under the model, it has probability

$$p(a_1 \dots a_N, x_1 \dots x_N) = \sum_{h_1 \dots h_N} p(a_1 \dots a_N, x_1 \dots x_N, h_1 \dots h_N)$$

An equivalent definition of an R-HMM is given by organizing the parameters in matrix form. Specifically, an R-HMM has parameters $\langle \pi^a, o^a_x, T^{b|a}, f^a \rangle$ where $\pi^a \in \mathbb{R}^m$ is a column vector, o^a_x is a row vector, $T^{b|a} \in \mathbb{R}^{m \times m}$ is a matrix, and $f^a \in \mathbb{R}^m$ is a row vector, defined for all $a, b \in [l]$ and $x \in [n]$. Their entries are set to

- $[\pi^a]_h = \pi(a, h)$ for $h \in [m]$
- $[o^a_x]_h = o(x|a, h)$ for $h \in [m]$
- $[T^{b|a}]_{h',h} = t(b, h'|a, h)$ for $h, h' \in [m]$
- $[f^a]_h = f(*|a, h)$ for $h \in [m]$

4 The Forward-Backward Algorithm

Given an observation sequence $x_1 \dots x_N$, we want to infer the associated sequence of labels under an R-HMM. This can be done by computing the *marginals* of $x_1 \dots x_N$

$$\mu(a, i) = \sum_{a_1 \dots a_N :\, a_i = a} p(a_1 \dots a_N, x_1 \dots x_N)$$

for all labels $a \in [l]$ and positions $i \in [N]$. Then the most likely label at each position i is given by

$$a^*_i = \arg\max_{a \in [l]} \mu(a, i)$$

The marginals can be computed using a tensor variant of the forward-backward algorithm, shown in figure 2. The algorithm takes additional quantities $\langle C^{b|a}, C^{*|a}, c^1_a, c^a_x \rangle$ called the *operators*:

- Tensors $C^{b|a} \in \mathbb{R}^{m \times m \times m}$ for $a, b \in [l]$
- Tensors $C^{*|a} \in \mathbb{R}^{1 \times m \times m}$ for $a \in [l]$
- Column vectors $c^1_a \in \mathbb{R}^m$ for $a \in [l]$
- Row vectors $c^a_x \in \mathbb{R}^m$ for $a \in [l]$ and $x \in [n]$

The following proposition states that these operators can be defined in terms of the R-HMM parameters to guarantee the correctness of the algorithm.

Proposition 4.1. *Given an R-HMM with parameters $\langle \pi^a, o^a_x, T^{b|a}, f^a \rangle$, for any vector $v \in \mathbb{R}^m$ define the operators:*

$$C^{b|a}(v) = T^{b|a} \mathit{diag}(v) \qquad c^1_a = \pi^a$$
$$C^{*|a}(v) = f^a \mathit{diag}(v) \qquad c^a_x = o^a_x$$

Then the algorithm in figure 2 correctly computes marginals $\mu(a, i)$ under the R-HMM.

The proof is an algebraic verification and deferred to the appendix. Note that the running time of the algorithm as written is $O(l^2 m^3 N)$.[1]

Proposition 4.1 can be generalized to the following theorem. This theorem implies that the operators can be linearly transformed by some invertible matrices as long as the transformation leaves the embedded R-HMM parameters intact. This observation is central to the derivation of the spectral algorithm which estimates the linearly transformed operators but not the actual R-HMM parameters.

Theorem 4.1. *Given an R-HMM with parameters $\langle \pi^a, o^a_x, T^{b|a}, f^a \rangle$, assume that for each $a \in [l]$ we have invertible $m \times m$ matrices G^a and H^a. For any vector $v \in \mathbb{R}^m$ define the operators:*

$$C^{b|a}(v) = G^b T^{b|a} \mathit{diag}(vH^a)(G^a)^{-1} \quad c^1_a = G^a \pi^a$$
$$C^{*|a}(v) = f^a \mathit{diag}(vH^a)(G^a)^{-1} \qquad c^a_x = o^a_x (H^a)^{-1}$$

Then the algorithm in figure 2 correctly computes marginals $\mu(a, i)$ under the R-HMM.

The proof is similar to that of Cohen et al. (2012).

[1] We can reduce the complexity to $O(l^2 m^2 N)$ by precomputing the matrices $C^{b|a}(c^a_x)$ for all $a, b \in [l]$ and $x \in [n]$ after parameter estimation.

5 Spectral Estimation of R-HMMs

In this section, we derive a consistent estimator for the operators $\langle C^{b|a}, C^{*|a}, c_a^1, c_x^a \rangle$ in theorem 4.1 through the use of singular-value decomposition (SVD) followed by the method of moments.

Section 5.1 describes the decomposition of the R-HMM model into random variables which are used in the final algorithm. Section 5.2 can be skimmed through on the first reading, especially if the reader is familiar with other spectral algorithms. It includes a detailed account of the derivation of the R-HMM algorithm.

For a first reading, note that an R-HMM sequence can be seen as a right-branching L-PCFG tree. Thus, in principle, one can convert a sequence into a tree and run the inside-outside algorithm of Cohen et al. (2012) to learn the parameters of an R-HMM. However, projecting this transformation into the spectral algorithm for L-PCFGs is cumbersome and unintuitive. This is analogous to the case of the Baum-Welch algorithm for HMMs (Rabiner, 1989), which is a special case of the inside-outside algorithm for PCFGs (Lari and Young, 1990).

5.1 Random Variables

We first introduce the random variables underlying the approach then describe the operators based on these random variables. From $p(a_1 \dots a_N, x_1 \dots x_N, h_1 \dots h_N)$, we draw an R-HMM sequence $(a_1 \dots a_N, x_1 \dots x_N, h_1 \dots h_N)$ and choose a time step i uniformly at random from $[N]$. The random variables are then defined as

$$
\begin{aligned}
X &= x_i \\
A_1 &= a_i \text{ and } A_2 = a_{i+1} && \text{(if } i = N, A_2 = *) \\
H_1 &= h_i \text{ and } H_2 = h_{i+1} \\
F_1 &= (a_i \dots a_N, x_i \dots x_N) && \text{(future)} \\
F_2 &= (a_{i+1} \dots a_N, x_{i+1} \dots x_N) && \text{(skip-future)} \\
P &= (a_1 \dots a_i, x_1 \dots x_{i-1}) && \text{(past)} \\
R &= (a_i, x_i) && \text{(present)} \\
D &= (a_1 \dots a_N, x_1 \dots x_{i-1}, x_{i+1} \dots x_N) && \text{(destiny)} \\
B &= [[i = 1]]
\end{aligned}
$$

Figure 3 shows the relationship between the random variables. They are defined in such a way that the future is independent of the past and the present is independent of the destiny conditioning on the current node's label and hidden state.

Next, we require a set of feature functions over the random variables.

- ϕ maps F_1, F_2 to $\phi(F_1), \phi(F_2) \in \mathbb{R}^{d_1}$.

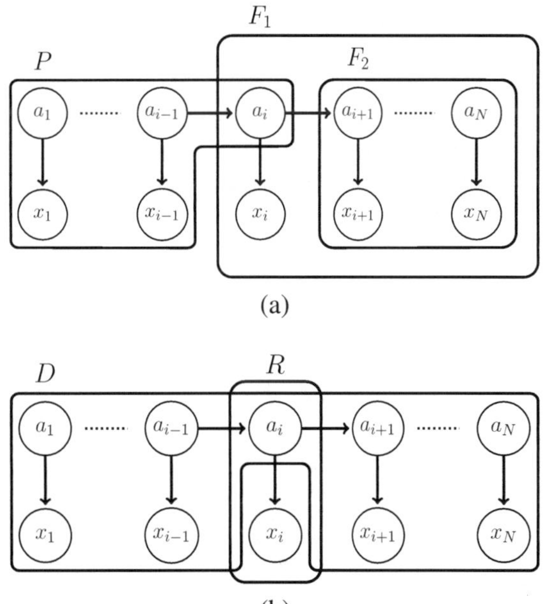

Figure 3: Given an R-HMM sequence, we define random variables over observed quantities so that conditioning on the current node, (a) the future F_1 is independent of the past P and (b) the present R is independent of the density D.

- ψ maps P to $\psi(P) \in \mathbb{R}^{d_2}$.
- ξ maps R to $\xi(R) \in \mathbb{R}^{d_3}$.
- υ maps D to $\upsilon(D) \in \mathbb{R}^{d_4}$.

We will see that the feature functions should be chosen to capture the influence of the hidden states. For instance, they might track the next label, the previous observation, or important combinations of labels and observations.

Finally, we require projection matrices

$$
\Phi^a \in \mathbb{R}^{m \times d_1} \qquad \Psi^a \in \mathbb{R}^{m \times d_2}
$$
$$
\Xi^a \in \mathbb{R}^{m \times d_3} \qquad \Upsilon^a \in \mathbb{R}^{m \times d_4}
$$

defined for all labels $a \in [l]$. These matrices will project the feature vectors of ϕ, ψ, ξ, and υ from (d_1, d_2, d_3, d_4)-dimensional spaces to an m-dimensional space. We refer to this reduced dimensional representation by the following random variables:

$$
\begin{aligned}
\underline{F}_1 &= \Phi^{A_1} \phi(F_1) && \text{(projected future)} \\
\underline{F}_2 &= \Phi^{A_2} \phi(F_2) && \text{(projected skip-future: if } i = N, \underline{F}_2 = 1) \\
\underline{P} &= \Psi^{A_1} \psi(P) && \text{(projected past)} \\
\underline{R} &= \Xi^{A_1} \xi(R) && \text{(projected present)} \\
\underline{D} &= \Upsilon^{A_1} \upsilon(D) && \text{(projected destiny)}
\end{aligned}
$$

Note that they are all vectors in $\mathbb{R}^m$.

5.2 Estimation of the Operators

Since $\underline{F}_1$, $\underline{F}_2$, $\underline{P}$, $\underline{R}$, and $\underline{D}$ do not involve hidden variables, the following quantities can be directly estimated from the training data of skeletal sequences. For this reason, they are called *observable blocks*:

$$\Sigma^a = \mathbf{E}[\underline{F}_1\underline{P}^\top | A_1 = a] \qquad \forall a \in [l]$$
$$\Lambda^a = \mathbf{E}[\underline{R}\ \underline{D}^\top | A_1 = a] \qquad \forall a \in [l]$$
$$D^{b|a} = \mathbf{E}[[[A_2 = b]]\underline{F}_2\underline{P}^\top \underline{R}^\top | A_1 = a] \qquad \forall a, b \in [l]$$
$$d_x^a = \mathbf{E}[[[X = x]]\underline{D}^\top | A_1 = a] \qquad \forall a \in [l], x \in [n]$$

The main result of this paper is that under certain conditions, matrices Σ^a and Λ^a are invertible and the operators $\langle C^{b|a}, C^{*|a}, c_a^1, c_x^a \rangle$ in theorem 4.1 can be expressed in terms of these observable blocks.

$$C^{b|a}(v) = D^{b|a}(v)(\Sigma^a)^{-1} \quad (1)$$
$$C^{*|a}(v) = D^{*|a}(v)(\Sigma^a)^{-1} \quad (2)$$
$$c_x^a = d_x^a(\Lambda^a)^{-1} \quad (3)$$
$$c_a^1 = \mathbf{E}[[[A_1 = a]]\underline{F}_1 | B = 1] \quad (4)$$

To derive this result, we use the following definition to help specify the conditions on the expectations of the feature functions.

Definition. *For each $a \in [l]$, define matrices $I^a \in \mathbb{R}^{d_1 \times m}$, $J^a \in \mathbb{R}^{d_2 \times m}$, $K^a \in \mathbb{R}^{d_3 \times m}$, $W^a \in \mathbb{R}^{d_4 \times m}$ by*

$$[I^a]_{k,h} = \boldsymbol{E}[[\phi(F_1)]_k | A_1 = a, H_1 = h]$$
$$[J^a]_{k,h} = \boldsymbol{E}[[\psi(P)]_k | A_1 = a, H_1 = h]$$
$$[K^a]_{k,h} = \boldsymbol{E}[[\xi(R)]_k | A_1 = a, H_1 = h]$$
$$[W^a]_{k,h} = \boldsymbol{E}[[\upsilon(D)]_k | A_1 = a, H_1 = h]$$

In addition, let $\Gamma^a \in \mathbb{R}^{m \times m}$ be a diagonal matrix with $[\Gamma^a]_{h,h} = P(H_1 = h | A_1 = a)$.

We now state the conditions for the correctness of Eq. (1-4). For each label $a \in [l]$, we require that

Condition 6.1 I^a, J^a, K^a, W^a have rank m.

Condition 6.2 $[\Gamma^a]_{h,h} > 0$ for all $h \in [m]$.

The conditions lead to the following proposition.

Proposition 5.1. *Assume Condition 6.1 and 6.2 hold. For all $a \in [l]$, define matrices*

$$\Omega_1^a = \boldsymbol{E}[\phi(F_1)\psi(P)^\top | A_1 = a] \in \mathbb{R}^{d_1 \times d_2}$$
$$\Omega_2^a = \boldsymbol{E}[\xi(R)\upsilon(D)^\top | A_1 = a] \in \mathbb{R}^{d_3 \times d_4}$$

Let $u_1^a \dots u_m^a \in \mathbb{R}^{d_1}$ and $v_1^a \dots v_m^a \in \mathbb{R}^{d_2}$ be the top m left and right singular vectors of Ω^a. Similarly, let $l_1^a \dots l_m^a \in \mathbb{R}^{d_3}$ and $r_1^a \dots r_m^a \in \mathbb{R}^{d_4}$ be the top m left and right singular vectors of Ψ^a. Define projection matrices

$$\Phi^a = [u_1^a \dots u_m^a]^\top \qquad \Psi^a = [v_1^a \dots v_m^a]^\top$$
$$\Xi^a = [l_1^a \dots l_m^a]^\top \qquad \Upsilon^a = [r_1^a \dots r_m^a]^\top$$

Then the following $m \times m$ matrices

$$G^a = \Phi^a I^a \qquad \mathcal{G}^a = \Psi^a J^a$$
$$H^a = \Xi^a K^a \qquad \mathcal{H}^a = \Upsilon^a W^a$$

are invertible.

The proof resembles that of lemma 2 of Hsu et al. (2012). Finally, we state the main result that shows $\langle C^{b|a}, C^{*|a}, c_a^1, c_x^a \rangle$ in Eq. (1-4) using the projections from proposition 5.1 satisfy theorem 4.1. A sketch of the proof is deferred to the appendix.

Theorem 5.1. *Assume conditions 6.1 and 6.2 hold. Let $\langle \Phi^a, \Psi^a, \Xi^a, \Upsilon^a \rangle$ be the projection matrices from proposition 5.1. Then the operators in Eq. (1-4) satisfy theorem 4.1.*

In summary, these results show that with the proper selection of feature functions, we can construct projection matrices $\langle \Phi^a, \Psi^a, \Xi^a, \Upsilon^a \rangle$ to obtain operators $\langle C^{b|a}, C^{*|a}, c_a^1, c_x^a \rangle$ which satisfy the conditions of theorem 4.1.

6 The Spectral Estimation Algorithm

In this section, we give an algorithm to estimate the operators $\langle C^{b|a}, C^{*|a}, c_a^1, c_x^a \rangle$ from samples of skeletal sequences. Suppose the training set consists of M skeletal sequences $(a^{(j)}, x^{(j)})$ for $j \in [M]$. Then M samples of the random variables can be derived from this training set as follows

- At each $j \in [M]$, choose a position i_j uniformly at random from the positions in $(a^{(j)}, x^{(j)})$. Sample the random variables $(X, A_1, A_2, F_1, F_2, P, R, D, B)$ using the procedure defined in section 5.1.

This process yields M samples

$$(x^{(j)}, a_1^{(j)}, a_2^{(j)}, f_1^{(j)}, f_2^{(j)}, p^{(j)}, r^{(j)}, d^{(j)}, b^{(j)}) \text{ for } j \in [M]$$

Assuming $(a^{(j)}, x^{(j)})$ are i.i.d. draws from the PMF $p(a_1 \dots a_N, x_1 \dots x_N)$ over skeletal sequences under an R-HMM, the tuples obtained through this process are i.i.d. draws from the joint PMF over $(X, A_1, A_2, F_1, F_2, P, R, D, B)$.

Input: samples of $(X, A_1, A_2, F_1, F_2, P, R, D, B)$; feature functions ϕ, ψ, ξ, and υ; number of hidden states m
Output: estimates $\left\langle \hat{C}^{b|a}, \hat{C}^{*|a}, \hat{c}^1_a, \hat{c}^a_x \right\rangle$ of the operators used in algorithm 2

[Singular Value Decomposition]

- For each label $a \in [l]$, compute empirical estimates of

$$\Omega_1^a = \mathbf{E}[\phi(F_1)\psi(P)^\top | A_1 = a]$$
$$\Omega_2^a = \mathbf{E}[\xi(R)\upsilon(D)^\top | A_1 = a]$$

and obtain their singular vectors via an SVD. Use the top m singular vectors to construct projections $\left\langle \hat{\Phi}^a, \hat{\Psi}^a, \hat{\Xi}^a, \hat{\Upsilon}^a \right\rangle$.

[Sample Projection]

- Project (d_1, d_2, d_3, d_4)-dimensional samples of

$$(\phi(F_1), \phi(F_2), \psi(P), \xi(R), \upsilon(D))$$

with matrices $\left\langle \hat{\Phi}^a, \hat{\Psi}^a, \hat{\Xi}^a, \hat{\Upsilon}^a \right\rangle$ to obtain m-dimensional samples of

$$(\underline{F}_1, \underline{F}_2, \underline{P}, \underline{R}, \underline{D})$$

[Method of Moments]

- For each $a, b \in [l]$ and $x \in [n]$, compute empirical estimates $\left\langle \hat{\Sigma}^a, \hat{\Lambda}^a, \hat{D}^{b|a}, \hat{d}^a_x \right\rangle$ of the observable blocks

$$\Sigma^a = \mathbf{E}[\underline{F}_1 \underline{P}^\top | A_1 = a]$$
$$\Lambda^a = \mathbf{E}[\underline{R}\ \underline{D}^\top | A_1 = a]$$
$$D^{b|a} = \mathbf{E}[[[A_2 = b]]\underline{F}_2 \underline{P}^\top \underline{R}^\top | A_1 = a]$$
$$d^a_x = \mathbf{E}[[[X = x]]\underline{D}^\top | A_1 = a]$$

and also $\hat{c}^1_a = \mathbf{E}[[[A_1 = a]]\underline{F}_1 | B = 1]$. Finally, set

$$\hat{C}^{b|a}(v) \leftarrow \hat{D}^{b|a}(v)(\hat{\Sigma}^a)^{-1}$$
$$\hat{C}^{*|a}(v) \leftarrow \hat{D}^{*|a}(v)(\hat{\Sigma}^a)^{-1}$$
$$\hat{c}^a_x \leftarrow \hat{d}^a_x(\hat{\Lambda}^a)^{-1}$$

Figure 4: The spectral estimation algorithm

The algorithm in figure 4 shows how to derive estimates of the observable representations from these samples. It first computes the projection matrices $\langle \Phi^a, \Psi^a, \Xi^a, \Upsilon^a \rangle$ for each label $a \in [l]$ by computing empirical estimates of Ω_1^a and Ω_2^a in proposition 5.1, calculating their singular vectors via an SVD, and setting the projections in terms of these singular vectors. These projection matrices are then used to project (d_1, d_2, d_3, d_4)-dimensional feature vectors

$$\left(\phi(f_1^{(j)}), \phi(f_2^{(j)}), \psi(p^{(j)}), \xi(r^{(j)}), \upsilon(d^{(j)})\right)$$

down to m-dimensional vectors

$$\left(\underline{f}_1^{(j)}, \underline{f}_2^{(j)}, \underline{p}^{(j)}, \underline{r}^{(j)}, \underline{d}^{(j)}\right)$$

for all $j \in [M]$. It then computes correlation between these vectors in this lower dimensional space to estimate the observable blocks which are used to obtain the operators as in Eq. (1-4). These operators can be used in algorithm 2 to compute marginals.

As in other spectral methods, this estimation algorithm is consistent, i.e., the marginals $\hat{\mu}(a, i)$ computed with the estimated operators approach the true marginal values given more data. For details, see Cohen et al. (2012) and Foster et al. (2012).

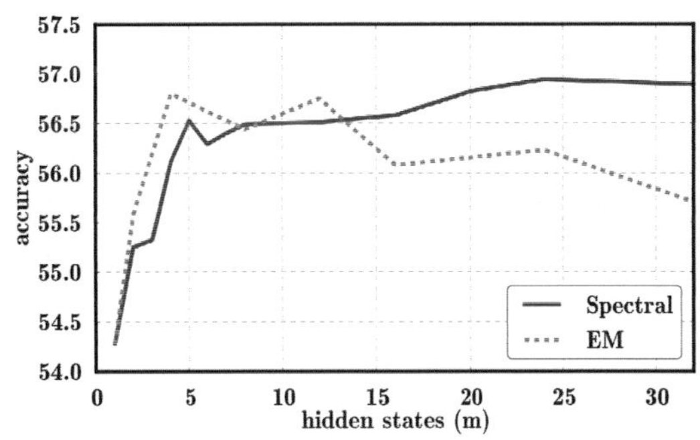

Figure 5: Accuracy of the spectral algorithm and EM on TIMIT development data for varying numbers of hidden states m. For EM, the highest scoring iteration is shown.

7 Experiments

We apply the spectral algorithm for learning R-HMMs to the task of phoneme recognition. The goal is to predict the correct sequence of phonemes $a_1 \dots a_N$ for a given a set of speech frames $x_1 \dots x_N$. Phoneme recognition is often modeled with a fixed-structure HMM trained with EM, which makes it a natural application for spectral training.

We train and test on the TIMIT corpus of spoken language utterances (Garofolo and others, 1988). The label set consists of $l = 39$ English phonemes following a standard phoneme set (Lee and Hon, 1989). For training, we use the `sx` and `si` utterances of the TIMIT training section made up of

$\phi(F_1)$	$a_{i+1} \times x_i$, a_{i+1}, x_i, $\mathtt{np}(a_i \dots a_N)$
$\psi(P)$	(a_{i-1}, x_{i-1}), a_{i-1}, x_{i-1}, $\mathtt{pp}(a_1 \dots a_i)$
$\xi(R)$	x_i
$\upsilon(D)$	$a_{i-1} \times x_{i-1}$, a_{i-1}, x_{i-1}, $\mathtt{pp}(a_1 \dots a_i)$, $\mathtt{pos}(a_1 \dots a_N)$

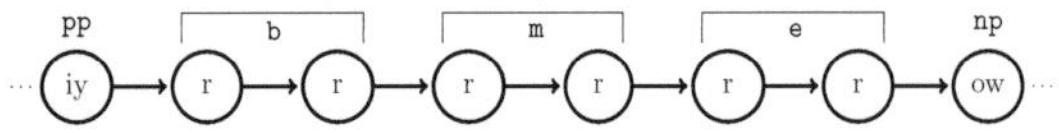

Figure 6: The feature templates for phoneme recognition. The simplest features look only at the current label and observation. Other features indicate the previous phoneme type used before a_i (pp), the next phoneme type used after a_i (np), and the relative position (beginning, middle, or end) of a_i within the current phoneme (pos). The figure gives a typical segment of the phoneme sequence $a_1 \dots a_N$

$M = 3696$ utterances. The parameter estimate is smoothed using the method of Cohen et al. (2013).

Each utterance consists of a speech signal aligned with phoneme labels. As preprocessing, we divide the signal into a sequence of N overlapping frames, 25ms in length with a 10ms step size. Each frame is converted to a feature representation using MFCC with its first and second derivatives for a total of 39 continuous features. To discretize the problem, we apply vector quantization using euclidean k-means to map each frame into $n = 10000$ observation classes. After preprocessing, we have 3696 skeletal sequence with $a_1 \dots a_N$ as the frame-aligned phoneme labels and $x_1 \dots x_N$ as the observation classes.

For testing, we use the `core` test portion of TIMIT, consisting of 192 utterances, and for development we use 200 additional utterances. Accuracy is measured by the percentage of frames labeled with the correct phoneme. During inference, we calculate marginals μ for each label at each position i and choose the one with the highest marginal probability, $a_i^* = \arg\max_{a \in [l]} \mu(a, i)$.

The spectral method requires defining feature functions ϕ, ψ, ξ, and υ. We use binary-valued feature vectors which we specify through features templates, for instance the template $a_i \times x_i$ corresponds to binary values for each possible label and output pair (ln binary dimensions).

Figure 6 gives the full set of templates. These feature functions are specially for the phoneme labeling task. We note that the HTK baseline explicitly models the position within the current phoneme as part of the HMM structure. The spectral method is able to encode similar information naturally through the feature functions.

Method	Accuracy
EM(4)	56.80
EM(24)	56.23
SPECTRAL(24), no np, pp, pos	55.45
SPECTRAL(24), no pos	56.56
SPECTRAL(24)	56.94

Figure 7: Feature ablation experiments on TIMIT development data for the best spectral model ($m = 24$) with comparisons to the best EM model ($m = 4$) and EM with $m = 24$.

Method	Accuracy
UNIGRAM	48.04
HMM	54.08
EM(4)	55.49
SPECTRAL(24)	55.82
HTK	55.70

Figure 8: Performance of baselines and spectral R-HMM on TIMIT test data. Number of hidden states m optimized on development data (see figure 5). The improvement of the spectral method over the EM baseline is significant at the $p \leq 0.05$ level (and very close to significant at $p \leq 0.01$, with a precise value of $p \leq 0.0104$).

We implement several baseline for phoneme recognition: UNIGRAM chooses the most likely label, $\arg\max_{a \in [l]} p(a|x_i)$, at each position; HMM is a standard HMM trained with maximum-likelihood estimation; EM(m) is an R-HMM with m hidden states estimated using EM; and SPECTRAL(m) is an R-HMM with m hidden states estimated with the spectral method described in this paper. We also compare to HTK, a fixed-structure HMM with three segments per phoneme estimated using EM with the HTK speech toolkit. See Young et al. (2006) for more details on this method.

An important consideration for both EM and the spectral method is the number of hidden states m in the R-HMM. More states allow for greater label refinement, with the downside of possible overfitting and, in the case of EM, more local optima. To determine the best number of hidden states, we optimize both methods on the development set for a range of m values between 1 to 32. For EM, we run 200 training iterations on each value of m and choose the iteration that scores best on the development set. As the spectral algorithm is non-iterative, we only need to evaluate the development set once per m value. Figure 5 shows the development accuracy of the two method as we adjust the value of m. EM accuracy peaks at 4 hidden states and then starts degrading, whereas the spectral method continues to improve until 24 hidden states.

Another important consideration for the spectral method is the feature functions. The analysis suggests that the best feature functions are highly informative of the underlying hidden states. To test this empirically we run spectral estimation with a reduced set of features by ablating the templates indicating adjacent phonemes and relative position. Figure 7 shows that removing these features does have a significant effect on development accuracy. Without either type of feature, development accuracy drops by 1.5%.

We can interpret the effect of the features in a more principled manner. Informative features yield greater singular values for the matrices Ω_1^a and Ω_2^a, and these singular values directly affect the sample complexity of the algorithm; see Cohen et al. (2012) for details. In sum, good feature functions lead to well-conditioned Ω_1^a and Ω_2^a, which in turn require fewer samples for convergence.

Figure 8 gives the final performance for the baselines and the spectral method on the TIMIT test set. For EM and the spectral method, we use best performing model from the development data, 4 hidden states for EM and 24 for the spectral method. The experiments show that R-HMM models score significantly better than a standard HMM and comparatively to the fixed-structure HMM. In training the R-HMM models, the spectral method performs competitively with EM while avoiding the problems of local optima.

8 Conclusion

This paper derives a spectral algorithm for the task of supervised sequence labeling using an R-HMM. Unlike EM, the spectral method is guaranteed to provide a consistent estimate of the parameters of the model. In addition, the algorithm is simple to implement, requiring only an SVD of the observed counts and other standard matrix operations. We show empirically that when equipped with informative feature functions, the spectral method performs competitively with EM on the task of phoneme recognition.

Appendix

Proof of proposition 4.1. At any time step $i \in [N]$ in the algorithm in figure 2, for all label $a \in [l]$ we have a column vector $\alpha_a^i \in \mathbb{R}^m$ and a row vector $\beta_a^i \in \mathbb{R}^m$. The value of these vectors at each index $h \in [m]$ can be verified as

$$[\alpha_a^i]_h = \sum_{\substack{a_1 \ldots a_i, h_1 \ldots h_i: \\ a_i = a, h_i = h}} p(a_1 \ldots a_i, x_1 \ldots x_{i-1}, h_1 \ldots h_i)$$

$$[\beta_a^i]_h = \sum_{\substack{a_i \ldots a_N, h_i \ldots h_N: \\ a_i = a, h_i = h}} p(a_{i+1} \ldots a_N, x_i \ldots x_N, h_{i+1} \ldots h_N | a_i, h_i)$$

Thus $\beta_a^i \alpha_a^i$ is a scalar equal to

$$\sum_{\substack{a_1 \ldots a_N, h_1 \ldots h_N: \\ a_i = a}} p(a_1 \ldots a_N, x_1 \ldots x_N, h_1 \ldots h_N)$$

which is the value of the marginal $\mu(a, i)$. □

Proof of theorem 5.1. It can be verified that $c_a^1 = G^a \pi^a$. For the others, under the conditional independence illustrated in figure 3 we can decompose the observable blocks in terms of the R-HMM parameters and invertible matrices

$$\Sigma^a = G^a \Gamma^a (\mathcal{G}^a)^\top \qquad \Lambda^a = H^a \Gamma^a (\mathcal{H}^a)^\top$$

$$D^{b|a}(v) = G^b T^{b|a} \text{diag}(v H^a) \Gamma^a (\mathcal{G}^a)^\top$$

$$D^{*|a}(v) = f^a \text{diag}(v H^a) \Gamma^a (\mathcal{G}^a)^\top \qquad d_x^a = o_x^a \Gamma^a (\mathcal{H}^a)^\top$$

using techniques similar to those sketched in Cohen et al. (2012). By proposition 5.1, Σ^a and Λ^a are invertible, and these observable blocks yield the operators that satisfy theorem 4.1 when placed in Eq. (1-3). □

References

A. Anandkumar, D. P. Foster, D. Hsu, S.M. Kakade, and Y.K. Liu. 2012a. Two svds suffice: Spectral decompositions for probabilistic topic modeling and latent dirichlet allocation. *Arxiv preprint arXiv:1204.6703*.

A. Anandkumar, D. Hsu, and S.M. Kakade. 2012b. A method of moments for mixture models and hidden markov models. *Arxiv preprint arXiv:1203.0683*.

B. Balle, A. Quattoni, and X. Carreras. 2011. A spectral learning algorithm for finite state transducers. *Machine Learning and Knowledge Discovery in Databases*, pages 156–171.

S. B. Cohen, K. Stratos, M. Collins, D. P. Foster, and L. Ungar. 2012. Spectral learning of latent-variable PCFGs. In *Proceedings of the 50th Annual Meeting of the Association for Computational Linguistics*. Association for Computational Linguistics.

S. B. Cohen, K. Stratos, M. Collins, D. P. Foster, and L. Ungar. 2013. Experiments with spectral learning of latent-variable pcfgs. In *Proceedings of the 2013 Conference of the North American Chapter of the Association for Computational Linguistics: Human Language Technologies*.

D. P. Foster, J. Rodu, and L.H. Ungar. 2012. Spectral dimensionality reduction for hmms. *Arxiv preprint arXiv:1203.6130*.

J. S. Garofolo et al. 1988. Getting started with the darpa timit cd-rom: An acoustic phonetic continuous speech database. *National Institute of Standards and Technology (NIST), Gaithersburgh, MD*, 107.

D. Hsu, S.M. Kakade, and T. Zhang. 2012. A spectral algorithm for learning hidden markov models. *Journal of Computer and System Sciences*.

H. Jaeger. 2000. Observable operator models for discrete stochastic time series. *Neural Computation*, 12(6):1371–1398.

K. Lari and S. J. Young. 1990. The estimation of stochastic context-free grammars using the inside-outside algorithm. *Computer speech & language*, 4(1):35–56.

K.F. Lee and H.W. Hon. 1989. Speaker-independent phone recognition using hidden markov models. *Acoustics, Speech and Signal Processing, IEEE Transactions on*, 37(11):1641–1648.

F. M. Luque, A. Quattoni, B. Balle, and X. Carreras. 2012. Spectral learning for non-deterministic dependency parsing. In *EACL*, pages 409–419.

T. Matsuzaki, Y. Miyao, and J. Tsujii. 2005. Probabilistic cfg with latent annotations. In *Proceedings of the 43rd Annual Meeting on Association for Computational Linguistics*, pages 75–82. Association for Computational Linguistics.

A. Parikh, L. Song, and E.P. Xing. 2011. A spectral algorithm for latent tree graphical models. In *Proceedings of the 28th International Conference on Machine Learning*.

F. Pereira and Y. Schabes. 1992. Inside-outside reestimation from partially bracketed corpora. In *Proceedings of the 30th annual meeting on Association for Computational Linguistics*, pages 128–135. Association for Computational Linguistics.

S. Petrov, L. Barrett, R. Thibaux, and D. Klein. 2006. Learning accurate, compact, and interpretable tree annotation. In *Proceedings of the 21st International Conference on Computational Linguistics and the 44th annual meeting of the Association for Computational Linguistics*, pages 433–440. Association for Computational Linguistics.

Slav Petrov, Adam Pauls, and Dan Klein. 2007. Learning structured models for phone recognition. In *Proc. of EMNLP-CoNLL*.

L. R. Rabiner. 1989. A tutorial on hidden markov models and selected applications in speech recognition. *Proceedings of the IEEE*, 77(2):257–286.

S. Siddiqi, B. Boots, and G. J. Gordon. 2010. Reduced-rank hidden Markov models. In *Proceedings of the Thirteenth International Conference on Artificial Intelligence and Statistics (AISTATS-2010)*.

L. Song, B. Boots, S. Siddiqi, G. Gordon, and A. Smola. 2010. Hilbert space embeddings of hidden markov models. In *Proceedings of the 27th International Conference on Machine Learning*. Citeseer.

S. Young, G. Evermann, M. Gales, T. Hain, D. Kershaw, XA Liu, G. Moore, J. Odell, D. Ollason, D. Povey, et al. 2006. The htk book (for htk version 3.4).

Sentence Compression with Joint Structural Inference

Kapil Thadani and **Kathleen McKeown**
Department of Computer Science
Columbia University
New York, NY 10025, USA
{kapil,kathy}@cs.columbia.edu

Abstract

Sentence compression techniques often assemble output sentences using fragments of lexical sequences such as n-grams or units of syntactic structure such as edges from a dependency tree representation. We present a novel approach for discriminative sentence compression that unifies these notions and jointly produces sequential *and* syntactic representations for output text, leveraging a compact integer linear programming formulation to maintain structural integrity. Our supervised models permit rich features over heterogeneous linguistic structures and generalize over previous state-of-the-art approaches. Experiments on corpora featuring human-generated compressions demonstrate a 13-15% relative gain in 4-gram accuracy over a well-studied language model-based compression system.

1 Introduction

Recent years have seen increasing interest in text-to-text generation tasks such as paraphrasing and text simplification, due in large part to their direct utility in high-level natural language tasks such as abstractive summarization. The task of sentence compression in particular has benefited from the availability of a number of useful resources such as the the Ziff-Davis compression corpus (Knight and Marcu, 2000) and the Edinburgh compression corpus (Clarke and Lapata, 2006b) which make compression problems highly relevant for data-driven approaches involving language generation.

The sentence compression task addresses the problem of minimizing the lexical footprint of a sentence, i.e., the number of words or characters in it, while preserving its most salient information. This is illustrated in the following example from the compression corpus of Clarke and Lapata (2006b):

> **Original:** In 1967 Chapman, who had cultivated a conventional image with his ubiquitous tweed jacket and pipe, by his own later admission stunned a party attended by his friends and future Python colleagues by coming out as a homosexual.
>
> **Compressed:** In 1967 Chapman, who had cultivated a conventional image, stunned a party by coming out as a homosexual.

Compression can therefore be viewed as analogous to text summarization[1] defined at the sentence level. Unsurprisingly, independent selection of tokens for an output sentence does not lead to fluent or meaningful compressions; thus, compression systems often assemble output text from units that are larger than single tokens such as n-grams (McDonald, 2006; Clarke and Lapata, 2008) or edges in a dependency structure (Filippova and Strube, 2008; Galanis and Androutsopoulos, 2010). These systems implicitly rely on a structural representation of text—as a sequence of tokens or as a dependency tree respectively—to to underpin the generation of an output sentence.

In this work, we present *structured transduction*: a novel supervised framework for sentence compression which employs a joint inference strategy to simultaneously recover sentence compressions under *both* these structural representations of text—a token sequence as well as a tree of syntactic dependencies. Sentence generation is treated as a discriminative structured prediction task in which rich linguistically-motivated

[1] To further the analogy, compression is most often formulated as a word deletion task which parallels the popular view of summarization as a sentence extraction task.

features can be used to predict the informativeness of specific tokens within the input text as well as the fluency of n-grams and dependency relationships in the output text. We present a novel constrained integer linear program that optimally solves the joint inference problem, using the notion of *commodity flow* (Magnanti and Wolsey, 1994) to ensure the production of valid acyclic sequences and trees for an output sentence.

The primary contributions of this work are:

- A supervised sequence-based compression model which outperforms Clarke & Lapata's (2008) state-of-the-art sequence-based compression system without relying on any hard syntactic constraints.
- A formulation to jointly infer tree structures alongside sequentially-ordered n-grams, thereby permitting features that factor over both phrases and dependency relations.

The structured transduction models offer additional flexibility when compared to existing models that compress via n-gram or dependency factorizations. For instance, the use of commodity flow constraints to ensure well-formed structure permits arbitrary reorderings of words in the input and is not restricted to producing text in the same order as the input like much previous work (McDonald, 2006; Clarke and Lapata, 2008; Filippova and Strube, 2008) *inter alia.*[2]

We ran compression experiments with the proposed approaches on well-studied corpora from the domains of written news (Clarke and Lapata, 2006b) and broadcast news (Clarke and Lapata, 2008). Our supervised approaches show significant gains over the language model-based compression system of Clarke and Lapata (2008) under a variety of performance measures, yielding 13-15% relative F_1 improvements for 4-gram retrieval over Clarke and Lapata (2008) under identical compression rate conditions.

2 Joint Structure Transduction

The structured transduction framework is driven by the fundamental assumption that generating fluent text involves considerations of diverse structural relationships between tokens in both input and output sentences. Models for sentence compression often compose text from units that are larger than individual tokens, such as n-grams which describe a token sequence or syntactic relations which comprise a dependency tree. However, our approach is specifically motivated by the perspective that *both* these representations of a sentence—a sequence of tokens and a tree of dependency relations—are equally meaningful when considering its underlying fluency and integrity. In other words, models for compressing a token sequence must also account for the compression of its dependency representation and vice versa.

In this section, we discuss the problem of recovering an optimal compression from a sentence as a linear optimization problem over heterogenous substructures (cf. §2.1) that can be assembled into valid and consistent representations of a sentence (cf. §2.2). We then consider rich linguistically-motivated features over these substructures (cf. §2.3) for which corresponding weights can be learned via supervised structured prediction (cf. §2.4).

2.1 Linear Objective

Consider a single compression instance involving a source sentence S containing m tokens. The notation $\widehat{S}$ is used to denote a well-formed compression of S. In this paper, we follow the standard assumption from compression research in assuming that candidate compressions $\widehat{S}$ are assembled from the tokens in S, thereby treating compression as a word-deletion task. The inference step aims to retrieve the output sentence $\widehat{S}^*$ that is the most likely compression of the given input S, i.e., the $\widehat{S}$ that maximizes $p(\widehat{S}|S) \propto p(\widehat{S}, S)$ or, in an equivalent discriminative setting, the $\widehat{S}$ that maximizes a feature-based score for compression

$$\widehat{S}^* \triangleq \arg\max_{\widehat{S}} \mathbf{w}^\top \boldsymbol{\Phi}(S, \widehat{S}) \qquad (1)$$

where $\boldsymbol{\Phi}(S, \widehat{S})$ denotes some feature map parameterized by a weight vector $\mathbf{w}$.

Let $T \triangleq \{t_i : 1 \leq i \leq m\}$ represent the set of tokens in S and let $x_i \in \{0, 1\}$ represent a token indicator variable whose value corresponds to whether token t_i is present in the output sentence $\widehat{S}$. The incidence vector $\mathbf{x} \triangleq \langle x_1, \ldots, x_m \rangle^\top$ therefore represents an entire token configuration that is equivalent to some subset of T.

If we were to consider a simplistic bag-of-tokens scenario in which the features factor entirely over the tokens from T, the highest-scoring

[2] We do not evaluate token reordering in the current work as the corpus used for experiments in §3 features human-generated compressions that preserve token ordering.

compression under (1) would simply be the token configuration that maximizes a linear combination of per-token scores, i.e., $\sum_{t_i \in T} x_i \cdot \theta_{\text{tok}}(i)$ where $\theta_{\text{tok}} : \mathbb{N} \rightarrow \mathbb{R}$ denotes a linear scoring function which measures the relative value of retaining t_i in a compression of S based on its features, i.e., $\theta_{\text{tok}}(i) \triangleq \boldsymbol{w}_{\text{tok}}^{\top} \boldsymbol{\phi}_{\text{tok}}(t_i)$. Although this can be solved efficiently under compression-rate constraints, the strong independence assumption used is clearly unrealistic: a model that cannot consider any relationship between tokens in the output does not provide a token ordering or ensure that the resulting sentence is grammatical.

The natural solution is to include higher-order factorizations of linguistic structures such as n-grams in the objective function. For clarity of exposition, we assume the use of trigrams without loss of generality. Let U represent the set of all possible trigrams that can be constructed from the tokens of S; in other words $U \triangleq \{\langle t_i, t_j, t_k \rangle : t_i \in T \cup \{\text{START}\}, t_j \in T, t_k \in T \cup \{\text{END}\}, i \neq j \neq k\}$. Following the notation for token indicators, let $y_{ijk} \in \{0, 1\}$ represent a trigram indicator variable for whether the contiguous sequence of tokens $\langle t_i, t_j, t_k \rangle$ is in the output sentence. The incidence vector $\mathbf{y} \triangleq \langle y_{ijk} \rangle_{\langle t_i, t_j, t_k \rangle \in U}$ hence represents some subset of the trigrams in U. Similarly, let V represent the set of all possible dependency edges that can be established among the tokens of S and the pseudo-token ROOT, i.e., $V \triangleq \{\langle i, j \rangle : i \in T \cup \{\text{ROOT}\}, j \in T, t_j \text{ is a dependent of } t_i \text{ in } S\}$. As before, $z_{ij} \in \{0, 1\}$ represents a dependency arc indicator variable indicating whether t_j is a direct dependent of t_i in the dependency structure of the output sentence, and $\mathbf{z} \triangleq \langle z_{ij} \rangle_{\langle t_i, t_j \rangle \in V}$ represents a subset of the arcs from V.

Using this notation, any output sentence $\widehat{S}$ can now be expressed as a combination of some token, trigram and dependency arc configurations $\langle \mathbf{x}, \mathbf{y}, \mathbf{z} \rangle$. Defining θ_{ngr} and θ_{dep} analogously to θ_{tok} for trigrams and dependency arcs respectively, we rewrite (1) as

$$\begin{aligned}
\widehat{S}^* = \arg\max_{\mathbf{x},\mathbf{y},\mathbf{z}} & \sum_{t_i \in T} x_i \cdot \theta_{\text{tok}}(i) \\
&+ \sum_{\langle t_i, t_j, t_k \rangle \in U} y_{ijk} \cdot \theta_{\text{ngr}}(i, j, k) \\
&+ \sum_{\langle t_i, t_j \rangle \in V} z_{ij} \cdot \theta_{\text{dep}}(i, j) \\
= \arg\max_{\mathbf{x},\mathbf{y},\mathbf{z}} & \; \mathbf{x}^{\top} \boldsymbol{\theta}_{\text{tok}} + \mathbf{y}^{\top} \boldsymbol{\theta}_{\text{ngr}} + \mathbf{z}^{\top} \boldsymbol{\theta}_{\text{dep}} \qquad (2)
\end{aligned}$$

where $\boldsymbol{\theta}_{\text{tok}} \triangleq \langle \theta_{\text{tok}}(i) \rangle_{t_i \in T}$ denotes the vector of token scores for all tokens $t_i \in T$ and $\boldsymbol{\theta}_{\text{ngr}}$ and $\boldsymbol{\theta}_{\text{dep}}$ represent vectors of scores for all trigrams and dependency arcs in U and V respectively. The joint objective in (2) is an appealingly straightforward and yet general formulation for the compression task. For instance, the use of standard substructures like n-grams permits scoring of the output sequence configuration $\mathbf{y}$ under probabilistic n-gram language models as in Clarke and Lapata (2008). Similarly, consideration of dependency arcs allows the compressed dependency tree $\mathbf{z}$ to be scored using a rich set of indicator features over dependency labels, part-of-speech tags and even lexical features as in Filippova and Strube (2008).

However, unlike the bag-of-tokens scenario, these output structures cannot be constructed efficiently due to their interdependence. Specifically, we need to maintain the following conditions in order to obtain an interpretable token sequence $\mathbf{y}$:

- Trigram variables y_{ijk} must be non-zero if and only if their corresponding word variables x_i, x_j and x_k are non-zero.
- The non-zero y_{ijk} must form a sentence-like linear ordering, avoiding disjoint structures, cycles and branching.

Similarly, a well-formed dependency tree $\mathbf{z}$ will need to satisfy the following conditions:

- Dependency variables z_{ij} must be non-zero if and only if the corresponding word variables x_i and x_j are.
- The non-zero z_{ij} must form a directed tree with one parent per node, a single root node and no cycles.

2.2 Constrained ILP Formulation

We now discuss an approach to recover exact solutions to (2) under the appropriate structural constraints, thereby yielding globally optimal compressions $\widehat{S} \equiv \langle \mathbf{x}, \mathbf{y}, \mathbf{z} \rangle$ given some input sentence S and model parameters for the scoring functions. For this purpose, we formulate the inference task for joint structural transduction as an integer linear program (ILP)—a type of linear program (LP) in which some or all of the decision variables are restricted to integer values. A number of highly optimized general-purpose solvers exist for solving ILPs thereby making them tractable for sentence-level natural language problems in which the number of variables and constraints is described by a low-order polynomial over the size of the input.

Recent years have seen ILP applied to many structured NLP applications including dependency parsing (Riedel and Clarke, 2006; Martins et al., 2009), text alignment (DeNero and Klein, 2008; Chang et al., 2010; Thadani et al., 2012) and many previous approaches to sentence and document compression (Clarke and Lapata, 2008; Filippova and Strube, 2008; Martins and Smith, 2009; Clarke and Lapata, 2010; Berg-Kirkpatrick et al., 2011; Woodsend and Lapata, 2012).

2.2.1 Basic structural constraints

We start with constraints that define the behavior of terminal tokens. Let y_{*jk}, y_{ij*} and z_{*j} denote indicator variables for the sentence-starting trigram $\langle \text{START}, t_j, t_k \rangle$, the sentence-ending trigram $\langle t_i, t_j, \text{END} \rangle$ and the root dependency $\langle \text{ROOT}, t_j \rangle$ respectively. A valid output sentence will started and terminate with exactly one trigram (perhaps the same); similarly, exactly one word should act as the root of the output dependency tree.

$$\sum_{j,k} y_{*jk} = 1 \tag{3}$$

$$\sum_{i,j} y_{ij*} = 1 \tag{4}$$

$$\sum_{j} z_{*j} = 1 \tag{5}$$

Indicator variables for any substructure, i.e., n-gram or dependency arc, must be kept consistent with the token variables that the substructure is defined over. For instance, we require constraints which specify that tokens can only be active (non-zero) in the solution when, for $1 \leq p \leq n$, there is exactly one active n-gram in the solution which contains this word in position p.[3] Tokens and dependency arcs can similarly be kept consistent by ensuring that a word can only be active when one incoming arc is active.

$$x_l - \sum_{\substack{i,j,k:\\ l \in \{i,j,k\}}} y_{ijk} = 0, \quad \forall t_l \in T \tag{6}$$

$$x_j - \sum_{i} z_{ij} = 0, \quad \forall t_j \in T \tag{7}$$

[3]Note that this does not always hold for n-grams of order $n > 2$ due to the way terminal n-grams featuring START and END are defined. Specifically, in a valid linear ordering of tokens and $\forall r \in 1 \ldots n-2$, there can be no n-grams that feature the last $n-r-1$ tokens in the r'th position or the first $n-r-1$ tokens in the $(n-r+1)$'th position. However, this is easily tackled computationally by assuming that the terminal n-gram replaces these missing n-grams for near-terminal tokens in constraint (6).

2.2.2 Flow-based structural constraints

A key challenge for structured transduction models lies in ensuring that output token sequences and dependency trees are well formed. This requires that output structures are fully connected and that cycles are avoided. In order to accomplish this, we introduce additional variables to establish *single-commodity flow* (Magnanti and Wolsey, 1994) between all pairs of tokens, inspired by recent work in dependency parsing (Martins et al., 2009). Linear token ordering is maintained by defining real-valued *adjacency* commodity flow variables γ_{ij}^{adj} which must be non-zero whenever t_j directly follows t_i in an output sentence. Similarly, tree-structured dependencies are enforced using additional *dependency* commodity flow variables γ_{ij}^{dep} which must be non-zero whenever t_j is the dependent of t_i in the output sentence. As with the structural indicators, flow variables γ_{*j}^{adj}, γ_{i*}^{adj}, γ_{*j}^{dep} are also defined for the terminal pseudo-tokens START, END and ROOT respectively.

Each active token in the solution *consumes* one unit of each commodity from the flow variables connected to it. In conjunction with the consistency constraints from equations (6) and (7), this ensures that cycles cannot be present in the flow structure for either commodity.

$$\sum_{i} \gamma_{ij}^{c} - \sum_{k} \gamma_{jk}^{c} = x_j, \quad \forall t_j \in T, \quad \forall c \in \{\text{adj, dep}\} \tag{8}$$

By itself, (8) would simply set all token indicators x_i simultaneously to 0. However, since START and ROOT have no incoming flow variables, the amount of commodity in the respective outgoing flow variables γ_{*j}^{adj} and γ_{*j}^{dep} remains unconstrained. These flow variables therefore provide a point of origin for their respective commodities.

In order for commodity flow to be meaningful, it should be confined to mirroring active structural indicators; for this, we first restrict the amount of commodity in any γ_{ij}^{c} to be non-negative.

$$\gamma_{ij}^{c} \geq 0, \quad \forall t_i, t_j \in T \quad \forall c \in \{\text{adj, dep}\} \tag{9}$$

The adjacency commodity is then linked to the n-grams that would actually establish an adjacency relationship between two tokens, while the dependency commodity is linked to its corresponding dependency arcs. In conjunction with (8–9), these

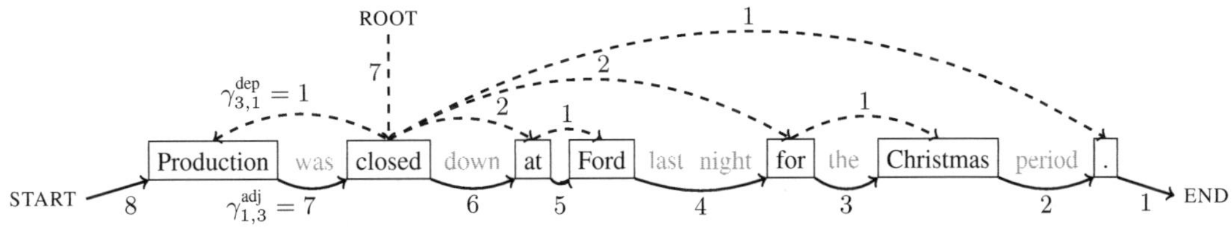

Figure 1: An illustration of commodity values for a valid solution of the program. The adjacency commodity γ^{adj} and dependency commodity γ^{dep} are denoted by solid and dashed lines respectively.

constraints also serve to establish *connectivity* for their respective structures.

$$\gamma^{\text{adj}}_{ij} - C_{\max} \sum_k y_{ijk} \leq 0, \quad \forall t_i, t_j \in T \quad (10)$$

$$\gamma^{\text{adj}}_{jk} - C_{\max} \sum_i y_{ijk} \leq 0, \quad \forall t_j, t_k \in T \quad (11)$$

$$\gamma^{\text{dep}}_{ij} - C_{\max} z_{ij} \leq 0, \quad \forall t_i, t_j \in T \quad (12)$$

where $C_{\max}$ is the maximum amount of commodity that the γ_{ij} variables may carry and serves as an upper bound on the number of tokens in the output sentence. Since we use commodity flow to avoid cyclical structure and not to specify spanning arborescences (Martins et al., 2009), $C_{\max}$ can simply be set to an arbitrary large value.

2.2.3 Compression rate constraints

The constraints specified above are adequate to enforce structural soundness in an output compression. In addition, compression tasks often involve a restriction on the size of the output sentence. When measured in tokens, this can simply be expressed via constraints over token indicators.

$$\sum_i x_i \geq R_{\min} \quad (13)$$

$$\sum_i x_i \leq R_{\max} \quad (14)$$

where the compression rate is enforced by restricting the number of output tokens to $[R_{\min}, R_{\max}]$.

2.3 Features

The scoring functions θ that guide inference for a particular compression instance are defined above as linear functions over structure-specific features. We employ the following general classes of features for tokens, trigrams and dependency arcs.

1. **Informativeness**: Good compressions might require specific words or relationships between words to be preserved, highlighted, or perhaps explicitly rejected. This can be expressed through features on token variables that indicate *a priori* salience.[4] For this purpose, we rely on indicator features for part-of-speech (POS) sequences of length up to 3 that surround the token and the POS tag of the token's syntactic governor conjoined with the label. Inspired by McDonald (2006), we also maintain indicator features for stems of verbs (at or adjacent to the token) as these can be useful indications of salience in compression. Finally, we maintain features for whether tokens are negation words, whether they appear within parentheses and if they are part of a capitalized sequence of tokens (an approximation of named entities).
2. **Fluency**: These features are intended to capture how the presence of a given substructure contributes to the overall fluency of a sentence. The n-gram variables are scored with a feature expressing their log-likelihood under an LM. For n-gram variables, we include features that indicate the POS tags and dependency labels corresponding to the tokens it covers. Dependency variable features involve indicators for the governor POS tag conjoined with the dependency direction. In addition, we also use lexical features for prepositions in the governor position of dependency variables in order to indicate whether certain prepositional phrases are likely to be preserved in compressions.
3. **Fidelity**: One might reasonably expect that many substructures in the input sentence will appear unchanged in the output sentence. Therefore, we propose boolean features that indicate that a substructure was seen in the input. Fidelity scores are included for all n-gram variables alongside label-specific fi-

[4] Many compression systems (Clarke and Lapata, 2008; Filippova and Strube, 2008) use a measure based on *tf*idf* which derives from informativeness score of Hori and Furui (2004), but we found this to be less relevant here.

delity scores for dependency arc variables, which can indicate whether particular labels are more or less likely to be dropped.

4. **Pseudo-normalization**: A drawback of using linear models for generation problems is an inability to employ output sentence length normalization in structure scoring. For this purpose, we use the common machine translation (MT) strategy of employing word penalty features. These are essentially word counts whose parameters are intended to balance out the biases in output length which are induced by other features.

Each scale-dependent feature is recorded both absolutely as well as normalized by the length of the input sentence. This is done in order to permit the model to acquire some robustness to variation in input sentence length when learning parameters.

2.4 Learning

In order to leverage a training corpus to recover weight parameters $\mathbf{w}^*$ for the above features that encourage good compressions for unseen data, we rely on the structured perceptron of Collins (2002). A fixed learning rate is used and parameters are averaged to limit overfitting.[5] In our experiments, we observed fairly stable convergence for compression quality over held-out development corpora, with peak performance usually encountered by 10 training epochs.

3 Experiments

In order to evaluate the performance of the structured transduction framework, we ran compression experiments over the newswire (NW) and broadcast news transcription (BN) corpora collected by Clarke and Lapata (2008). Sentences in these datasets are accompanied by gold compressions—one per sentence for NW and three for BN—produced by trained human annotators who were restricted to using word deletion, so paraphrasing and word reordering do not play a role. For this reason, we chose to evaluate the systems using n-gram precision and recall (among other metrics), following Unno et al. (2006) and standard MT evaluations.

We filtered the corpora to eliminate instances with less than 2 and more than 110 tokens and used the same training/development/test splits from Clarke and Lapata (2008), yielding 953/63/603 sentences respectively for the NW corpus and 880/78/404 for the BN corpus. Dependency parses were retrieved using the Stanford parser[6] and ILPs were solved using Gurobi.[7] As a state-of-the-art baseline for these experiments, we used a reimplementation of the LM-based system of Clarke and Lapata (2008), which we henceforth refer to as CL08. This is equivalent to a variant of our proposed model that excludes variables for syntactic structure, uses LM log-likelihood as a feature for trigram variables and a *tf*idf*-based significance score for token variables, and incorporates several targeted syntactic constraints based on grammatical relations derived from RASP (Briscoe et al., 2006) designed to encourage fluent output.

Due to the absence of word reordering in the gold compressions, trigram variables y that were considered in the structured transduction approach were restricted to only those for which tokens appear in the same order as the input as is the case with CL08. Furthermore, in order to reduce computational overhead for potentially-expensive ILPs, we also excluded dependency arc variables which inverted an existing governor-dependent relationship from the input sentence parse.

A recent analysis of approaches to evaluating compression (Napoles et al., 2011b) has shown a strong correlation between the compression rate and human judgments of compression quality, thereby concluding that comparisons of systems which compress at different rates are unreliable. Consequently, all comparisons that we carry out here involve a restriction to a particular compression rate to ensure that observed differences can be interpreted meaningfully.

3.1 Results

Table 1 summarizes the results from compression experiments in which the target compression rate is set to the average gold compression rate for each instance. We observe a significant gain for the joint structured transduction system over the Clarke and Lapata (2008) approach for n-gram F_1. Since n-gram metrics do not distinguish between content words and function words, we also include an evaluation metric that observes the precision, recall and F-measure of nouns and verbs

[5] Given an appropriate loss function, large-margin structured learners such as k-best MIRA (McDonald et al., 2005) can also be used as shown in Clarke and Lapata (2008).

[6] `http://nlp.stanford.edu/software/`

[7] `http://www.gurobi.com`

Corpus	System	n-grams $F_1\%$				Content words			Syntactic relations $F_1\%$	
		$n = 1$	2	3	4	P%	R%	$F_1\%$	Stanford	RASP
NW	CL08	66.65	53.08	40.35	31.02	73.84	66.41	69.38	51.51	50.21
	Joint ST	**71.91**	**58.67**	**45.84**	**35.62**	**76.82**	**76.74**	**76.33**	**55.02**	50.81
BN	CL08	75.08	61.31	46.76	37.58	80.21	75.32	76.91	60.70	57.27
	Joint ST	**77.82**	**66.39**	**52.81**	**42.52**	80.77	**81.93**	**80.75**	61.38	56.47

Table 1: Experimental results under various quality metrics (see text for descriptions). Systems were restricted to produce compressions that matched their average gold compression rate. Boldfaced entries indicate significant differences ($p < 0.0005$) under the paired t-test and Wilcoxon's signed rank test.

as a proxy for the content in compressed output. From these, we see that the primary contribution of the supervised joint approach is in enhancing the recall of meaning-bearing words.

In addition to the direct measures discussed above, Napoles et al. (2011b) indicate that various other metrics over syntactic relations such as those produced by RASP also correlate significantly with human judgments of compression quality. Compressed sentences were therefore parsed with RASP as well as the Stanford dependency parser and their resulting dependency graphs were compared to those of the gold compressions. These metrics show statistically insignificant differences except in the case of F_1 over Stanford dependencies for the NW corpus.[8]

Comparisons with CL08 do not adequately address the question of whether the performance gain observed is driven by the novel joint inference approach or the general power of discriminative learning. To investigate this, we also studied a variant of the proposed model which eliminates the dependency variables $\mathbf{z}$ and associated commodity flow machinery, thereby bridging the gap between the two systems discussed above. This system, which we refer to as Seq ST, is otherwise trained under similar conditions as Joint ST. Table 2 contains an example of incorrect system output for the three systems under study and illustrates some specific quirks of each, such as the tendency of CL08 to preserve deeply nested noun phrases, the limited ability of Seq ST to identify heads of constituents and the potential for plausible but unusual output parses from Joint ST.

Figure 2 examines the variation of content word $F_1\%$ when the target compression rate is varied for the BN corpus, which contains three reference compressions per instance. Although the gold compressions are often unreachable under low rates, this provides a view into a model's ability to select meaningful words under compression constraints. We observe that the Joint ST model consistently identifies content words more accurately than the sequence-only models despite sharing all token and trigram features with Seq ST.

Input	When Los Angeles hosted the Olympics in 1932 , Kurtz competed in high platform diving.
Gold	When Los Angeles hosted the Olympics , Kurtz competed in high diving .
CL08	When Los Angeles hosted Olympics in 1932 , in high platform diving .
Seq ST	When Los Angeles hosted the Olympics , Kurtz competed in high platform
Joint ST	When Los Angeles hosted the Olympics in 1932 , Kurtz competed diving .

Table 2: Examples of erroneous system compressions for a test instance from the NW corpus.

Figure 3 studies the variation of RASP grammatical relation $F_1\%$ with compression rate as an approximate measure of grammatical robustness. As all three systems track each other fairly closely, the plot conveys the absolute difference of the ST systems from the CL08 baseline, which reveals that Joint ST largely outperforms Seq ST under different compression conditions. We also note that a high compression rate, i.e., minimal compression, is generally favorable to CL08 under the RASP F_1 measure and conjecture that this may be due to the hard syntactic constraints employed by CL08, some of which are defined over RASP relations. At higher compression rates, these constraints largely serve to prevent the loss of meaningful syntactic relationships, e.g., that between a preposition and its prepositional phrase; however, a restrictive compression rate would likely result in all such mutually-constrained components being dropped rather than simultaneously preserved.

[8] Our RASP F_1 results for Clarke and Lapata (2008) in Table 1 outperform their reported results by about 10% (absolute) which may stem from our Gigaword-trained LM or improvements in recent versions of RASP.

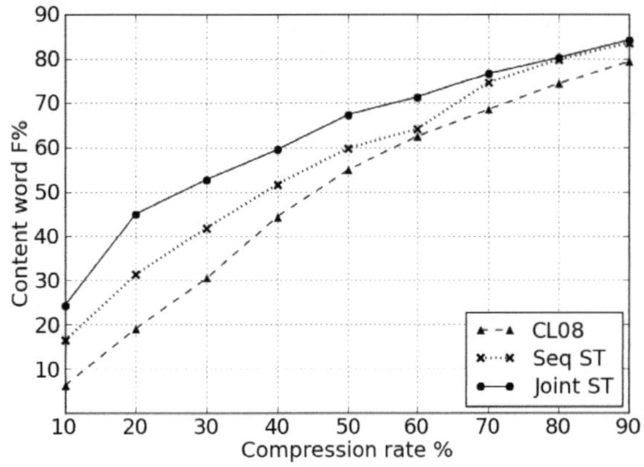

Figure 2: Informativeness of compressions in the BN test corpus indicated by noun and verb $F_1\%$ with respect to gold at different compression rates.

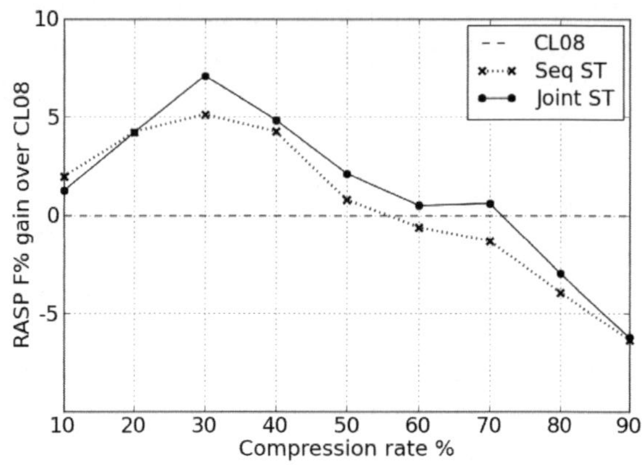

Figure 3: Relative grammaticality of BN test corpus compressions indicated by the absolute difference of RASP relation $F_1\%$ from that of CL08.

4 Related Work

An early notion of compression was proposed by Dras (1997) as reluctant sentence paraphrasing under length constraints. Jing and McKeown (2000) analyzed human-generated summaries and identified a heavy reliance on sentence reduction (Jing, 2000). The extraction by Knight and Marcu (2000) of a dataset of natural compression instances from the Ziff-Davis corpus spurred interest in supervised approaches to the task (Knight and Marcu, 2002; Riezler et al., 2003; Turner and Charniak, 2005; McDonald, 2006; Unno et al., 2006; Galley and McKeown, 2007; Nomoto, 2007). In particular, McDonald (2006) expanded on Knight & Marcu's (2002) transition-based model by using dynamic programming to recover optimal transition sequences, and Clarke and Lapata (2006a) used ILP to replace pairwise transitions with trigrams. Other recent work (Filippova and Strube, 2008; Galanis and Androutsopoulos, 2010) has used dependency trees directly as sentence representations for compression. Another line of research has attempted to broaden the notion of compression beyond mere word deletion (Cohn and Lapata, 2009; Ganitkevitch et al., 2011; Napoles et al., 2011a). Finally, progress on standalone compression tasks has also enabled document summarization techniques that jointly address sentence selection and compression (Daumé and Marcu, 2002; Clarke and Lapata, 2007; Martins and Smith, 2009; Berg-Kirkpatrick et al., 2011; Woodsend and Lapata, 2012), a number of which also rely on ILP-based inference.

Monolingual text-to-text generation research also faces many obstacles common to MT. Recent work in MT decoding has proposed more efficient approaches than ILP to produced text optimally under syntactic and sequential models of language (Rush and Collins, 2011). We are currently exploring similar ideas for compression and other text-to-text generation problems.

5 Conclusion

We have presented a supervised discriminative approach to sentence compression that elegantly accounts for two complementary aspects of sentence structure—token ordering and dependency syntax. Our inference formulation permits rich, linguistically-motivated features that factor over the tokens, n-grams and dependencies of the output. Structural integrity is maintained by linear constraints based on commodity flow, resulting in a flexible integer linear program for the inference task. We demonstrate that this approach leads to significant performance gains over a state-of-the-art baseline compression system without resorting to hand-picked constraints on output content.

Acknowledgments

This work was supported by the Intelligence Advanced Research Projects Activity (IARPA) via Department of Interior National Business Center (DoI/NBC) contract number D11PC20153. The U.S. Government is authorized to reproduce and distribute reprints for Governmental purposes notwithstanding any copyright annotation thereon. The views and conclusions contained herein are those of the authors and should not be interpreted as necessarily representing the official policies or endorsements, either expressed or implied, of IARPA, DoI/NBC, or the U.S. Government.

References

Taylor Berg-Kirkpatrick, Dan Gillick, and Dan Klein. 2011. Jointly learning to extract and compress. In *Proceedings of ACL-HLT*, pages 481–490.

Ted Briscoe, John Carroll, and Rebecca Watson. 2006. The second release of the RASP system. In *Proceedings of the ACL-COLING Interactive Presentation Sessions*.

Ming-Wei Chang, Dan Goldwasser, Dan Roth, and Vivek Srikumar. 2010. Discriminative learning over constrained latent representations. In *Proceedings of HLT-NAACL*, pages 429–437.

James Clarke and Mirella Lapata. 2006a. Constraint-based sentence compression: an integer programming approach. In *Proceedings of ACL-COLING*, pages 144–151.

James Clarke and Mirella Lapata. 2006b. Models for sentence compression: a comparison across domains, training requirements and evaluation measures. In *Proceedings of ACL-COLING*, pages 377–384.

James Clarke and Mirella Lapata. 2007. Modelling compression with discourse constraints. In *Proceedings of EMNLP-CoNLL*, pages 1–11.

James Clarke and Mirella Lapata. 2008. Global inference for sentence compression: an integer linear programming approach. *Journal for Artificial Intelligence Research*, 31:399–429, March.

James Clarke and Mirella Lapata. 2010. Discourse constraints for document compression. *Computational Linguistics*, 36(3):411–441.

Trevor Cohn and Mirella Lapata. 2009. Sentence compression as tree transduction. *Journal of Artificial Intelligence Research*, 34(1):637–674, April.

Michael Collins. 2002. Discriminative training methods for hidden Markov models. In *Proceedings of EMNLP*, pages 1–8.

Hal Daumé, III and Daniel Marcu. 2002. A noisy-channel model for document compression. In *Proceedings of ACL*, pages 449–456.

John DeNero and Dan Klein. 2008. The complexity of phrase alignment problems. In *Proceedings of ACL-HLT*, pages 25–28.

Mark Dras. 1997. Reluctant paraphrase: Textual restructuring under an optimisation model. In *Proceedings of PacLing*, pages 98–104.

Katja Filippova and Michael Strube. 2008. Dependency tree based sentence compression. In *Proceedings of INLG*, pages 25–32.

Dimitrios Galanis and Ion Androutsopoulos. 2010. An extractive supervised two-stage method for sentence compression. In *Proceedings of HLT-NAACL*, pages 885–893.

Michel Galley and Kathleen McKeown. 2007. Lexicalized Markov grammars for sentence compression. In *Proceedings of HLT-NAACL*, pages 180–187, April.

Juri Ganitkevitch, Chris Callison-Burch, Courtney Napoles, and Benjamin Van Durme. 2011. Learning sentential paraphrases from bilingual parallel corpora for text-to-text generation. In *Proceedings of EMNLP*, pages 1168–1179.

Chiori Hori and Sadaoki Furui. 2004. Speech summarization: an approach through word extraction and a method for evaluation. *IEICE Transactions on Information and Systems*, E87-D(1):15–25.

Hongyan Jing and Kathleen R. McKeown. 2000. Cut and paste based text summarization. In *Proceedings of NAACL*, pages 178–185.

Hongyan Jing. 2000. Sentence reduction for automatic text summarization. In *Proceedings of the Conference on Applied Natural Language Processing*, pages 310–315.

Kevin Knight and Daniel Marcu. 2000. Statistics-based summarization - step one: Sentence compression. In *Proceedings of AAAI*, pages 703–710.

Kevin Knight and Daniel Marcu. 2002. Summarization beyond sentence extraction: a probabilistic approach to sentence compression. *Artificial Intelligence*, 139(1):91–107, July.

Thomas L. Magnanti and Laurence A. Wolsey. 1994. Optimal trees. In *Technical Report 290-94, Massechusetts Institute of Technology, Operations Research Center*.

André F. T. Martins and Noah A. Smith. 2009. Summarization with a joint model for sentence extraction and compression. In *Proceedings of the Workshop on Integer Linear Programming for Natural Langauge Processing*, pages 1–9.

André F. T. Martins, Noah A. Smith, and Eric P. Xing. 2009. Concise integer linear programming formulations for dependency parsing. In *Proceedings of ACL-IJCNLP*, pages 342–350.

Ryan McDonald, Koby Crammer, and Fernando Pereira. 2005. Online large-margin training of dependency parsers. In *Proceedings of ACL*, pages 91–98.

Ryan McDonald. 2006. Discriminative sentence compression with soft syntactic evidence. In *Proceedings of EACL*, pages 297–304.

Courtney Napoles, Chris Callison-Burch, Juri Ganitkevitch, and Benjamin Van Durme. 2011a. Paraphrastic sentence compression with a character-based metric: tightening without deletion. In *Proceedings of the Workshop on Monolingual Text-To-Text Generation*, pages 84–90.

Courtney Napoles, Benjamin Van Durme, and Chris Callison-Burch. 2011b. Evaluating sentence compression: pitfalls and suggested remedies. In *Proceedings of the Workshop on Monolingual Text-To-Text Generation*, pages 91–97.

Tadashi Nomoto. 2007. Discriminative sentence compression with conditional random fields. *Information Processing and Management*, 43(6):1571–1587, November.

Sebastian Riedel and James Clarke. 2006. Incremental integer linear programming for non-projective dependency parsing. In *Proceedings of EMNLP*, pages 129–137.

Stefan Riezler, Tracy H. King, Richard Crouch, and Annie Zaenen. 2003. Statistical sentence condensation using ambiguity packing and stochastic disambiguation methods for lexical-functional grammar. In *Proceedings of HLT-NAACL*, pages 118–125.

Alexander M. Rush and Michael Collins. 2011. Exact decoding of syntactic translation models through lagrangian relaxation. In *Proceedings of ACL-HLT*, pages 72–82.

Kapil Thadani, Scott Martin, and Michael White. 2012. A joint phrasal and dependency model for paraphrase alignment. In *Proceedings of COLING*, pages 1229–1238.

Jenine Turner and Eugene Charniak. 2005. Supervised and unsupervised learning for sentence compression. In *Proceedings of ACL*, pages 290–297.

Yuya Unno, Takashi Ninomiya, Yusuke Miyao, and Jun'ichi Tsujii. 2006. Trimming CFG parse trees for sentence compression using machine learning approaches. In *Proceedings of ACL-COLING*, pages 850–857.

Kristian Woodsend and Mirella Lapata. 2012. Multiple aspect summarization using integer linear programming. In *Proceedings of EMNLP*, pages 233–243.

Learning Adaptable Patterns for Passage Reranking

Aliaksei Severyn[(1)] and **Massimo Nicosia**[(1)] and **Alessandro Moschitti**[1,2]
[(1)]DISI, University of Trento, 38123 Povo (TN), Italy
{severyn,m.nicosia,moschitti}@disi.unitn.it
[(2)]QCRI, Qatar Foundation, 5825 Doha, Qatar
amoschitti@qf.org.qa

Abstract

This paper proposes passage reranking models that (i) do not require manual feature engineering and (ii) greatly preserve accuracy, when changing application domain. Their main characteristic is the use of relational semantic structures representing questions and their answer passages. The relations are established using information from automatic classifiers, i.e., question category (QC) and focus classifiers (FC) and Named Entity Recognizers (NER). This way (i) effective structural relational patterns can be automatically learned with kernel machines; and (ii) structures are more invariant w.r.t. different domains, thus fostering adaptability.

1 Introduction

A critical issue for implementing Question Answering (QA) systems is the need of designing answer search and extraction modules specific to the target application domain. These modules encode handcrafted rules based on syntactic patterns that detect the relations between a question and its candidate answers in text fragments. Such rules are triggered when patterns in the question and the passage are found. For example, given a question[1]:

> *What is Mark Twain's real name?*

and a relevant passage, e.g., retrieved by a search engine:

> *Samuel Langhorne Clemens, better known as Mark Twain.*

the QA engineers typically apply a syntactic parser to obtain the parse trees of the above two sentences, from which, they extract rules like:

> **if** *the pattern* "`What is` NP_2's `ADJ name`" *is in the question* **and** *the pattern* "NP_1 `better known as` NP_2" *is in the answer passage* **then** *associate the passage with a high score*[2].

Machine learning has made easier the task of QA engineering by enabling the automatic learning of answer extraction modules. However, new features and training data have to be typically developed when porting a QA system from a domain to another. This is even more critical considering that effective features tend to be as much complex and similar as traditional handcrafted rules.

To reduce the burden of manual feature engineering for QA, we proposed structural models based on kernel methods, (Moschitti et al., 2007; Moschitti and Quarteroni, 2008; Moschitti, 2008) with passages limited to one sentence. Their main idea is to: (i) generate question and passage pairs, where the text passages are retrieved by a search engine; (ii) assuming those containing the correct answer as positive instance pairs and all the others as negative ones; (iii) represent such pairs with two syntactic trees; and (ii) learn to rank answer passages by means of structural kernels applied to two trees. This enables the automatic engineering of structural/lexical semantic patterns.

More recently, we showed that such models can be learned for passages constituted by multiple sentences on very large-scale (Severyn and Moschitti, 2012). For this purpose, we designed a shallow syntactic representation of entire paragraphs by also improving the pair representation using relational tags.

In this paper, we firstly use our model in (Severyn and Moschitti, 2012) as the current baseline and compare it with more advanced structures derived from dependency trees.

[1]We use this question/answer pair from TREC QA as a running example in the rest of the paper.

[2]If the point-wise answer is needed rather than the entire passage, the rule could end with: **returns** NP_1

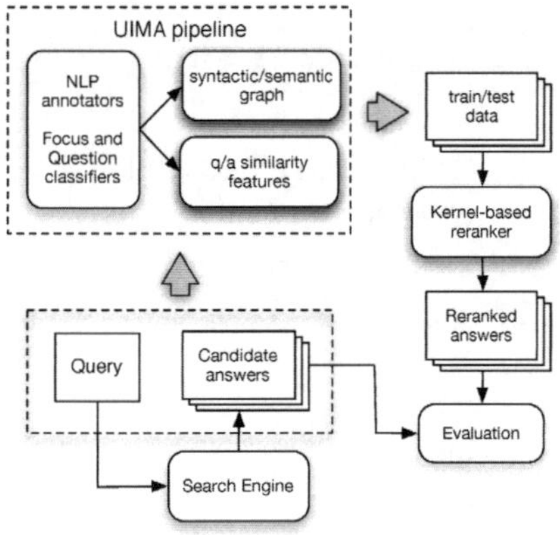

Figure 1: Kernel-based Answer Passage Reranking system

Secondly, we enrich the semantic representation of QA pairs with the categorical information provided by automatic classifiers, i.e., question category (QC) and focus classifiers (FC) and Named Entity Recognizers (NER). FC determines the constituent of the question to be linked to the named entities (NEs) of the answer passage. The target NEs are selected based on their compatibility with the category of the question, e.g., an NE of type PERSON is compatible with a category of a question asking for a human (HUM).

Thirdly, we tested our models in a cross-domain setting since we believe that: (i) the enriched representation is supposed to increase the capability of learning effective structural relational patterns through kernel machines; and (ii) such structural features are more invariant with respect to different domains, fostering their adaptability.

Finally, the results show that our methods greatly improve on IR baseline, e.g., BM25, by 40%, and on previous reranking models, up to 10%. In particular, differently from our previous work such models can effectively use NERs and the output of different automatic modules.

The rest of the paper is organized as follows, Sec. 2 describes our kernel-based reranker, Sec. 3 illustrates our question/answer relational structures; Sec. 5 briefly describes the feature vectors, and finally Sec. 6 reports the experimental results on TREC and Answerbag data.

2 Learning to rank with kernels

2.1 QA system

Our QA system is based on a rather simple reranking framework as displayed in Figure 1: given a query question a search engine retrieves a list of candidate passages ranked by their relevancy. Various NLP components embedded in the pipeline as UIMA[3] annotators are then used to analyze each question together with its candidate answers, e.g., part-of-speech tagging, chunking, named entity recognition, constituency and dependency parsing, etc. These annotations are then used to produce structural models (described in Sec. 3), which are further used by a question focus detector and question type classifiers to establish relational links for a given question/answer pair. The resulting tree pairs are then used to train a kernel-based reranker, which outputs the model to refine the initial ordering of the retrieved answer passages.

2.2 Tree kernels

We use tree structures as our base representation since they provide sufficient flexibility in representation and allow for easier feature extraction than, for example, graph structures. We rely on the Partial Tree Kernel (PTK) (Moschitti, 2006) to handle feature engineering over the structural representations. The choice of PTK is motivated by its ability to generate rich feature spaces over both constituency and dependency parse trees. It generalizes a subset tree kernel (STK) (Collins and Duffy, 2002) that maps a tree into the space of all possible tree fragments constrained by the rule that the sibling nodes from their parents cannot be separated. Different from STK where the nodes in the generated tree fragments are constrained to include none or all of their direct children, PTK fragments can contain any subset of the features, i.e., PTK allows for breaking the production rules. Consequently, PTK generalizes STK, thus generating an extremely rich feature space, which results in higher generalization ability.

2.3 Preference reranking with kernels

To enable the use of kernels for learning to rank with SVMs, we use preference reranking (Joachims, 2002), which reduces the task to binary classification. More specifically, the problem of learning to pick the correct candidate h_i from a candidate set $\{h_1, \ldots, h_k\}$ is reduced to a binary classification problem by creating *pairs*: positive training instances $\langle h_1, h_2\rangle, \ldots, \langle h_1, h_k\rangle$ and negative instances $\langle h_2, h_1\rangle, \ldots, \langle h_k, h_1\rangle$. This set can then be used to train a binary classifier. At classification time the standard one-versus-all binarization method is applied to form all possible

[3] http://uima.apache.org/

pairs of hypotheses. These are ranked according to the number of *classifier votes* they receive: a positive classification of $\langle h_k, h_i \rangle$ gives a vote to h_k whereas a negative one votes for h_i.

A vectorial representation of such pairs is the difference between the vectors representing the hypotheses in a pair. However, this assumes that features are explicit and already available whereas we aim at automatically generating implicit patterns with kernel methods. Thus, for keeping implicit the difference between such vectors we use the following preference kernel:

$$P_K(\langle h_1, h_2 \rangle, \langle h'_1, h'_2 \rangle) = K(h_1, h'_1) + K(h_2, h'_2) - K(h_1, h'_2) - K(h_2, h'_1), \quad (1)$$

where h_i and h'_i refer to two sets of hypotheses associated with two rankings and K is a kernel applied to pairs of hypotheses. We represent the latter as pairs of question and answer passage trees. More formally, given two hypotheses, $h_i = \langle h_i(q), h_i(a) \rangle$ and $h_i = \langle h'_i(q), h'_i(a) \rangle$, whose members are the question and answer passage trees, we define $K(h_i, h'_i)$ as $TK(h_i(q), h'_i(q)) + TK(h_i(a), h'_i(a))$, where TK can be any tree kernel function, e.g., STK or PTK.

To enable traditional feature vectors it is enough to add the product $(\vec{x}_{h_1} - \vec{x}_{h_2}) \cdot (\vec{x}_{h'_1} - \vec{x}_{h'_2})$ to the structural kernel P_K, where $\vec{x}_h$ is the feature vector associated with the hypothesis h.

We opted for a simple kernel sum over a product, since the latter rarely works in practice. Although in (Moschitti, 2004) the kernel product has been shown to provide some improvement when applied to tree kernels over a subcategorization frame structure, in general, it seems to work well only when the tree structures are small and derived rather accurately (Giordani and Moschitti, 2009; Giordani and Moschitti, 2012).

3 Structural models of Q/A pairs

First, we briefly describe a shallow tree representation that we use as our baseline model and then propose a new dependency-based representation.

3.1 Shallow tree structures

In a shallow syntactic representation first explored for QA in (Severyn and Moschitti, 2012) each question and its candidate answer are encoded into a tree where part-of-speech tags are found at the pre-terminal level and word lemmas at the leaf level. To encode structural relationships for a given q/a pair a special **REL** tag is used to link the related structures. The authors adopt a simple strategy to establish such links: lemmas shared between a question and and answer get their parents (POS tags) and grandparents (chunk labels) marked by a **REL** tag.

3.2 Dependency-based structures

Given the ability of PTK to generate a rich set of structural features from a relatively flat shallow tree representation, we propose to use dependency relations between words to derive an alternative structural model. In particular, we use a variation of the dependency tree, where dependency relations are altered in such a way that the words are always at the leaf level. This reordering of the nodes in the dependency tree, s.t. words do not form long chains, which is typical in the standard dependency tree representation, is essential for PTK to extract meaningful fragments. We also add part-of-speech tags between the words and the nodes encoding their grammatical roles (provided by the original dependency parse tree). Again a special **REL** tag is used in the same manner as in the shallow representation to establish structural links between a question and an answer. Fig. 2 (top) gives an example of a dependency-based structure for our example q/a pair.

4 Relational Linking

The use of a special tag to mark the related fragments in the question and answer tree representations has been shown to yield more accurate relational models (Severyn and Moschitti, 2012). However, previous approach was based on a naïve hard matching between word lemmas.

Below we propose a novel strategy to establish relational links using named entities extracted from the answer along with question focus and category classifiers. In particular, we use a question category to link the focus word of a question with the named entities extracted from the candidate answer. For this purpose, we first introduce our tree kernel-based models for building a question focus and category classifiers.

4.1 Question focus detection

The question focus is typically a simple noun representing the entity or property being sought by the question (Prager, 2006). It can be used to search for semantically compatible candidate an-

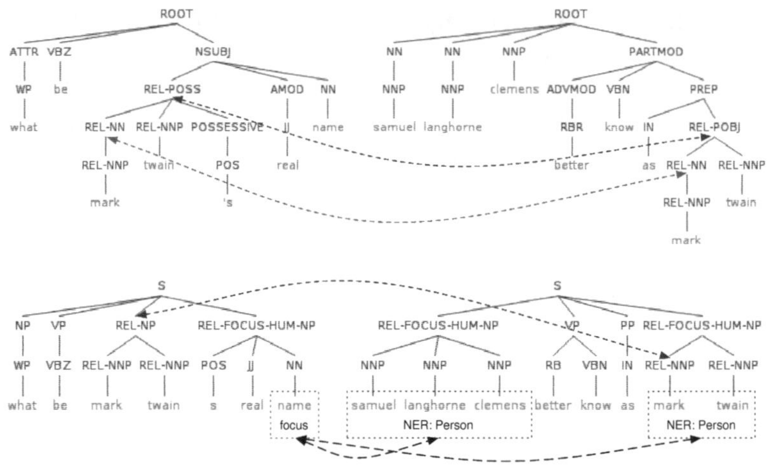

Figure 2: Dependency-based structure DEP (**top**) for the q/a pair. *Q: What is Mark Twain's real name? A: Samuel Langhorne Clemens, better known as Mark Twain.* Arrows indicate the tree fragments in the question and its answer passage linked by the relational **REL** tag. Shallow tree structure CH (**bottom**) with a typed relation tag **REL-FOCUS-HUM** to link a question focus word *name* with the named entities of type *Person* corresponding to the question category (HUM).

swers in document passages, thus greatly reducing the search space (Pinchak, 2006). While several machine learning approaches based on manual features and syntactic structures have been recently explored, e.g. (Quarteroni et al., 2012; Damljanovic et al., 2010; Bunescu and Huang, 2010), we opt for the latter approach where tree kernels handle automatic feature engineering.

In particular, to detect the question focus word we train a binary SVM classifier with tree kernels applied to the constituency tree representation. For each given question we generate a set of candidate trees where the parent (node with the POS tag) of each candidate focus word is annotated with a special **FOCUS** tag. Trees with the correctly tagged focus word constitute a positive example, while the others are negative examples. To detect the focus for an unseen question we classify the trees obtained after tagging each candidate focus word. The tree yielding the highest classification score reveals the target focus word.

4.2 Question classification

Question classification is the task of assigning a question to one of the pre-specified categories. We use the coarse-grain classes described in (Li and Roth, 2002): six non-overlapping classes: Abbreviations (ABBR), Descriptions (DESC, e.g. definitions or explanations), Entity (ENTY, e.g. animal, body or color), Human (HUM, e.g. group or individual), Location (LOC, e.g. cities or countries) and Numeric (NUM, e.g. amounts or dates). These categories can be used to determine the Expected Answer Type for a given question and find the appropriate entities found in the candidate answers. Imposing such constraints on the potential answer keys greatly reduces the search space.

Previous work in Question Classification reveals the power of syntactic/semantic tree representations coupled with tree kernels to train the state-of-the-art models (Bloehdorn and Moschitti, 2007). Hence, we opt for an SVM multi-classifier using tree kernels to automatically extract the question class. To build a multi-class classifier we train a binary SVM for each of the classes and apply a one-vs-all strategy to obtain the predicted class. We use constituency trees as our input representation.

4.3 Linking focus word with named entities using question class

Question focus captures the target information need posed by a question, but to make this piece of information effective, the focus word needs to be linked to the target candidate answer. The focus word can be lexically matched with words present in an answer, or the match can be established using semantic information. Clearly, the latter approach is more appealing since it helps to alleviate the lexical gap problem which makes the näive string matching of words between a question and its answer less reliable.

Hence, we propose to exploit a question category (automatically identified by a question type classifier) along with named entities found in the answer to establish relational links between the tree structures of a given q/a pair. In particular, once the question focus and question category

Table 1: Question classes → named entity types.

Question Category	Named Entity types
HUM	Person
LOC	Location
NUM	Date, Time, Money, Percentage
ENTY	Organization, Person

are determined, we link the focus word w_{focus} in the question, with all the named entities whose type matches the question class. Table 1 provides the correspondence between question classes and named entity types. We perform tagging at the chunk level and use two types of relational tags: plain **REL-FOCUS** and a tag typed with a question class, e.g., **REL-FOCUS-HUM**. Fig. 2 (bottom) shows an example q/a pair where the typed relational tag is used in the shallow syntactic tree representation to link the chunk containing the question focus *name* with the named entities of the corresponding type *Person* (according to the mapping defined in Table 1), i.e. *samuel langhorne clemens* and *mark twain*.

5 Feature vector representation

While the primary focus of our study is on the structural representations and relations between q/a pairs we also include basic features widely used in QA:

Term-overlap features. A cosine similarity between a question and an answer: $sim_{COS}(q, a)$, where the input vectors are composed of: (i) n-grams (up to tri-grams) of word lemmas and part-of-speech tags, and (ii) dependency triplets. For the latter, we simply hash the string value of the predicate defining the triple together with its argument, e.g. *poss(name, twain)*.

PTK score. For the structural representations we also define a similarity based on the PTK score: $sim_{PTK}(q, a) = PTK(q, a)$, where the input trees can be both dependency trees and shallow chunk trees. Note that this similarity is computed between the members of a q/a pair, thus, it is very different from the one defined in Eq. 1.

NER relatedness represents a match between a question category and the related named entity types extracted from the candidate answer. It counts the proportion of named entities in the answer that correspond to the question type returned by the question classifier.

In our study feature vectors serve a complementary purpose, while the main focus is to study the virtue of structural representations for reranking. The effect of a more extensive number of pairwise similarity features in QA has been studied elsewhere, e.g., (Surdeanu et al., 2008).

6 Experiments

We report the results on two QA collections: factoid open-domain QA corpus from TREC and a community QA corpus Answerbag. Since we focus on passage reranking we do not carry out answer extraction. The goal is to rank the passage containing the right answer in the top position.

6.1 Corpora

TREC QA. In the TREC QA tasks, answer passages containing correct information nuggets, i.e. answer keys, have to be extracted from a given text corpus, typically a large corpus from newswire. In our experiments, we opted for questions from 2002 and 2003 years, which totals to 824 questions. AQUAINT newswire corpus[4] is used for searching the supporting answers.

Answerbag is a community-driven QA collection that contains a large portion of questions that have "professionally researched" answers. Such answers are provided by the website moderators and allow for training high quality models. From the original corpus containing 180k question/answer pairs, we use 1k randomly sampled questions for testing and 10k for training.

Question Focus. We use 3 datasets for training and evaluating the performance of our focus detector: SeCo-600 (Quarteroni et al., 2012), Mooney GeoQuery (Damljanovic et al., 2010) and the dataset from (Bunescu and Huang, 2010). The SeCo dataset contains 600 questions from which we discarded a subset of multi-focus questions and non-interrogative queries. The Mooney GeoQuery contains 250 question targeted at geographical information in the U.S. The first two datasets are very domain specific, so we also carried out experiments with the dataset from (Bunescu and Huang, 2010), which contains the first 2000 questions from the answer type dataset from Li and Roth annotated with focus words. We removed questions with implicit and multiple focuses.

Question Classification. We used the UIUIC dataset (Li and Roth, 2002)[5] which contains 5952

[4] http://www.ldc.upenn.edu/Catalog/docs/LDC2002T31/

[5] although the QC dataset from (Li and Roth, 2002) includes additional 50 fine grain classes we opted for using only 6 coarse classes that are sufficient to capture the coarse semantic answer type of the candidate answer. This choice also results in a more accurate multi-class classifier.

factoid questions from different sources (USC, TREC 8, TREC 9, TREC 10). For training the classifiers we excluded questions from TREC 8 to ensure there is no overlap with the data used for testing models trained on TREC QA.

6.2 Models and Metrics

Our models are built applying a kernel-based reranker to the output of a search engine.

6.2.1 BM25

We use Terrier[6] search engine, which provides BM25 scoring model for indexing and retrieval. For the TREC QA 2002 and 2003 task we index AQUAINT corpus treating paragraphs as documents. The resulting index contains about 12 million items. For the Answerbag we index the entire collection of 180k answers. We retrieve a list of top 50 candidate answers for each question.

6.2.2 Reranking models

To train our reranking models we used SVM-light-TK[7], which encodes structural kernels in SVM-light (Joachims, 2002) solver. In particular, we use PTK on the relational tree structures combined with the polynomial kernel of degree 3 applied to the feature vectors. Therefore, different representations lead to different models described below.

CH - our basic shallow chunk tree (Severyn and Moschitti, 2012) used as a **baseline** structural reranking model.

DEP - dependency tree augmented with POS tags and reorganized relations suitable for PTK.

V - reranker model using similarity features defined in Sec. 5.

DEP+V, CH+V - a combination of tree structures and similarity feature vectors.

+FC+QC - relational linking of the question focus word and named entities of the corresponding type using Focus and Question classifiers.

+TFC+QC - a typed relational link refined a question category.[8]

6.2.3 Metrics

We report the following metrics, most commonly used in QA: Precision at rank 1 (P@1), i.e., the percentage of questions with a correct answer at rank 1, Mean Reciprocal Rank (MRR), and Mean Average Precision (MAP). The reported metrics are averages after performing a 5-fold cross-validation. We used a paired t-test at 95% confidence to compare the performance of our models to a baseline.

[6]http://terrier.org/

[7]http://disi.unitn.it/moschitti/Tree-Kernel.htm

[8]† is used for showing the results of DEP, DEP+V and CH+V structural representations that are significantly better than the baseline model CH, while ‡ indicates improvement of +QC+FC and +QC+TFC tagging applied to basic structural representations, e.g. CH+V and DEP+V.

Table 2: Structural representations on TREC QA.

Models	MAP	MRR	P@1
BM25	0.22	28.02	18.17
V	0.22	28.40	18.54
Structural representations			
CH (S&M, 2012)	0.28	35.63	24.88
CH+V	0.30†	37.45†	27.91†
DEP	0.30†	37.87†	28.05†
DEP+V	0.30†	37.64†	28.05†
Refined relational tag			
CH+V+QC+FC	0.32‡	39.48‡	29.63‡
CH+V+QC+TFC	0.32‡	39.49‡	30.00‡
DEP+V+QC+FC	0.31‡	37.49	28.56
DEP+V+QC+TFC	0.31‡	38.05‡	28.93‡

6.3 Passage Reranking Results

We first evaluate the impact of two different syntactic representations using shallow and dependency trees. Then, we evaluate the accuracy boost when such structures are enriched with automatically derived tags, e.g., question focus and question category and NEs found in the answer passage.

6.3.1 Structural representations

Table 2 reveals that using V model results in a small improvement over BM25 baseline. Indeed, similarity scores that are most often based on word-overlap measures even when computed over various q/a representations are fairly redundant to the search engine similarity score. Instead, using the structural representations, CH and DEP, gives a bigger boost in the performance. Interestingly, having more features in the CH+V model results in further improvement while DEP+V seems to remain insensitive to additional features provided by the V model.

6.3.2 Semantically Enriched Structures

In the following set of experiments we explore another strategy for linking structures for a given q/a pair. We automatically detect the question focus word and link it to the related named entities in the answer, selected accordingly to the question category identified by the question classifier (QC+FC). Further refining the relational link

Table 3: Accuracy (%) of focus classifiers.

DATASET	ST	STK	STK+BOW	PTK
MOONEY	73.0	81.9	81.5	80.5
SECO-600	90.0	94.5	94.5	90.0
BUNESCU	89.7	98.3	98.2	96.9

Table 4: Accuracy (%) of question classifiers.

DATASET	STK+BOW	PTK
LI & ROTH	86.1	82.2
TREC TEST	79.3	78.1

with the question category yields QC+TFC model. First, we report the results of training our question focus detector and question category classifier.

Focus classifier results. Table 3 displays the accuracies obtained by the question focus detector on 3 datasets using different kernels: the ST (subtree kernel where fragments contain full subtrees including leaves), STK, STK+bow (bag-of-words feature vector is added) and PTK. As we can see, using STK model yields the best accuracy and we use it in our pipeline to automatically detect the focus.

Question classifier results. Table 4 contains the accuracies of the question classifier on the UIUIC dataset and the TREC questions that we also use for testing our reranker models. STK+bow performs better than PTK, since here the input representation is a plain constituency tree, for which STK is particularly suited. Hence, we use this model to predict the question category.

Ranking results. Table 2 (bottom) summarizes the performance of the CH+V and DEP+V models when coupled with QC+FC and QC+TFC strategies to establish the links between the structures in a given q/a pair. CH structural representation with QC+FC yields an interesting improvement, while further refining the relational tag by adding a question category (QC+TFC) gives slightly better results.

Integrating the refined relational tag into the DEP based structures results more problematic, since the dependency tree is less suitable for representing multi-word expressions, named entities in our case. Hence, using the relational tag to mark the nodes spanning such multi-word entities in the dependency structure may result in less meaningful features than in CH model, where words in a phrase are naturally grouped under a chunk node. A more detailed discussion on the merits of each model is provided in the Sec. 6.5.

Table 5: Cross-domain experiment: training on Answerbag and testing on TREC QA.

MODELS	MAP	MRR	P@1
BM25	0.22	27.91	18.08
V	0.23	28.86	18.90
BASIC STRUCTURAL REPRESENTATIONS			
CH (S&M, 2012)	0.24	30.25	20.42
CH+V	0.25†	31.31†	21.28†
DEP+V	0.26†	33.26†	22.21†
REFINED RELATIONAL TAG			
CH+V+QC+TFC	0.27‡	33.53‡	22.81‡
DEP+V+QC+TFC	0.29‡	34.25‡	23.45‡

6.4 Learning cross-domain pairwise structural relationships

To test the robustness of the syntactic patterns automatically learned by our structural models, we conduct a cross-domain experiment, i.e. we train a model on Answerbag data and test it on TREC. It should be noted that unlike TREC data, where the answers are simply passages containing the correct answer phrase, answers in Answerbag specifically address a given question and are generated by humans. Additionally, TREC QA contains only factoid questions, while Answerbag is a community QA corpus with a large portion of non-factoid questions. Interestingly, the results demonstrate the robustness of our syntactic relational model which captures patterns shared across different domains, e.g. TREC and Answerbag data.

Table 5 shows that: (i) models based on dependency structures result in a better generalization ability extracting more robust syntactic patterns; and (ii) the strategy to link the question focus with the related named entities in the answer provides an interesting improvement over the basic structural representations.

6.5 Error Analysis

Consider our running example q/a pair from Sec. 1. As the first candidate answer, the search engine retrieves the following incorrect passage: *"The autobiography of Mark Twain", Mark Twain.* It is relatively short and mentions the keywords {*Mark, Twain*} twice, which apparently results in a high score for the BM25 model. Instead, the search engine ranks the correct answer at position 34. After reranking using the basic CH+V model the correct answer is promoted by 20 positions. While using the CH+V+QC+FC model the correct answer advances to position 6. Below, we provide the intuition behind the merits of QC+FC and QC+TFC encoding question focus and question category into the basic models.

The model learned by the reranker represents a collection of q/a pairs from the training set (support vectors) which are matched against each candidate q/a pair. We isolated the following pair from the model that has a high structural similarity with our running example:

Q: What is Barbie's full name?

A: The toy is called after Barbie Millicent Roberts from Willows.

Despite differences in the surface forms of the words, PTK extracts matching patterns, e.g. `[S NP [VP VBN] [PP IN] REL-NP]`, which yields a high similarity score boosting the rank of the correct candidate. However, we note that at the same time an incorrect candidate answer, e.g. *Mark Twain was accused of racist language.*, exhibits similar patterns and also gets a high rank. The basic structural representation is not able to encode essential differences from the correct answer candidate. This poses a certain limitation on the discriminative power of CH and DEP representations. Introducing a focus tag changes the structural representation of both q/a pairs, s.t. the correct q/a pair preserves the pattern (after identifying word *name* as focus and question category as HUM, it is transformed to `[S REL-FOCUS-NP [VP VBN] [PP IN] REL-FOCUS-NP]`), while it is absent in the incorrect candidate. Thus, linking the focus word with the related NEs in the answer helps to discriminate between structurally similar yet semantically different candidates.

Another step towards a more fine-grained structural representation is to specialize the relational focus tag (QC+TFC model). We propose to augment the focus tag with the question category to avoid matches with other structurally similar but semantically different candidates. For example, a q/a pair found in the list of support vectors:

Q: What is Mark Twain's place of birth?

A: Mark Twain was raised in Hannibal Missouri.

would exhibit high structural similarity even when relational focus is used (since the relational tag does not incorporate the question class LOC), but refining the focus tag with the question class eliminates such cases.

7 Related Work

Previous studies similar to ours carry out passage reranking by exploiting structural information, e.g. using subject-verb-object relations (Attardi et al., 2001; Katz and Lin, 2003). Unfortunately, the large variability of natural language makes such triples rather sparse thus different methods explore soft matching (i.e., lexical similarity) based on answer types and named entity types (Aktolga et al., 2011). Passage reranking using classifiers of question and answer pairs were proposed in (Radlinski and Joachims, 2006; Jeon et al., 2005).

Regarding kernel methods, our work in (Moschitti et al., 2007; Severyn and Moschitti, 2012) was the first to exploit tree kernels for modeling answer reranking. However, such method lacks the use of important relational information between a question and a candidate answer, which is essential to learn accurate relational patterns. In contrast, this paper relies on shallow and dependency trees encoding the output of question and focus classifiers to connect focus word and NEs of the answer passage. This provides more effective relational information, which allows our model to significantly improve on previous rerankers.

8 Conclusions

This paper shows a viable research direction in the automatic QA engineering. One of its main characteristics is the use of structural kernel technology to induce features from structural semantic representations of question and answer passage pairs. The same technology is also used to construct question and focus classifiers, which are used to derive relational structures.

An interesting result of this paper is that to design an answer passage reranker for a new domain, we can use off-the-shelf syntactic parsers and NERs along with little training data for the QC and FC classifiers. This is due to the fact that: (i) the kernel technology is able to automatically extract effective structural patterns; and (ii) the extracted patterns are rather robust, e.g., models learned on Answerbag improve accuracy on TREC test data.

Acknowledgements

This research is partially supported by the EU's 7th Framework Program (FP7/2007-2013) (#288024 LiMoSINe project) and an Open Collaborative Research (OCR) award from IBM Research.

References

Elif Aktolga, James Allan, and David A. Smith. 2011. Passage reranking for question answering using syntactic structures and answer types. In *ECIR*.

Giuseppe Attardi, Antonio Cisternino, Francesco Formica, Maria Simi, and Ro Tommasi. 2001. Piqasso: Pisa question answering system. In *TREC*, pages 599–607.

Stephan Bloehdorn and Alessandro Moschitti. 2007. Combined syntactic and semantic kernels for text classification. In *ECIR*.

Razvan Bunescu and Yunfeng Huang. 2010. Towards a general model of answer typing: Question focus identification. In *CICLing*.

Michael Collins and Nigel Duffy. 2002. New Ranking Algorithms for Parsing and Tagging: Kernels over Discrete Structures, and the Voted Perceptron. In *ACL*.

Danica Damljanovic, Milan Agatonovic, and Hamish Cunningham. 2010. Identification of the question focus: Combining syntactic analysis and ontology-based lookup through the user interaction. In *LREC*.

Alessandra Giordani and Alessandro Moschitti. 2009. Syntactic structural kernels for natural language interfaces to databases. In *Proceedings of ECML PKDD*, ECML PKDD '09. Springer-Verlag.

Alessandra Giordani and Alessandro Moschitti. 2012. Translating questions to sql queries with generative parsers discriminatively reranked. In *Proceedings of The 24rd International Conference on Computational Linguistics*, India. Coling 2012.

Jiwoon Jeon, W. Bruce Croft, and Joon Ho Lee. 2005. Finding similar questions in large question and answer archives. In *CIKM*.

T. Joachims. 2002. Optimizing search engines using clickthrough data. In *ACM SIGKDD Conference on Knowledge Discovery and Data Mining (KDD)*, pages 133–142.

Boris Katz and Jimmy Lin. 2003. Selectively using relations to improve precision in question answering.

Xin Li and Dan Roth. 2002. Learning question classifiers. In *COLING*.

Alessandro Moschitti and Silvia Quarteroni. 2008. Kernels on linguistic structures for answer extraction. In *ACL*.

Alessandro Moschitti, Silvia Quarteroni, Roberto Basili, and Suresh Manandhar. 2007. Exploiting syntactic and shallow semantic kernels for question/answer classification. In *ACL*.

Alessandro Moschitti. 2004. A study on convolution kernels for shallow statistic parsing. In *Proceedings of the 42nd Meeting of the Association for Computational Linguistics (ACL'04), Main Volume*, pages 335–342, Barcelona, Spain, July.

Alessandro Moschitti. 2006. Efficient convolution kernels for dependency and constituent syntactic trees. In *ECML*.

Alessandro Moschitti. 2008. Kernel methods, syntax and semantics for relational text categorization. In *CIKM*.

Christopher Pinchak. 2006. A probabilistic answer type model. In *In EACL*.

John M. Prager. 2006. Open-domain question-answering. *Foundations and Trends in Information Retrieval*, 1(2):91–231.

Silvia Quarteroni, Vincenzo Guerrisi, and Pietro La Torre. 2012. Evaluating multi-focus natural language queries over data services. In *LREC*.

Filip Radlinski and Thorsten Joachims. 2006. Query chains: Learning to rank from implicit feedback. *CoRR*.

Aliaksei Severyn and Alessandro Moschitti. 2012. Structural relationships for large-scale learning of answer re-ranking. In *SIGIR*.

M. Surdeanu, M. Ciaramita, and H. Zaragoza. 2008. Learning to rank answers on large online QA collections. In *Proceedings of ACL-HLT*.

Documents and Dependencies: an Exploration of Vector Space Models for Semantic Composition

Alona Fyshe, Partha Talukdar, Brian Murphy and Tom Mitchell
Machine Learning Department &
Center for the Neural Basis of Cognition
Carnegie Mellon University, Pittsburgh
{afyshe|ppt|bmurphy|tom.mitchell}@cs.cmu.edu

Abstract

In most previous research on distributional semantics, Vector Space Models (VSMs) of words are built either from *topical* information (e.g., documents in which a word is present), or from syntactic/semantic *types* of words (e.g., dependency parse links of a word in sentences), but not both. In this paper, we explore the utility of combining these two representations to build VSM for the task of semantic composition of adjective-noun phrases. Through extensive experiments on benchmark datasets, we find that even though a type-based VSM is effective for semantic composition, it is often outperformed by a VSM built using a combination of topic- and type-based statistics. We also introduce a new evaluation task wherein we predict the composed vector representation of a phrase from the brain activity of a human subject reading that phrase. We exploit a large syntactically parsed corpus of 16 billion tokens to build our VSMs, with vectors for both phrases and words, and make them publicly available.

1 Introduction

Vector space models (VSMs) of word semantics use large collections of text to represent word meanings. Each word vector is composed of features, where features can be derived from global corpus co-occurrence patterns (e.g. how often a word appears in each document), or local corpus co-occurrence patterns patterns (e.g. how often two words appear together in the same sentence, or are linked together in dependency parsed sentences). These two feature types represent different aspects of word meaning (Murphy et al., 2012c), and can be compared with the paradigmatic/syntagmatic distinction (Sahlgren, 2006). Global patterns give a more *topic-based* meaning (e.g. *judge* might appear in documents also containing *court* and *verdict*). Certain local patterns give a more *type-based* meaning (e.g. the noun *judge* might be modified by the adjective *harsh*, or be the subject of *decide*, as would related and substitutable words such as *referee* or *conductor*). Global patterns have been used in Latent Semantic Analysis (Landauer and Dumais, 1997) and LDA Topic models (Blei et al., 2003). Local patterns based on word co-occurrence in a fixed width window were used in Hyperspace Analogue to Language (Lund and Burgess, 1996). Subsequent models added increasing linguistic sophistication, up to full syntactic and dependency parses (Lin, 1998; Padó and Lapata, 2007; Baroni and Lenci, 2010).

In this paper we systematically explore the utility of a global, topic-based VSM built from what we call *Document* features, and a local, type-based VSM built from *Dependency* features. Our Document VSM represents each word w by a vector where each feature is a specific document, and the feature value is the number of mentions of word w in that document. Our Dependency VSM represents word w with a vector where each feature is a dependency parse link (e.g., the word w is the subject of the verb "eat"), and the feature value is the number of instances of this dependency feature for word w across a large text corpus. We also consider a third *Combined* VSM in which the word vector is the concatenation of its Document and Dependency features. All three models subsequently normalize frequencies using positive pointwise mutual-information (PPMI), and are dimensionality reduced using singular value decomposition (SVD). This is the first systematic study of the utility of Document and Dependency features for semantic composition. We construct all three VSMs (Dependencies, Documents, Combined) using the same text corpus and preprocessing pipeline, and make the resulting VSMs available for download (`http://www.cs.cmu.edu/~afyshe/papers/conll2013/`). To our knowledge, this is the first freely available VSM that includes entries for both words and adjective-noun phrases, and it is built from a much larger corpus than previously shared resources (16 billion words, 50 million documents). Our main contributions include:

- We systematically study complementarity of topical (Document) and type (Dependency) features in Vector Space Model (VSM) for semantic composition of adjective-noun phrases. To the best of our knowledge, this is one of the first studies of this kind.
- Through extensive experiments on standard benchmark datasets, we find that a VSM built from a combination of topical and type features is more effective for semantic composition, compared to a VSM built from Document and Dependency features alone.
- We introduce a novel task: to predict the vector representation of a composed phrase from the brain activity of human subjects reading that phrase.
- We explore two composition methods, addition and dilation, and find that while addition performs well on corpus-only tasks, dilation performs best on the brain activity task.
- We build our VSMs, for both phrases and words, from a large syntactically parsed text corpus of 16 billion tokens. We also make the resulting VSM publicly available.

2 Related Work

Mitchell and Lapata (2010) explored several methods of combining adjective and noun vectors to estimate phrase vectors, and compared the similarity judgements of humans to the similarity of their predicted phrase vectors. They found that for adjective-noun phrases, type-based models outperformed Latent Dirichlet Allocation (LDA) topic models. For the type-based models, multiplication performed the best, followed by weighted addition and a dilation model (for details on composition functions see Section 4.2). However, Mitchell and Lapata did not combine the topic- and type-based models, an idea we explore in detail in this paper.

Baroni and Zamparelli (2010) extended the typical vector representation of words. Their model used matrices to represent adjectives, while nouns were represented with column vectors. The vectors for nouns and adjective-noun phrases were derived from local word co-occurrence statistics. The matrix to represent the adjective was estimated with partial least squares regression where the product of the learned adjective matrix and the observed noun vector should equal the observed adjective-noun vector. Socher et al. (2012) also extended word representations beyond simple vectors. Their model assigns each word a vector and a matrix, which are composed via an non-linear function (e.g. tanh) to create phrase representations consisting of another vector/matrix pair. This process can proceed recursively, following a parse tree to produce a composite sentence meaning. Other general semantic composition frameworks have been suggested, e.g. (Sadrzadeh and Grefenstette, 2011) who focus on the operational nature of composition, rather than the representations that are supplied to the framework. Here we focus on creating word representations that are useful for semantic composition.

Turney (2012) published an exploration of the impact of domain- and function-specific vector space models, analogous to the topic and type meanings encoded by our Document and Dependency models respectively. In Turney's work, domain-specific information was represented by noun token co-occurrence statistics within a local window, and functional roles were represented by generalized token/part-of-speech co-occurrence patterns with verbs - both of which are relatively local and shallow when compared with this work. Similar local context-based features were used to cluster phrases in (Lin and Wu, 2009). Though the models discussed here are not entirely comparable to it, a recent comparison suggested that broader, deeper features such as ours may result in representations that are superior for tasks involving neural activation data (Murphy et al., 2012b).

In contrast to the composite model in (Griffiths et al., 2005), in this paper we explore the complementarity of semantics captured by topical information and syntactic/semantic types. We focus on learning VSMs (involving both words and phrases) for semantic composition, and use more expressive dependency-based features in our type-based VSM. A comparison of vector-space representations was recently published (Blacoe and Lapata, 2012), in which the authors compared several methods of combining single words vectors to create phrase vectors. They found that the best performance for adjective-noun composition used point-wise multiplication and a model based on type-based word co-occurrence patterns.

3 Creating a Vector-Space

To create the Dependency vectors, a 16 billion word subset of ClueWeb09 (Callan and Hoy, 2009) was dependency parsed using the Malt parser (Hall et al., 2007). Dependency statistics were then collected for a predetermined list of target words and adjective-noun phrases, and for arbitrary adjective-noun phrases observed in the corpus. The list was composed of the 40 thousand most frequent single tokens in the American National Corpus (Ide and Suderman, 2006), and a small number of words and phrases used as stimuli in our brain imaging experiments. Additionally, we included any phrase found in the corpus whose maximal token span matched the PoS pattern *J+N+*, where *J* and *N* denote adjective and noun PoS tags respectively. For each *unit* (i.e., word or phrase) in this augmented list, counts of all unit-external dependencies incident on the head word were aggregated across the corpus, while unit-internal dependencies were ignored. Each token was appended with its PoS tag, and the dependency edge label was also included. This resulted in the extraction of 498 million dependency tuples. For example, the dependency tuple *(a/DT, NMOD, 27-inch/JJ television/NN,14)*, indicates that *a/DT* was found as a child of *27-inch/JJ television/NN* with a frequency of 14 in the corpus.

To create Document vectors, word-document co-occurrence counts were taken from the same subset of Clueweb, which covered 50 million documents. We applied feature-selection for computational efficiency reasons, ranking documents by the number of target word/phrase types they contained and choosing the top 10 million.

A series of three additional filtering steps selected target words/phrases, and Document/Dependency features for which there was adequate data.[1] First, a co-occurrence frequency cut-off was used to reduce the dimensionality of the matrices, and to discard noisy estimates. A cutoff of 20 was applied to the dependency counts, and of 2 to document counts. Positive pointwise-mutual-information (PPMI) was used as an association measure to normalize the observed co-occurrence frequency for the varying frequency of the target word and its features, and to discard negative associations. Second, the target list was filtered to the 57 thousand words and phrases which had at least 20 non-"stop word" Dependency co-occurrence types, where a "stop word" was one of the 100 most frequent Dependency features observed (so named because the dependencies were largely incident on function words). Third, features observed for no more than one target were removed, as were empty target entries. The result was a Document co-occurrence matrix of 55 thousand targets by 5.2 million features (total 172 million non-zero entries), and a Dependency matrix of 57 thousand targets by 1.25 million features (total 35 million non-zero entries).

A singular value decomposition (SVD) matrix factorization was computed separately on the Dependency and Document statistics matrices, with 1000 latent dimensions retained. For this step we used Python/Scipy implementation of the Implicitly Restarted Arnoldi method (Lehoucq et al., 1998; Jones et al., 2001). This method is compatible with PPMI normalization, since a zero value represents both negative target-feature associations, and those that were not observed or fell below the frequency cut-off. To combine Document and Dependency information, we concatenate vectors.

4 Experiments

To evaluate how Document and Dependency dimensions can interact and compliment each other,

[1] In earlier experiments with more than 500 thousand phrasal entries, we found that the majority of targets were dominated by non-distinctive stop word co-occurrences, resulting in semantically vacuous representations.

Table 1: The nearest neighbors of three queries under three VSMs: all 2000 dimensions (Deps & Docs); 1000 Document dimensions (Docs); 1000 Dependency dimensions (Deps).

Query	Deps & Docs	Docs	Deps
beautiful/JJ	wonderful/JJ lovely/JJ excellent/JJ	wonderful/JJ fantastic/JJ unspoiled/JJ	lovely/JJ gorgeous/JJ wonderful/JJ
dog/NN	cat/NN dogs/NNS pet/NN	dogs/NNS vet/NN leash/NN	cat/NN the/DT_dog/NN dogs/NNS
bad/JJ_publicity/NN	negative/JJ_publicity/NN bad/JJ_press/NN unpleasantness/NN	fast/JJ_cash/NN_loan/NN small/JJ_business/NN_loan/NN important/JJ_cities/NNS	negative/JJ_publicity/NN bad/JJ_press/NN unpleasantness/NN

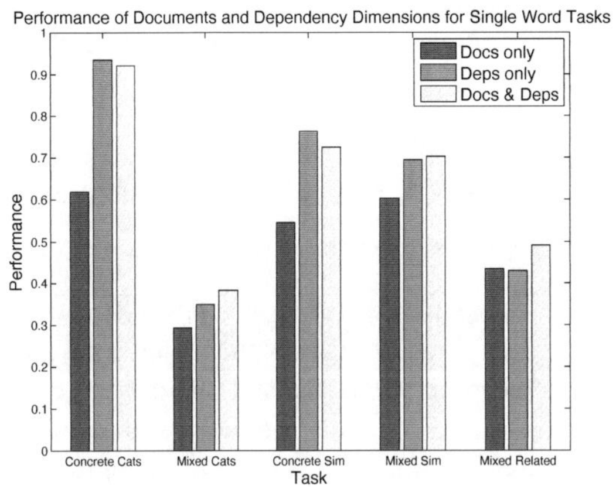

Figure 1: Performance of VSMs for single word behavioral tasks as we vary Document and Dependency inclusion.

we can perform a qualitative comparison between the nearest neighbors (NNs) of words and phrases in the three VSMs – Dependency, Document, and Combined (Dependency & Document). Results appear in Table 1. Note that single words and phrases can be neighbors of each other, demonstrating that our VSMs can generalize across syntactic types. In the Document VSM, we get more topically related words as NNs (e.g., *vet* and *leash* for *dog*); and in the Dependency VSM, we see words that might substitute for one another in a sentence (e.g., *gorgeous* for *beautiful*). The two feature sets can work together to up-weight the most suitable NNs (as in *beautiful*), or help to drown out noise (as in the NNs for *bad publicity* in the Document VSM).

4.1 Judgements of Word Similarity

As an initial test of the informativeness of Document and Dependency features, we evaluate the representation of single words. Behavioral judgement benchmarks have been widely used to evaluate vector space representations (Lund and Burgess, 1996; Rapp, 2003; Sahlgren, 2006). Here we used five such tests. Two tests are categorization tests, where we evaluate how well an automatic clustering of our word vectors correspond to pre-defined word categories. The first "Concrete Categories" test-set consists of 82 nouns, each assigned to one of 10 concrete classes (Battig and Montague, 1969). The second "Mixed Categories" test-set contains 402 nouns in a range of 21 concrete and abstract classes from WordNet (Almuhareb and Poesio, 2004; Miller et al., 1990). Both categorization tests were performed with the Cluto clustering package (Karypis, 2003) using cosine distances. Success was measured as percentage purity over clusters based on their plurality class, with chance performance at 10% and 5% respectively for the "Concrete Categories" and "Mixed Categories" tests.

The remaining three tests use group judgements of similarity: the "Concrete Similarity" set of 65 concrete word pairs (Rubenstein and Goodenough, 1965); and two variations on the WordSim353 test-set (Finkelstein et al., 2002), partitioned into subsets corresponding to strict attributional similarity ("Mixed Similarity", 203 noun pairs), and broader topical "relatedness" ("Mixed Relatedness", 252 noun pairs) (Agirre et al., 2009). Performance on these benchmarks is Spearman correlation between the aggregate human judgements and pairwise cosine distances of word vectors in a VSM.

The results in Figure 1 show that the Dependency VSM substantially outperforms the Document VSM when predicting human judgements of strict attributional (categorial) similarity ("Similarity" as opposed to "Relatedness") for concrete nouns. Conversely the Document VSM is compet-

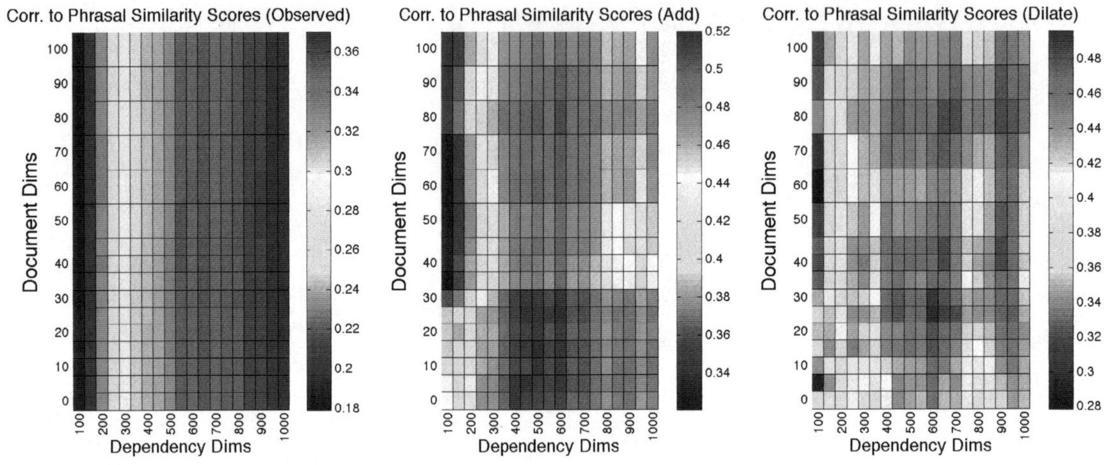

Figure 2: The performance of three phrase representations for predicting the behavioral phrasal similarity scores from Mitchell and Lapata (2010). The highest correlation is 0.5033 and uses 25 Document dimensions, 600 Dependency dimensions and the addition composition function.

itive for less concrete word types, and for judgements of broader topical relatedness.

4.2 Judgements of Phrase Similarity

We also evaluated our system on behavioral data of phrase similarity judgements gathered from 18 human informants. The adjective-noun phrase pairs are divided into 3 groups: high, medium and low similarity (Mitchell and Lapata, 2010). For each pair of phrases, informants rated phrase similarity on a Likert scale of 1-7. There are 36 phrase pairs in each of the three groups for a total of 108 phrase pairs. Not all of the phrases occurred frequently enough in our corpus to pass our thresholds, and so were omitted from our analysis. In several cases we also used pluralizations of the test phrases (e.g."dark eyes") where the singular form was not found in our VSM. After these changes we were left with 28, 24 and 28 in the high, medium and low groups respectively. In total we have 80 *observed* vectors for the 108 phrase pairs. These adjective-noun phrases were included in the list of targets, so their statistics were gathered in the same way as for single words. This does not impact results for composed vectors, as all of the single words in the phrases do appear in our VSMs. A full list of the phrase pairs can be found in Mitchell and Lapata (2010).

To evaluate, we used three different representations of phrases. For phrase pairs that passed our thresholds, we can test the similarity of observed representations by comparing the VSM representation of the phrase (no composition function). For all 108 phrase pairs we can test the composed phrase representations, derived by applying addition and dilation operations to word vectors. Multiplication is not used as SVD representations include negative values, and so the product of two negative values would be positive.

Addition is the element-wise sum of two semantic feature vectors $s_i^{add} = s_i^{adj} + s_i^{noun}$, where s_i^{noun}, s_i^{adj}, and s_i^{add} are the ith element of the noun, adjective, and predicted phrase vectors, respectively. Dilation of two semantic feature vectors s^{adj} and s^{noun} is calculated by first decomposing the noun into a component parallel to the adjective (x) and a component perpendicular to the adjective (y) so that $s^{noun} = x + y$. Dilation then enhances the adjective component by multiplying it by a scalar (γ): $s^{dilate} = \gamma x + y$. This can be viewed as taking the representation of the noun, and up-weighting the elements it shares with the adjective, which is coherent with the notion of co-composition (Pustejovsky, 1995). Previous work (Mitchell and Lapata, 2010) tuned the γ parameter ($\gamma = 16.7$). We use that value here, though further optimization might increase performance.

For our evaluation we calculated the cosine distance between pairs of phrases in the three different representation spaces: observed, addition and dilation. Results for a range of dimensionality settings appear in Figure 2. In the observed space, we maximized performance when we included all 1000 of the Document and 350 Dependency dimensions. For consistency the y axis in Figure 2 extends only to 100 Document dimensions: changes beyond 100 dimensions for observed vectors were minimal. By design, SVD will tend to use lower dimensions to represent the strongest signals in the input statistics, which typically originate in the types of targets that are most frequent – in this case single words. We have observed that less frequent and noisier counts, as might be found for many phrases, are displaced to the higher dimensions. Consistent with this observation, maximum performance occurs using a high number of dimensions (correlation of 0.37 to human judgements of phrase similarity).

Interestingly, using the single word vectors to predict the phrase vectors via the addition function gives the best correlation of any of the representations, outperforming even the observed phrase representations. When using 25 Document dimensions and 600 Dependency dimensions the correlation is 0.52, compared to the best performance of 0.51 using Dependency dimensions only. We speculate that the advantage of composed vectors over observed vectors is due to sparseness and resulting noise/variance in the observed phrase vectors, as phrases are necessarily less frequent than their constituent words.

The dilation composition function performs slightly worse than addition, but shows best performance at the same point as addition. Here, the highest correlation (0.46) is substantially lower than that attained by addition, and uses 25 dimensions of the Document, and 600 dimensions of the Dependency VSM.

To summarize, without documents, {observed, addition and dilation} phrase vectors have maximal correlations {0.37, 0.51 and 0.46}. With documents, {observed, addition and dilation} phrase vectors have maximal correlations {0.37, 0.52 and 0.50}. Our results using the addition function (0.52) outperform the results in two previous studies (Mitchell and Lapata, 2010; Blacoe and Lapata, 2012): (0.46 and 0.48 respectively). This is evidence that a VSM built from a larger corpus, and with both Document and Dependency information can yield superior results.

4.3 Composed vs Observed Phrase Vectors

Next we tested how well our representations and semantic composition functions could predict the *observed* vector statistics for phrases from the vectors of their component words. Again, we explored addition and dilation composition functions. For testing we have $13,575$ vectors for which both the adjective and noun passed our thresholds. We predicted a composed phrase vector using the statistics of the single words and one of the two composition functions (addition or dilation). We then sorted the list of *observed* phrase vectors by their distance to the *composed* phrase vector and recorded the position of the corresponding observed vector in the list. From this we calculated percentile rank, the percent of phrases that are further from the predicted vector than the observed vector. Percentile rank is: $100 \times (1 - \mu_{rank}/N)$ where μ_{rank} is the average position of the correct observed vector in the sorted list and $N = 13,575$ is the size of the list.

Figure 3 shows the changes in percentile rank in response to varying dimensions of Documents and Dependencies for the addition function. Dilation results are not shown, but the pattern of performance is very similar. In general, when one includes more Document dimensions, the percentile rank increases. For both the dilation and addition composition functions the peak performance is with 750 Dependency dimensions and 1000 Document dimensions. Dilation's peak performance is 97.87; addition peaks at 98.03 percentile rank. As in Section 4.2, we see that the accurate representation of phrases requires higher SVD dimensions.

To evaluate when composition fails, we examined the cases where the percentile rank was $< 25\%$. Amongst these words we found an over-representation of operational adjectives like "better" and "more". As observed previously, it is possible that such adjectives could be better represented with a matrix or function (Socher et al., 2012; Baroni and Zamparelli, 2010). Composition may also be failing when the adjective-noun phrase is non-compositional (e.g. lazy susan); filtering such phrases could improve performance.

4.4 Brain Activity Data

Here we explore the relationship between the neural activity observed when a person reads a phrase,

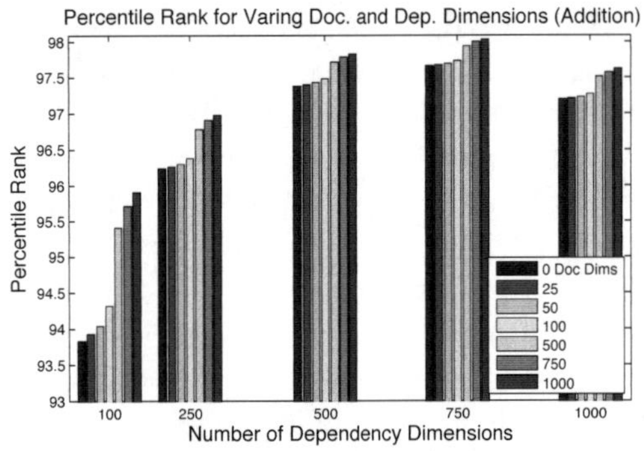

Figure 3: The percentile rank of observed phrase vectors compared to vectors created using the addition composition function.

and our predicted composed VSM for that phrase. We collected brain activity data using Magnetoencephalography (MEG). MEG is a brain imaging method with much higher temporal resolution (1 ms) than fMRI ($\sim$2 sec). Since words are naturally read at a rate of about 2 per second, MEG is a better candidate for capturing the fast dynamics of semantic composition in the brain. Some previous work has explored adjective-noun composition in the brain (Chang et al., 2009), but used fMRI and corpus statistics based only on co-occurrence with 5 hand-selected verbs.

Our MEG data was collected while 9 participants viewed 38 phrases, each repeated 20 times (randomly interleaved). The stimulus nouns were chosen because previous research had shown them to be decodable from MEG recordings, and the adjectives were selected to modulate their most decodable semantic properties (e.g. edibility, manipulability) (Sudre et al., 2012). The 8 adjectives selected are ("big", "small", "ferocious", "gentle", "light", "heavy", "rotten", "tasty"), and the 6 nouns are ("dog", "bear", "tomato", "carrot", "hammer", "shovel"). The words "big" and "small" are paired with every noun, "ferocious" and "gentle" with animals, "light" and "heavy" with tools and "rotten" and "tasty" with foods. We also included the words "the" and the word "thing" as semantically neutral fillers, to present each of the words in a condition without semantic modulation. In total there are 38 phrases (e.g. "rotten carrot", "big hammer").

In the MEG experiment, the adjective and paired noun were each shown for 500ms, with a 300ms interval between them, and there were 3 seconds in total time between the onset of subsequent phrases. Data was preprocessed to maximize the signal/noise ratio as is common practice – see Gross et al., (2012). The 20 repeated trials for each phrase were averaged together to create one average brain image per phrase.

Figure 4: Results for predicting composed phrase vectors (addition [4a] and dilation [4b]) from MEG recordings. Results shown are the average over 9 subjects viewing 38 adjective-noun phrases. This is the one task on which dilation outperforms addition.

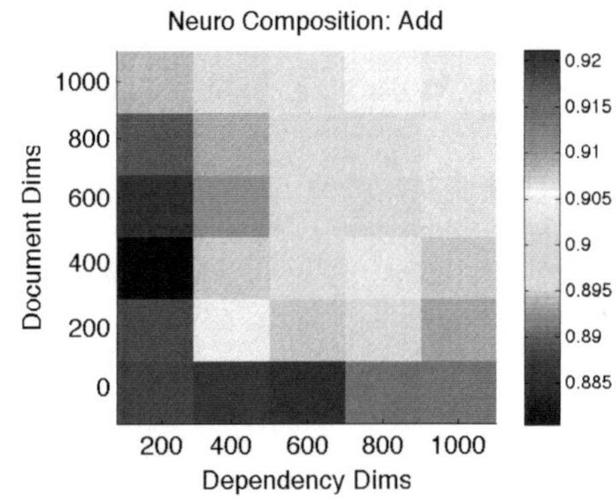

(a) Addition composition function results.

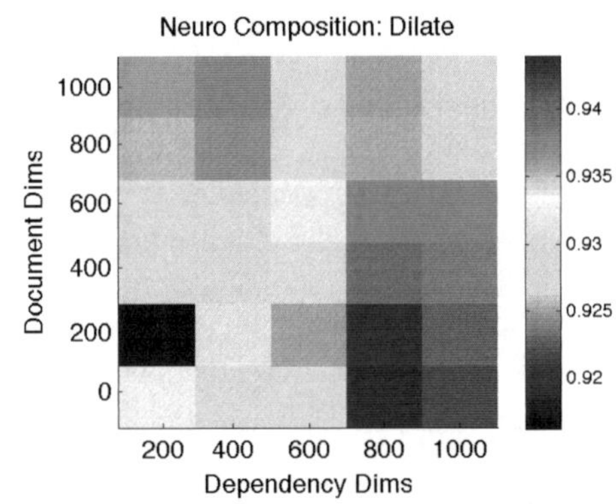

(b) Dilation composition function results.

To determine if the recorded MEG data can be used to predict our composed vector space representations, we devised the following classification framework.[2] The training data is comprised of the averaged MEG signal for each of the 38 phrases for one subject, and the labels are the 38 phrases. We use our VSMs and composition functions to form a mapping of the 38 phrases to com-

[2]Predicting brain activity from VSM representations is also possible, but provides additional challenges, as parts of the observed brain activity are not driven by semantics.

posed semantic feature vectors $w \rightarrow \{s_1 \dots s_m\}$. The mapping allows us to use Zero Shot Learning (Palatucci et al., 2009) to predict novel phrases (not seen during training) from a MEG recording. This is a particularly attractive characteristic for the task of predicting words, as there are many words and many more phrases in the English language, and one cannot hope to collect MEG recordings for all of them.

Formally, let us define the semantic representation of a phrase w as semantic feature vector $\vec{s_w} = \{s_1 ... s_m\}$, where the semantic space has dimension m that varies depending on the number of Document and/or Dependency dimensions we include. We utilize the mapping $w \rightarrow \{s_1 \dots s_m\}$ to train m independent functions $f_1(X) \rightarrow s'_1, \dots, f_m(X) \rightarrow s'_m$ where s' represents the value of a predicted composed semantic feature. We combine the output of $f_1 \dots f_m$ to create the final predicted semantic vector $\vec{s'} = \{s'_1 \dots s'_m\}$. We use cosine distance to quantify the distance between true and predicted semantic vectors.

To measure performance we use the **2 vs. 2 test**. For each test we withhold two phrases and train regressors on the remaining 36. We use the regressors f and MEG data from the two held out phrases to create two predicted semantic vectors. We then choose the assignment of predicted semantic vectors ($\vec{s'_i}$ and $\vec{s'_j}$) to true semantic vectors ($\vec{s_i}$ and $\vec{s_j}$) that minimizes the sum of cosine distances. If we choose the correct assignment ($\vec{s'_i} \mapsto \vec{s_i}$ and $\vec{s'_j} \mapsto \vec{s_j}$) we mark the test as correct. **2 vs. 2 accuracy** is the number of 2 vs. 2 tests with correct assignments divided by the total number of tests. There are (38 choose 2) $=$ 703 distinct 2 vs. 2 tests, and we evaluate on the subset for which neither the adjective nor noun are shared (540 pairs). Chance performance is 0.50.

For each f we trained a regressor with L_2 penalty. We tune the regularization parameter with leave-one-out-cross-validation on training data. We train regressors using the first 800 ms of MEG signal after the noun stimulus appears, when we assume semantic composition is taking place.

Results appear in Figure 4. The best performance (2 vs. 2 accuracy of 0.9440) is achieved with dilation, 800 dimensions of Dependencies and zero Document dimensions. When we use the addition composition function, optimal performance is 0.9212, at 600 Dependency and zero Document dimensions. Note, however, that the parameter search here was much coarser that in Sections 4.2 and 4.3, due to the computation required. We used a finer grid around the peaks in performance for addition and dilation and found minimal improvement ($\pm 0.5\%$) with the addition of a small number of Document dimensions.

It is intriguing that this neurosemantic task is the only task for which dilation outperforms addition. All other composition tasks explored in this study were concerned with matching composed word vectors to observed or composed word vectors, whereas here we are interested in matching composed word vectors to observed *brain activity*. Perhaps the brain works in a manner more akin to the emphasis of elements as modeled by dilation, rather than a summing of features. Further work is required to fully understand this phenomenon, but this is surely a thought-provoking result.[3]

5 Conclusion

We have performed a systematic study of complementarity of topical (Document) and type (Dependency) features in Vector Space Model (VSM) for semantic composition of adjective-noun phrases. To the best of our knowledge, this is one of the first such studies of this kind. Through experiments on multiple real world benchmark datasets, we demonstrated the benefit of combining topic- and type-based features in a VSM. Additionally, we introduced a novel task of predicting vector representations of composed phrases from the brain activity of human subjects reading those phrases. We exploited a large syntactically parsed corpus to build our VSM models, and make them publicly available. We hope that the findings and resources from this paper will serve to inform future work on VSMs and semantic composition.

Acknowledgment

We are thankful to the anonymous reviewers for their constructive comments. We thank CMUs Parallel Data Laboratory (PDL) for making the OpenCloud cluster available, Justin Betteridge (CMU) for his help with parsing the corpus, and Yahoo! for providing the M45 cluster. This research has been supported in part by DARPA (under contract number FA8750-13-2-0005), NIH (NICHD award 1R01HD075328-01), Keck Foundation (DT123107), NSF (IIS0835797), and Google. Any opinions, findings, conclusions and recommendations expressed in this paper are the authors and do not necessarily reflect those of the sponsors.

[3]No pun intended.

References

Eneko Agirre, Enrique Alfonseca, Keith Hall, Jana Kravalova, and Marius Pas. 2009. A study on similarity and relatedness using distributional and WordNet-based approaches. *Proceedings of NAACL-HLT 2009.*

Abdulrahman Almuhareb and Massimo Poesio. 2004. Attribute-based and value-based clustering: An evaluation. In *Proceedings of EMNLP*, pages 158–165.

Marco Baroni and Alessandro Lenci. 2010. Distributional memory: A general framework for corpus-based semantics. *Computational Linguistics*, 36(4):673–721.

Marco Baroni and Roberto Zamparelli. 2010. Nouns are vectors, adjectives are matrices: Representing adjective-noun constructions in semantic space. In *Proceedings of the 2010 Conference on Empirical Methods in Natural Language Processing*, pages 1183–1193. Association for Computational Linguistics.

W F Battig and W E Montague. 1969. Category Norms for Verbal Items in 56 Categories: A Replication and Extension of the Connecticut Category Norms. *Journal of Experimental Psychology Monographs*, 80(3):1–46.

William Blacoe and Mirella Lapata. 2012. A Comparison of Vector-based Representations for Semantic Composition. In *Proceedings of the 2012 Joint Conference on Empirical Methods in Natural Language Processing and Computational Natural Language Learning*, pages 546–556, Jeju Island, Korea.

David M Blei, Andrew Y Ng, and Michael I Jordan. 2003. Latent Dirichlet Allocation. *Journal of Machine Learning Research*, 3(4-5):993–1022.

Jamie Callan and Mark Hoy. 2009. The ClueWeb09 Dataset. *http://boston.lti.cs.cmu.edu/Data/clueweb09/.*

Kai-min Chang, Vladimir L. Cherkassky, Tom M Mitchell, and Marcel Adam Just. 2009. Quantitative modeling of the neural representation of adjective-noun phrases to account for fMRI activation. In *Proceedings of the Annual Meeting of the ACL and the 4th IJCNLP of the AFNLP*, pages 638–646.

Lev Finkelstein, Evgeniy Gabrilovich, Yossi Matias, Ehud Rivlin, Zach Solan, Gadi Wolfman, and Eytan Ruppin. 2002. Placing search in context: the concept revisited. *ACM Transactions on Information Systems*, 20(1):116–131.

Thomas L Griffiths, Mark Steyvers, David M Blei, and Joshua B Tenenbaum. 2005. Integrating topics and syntax. *Advances in neural information processing systems*, 17.

Joachim Gross, Sylvain Baillet, Gareth R. Barnes, Richard N. Henson, Arjan Hillebrand, Ole Jensen, Karim Jerbi, Vladimir Litvak, Burkhard Maess, Robert Oostenveld, Lauri Parkkonen, Jason R. Taylor, Virginie van Wassenhove, Michael Wibral, and Jan-Mathijs Schoffelen. 2012. Good-practice for conducting and reporting MEG research. *NeuroImage*, October.

J Hall, J Nilsson, J Nivre, G Eryigit, B Megyesi, M Nilsson, and M Saers. 2007. Single Malt or Blended? A Study in Multilingual Parser Optimization. In *Proceedings of the CoNLL Shared Task Session of EMNLPCoNLL 2007*, volume s. 19-33, pages 933–939. Association for Computational Linguistics.

Nancy Ide and Keith Suderman. 2006. The American National Corpus First Release. *Proceedings of the Fifth Language Resources and Evaluation Conference (LREC).*

Eric Jones, Travis Oliphant, Pearu Peterson, and others. 2001. SciPy: Open source scientific tools for Python.

George Karypis. 2003. CLUTO: A Clustering Toolkit. Technical Report 02-017, Department of Computer Science, University of Minnesota.

T Landauer and S Dumais. 1997. A solution to Plato's problem: the latent semantic analysis theory of acquisition, induction, and representation of knowledge. *Psychological Review*, 104(2):211–240.

R B Lehoucq, D C Sorensen, and C Yang. 1998. *Arpack users' guide: Solution of large scale eigenvalue problems with implicitly restarted Arnoldi methods.* SIAM.

Dekang Lin and Xiaoyun Wu. 2009. Phrase clustering for discriminative learning. In *Proceedings of the ACL.*

Dekang Lin. 1998. Automatic Retrieval and Clustering of Similar Words. In *COLING-ACL*, pages 768–774.

K Lund and C Burgess. 1996. Producing high-dimensional semantic spaces from lexical co-occurrence. *Behavior Research Methods, Instruments, and Computers*, 28:203–208.

George A Miller, Richard Beckwith, Christiane Fellbaum, Derek Gross, and Katherine Miller. 1990. Introduction to WordNet: an on-line lexical database. *International Journal of Lexicography*, 3(4):235–244.

Jeff Mitchell and Mirella Lapata. 2010. Composition in distributional models of semantics. *Cognitive science*, 34(8):1388–429, November.

Brian Murphy, Partha Talukdar, and Tom Mitchell. 2012a. Comparing Abstract and Concrete Conceptual Representations using Neurosemantic Decoding. In *NAACL Workshop on Cognitive Modelling and Computational Linguistics.*

Brian Murphy, Partha Talukdar, and Tom Mitchell. 2012b. Selecting Corpus-Semantic Models for Neurolinguistic Decoding. In *First Joint Conference on Lexical and Computational Semantics (*SEM)*, pages 114–123, Montreal, Quebec, Canada.

Brian Murphy, Partha Pratim Talukdar, and Tom Mitchell. 2012c. Learning Effective and Interpretable Semantic Models using Non-Negative Sparse Embedding. In *International Conference on Computational Linguistics (COLING 2012), Mumbai, India.*

S Padó and M Lapata. 2007. Dependency-based construction of semantic space models. *Computational Linguistics*, 33(2):161–199.

Mark Palatucci, Geoffrey Hinton, Dean Pomerleau, and Tom M Mitchell. 2009. Zero-Shot Learning with Semantic Output Codes. *Advances in Neural Information Processing Systems*, 22:1410–1418.

James Pustejovsky. 1995. *The Generative Lexicon*. MIT Press, Cambridge.

Reinhard Rapp. 2003. Word Sense Discovery Based on Sense Descriptor Dissimilarity. *Proceedings of the Ninth Machine Translation Summit*, pp:315–322.

Herbert Rubenstein and John B. Goodenough. 1965. Contextual correlates of synonymy. *Communications of the ACM*, 8(10):627–633, October.

Mehrnoosh Sadrzadeh and Edward Grefenstette. 2011. A Compositional Distributional Semantics Two Concrete Constructions and some Experimental Evaluations. *Lecture Notes in Computer Science*, 7052:35–47.

Magnus Sahlgren. 2006. *The Word-Space Model: Using distributional analysis to represent syntagmatic and paradigmatic relations between words in high-dimensional vector spaces*. Dissertation, Stockholm University.

Richard Socher, Brody Huval, Christopher D. Manning, and Andrew Y. Ng. 2012. Semantic Compositionality through Recursive Matrix-Vector Spaces. In *Conference on Empirical Methods in Natural Language Processing and Computational Natural Language Learning*.

Gustavo Sudre, Dean Pomerleau, Mark Palatucci, Leila Wehbe, Alona Fyshe, Riitta Salmelin, and Tom Mitchell. 2012. Tracking Neural Coding of Perceptual and Semantic Features of Concrete Nouns. *NeuroImage*, 62(1):463–451, May.

Peter D Turney. 2012. Domain and Function : A Dual-Space Model of Semantic Relations and Compositions. *Journal of Artificial Intelligence Research*, 44:533–585.

Hidden Markov tree models for semantic class induction

Édouard Grave
Inria - Sierra Project-Team
École Normale Supérieure
Paris, France
Edouard.Grave
@inria.fr

Guillaume Obozinski
Université Paris-Est, LIGM
École des Ponts - ParisTech
Marne-la-Vallée, France
Guillaume.Obozinski
@imagine.enpc.fr

Francis Bach
Inria - Sierra Project-Team
École Normale Supérieure
Paris, France
Francis.Bach
@ens.fr

Abstract

In this paper, we propose a new method for semantic class induction. First, we introduce a generative model of sentences, based on dependency trees and which takes into account homonymy. Our model can thus be seen as a generalization of Brown clustering. Second, we describe an efficient algorithm to perform inference and learning in this model. Third, we apply our proposed method on two large datasets (10^8 tokens, 10^5 words types), and demonstrate that classes induced by our algorithm improve performance over Brown clustering on the task of semi-supervised supersense tagging and named entity recognition.

1 Introduction

Most competitive learning methods for computational linguistics are supervised, and thus require labeled examples, which are expensive to obtain. Moreover, those techniques suffer from data scarcity: many words only appear a small number of time, or even not at all, in the training data. It thus helps a lot to first learn word clusters on a large amount of unlabeled data, which are cheap to obtain, and then to use this clusters as features for the supervised task. This scheme has proven to be effective for various tasks such as named entity recognition (Freitag, 2004; Miller et al., 2004; Liang, 2005; Faruqui et al., 2010), syntactic chunking (Turian et al., 2010) or syntactic dependency parsing (Koo et al., 2008; Haffari et al., 2011; Tratz and Hovy, 2011). It was also successfully applied for transfer learning of multilingual structure by Täckström et al. (2012).

The most commonly used clustering method for semi-supervised learning is the one proposed by Brown et al. (1992), and known as Brown clustering. While still being one of the most efficient word representation method (Turian et al., 2010), Brown clustering has two limitations we want to address in this work. First, since it is a hard clustering method, homonymy is ignored. Second, it does not take into account syntactic relations between words, which seems crucial to induce semantic classes. Our goal is thus to propose a method for semantic class induction which takes into account both syntax and homonymy, and then to study their effects on semantic class learning.

In this paper, we start by introducing a new unsupervised method for semantic classes induction. This is achieved by defining a generative model of sentences with latent variables, which aims at capturing semantic roles of words. We require our method to be scalable, in order to learn models on large datasets containing tens of millions of sentences. More precisely, we make the following contributions:

- We introduce a generative model of sentences, based on dependency trees, which can be seen as a generalization of Brown clustering,
- We describe a fast approximate inference algorithm, based on message passing and online EM for scaling to large datasets. It allowed us to learn models with 512 latent states on a dataset with hundreds of millions of tokens in less than two days on a single core,
- We learn models on two datasets, Wikipedia articles about musicians and the NYT corpus,

and evaluate them on two semi-supervised tasks, namely supersense tagging and named entity recognition.

1.1 Related work

Brown clustering (Brown et al., 1992) is the most commonly used method for word cluster induction for semi-supervised learning. The goal of this algorithm is to discover a clustering function $\mathcal{C}$ from words to clusters which maximizes the likelihood of the data, assuming the following sequential model of sentences:

$$\prod_{k} p(w_k \mid \mathcal{C}(w_k))p(\mathcal{C}(w_k) \mid \mathcal{C}(w_{k-1})).$$

It can be shown that the best clustering is actually maximizing the mutual information between adjacent clusters. A greedy agglomerative algorithm was proposed by Brown et al. (1992) in order to find the clustering $\mathcal{C}$, while Clark (2003) proposed to use the exchange clustering algorithm (Kneser and Ney, 1993) to maximize the previous likelihood. One of the limitations of this model is the fact that it neither takes into account homonymy or syntax.

Another limitation of this method is the complexity of the algorithms proposed to find the best clustering. This led Uszkoreit and Brants (2008) to consider a slightly different model, where the class-to-class transitions are replaced by word-to-class transitions:

$$\prod_{k} p(w_k \mid \mathcal{C}(w_k))p(\mathcal{C}(w_k) \mid w_{k-1}).$$

Thanks to that modification, Uszkoreit and Brants (2008) designed an efficient variant of the exchange algorithm, allowing them to train models on very large datasets. This model was then extended to the multilingual setting by Täckström et al. (2012).

Semantic space models are another family of methods, besides clustering, that can be used as features for semi-supervised learning. In those techniques, words are represented as vectors in a high-dimensional space. These vectors are obtained by representing the unlabeled corpus as a word-document co-occurrence matrix in the case of *latent semantic analysis* (LSA) (Deerwester et al., 1990), or word-word co-occurrence matrix in the case of the *hyperspace analog to language* model (HAL) (Lund and Burgess, 1996). Dimension reduction is then performed, by taking the singular value decomposition of the co-occurrence matrix, in order to obtained the so-called semantic space. Hofmann (1999) proposed a variant of LSA, which corresponds to a generative model of document. More recently, Dhillon et al. (2011) proposed a method based on canonical correlation analysis to obtained a such word embeddings.

A last approach to word representation is latent Dirichlet allocation (LDA), proposed by Blei et al. (2003). LDA is a generative model where each document is viewed as a mixture of topics. The major difference between LDA and our model is the fact that LDA treats documents as bags of words, while we introduce a model of sentences, taking into account the syntax. Griffiths et al. (2005) defined a composite model, using LDA for topic modeling and an HMM for syntax modeling. This model, HMM-LDA, was used by Li and McCallum (2005) for semi-supervised learning and applied to part-of-speech tagging and Chinese word segmentation. Séaghdha (2010) proposed to use topic models, such as LDA, to perform selectional preference induction.

Finally, Boyd-Graber and Blei (2009) proposed a variant of LDA, using parse trees to include the syntax. Given that we aim for our classes to capture as much of the word semantics reflected by the syntax, such as the semantic roles of words, we believe that it is not necessarily useful or even desirable that the latent variables should be determined, even in part, by topic parameters that are sharing information at the document level. Moreover, our model being significantly simpler, we were able to design fast and efficient algorithms, making it possible to use our model on much larger datasets, and with many more latent classes.

2 Model

In this section, we introduce our probabilistic generative model of sentences. We start by setting up some notations. A sentence is represented by a K-tuple $\mathbf{w} = (w_1, ..., w_K)$ where each $w_k \in \{1, ..., V\}$ is an integer representing a word and V is the size of the vocabulary. Our goal will be to infer a K-tuple $\mathbf{c} = (c_1, ..., c_K)$ of semantic classes, where each $c_k \in \{1, ..., C\}$ is an integer representing a semantic class, corresponding to the word w_k.

The generation of a sentence can be decomposed in two steps: first, we generate the semantic classes according to a Markov process, and

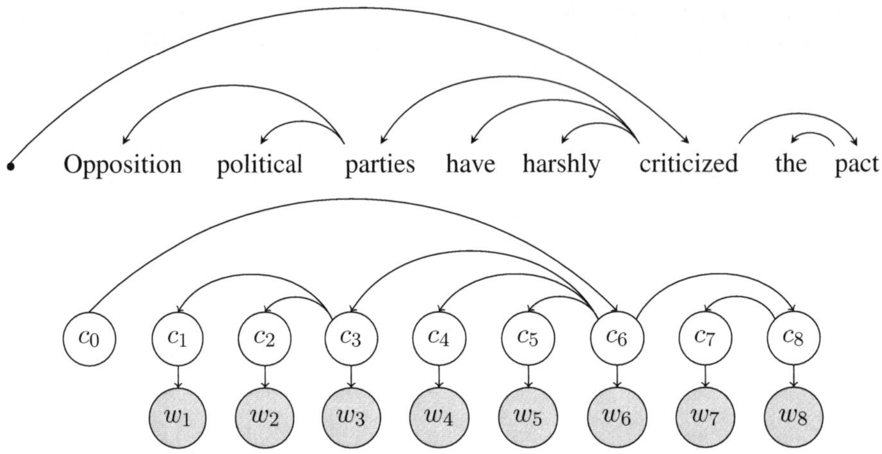

Figure 1: Example of a dependency tree and its corresponding graphical model.

then, given each class c_k, we generate the corresponding word w_k independently of other words. The Markov process used to generate the semantic classes will take into account selectional preference. Since we want to model homonymy, each word can be generated by multiple classes.

We now describe the Markov process we propose to generate the semantic classes. We assume that we are given a directed tree defined by the function $\pi : \{1, ..., K\} \mapsto \{0, ..., K\}$, where $\pi(k)$ represents the unique parent of the node k and 0 is the root of the tree. Each node, except the root, corresponds to a word of the sentence. First, we generate the semantic class corresponding to the root of the tree and then generate recursively the class for the other nodes. The classes are conditionally independent given the classes of their parents. Using the language of probabilistic graphical models, this means that the distribution of the semantic classes factorizes in the tree defined by π (See Fig. 1 for an example). We obtain the following distribution on pairs $(\mathbf{w}, \mathbf{c})$ of words and semantic classes:

$$p(\mathbf{w}, \mathbf{c}) = \prod_{k=1}^{K} p(c_k \mid c_{\pi(k)}) p(w_k \mid c_k),$$

with c_0 being equal to a special symbol denoting the root of the tree.

In order to fully define our model, we now need to specify the observation probability distribution $p(w_k \mid c_k)$ of a word given the corresponding class and the transition probability distribution $p(c_k \mid c_{\pi(k)})$ of a class given the class of the parent. Both these distributions will be categorical (and thus multinomial with one trial). The corresponding parameters will be represented by the stochastic matrices $\mathbf{O}$ and $\mathbf{T}$ (i.e. matrices with non-negative elements and unit-sum columns):

$$p(w_k = i \mid c_k = j) = O_{ij},$$
$$p(c_k = i \mid c_{\pi(k)} = j) = T_{ij}.$$

Finally, we introduce the trees that we consider to define the distribution on semantic classes. (We recall that the trees are assumed given, and not a part of the model.)

2.1 Markov chain model

The simplest structure we consider on the semantic classes is a Markov chain. In this special case, our model reduces to a hidden Markov model. Each semantic class only depends on the class of the previous word in the sentence, thus failing to capture selectional preference of semantic class. But because of its simplicity, it may be more robust, and does not rely on external tools. It can be seen as a generalization of the Brown clustering algorithm (Brown et al., 1992) taking into account homonymy.

2.2 Dependency tree model

The second kind of structure we consider to model interactions between semantic classes is a syntactic dependency tree corresponding to the sentence. A dependency tree is a labeled tree in which nodes correspond to the words of a sentence, and edges represent the grammatical relations between those words, such as *nominal subject*, *direct object* or *determiner*. We use the Stanford typed dependencies basic representations, which always form a tree (De Marneffe and Manning, 2008).

We believe that a dependency tree is a better structure than a Markov chain to learn semantic classes, with no additional cost for inference and learning compared to a chain. First, syntactic dependencies can capture long distance interactions between words. See Fig. 1 and the dependency between `parties` and `criticized` for an example. Second, the syntax is important to model selectional preference. Third, we believe that syntactic trees could help much for languages which do not have a strict word order, such as Czech, Finnish, or Russian. One drawback of this model is that all the children of a particular node share the same transition probability distribution. While this is not a big issue for nouns, it is a bigger concern for verbs: subject and object should not share the same transition probability distribution.

A potential solution would be to introduce a different transition probability distribution for each type of dependency. This possibility will be explored in future work.

2.3 Brown clustering on dependency trees

As for Brown clustering, we can assume that words are generated by a single class. In that case, our model reduces to finding a deterministic clustering function $\mathcal{C}$ which maximizes the following likelihood:

$$\prod_k p(w_k \mid \mathcal{C}(w_k))p(\mathcal{C}(w_k) \mid \mathcal{C}(w_{\pi(k)})).$$

In that case, we can use the algorithm proposed by Brown et al. (1992) to greedily maximize the likelihood of the data. This model can be seen as a generalization of Brown clustering taking into account the syntactic relations between words.

3 Inference and learning

In this section, we present the approach used to perform learning and inference in our model. Our goal here is to have efficient algorithms, in order to apply our model to large datasets (10^8 tokens, 10^5 words types). The parameters $\mathbf{T}$ and $\mathbf{O}$ of the model will be estimated with the maximum likelihood estimator:

$$\hat{\mathbf{T}}, \hat{\mathbf{O}} = \arg\max_{\mathbf{T},\mathbf{O}} \prod_{n=1}^{N} p(\mathbf{w}^{(n)} \mid \mathbf{T}, \mathbf{O}),$$

where $(\mathbf{w}^{(n)})_{n\in\{1,\ldots,N\}}$ represents our training set of N sentences.

First, we present an online variant of the well-known expectation-maximization (EM) algorithm, proposed by Cappé and Moulines (2009), allowing our method to be scalable in term of numbers of examples. Then, we present an approximate message passing algorithm which has a linear complexity in the number of classes, instead of the quadratic complexity of the exact inference algorithm. Finally, we describe a state-splitting strategy to speed up the learning.

3.1 Online EM

In the batch EM algorithm, the E-step consists in computing the expected sufficient statistics τ and ω of the model, sometimes referred as pseudocounts, corresponding respectively to $\mathbf{T}$ and $\mathbf{O}$:

$$\tau_{ij} = \sum_{n=1}^{N}\sum_{k=1}^{K_n} \mathbb{E}\left[\delta(c_k^{(n)} = i,\, c_{\pi(k)}^{(n)} = j)\right],$$
$$\omega_{ij} = \sum_{n=1}^{N}\sum_{k=1}^{K_n} \mathbb{E}\left[\delta(w_k^{(n)} = i,\, c_k^{(n)} = j)\right].$$

On large datasets, N which is the number of sentences can be very large, and so, EM is inefficient because it requires that inference is performed on the entire dataset at each iteration. We therefore consider the online variant proposed by Cappé and Moulines (2009): instead of recomputing the pseudocounts on the whole dataset at each iteration t, those pseudocounts are updated using only a small subset $\mathcal{B}_t$ of the data, to get

$$\tau_{ij}^{(t)} = (1-\alpha_t)\tau_{ij}^{(t-1)} + \alpha_t \sum_{n\in\mathcal{B}_t}\sum_{k=1}^{K_n} \mathbb{E}\left[\delta(c_k^{(n)} = i,\, c_{\pi(k)}^{(n)} = j)\right],$$

and

$$\omega_{ij}^{(t)} = (1-\alpha_t)\omega_{ij}^{(t-1)} + \alpha_t \sum_{n\in\mathcal{B}_t}\sum_{k=1}^{K_n} \mathbb{E}\left[\delta(w_k^{(n)} = i,\, c_k^{(n)} = j)\right],$$

where the scalars α_t are defined by $\alpha_t = 1/(a+t)^\gamma$ with $0.5 < \gamma \leq 1$. In the experiments, we used $a = 4$. We chose γ in the set $\{0.5, 0.6, 0.7, 0.8, 0.9, 1.0\}$.

3.2 Approximate inference

Inference is performed on trees using the sum-product message passing algorithm, a.k.a. belief

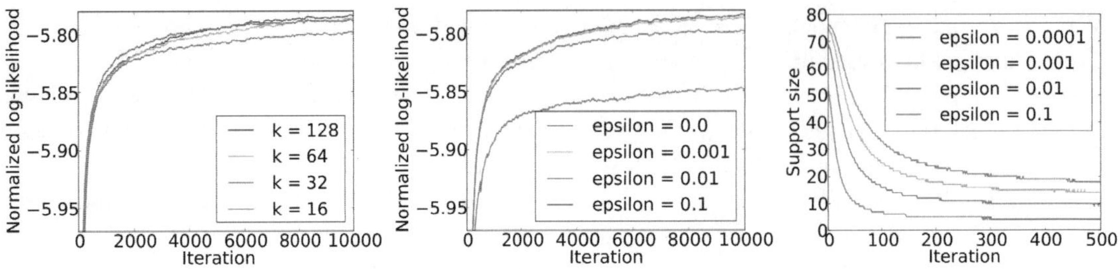

Figure 2: Comparison of the two projection methods for approximating vectors, for a model with 128 latent classes. The first two plots are the log-likelihood on a held-out set as a function of the iterates of online EM. Green curves ($k = 128$ and $\varepsilon = 0$) correspond to learning without approximation.

propagation, which extends the classical $\alpha - \beta$ recursions used for chains, see e.g. Wainwright and Jordan (2008). We denote by $\mathcal{N}(k)$ the set containing the children and the father of node k. In the exact message-passing algorithm, the message $\mu_{k\to\pi(k)}$ from node k to node $\pi(k)$ takes the form:

$$\mu_{k\to\pi(k)} = \mathbf{T}^\top \mathbf{u},$$

where $\mathbf{u}$ is the vector obtained by taking the elementwise product of all the messages received by node k except the one from node $\pi(k)$, i.e.,

$$u_i = \prod_{k' \in \mathcal{N}(k)\setminus\{\pi(k)\}} \mu_{k'\to k}(i).$$

Similarly, the pseudocounts can be written as

$$\mathbb{E}\left[\delta(c_k^{(n)} = i, c_{\pi(k)}^{(n)} = j)\right] \propto u_i T_{ij} v_j,$$

where $\mathbf{v}$ is the vector obtained by taking the elementwise product of all the messages received by node $\pi(k)$, except the one from node k, i.e.,

$$v_j = \prod_{k' \in \mathcal{N}(\pi(k))\setminus\{k\}} \mu_{k'\to\pi(k)}(j).$$

Both these operations thus have quadratic complexity in the number of semantic classes. In order to reduce the complexity of those operations, we propose to start by projecting the vectors $\mathbf{u}$ and $\mathbf{v}$ on a set of sparse vectors, and then, perform the operations with the sparse approximate vectors. We consider two kinds of projections:

- *k-best projection*, where the approximate vector is obtained by keeping the k largest coefficients,

- *ε-best projection*, where the approximate vector is obtained by keeping the smallest set of larger coefficients such that their sum is greater than $(1 - \varepsilon)$ times the ℓ_1-norm of the original vector.

This method is similar to the one proposed by Pal et al. (2006). The advantage of the k-best projection is that we control the complexity of the operations, but not the error, while the advantage of the ε-best projection is that we control the error but not the complexity. As shown in Fig. 2, good choices for ε and k are respectively 0.01 and 16. We use these values in the experiments. We also note, on the right plot of Fig. 2, that during the first iterations of EM, the sparse vectors obtained with the ε-best projection have a large number of non-zero elements. Thus, this projection is not adequate to directly learn large latent class models. This issue is addressed in the next section, where we present a state splitting strategy in order to learn models with a large number of latent classes.

3.3 State splitting

A common strategy to speed up the learning of large latent state space models, such as ours, is to start with a small number of latent states, and split them during learning (Petrov, 2009). As far as we know, there are still no good heuristics to choose which states to split, or how to initialize the parameters corresponding to the new states. We thus apply the simple, yet effective method, consisting in splitting all states into two and in breaking the symmetry by adding a bit of randomness to the emission probabilities of the new states. As noted by Petrov (2009), state splitting could also improve the quality of learnt models.

3.4 Initialization

Because the negative log-likelihood function is not convex, initialization can greatly change the quality of the final model. Initialization for online EM is done by setting the initial pseudocounts, and then performing an M-step. We have considered the following strategies to initialize our model:

- *random initialization:* the initial pseudo-counts τ_{ij} and ω_{ij} are sampled from a uniform distribution on $[0, 1]$,
- *Brown initialization:* the model is initialized using the (normalized) pseudocounts obtained by the Brown clustering algorithm. Because a parameter equal to zero remains equal to zero when using the EM algorithm, we replace null pseudocounts by a small smoothing value, e.g., for observation i, we use $10^{-5} \times \max_j \omega_{ij}$,

4 Experiments

In this section, we present the datasets used for the experiments, and the two semi-supervised tasks on which we evaluate our models: named entity recognition and supersense tagging.

4.1 Datasets

We considered two datasets: the first one, which we refer to as the *music dataset*, corresponds to all the Wikipedia articles refering to a musical artist. They were extracted using the Freebase database[1]. This dataset comprises 2.22 millions sentences and 56 millions tokens. We choose this dataset because it corresponds to a restricted domain.

The second dataset are the articles of the NYT corpus (Sandhaus, 2008) corresponding to the period 1987-1997 and labeled as *news*. This dataset comprises 14.7 millions sentences and 310 millions tokens.

We parsed both datasets using the Stanford parser, and converted parse trees to dependency trees (De Marneffe et al., 2006). We decided to discard sentences longer than 50 tokens, for parsing time reasons, and then lemmatized tokens using Wordnet. Each word of our vocabulary is then a pair of lemma and its associated part-of-speech. This means that the noun *attack* and the verb *attack* are two different words. Finally, we introduced a special token, -*-, for infrequent (lemma, part-of-speech) pairs, in order to perform smoothing. For the music dataset, we kept the 25 000 most frequent words, while for the NYT corpus, we kept the 100 000 most frequent words. For the music dataset we set the number of latent states to 256, while we set it to 512 for the NYT corpus.

[1] www.freebase.com

4.2 Qualitative results

Before moving on to the quantitative evaluation of our model, we discuss qualitatively the induced semantic classes. Examples of semantic classes are presented in Tables 1, 2 and 3. Tree models with random initialization were used to obtain those semantic classes. First we observe that most classes can be easily given natural semantic interpretation. For example class 196 of Table 1 contains musical instruments, while class 116 contains musical genres.

Table 2 presents groups of classes that contain a given homonymous word; it seems that the different classes capture rather well the different senses of each word. For example, the word *head* belongs to the class 116, which contains body parts and to the class 127, which contains words referring to leaders.

4.3 Semi-supervised learning

We propose to evaluate and compare the different models in the following semi-supervised learning setting: we start by learning a model on the NYT corpus in an unsupervised way, and then use it to define features for a supervised classifier. We now introduce the tasks we considered.

4.3.1 Named entity recognition

The first supervised task on which we evaluate the different models, is named entity recognition. We cast it as a sequence tagging problem, and thus, we use a linear conditional random field (CRF) (Lafferty et al., 2001) as our supervised classifier. For each sentence, we apply the Viterbi algorithm in order to obtain the most probable sequence of semantic classes, and use this as features for the CRF. The only other feature we use is a binary feature indicating if the word is capitalized or not. Results of experiments performed on the MUC7 dataset are reported in table 4. The baseline for this task is assigning named entity classes to word sequences that occur in the training data.

4.3.2 Supersense tagging

Supersense tagging consists in identifying, for each word of a sentence, its corresponding supersense, a.k.a. lexicographer class, as defined by Wordnet (Ciaramita and Altun, 2006). Because each Wordnet synset belongs to one lexicographer class, supersense tagging can be seen as a coarse disambiguation task for nouns and verbs. We decided to evaluate our models on this task to

# 54	radio BBC television station tv stations channel 1 MTV program network fm music
# 52	chart billboard uk top top singles 100 Hot album country 40 10 R&B 200 US song u.s.
# 78	bach mozart liszt beethoven wagner chopin brahms stravinsky haydn debussy tchaikovsky
# 69	sound style instrument elements influence genre theme form lyric audience direction
#215	tour show concert performance appearance gig date tours event debut session set night party
#116	rock pop jazz classical folk punk metal roll hip country traditional -*- blues dance
#123	win receive sell gain earn award achieve garner give enjoy have get attract bring include
#238	reach peak hit chart go debut make top platinum fail enter gold become with certify
#203	piano concerto -*- for violin symphony in works sonata string of quartet orchestra no.
#196	guitar bass vocal drum keyboard piano saxophone percussion violin player trumpet organ
#243	leave join go move form return sign tour begin decide continue start attend meet disband
#149	school university college hall conservatory academy center church institute cathedral

Table 1: Selected semantic classes corresponding to the music dataset. Like LDA, our model is a probabilistic model which generates words from latent classes. Unlike LDA though, rather than treating words as exchangeable, it accounts for syntax and semantic relations between words. As a consequence, instead of grouping words with same topic but various semantic roles or grammatical functions, our model tends to group words that tend to be syntactically and semantically equivalent.

#116	**head** hand hands foot face shoulder way knee eyes back body finger car arms arm
#127	president member director chairman executive **head** editor professor manager secretary
#360	company corporation group industry fund **bank** association institute trust system
#480	street avenue side **bank** square precinct coast broadway district strip bridge station
#87	pay base sell use available buy depend make provide receive get lose spend **charge** offer
#316	**charge** arrest convict speak tell found accuse release die indict ask responsible suspend
#263	system computer machine technology plant product **program** equipment line network
#387	plan agreement contract effort **program** proposal deal offer bill bid order campaign request
#91	have be win score play lead hit make run -*- lose finish pitch start miss come go **shoot** take
#198	kill **shoot** die wound injure found arrest fire report take dead attack beat leave strike carry

Table 2: Semantic classes containing homonymous words. Different classes capture different senses of each word.

demonstrate the effect of homonymy. We cast supersense tagging as a classification problem and use posterior distribution of semantic classes as features for a support vector machine with the Hellinger kernel, defined by

$$K(\mathbf{p}, \mathbf{q}) = \sum_{c=1}^{C} \sqrt{p_c q_c},$$

where $\mathbf{p}$ and $\mathbf{q}$ are posterior distributions. We train and test the SVM classifier on the section A, B and C of the Brown corpus, tagged with Wordnet supersenses (SemCor). All the considered methods predict among the possible supersenses according to Wordnet, or among all the supersenses if the word does not appear in Wordnet. We report results in Table 5. The baseline predicts the most common supersense of the training set.

4.4 Discussion of results

First, we observe that hidden Markov models improve performances over Brown clustering, on both chains and trees. This seems to indicate that taking into account homonymy leads to richer models which is beneficial for both tasks. We also note that Brown clustering on dependency trees always outperforms Brown clustering on chains for the two tasks we consider, confirming that syntactic dependencies are a better structure to induce semantic classes than a linear chain.

Hidden Markov tree models also outperform hidden Markov chain models, except for supersense tagging on verbs. We believe that this drop in performance on verbs can be explained because in English the word order (Subject-Verb-Object) is strict, and thus, the chain model is able to dif-

#484	rise fell be close offer drop gain trade price jump slip end decline unchanged sell total lose
#352	it have would But be not nt will get may too make So see might can always still probably
#115	coach manager bill Joe george don pat Jim bob Lou al general mike Dan tom owner ray
#131	San St. santa Notre s Francisco calif. green tampa Diego louis class AP bay &aaa Fla. Jose
#350	strong short score good better hit second leave fast close impressive easy high quick enough
#274	A Another an new second single free -*- special fair national strong long major political big
#47	gogh rushdie pan guardia vega freud Prensa miserable picasso jesus Armani Monde Niro
#489	health public medical right care human civil community private social research housing
#238	building house home store apartment area space restaurant site neighborhood town park
#38	more very too as so much less enough But seem even because if particularly relatively pretty

Table 3: Randomly selected semantic classes corresponding to the news dataset.

	F1 score
Baseline	71.66
Brown clustering	82.57
tree Brown clustering	82.93
chain HMM, random init	84.66
chain HMM, Brown init	84.47
tree HMM, random init	84.07
tree HMM, Brown init	**85.49**

Table 4: Results of semi-supervised named entity recognition.

	nouns	verbs
Baseline	61.9 (0.2)	43.1 (0.2)
Brown clustering	73.9 (0.1)	63.7 (0.2)
tree Brown clustering	75.0 (0.2)	65.2 (0.2)
HMM (random)	76.1 (0.1)	63.0 (0.2)
HMM (Brown)	76.8 (0.1)	**66.6 (0.3)**
tree HMM (random)	76.7 (0.1)	61.5 (0.2)
tree HMM (Brown)	**77.9 (0.1)**	66.0 (0.2)

Table 5: Results of semi-supervised supersense tagging: prediction accuracies with confidence intervals, obtained on 50 random splits of the data.

ferentiate between subject and object, while the tree model treats subject and object in the same way (both are children of the verb). Moreover, in the tree model, verbs have a lot of children, such as adverbial clauses and auxiliary verbs, which share their transition probability distribution with the subject and the object. These two effects make the disambiguation of verbs more noisy for trees than for chains. Another possible explanation of this drop of performance is that it is due to errors made by the syntactic parser.

4.5 On optimization parameters

We briefly discuss the different choices that can influence learning efficiency in the proposed models. In practice, we have not observed noticeable differences between *ε-best projection* and *k-best projection* for the approximate inference, and we thus advise to use the latter as its complexity is controled. By contrast, as illustrated by results in tables 4 and 5, initialization can greatly change the performance in semi-supervised learning, in particular for tree models. We thus advise to initialize with Brown clusters. Finally, as noted by Liang and Klein (2009), the step size of online EM also has a significant impact on performance.

5 Conclusion

In this paper, we considered an arguably natural generative model of sentences for semantic class induction. It can be seen as a generalization of Brown clustering, taking into account homonymy and syntax, and thus allowed us to study their impact on semantic class induction. We developed an efficient algorithm to perform inference and learning, which makes it possible to learn in this model on large datasets, such as the New York Times corpus. We showed that this model induces relevant semantic classes and that it improves performance over Brown clustering on semi-supervised named entity recognition and supersense tagging. We plan to explore in future work better ways to model verbs, and in particular how to take into account the type of dependencies between words.

Acknowledgments

Francis Bach is supported in part by the European Research Council (SIERRA ERC-239993).

References

D. M. Blei, A. Y. Ng, and M. I. Jordan. 2003. Latent dirichlet allocation. *The Journal of Machine Learning Research*.

J. L. Boyd-Graber and D. Blei. 2009. Syntactic topic models. In *Advances in Neural Information Processing Systems 21*.

P. F. Brown, P. V. deSouza, R. L. Mercer, V. J. Della Pietra, and J. C. Lai. 1992. Class-based n-gram models of natural language. *Computational linguistics*.

O. Cappé and E. Moulines. 2009. On-line expectation–maximization algorithm for latent data models. *Journal of the Royal Statistical Society: Series B (Statistical Methodology)*.

M. Ciaramita and Y. Altun. 2006. Broad-coverage sense disambiguation and information extraction with a supersense sequence tagger. In *Proceedings of the 2006 Conference on Empirical Methods in Natural Language Processing*.

Alexander Clark. 2003. Combining distributional and morphological information for part of speech induction. In *Proceedings of the tenth conference of European chapter of the Association for Computational Linguistics*.

M. C. De Marneffe and C. D. Manning. 2008. The Stanford typed dependencies representation. In *Coling 2008: Proceedings of the workshop on Cross-Framework and Cross-Domain Parser Evaluation*.

M. C. De Marneffe, B. MacCartney, and C. D. Manning. 2006. Generating typed dependency parses from phrase structure parses. In *Proceedings of LREC*.

S. Deerwester, S. T. Dumais, G. W. Furnas, T. K. Landauer, and R. Harshman. 1990. Indexing by latent semantic analysis. *Journal of the American society for information science*.

P. S. Dhillon, D. Foster, and L. Ungar. 2011. Multi-view learning of word embeddings via CCA. *Advances in Neural Information Processing Systems*.

M. Faruqui, S. Padó, and M. Sprachverarbeitung. 2010. Training and evaluating a German named entity recognizer with semantic generalization. *Semantic Approaches in Natural Language Processing*.

D. Freitag. 2004. Trained named entity recognition using distributional clusters. In *Proceedings of the 2004 Conference on Empirical Methods in Natural Language Processing*.

T. L. Griffiths, M. Steyvers, D. M. Blei, and J. B. Tenenbaum. 2005. Integrating topics and syntax. *Advances in Neural Information Processing Systems*.

G. Haffari, M. Razavi, and A. Sarkar. 2011. An ensemble model that combines syntactic and semantic clustering for discriminative dependency parsing. In *Proceedings of the 49th Annual Meeting of the Association for Computational Linguistics*.

T. Hofmann. 1999. Probabilistic latent semantic analysis. In *Proceedings of the Fifteenth conference on Uncertainty in artificial intelligence*.

R. Kneser and H. Ney. 1993. Improved clustering techniques for class-based statistical language modelling. In *Third European Conference on Speech Communication and Technology*.

T. Koo, X. Carreras, and M. Collins. 2008. Simple semi-supervised dependency parsing. In *Proceedings of ACL-08: HLT*.

J. Lafferty, A. McCallum, and F. Pereira. 2001. Conditional random fields: Probabilistic models for segmenting and labeling sequence data. *Proceedings of the 18th International Conference on Machine Learning*.

W. Li and A. McCallum. 2005. Semi-supervised sequence modeling with syntactic topic models. In *Proceedings of the National Conference on Artificial Intelligence*.

P. Liang and D. Klein. 2009. Online EM for unsupervised models. In *Human Language Technologies: The 2009 Annual Conference of the North American Chapter of the Association for Computational Linguistics*.

P. Liang. 2005. Semi-supervised learning for natural language. Master's thesis, Massachusetts Institute of Technology.

K. Lund and C. Burgess. 1996. Producing high-dimensional semantic spaces from lexical co-occurrence. *Behavior Research Methods, Instruments, & Computers*.

S. Miller, J. Guinness, and A. Zamanian. 2004. Name tagging with word clusters and discriminative training. In *Proceedings of HLT-NAACL*.

C. Pal, C. Sutton, and A. McCallum. 2006. Sparse forward-backward using minimum divergence beams for fast training of conditional random fields. In *ICASSP 2006 Proceedings*.

S. Petrov. 2009. *Coarse-to-Fine Natural Language Processing*. Ph.D. thesis, University of California at Bekeley.

E. Sandhaus. 2008. The New York Times annotated corpus. *Linguistic Data Consortium, Philadelphia*.

D. O. Séaghdha. 2010. Latent variable models of selectional preference. In *Proceedings of the 48th Annual Meeting of the Association for Computational Linguistics*.

O. Täckström, R. McDonald, and J. Uszkoreit. 2012. Cross-lingual word clusters for direct transfer of linguistic structure. In *Proceedings of the 2012 Conference of the North American Chapter of the Association for Computational Linguistics*.

S. Tratz and E. Hovy. 2011. A fast, accurate, non-projective, semantically-enriched parser. In *Proceedings of the 2011 Conference on Empirical Methods in Natural Language Processing*.

J. Turian, L. Ratinov, and Y. Bengio. 2010. Word representations: a simple and general method for semi-supervised learning. In *Proceedings of the 48th Annual Meeting of the Association for Computational Linguistics*.

J. Uszkoreit and T. Brants. 2008. Distributed word clustering for large scale class-based language modeling in machine translation. *Proceedings of ACL-08: HLT*.

M. J. Wainwright and M. I. Jordan. 2008. Graphical models, exponential families, and variational inference. *Foundations and Trends® in Machine Learning*.

Better Word Representations with Recursive Neural Networks for Morphology

Minh-Thang Luong **Richard Socher** **Christopher D. Manning**
Computer Science Department Stanford University, Stanford, CA, 94305
{lmthang, manning}@stanford.edu richard@socher.org

Abstract

Vector-space word representations have been very successful in recent years at improving performance across a variety of NLP tasks. However, common to most existing work, words are regarded as independent entities without any explicit relationship among morphologically related words being modeled. As a result, rare and complex words are often poorly estimated, and all unknown words are represented in a rather crude way using only one or a few vectors. This paper addresses this shortcoming by proposing a novel model that is capable of building representations for morphologically complex words from their morphemes. We combine recursive neural networks (RNNs), where each morpheme is a basic unit, with neural language models (NLMs) to consider contextual information in learning morphologically-aware word representations. Our learned models outperform existing word representations by a good margin on word similarity tasks across many datasets, including a new dataset we introduce focused on rare words to complement existing ones in an interesting way.

1 Introduction

The use of word representations or word clusters pretrained in an unsupervised fashion from lots of text has become a key "secret sauce" for the success of many NLP systems in recent years, across tasks including named entity recognition, part-of-speech tagging, parsing, and semantic role labeling. This is particularly true in deep neural network models (Collobert et al., 2011), but it is also true in conventional feature-based models (Koo et al., 2008; Ratinov and Roth, 2009).

Deep learning systems give each word a distributed representation, i.e., a dense low-dimensional real-valued vector or an embedding. The main advantage of having such a distributed representation over word classes is that it can capture various dimensions of both semantic and syntactic information in a vector where each dimension corresponds to a latent feature of the word. As a result, a distributed representation is compact, less susceptible to data sparsity, and can implicitly represent an exponential number of word clusters.

However, despite the widespread use of word clusters and word embeddings, and despite much work on improving the learning of word representations, from feed-forward networks (Bengio et al., 2003) to hierarchical models (Morin, 2005; Mnih and Hinton, 2009) and recently recurrent neural networks (Mikolov et al., 2010; Mikolov et al., 2011), these approaches treat each full-form word as an independent entity and fail to capture the explicit relationship among morphological variants of a word.[1] The fact that morphologically complex words are often rare exacerbates the problem. Though existing clusterings and embeddings represent well frequent words, such as "distinct", they often badly model rare ones, such as "distinctiveness".

In this work, we use recursive neural networks (Socher et al., 2011b), in a novel way to model morphology and its compositionality. Essentially, we treat each morpheme as a basic unit in the RNNs and construct representations for morphologically complex words on the fly from their morphemes. By training a neural language model (NLM) and integrating RNN structures for complex words, we utilize contextual information in

[1] An almost exception is the word clustering of (Clark, 2003), which does have a model of morphology to encourage words ending with the same suffix to appear in the same class, but it still does not capture the relationship between a word and its morphologically derived forms.

an interesting way to learn morphemic semantics and their compositional properties. Our model has the capability of building representations for any new unseen word comprised of known morphemes, giving the model an infinite (if still incomplete) covered vocabulary.

Our learned representations outperform publicly available embeddings by a good margin on word similarity tasks across many datasets, which include our newly released dataset focusing on rare words (see Section 5). The detailed analysis in Section 6 reveals that our models can blend well syntactic information, i.e., the word structure, and the semantics in grouping related words.[2]

2 Related Work

Neural network techniques have found success in several NLP tasks recently such as sentiment analysis at the sentence (Socher et al., 2011c) and document level (Glorot et al., 2011), language modeling (Mnih and Hinton, 2007; Mikolov and Zweig, 2012), paraphrase detection (Socher et al., 2011a), discriminative parsing (Collobert, 2011), and tasks involving semantic relations and compositional meaning of phrases (Socher et al., 2012).

Common to many of these works is use of a distributed word representation as the basic input unit. These representations usually capture local cooccurrence statistics but have also been extended to include document-wide context (Huang et al., 2012). Their main advantage is that they can both be learned unsupervisedly as well as be tuned for supervised tasks. In the former training regiment, they are evaluated by how well they can capture human similarity judgments. They have also been shown to perform well as features for supervised tasks, e.g., NER (Turian et al., 2010).

While much work has focused on different objective functions for training single and multi-word vector representations, very little work has been done to tackle sub-word units and how they can be used to compute syntactic-semantic word vectors. Collobert et al. (2011) enhanced word vectors with additional character-level features such as capitalization but still can not recover more detailed semantics for very rare or unseen words, which is the focus of this work.

This is somewhat ironic, since working out correct morphological inflections was a very central problem in early work in the parallel distributed processing paradigm and criticisms of it (Rumelhart and McClelland, 1986; Plunkett and Marchman, 1991), and later work developed more sophisticated models of morphological structure and meaning (Gasser and Lee, 1990; Gasser, 1994), while not providing a compositional semantics nor working at the scale of what we present.

To the best of our knowledge, the work closest to ours in terms of handing unseen words are the factored NLMs (Alexandrescu and Kirchhoff, 2006) and the compositional distributional semantic models (DSMs) (Lazaridou et al., 2013). In the former work, each word is viewed as a vector of features such as stems, morphological tags, and cases, in which a single embedding matrix is used to look up all of these features.[3] Though this is a principled way of handling new words in NLMs, the by-product word representations, i.e. the concatenations of factor vectors, do not encode in them the compositional information (they are stored in the NN parameters). Our work does not simply concatenate vectors of morphemes, but rather combines them using RNNs, which captures morphological compositionality.

The latter work experimented with different compositional DSMs, originally designed to learn meanings of phrases, to derive representations for complex words, in which the base unit is the morpheme similar to ours. However, their models can only combine a stem with an affix and does not support recursive morpheme composition. It is, however, interesting to compare our neural-based representations with their DSM-derived ones and cross test these models on both our rare word similarity dataset and their nearest neighbor one, which we leave as future work.

Mikolov et al. (2013) examined existing word embeddings and showed that these representations already captured meaningful syntactic and semantic regularities such as the singular/plural relation that x_{apple} - $x_{\text{apples}} \approx x_{\text{car}}$ - x_{cars}. However, we believe that these nice relationships will not hold for rare and complex words when their vectors are poorly estimated as we analyze in Section 6. Our model, on the other hand, explicitly represents these regularities through morphological structures of words.

[2]The rare word dataset and trained word vectors can be found at `http://nlp.stanford.edu/~lmthang/morphoNLM`.

[3](Collobert et al., 2011) used multiple embeddings, one per discrete feature type, e.g., POS, Gazeteer, etc.

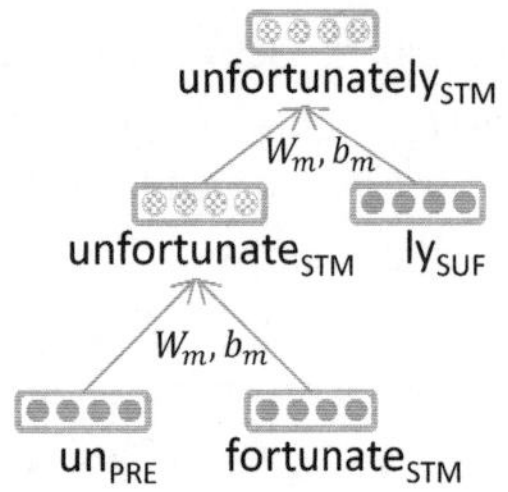

Figure 1: **Morphological Recursive Neural Network**. A vector representation for the word "unfortunately" is constructed from morphemic vectors: *un*$_{\texttt{pre}}$, *fortunate*$_{\texttt{stm}}$, *ly*$_{\texttt{suf}}$. Dotted nodes are computed on-the-fly and not in the lexicon.

3 Morphological RNNs

Our morphological Recursive Neural Network (*morphoRNN*) is similar to (Socher et al., 2011b), but operates at the morpheme level instead of at the word level. Specifically, morphemes, the minimum meaning-bearing unit in languages, are modeled as real-valued vectors of parameters, and are used to build up more complex words. We assume access to a dictionary of morphemic analyses of words, which will be detailed in Section 4.

Following (Collobert and Weston, 2008), distinct morphemes are encoded by column vectors in a morphemic embedding matrix $\boldsymbol{W_e} \in \mathbb{R}^{d \times |\mathbb{M}|}$, where d is the vector dimension and $\mathbb{M}$ is an ordered set of all morphemes in a language.

As illustrated in Figure 1, vectors of morphologically complex words are gradually built up from their morphemic representations. At any local decision (a dotted node), a new parent word vector ($\boldsymbol{p}$) is constructed by combining a stem vector ($\boldsymbol{x}_{\texttt{stem}}$) and an affix vector ($\boldsymbol{x}_{\texttt{affix}}$) as follow:

$$\boldsymbol{p} = f(\boldsymbol{W_m}[\boldsymbol{x}_{\texttt{stem}}; \boldsymbol{x}_{\texttt{affix}}] + \boldsymbol{b_m}) \quad (1)$$

Here, $\boldsymbol{W_m} \in \mathbb{R}^{d \times 2d}$ is a matrix of morphemic parameters while $\boldsymbol{b_m} \in \mathbb{R}^{d \times 1}$ is an intercept vector. We denote an element-wise activation function as f, such as $\tanh$. This forms the basis of our morphoRNN models with $\boldsymbol{\theta} = \{\boldsymbol{W_e}, \boldsymbol{W_m}, \boldsymbol{b_m}\}$ being the parameters to be learned.

3.1 Context-insensitive Morphological RNN

Our first model examines how well morphoRNNs could construct word vectors simply from the morphemic representation *without referring to any context information*. Input to the model is a reference embedding matrix, i.e. word vectors trained by an NLM such as (Collobert and Weston, 2008) and (Huang et al., 2012). By assuming that these reference vectors are right, the goal of the model is to construct new representations for morphologically complex words from their morphemes that closely match the corresponding reference ones.

Specifically, the structure of the context-insensitive morphoRNN (*cimRNN*) is the same as the basic morphoRNN. For learning, we first define a cost function s for each word x_i as the squared Euclidean distance between the newly-*constructed* representation $\boldsymbol{p}_c(x_i)$ and its *reference* vector $\boldsymbol{p}_r(x_i)$: $s(x_i) = \|\boldsymbol{p}_c(x_i) - \boldsymbol{p}_r(x_i)\|_2^2$.

The objective function is then simply the sum of all individual costs over N training examples, plus a regularization term, which we try to minimize:

$$J(\boldsymbol{\theta}) = \sum_{i=1}^{N} s(x_i) + \frac{\lambda}{2}\|\boldsymbol{\theta}\|_2^2 \quad (2)$$

3.2 Context-sensitive Morphological RNN

The cimRNN model, though simple, is interesting to attest if morphemic semantics could be learned solely from an embedding. However, it is limited in several aspects. Firstly, the model has no chance of improving representations for rare words which might have been poorly estimated. For example, "distinctness" and "unconcerned" are very rare, occurring only 141 and 340 times in Wikipedia documents, even though their corresponding stems "distinct" and "concern" are very frequent (35323 and 26080 respectively). Trying to construct exactly those poorly-estimated word vectors might result in a bad model with parameters being pushed in wrong directions.

Secondly, though word embeddings learned from an NLM could, in general, blend well both the semantic and syntactic information, it would be useful to explicitly model another kind of syntactic information, the word structure, as we train our embeddings. Motivated by these limitations, we propose a context-sensitive morphoRNN (*csmRNN*) which integrates RNN structures into NLM training, allowing for contextual information being taken into account in learning morphemic compositionality. Specifically, we adopt the NLM training approach proposed in (Collobert et al., 2011) to learn word embeddings, but build representations for complex words from their morphemes. During learning, updates at the top level of the neural network will be back-propagated all the way till the morphemic layer.

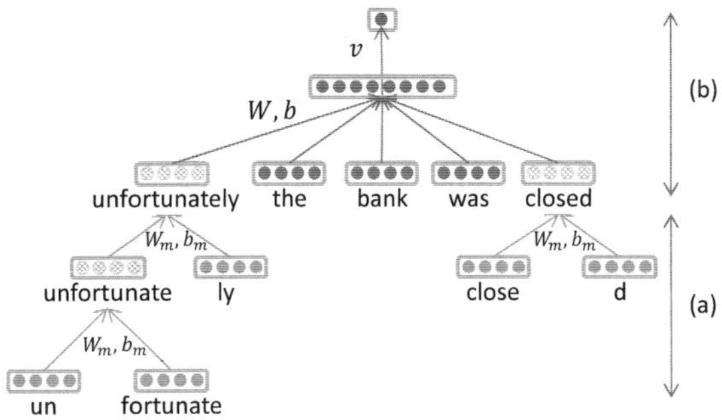

Figure 2: **Context-sensitive morphological RNN** has two layers: (a) the *morphological* RNN, which constructs representations for words from their morphemes and (b) the *word-based* neural language which optimizes scores for relevant ngrams.

Structure-wise, we stack the NLM on top of our morphoRNN as illustrated in Figure 2. Complex words like "unfortunately" and "closed" are constructed from their morphemic vectors, $un_{\texttt{pre}}$ + $fortunate_{\texttt{stm}}$ + $ly_{\texttt{suf}}$ and $close_{\texttt{stm}}$ + $d_{\texttt{suf}}$, whereas simple words[4], i.e. stems, and affixes could be looked up from the morphemic embedding matrix $\boldsymbol{W_e}$ as in standard NLMs. Once vectors of all complex words have been built, the NLM assigns a score for each ngram n_i consisting of words $x_1, \ldots, x_n$ as follows:

$$s(n_i) = \boldsymbol{v}^\top f(\boldsymbol{W}[\boldsymbol{x}_1; \ldots; \boldsymbol{x}_n] + \boldsymbol{b})$$

Here, $\boldsymbol{x}_j$ is the vector representing the word x_j. We follow (Huang et al., 2012) to use a simple feed-forward network with one h-dimensional hidden layer. $\boldsymbol{W} \in \mathbb{R}^{h \times nd}$, $\boldsymbol{b} \in \mathbb{R}^{h \times 1}$, and $\boldsymbol{v} \in \mathbb{R}^{h \times 1}$ are parameters of the NLM, and f is an element-wise activation function as in Eq. (1). We adopt a ranking-type cost in defining our objective function to minimize as below:

$$J(\boldsymbol{\theta}) = \sum_{i=1}^{N} \max\{0, 1 - s(n_i) + s(\overline{n}_i)\} \quad (3)$$

Here, N is the number of all available ngrams in the training corpus, whereas $\overline{n}_i$ is a "corrupted" ngram created from n_i by replacing its last word with a random word similar in spirit to (Smith and Eisner, 2005). Our model parameters are $\boldsymbol{\theta} = \{\boldsymbol{W_e}, \boldsymbol{W_m}, \boldsymbol{b_m}, \boldsymbol{W}, \boldsymbol{b}, \boldsymbol{v}\}$.

Such a ranking criterion influences the model to assign higher scores to valid ngrams than to invalid ones and has been demonstrated in (Collobert et al., 2011) to be both efficient and effective in learning word representations.

[4]"fortunate", "the", "bank", "was", and "close".

3.3 Learning

Our models alternate between two stages: (1) *forward pass* – recursively construct morpheme trees (cimRNN, csmRNN) and language model structures (csmRNN) to derive scores for training examples and (2) *back-propagation pass* – compute the gradient of the corresponding object function with respect to the model parameters.

For the latter pass, computing the objective gradient amounts to estimating the gradient for each individual cost $\frac{\partial s(x)}{\partial \boldsymbol{\theta}}$, where x could be either a word (cimRNN) or an ngram (csmRNN). We have the objective gradient for the cimRNN derived as:

$$\frac{\partial J(\boldsymbol{\theta})}{\partial \boldsymbol{\theta}} = \sum_{i=1}^{N} \frac{\partial s(x_i)}{\partial \boldsymbol{\theta}} + \lambda \boldsymbol{\theta}$$

In the case of csmRNN, since the objective function in Eq. (3) is not differentiable, we use the subgradient method (Ratliff et al., 2007) to estimate the objective gradient as:

$$\frac{\partial J(\boldsymbol{\theta})}{\partial \boldsymbol{\theta}} = \sum_{i:1-s(n_i)+s(\overline{n}_i)>0} -\frac{\partial s(n_i)}{\partial \boldsymbol{\theta}} + \frac{\partial s(\overline{n}_i)}{\partial \boldsymbol{\theta}}$$

Back-propagation through structures (Goller and Küchler, 1996) is employed to compute the gradient for each individual cost with similar formulae as in (Socher et al., 2010). Unlike their RNN structures over sentences, where each sentence could have an exponential number of derivations, our morphoRNN structure per word is, in general, deterministic. Each word has a single morphological tree structure which is constructed from the main morpheme (the stem) and gradually appended affixes in a fixed order (see Section 4 for more details). As a result, both our forward and backward passes over morphological structures are efficient with no recursive calls implementation-wise.

4 Unsupervised Morphological Structures

We utilize an unsupervised morphological segmentation toolkit, named Morfessor by Creutz and Lagus (2007), to obtain segmentations for words in our vocabulary. Morfessor segments words in two stages: (a) it recursively splits words to minimize an objective inspired by the minimum description length principle and (b) it labels morphemes with tags `pre` (prefixes), `stm` (stems), and `suf` (suffixes) using hidden Markov models.

Morfessor captures a general word structure of the form $(\texttt{pre}^* \ \texttt{stm} \ \texttt{suf}^*)^+$, which is handy for words in morphologically rich languages like Finnish or Turkish. However, such general form is currently unnecessary in our models as the morphoRNNs assume input of the form $\texttt{pre}^* \ \texttt{stm} \ \texttt{suf}^*$ for efficient learning of the RNN structures: a stem is always combined with an affix to yield a new stem.[5] We, thus, postprocess as follows:

(1) Restrict segmentations to the form $\texttt{pre}^* \ \texttt{stm}\{1,2\} \ \texttt{suf}^*$: allow us to capture compounds.

(2) Split hyphenated words *A-B* as $A_{\texttt{stm}} \ B_{\texttt{stm}}$.

(3) For a segmentation with two stems, $\texttt{pre}^* \ A_{\texttt{stm}} \ B_{\texttt{stm}} \ \texttt{suf}^*$, we decide if one could be a main stem while the other could functions as an affix.[6] Otherwise, we reject the segmentation. This will provide us with more interesting morphemes such as $al_{\texttt{pre}}$ in Arabic names (al-jazeera, al-salem) and $related_{\texttt{suf}}$ in compound adjectives (health-related, government-related).

(4) To enhance precision, we reject a segmentation if it has either an affix or an unknown stem (not a word by itself) whose type count is below a predefined *threshold*[7].

The final list of affixes produced is given in Table 1. Though generally reliable, our final segmentations do contain errors, most notably non-compositional ones, e.g. $de_{\texttt{pre}} \ fault_{\texttt{stm}} \ ed_{\texttt{suf}}$ or $re_{\texttt{pre}} \ turn_{\texttt{stm}} \ s_{\texttt{suf}}$. With a sufficiently large number of segmentation examples, we hope that the model would be able to pick up general trends from the data. In total, we have about 22K complex words out of a vocabulary of 130K words.

Examples of words with interesting affixes are given in Table 2. Beside conventional affixes, non-conventional ones like "0" or "mc" help further categorize rare or unknown words into meaningful groups such as measurement words or names.

[5]When multiple affixes are present, we use a simple heuristic to first merge suffixes into stems and then combine prefixes. Ideally, we would want to learn and generate an order for such combination, which we leave for future work.

[6]We first aggregate type counts of pairs (*A*, left) and (*B*, right) across all segmentations with two stems. Once done, we label A as `stm` and B as `suf` if count (*B*, right) $> 2 \times$ count (*A*, left), and conversely, we label them as $A_{\texttt{pre}} \ B_{\texttt{stm}}$ if count (*A*, left) $> 2 \times$ count(*B*, right). Our rationale was that affixes occur more frequently than stems.

Prefixes	**Suffixes**
0 *al* all *anti auto co counter cross de dis* electro end *ex* first five focus four half high hyper ill *im in inter ir* jan jean long low market mc micro mid *multi* neuro newly no *non* off one *over post pre pro re* second *self semi* seven short six state *sub super* third three top *trans* two *un under* uni well	*able al ally* american *ance ate ation* backed bank based born controlled *d* dale down *ed en er es* field ford free *ful* general head *ia ian ible ic* in *ing isation ise ised ish ism ist ity ive ization ize ized izing* land led *less* ling listed *ly* made making man *ment ness* off on out owned related *s* ship shire style ton town up us ville wood

Table 1: List of prefixes and suffixes discovered – conventional affixes in English are italicized.

Affix	**Words**
0	0-acre, 0-aug, 0-billion, 0-centistoke
anti	anti-immigrant, antipsychotics
counter	counterexample, counterinsurgency
hyper	hyperactivity, hypercholesterolemia
mc	mcchesney, mcchord, mcdevitt
bank	baybank, brockbank, commerzbank
ford	belford, blandford, carlingford
land	adventureland, bodoland, bottomland
less	aimlessly, artlessness, effortlessly
owned	bank-owned, city-owned disney-owned

Table 2: Sample affixes and corresponding words.

5 Experiments

As our focus is in learning morphemic semantics, we do not start training from scratch, but rather, initialize our models with existing word representations. In our experiments, we make use of two publicly-available embeddings (50-dimensional) provided by(Collobert et al., 2011) (denoted as *C&W*)[8] and Huang et al. (2012) (referred as *HSMN*)[9].

Both of these representations are trained on Wikipedia documents using the same ranking-type cost function as in Eq. (3). The latter further utilizes global context and adopts a multi-prototype approach, i.e. each word is represented by multiple vectors, to better capture word semantics in various contexts. However, we only use their single-prototype embedding[10] and as we train, we

[7]Set to 15 and 3 for affixes and stems respectively.

[8]`http://ronan.collobert.com/senna/`.

[9]`http://www-nlp.stanford.edu/~ehhuang/`.

[10]The embedding obtained just before the clustering step to build multi-prototype representation.

do not consider the global sentence-level context information. It is worth to note that these aspects of the HSMN embedding – incorporating global context and maintaining multiple prototypes – are orthogonal to our approach, which would be interesting to investigate in future work.

For the context-sensitive morphoRNN model, we follow Huang et al. (2012) to use the April 2010 snapshot of the Wikipedia corpus (Shaoul and Westbury, 2010). All paragraphs containing non-roman characters are removed while the remaining text are lowercased and then tokenized. The resulting clean corpus contains about 986 million tokens. Each digit is then mapped into 0, i.e. 2013 will become 0000. Other rare words not in the vocabularies of C&W and HSMN are mapped to an UNKNOWN token, and we use <s> and </s> for padding tokens representing the beginning and end of each sentence.

Follow (Huang et al., 2012)'s implementation, which our code is based on initially, we use 50-dimensional vectors to represent morphemic and word embeddings. For cimRNN, the regularization weight λ is set to 10^{-2}. For csmRNN, we use 10-word windows of text as the local context, 100 hidden units, and no weight regularization.

5.1 Word Similarity Task

Similar to (Reisinger and Mooney, 2010) and (Huang et al., 2012), we evaluate the quality of our morphologically-aware embeddings on the popular *WordSim-353* dataset (Finkelstein et al., 2002), WS353 for short. In this task, we compare correlations between the similarity scores given by our models and those rated by human.

To avoid overfitting our models to a single dataset, we benchmark our models on a variety of others including *MC* (Miller and Charles, 1991), *RG* (Rubenstein and Goodenough, 1965), *SCWS**[11] (Huang et al., 2012), and our new rare word (*RW*) dataset (details in §5.1.1). Information about these datasets are summarized in Table 3

We also examine these datasets from the "rareness" aspect by looking at distributions of words across frequencies as in Table 4. The first bin counts unknown words in each dataset, while the remaining bins group words based on their frequencies extracted from Wikipedia documents. It is interesting to observe that WS353, MC, RG contain very frequent words and have few complex words (only WS353 has).[12] SCWS* and RW have a more diverse set of words in terms of frequencies and RW has the largest number of unknown and rare words, which makes it a challenging dataset.

	pairs	**type**	**raters**	**scale**	**Complex words** token	type
WS353	353	437	13-16	0-10	24	17
MC	30	39	38	0-4	0	0
RG	65	48	51	0-4	0	0
SCWS*	1762	1703	10	0-10	190	113
RW (new)	2034	2951	10	0-10	987	686

Table 3: **Word similarity datasets** and their statistics: number of pairs/raters/type counts as well as rating scales. The number of complex words are shown as well (both type and token counts). RW denotes our new rare word dataset.

	All words	**Complex words**
WS353	0 | 0 / 9 / 87 / 341	0 | 0 / 1 / 6 / 10
MC	0 | 0 / 1 / 17 / 21	0 | 0 / 0 / 0 / 0
RG	0 | 0 / 4 / 22 / 22	0 | 0 / 0 / 0 / 0
SCWS*	26 | 2 / 140 / 472 / 1063	8 | 2 / 22 / 44 / 45
RW	801 | 41 / 676 / 719 / 714	621 | 34 / 311 / 238 / 103

Table 4: **Word distribution by frequencies** – distinct words in each dataset are grouped based on frequencies and counts are reported for the following bins : unknown | [1, 100] / [101, 1000] / [1001, 10000] / [10001, ∞). We report counts for all words in each dataset as well as complex ones.

5.1.1 Rare Word Dataset

As evidenced in Table 4, most existing word similarity datasets contain frequent words and few of them possesses enough rare or morphologically complex words that we could really attest the expressiveness of our morphoRNN models. In fact, we believe a good embedding in general should be able to learn useful representations for not just frequent words but also rare ones. That motivates us to construct another dataset focusing on rare words to complement existing ones.

Our dataset construction proceeds in three stages: (1) select a list of rare words, (2) for each of the rare words, find another word (not necessarily rare) to form a pair, and (3) collect human judgments on how similar each pair is.

[11] SCWS* is a modified version of the Stanford's contextual word similarities dataset. The original one utilizes surrounding contexts in judging word similarities and includes pairs of identical words, e.g. financial *bank* vs. river *bank*. We exclude these pairs and ignore the provided contexts.

[12] All these counts are with respect to the vocabulary list in the C&W embedding (we obtain similar figures for HSMN).

	(5, 10]	(10, 100]	(100, 1000]
un-	untracked unrolls undissolved	unrehearsed unflagging unfavourable	unprecedented unmarried uncomfortable
-al	apocalyptical traversals bestowals	acoustical extensional organismal	directional diagonal spherical
-ment	obtainment acquirement retrenchments	discernment revetment rearrangements	confinement establishment management

word$_1$	untracked	unflagging	unprecedented	apocalyptical	organismal	diagonal	obtainment	discernment	confinement
word$_2$	inaccessible	constant	new	prophetic	system	line	acquiring	knowing	restraint

Table 5: **Rare words** (top) – *word*$_1$ by affixes and frequencies and sample **word pairs** (bottom).

Rare word selection: our choices of rare words (*word*$_1$) are based on their frequencies – based on five bins (5, 10], (10, 100], (100, 1000], (1000, 10000], and the affixes they possess. To create a diverse set of candidates, we randomly select 15 words for each configuration (a frequency bin, an affix). At the scale of Wikipedia, a word with frequency of 1-5 is most likely a junk word, and even restricted to words with frequencies above five, there are still many non-English words. To counter such problems, each word selected is required to have a non-zero number of synsets in WordNet(Miller, 1995).

Table 5 (top) gives examples of rare words selected and organized by frequencies and affixes. It is interesting to find out that words like *obtainment* and *acquirement* are extremely rare (not in traditional dictionaries) but are perfectly understandable. We also have less frequent words like *revetment* from French or *organismal* from biology.

Pair construction: following (Huang et al., 2012), we create pairs with interesting relationships for each *word*$_1$ as follow. First, a WordNet synset of *word*$_1$ is randomly selected, and we construct a set of candidates which connect to that synset through various relations, e.g., hypernyms, hyponyms, holonyms, meronyms, and attributes. A *word*$_2$ is then randomly selected from these candidates, and the process is repeated another time to generate a total of two pairs for each *word*$_1$. Sample word pairs are given in Table 5 in which *word*$_2$ includes mostly frequent words, implying a balance of words in terms of frequencies in our dataset. We collected 3145 pairs after this stage

Human judgment: we use Amazon Mechanical Turk to collect 10 human similarity ratings on a scale of [0, 10] per word pair.[13] Such procedure has been demonstrated by Snow et al. (2008) in replicating ratings for the MC dataset, achieving close inter-annotator agreement with expert raters. Since our pairs contain many rare words which are challenging even to native speakers, we ask raters to indicate for each pair if they do not know the first word, the second word, or both. We use such information to collect reliable ratings by either discard pairs which many people do not know or collect additional ratings to ensure we have 10 ratings per pair.[14] As a result, only 2034 pairs are retained.

5.2 Results

We evaluate the quality of our morphoRNN embeddings through the word similarity task discussed previously. The Spearman's rank correlation is used to gauge how well the relationship between two variables, the similarity scores given by the NLMs and the human annotators, could be described using a monotonic function.

Detailed performance of the morphoRNN embeddings trained from either the HSMN or the C&W embeddings are given in Table 7 for all datasets. We also report baseline results (rows *HSMN, C&W*) using these initial embeddings alone, which interestingly reveals strengths and weaknesses of existing embeddings. While HSMN is good for datasets with frequent words (WS353, MC, and RG), its performances for those with more rare and complex words (SCWS* and RW) are much inferior than those of C&W, and vice versa. Additionally, we consider two slightly more competitive baselines (rows *+stem*) based on the morphological segmentation of unknown words: instead of using a universal vector representing all unknown words, we use vectors representing the stems of unknown words. These baselines yield slightly better performance for the SCWS* and RW datasets while the trends we mentioned earlier remain the same.

Our first model, the context-insensitive morphoRNN (cimRNN), outperforms its corresponding baseline significantly over the rare word

[13]We restrict to only US-based workers with 95% approval rate and ask for native speakers to rate 20 pairs per hit.

[14]In our later experiments, an aggregated rating is derived for each pair. We first discard ratings not within one standard deviation of the mean, and then estimate a new mean from the remaining ones to use as an aggregated rating.

Words	C&W	C&W + cimRNN	C&W + csmRNN
commenting	insisting insisted focusing hinted	republishing accounting expounding	commented comments criticizing
comment	commentary rant statement remark	commentary rant statement remark	rant commentary statement anecdote
distinctness	morphologies pesawat clefts	modality indistinct tonality spatiality	indistinct distinctiveness largeness uniqueness
distinct	different distinctive broader narrower	different distinctive broader divergent	divergent diverse distinctive homogeneous
unaffected	unnoticed dwarfed mitigated	disaffected unconstrained uninhibited	undesired unhindered unrestricted
affected	caused plagued impacted damaged	disaffected unaffected mitigated disturbed	complicated desired constrained reasoned
unaffect	∅	affective affecting affectation unobserved	affective affecting affectation restrictive
affect	exacerbate impacts characterize	affects affectation exacerbate characterize	decrease arise complicate exacerbate
heartlessness	∅	fearlessness vindictiveness restlessness	depersonalization terrorizes sympathizes
heartless	merciless sadistic callous mischievous	merciless sadistic callous mischievous	sadistic callous merciless hideous
heart	death skin pain brain life blood	death skin pain brain life blood	death brain blood skin lung mouth
saudi-owned	avatar mohajir kripalani fountainhead	saudi-based somaliland al-jaber	saudi-based syrian-controlled syrian-backed
short-changed	kindled waylaid endeared peopled	conformal conformist unquestionable	short-termism short-positions self-sustainable

Table 6: **Nearest neighbors**. We show morphologically related words and their closest words in different representations ("unaffect" is a pseudo-word; ∅ marks no results due to unknown words).

	WS353	MC	RG	SCWS*	RW
HSMN	62.58	65.90	62.81	32.11	1.97
+stem	62.58	65.90	62.81	32.11	3.40
+cimRNN	62.81	65.90	62.81	32.97	14.85
+csmRNN	**64.58**	**71.72**	**65.45**	**43.65**	**22.31**
C&W	49.77	57.37	49.30	48.59	26.75
+stem	49.77	57.37	49.30	**49.05**	28.03
+cimRNN	51.76	57.37	49.30	47.00	33.24
+csmRNN	**57.01**	**60.20**	**55.40**	48.48	**34.36**

Table 7: **Word similarity task** – shown are Spearman's rank correlation coefficient ($\rho \times 100$) between similarity scores assigned by neural language models and by human annotators. *stem* indicates baseline systems in which unknown words are represented by their stem vectors. *cimRNN* and *csmRNN* refer to our context insensitive and sensitive morphological RNNs respectively.

dataset. The performance is constant for MC and RG (with no complex words) and modestly improved for MC (with some complex words – see Table 4). This is expected since the cimRNN model only concerns about reconstructing the original embedding (while learning word structures), and the new representation mostly differs at morphologically complex words. For SCWS*, the performance, however, decreases when training with C&W, which perhaps is due to: (a) the baseline performance of C&W for SCWS* is competitive and (b) the model trades off between learning syntactics (the word structure) and capturing semantics, which requires context information.

On the other hand, the context-sensitive morphoRNN (csmRNN) consistently improves correlations over the cimRNN model for all datasets, demonstrating the effectiveness of using surrounding contexts in learning both morphological syntactics and semantics. It also outperforms the corresponding baselines by a good margin for all datasets (except for SCWS*). This highlights the fact that our method is reliable and potentially applicable for other embeddings.

6 Analysis

To gain a deeper understanding of how our morphoRNN models have "moved" word vectors around, we look at nearest neighbors of several complex words given by various embeddings, where cosine similarity is used as a distance metric. Examples are shown in Table 6 for three representations: C&W and the context-insensitive/sensitive morphoRNN models trained on the C&W embedding.[15]

Syntactically, it is interesting to observe that the cimRNN model could well enforce structural agreement among related words. For example, it returns *V-ing* as nearest neighbors for "commenting" and similarly, *JJ-ness* for "fearlessness", an unknown word that C&W cannot handle. However, for those cases, the nearest neighbors are badly unrelated.

On the semantic side, we notice that when structural agreement is not enforced, the cimRNN model tends to cluster words sharing the same stem together, e.g., rows with words of the form *__affect__*.[16] This might be undesirable when we want to differentiate semantics of words sharing the same stem, e.g. "affected" and "unaffected".

The csmRNN model seems to balance well between the two extremes (syntactic and semantic) by taking into account contextual information

[15]Results of HSMN-related embeddings are not shown, but similar trends follow.

[16]"unaffect" is a pseudo-word that we inserted.

when learning morphological structures. It returns neighbors of the same structure *un__ed* for "unaffected", but does not include any negation of "affected" in the top 10 results when "affected" is queried.[17] Even better, the answers for "distinctness" have blended well both types of results.

7 Conclusion

This paper combines recursive neural networks (RNNs) and neural language models (NLMs) in a novel way to learn better word representations. Each of these components contributes to the learned syntactic-semantic word vectors in a unique way. The RNN explicitly models the morphological structures of words, i.e., the syntactic information, to learn morphemic compositionality. This allows for better estimation of rare and complex words and a more principled way of handling unseen words, whose representations could be constructed from vectors of known morphemes.

The NLMs, on the other hand, utilize surrounding word contexts to provide further semantics to the learned morphemic representations. As a result, our context-sensitive morphoRNN embeddings could significantly outperform existing embeddings on word similarity tasks for many datasets. Our analysis reveals that the model could blend well both the syntactic and semantic information in clustering related words. We have also made available a word similarity dataset focusing on rare words to complement existing ones which tend to include frequent words.

Lastly, as English is still considered limited in terms of morphology, our model could potentially yield even better performance when applied to other morphologically complex languages such as Finnish or Turkish, which we leave for future work. Also, even within English, we expect our model to be value to other domains, such as bio-NLP with complicated but logical taxonomy.

Acknowledgements

We thank the anonymous reviewers for their feedback and Eric Huang for making his various pieces of code available to us as well as answering our questions on different datasets. Stanford University gratefully acknowledges the support of the Defense Advanced Research Projects Agency (DARPA) Deep Exploration and Filtering of Text (DEFT) Program under Air Force Research Laboratory (AFRL) contract no. FA8750-13-2-0040 and the DARPA Broad Operational Language Translation (BOLT) program through IBM. Any opinions, findings, and conclusion or recommendations expressed in this material are those of the authors and do not necessarily reflect the view of the DARPA, AFRL, or the US government.

[17]"disaffected" is ranked 5th for the first query while "affecting" occurs at position 8 for the latter.

References

Andrei Alexandrescu and Katrin Kirchhoff. 2006. Factored neural language models. In *NAACL*.

Y. Bengio, R. Ducharme, P. Vincent, and C. Janvin. 2003. A neural probabilistic language model. *Journal of Machine Learning Research*, 3:1137–1155.

Alexander Clark. 2003. Combining distributional and morphological information for part of speech induction. In *EACL*.

R. Collobert and J. Weston. 2008. A unified architecture for natural language processing: deep neural networks with multitask learning. In *ICML*.

R. Collobert, J. Weston, L. Bottou, M. Karlen, K. Kavukcuoglu, and P. Kuksa. 2011. Natural language processing (almost) from scratch. *Journal of Machine Learning Research*, 12:2493–2537.

R. Collobert. 2011. Deep learning for efficient discriminative parsing. In *AISTATS*.

Mathias Creutz and Krista Lagus. 2007. Unsupervised models for morpheme segmentation and morphology learning. *ACM Transactions on Speech and Language Processing*, 4:3:1–3:34.

Lev Finkelstein, Evgeniy Gabrilovich, Yossi Matias, Ehud Rivlin, Zach Solan, Gadi Wolfman, and Eytan Ruppin. 2002. Placing search in context: the concept revisited. *ACM Transactions on Information Systems*, 20(1):116–131.

Michael Gasser and Chan-Do Lee. 1990. A short-term memory architecture for the learning of morphophonemic rules. In *NIPS*.

Michael Gasser. 1994. Acquiring receptive morphology: A connectionist model. In *ACL*.

X. Glorot, A. Bordes, and Y. Bengio. 2011. Domain adaptation for large-scale sentiment classification: A deep learning approach. In *ICML*.

C. Goller and A. Küchler. 1996. Learning task-dependent distributed representations by backpropagation through structure. *IEEE Transactions on Neural Networks*, 1:347–352.

E. H. Huang, R. Socher, C. D. Manning, and A. Y. Ng. 2012. Improving word representations via global context and multiple word prototypes. In *Annual Meeting of the Association for Computational Linguistics (ACL)*.

Terry Koo, Xavier Carreras, and Michael Collins. 2008. Simple semi-supervised dependency parsing. In *ACL*.

Angeliki Lazaridou, Marco Marelli, Roberto Zamparelli, and Marco Baroni. 2013. Compositional-ly derived representations of morphologically complex words in distributional semantics. In *ACL*.

Tomas Mikolov and Geoffrey Zweig. 2012. Context dependent recurrent neural network language model. In *SLT*.

Tomas Mikolov, Martin Karafiát, Lukas Burget, Jan Cernocký, and Sanjeev Khudanpur. 2010. Recurrent neural network based language model. In *INTERSPEECH*.

Tomas Mikolov, Stefan Kombrink, Lukas Burget, Jan Cernocký, and Sanjeev Khudanpur. 2011. Extensions of recurrent neural network language model. In *ICASSP*.

Tomas Mikolov, Wen-tau Yih, and Geoffrey Zweig. 2013. Linguistic regularities in continuous space word representations. In *NAACL-HLT*.

George A. Miller and Walter G. Charles. 1991. Contextual correlates of semantic similarity. *Language and Cognitive Processes*, 6(1):1–28.

G.A. Miller. 1995. WordNet: A Lexical Database for English. *Communications of the ACM*.

Andriy Mnih and Geoffrey Hinton. 2007. Three new graphical models for statistical language modelling. In *ICML*.

Andriy Mnih and Geoffrey Hinton. 2009. A scalable hierarchical distributed language model. In *NIPS*.

Frederic Morin. 2005. Hierarchical probabilistic neural network language model. AIstats'05. In *AISTATS*.

K. Plunkett and V. Marchman. 1991. U-shaped learning and frequency effects in a multi-layered perceptron: implications for child language acquisition. *Cognition*, 38(1):43–102.

Lev Ratinov and Dan Roth. 2009. Design challenges and misconceptions in named entity recognition. In *CoNLL*.

Nathan D. Ratliff, J. Andrew Bagnell, and Martin A. Zinkevich. 2007. Online subgradient methods for structured prediction.

Joseph Reisinger and Raymond J. Mooney. 2010. Multi-prototype vector-space models of word meaning. In *NAACL*.

Herbert Rubenstein and John B. Goodenough. 1965. Contextual correlates of synonymy. *Communications of the ACM*, 8(10):627–633.

David E. Rumelhart and James L. McClelland. 1986. On learning the past tenses of English verbs. In J. L. McClelland, D. E. Rumelhart, and PDP Research Group, editors, *Parallel Distributed Processing. Volume 2: Psychological and Biological Models*, pages 216–271. MIT Press.

Cyrus Shaoul and Chris Westbury. 2010. The Westbury lab wikipedia corpus. Edmonton, AB: University of Alberta.

Noah A. Smith and Jason Eisner. 2005. Contrastive estimation: training log-linear models on unlabeled data. In *ACL*.

Rion Snow, Brendan O'Connor, Daniel Jurafsky, and Andrew Y. Ng. 2008. Cheap and fast—but is it good?: Evaluating non-expert annotations for natural language tasks. In *EMNLP*.

Richard Socher, Christopher Manning, and Andrew Ng. 2010. Learning continuous phrase representations and syntactic parsing with recursive neural networks. In *NIPS*2010 Workshop on Deep Learning and Unsupervised Feature Learning*.

R. Socher, E. H. Huang, J. Pennington, A. Y. Ng, and C. D. Manning. 2011a. Dynamic pooling and unfolding recursive autoencoders for paraphrase detection. In *NIPS*.

R. Socher, Cliff C. Lin, A. Y. Ng, and C. D. Manning. 2011b. Parsing natural scenes and natural language with recursive neural networks. In *ICML*.

R. Socher, J. Pennington, E. H. Huang, A. Y. Ng, and C. D. Manning. 2011c. Semi-supervised recursive autoencoders for predicting sentiment distributions. In *EMNLP*.

R. Socher, B. Huval, C. D. Manning, and A. Y. Ng. 2012. Semantic compositionality through recursive matrix-vector spaces. In *EMNLP*.

J. Turian, L. Ratinov, and Y. Bengio. 2010. Word representations: a simple and general method for semi-supervised learning. In *ACL*.

Separating Disambiguation from Composition in Distributional Semantics

Dimitri Kartsaklis
University of Oxford
Dept of Computer Science
Wolfson Bldg, Parks Road
Oxford, OX1 3QD, UK
dimitri.kartsaklis@cs.ox.ac.uk

Mehrnoosh Sadrzadeh
Queen Mary Univ. of London
School of Electr. Engineering
and Computer Science
Mile End Road
London, E1 4NS, UK
mehrs@eecs.qmul.ac.uk

Stephen Pulman
University of Oxford
Dept of Computer Science
Wolfson Bldg, Parks Road
Oxford, OX1 3QD, UK
stephen.pulman@cs.ox.ac.uk

Abstract

Most compositional-distributional models of meaning are based on ambiguous vector representations, where all the senses of a word are fused into the same vector. This paper provides evidence that the addition of a vector disambiguation step prior to the actual composition would be beneficial to the whole process, producing better composite representations. Furthermore, we relate this issue with the current evaluation practice, showing that disambiguation-based tasks cannot reliably assess the quality of composition. Using a word sense disambiguation scheme based on the generic procedure of Schütze (1998), we first provide a proof of concept for the necessity of separating disambiguation from composition. Then we demonstrate the benefits of an "unambiguous" system on a composition-only task.

1 Introduction

Compositional and distributional semantic models seem to provide complementary solutions for solving the same problem, that of assigning a proper "meaning" to a text segment. Specifically, while compositional models deal with the recursive nature of the language, providing a way to address its inherent ability to create infinite sentences from finite resources (words), they leave words as unexplained primitives whose meanings have somehow already been set before the compositional process. On the other hand, distributional models have been especially successful in providing concrete representations for the meaning of words as vectors in a vector space, created by taking into account the context in which each word appears. Despite its success for smaller language units, the distributional hypothesis does not naturally lend itself to compounds of words. Hence these models do not canonically scale in tasks requiring the creation of vector representations for text constituents larger than words, i.e. for phrases and sentences.

Given the complementary nature of those two semantic models, it is not surprising that considerable research activity has been dedicated on combining them into a single framework that would benefit from the best of both worlds in a unified manner: Mitchell and Lapata (2008) experiment with intransitive sentences, applying simple compositional models based on vector addition and point-wise multiplication in a disambiguation task; Baroni and Zamparelli (2010) and Guevara (2010) use regression models in order to build vectors for adjective-noun compounds; Erk and Padó (2008) work on transitive sentences using structured vector spaces; Socher et al. (2010, 2011, 2012) use neural networks to combine vectors following the grammatical structure; Grefenstette and Sadrzadeh (2011a,b) apply the categorical framework of Coecke et al. (2010) on the disambiguation task of Mitchell and Lapata (2008); and Kartsaklis et al. (2012) and Grefenstette et al. (2013) build upon previous implementations by adding specific algebraic operations and machine learning techniques to further improve the concrete abilities of the abstract categorical models.

A common strand in all of the above models is that they are based on "ambiguous" vector representations, where a polysemous word is represented by a single vector regardless of the number of its actual senses. For example, the word 'bank' has at least two meanings (financial institution and land alongside a river), both of which will be fused into a single vector representation. And, although it is generally true that compositional models following the formal semantics view of Montague do not care about disambiguation (meanings of words in such models are represented by logical constants explicitly set before the compositional process), the story changes when one moves to a vector space model with ambiguous vector representations. The main problem is that, when acting on ambiguous vector spaces, compositional models seem to perform two tasks at the same time, composition *and* disambiguation, leaving the resulting vector hard to interpret: it is not clear if this vector is a proper meaning representation for the composed compound or just a disambiguated version of one of the words therein. This problem escapes the evaluation schemes, especially when disambiguation tasks are used as a criterion for evaluating compositional models—a common practice in current research for compositional-distributional semantics. Indeed, Pulman (2013) argues that although disambiguation can emerge as a welcome side-effect of the compositional process, it is not clear if compositionality is either a necessary or sufficient condition for disambiguation to happen. On the contrary, it seems that the form of most current vector space models and the compositional operations used on them (quite often some form of vector point-wise multiplication) mainly achieve disambiguation, but not composition.

The purpose of this paper is to further investigate the potential of a compositional-distributional model based on disambiguated vector representations, where each word can have one or more distinct senses. More specifically, we aim to show that (a) compositionality is not a necessary condition for disambiguation, so the quite common practice of using a disambiguation task as a criterion for evaluating the performance of compositional-distributional models is questionable; and (b) the introduction of a separate disambiguation step in the compositional process of distributional models can be indeed beneficial for the quality of the resulting composed vectors.

We train our models from BNC, a 100-million words corpus created from samples of written and spoken English. We perform word sense induction by following the generic algorithm of Schütze (1998), in which the senses of a word are represented by distinct clusters created by taking into account the various contexts in which this specific word occur in the corpus. For the actual clustering step we use a combination of hierarchical agglomerative clustering and the Caliński-Harabasz index (Caliński and Harabasz, 1974). The parameters of the models are fine-tuned on the noun set of SEMEVAL 2010 Word Sense Induction and Disambiguation task (Manandhar et al., 2010).

Equipped with a disambiguated vector space, we use it on a verb disambiguation experiment, similar in style to that of Mitchell and Lapata (2008), but applied on a more linguistically motivated dataset, based on the work of Pickering and Frisson (2001). We find that the application of a simple disambiguation algorithm, *without* any compositional steps, is proven more effective than a number of compositional models. We consider this as an indication for the necessity of separating disambiguation from composition, since it implies that the latter is not necessary for achieving the former. Next, we demonstrate that a compositional model based on disambiguated vectors can indeed produce composite vector representations of better quality, by applying the model on a phrase similarity task (Mitchell and Lapata, 2010). The goal here is to evaluate the similarity of short verb phrases, based on the distance of their composite vectors.

2 Composition in distributional models

The transition from word meaning to sentence meaning, a task easily done by human subjects based on the rules of grammar, implies the existence of a composition operation applied to primitive text units in order to build compound ones. Various solutions have been proposed with different levels of sophistication for this problem in the context of vector space models of meaning.

At one end of the spectrum the simple models of Mitchell and Lapata (2008) address composition as the point-wise multiplication or addition of the involved word vectors. This bag-of-words approach has been proven a hard-to-beat baseline for many of the more sophisticated models. At the other end, composition in the work of Socher et al. (2010, 2011, 2012) is served by the advanced machinery of recurring neural networks, where the output of the network is used again as input in a recurring fashion, for composing vectors of larger constituents. Following a different path, the categorical framework of Coecke et al. (2010) exploits a structural homomorphism between grammar and vector spaces in order to treat words with special meanings, such as verb and adjectives, as functions (tensors of rank-n) that apply to their arguments. This application has the form of inner product, generalising the familiar notion of matrix multiplication to tensors of higher rank.

Regardless of their level of sophistication, most of the models which aim to apply compositionality on word vector representations fail to address the problem of handling the polysemous nature of words. Even more importantly, many of the models are evaluated on their ability to *disambiguate* the meaning of specific words, following an idea first introduced by Kintsch (2001) and later adopted by Mitchell and Lapata (2008) and others. For example, in this latter work the authors test their multiplicative and additive models as follows: given an ambiguous intransitive verb, say 'run' (with the two senses to be those of moving fast and of a liquid dissolving), they examine to what extent the composition of the verb with an appropriate subject (e.g. 'horse' or 'colour') will disambiguate the intended sense of the verb within the specific context. Each row in the dataset consists of a subject (e.g. 'horse'), a verb ('run'), a high-similarity landmark verb ('gallop'), and a low-similarity landmark verb ('dissolve'). The subject is combined with the main verb to form a simple intransitive sentence, and the vector of this sentence is then compared with the vectors of the landmark verbs. The goal is to evaluate the degree to which the composed sentence vector is closer to the high landmark than to the vector of the low landmark, and this is considered an indication of successful composition.

However, although it is generally true that multiplying $\overrightarrow{run}$ with $\overrightarrow{horse}$ will filter out most of the components of $\overrightarrow{run}$ that are irrelevant to 'dissolve' (since the 'dissolve'-related elements of $\overrightarrow{horse}$ should have values close to zero) and will produce a disambiguated version of this verb under the context of 'horse', it is not at all clear if this vector will also constitute an appropriate representation for the meaning of the intransitive sentence 'horse runs'. In other words, here we have two tasks taking place at the same time: (a) disambiguation of the ambiguous word given its context; and (b) composition that produces a meaning vector for the whole sentence. The extent to which the latter is a necessary condition for the former remains unclear, and constitutes a factor that complicates the evaluation and assessment of such systems. In this paper we argue that as long as the above distinct tasks are interwoven into a single step, claims of compositionality in distributional systems cannot be reliably assessed. We therefore propose the addition of a disambiguation step in the generic methodology of compositional-distributional models.

3 Related work

Although in general word sense induction is a popular topic in the natural language processing literature, little has been done to address polysemy specifically in the context of compositional-distributional models of meaning. In fact, the only works relevant to ours we are aware of are that of Erk and Padó (2008) and Reddy et al. (2011). The structured vector space of Erk and Padó (2008) is designed to handle ambiguity in an implicit way, showing promising results on the Mitchell and Lapata (2008) task. The work of Reddy et al. (2011) is closer to our research: the authors evaluate two word sense disambiguation approaches on the noun-noun compound similarity task introduced by Mitchell and Lapata (2010), using simple multiplicative and additive models for composition. The reported results are also promising, where at least one of their models performs better than the current practice of using ambiguous vector representations.

Compared to both of the above works, the scope of the current paper is broader: it does not solely aim to demonstrate the positive effect of a "cleaner" vector space on the compositional process, but it also proceeds one step further and relates this issue with the current evaluation practice, showing that a number of verb disambiguation tasks that have been invariantly used for the assessment of compositional-distributional models might be in fact based on a wrong criterion.

4 Disambiguation scheme

Our word sense induction method is based on the effective procedure first presented by Schütze (1998). For the ith occurrence of a target word w_t in the corpus with context $C_i = \{w_1, \ldots, w_n\}$, we calculate the centroid of the context as $\overrightarrow{c_i} = \frac{1}{n}(\overrightarrow{w_1} + \ldots + \overrightarrow{w_n})$, where $\overrightarrow{w}$ is the lexical (or *first order*) vector of word w as it is created by the usual distributional practice (more details in Section 5). Then, we cluster these centroids in order to form a number of sense clusters. Each sense of the word is represented by the centroid of the corresponding cluster. Following Schütze, we will refer to these sense vectors as *second-order vectors*, in order to distinguish them from the lexical (first-order) vectors. So, in our model each word is represented by a tuple $\langle \overrightarrow{w}, S \rangle$, where $\overrightarrow{w}$ is the 1st-order vector of the word and S the set of 2nd-order vectors created by the above procedure.

We are now able to disambiguate the sense of a target word w_t given a context C by calculating a context vector $\overrightarrow{c}$ for C as above, and then comparing this with every 2nd-order vector of w_t; the word is assigned to the sense that corresponds to the closest 2nd-order vector. That is,

$$\overrightarrow{s_{pref}} = \arg\min_{\overrightarrow{s} \in S} d(\overrightarrow{s}, \overrightarrow{c}) \qquad (1)$$

where S is the set of 2nd-order vectors for w_t and $d(\overrightarrow{u}, \overrightarrow{v})$ the vector distance metric we use.

For the clustering step, we use an iterative bottom-up approach known as hierarchical agglomerative clustering (HAC). Hierarchical clus-

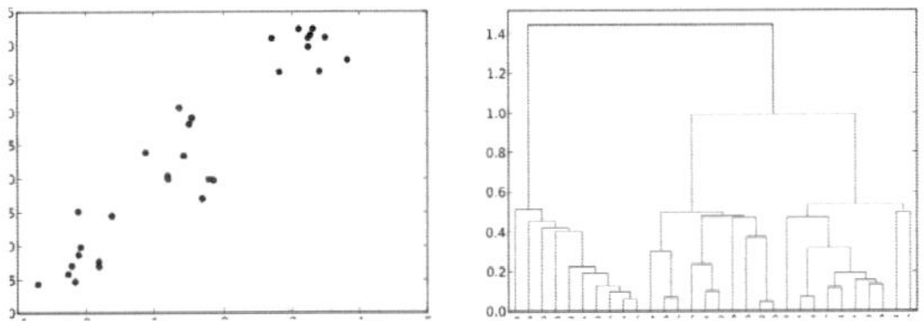

Figure 1: Hierarchical agglomerative clustering.

tering has been invariably applied to unsupervised word sense induction on a variety of languages, generally showing good performance—see, for example, the comparative study of Broda and Mazur (2012) for English and Polish. Compared to k-means clustering, this approach has the major advantage that it does not require us to define in advance a specific number of clusters. Compared to more advanced probabilistic techniques, such as Bayesian mixture models, it is much more straightforward and simple to implement, yet powerful enough to demonstrate the necessity of factoring out ambiguity from compositional-distributional models.

HAC is a bottom-up method of cluster analysis, starting with each data point (context vector in our case) forming its own cluster; then, in each iteration the two closest clusters are merged into a new cluster, until all points are finally merged under the same cluster. This process produces a *dendrogram* (i.e. a tree diagram), which essentially embeds every possible clustering of the dataset. As an example, Figure 1 shows a small dataset produced by three distinct Gaussian distributions, and the dendrogram derived by the above algorithm. Implementation-wise, the clustering part in this work is served by the efficient FASTCLUSTER library (Müllner, 2013).

Choosing a number of senses In HAC, one still needs to decide where exactly to cut the tree in order to get the best possible partitioning of the data. Although the right answer to this problem might depend on many factors, we can safely assume that the optimal partitioning is the one that provides the most compact and maximally separated clusters. One way to measure the quality of a clustering based on this criterion is the Caliński/Harabasz index (Caliński and Harabasz, 1974), also known as variance ratio criterion (VRC). Given a set of N data points and a partitioning of k disjoint clusters, VRC is computed as follows:

$$VRC_k = \frac{trace(B)}{trace(W)} \times \frac{N-k}{k-1} \quad (2)$$

Here, W and B are the intra-cluster and inter-cluster dispersion matrices, respectively:

$$W = \sum_{i=1}^{k}\sum_{l=1}^{N_i}(\overrightarrow{x_i}(l) - \bar{x}_i)(\overrightarrow{x_i}(l) - \bar{x}_i)^{\mathsf{T}} \quad (3)$$

$$B = \sum_{i=1}^{k} N_i(\bar{x}_i - \bar{x})(\bar{x}_i - \bar{x})^{\mathsf{T}} \quad (4)$$

where N_i is the number of data points assigned to cluster i, $\overrightarrow{x_i}(l)$ is the lth point assigned to this cluster, $\bar{x}_i$ is the centroid of ith cluster (the mean), and $\bar{x}$ is the data centroid of the overall dataset. Given the above formulas, the trace of B is the sum of inter-cluster variances, while the trace of W is the sum of intra-cluster variances. A good partitioning should have high values for B (which is an indication for well-separated clusters) and low values for W (an indication for compact clusters), so the higher the quality of the partitioning the greater the value of this ratio.

Compared to other criteria, VRC has been found to be one of the most effective approaches for clustering validity—see the comparative studies of Milligan and Cooper (1985) and Vendramin et al. (2009). Furthermore, it has been previously applied to word sense discrimination successfully, returning the best results among a number of other measures (Savova et al., 2006). For this work, we calculate VRC for a number of different partitionings (ranged from 2 to 10 clusters), and we keep the partitioning that results in the highest VRC value as the optimal number of senses for the specific word. Note that since the HAC dendrogram already embeds all possible clusterings, the cutting of the tree in order to get a different partitioning is performed in constant time.

5 Experimental setting

The choice of our 1st-order vector space is based on empirical tests, where we found out that a basis with elements of the form $\langle word, class \rangle$ presents the right balance for our purposes among simpler techniques, such as word-based spaces, and more complex ones, such as dependency-based approaches. In our vector space, each word has a distinct vector representation for every word class under which occurs in the corpus (e.g. 'suit' will have a noun vector and a verb vector). As our basis elements we use the 2000 most frequent content words in BNC, with weights being calculated as the ratio of the probability of the context word given the target word to the probability of the context word overall. The context here is a 5-word window on both sides of the target word.

The parameters of the clustering scheme are optimized on the noun set of SEMEVAL 2010 Word

Sense Induction & Disambiguation Task (Manandhar et al., 2010). Specifically, when using HAC one has to decide how to measure the distance between the clusters, which is the merging criterion applied in every iteration of the algorithm, as well as the measure between the data points, i.e. the individual vectors. Based on empirical tests we limit our options to two inter-cluster measures: complete-link and Ward's methods. In the complete-link method the distance between two clusters X and Y is the distance between their two most remote elements:

$$D(X,Y) = \max_{x \in X, y \in Y} d(x,y) \quad (5)$$

In Ward's method, two clusters are selected for merging if the new partitioning exhibits the minimum increase in the overall intra-cluster variance. The cluster distance is given by:

$$D(X,Y) = \frac{2|X||Y|}{|X|+|Y|} \|\overrightarrow{c_X} - \overrightarrow{c_Y}\|^2 \quad (6)$$

where $\overrightarrow{c_X}$ and $\overrightarrow{c_Y}$ are the centroids of X and Y.

We test these *linkage* methods in combination with three vector distance measures: euclidean, cosine, and Pearson's correlation (6 models in total). The metrics were chosen to represent progressively more relaxed forms of vector comparison, with the strictest form to be the euclidean distance and correlation as the most relaxed. For sense detection we use the disambiguation algorithm described in Section 4, considering as context the whole sentence in which a target word appears. The distance metric used for the disambiguation process in each model is identical to the metric used for the clustering process, so in the Ward/euclidean model the disambiguation is based on the euclidean distance, in complete-link/cosine model on the cosine distance, and so on. We evaluate the models using V-measure, an entropy-based metric that addresses the so-called *matching problem* of F-score (Rosenberg and Hirschberg, 2007). Table 1 shows the results.

Model	V-Meas.	Avg clust.
Ward/Euclidean	0.05	1.44
Ward/Correlation	**0.14**	**3.14**
Ward/Cosine	0.08	1.94
Complete/Euclidean	0.00	1.00
Complete/Correlation	0.11	2.66
Complete/Cosine	0.06	1.74
Most frequent sense	0.00	1.00
1 cluster/instance	0.36	89.15
Gold standard	1.0	4.46

Table 1: Results on the noun set of SEMEVAL 2010 WSI&D task.

keyboard: 1105 contexts, 2 senses
COMPUTER (665 contexts): program dollar disk power enter port graphic card option select language drive pen application corp external editor woman price page design sun cli amstrad lock interface lcd slot notebook
MUSIC (440 contexts): drummer instrumental singer german father fantasia english generation wolfgang wayne cello body join ensemble mike chamber gary saxophone sax ricercarus apply form son metal guy clean roll barry orchestra

Table 2: Derived senses for word 'keyboard'.

Ward's method in combination with correlation distance provided the highest V-measure, followed by the combination of complete-link with (again) correlation. Although a direct comparison of our models with the models participating in this task would not be quite sound (since these models were trained on a special corpus provided by the organizers, while our model was trained on the BNC), it is nevertheless enlightening to mention that the 0.14 V-measure places the Ward-correlation model at the 4th rank among 28 systems for the noun set of the task, while at the same time provides a reasonable average number of clusters per word (3.14), close to that of the human-annotated gold standard (4.46). Compare this, for example, with the best-performing system that achieved a V-measure of 0.21, a score that was largely due to the fact that the model assigned the unrealistic number of 11.54 senses per word on average (since V-measure tends to favour higher numbers of senses, as the baseline *1 cluster/instance* shows in Table 1).[1]

Table 2 provides an example of the results, showing the senses for the noun 'keyboard' learnt by the best model of Ward's method and correlation measure. Each sense is visualized as a list of the most dominant words in the cluster, ranked by their TF-ICF values. Furthermore, Figure 2 shows the dendrograms produced by four linkage methods for the word 'keyboard', demonstrating the superiority of Ward's method.

6 Disambiguation vs composition

A number of models that aim to equip distributional semantics with compositionality are evaluated on some form of the disambiguation task presented in Section 2. Versions of this task can be found, for example, in Mitchell and Lapata (2008),

[1]The results of SEMEVAL 2010 can be found online at http://www.cs.york.ac.uk/semeval2010_WSI/task_14_ranking.html.

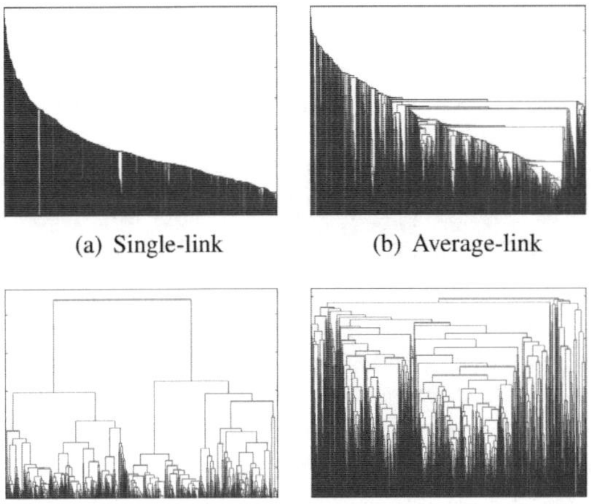

(a) Single-link (b) Average-link

(c) Ward's method (d) Complete-link

Figure 2: Dendrograms produced for word 'keyboard' according to 4 different linkage methods.

Erk and Padó (2008), Grefenstette and Sadrzadeh (2011a,b), Kartsaklis et al. (2012) and Grefenstette et al. (2013). We briefly remind that the goal is to assess how well a compositional model can disambiguate the meaning of an ambiguous verb, given a specific context. This kind of evaluation involves two distinct tasks: the composition of sentence vectors, and the disambiguation of the verbs. And, although the evaluation of a model against human judgements provides some indication for the success of the latter task, it leaves unclear to what extent the former has been achieved. In this section we perform two experiments in order to address this question. The first of them aims to support the following argument: that although disambiguation can emerge as a side-effect of a compositional process, compositionality is not a necessary condition for this to happen. The second experiment is based on a more appropriate task that requires genuine compositional abilities, and demonstrates the good performance of a compositional model based on the disambiguated vector space of Section 5.

As our compositional method for the following tasks we use the multiplicative and additive models of Mitchell and Lapata (2008). Despite the simple nature of these models, there is a number of reasons that make them good candidates for demonstrating the main ideas of this paper. First, for better or worse "simple" does not necessarily mean "ineffective". The comparative study of Blacoe and Lapata (2012) shows that for certain tasks these "baselines" perform equally well or even better than other more sophisticated models. And second, it is reasonable to expect that better compositional models would only work in favour of our arguments, and not the other way around.

6.1 Evaluating disambiguation

One potential problem with the datasets used for the disambiguation task of Section 2, similar to the one of Grefenstette and Sadrzadeh (2011a), is that ambiguous verbs are usually collected from a corpus based on some automated method. And, although they do exhibit variations in their senses (as most verbs do), in many cases these meanings are actually related—for example, the meanings of 'write' in G&S dataset are *spell* and *publish*. To overcome this problem, we used the work of Pickering and Frisson (2001), which provides a list of genuinely ambiguous verbs obtained from careful manual selection and ranking from human evaluators. The evaluators assessed the relatedness of each verb's different meanings using a scale of 0 (totally unrelated) to 7 (highly related). From these verbs, we picked 10 with an average mark < 1. An example is 'file', which means 'smooth' in 'file nails' and 'register' as in 'file an application'. For each verb we picked the 10 most occurring subjects and objects from the BNC (5 for each landmark). In the case of verb 'file', for example, among these were 'woman' and 'nails' for landmark 'smooth', and 'union' and 'lawsuit' for landmark 'register'. Each subject and object was modified by its most occurring adjective in the corpus. This resulted in triples of sentences of the following form:

(1) *main*: young woman filed long nails
high: young woman smoothed long nails
low: young woman registered long nails

(2) *main*: monetary union filed civil lawsuit
high: mon. union registered civil lawsuit
low: mon. union smoothed civil lawsuit

The main sentence was paired with both high and low landmark sentences, creating a dataset[2] of 200 sentence pairs (10 main verbs $\times$ 10 contexts $\times$ 2 landmarks)[3]. These were randomly presented to 43 human annotators, whose duty was to judge the similarity between the sentences of each pair. The human scores were compared with scores produced by a number of models (Table 3).

The most successful model (M1) does not apply any form of composition. Instead, the comparison of a sentence with a "landmark" sentence is simply based on disambiguated versions of the

[2]The dataset will be available at http://www.cs.ox.ac.uk/activities/compdistmeaning/.

[3]As a comparison, the Mitchell and Lapata (2008) dataset consists of 15 main verbs $\times$ 4 contexts $\times$ 2 landmarks $= 120$ sentence pairs, while the Grefenstette and Sadrzadeh (2011a) dataset has the same configuration and size with ours.

verbs alone. Specifically, the main verb and the landmark verb are disambiguated given the context (subjects, objects, and adjectives that modify them) according to Equation 1; this produces two 2nd-order vectors, one for the main verb and one for the landmark. The degree of similarity between the two sentences is then calculated by measuring the similarity between the two sense vectors of the verbs, without any compositional step. The score of 0.28 achieved by this model is impressive, given that the inter-annotator agreement (which serves as an upper-bound) is 0.38.

A number of interesting observations can be made based on the results of Table 3. First of all, the 'verbs-only' model outperforms the two baselines (which use composition but not disambiguation) by a large margin, and indeed also the other compositional models. This is an indication that this kind of disambiguation task might not be the best way to evaluate a compositional model. The fact that the most important condition for success is the proper disambiguation of the verb, means that the good performance of a compositional model demonstrates only this: how well the model is able to *disambiguate* an ambiguous verb. This is different from how well the composed representation reflects the meaning of the larger constituent; that is, it has very little to say about the extent to which an operation like $\overrightarrow{woman} \odot \overrightarrow{file} \odot \overrightarrow{nails}$ ($\odot$ denotes point-wise multiplication) results in a faithful representation of the meaning of sentence 'woman filed nails'.

M2 to M5 represent different versions of the compositional models that use disambiguation in a distinct step. All these models compose both the main verb and the landmark with a given context, and then perform the comparison at sentence level. In M2 and M3 all words are first disambiguated prior to composition, while in M4 and M5 the 2nd-order vector of the verb is composed with the 1st-order vectors of the other words. The most impressive observation here is that the separation of disambiguation results in a tremendous improvement for the additive model, from 0.04 to 0.21. This is not surprising since, when using magnitude invariant measures between vectors (such as cosine distance), the resulting vector is nothing more than the average of the involved word vectors. The introduction of the disambiguation step before the composition, therefore, makes a great difference since it provides much more accurate starting points to be averaged.

	Disambig.	Composition	ρ	
M1	**Only verbs**	**No**	**0.282**	*
M2	All words	Multiplicative	0.118	
M3	All words	Additive	0.210	
M4	Only verbs	Multiplicative	0.110	
M5	Only verbs	Additive	0.234	*
B1	No	Multiplicative	0.143	
B2	No	Additive	0.042	
	Inter-annotator agreement		0.383	

* The difference between M1 and M5 is highly statistically significant with $p < 0.0001$

Table 3: Spearman's ρ for the Pickering and Frisson dataset.

On the other hand, the disambiguated version of multiplicative model (M2) presents inferior performance compared to the "ambiguous" version (B1). We argue that the reason behind this is that the two models perform different jobs: the result of B1 is a "mixing" of composition and disambiguation of the most ambiguous word (i.e. the verb), since this is the natural effect of the point-wise multiplication operation (see discussion in Section 2); on the other hand, M2 is designed to construct an appropriate composite meaning for the whole sentence. We will try to support this argument by the experiment of the next section.

6.2 A better test of compositionality

Although there might not exists such a thing as *the* best evaluation method for compositional-distributional semantics, it is safe to assume that a phrase similarity task avoids many of the pitfalls of tasks such as the one of Section 6.1. Given pairs of short phrases, the goal is to assess the similarity of the phrases by constructing composite vectors for them and computing their distance. No assumptions about disambiguation abilities regarding a specific word (e.g. the verb) are made here; the only criterion is to what extent the composite vector representing the meaning of a phrase is similar or dissimilar to the vector of another phrase. From this perspective, this task seems the ideal choice for evaluating a model aiming to provide appropriate phrasal semantics. The scores given by the models are compared to those of human evaluators using Spearman's ρ.

For this experiment, we use the "verb-object" part of the dataset presented in the work of Mitchell and Lapata (2010), which consists of 108 pairs of short verb phrases exhibiting three degrees of similarity. A high similarity pair for example, is *produce effect/achieve result*, a medium one is *pour tea/join party*, and a low one is *close eye/achieve end*. The original dataset also con-

	Disambig.	Composition	ρ	
M1	Only verbs	No	0.318	
M2	**All words**	**Multiplicative**	**0.412**	*
M3	**All words**	**Additive**	**0.414**	†
M4	Only verbs	Multiplicative	0.352	
M5	Only verbs	Additive	0.324	
B1	No	Multiplicative	0.379	*†
B2	No	Additive	0.334	
	Inter-annotator agreement		0.550	

* Difference between M2/B1 is stat. sign. with $p \leq 0.07$

† Difference between M3/B1 is stat. sign. with $p \leq 0.06$

Table 4: Phrase similarity results.

tains noun-noun and adjective-noun compounds. However, the verb-object part serves the purposes of this paper much better, for two reasons. First, since by definition the proposed methodology suits better circumstances involving at least some level of word ambiguity, a dataset based on the most ambiguous part of speech (verbs) seems a reasonable choice. Second, this part of the dataset allows us to do some meaningful comparisons with the task of Section 6.1, which is again around verb structures. The results are shown in Table 4.

This time, the disambiguation step provides solid benefits for both multiplicative (M2) and additive (M3) models, with differences that are statistically significant from the best baseline B1 (with $p \leq 0.07$ and $p \leq 0.06$, respectively). Note that the 'verbs-only' model (M1), which was by a large margin the most successful for the task of Section 6.1, now shows the worst performance. For comparison, the best result reported by Mitchell and Lapata (2010) on a 1st-order space similar to ours (regarding dimensions and weights) was 0.38 ("dilation" model).

7 Discussion

This paper is based on the observation that any compositional operation between two vectors is essentially a hybrid process consisting of two "components" that, depending on the form of the underlying vector space, can have different "magnitudes". One of the components results in a certain amount of disambiguation for the most ambiguous original word, while the other one works towards a composite representation for the meaning of the whole phrase or sentence. The tasks of Section 6 are designed so that each one of them assesses a different aspect of this hybrid process: the task of Section 6.1 is focused on the disambiguation aspect, while the task of Section 6.2 addresses the compositionality part. One of our main arguments is the observation that, in order the get better compositional representations, it is essential to first eliminate (or at least reduce as much as possible the magnitude of) the disambiguation "component" that might show up as a by-product of the compositional process, so that the result is mainly a product of pure composition—this is what the "unambiguous" models do achieve in the task of Section 6.2. Based on the experimental work conducted in this paper, our first concluding remark is that the elimination of the ambiguity factor can be essential for the quality of the composed vectors.

But, if Table 4 provides a proof that the separation of disambiguation and composition can indeed produce better compositional representations, what is the meaning of the inferior performance of all "unambiguous" models (M2 to M5) compared to verbs-only version (M1) in the task of Section 6.1? Why disambiguation is not always effective (as in the case of multiplicative model) for that task? These are strong indications that the quality of composition is not crucial for disambiguation tasks of this sort, whose only achievement is that they measure the disambiguation side-effects generated by the compositional process. In other words, the practice of evaluating the quality of composition by using disambiguation tasks is problematic. As the topic of compositionality in distributional models of meaning increasingly gains popularity in the recent years, this second concluding remark is equally important since it can contribute towards better evaluation schemes of such models.

8 Future work

A next step to take in the future is the application of these ideas on more complex spaces, such as those based on the categorical framework of Coecke et al. (2010). The challenge here is the effective generalization of a disambiguation scheme on tensors of rank greater than 1. Additionally, we would expect this method to benefit from more robust probabilistic clustering techniques. An appealing option is the use of a non-parametric method, such as a hierarchical Dirichlet process (Yao and Van Durme, 2011).

Acknowledgements

We would like to thank Daniel Müllner for his comments on the use of FASTCLUSTER library, as well as the three anonymous reviewers for their fruitful suggestions. Support by EPSRC grant EP/F042728/1 is gratefully acknowledged by the first two authors.

References

Baroni, M. and Zamparelli, R. (2010). Nouns are Vectors, Adjectives are Matrices. In *Proceedings of Conference on Empirical Methods in Natural Language Processing (EMNLP)*.

Blacoe, W. and Lapata, M. (2012). A comparison of vector-based representations for semantic composition. In *Proceedings of the 2012 Joint Conference on Empirical Methods in Natural Language Processing and Computational Natural Language Learning*, pages 546–556, Jeju Island, Korea. Association for Computational Linguistics.

Broda, B. and Mazur, W. (2012). Evaluation of clustering algorithms for word sense disambiguation. *International Journal of Data Analysis Techniques and Strategies*, 4(3):219–236.

Caliński, T. and Harabasz, J. (1974). A Dendrite Method for Cluster Analysis. *Communications in Statistics-Theory and Methods*, 3(1):1–27.

Coecke, B., Sadrzadeh, M., and Clark, S. (2010). Mathematical Foundations for Distributed Compositional Model of Meaning. Lambek Festschrift. *Linguistic Analysis*, 36:345–384.

Erk, K. and Padó, S. (2008). A Structured Vector-Space Model for Word Meaning in Context. In *Proceedings of Conference on Empirical Methods in Natural Language Processing (EMNLP)*, pages 897–906.

Grefenstette, E., Dinu, G., Zhang, Y.-Z., Sadrzadeh, M., and Baroni, M. (2013). Multistep regression learning for compositional distributional semantics.

Grefenstette, E. and Sadrzadeh, M. (2011a). Experimental Support for a Categorical Compositional Distributional Model of Meaning. In *Proceedings of Conference on Empirical Methods in Natural Language Processing (EMNLP)*.

Grefenstette, E. and Sadrzadeh, M. (2011b). Experimenting with Transitive Verbs in a DisCoCat. In *Proceedings of Workshop on Geometrical Models of Natural Language Semantics (GEMS)*.

Guevara, E. (2010). A Regression Model of Adjective-Noun Compositionality in Distributional Semantics. In *Proceedings of the ACL GEMS Workshop*.

Kartsaklis, D., Sadrzadeh, M., and Pulman, S. (2012). A unified sentence space for categorical distributional-compositional semantics: Theory and experiments. In *Proceedings of 24th International Conference on Computational Linguistics (COLING 2012): Posters*, pages 549–558, Mumbai, India. The COLING 2012 Organizing Committee.

Kintsch, W. (2001). Predication. *Cognitive Science*, 25(2):173–202.

Manandhar, S., Klapaftis, I., Dligach, D., and Pradhan, S. (2010). Semeval-2010 task 14: Word sense induction & disambiguation. In *Proceedings of the 5th International Workshop on Semantic Evaluation*, pages 63–68. Association for Computational Linguistics.

Milligan, G. and Cooper, M. (1985). An Examination of Procedures for Determining the Number of Clusters in a Data Set. *Psychometrika*, 50(2):159–179.

Mitchell, J. and Lapata, M. (2008). Vector-based Models of Semantic Composition. In *Proceedings of the 46th Annual Meeting of the Association for Computational Linguistics*, pages 236–244.

Mitchell, J. and Lapata, M. (2010). Composition in distributional models of semantics. *Cognitive Science*, 34(8):1388–1439.

Müllner, D. (2013). fastcluster: Fast Hierarchical Clustering Routines for R and Python. *Journal of Statistical Software*, 9(53):1–18.

Pickering, M. and Frisson, S. (2001). Processing ambiguous verbs: Evidence from eye movements. *Journal of Experimental Psychology: Learning, Memory, and Cognition*, 27(2):556.

Pulman, S. (2013). Combining Compositional and Distributional Models of Semantics. In Heunen, C., Sadrzadeh, M., and Grefenstette, E., editors, *Quantum Physics and Linguistics: A Compositional, Diagrammatic Discourse*. Oxford University Press.

Reddy, S., Klapaftis, I., McCarthy, D., and Manandhar, S. (2011). Dynamic and static prototype vectors for semantic composition. In *Proceedings of 5th International Joint Conference on Natural Language Processing*, pages 705–713.

Rosenberg, A. and Hirschberg, J. (2007). V-measure: A conditional entropy-based external cluster evaluation measure. In *Proceedings of the 2007 Joint Conference on Empirical Methods in Natural Language Processing and Computational Natural Language Learning*, pages 410–420.

Savova, G., Therneau, T., and Chute, C. (2006). Cluster Stopping Rules for Word Sense Discrimination. In *Proceedings of the workshop on Making Sense of Sense: Bringing Psycholinguistics and Computational Linguistics Together*, pages 9–16.

Schütze, H. (1998). Automatic Word Sense Discrimination. *Computational Linguistics*, 24:97–123.

Socher, R., Huang, E., Pennington, J., Ng, A., and Manning, C. (2011). Dynamic Pooling and Unfolding Recursive Autoencoders for Paraphrase Detection. *Advances in Neural Information Processing Systems*, 24.

Socher, R., Huval, B., Manning, C., and A., N. (2012). Semantic compositionality through recursive matrix-vector spaces. In *Conference on Empirical Methods in Natural Language Processing 2012*.

Socher, R., Manning, C., and Ng, A. (2010). Learning Continuous Pphrase Representations and Syntactic Parsing with recursive neural networks. In *Proceedings of the NIPS-2010 Deep Learning and Unsupervised Feature Learning Workshop*.

Vendramin, L., Campello, R., and Hruschka, E. (2009). On the Comparison of Relative Clustering Validity Criteria. In *Proceedings of the SIAM International Conference on Data Mining, SIAM*, pages 733–744.

Yao, X. and Van Durme, B. (2011). Nonparametric bayesian word sense induction. *ACL HLT 2011*, page 10.

Frame Semantics for Stance Classification

Kazi Saidul Hasan and **Vincent Ng**
Human Language Technology Research Institute
University of Texas at Dallas
Richardson, TX 75083-0688
{saidul,vince}@hlt.utdallas.edu

Abstract

Determining the stance expressed by an author from a post written for a two-sided debate in an online debate forum is a relatively new problem in opinion mining. We extend a state-of-the-art learning-based approach to debate stance classification by (1) inducing lexico-syntactic patterns based on syntactic dependencies and semantic frames that aim to capture the meaning of a sentence and provide a generalized representation of it; and (2) improving the classification of a test post via a novel way of exploiting the information in other test posts with the same stance. Empirical results on four datasets demonstrate the effectiveness of our extensions.

1 Introduction

Given a post written for a *two-sided* topic in an online debate forum (e.g., *"Should abortion be allowed?"*), the task of *debate stance classification* involves determining which of the two sides (i.e., *for* or *against*) its author is taking. For example, a stance classification system should determine that the author of the following post is anti-abortion.

Post 1: *Abortion has been legal for decades and no one seems to have a problem with it. That's ridiculous! There are millions of people in the world who would love to have children but can't.*

Previous approaches to debate stance classification have focused on three debate settings, namely congressional floor debates (Thomas et al., 2006; Bansal et al., 2008; Balahur et al., 2009; Yessenalina et al., 2010; Burfoot et al., 2011), company-internal discussions (Murakami and Raymond, 2010), and online social, political, and ideological debates in public forums (Agrawal et al., 2003; Somasundaran and Wiebe, 2010; Wang and Rosé, 2010; Biran and Rambow, 2011; Hasan and Ng, 2012). As Walker et al. (2012) point out, debates in public forums differ from congressional debates and company-internal discussions in terms of language use. Specifically, online debaters use colorful and emotional language to express their points, which may involve sarcasm, insults, and questioning another debater's assumptions and evidence. These properties can potentially make stance classification of online debates more challenging than that of the other two types of debates.

Our goal in this paper is to improve the state of the art in stance classification of online debates, focusing in particular on *ideological debates.* Specifically, we present two extensions, one linguistic and the other extra-linguistic, to the state-of-the-art supervised learning approach to this task proposed by Anand et al. (2011). In our linguistic extension, we induce patterns from each sentence in the training set using *syntactic dependencies* and *semantic frames* that aim to capture the *meaning* of a sentence and provide a *generalized representation* of it. Note that while Anand et al.'s lexico-syntactic approach aims to generalize from a sentence using syntactic dependencies, we aim to generalize using semantic frames. As we will see in Section 4, not only is there no guarantee that syntactic dependencies can retain or sufficiently capture the meaning of a sentence during the generalization process, it is in fact harder to generalize from syntactic dependencies than from semantic frames. In our extra-linguistic extension, we improve the classification of a test post via a novel way of exploiting the information in other test posts with the same stance.

We evaluate our approach to stance classification of ideological debates on datasets collected for four domains from online debate forums. Experimental results demonstrate the effectiveness of our approach: it outperforms an improved version of Anand et al.'s approach by 2.6–7.0 accuracy points on the four domains.

Domain	Number of posts	% of "for" posts
ABO	1741	54.9
GAY	1376	63.4
OBA	985	53.9
MAR	626	69.5

Table 1: Statistics of the four datasets.

The rest of the paper is organized as follows. We first present our datasets in Section 2. Section 3 describes our two learning-based baseline systems for stance classification. Sections 4 and 5 discuss our two extensions. Finally, we show evaluation results in Section 6 and present conclusions in Section 7.

2 Datasets

For our experiments, we collect debate posts from four popular *domains*, Abortion (ABO), Gay Rights (GAY), Obama (OBA), and Marijuana (MAR). Each post should receive one of two *domain labels*, *for* or *against*, depending on whether the author of the post *supports* or *opposes* abortion, gay rights, Obama, or the legalization of marijuana. To see how we obtain these domain labels, let us first describe the data collection process in more detail.

We collect our debate posts for the four domains from an online debate forum[1]. In each domain, there are several two-sided debates. Each debate has a subject (e.g., "Abortion should be banned") for which a number of posts were written by different authors. Each post is manually tagged with its author's stance (i.e., *yes* or *no*) on the debate subject. Since the label of each post represents the subject stance but not the domain stance, we need to automatically convert the former to the latter. For example, for the subject "Abortion should be banned", the subject stance *yes* implies that the author opposes abortion, and hence the domain label for the corresponding label should be *against*.

We construct one dataset for each domain. Statistics of these datasets are shown in Table 1.

3 Baseline Systems

We employ as baselines two stance classification systems, Anand et al.'s (2011) approach and an enhanced version of it, as described below.

Our first baseline, Anand et al.'s approach, is a supervised method that trains a stance classifier for determining whether the stance expressed in a debate post is *for* or *against*. Hence, we create one training instance from each post in the training set, using the stance it expresses as its class label. Following Anand et al., we represent a training instance using five types of features: n-grams, document statistics, punctuations, syntactic dependencies, and, if applicable, the set of features computed for the immediately preceding post in its thread. Their n-gram features include both the unigrams and bigrams in a post, as well as its first unigram, first bigram, and first trigram. The features based on document statistics include the post length, the number of words per sentence, the percentage of words with more than six letters, and the percentage of words as pronouns and sentiment words. The punctuation features are composed of the repeated punctuation symbols in a post. The dependency-based features have three variants. In the first variant, the pair of arguments involved in each dependency relation extracted by a dependency parser is used as a feature. The second variant is the same as the first except that the head (i.e., the first argument in a relation) is replaced by its part-of-speech (POS) tag. The features in the third variant, the *topic-opinion features*, are created by replacing each feature from the first two types that contains a sentiment word with the corresponding polarity label (i.e., $+$ or $-$). For instance, given the sentence "John hates guns", the topic-opinion features $John^-$ and $guns^-$ are generated, since "hate" has a negative polarity and it is connected to "John" and "guns" via the *nsubj* and *dobj* relations, respectively. In our implementation, we train the stance classifier using SVM^{light} (Joachims, 1999). After training, we can apply the stance classifier to classify the test instances, which are generated in the same way as the training instances.

Related work on stance classification of *congressional debates* has found that enforcing *author constraints* (ACs) can improve classification performance (e.g., Thomas et al. (2006), Burfoot et al. (2011), Lu et al. (2012)). ACs are a type of inter-post constraints that specify that two posts written by the same author for the same debate domain should have the same stance. We hypothesize that ACs could similarly be used to improve stance classification of ideological debates, and therefore propose a second baseline where we enhance the first baseline with ACs. Enforcing ACs is simple.

[1] `http://www.createdebate.com/`

We first use the learned stance classifier to classify the test posts as in the first baseline, and then *post-process* the labels of the test posts. Specifically, we sum up the confidence values[2] assigned to the set of test posts written by the same author for the same debate domain. If the sum is positive, then we label *all* the posts in this set as *for*; otherwise we label them as *against*.

4 Semantic Generalization

Our first extension to Anand et al.'s (2011) approach involves semantic generalization.

To motivate this extension, let us take a closer look at Anand et al.'s attempt to generalize using syntactic dependencies. Note that any approach that aims to generalize using syntactic dependencies suffers from several weaknesses. First, the semantic relationship between the pair of lexical items involved in each of these features is not encoded. This means that the resulting features do not adequately capture the meaning of the underlying sentence. Second, replacing a word with its POS tag is a syntactic, not semantic, generalization, and doing so further abstracts the resulting feature from the meaning of the underlying sentence. Above all, while the resulting features are intended to improve generalizations, they can provide very limited generalizations. To see why, consider two semantically similar sentences "I hate arrogant people" and "I dislike arrogant people". Ideally, any features that intend to provide a generalized representation of these sentences should be able to encode the fact that they are semantically similar. However, Anand et al.'s features would fail to do so because they cannot capture the fact that "hate" and "dislike" are semantically similar.

In the rest of this section we describe how we generate a *semantic generalization* of a sentence to capture its *meaning*. Our approach to semantic generalization involves (1) inducing from the training data a set of patterns that aim to provide a semantic generalization of the sentences in the training posts and (2) using them in combination with the baseline systems to classify a test post. Below we describe these two steps in detail.

4.1 Step 1: Pattern Induction

This step is composed of two sub-steps.

[2]We use as the confidence value the signed distance of the associated test point from the SVM hyperplane.

4.1.1 Sub-step 1: Topic Extraction

For each domain, we extract a list of *topics*. We define a topic as a word sequence that (1) starts with zero or more adjectives and ends with one or more nouns and (2) appears in at least five posts from the domain. Using this method, for example, we can extract "abortion", "partial-birth abortion", "birth control", etc., as the topics for Abortion.

4.1.2 Sub-step 2: Pattern Creation

Given a sentence, we create patterns to capture its information using syntactic dependencies and semantic frames.[3] These patterns can be divided into three types, as described below. For ease of exposition, we will use the two (semantically equivalent) sentences below as our running examples and see what patterns are created from them.

(1) Some people hate guns.
(2) Some people do not like guns.

Subject-Frame-Object (SFO) patterns. We create a set of SFO patterns for a transitive verb if (1) it is a frame target[4]; (2) its subject (respectively object) is a topic; and (3) its object (respectively subject) is a frame target. In sentence (1), *hate* is the target of the frame *Experiencer_focus* (henceforth EF), its subject, *people*, is a topic, and its object, *guns* is the target of the frame *Weapon*. As a result, we create a set of SFO patterns, each of which is represented as a 6-tuple. More specifically, we create the 8 SFO patterns shown in the first column of Table 2. Pattern 1 says that (1) this is an SFO pattern; (2) the subject is the word *people*; (3) the frame name of the verb is EF; (4) the frame name of the object is Weapon; (5) the verb is *not* negated (POS); and (6) we *don't care* (DC) whether the verb is sentiment-bearing. If the verb is sentiment-bearing (in this case, *hate* has a negative sentiment), we create another pattern that is the same as the first one, except that DC is replaced with its sentiment value (see Pattern 2).

Next, note that since the subject of *hate* is the target of the frame *People* and its object is a topic, we need to create patterns in a similar manner, resulting in Patterns 3 and 4. Note that *People* in these two patterns (with 'P' capitalized) is the

[3]We use the Stanford parser (de Marneffe and Manning, 2008) and SEMAFOR (Das et al., 2010) to obtain dependency relations and semantic frames, respectively.

[4]A word w is the target of a frame f if f is assigned to w to generalize its meaning. For example, *assassination*, *kill*, and *terminate* are the targets of the frame *Killing*.

1 <SFO:people:EF:Weapon:POS:DC>	9 <SFO:people:EF:Weapon:NEG:DC>	17 <DF:dobj:EF:Weapon:POS:DC>
2 <SFO:people:EF:Weapon:POS:−>	10 <SFO:people:EF:Weapon:POS:−>	18 <DF:dobj:EF:Weapon:POS:−>
3 <SFO:People:EF:guns:POS:DC>	11 <SFO:People:EF:guns:NEG:DC>	19 <DF:dobj:EF:guns:POS:DC>
4 <SFO:People:EF:guns:POS:−>	12 <SFO:People:EF:guns:POS:−>	20 <DF:dobj:EF:guns:POS:−>
5 <SFO:people:EF:DC:POS:DC>	13 <SFO:people:EF:DC:NEG:DC>	21 <FET:people:Experiencer:EF:POS:DC>
6 <SFO:people:EF:DC:POS:−>	14 <SFO:people:EF:DC:POS:−>	22 <FET:people:Experiencer:EF:POS:−>
7 <SFO:DC:EF:guns:POS:DC>	15 <SFO:DC:EF:guns:NEG:DC>	23 <FET:guns:Content:EF:POS:DC>
8 <SFO:DC:EF:guns:POS:−>	16 <SFO:DC:EF:guns:POS:−>	24 <FET:guns:Content:EF:POS:−>

Table 2: Sample patterns created for sentences (1) and (2).

name of the frame *People*, not the word *people* appearing in the sentence.

To provide better generalization, we create a simplified version of each SFO pattern by replacing the frame name representing subject/object with the value DC. This results in Patterns 5–8.

For sentence (2), we can generate patterns in a similar manner, resulting in Patterns 9–16. For example, Pattern 9 contains the element NEG, which encodes the fact that the verb *like* is negated. Pattern 10 deserves discussion. Since the positive sentiment-bearing verb *like* is negated, the sentiment value of Pattern 10 is −, which encodes the fact that *not like* has a negative sentiment. The negation value of Pattern 10 is POS rather than NEG, reflecting the fact that *not like* does not appear in a negative context. In other words, the sentiment value needs to be flipped if the verb is negated, and so may the negation value. It is worth noting that Patterns 2 and 10 are identical, which provides suggestive evidence that sentences (1) and (2) are semantically equivalent.

Dependency-Frame (DF) patterns. We create a set of DF patterns for a dependency relation d if (1) both arguments of d are frame targets or (2) the head is a frame target and the dependent is a topic. For example, in the dependency relation *dobj(hate,guns)*, both *hate* and *guns* are frame targets, as discussed above, and *guns* is a topic, so a set of DF patterns (Patterns 17–20 in Table 2) will be created from it. A DF pattern is represented as a 6-tuple. For example, Pattern 17 says that (1) this is a DF pattern; (2) the relation type is *dobj*; (3) the frame name of the head is EF; (4) the frame name of the dependent is *Weapon*; (5) the head is not negated; and (6) we don't care about the sentiment of the head. Pattern 18 is the same as Pattern 17, except that it takes into account the sentiment value of the verb. Patterns 19 and 20 replaces the frame name of the dependent with the topic name, which is *guns*. The negation and sentiment values are computed in the same way as those in the SFO patterns.

Frame-Element-Topic (FET) patterns. We create one FET pattern for every (v,fe) pair in a sentence where v is a verb *and* a frame target, and fe is a topic *and* a frame element of v's frame.[5] In sentence (1), *people* is a topic and it is assigned the role *Experiencer*, so two FET patterns (Patterns 21 and 22) are created. Also, since *guns* is a topic and it is assigned the role *Content*, two additional FET patterns (Patterns 23 and 24) are created. The negation and sentiment values are computed in the same way as those in the SFO patterns.

4.2 Step 2: Classification

In this step, we will use the patterns learned in Step 1 in combination with the baseline systems to classify a test post. A simple way to combine the learned patterns with the baseline systems would be to augment the feature set they employ with the learned patterns. One potential weakness of this method is that the impact of these patterns could be undermined by the fact that they are significantly outnumbered by the baseline features, particularly the n-gram features.

For this reason, we decided to train another stance classifier, which we will refer to as the semantics-based classifier, c_s. Like the baseline stance classifier c_b, (1) c_s is trained using SVM^{light}, (2) each training instance for c_s corresponds to a training post, and (3) its class label is the stance the post expresses. Unlike c_b, however, the features employed by c_s are created from the learned patterns. Specifically, from each pattern we create one binary feature whose value is 1 if and only if the corresponding pattern is applicable to the training post under consideration.

A natural question, then, is: how can we combine the decisions made by c_b and c_s? To answer this question, we applied both classifiers to the de-

[5]Note that since fe is a frame element of v's frame, it is assigned a semantic role.

System	ABO	GAY	OBA	MAR
c_b	60.3	63.2	59.5	67.1
c_s	56.1	58.7	56.0	65.2

Table 3: Development set accuracies.

System	ABO	GAY	OBA	MAR
c_b	22.9	18.5	24.1	9.6
c_s	17.6	14.3	19.4	7.2

Table 4: Percentage of posts predicted correctly by one but not both classifiers on the development set.

velopment set for each domain and obtained the results in Table 3. As we can see, c_s performs significantly worse than c_b for all domains.[6]

At first glance, we should just abandon c_s because of its consistently poorer performance. However, since the two classifiers are trained on disjoint feature sets (one is lexico-syntactic and the other semantic), we hypothesize that the mistakes they made on the development set could be *complementary*. To confirm this hypothesis, we compute the percentage of posts in the development set that are correctly classified by one but not the other. Results of this experiment are shown in Table 4. As we can see, these results are largely consistent with our hypothesis. For instance, for ABO, 22.9% of the posts are classified correctly only by c_b but not c_s, whereas 17.6% of them are classified correctly only by c_s but not c_b.

Given these results, we hypothesize that performance could be improved by combining the predictions made by c_b and c_s. Since c_b consistently outperforms c_s on all datasets, we use c_s to make a prediction if and only if (1) c_b cannot predict confidently and (2) c_s can predict confidently. This preference for c_b is encoded in the following rule-based strategy for classifying a test post p, where the rules are applied in the order in which they are listed.

Rule 1: if c_b can classify p confidently, then use c_b's prediction.

Rule 2: if c_s can classify p confidently, use c_s's prediction.

Rule 3: use c_b's prediction.

The next question is: how do we define *confidence*? Since c_b and c_s are SVM-based classifiers, the data points that are closer to the hyperplane are those whose labels the SVM is less confident about. Hence, we define confidence for classifier c_i by the interval $[conf_l^i, conf_u^i]$, where $conf_l^i < 0$ and $conf_u^i > 0$ are signed distances from the hyperplane defining c_i. Specifically, we say that a point p is confidently classified by c_i if and only if p lies outside the interval defined by $conf_l^i$ and $conf_u^i$. Since we have two classifiers, c_b and c_s, we need to define two intervals (i.e., four numbers). Rather than defining these four numbers by hand, we tune them jointly so that the accuracy of our combination strategy on the development set is maximized.[7]

There is a caveat, however. Recall that when applying this extension, we need to compute the signed distances of every post p from c_b and c_s to determine which classifier will be used to classify p. The question, then, is: when applying this extension to the second baseline (the Anand et al. baseline extended with ACs) where all the posts written by the same author for the same domain should have the same stance, how should their signed distances be computed? We adopt a simple solution: we take the average of the signed distances of all such posts from the corresponding hyperplane and set the signed distance of each such post to the average value.

5 Exploiting Same-Stance Posts

To classify a debate post p in the test set, we have so far exploited only the information extracted from p itself. However, it is conceivable that we can improve the classification of p by exploiting the information extracted from other test posts that have the same stance as p. This is the goal of our second extension.

To see why doing so can improve the classification of p, we make a simple observation: some posts are easier to classify than the others. Typically, posts containing expressions that are strong indicators of the stance label are easier to classify than those that do not. As an example, consider the following posts:

Post 2: *I don't think abortion should be illegal.*

Post 3: *What will you do if a woman's life is in danger while she's pregnant? Do you still want to sacrifice her life simply because the fetus is alive?*

It should be fairly easy for a human to see that the authors of both posts support abortion. However, Post 2 is arguably easier to classify than

[6]All significance tests are paired t-tests, with $p < 0.05$.

[7]For parameter tuning, for each of the four numbers we tried the values from -0.5 to $+0.5$ with a step value of 0.001.

Post 3: Post 2 has an easy-to-determine stance, whereas Post 3 has a couple of rhetorical questions that may be difficult for a machine to understand. Hence, we might be able to improve the classification of Post 3 by exploiting information from other posts that have the same stance as itself (which in this case would be Post 2).

In practice, however, we are not given the information of which posts have the same stance. In the two subsections below, we discuss two simple methods of determining whether two posts are *likely* to have the same stance.

5.1 Using Same-Author Information

The first method, which we will refer to as M_1, is fairly straightforward: we posit that two posts are likely to have the same stance if they are written by the same author. Given a test post p to be classified, we can use this method to identify a subset of p's same-stance posts. For convenience, we denote this set as SameStancePosts(p). The question, then, is: how can we exploit information in SameStancePosts(p) to improve the classification of p? One way would be to *combine* the content of the posts in SameStancePosts(p) with that of p (i.e., by taking the union of all the binary-valued feature vectors), and use the class value of the combined post as the class value of p. However, rather than simply combining all the posts to form one big post, we generalize this idea by (1) generating all possible combinations of posts in SameStancePosts(p); (2) for each such combination, combine it with p; (3) classify each combination obtained in (2) using the SVM classifier; (4) sum the confidence values of all the combinations; and (5) use the signed value as the class value of p. Note that if SameStancePosts(p) contains n posts, the number of possible combinations is $\sum_{i=0}^{n} \binom{n}{i}$. For efficiency reasons, we allow each combination to contain at most 10 posts.

At first glance, it seems that the combination method described in the previous paragraph is an alternative implementation of ACs. (Recall that ACs are inter-post constraints that ensure that two posts written by the same author for the same domain should receive the same label.) Nevertheless, there are two major differences between our combination method and ACs. First, in ACs, the same-author posts can only interact via the confidence values assigned to them. On the other hand, in our proposal, the same-author posts interact via feature sharing. In other words, in ACs, the same-author posts interact *after* they are classified by the stance classifier, whereas in our proposal, the interaction occurs *before* the posts are classified. Second, in ACs, all the same-author posts receive the same stance label. On the other hand, this is not necessarily the case in our proposal, because two same-author posts can be classified using different combinations. In other words, ACs and our combination method are not the same. In fact, they can be used in conjunction with each other.

Feature	Definition
SameDebate	whether authors posted in same debate
SameThread	whether authors posted in same thread
Replied	whether one author replied to the other

Table 5: Interaction features for the author-agreement classifier.

5.2 Finding Similar-Minded Authors

Using M_1 to identify same-stance posts has a potential weakness. If an author has composed a small number of posts, then the number of combinations that can be generated will be small. In the extreme case, if an author has composed just one post p, then no combinations will be generated using M_1.

To enable p to benefit from our idea of exploiting same-stance posts, we propose another method to identify same-stance posts, M_2, which is a generalization of M_1. In M_2, we posit that two posts are likely to have the same stance if they are written by the same author or by *similar-minded* authors. Given test post p, we can compute SameStancePosts(p) using the definition of M_2, and apply the same 5-step combination method described in the previous subsection to SameStancePosts(p) to classify p.

The remaining question is: given an author, a, in the test set, how do we compute his set of similar-minded authors, $A_{similar}$? To do this, we train a binary author-agreement classifier on the training set to generate $A_{similar}$ for a. Specifically, each training instance corresponds to a pair of authors in the training set having one of two class labels, *agree* (i.e., authors have the same stance) and *disagree* (i.e., authors have opposing stances). We represent each instance with two types of features. Features of the first type are obtained by taking the *difference* of the feature vectors corresponding to the two authors under consideration, where the feature vector of an author is obtained by taking the union of the feature vectors corresponding to all of the posts written by her. Taking the difference would allow the learner to focus on those features whose values differ in the feature vectors. For the second type of features, we use *author interaction* information encoded as three binary features (see Table 5 for their definitions), which capture how authors interact with each other in a debate thread. After training the classifier, we apply it to classify the author-pairs in the test set. Then, for each author a, we compute her k-nearest authors based on the magnitude of their agreement, where k is tuned to maximize accuracy on the development data.[8] Finally, we take $A_{similar}$ to be the set of k-nearest authors.

6 Evaluation

6.1 Experimental Setup

Results are expressed in terms of *accuracy* obtained via 5-fold cross validation, where accuracy is the percentage of test instances correctly classified. Since all experiments require the use of development data for parameter tuning, we use three folds for model training, one fold for development, and one fold for testing in each fold experiment.

6.2 Results

Results are shown in Table 6. Row 1 shows the results of the Anand et al. (2011) baseline on the four datasets, obtained by training a stance classifier using the SVM^{light} package.[9] Row 2 shows the results of the second baseline, Anand et al.'s system enhanced with ACs. As we can see, incorporating ACs into Anand et al.'s system improves its performance significantly on all datasets and yields a system that achieves an average improvement of 4.6 accuracy points.

Next, we incorporate our first extension, pattern induction, into the better of the two baselines (i.e., the second baseline). Results of combining c_b and c_s to classify the test posts (together with the ACs) are shown in row 3 of Table 6. As we can see, incorporating pattern induction into the second baseline significantly improves its performance on all four datasets and yields a system that achieves an average improvement of 2.48 accuracy points.

Before incorporating our second extension, let us recall our earlier hypothesis that combining c_b and c_s using our method would be better than training just one classifier that combines the features used by c_b and c_s. The reason behind our hypothesis was that simply combining the feature sets would undermine the impact of pattern-based features because they would be significantly outnumbered by the features in c_b. To confirm this hypothesis, we showed in row 4 of Table 6 the results of this experiment, where we trained one classifier on all the features used by c_b and c_s. As we can see, this classifier (referred to as c_{bs} in the table) together with the ACs performs significantly worse than the c_b+c_s+AC system (row 3) on all datasets. In fact, the c_b+AC system (row 2) outperforms the c_{bs}+AC system on OBA, but they are statistically indistinguishable on the remaining datasets. These results suggest that combining the pattern-based features with the baseline features into one feature set renders the former ineffective.

System	ABO	GAY	OBA	MAR
c_b	61.4	62.6	58.1	66.9
c_b+AC	72.0	64.9	62.7	67.8
c_b+c_s+AC	73.2	68.0	64.2	71.9
c_{bs}+AC	71.8	65.0	60.2	67.9
c_b+c_s+M_1+AC	74.8	69.1	69.7	73.2
c_b+c_s+M_2+AC	**75.9**	**70.6**	**71.2**	**75.3**

Table 6: 5-fold cross-validation accuracies.

Finally, we incorporate our second extension, the one that involves generating combinations of test posts written by the same author (M_1) and by both the same author and similar-minded authors (M_2). Results of these experiments are shown in rows 5–6 of Table 6. The M_1-based system significantly outperforms c_b+c_s+AC on all four domains, yielding an average improvement of 2.4 accuracy points. The M_2-based system further beats the M_1-based system by 1.5 accuracy points on average, and their performance difference is significant on all but the ABO domain.

Overall, our two extensions yield a stance classification system that significantly outperforms the better baseline on all four datasets, with an average improvement of 6.4 accuracy points.

Given the better performance of the combination-based systems, a natural question is: can we further improve performance by applying our combination methods to generate artificial posts and use them as additional training instances? To answer this question, we apply both M_1 and M_2 to generate additional

[8]We tested values of k from 1 to 7.

[9]For all SVM experiments, the regularization parameter C is tuned using development data, but the remaining learning parameters are set to their default values.

training instances, using a random selection of same-stance authors in place of M_2's k-nearest neighbor method. However, neither method yields an improvement in performance over the method on which it is based. We speculate that since all the posts in the training combinations are already present in the training set as individual posts, they are more likely to be farther away from the hyperplane than the individual posts, meaning that they are less likely to be support vectors. This in turn implies that they are less likely to affect classification performance.

6.3 Error Analysis

To gain additional insights into our approach, we performed a qualitative analysis of the errors produced by our best-performing system below.

Failure to accumulate decisions from several clues. Authors often express their stance using a group of sentences where the latter sentence(s) indicate the actual stance and the initial sentence(s) may give a false impression about the author's stance. Consider Post 1 (see Section 1) and Post 4.

Post 4: *I agree abortion creates stress and pain. I agree it kills a potential life. That does not mean it is right to ban abortion.*

In Post 1, the author is anti-abortion, whereas in Post 4, the author is pro-abortion. However, the first sentence in Post 1 gives a misleading clue about the author's stance, and so do the first two sentences in Post 4. Since all the systems discussed in the paper operate on one sentence at a time, they are all prone to such errors. One way to address this problem could be to determine how adjacent sentences are related to each other via the use of discourse relations.

Presence of materials irrelevant to stance. Because of the informal style of writing, we often find long posts with one or two sentences indicating the actual stance of the author. The rest of such posts often include descriptions of an author's personal experience, comments or questions directed to other authors etc. Such long posts are frequently misclassified for all four domains. Consider the following example.

Post 5: *Marijuana should at least be decriminalized. Driving stoned, however, is something totally different and should definitely be a crime. Also, weed can't kill you, unlike cigarettes and alcohol. In my opinion cigarettes should definitely be illegal, but they're so ingrained into our culture that I doubt that is going to happen any time soon.*

In this post, the author supports the legalization of marijuana. However, the only useful hints about her stance are "marijuana should at least be decriminalized" and "weed can't kill you". The rest of the post is not helpful for stance classification.

Convoluted posts appearing later in long post sequences. As a post sequence gets longer, authors tend to focus on specific aspects of a debate and consequently, it becomes more difficult to classify their stances, even with the context-based features (features taken from the immediately preceding post) proposed by Anand et al. Consider the following post sequence, where only the first post (P1) and the nth post (Pn) are shown due to space limitations.

[P1: Anti-Obama] Obama is a pro-abortionist. Killing babies is wrong so stop doing it. The new health reform bill is not good. There are some good things but more worse than good. You could have just passed some laws instead of making a whole bill.

...

[Pn: Pro-Obama] Killing fetuses isn't wrong. Besides, we could use those fetuses for stem cell research.

As we can see, the author of P1 does not support Obama because of his pro-abortion views. In Pn, a pro-Obama author explains why she thinks abortion is not wrong. However, without the context from P1 that Obama is pro-abortion, it is not easy for a machine to classify Pn correctly. This problem is more serious in ABO and GAY than in the other domains as the average length of a post sequence in these two domains is larger.

7 Conclusions

We examined the under-studied task of stance classification of ideological debates. Employing our two extensions yields a system that outperforms an improved version of Anand et al.'s approach by 2.6–7.0 accuracy points. In particular, while existing approaches to debate stance classification have primarily employed lexico-syntactic features, to our knowledge this is the first attempt to employ FrameNet for this task to induce features that aim to capture the meaning and provide semantic generalizations of a sentence. In addition, our method for identifying and exploiting same-stance posts during the inference procedure provides further gains when used on top of our FrameNet extension.

References

Rakesh Agrawal, Sridhar Rajagopalan, Ramakrishnan Srikant, and Yirong Xu. 2003. Mining newsgroups using networks arising from social behavior. In *Proceedings of the 12th international conference on World Wide Web*, WWW '03, pages 529–535.

Pranav Anand, Marilyn Walker, Rob Abbott, Jean E. Fox Tree, Robeson Bowmani, and Michael Minor. 2011. Cats rule and dogs drool!: Classifying stance in online debate. In *Proceedings of the 2nd Workshop on Computational Approaches to Subjectivity and Sentiment Analysis (WASSA 2011)*, pages 1–9.

Alexandra Balahur, Zornitsa Kozareva, and Andrés Montoyo. 2009. Determining the polarity and source of opinions expressed in political debates. In *Proceedings of the 10th International Conference on Computational Linguistics and Intelligent Text Processing*, CICLing '09, pages 468–480.

Mohit Bansal, Claire Cardie, and Lillian Lee. 2008. The power of negative thinking: Exploiting label disagreement in the min-cut classification framework. In *Proceedings of the 22nd International Conference on Computational Linguistics: Companion volume: Posters*, pages 15–18.

Or Biran and Owen Rambow. 2011. Identifying justifications in written dialogs. In *Proceedings of the 2011 IEEE Fifth International Conference on Semantic Computing*, ICSC '11, pages 162–168.

Clinton Burfoot, Steven Bird, and Timothy Baldwin. 2011. Collective classification of congressional floor-debate transcripts. In *Proceedings of the 49th Annual Meeting of the Association for Computational Linguistics: Human Language Technologies*, pages 1506–1515.

Dipanjan Das, Nathan Schneider, Desai Chen, and Noah A. Smith. 2010. Probabilistic frame-semantic parsing. In *Human Language Technologies: The 2010 Annual Conference of the North American Chapter of the Association for Computational Linguistics*, pages 948–956.

Marie-Catherine de Marneffe and Christopher D. Manning. 2008. The Stanford typed dependencies representation. In *Proceedings of the COLING Workshop on Cross-Framework and Cross-Domain Parser Evaluation*, CrossParser '08, pages 1–8.

Kazi Saidul Hasan and Vincent Ng. 2012. Predicting stance in ideological debate with rich linguistic knowledge. In *Proceedings of the 24th International Conference on Computational Linguistics: Posters*, pages 451–460.

Thorsten Joachims. 1999. Making large-scale SVM learning practical. In Bernhard Scholkopf and Alexander Smola, editors, *Advances in Kernel Methods - Support Vector Learning*, pages 44–56. MIT Press.

Yue Lu, Hongning Wang, ChengXiang Zhai, and Dan Roth. 2012. Unsupervised discovery of opposing opinion networks from forum discussions. In *Proceedings of the 21st ACM International Conference on Information and Knowledge Management*, CIKM '12, pages 1642–1646.

Akiko Murakami and Rudy Raymond. 2010. Support or oppose? Classifying positions in online debates from reply activities and opinion expressions. In *Proceedings of the 23rd International Conference on Computational Linguistics: Posters*, pages 869–875.

Swapna Somasundaran and Janyce Wiebe. 2010. Recognizing stances in ideological on-line debates. In *Proceedings of the NAACL HLT 2010 Workshop on Computational Approaches to Analysis and Generation of Emotion in Text*, CAAGET '10, pages 116–124.

Matt Thomas, Bo Pang, and Lillian Lee. 2006. Get out the vote: Determining support or opposition from Congressional floor-debate transcripts. In *Proceedings of the 2006 Conference on Empirical Methods in Natural Language Processing*, pages 327–335.

Marilyn Walker, Pranav Anand, Rob Abbott, and Ricky Grant. 2012. Stance classification using dialogic properties of persuasion. In *Proceedings of the 2012 Conference of the North American Chapter of the Association for Computational Linguistics: Human Language Technologies*, pages 592–596.

Yi-Chia Wang and Carolyn P. Rosé. 2010. Making conversational structure explicit: Identification of initiation-response pairs within online discussions. In *Human Language Technologies: The 2010 Annual Conference of the North American Chapter of the Association for Computational Linguistics*, pages 673–676.

Ainur Yessenalina, Yisong Yue, and Claire Cardie. 2010. Multi-level structured models for document-level sentiment classification. In *Proceedings of the 2010 Conference on Empirical Methods in Natural Language Processing*, pages 1046–1056.

Philosophers are Mortal: Inferring the Truth of Unseen Facts

Gabor Angeli
Stanford University
Stanford, CA 94305
angeli@stanford.edu

Christopher D. Manning
Stanford University
Stanford, CA 94305
manning@stanford.edu

Abstract

Large databases of facts are prevalent in many applications. Such databases are accurate, but as they broaden their scope they become increasingly incomplete. In contrast to extending such a database, we present a system to query whether it contains an arbitrary fact. This work can be thought of as re-casting open domain information extraction: rather than growing a database of known facts, we smooth this data into a database in which *any* possible fact has membership with some confidence. We evaluate our system predicting held out facts, achieving 74.2% accuracy and outperforming multiple baselines. We also evaluate the system as a common-sense filter for the ReVerb Open IE system, and as a method for answer validation in a Question Answering task.

1 Introduction

Databases of facts, such as Freebase (Bollacker et al., 2008) or Open Information Extraction (Open IE) extractions, are useful for a range of NLP applications from semantic parsing to information extraction. However, as the domain of a database grows, it becomes increasingly impractical to collect completely, and increasingly unlikely that all the elements intended for the database are explicitly mentioned in the source corpus. In particular, common-sense facts are rarely explicitly mentioned, despite their abundance. It would be useful to infer the truth of such unseen facts rather than assuming them to be implicitly false.

A growing body of work has focused on automatically extending large databases with a finite set of additional facts. In contrast, we propose a system to generate the (possibly infinite) completion of such a database, with a degree of confidence for each unseen fact. This task can be cast as querying whether an arbitrary element is a member of the database, with an informative degree of confidence. Since often the facts in these databases are devoid of context, we refine our notion of *truth* to reflect whether we would assume a fact to be true without evidence to the contrary. In this vein, we can further refine our task as determining whether an arbitrary fact is *plausible* – true in the absence contradictory evidence.

In addition to general applications of such large databases, our approach can further be integrated into systems which can make use of probabilistic membership. For example, certain machine translation errors could be fixed by determining that the target translation expresses an implausible fact. Similarly, the system can be used as a soft feature for semantic compatibility in coreference; e.g., the types of phenomena expressed in Hobbs' selectional constraints (Hobbs, 1978). Lastly, it is useful as a common-sense filter; we evaluate the system in this role by filtering implausible facts from Open IE extractions, and filtering incorrect responses for a question answering system.

Our approach generalizes word similarity metrics to a notion of *fact similarity*, and judges the membership of an unseen fact based on the aggregate similarity between it and existing members of the database. For instance, if we have not seen the fact that philosophers are mortal[1] but we know that Greeks are mortal, and that philosophers and Greeks are similar, we would like to infer that the fact is nonetheless plausible.

We implement our approach on both a large open-domain database of facts extracted from the Open IE system ReVerb (Fader et al., 2011), and ConceptNet (Liu and Singh, 2004), a hand curated database of common sense facts.

[1] This is an unseen fact in http://openie.cs.washington.edu.

2 Related Work

Many NLP applications make use of a knowledge base of facts. These include semantic parsing (Zelle and Mooney, 1996; Zettlemoyer and Collins, 2005; Kate et al., 2005; Zettlemoyer and Collins, 2007) question answering (Voorhees, 2001), information extraction (Hoffmann et al., 2011; Surdeanu et al., 2012), and recognizing textual entailment (Schoenmackers et al., 2010; Berant et al., 2011).

A large body of work has been devoted to creating such knowledge bases. In particular, Open IE systems such as TextRunner (Yates et al., 2007), ReVerb (Fader et al., 2011), Ollie (Mausam et al., 2012), and NELL (Carlson et al., 2010) have tackled the task of compiling an open-domain knowledge base. Similarly, the MIT Media Lab's ConceptNet project (Liu and Singh, 2004) has been working on creating a large database of common sense facts.

There have been a number of systems aimed at automatically extending these databases. That is, given an existing database, they propose new relations to be added. Snow et al. (2006) present an approach to enriching the WordNet taxonomy; Tandon et al. (2011) extend ConceptNet with new facts; Soderland et al. (2010) use ReVerb extractions to enrich a domain-specific ontology. We differ from these approaches in that we aim to provide an exhaustive completion of the database; we would like to respond to a query with either membership or lack of membership, rather than extending the set of elements which are members.

Yao et al. (2012) and Riedel et al. (2013) present a similar task of predicting novel relations between Freebase entities by appealing to a large collection of Open IE extractions. Our work focuses on arguments which are not necessarily named entities, at the expense of leveraging less entity-specific information.

Work in classical artificial intelligence has tackled the related task of loosening the closed world assumption and monotonicity of logical reasoning, allowing for modeling of unseen propositions. Reiter (1980) presents an approach to leveraging default propositions in the absence of contradictory evidence; McCarthy (1980) defines a means of overriding the truth of a proposition in abnormal cases. Perhaps most similar to this work is Pearl (1989), who proposes approaching non-monotonicity in a probabilistic framework, and in particular presents a framework for making inferences which are not strictly entailed but can be reasonably assumed. Unlike these works, our approach places a greater emphasis on working with large corpora of open-domain predicates.

3 Approach

At a high level, we are provided with a large database of facts which we believe to be true, and a query fact not in the database. The task is to output a judgment on whether the fact is plausible (true unless we have reason to believe otherwise), with an associated confidence. Although our approach is robust to unary relations, we evaluate only against binary relations.

We decompose this decision into three parts, as illustrated in Figure 1: (i) we find candidate facts that are similar to our query, (ii) we define a notion of similarity between these facts and our query, and (iii) we define a method for aggregating a collection of these similarity values into a single judgment. The first of these parts can be viewed as an information retrieval component. The second part can be viewed as an extension of word similarity to fact similarity. The third part is cast as a classification task, where the input is a set of similar facts, and the decision is the confidence of the query being plausible.

We define a fact as a triple of two arguments and a relation. We denote a fact in our database as $f = (a_1, r, a_2)$. A fact which we are querying is denoted by f_q – as our focus is on unseen facts, this query is generally not in the database.

3.1 Finding Candidate Facts

Naïvely, when determining the correctness of a query fact, it would be optimal to compare it to the entire database of known facts. However, this approach poses significant problems:

1. The computational cost becomes unreasonable with a large database, and only a small portion of the database is likely to be relevant.
2. The more candidates we consider the more opportunities we create for false positives in finding similar facts. For a sufficiently large database, even a small false positive rate could hurt performance.

To address these two problems, we consider only facts which match the query fact in two of their three terms. Formally, we define

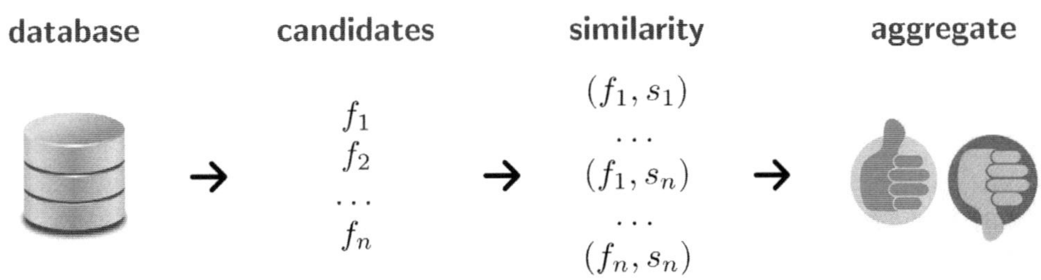

Figure 1: An overview of our approach. A large database of facts is queried for candidate entries that may be similar to the query fact (see Section 3.1); the similarity of each of these facts to the query fact is computed using a number of word similarity metrics (see Section 3.2); finally, these similarity judgments are aggregated into a single judgment per metric, and then a single overall judgment (see Section 3.3).

functions: $\text{cand}(f_q, f_i; a_1)$, $\text{cand}(f_q, f_i; r)$, and $\text{cand}(f_q, f_i; a_2)$ for whether the query f_q matches a fact in our database f_i on all but one of the arguments (or relation). For efficiency, the total number of candidates returned by each of these three functions was limited to 100, creating up to 300 similar facts overall.

The simplest implementation of this cand function would be exact match ($\text{cand}_{\text{exact}}$); however, this is liable to return few results. As an example, suppose our query is (*private land, be sold to, government*). We would like to consider a fact in our database (***his** land, be sold to, United States*) as similar except for second argument (*government* versus *United States*), despite the first argument not matching exactly. To account for this, we define a class of functions which match the head word of the two phrases, and as many of the following stricter criteria as possible while maintaining at least 40 candidate facts:[2]

$\text{cand}_{\text{head}}$ Match the head word of the two phrases only. Head words were extracted using the Stanford Parser (Klein and Manning, 2003), treating each argument and relation as a sentence.

cand_{vn} Match all verbs and nouns in the two phrases; This prunes candidates such as (*land **of our ancestors**, be sold to, Prussia*). Tagging was done with the Stanford Tagger (Toutanova et al., 2003).

$\text{cand}_{\text{open}}$ Match the open-class words between the two phrases. More precisely, it matches every word which is not a pronoun, determiner, preposition, or form of the verb *be*. This prunes candidates such as (***worthless** land, be sold to, gullible investors*).

We proceed to describe our notion of similarity between facts, which will be applied to the set of candidate similar facts retrieved.

3.2 Similarity Between Facts

Determining the similarity between two facts is in general difficult. For sufficiently complicated facts, it can be has hard as recognizing textual entailment (RTE); for instance, determining that *every philosopher is mortal* and *Socrates is mortal* are similar requires fairly sophisticated inference. We choose a simple approach, in order to avoid fitting to a particular corpus or weakening our ability to generalize to arbitrary phrases.

Our approach casts fact similarity in terms of assessing word similarity. The candidate facts from Section 3.1 differ from the query fact by a single phrase; we define the similarity between the candidate and query fact to be the similarity between the differing term.

The word similarity metrics are summarized in Table 1. They fall into two broad classes: information-theoretic thesaurus based metrics, and distributional similarity metrics.

Thesaurus Based Metrics We adopt many of the thesaurus based similarity metrics described in Budanitsky and Hirst (2006). For each metric, we use the WordNet ontology (Miller, 1995) combined with n-gram counts retrieved from Google n-grams (Brants and Franz, 2006). Every word form was assigned a minimum count of 1; 2265 entries had no counts and were assigned this minimum (1.5%). 167 of these were longer than 5 words; the remaining did not appear in the corpus.

Since WordNet is a relatively sparse resource,

[2]This threshold is chosen in conjunction with the aggregation threshold in Section 3.3, to allow for at least two facts in the 95% threshold.

if a query phrase is not found a number of simple variants are also tried. These are, in order of preference: a lemmatized version of the phrase, the head word of the phrase, and the head lemma of the phrase. If none of these are found, then the named entities in the sentence were replaced with their types. If that fails as well, acronyms[3] were expanded. For words with multiple sense, the maximum similarity for any pair of word senses was used.

Distributional Similarity Based Metrics We define a number of similarity metrics on the 50 dimensional word vectors of Huang et al. (2012). These cover a vocabulary of 100,231 words; a special vector is defined for unknown words.

Compound phrases are queried by treating the phrase as a bag of words and averaging the word vectors of each word in the phrase, pruning out unknown words. If the phrase contains no known words, the same relaxation steps are tried as the thesaurus based metrics.

3.3 Aggregating Similarity

At this stage, we are presented with a set of candidate facts which may be similar to our query, and a set of similarity judgments for each of these candidate facts. Intuitively, we would like to mark a fact as plausible if it has enough sufficiently similar candidate facts based on a large number of metrics. This is a two-dimensional aggregation task: (i) we aggregate judgments for a single similarity metric, and (ii) we aggregate these aggregate judgments across similarity metrics. We accomplish the first half with a thresholded average similarity; the second half we accomplish by using the aggregate similarity judgments as features for a logistic regression model.

Thresholded Average Similarity Given a set of similarity values, we average the top 5% of the values and use this as the aggregate similarity judgment. This approach incorporates the benefit of two simpler aggregation techniques: averaging and taking the maximum similarity.

Averaging similarity values has the advantage of robustness – given a set of candidate facts, we would like as many of those facts to be as similar to the query as possible. To illustrate, we should be more certain that (*philosophers*, *are*, *mortal*)

	Name	Formula
Thesaurus Based	Path	$-\log \text{len}(w_1, \text{lcs}, w_2)$
	Resnik	$-\log P(\text{lcs})$
	Lin	$\frac{\log(P(\text{lcs})^2)}{\log(P(w_1) \cdot P(w_2))}$
	Jiang-Conrath	$\log\left(\frac{P(\text{lcs})^2}{P(w_1) \cdot P(w_2)}\right)^{-1}$
	Wu-Palmer	$\frac{2 \cdot \text{depth}(\text{lcs})}{2 \cdot \text{depth}(\text{lcs}) + \text{len}(w_1, \text{lcs}, w_2)}$
Distributional	Cosine	$\frac{w_1 \cdot w_2}{\|w_1\|\|w_2\|}$
	Angle	$\arccos\left(\frac{w_1 \cdot w_2}{\|w_1\|\|w_2\|}\right)$
	Jensen-Shannon	$\frac{(KL(p_1\|p_2) + KL(p_2\|p_1))}{2}$
	Hellinger	$\frac{1}{\sqrt{2}}\|\sqrt{p_1} - \sqrt{p_2}\|$
	Jaccard	$\frac{\|\min(w_1, w_2)\|_1}{\|\max(w_1, w_2)\|_1}$
	Dice	$\frac{\|\min(w_1, w_2)\|_1}{\frac{1}{2}\|w_1 + w_2\|_1}$

Table 1: A summary of similarity metrics used to calculate fact similarity. For the thesaurus based metrics, the two synsets being compared are denoted by w_1 and w_2; the lowest common subsumer is denoted as lcs. For distributional similarity metrics, the two word vectors are denoted by w_1 and w_2. For metrics which require a probability distribution, we pass the vectors through a sigmoid to obtain $p_i = \frac{1}{1+e^{-w_i}}$.

if we know both that (*Greeks*, *are*, *mortal*) and (*men*, *are*, *mortal*). However, since the number of similar facts is likely to be small relative the number of candidate facts considered, this approach has the risk of losing the signal in the noise of uninformative candidates. Taking the maximum similarity judgment alleviates this concern, but constrains the use of only one element in our aggregate judgment.

If fewer than 20 candidates are returned, our combination approach reduces to taking the maximum similarity value. Note also that the 40 fact threshold in the candidate selection phase is chosen to provide at least two similarity values to be averaged together. The threshold was chosen empirically, although varying it does not have a significant effect on performance.

Aggregate Similarity Values At this point, we have a number of distinct notions of similarity: for each metric, for each differing term, we have a judgment for whether the query fact is similar to the list of candidates. We combine these using

[3] 6053 acronyms and initialisms were scraped from `http://en.wikipedia.org/wiki/List_of_acronyms_and_initialisms`

a simple logistic regression model, treating each judgment over different metrics and terms as a feature with weight given by the judgment. For example, cosine similarity may judge candidate facts differing on their first argument to have a similarity of 0.2. As a result, a feature would be created with weight 0.2 for the pair (cosine, argument 1). In addition, features are created which are agnostic to which term differs (e.g., the cosine similarity on whichever term differs), bringing the total feature count to 44 for 11 similarity metrics.

Lastly, we define 3 auxiliary feature classes:

- **Argument Similarity**: We define a feature for the similarity between the two arguments in the query fact. Similarity metrics (particularly distributional similarity metrics) often capture a notion more akin to relatedness than similarity (Budanitsky and Hirst, 2006); the subject and object of a relation are, in many cases, related in this sense.
- **Bias**: A single bias feature is included to account for similarity metrics which do not center on zero.
- **No Support Bias**: A feature is included for examples which have no candidate facts in the knowledge base.

4 Data

Our approach is implemented using two datasets. The first, described in Section 4.1, is built using facts retrieved from running the University of Washington's ReVerb system run over web text. To showcase the system within a cleaner environment, we also build a knowledge base from the MIT Media Lab's ConceptNet.

4.1 ReVerb

We created a knowledge base of facts by running ReVerb over ClueWeb09 (Callan et al., 2009). Extractions rated with a confidence under 0.5 were discarded; the first billion undiscarded extractions were used in the final knowledge base. This resulted in approximately 500 million unique facts.

Some examples of facts extracted with ReVerb are given in Table 2. Note that our notion of plausibility is far more unclear than in the ConceptNet data; many facts extracted from the internet are explicitly false, and others are true only in specific contexts, or are otherwise underspecified.

Argument 1	Relation	Argument 2
cat	Desires	tuna fish
air	CapableOf	move through tiny hole
sneeze	HasA	allergy
person who	IsA	not wage-slaves get more sleep

Table 3: Example ConceptNet extractions. The top rows correspond to characteristic correct extractions; the bottom rows characterize the types of noise in the data.

4.2 ConceptNet

We also created a dataset using a subset of ConceptNet. ConceptNet is a hand-curated common sense database, taking information from multiple sources (including ReVerb) and consolidating them in a consistent format. We focus on the manually created portion of the database, extracted from sources such as the Open Mind Common Sense[4] (Singh et al., 2002).

The knowledge base consists of 597,775 facts, each expressing one of 34 relations. Examples of facts in the ConceptNet database are given in Table 3. While the arguments are generally cleaner than the ReVerb corpus, there are nonetheless instances of fairly complex facts.

4.3 Training Data

Our training data consists of a set of tuples, each consisting of a fact f and a database d which does not contain f. We create artificial negative training instances in order to leverage the standard classification framework. We would like negative examples which are likely to be implausible, but which are close enough to known facts that we can learn a reasonable boundary for discriminating between the two. To this end, we sample negative instances by modifying a single argument (or the relation) of a corresponding positive training instance. In more detail: we take a positive training instance (a_1, r, a_2) and a fact from our database (a'_1, r', a'_2), and compute the cosine similarity $\text{sim}_{\cos}(a_1, a'_1)$, $\text{sim}_{\cos}(r, r')$, and $\text{sim}_{\cos}(a_2, a'_2)$. Our negative instance will be one of (a'_1, r, a_2), (a_1, r', a_2), or (a_1, r, a'_2) corresponding to the entry whose similarity was the largest. Negative facts which happen to be in the database are ignored.

[4] http://openmind.media.mit.edu/

Argument 1	Relation	Argument 2
officials	contacted	students
food riots	have recently taken place in	many countries
turn	left on	Front Street
animals	have not been performed to evaluate	the carcinogenic potential of adenosine

Table 2: Example ReVerb extractions. The top rows correspond to characteristic correct extractions; the bottom rows shows examples of the types of noise in the data. Note that in general, both the arguments and the predicate can be largely unconstrained text.

To simulate unseen facts, we construct training instances by predicting the plausibility of a fact held out from the database. That is, if our database consists of $d = \{f_0, f_1, \dots f_n\}$ we construct training instances $(f_i, d \setminus \{f_i\})$. Negative examples are likewise constrained to not occur in the database, as are the facts used in their construction.

5 Results

We evaluate our system with three experiments. The first, described in Section 5.2, evaluates the system's ability to discriminate plausible facts from sampled implausible facts, mirroring the training regime. The second evaluates the system as a semantic filter for ReVerb extractions, tested against human evaluations. The third uses our system for validating question answering responses.

5.1 Baselines

We define a number of baselines to compare against. Many of these are subsets of our system, to justify the inclusion of additional complexity.

Similar Fact Count This baseline judges the truth of a fact by tuning a threshold on the total number of similar facts in the database. This baseline would perform well if our negative facts were noticeably disconnected from our database.

Argument Similarity A key discriminating feature may be the similarity between a_1 and a_2 in true versus false facts. This baseline thresholds the cosine similarity between arguments, tuned on the training data to maximize classification accuracy.

Cosine Similarity At its core, our model judges the truth of a fact based on its similarity to facts in the database; we create a baseline to capture this intuition. For every candidate fact (differing in either an argument or the relation), we compute the cosine similarity between the query and the candidate, evaluated on the differing terms. This baseline outputs the maximum similarity between a query and any candidate; a threshold on this similarity is tuned on the training data to maximize classification accuracy.

System	ReVerb		ConceptNet	
	Train	Test	Train	Test
random	50.0	50.0	50.0	50.0
count	51.9	52.3	51.0	51.6
argsim	52.0	52.6	62.1	60.0
cos	71.4	70.6	71.9	70.5
system	**74.3**	**74.2**	**76.5**	**74.3**

Table 4: Classification accuracy for ReVerb and ConceptNet data. The three baselines are described above the line as described in Section 5.1; random chance would get an accuracy of 50%.

5.2 Automatic Evaluation

A natural way to evaluate our system is to use the same regime as our training, evaluating on held out facts. For both domains we train on a balanced dataset of 20,000 training and 10,000 test examples. Performance is measured in terms of classification accuracy, with a random baseline of 50%.

Table 4 summarizes our results. The similar fact count baseline performs nearly at random chance, suggesting that our sampled negative facts cannot be predicted solely on the basis of connectedness with the rest of the database. Furthermore, we outperform the cosine baseline, supporting the intuition that aggregating similarity metrics is useful.

To evaluate the informativeness of the confidence our system produces, we can allow our system to abstain from unsure judgments. Recall refers to the percentage of facts the system chooses to make a guess on; precision is the percentage of those facts which are classified correctly. From this, we can create a precision/recall curve – presented in Figure 2 for ReVerb and Figure 3 for ConceptNet. Our system achieves an area under

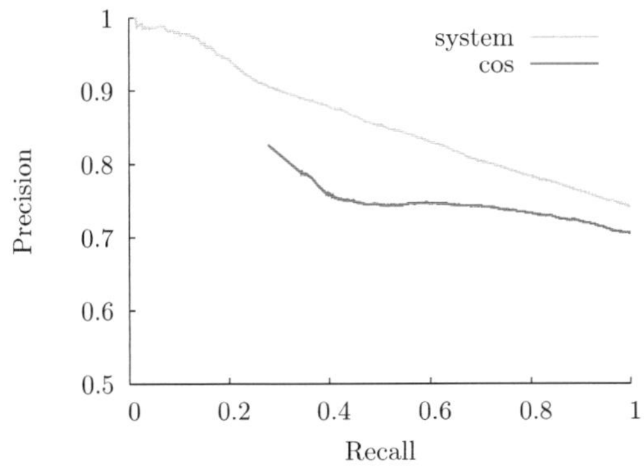

Figure 2: Accuracy of ReVerb classification, as a function of the percent of facts answered. The y axis begins at random chance (50%).

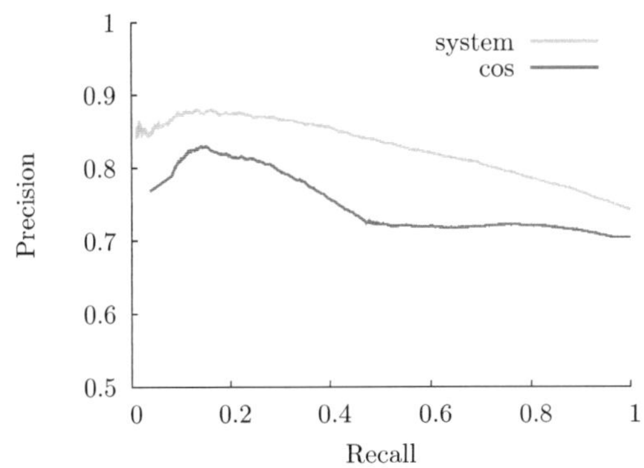

Figure 3: Accuracy of ConceptNet classification, as a function of the percent of facts answered. The y axis begins at random chance (50%).

the curve of 0.827 on ConceptNet (compared to the cosine baseline of 0.751). For ReVerb, we obtain an area of 0.860 (compared to 0.768 for the cosine baseline).[5]

5.3 ReVerb Filtering

In order to provide a grounded evaluation metric we evaluate our system as a confidence estimator for ReVerb extractions. Many ReVerb extractions are semantically implausible, or clash with common-sense intuition. We annotate a number of extractions on Mechanical Turk, and attempt to predict the extractions' feasibility.

This task is significantly more difficult than the intrinsic evaluations. Part of the difficulty stems

[5]Curves begin at the recall value given a system confidence of 1.0. For area under the curve calculations, this value is extended through to recall 0.

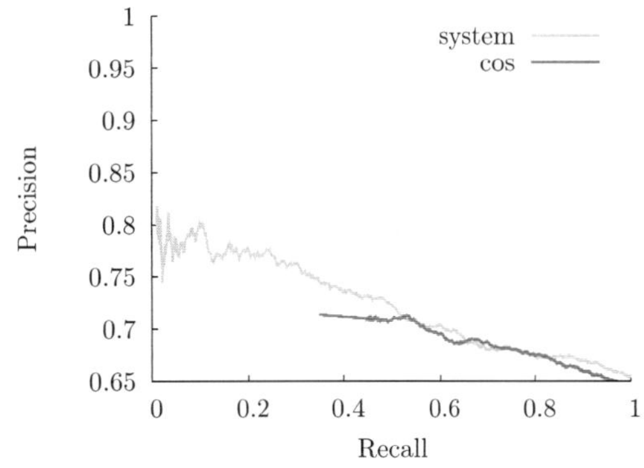

Figure 4: PR curve for ReVerb confidence estimation. The y axis of the graph is truncated at 65% – this corresponds to the majority class baseline.

from our database itself (and therefore our candidate similar facts) being unfiltered – our query facts empirically were and therefore in a sense *should* be in the database. Another part stems from these facts already having been filtered once by ReVerb's confidence estimator.

To collect training and test data, we asked workers on Amazon Mechanical Turk to rate facts as *correct*, *plausible*, or *implausible*. They were instructed that they need not research the facts, and that correct facts may be underspecified. Workers were given the following descriptions of the three possible responses:

- **Correct**: You would accept this fact if you read it in a reputable source (e.g., Wikipedia) in an appropriate context.
- **Plausible**: You would accept this fact if you read it in a storybook.
- **Implausible**: The fact is either dubious, or otherwise nonsense.

Below this, five examples were shown alongside one control (e.g., (*rock*, *float on*, *water*)). Workers who answered more than 20% of the controls incorrectly were discarded. In total, 9 workers and 117 of 1200 HITs were discarded.

Each example was shown to three separate workers; a final judgment was made by taking the majority vote between *correct* (corresponding to our notion of plausibility) and *implausible*, ignoring votes of *plausible*. In cases where all the votes were made for *plausible*, or there was a tie, the example was discarded.

The experiment was run twice on 2000 ReVerb extractions to collect training and test data. The training corpus consists of 1256 positive and 540 negative examples (1796 total; 70% positive). The test corpus consists of 1286 positive and 689 negative examples (1975 total; 65% positive)

Our system was retrained with the human evaluated training data; to account for class bias, our system's classification threshold was then tuned on the training data, optimizing for area under the precision/recall curve. Figure 4 illustrates our results, bounded below by majority choice. Our system achieves an area under the curve of 0.721; the cosine baseline has an area of 0.696.

Our system offers a viable trade-off of recall in favor of precision. For example, keeping only a third of the data can reduce the error rate by 25% – this can be appealing for large corpora where filtering is frequent anyways.

5.4 Answer Validation Exercise

The Answer Validation Exercise, organized as a track at CLEF between 2006 and 2008, focuses on filtering candidate answers from question answering systems (Peñas et al., 2007; Peñas et al., 2008; Rodrigo et al., 2009). Systems are presented with a question, and a set of answers along with their justification. The answers are either validated, rejected, or given an annotation of unknown and ignored during scoring. Since the proportion of correct answers is small (around 10%), the evaluation measures precision and recall over true answers predicted by each system.

Many answers in the task are incorrect because they violate common-sense intuition – for instance, one answer to *What is leprosy?* was *Africa clinic*. While any such specific mistake is easy to fix, our approach can be a means of handling a wide range of such mistakes elegantly.

To adapt our system to the task, we first heuristically converted the question into a query fact using the subject and object Stanford Dependency labels (de Marneffe and Manning, 2008). If either the subject or object specifies a type (e.g., *Which **party** does Bill Clinton belong to?*), the score of the fact encoding this relationship (e.g., (*Democrat*, *be*, *party*)) is averaged with the main query. Next, answers with very little n-gram overlap between the justification and either the question or answer are filtered; this filters answers which may be correct, but were not properly justified. Lastly, our system trained on Turk data (see Section 5.3), predicts an answer to be correct if it

System	**2007**			**2008**		
	P	R	F_1	P	R	F_1
all validated	11	100	19	8	100	14
filter only	16	95	27	14	100	24
median	–	–	35	–	–	20
best	–	–	55	–	–	64
system	31	62	41	16	43	23

Table 5: Classification accuracy for the Answer Validation Exercise task. The baseline is accepting all answers as correct (*all validated*); a second baseline (*filter only*) incorporates only the n-gram overlap threshold. The median and top performing scores for both years are provided for comparison.

scores above the 65th percentile of candidate response scores. Lastly, as our system has no principled way of handling numbers, any answer which is entirely numeric is considered invalid.

Results are shown in Table 5. We evaluate on the 2007 and 2008 datasets, outperforming the median score both years. Our system would place third out of the eight systems that competed in both the 2007 and 2008 tasks. As we are evaluating our system as a single component not trained on the task, we understandably fall well under the top performing systems; however, our performance is nonetheless an indication that the system provides a valuable signal for the task.

6 Conclusion

We have created a simple yet effective system to determine the plausibility of an arbitrary fact, both in terms of an intrinsic measure, and in downstream applications. Furthermore we have shown that the confidences returned by our system are informative, and that high-precision judgments can be obtained even at reasonable recall. We hope to devote future work to enriching the notion of fact similarity, and better handling the noise in the training data.

Acknowledgements We gratefully acknowledge the support of the Defense Advanced Research Projects Agency (DARPA) Deep Exploration and Filtering of Text (DEFT) Program under Air Force Research Laboratory (AFRL) contract no. FA8750-13-2-0040. Any opinions, findings, and conclusion or recommendations expressed in this material are those of the authors and do not necessarily reflect the view of the DARPA, AFRL, or the US government.

References

Jonathan Berant, Ido Dagan, and Jacob Goldberger. 2011. Global learning of typed entailment rules. In *Proceedings of ACL*, Portland, OR.

Kurt Bollacker, Colin Evans, Praveen Paritosh, Tim Sturge, and Jamie Taylor. 2008. Freebase: a collaboratively created graph database for structuring human knowledge. In *Proceedings of the 2008 ACM SIGMOD international conference on Management of data*, pages 1247–1250.

Thorsten Brants and Alex Franz. 2006. Web 1T 5-gram version 1. *Linguistic Data Consortium.*

A. Budanitsky and G. Hirst. 2006. Evaluating WordNet-based measures of lexical semantic relatedness. *Computational Linguistics*, pages 13–47.

Jamie Callan, Mark Hoy, Changkuk Yoo, and Le Zhao. 2009. The ClueWeb09 data set.

Andrew Carlson, Justin Betteridge, Bryan Kisiel, Burr Settles, Estevam R Hruschka Jr, and Tom M Mitchell. 2010. Toward an architecture for never-ending language learning. In *AAAI*, pages 3–3.

Marie-Catherine de Marneffe and Christopher D. Manning. 2008. The Stanford typed dependencies representation. In *Coling 2008: Proceedings of the workshop on Cross-Framework and Cross-Domain Parser Evaluation*, pages 1–8.

Anthony Fader, Stephen Soderland, and Oren Etzioni. 2011. Identifying relations for open information extraction. In *EMNLP*, pages 1535–1545.

Jerry R Hobbs. 1978. Resolving pronoun references. *Lingua*, pages 311–338.

Raphael Hoffmann, Congle Zhang, Xiao Ling, Luke Zettlemoyer, and Daniel S Weld. 2011. Knowledge-based weak supervision for information extraction of overlapping relations. In *ACL-HLT*, pages 541–550.

Eric H Huang, Richard Socher, Christopher D Manning, and Andrew Y Ng. 2012. Improving word representations via global context and multiple word prototypes. *ACL.*

Rohit J. Kate, Yuk Wah Wong, and Raymond J. Mooney. 2005. Learning to transform natural to formal languages. In *AAAI*, pages 1062–1068, Pittsburgh, PA.

Dan Klein and Christopher D Manning. 2003. Accurate unlexicalized parsing. In *ACL*, pages 423–430.

Hugo Liu and Push Singh. 2004. ConceptNet: a practical commonsense reasoning toolkit. *BT technology journal*, pages 211–226.

Mausam, Michael Schmitz, Robert Bart, Stephen Soderland, and Oren Etzioni. 2012. Open language learning for information extraction. In *EMNLP*.

John McCarthy. 1980. Circumscription—a form of non-monotonic reasoning. *Artificial intelligence*, pages 27–39.

George A. Miller. 1995. WordNet: a lexical database for English. *Communications of the ACM*, pages 39–41.

Judea Pearl. 1989. *Probabilistic semantics for non-monotonic reasoning: A survey.* Knowledge Representation and Reasoning.

Anselmo Peñas, Álvaro Rodrigo, Valentín Sama, and Felisa Verdejo. 2007. Overview of the answer validation exercise 2006. In *Evaluation of Multilingual and Multi-modal Information Retrieval*, pages 257–264.

Anselmo Peñas, Álvaro Rodrigo, and Felisa Verdejo. 2008. Overview of the answer validation exercise 2007. In *Advances in Multilingual and Multimodal Information Retrieval*, pages 237–248.

Raymond Reiter. 1980. A logic for default reasoning. *Artificial intelligence*, pages 81–132.

Sebastian Riedel, Limin Yao, Andrew McCallum, and Benjamin M Marlin. 2013. Relation extraction with matrix factorization and universal schemas. In *NAACL-HLT*, pages 74–84.

Álvaro Rodrigo, Anselmo Peñas, and Felisa Verdejo. 2009. Overview of the answer validation exercise 2008. In *Evaluating Systems for Multilingual and Multimodal Information Access*, pages 296–313.

Stefan Schoenmackers, Oren Etzioni, Daniel S Weld, and Jesse Davis. 2010. Learning first-order horn clauses from web text. In *EMNLP*, pages 1088–1098.

Push Singh, Thomas Lin, Erik Mueller, Grace Lim, Travell Perkins, and Wan Li Zhu. 2002. Open mind common sense: Knowledge acquisition from the general public. *On the Move to Meaningful Internet Systems 2002: CoopIS, DOA, and ODBASE*, pages 1223–1237.

Rion Snow, Daniel Jurafsky, and Andrew Y Ng. 2006. Semantic taxonomy induction from heterogenous evidence. In *ACL*, pages 801–808.

Stephen Soderland, Brendan Roof, Bo Qin, Shi Xu, Oren Etzioni, et al. 2010. Adapting open information extraction to domain-specific relations. *AI Magazine*, pages 93–102.

Mihai Surdeanu, Julie Tibshirani, Ramesh Nallapati, and Christopher D. Manning. 2012. Multi-instance multi-label learning for relation extraction. In *EMNLP*.

Niket Tandon, Gerard de Melo, and Gerhard Weikum. 2011. Deriving a web-scale common sense fact database. In *AAAI*.

Kristina Toutanova, Dan Klein, Christopher D Manning, and Yoram Singer. 2003. Feature-rich part-of-speech tagging with a cyclic dependency network. In *NAACL-HLT*, pages 173–180.

Ellen M Voorhees. 2001. Question answering in TREC. In *Proceedings of the tenth international conference on Information and knowledge management*, pages 535–537.

Limin Yao, Sebastian Riedel, and Andrew McCallum. 2012. Probabilistic databases of universal schema. In *Proceedings of the Joint Workshop on Automatic Knowledge Base Construction and Web-scale Knowledge Extraction*, pages 116–121.

Alexander Yates, Michael Cafarella, Michele Banko, Oren Etzioni, Matthew Broadhead, and Stephen Soderland. 2007. TextRunner: Open information extraction on the web. In *ACL-HLT*, pages 25–26.

John M. Zelle and Raymond J. Mooney. 1996. Learning to parse database queries using inductive logic programming. In *AAAI/IAAI*, pages 1050–1055, Portland, OR.

Luke S. Zettlemoyer and Michael Collins. 2005. Learning to map sentences to logical form: Structured classification with probabilistic categorial grammars. In *UAI*, pages 658–666. AUAI Press.

Luke S. Zettlemoyer and Michael Collins. 2007. Online learning of relaxed CCG grammars for parsing to logical form. In *EMNLP-CoNLL*, pages 678–687.

Towards Robust Linguistic Analysis Using OntoNotes

Sameer Pradhan[1], **Alessandro Moschitti**[2,3], **Nianwen Xue**[4], **Hwee Tou Ng**[5]
Anders Björkelund[6], **Olga Uryupina**[2], **Yuchen Zhang**[4] and **Zhi Zhong**[5]

[1] Boston Childrens Hospital and Harvard Medical School, Boston, MA 02115, USA
[2] University of Trento, University of Trento, 38123 Povo (TN), Italy
[3] QCRI, Qatar Foundation, 5825 Doha, Qatar
[4] Brandeis University, Brandeis University, Waltham, MA 02453, USA
[5] National University of Singapore, Singapore, 117417
[6] University of Stuttgart, 70174 Stuttgart, Germany

Abstract

Large-scale linguistically annotated corpora have played a crucial role in advancing the state of the art of key natural language technologies such as syntactic, semantic and discourse analyzers, and they serve as training data as well as evaluation benchmarks. Up till now, however, most of the evaluation has been done on monolithic corpora such as the Penn Treebank, the Proposition Bank. As a result, it is still unclear how the state-of-the-art analyzers perform in general on data from a variety of genres or domains. The completion of the OntoNotes corpus, a large-scale, multi-genre, multilingual corpus manually annotated with syntactic, semantic and discourse information, makes it possible to perform such an evaluation. This paper presents an analysis of the performance of publicly available, state-of-the-art tools on all layers and languages in the OntoNotes v5.0 corpus. This should set the benchmark for future development of various NLP components in syntax and semantics, and possibly encourage research towards an integrated system that makes use of the various layers jointly to improve overall performance.

1 Introduction

Roughly a million words of text from the Wall Street Journal newswire (WSJ), circa 1989, has had a significant impact on research in the language processing community — especially those in the area of syntax and (shallow) semantics, the reason for this being the seminal impact of the Penn Treebank project which first selected this text for annotation. Taking advantage of a solid syntactic foundation, later researchers who wanted to annotate semantic phenomena on a relatively large scale, also used it as the basis of their annotation. For example the Proposition Bank (Palmer et al., 2005), BBN Name Entity and Pronoun coreference corpus (Weischedel and Brunstein, 2005), the Penn Discourse Treebank (Prasad et al., 2008), and many other annotation projects, all annotate the same underlying body of text. It was also converted to dependency structures and other syntactic formalisms such as CCG (Hockenmaier and Steedman, 2002) and LTAG (Shen et al., 2008), thereby creating an even bigger impact through these additional syntactic resources. The most recent one of these efforts is the OntoNotes corpus (Weischedel et al., 2011). However, unlike the previous extensions of the Treebank, in addition to using roughly a third of the same WSJ subcorpus, OntoNotes also added several other genres, and covers two other languages — Chinese and Arabic: portions of the Chinese Treebank (Xue et al., 2005) and the Arabic Treebank (Maamouri and Bies, 2004) have been used to sample the genre of text that they represent.

One of the current hurdles in language processing is the problem of domain, or genre adaptation. Although genre or domain are popular terms, their definitions are still vague. In OntoNotes, "genre" means a type of source – newswire (NW), broadcast news (BN), broadcast conversation (BC), magazine (MZ), telephone conversation (TC), web data (WB) or pivot text (PT). Changes in the entity and event profiles across source types, and even in the same source over a time duration, as explicitly expressed by surface lexical forms, usually account for a lot of the decrease in performance of models trained on one source and tested on another, usually because these are the salient cues that are relied upon by statistical models.

Large-scale corpora annotated with multiple layers of linguistic information exist in various languages, but they typically consist of a single source or collection. The Brown corpus, which consists of multiple genres, have been usually used to investigate issues of genres of sensitivity, but it is relatively small and does not include any infor-

[1]A portion of the English data in the OntoNotes corpus is a selected set of sentences that were annotated for parse and word sense information. These sentences are present in a document of their own, and so the documents for parse layers for English are inflated by about 3655 documents and for the word sense are inflated by about 8797 documents.

Language	Parse		Proposition			Sense			Name		Coreference	
	Documents	Words	Documents	Verb Prop.	Noun Prop.	Documents	Verb Sense	Noun Sense	Documents	Words	Documents	Words
English	7,967[1]	2.6M	6,124	300K	18K	12K	173K	120K	3,637	2.0M	2,384 (3493)	1.7M
Chinese	2002	1.0M	1861	148K	7K	1573	83K	1K	1,911	988K	1,729 (2,280)	950K
Arabic	599	402K	599	30K	-	310	4.3K	8.7K	446	298K	447 (447)	300K

Table 1: Coverage for each layer in the OntoNotes v5.0 corpus, by number of documents, words, and some other attributes. The numbers in parenthesis are the total number of parts in the documents.

mal genres such as web data. Very seldom has it been the case that the exact same phenomena have been annotated on a broad cross-section of the same language before OntoNotes. The OntoNotes corpus thus provides an opportunity for studying the genre effect on different syntactic, semantic and discourse analyzers.

Parts of the OntoNotes Corpus have been used for various shared tasks organized by the language processing community. The word sense layer was the subject of prediction in two SemEval-2007 tasks, and the coreference layer was the subject of prediction in the SemEval-2010[2] (Recasens et al., 2010), CoNLL-2011 and 2012 shared tasks (Pradhan et al., 2011; Pradhan et al., 2012). The CoNLL-2012 shared task provided predicted information to the participants, however, that did not include a few layers such as the named entities for Chinese and Arabic, propositions for Arabic, and for better comparison of the English data with the CoNLL-2011 task, a smaller OntoNotes v4.0 portion of the English parse and propositions was used for training.

This paper is a first attempt at presenting a coherent high-level picture of the performance of various publicly available state-of-the-art tools on all the layers of OntoNotes in all three languages, so as to pave the way for further explorations in the area of syntax and semantics processing.

The possible avenues for exploratory studies on various fronts are enormous. However, given space considerations, in this paper, we will restrict our presentation of the performance on all layers of annotation in the data by using a stratified cross-section of the corpus for training, development, and testing. The paper is organized as follows: Section 2 gives an overview of the OntoNotes corpus. Section 3 explains the parameters of the evaluation and the various underlying assumptions. Section 4 presents the experimental results and discussion, and Section 5 concludes the paper.

2 OntoNotes Corpus

The OntoNotes project has created a large-scale corpus of accurate and integrated annotation of multiple layers of syntactic, semantic and discourse information in text. The English language portion comprises roughly 1.7M words and Chinese language portion comprises roughly 1M words of newswire, magazine articles, broadcast news, broadcast conversations, web data and conversational speech data[3]. The Arabic portion is smaller, comprising 300K words of newswire articles. This rich, integrated annotation covering many layers aims at facilitating the development of richer, cross-layer models and enabling better automatic semantic analysis. The corpus is tagged with syntactic trees, propositions for most verb and some noun instances, partial verb and noun word senses, coreference, and named entities. Table 1 gives an overview of the number of documents that have been annotated in the entire OntoNotes corpus.

2.1 Layers of Annotation

This section provides a very concise overview of the various layers of annotations in OntoNotes. For a more detailed description, the reader is referred to (Weischedel et al., 2011) and the documentation accompanying the v5.0[4] release.

2.1.1 Syntax

This represents the layer of syntactic annotation based on revised guidelines for the Penn Treebank (Marcus et al., 1993; Babko-Malaya et al., 2006), the Chinese Treebank (Xue et al., 2005) and the Arabic Treebank (Maamouri and Bies, 2004). There were two updates made to the parse trees as part of the OntoNotes project: i) the introduction of NML phrases, in the English portion, to mark nominal sub-constituents of flat NPs that do not follow the default right-branching structure, and ii) re-tokenization of hyphenated tokens into multiple tokens in English and Chinese. The Arabic Treebank on the other hand was also significantly revised in an effort to increase consistency.

2.1.2 Word Sense

Coarse-grained word senses are tagged for the most frequent polysemous verbs and nouns, in or-

[2] A small portion 125K words in English was used for this evaluation.

[3] These numbers are for the portion that has all layers of annotations. The word count for each layer is mentioned in Table 1

[4] For all the layers of data used in this study, the OntoNotes v4.99 pre-release that was used for the CoNLL-2012 shared task is identical to the v5.0 release.

der to maximize token coverage. The word sense granularity is tailored to achieve very high inter-annotator agreement as demonstrated by Palmer et al. (2007). These senses are defined in the sense inventory files. In the case of English and Arabic languages, the sense-inventories (and frame files) are defined separately for each part of speech that is realized by the lemma in the text. For Chinese, however the sense inventories (and frame files) are defined per lemma – independent of the part of speech realized in the text.

2.1.3 Proposition

The propositions in OntoNotes are PropBank-style semantic roles for English, Chinese and Arabic. Most English verbs and few nouns were annotated using the revised guidelines for the English PropBank (Babko-Malaya et al., 2006) as part of the OntoNotes effort. Some enhancements were made to the English PropBank and Treebank to make them synchronize better with each other: one of the outcomes of this effort was that two types of LINKs that represent pragmatic coreference (LINK-PCR) and selectional preferences (LINK-SLC) were added to the original PropBank (Palmer et al., 2005). More details can be found in the addendum to the PropBank guidelines[5] in the OntoNotes v5.0 release. A part of speech agnostic Chinese PropBank (Xue and Palmer, 2009) guidelines were used to annotate most frequent lemmas in Chinese. Many verbs and some nouns and adjectives were annotated using the revised Arabic PropBank guidelines (Palmer et al., 2008; Zaghouani et al., 2010).

2.1.4 Named Entities

The corpus was tagged with a set of 18 well-defined proper named entity types that have been tested extensively for inter-annotator agreement by Weischedel and Burnstein (2005).

2.1.5 Coreference

This layer captures general anaphoric coreference that covers entities and events not limited to noun phrases or a limited set of entity types (Pradhan et al., 2007). It considers all pronouns (PRP, PRP$), noun phrases (NP) and heads of verb phrases (VP) as potential mentions. Unlike English, Chinese and Arabic have dropped subjects and objects which were also considered during coreference annotation[6]. The mentions formed by these dropped pronouns total roughly about 11% for both Chinese and Arabic. Coreference is the only document-level phenomenon in OntoNotes. Some of the documents in the corpus — especially the ones in the broadcast conversation, web data, and telephone conversation genre — are very long which prohibited efficient annotation in their entirety. These are split into smaller parts, and each part is considered a separate document for the sake of coreference evaluation.

3 Evaluation Setting

Given the scope of the corpus and the multitude of settings one can run evaluations, we had to restrict this study to a relatively focused subset. There has already been evidence of models trained on WSJ doing poorly on non-WSJ data on parses (Gildea, 2001; McClosky et al., 2006), semantic role labeling (Carreras and Màrquez, 2005; Pradhan et al., 2008), word sense (Escudero et al., 2000; **?**), and named entities. The phenomenon of coreference is somewhat of an outlier. The winning system in the CoNLL-2011 shared task was one that was completely rule-based and not directly trained on the OntoNotes corpus. Given this overwhelming evidence, we decided not to focus on potentially complex cross-genre evaluations. Instead, we decided on evaluating the performance on each layer of annotation using an appropriately selected, stratified training, development and test set, so as to facilitate future studies.

3.1 Training, Development and Test Partitions

In this section we will have a brief discussion on the logic behind the partitioning of the data into training, development and test sets. Before we do that, it would help to know that given the range and peculiarities of the layers of annotation and presence of various resource and technical constraints, not all the documents in the corpus are annotated with all the layers of information, and token-centric phenomena (such as word sense and propositions of predicates) were not annotated with 100% coverage. Most of the proposition annotation in English and Arabic is for the verb predicates, with a few nouns annotated in English and some adjectives in Arabic. In Chinese, the selection is part of speech agnostic, and is based on the lemmas that can be considered predicates. Some documents in the corpora are actually snippets from larger documents, and have been annotated for a combination of parse, propositions, word sense and names, but not coreference. If one considers each layer independently, then an ideal partitioning scheme would create a separate partition for each layer such that it maximizes the number of examples that can be extracted for that layer from the corpus. The upside is that one would get as much data there is to train and estimate the performance of each layer across the entire corpus. The downside is that this might cover vari-

[5] doc/propbank/english-propbank.pdf

[6] As we will see later these are not used during the task.

ous cross sections of the documents in the corpus, and would not provide a clean picture when looking at the collective performance for all the layers. The documents that are annotated with coreference correspond to the intersection of all annotations. These are the documents that have also been annotated with all the other layers of information. The amount of data we can get together in such a test set is big enough to be representative. Therefore, we decided that it would be ideal to choose a portion of these documents as the test collection for all layers. An additional advantage is that it is the exact same test set used in the CoNLL-2012 shared task, and so in a way is already a standard. On the training and development side however, one can still imagine using all possible information for training models for a particular layer, and that is what we decided to do. The training and development data is generated by providing all documents with all available layers of annotation for input, however, the test set is generated by providing as input to the algorithm the set of documents in the corpus that have been annotated for coreference. This algorithm tries to reuse previously established partitions for English, i.e., the WSJ portion. Unfortunately, in the case of Chinese and Arabic, either the historical partitions were not in the selection used for OntoNotes, or were partially overlapping with the ones created using this scheme, and/or had a very small portion of OntoNotes covered in the test set. Therefore, we decided to create a fresh partition for the Chinese and Arabic data. Note, however, that the these test sets also match the ones used in the CoNLL-2012 evaluation. The algorithm for selecting the training, development and test partitions is described on the CoNLL-2012 shared task webpage, along with the list of training, development, and test document IDs[7].

3.2 Assumptions

Next we had to decide on a set of assumptions to use while designing the experiments to measure the automatic prediction accuracy for each of the layers. Since some of these decisions affect more than one layer of annotation, we will describe these in this section instead of in the section where we discuss the experiment with a particular layer of annotation.

[7] http://conll.cemantix.org/2012/download/ids/
For each language there are two sub-directories — "all" contains more general lists which include documents that had at least one of the layers of annotation, and "coref" contains the lists that include documents that have coreference annotation. The former were used to generate training, development, test sets for layers other than coreference, and the latter was used to generate training/development/test sets for the coreference layer used in the CoNLL-2012 shared task.

Word Segmentation The three languages that we are evaluating are from quite different language families. Arabic has a complex morphology, English has limited morphology, whereas Chinese has very little morphology. English word segmentation amounts to rule-based tokenization, and is close to perfect. In the case of Chinese and Arabic, although the tokenization/segmentation is not as good as English, the accuracies are in the high 90s. Given this we decided to use gold, Treebank segmentation for all languages. In the case of Chinese, the words themselves are lemmas, whereas in English they can be predicted with very high accuracy. For Arabic, by default written text is unvocalised, and lemmatization is a complex process which we considered out of the scope of this study, so we decided to use correct, gold standard lemmas, along with the correct vocalized version of the tokens.

Traces and Function Tags Treebank traces have hardly played a role in the mainstream parser and semantic role labeling evaluation. Function tags also have received similar treatment in the parsing community, and though they are important, there is also a significant information overlap between them and the proposition structure provided by the PropBank layer. Whereas in English, most traces represent syntactic phenomena such as movement and raising, in Chinese and Arabic, they can also represent dropped subjects/objects. These subset of traces directly affect the coreference layer, since, unlike English, traces in Chinese and Arabic (***pro*** and * respectively) are legitimate targets of mentions and are considered for coreference annotation in OntoNotes. Recovering traces in text is a hard problem, and the most recently reported numbers in literature for Chinese are around a F-score of 50 (Yang and Xue, 2010; Cai et al., 2011). For Arabic there have not been much studies on recovering these. A study by Gabbard (2010) shows that these can be recovered with an F-score of 55 with automatic parses and roughly 65 using gold parses. Considering the low level of prediction accuracy of these tokens, and their relative low frequency, we decided to consider predicting traces in trees out of the scope of this study. In other words, we removed the manually identified traces and function tags from the Treebanks across all three languages, in all the three – training, development and test partitions. This meant removing any and all dependent annotation in layers such as PropBank and Coreference. In the case of PropBank these are the argument bearing traces, whereas in coreference these are the mentions formed by these elided subjects/objects.

Disfluencies One thing that needs to be dealt with in conversational data is the presence of disfluencies (restarts, etc.). In the English parses of the OntoNotes, disfluencies are marked using a special EDITED[8] phrase tag – as was the case for the Switchboard Treebank. Computing the accuracy of identifying disfluencies is also out of the scope of this study. Given the frequency of disfluencies and the performance with which one can identify them automatically,[9] a probable processing pipeline would filter them out before parsing. We decided to remove them using oracle information available in the English Treebank, and the coreference chains were remapped to trees without disfluencies. Owing to various technical constraints, we decided to retain the disfluencies in the Chinese data.

Spoken Genre Given the scope of this study, we make another significant assumption. For the spoken genres – BC, BN and TC – we use the manual transcriptions rather than the output of a speech recognizer, as would be the case in real world. The performance on various layers for these genres would therefore be artificially inflated, and should be taken into account while analyzing results. Not many studies have previously reported on syntactic and semantic analysis for spoken genre. Favre et al. (2010) report the performance on the English subset of an earlier version of OntoNotes.

Discourse The corpus contains information on the speaker for broadcast communication, conversation, telephone conversation and writer for the web data. This information provides an important clue for correctly linking anaphoric pronouns with the right antecedents. This information could be automatically deduced, but is also not within the scope of our study. Therefore, we decided to provide gold, instead of predicted, data both during training and testing. Table 2 lists the status of the layers.

Layer	English	Chinese	Arabic
Segmentation	•	•	•
Lemma	○	—	•
Parse	○	○	○[10]
Proposition	○	○	○
Predicate Frame	○	○	○
Word Sense	○	○	○
Name Entities	○	○	○
Coreference	○	○	○
Speaker	•	•	—
Number	○	×	×
Gender	○	×	×

Table 2: Status of layers used during prediction of other layers. A "•" indicates gold annotation, a "○" indicates predicted, a "×" indicates an absence of the predicted layer, and a "—" indicates that the layer is not applicable to the language.

4 Experiments

In this section, we will report on the experiments carried out using all available data in the training set for training models for a particular layer, and using the CoNLL-2012 test set as the test set.

The predicted annotation layers input to downstream models were automatically annotated by using NLP processors learned with n-cross fold validation on the training data. This way, the n chunks of training data are annotated avoiding dependencies with the data used for training the NLP processors.

4.1 Syntax

Predicted parse trees for English were produced using the Charniak parser[11] (Charniak and Johnson, 2005). Some additional tag types used in the OntoNotes trees were added to the parser's tagset, including the nominal (NML) tag, and the rules used to determine head words were extended correspondingly. Chinese and Arabic parses were generated using the Berkeley parser (Petrov and Klein, 2007). In the case of Arabic, the parsing community uses a mapping from rich Arabic part of speech tags to Penn-style part of speech tags. We used the mapping that is included with the Arabic Treebank. The predicted parses for the training portion of the data were generated using 10-fold (5-folds for Arabic) cross-validation. For testing, we used a model trained on the entire training portion. Table 3 shows the precision, recall and F_1-scores of the re-trained parsers on the CoNLL-2012 test along with the part of speech accuracies (POS) using the standard `evalb` scorer.

The performance on the PT genre for English is the highest among other English genres. This is possibly because of the professional, clean translations of the underlying text, and are mostly shorter sentences. The MZ genre and the NW both of which contain well edited text, share similar scores. There is a few points gap between these and the other genres. As for Chinese, the performance on MZ is the highest followed by BN. Surprisingly, the WB genre has a similar score and the others are close behind except for TC. As expected, the Arabic parser performance is the low-

[8]There is another phrase type – EMBED in the telephone conversation genre which is similar to the EDITED phrase type, and sometimes identifies insertions, but sometimes contains logical continuation of phrases by different speakers, so we decided not to remove that from the data.

[9]A study by Charniak and Johnson (2001) shows that one can identify and remove edits from transcribed conversational speech with an F-score of about 78, with roughly 95 precision and 67 recall.

[10]The predicted part of speech for Arabic are a mapped down version of the richer gold version present in the Treebank

[11]http://bllip.cs.brown.edu/download/reranking-parserAug06.tar.gz

		All Sentences				
		N	POS	P	R	F
English	BC	2,211	97.33	86.36	86.11	86.23
	BN	1,357	97.32	87.61	87.03	87.32
	MZ	780	96.58	89.90	89.49	89.70
	NW	2,327	97.15	87.68	87.25	87.47
	TC	1,366	96.11	85.09	84.13	84.60
	WB	1,787	96.03	85.46	85.26	85.36
	PT	1,869	98.77	95.29	94.66	94.98
	Overall	11,697	97.09	88.08	87.65	87.87
Chinese	BC	885	94.79	80.17	79.35	79.76
	BN	929	93.85	83.49	80.13	81.78
	MZ	451	97.06	88.48	83.85	86.10
	NW	481	94.07	82.26	77.28	79.69
	TC	968	92.22	71.90	69.19	70.52
	WB	758	92.37	82.57	78.92	80.70
	Overall	4,472	94.12	82.23	78.93	80.55
Arabic	NW	1,003	94.12	74.71	75.67	75.19

Table 3: Parser performance on the CoNLL-2012 test set.

est among the three languages.

4.2 Word Sense

We used the IMS[12] (It Makes Sense) (Zhong and Ng, 2010) word sense tagger. IMS was trained on all the word sense data that is present in the training portion of the OntoNotes corpus using cross-validated predictions on the input layers similar to the proposition tagger. During testing, for English and Arabic, IMS must first use the automatic POS information to identify the nouns and verbs in the test data, and then assign senses to the automatically identified nouns and verbs. In the case of Arabic, IMS uses gold lemmas. Since automatic POS tagging is not perfect, IMS does not always output a sense to all word tokens that need to be sense tagged due to wrongly predicted POS tags. As such, recall is not the same as precision on the English and Arabic test data. For Chinese the measure of performance is just the accuracy since the senses are defined per lemma rather than per part of speech. Since we provide gold word segmentation, IMS attempts to sense tag all correctly segmented Chinese words, so recall and precision are the same and so is the F_1-score. Table 4 shows the performance of this classifier aggregated over both the verbs and nouns in the CoNLL-2012 test set and an overall score split by nouns and verbs for English and Arabic. For both nouns and verbs in English, the F_1-score is over 80%. The performance on English nouns is slightly higher than English verbs. Comparing to the other two languages, the performance on Arabic is relatively lower, especially the performance on Arabic verbs, whose F_1-score is less than 70%. For English, genres PT and TC, and for Chinese genres TC and WB, no gold standard senses were available, and so their accuracies could not be computed. Previously, Zhong et al. (2008) reported the word sense performance on the Wall Street Journal portion of an earlier version of OntoNotes, but the results are not directly comparable.

[12] http://www.comp.nus.edu.sg/~nlp/sw/IMS_v0.9.2.1.tar.gz

		Performance			
		P	R	F	A
English	BC	81.2	81.3	81.2	-
	BN	82.0	81.5	81.7	-
	MZ	79.1	78.8	79.0	-
	NW	85.7	85.7	85.7	-
	WB	77.5	77.6	77.5	-
	Overall	82.5	82.5	82.5	-
	Nouns	83.4	83.1	83.2	-
	Verbs	81.8	81.9	81.8	-
Chinese	BC	-	-	-	80.5
	BN	-	-	-	85.4
	MZ	-	-	-	82.4
	NW	-	-	-	89.1
	Overall	-	-	-	84.3
Arabic	NW	75.9	75.2	75.6	-
	Nouns	79.2	77.7	78.4	-
	Verbs	68.8	69.5	69.1	-

Table 4: Word sense performance on the CoNLL-2012 test set.

4.3 Proposition

The revised PropBank has introduced two new links — LINK-SLC and LINK-PCR. Since the community is not used to the new PropBank representation which (i) relies heavily on the trace structure in the Treebank and (ii) we decided to exclude, we *unfold* the LINKs back to their original representation as in the PropBank 1.0 release. We used ASSERT[15] (Pradhan et al., 2005) to predict the propositional structure for English. We made a small modification to ASSERT, and replaced the TinySVM classifier with a CRF[16] to speed up training the model on all the data. The Chinese propositional structure was predicted with the Chinese semantic role labeler described in (Xue, 2008), retrained on the OntoNotes v5.0 data. The Arabic propositional structure was predicted using the system described in Diab et al. (2008). (Diab et al., 2008) Table 5 shows the detailed per-

[14] The Frame ID column indicates the F-score for English and Arabic, and accuracy for Chinese for the same reasons as word sense.

[15] http://cemantix.org/assert.html

[16] http://leon.bottou.org/projects/sgd

		Frame ID	Total Sent.	Total Prop.	% Perfect Prop.	Argument ID + Class		
						P	R	F
English	BC	93.2	1994	5806	52.89	80.76	69.69	74.82
	BN	92.7	1218	4166	54.78	80.22	69.36	74.40
	MZ	90.8	740	2655	50.77	79.13	67.78	73.02
	NW	92.8	2122	6930	46.45	79.80	66.80	72.72
	TC	91.8	837	1718	49.94	79.85	72.35	75.91
	WB	90.7	1139	2751	42.86	80.51	69.06	74.35
	PT	96.6	1208	2849	67.53	89.35	84.43	86.82
	Overall	92.8	9,261	26,882	51.66	81.30	70.53	75.53
Chinese	BC	87.7	885	2,323	31.34	53.92	68.60	60.38
	BN	93.3	929	4,419	35.44	64.34	66.05	65.18
	MZ	92.3	451	2,620	31.68	65.04	65.40	65.22
	NW	96.6	481	2,210	27.33	69.28	55.74	61.78
	TC	82.2	968	1,622	32.74	48.70	59.12	53.41
	WB	87.8	758	1,761	35.21	62.35	68.87	65.45
	Overall	90.9	4,472	14,955	32.62	61.26	64.48	62.83
Arabic	NW	85.6	1,003	2337	24.18	52.99	45.03	48.68

Table 5: Proposition and frameset disambiguation performance[14] in the CoNLL-2012 test set.

formance numbers[17]. The CoNLL-2005 scorer[18] was used to compute the scores. At first glance, the performance on the English newswire genre is much lower than what has been reported for WSJ Section 23. This could be attributed to several factors: i) the newswire in OntoNotes not only contains WSJ data, but also Xinhua news, and some other newswire evaluation data, ii) The WSJ training and test portions in OntoNotes are a subset of the standard ones that have been used to report performance earlier; iii) the PropBank guidelines were significantly revised during the OntoNotes project in order to synchronize well with the Treebank, and finally iv) it includes propositions for *be* verbs missing from the original PropBank. It looks like the newly added Pivot Text data (comprised of the New Testament) shows very good performance. The Chinese and Arabic[19] accuracy is much worse. In addition to automatically predicting the arguments, we also trained the IMS system to tag PropBank frameset IDs.

Language	Genre	Entity Count	Performance P	R	F
English	BC	1671	80.17	77.20	78.66
	BN	2180	88.95	85.69	87.29
	MZ	1161	82.74	82.17	82.45
	NW	4679	86.79	84.25	85.50
	TC	362	74.09	61.60	67.27
	WB	1133	77.72	68.05	72.56
	Overall	11186	84.04	80.86	82.42
Chinese	BC	667	72.49	58.47	64.73
	BN	3158	82.17	71.50	76.46
	NW	1453	86.11	76.39	80.96
	MZ	1043	65.16	56.66	60.62
	TC	200	48.00	60.00	53.33
	WB	886	80.60	51.13	62.57
	Overall	7407	78.20	66.45	71.85
Arabic	NW	2550	74.53	62.55	68.02

Table 6: Performance of the named entity recognizer on the CoNLL-2012 test set.

4.4 Named Entities

We retrained the Stanford named entity recognizer[20] (Finkel et al., 2005) on the OntoNotes data. Table 6 shows the performance details for all the languages across all 18 name types broken down by genre. In English, BN has the highest performance followed by the NW genre. There is a significant drop from those and the TC and WB genre. Somewhat similar trend is observed in the Chinese data, with Arabic having the lowest scores. Since the Pivot Text portion (PT) of OntoNotes was not tagged with names, we could not compute the accuracy for that cross-section of the data. Previously Finkel and Manning (2009) performed a joint estimation of named entity and parsing. However, it was on an earlier version of the English portion of OntoNotes using a different cross-section for training and testing and therefore is not directly comparable.

4.5 Coreference

The task is to automatically identify mentions of entities and events in text and to link the coreferring mentions together to form entity/event chains. The coreference decisions are made using automatically predicted information on other structural and semantic layers including the parses, semantic roles, word senses, and named entities that were produced in the earlier sections. Each document part from the documents that were split into multiple parts during coreference annotation were treated as separate document.

We used the number and gender predictions generated by Bergsma and Lin (2006). Unfortunately neither Arabic, nor Chinese have comparable data available. Chinese, in particular, does not have number or gender inflections for nouns, but (Baran and Xue, 2011) look at a way to infer such information.

We trained the Björkelund and Farkas (2012) coreference system[21] which uses a combination of two pair-wise resolvers, the first is an incremental chain-based resolution algorithm (Björkelund and Farkas, 2012), and the second is a best-first resolver (Ng and Cardie, 2002). The two resolvers are combined by stacking, i.e., the output of the first resolver is used as features in the second one. The system uses a large feature set tailored for each language which, in addition to classic coreference features, includes both lexical and syntactic information.

Recently, it was discovered that there is possibly a bug in the official scorer used for the CoNLL 2011/2012 and the SemEval 2010 coreference tasks. This relates to the mis-implementation of the method proposed by (Cai and Strube, 2010) for scoring predicted mentions. This issue has also been recently reported in Recasens et al., (2013). As of this writing, the BCUBED metric has been fixed, and the correctness of the CEAF_m, CEAF_e and BLANC metrics is being verified. We will be updating the CoNLL shared task webpages[22] with more detailed information and also release the patched scripts as soon as they are available. We will also re-generate the scores for previous shared tasks, and the coreference layer in this paper and make them available along with the models and system outputs for other layers. Table 7 shows the performance of the system on the

[17] The number of sentences in this table are a subset of the ones in the table showing parser performance, since these are the sentences for which at least one predicate has been tagged with its arguments

[18] http://www.lsi.upc.es/~srlconll/srl-eval.pl

[19] The system could not not use the morphology features in Diab et al. (2008).

[20] http://nlp.stanford.edu/software/CRF-NER.shtml

[21] http://www.ims.uni-stuttgart.de/~anders/coref.html

[22] http://conll.cemantix.org

CoNLL-2012 test set, broken down by genre. The same metrics that were used for the CoNLL-2012 shared task are computed, with the CoNLL column being the official CoNLL measure.

Language	Genre	MD	MUC	BCUBED	CEAF$_m$	CEAF$_e$	BLANC	CONLL
				PREDICTED MENTIONS				
English	BC	73.43	63.92	61.98	54.82	42.68	73.04	56.19
	BN	73.49	63.92	65.85	58.93	48.14	72.74	59.30
	MZ	71.86	64.94	71.38	64.03	50.68	78.87	62.33
	NW	68.54	60.20	65.11	57.54	45.10	73.72	56.80
	PT	86.95	79.09	68.33	65.52	50.83	77.74	66.08
	TC	80.81	76.78	71.35	65.41	45.44	82.45	64.52
	WB	74.43	66.86	61.43	54.76	42.05	73.54	56.78
	Overall	75.38	67.58	65.78	59.20	45.87	75.8	59.74
Chinese	BC	68.02	59.6	59.44	53.12	40.77	73.63	53.27
	BN	68.57	61.34	67.83	60.90	48.10	77.39	59.09
	MZ	55.55	48.89	58.83	55.63	46.04	74.25	51.25
	NW	89.19	80.71	73.64	76.30	70.89	82.56	75.08
	TC	77.72	73.59	71.65	64.30	48.52	83.14	64.59
	WB	72.61	65.79	62.32	56.71	43.67	77.45	57.26
	Overall	66.37	58.61	66.56	59.01	48.19	76.07	57.79
Arabic	NW	60.55	47.82	61.16	53.42	44.30	69.63	51.09
				GOLD MENTIONS				
English	BC	85.63	76.09	68.70	61.73	49.87	76.24	64.89
	BN	82.11	73.56	71.52	63.67	52.29	75.70	65.79
	MZ	85.65	77.73	78.82	72.75	60.09	83.88	72.21
	NW	80.68	73.52	73.08	65.63	51.96	81.06	66.19
	PT	93.20	85.72	73.25	70.76	58.81	79.78	72.59
	TC	90.68	86.83	78.94	73.87	56.26	85.82	74.01
	WB	88.12	80.61	69.86	63.45	51.13	76.48	67.20
	Overall	86.16	78.7	72.67	66.32	53.23	79.22	68.2
Chinese	BC	84.88	76.34	69.89	62.02	49.29	76.89	65.17
	BN	80.97	74.89	76.88	68.91	55.56	81.94	69.11
	MZ	78.85	73.06	70.15	61.68	46.86	78.78	63.36
	NW	93.23	86.54	86.70	80.60	76.60	85.75	83.28
	TC	92.91	88.31	84.51	79.49	63.87	90.04	78.90
	WB	85.87	77.61	69.24	60.71	47.47	77.67	64.77
	Overall	83.47	76.85	76.30	68.30	56.61	81.56	69.92
Arabic	NW	76.43	60.81	67.29	59.50	49.32	74.61	59.14

Table 7: Performance of the coreference system on the CoNLL-2012 test set.

The varying results across genres mostly meet our expectations. In English, the system does best on TC and the PT genres. The text in the TC set often involve long chains where the speakers refer to themselves which, given speaker information, is fairly easy to resolve. The PT section includes many references to god (e.g. *god* and *the lord*) which the lexicalized resolver is quite good at picking up during training. The more difficult genres consist of texts where references to many entities are interleaved in the discourse and is as such harder to resolve correctly. For Chinese the numbers on the TC genre are also quite good, and the explanation above also holds here — many mentions refer to either of the speakers. For Chinese the NW section displays by far the highest scores, however, and the reason for this is not clear to us. Not surprisingly, restricting the set of mentions only to gold mentions gives a large boost across all genres and all languages. This shows that mention detection (MD) and singleton detection (which is not part of the annotation) remain a big source of errors for the coreference resolver. For these experiments we used a combination of training and development data for training — following the CoNLL-2012 shared task specification. Leaving out the development set has a very negligible effect on the CoNLL-score for all the languages (English: 0.14; Chinese 0.06; Arabic: 0.40 F-score respectively). The effect on Arabic is the most (0.40 F-score) most likely because of its much smaller size. To gauge the performance improvement between 2011 and 2012 shared tasks, we performed a clean comparison of over the best performing system and an earlier version of this system (Björkelund and Nugues, 2011) on the CoNLL 2011 test set using the CoNLL 2011 train and development set for training. The current system has a CoNLL score of 60.09 $(\frac{64.92+69.84+45.51}{3})$[23] as opposed to the 54.53 reported in *björkelund* (Björkelund and Nugues, 2011), and the 57.79 reported for the best performing system of CoNLL-2011. One caveat is that these score comparison are done using the earlier version (v4) of the CoNLL scorer. Nevertheless, it is encouraging to see that within a short span of a year, there has been significant improvement in system performance – partially owing to cross-pollination of research generated through the shared tasks.

5 Conclusion

In this paper we reported work on finding a reasonable training, development and test split for the various layers of annotation in the OntoNotes v5.0 corpus, which consists of multiple genres in three typologically very different languages. We also presented the performance of publicly available, state-of-the-art algorithms on all the different layers of the corpus for the different languages. The trained models as well as their output will be made publicly available[24] to serve as benchmarks for language processing community. Training so many different NLP components is very time-consuming, thus, we hope the work reported here has lifted the burden of having to create reasonable baselines for researchers who wish to use this corpus to evaluate their systems. We created just one data split in training, development and test set, covering a collection of genres for each layer of annotation in each language in order to keep the workload manageable However, the results do not discriminate the performance on individual genres: we believe such a setup is still a more realistic gauge for the performance of the state-of-the-art NLP components than a monolithic corpus such as the Wall Street Journal section of the Penn Treebank. It can be used as a starting point for developing the next generation of NLP components that are more robust and perform well on a multitude of genres for a variety of different languages.

[23] (MUC + BCUBED + CEAF$_e$)/3

[24] http://cemantix.org

6 Acknowledgments

We gratefully acknowledge the support of the Defense Advanced Research Projects Agency (DARPA/IPTO) under the GALE program, DARPA/CMO Contract No. HR0011-06-C-0022 for sponsoring the creation of the OntoNotes corpus. This work was partially supported by grants R01LM10090 and U54LM008748 from the National Library Of Medicine, and R01GM090187 from the National Institutes of General Medical Sciences. We are indebted to Slav Petrov for helping us to retrain his syntactic parser for Arabic. Alessandro Moschitti and Olga Uryupina have been partially funded by the European Community's Seventh Framework Programme (FP7/2007-2013) under the grant number 288024 (LIMOSINE). The content is solely the responsibility of the authors and does not necessarily represent the official views of the National Institutes of Health. Nianwen Xue and Yuchen Zhang are supported in part by the DAPRA via contract HR0011-11-C-0145 entitled "Linguistic Resources for Multilingual Processing."

References

Olga Babko-Malaya, Ann Bies, Ann Taylor, Szuting Yi, Martha Palmer, Mitch Marcus, Seth Kulick, and Libin Shen. 2006. Issues in synchronizing the English treebank and propbank. In *Workshop on Frontiers in Linguistically Annotated Corpora 2006*, July.

Elizabeth Baran and Nianwen Xue. 2011. Singular or plural? exploiting parallel corpora for Chinese number prediction. In *Proceedings of Machine Translation Summit XIII*, Xiamen, China.

Shane Bergsma and Dekang Lin. 2006. Bootstrapping path-based pronoun resolution. In *Proceedings of the 21st International Conference on Computational Linguistics and 44th Annual Meeting of the Association for Computational Linguistics*, pages 33–40, Sydney, Australia, July.

Anders Björkelund and Richárd Farkas. 2012. Data-driven multilingual coreference resolution using resolver stacking. In *Joint Conference on EMNLP and CoNLL - Shared Task*, pages 49–55, Jeju Island, Korea, July. Association for Computational Linguistics.

Anders Björkelund and Pierre Nugues. 2011. Exploring lexicalized features for coreference resolution. In *Proceedings of the Fifteenth Conference on Computational Natural Language Learning: Shared Task*, pages 45–50, Portland, Oregon, USA, June. Association for Computational Linguistics.

Jie Cai and Michael Strube. 2010. Evaluation metrics for end-to-end coreference resolution systems. In *Proceedings of the 11th Annual Meeting of the Special Interest Group on Discourse and Dialogue*, SIGDIAL '10, pages 28–36.

Shu Cai, David Chiang, and Yoav Goldberg. 2011. Language-independent parsing with empty elements. In *Proceedings of the 49th Annual Meeting of the Association for Computational Linguistics: Human Language Technologies*, pages 212–216, Portland, Oregon, USA, June. Association for Computational Linguistics.

Xavier Carreras and Lluís Màrquez. 2005. Introduction to the CoNLL-2005 shared task: Semantic role labeling. In *Proceedings of the Ninth Conference on Computational Natural Language Learning (CoNLL)*, Ann Arbor, MI, June.

Eugene Charniak and Mark Johnson. 2001. Edit detection and parsing for transcribed speech. In *Proceedings of the Second Meeting of the North American Chapter of the Association for Computational Linguistics*, June.

Eugene Charniak and Mark Johnson. 2005. Coarse-to-fine n-best parsing and maxent discriminative reranking. In *Proceedings of the 43rd Annual Meeting of the Association for Computational Linguistics (ACL)*, Ann Arbor, MI, June.

Mona Diab, Alessandro Moschitti, and Daniele Pighin. 2008. Semantic role labeling systems for Arabic using kernel methods. In *Proceedings of ACL-08: HLT*, pages 798–806, Columbus, Ohio, June. Association for Computational Linguistics.

Gerard Escudero, Lluis Marquez, and German Rigau. 2000. An empirical study of the domain dependence of supervised word disambiguation systems. In *2000 Joint SIGDAT Conference on Empirical Methods in Natural Language Processing and Very Large Corpora*, pages 172–180, Hong Kong, China, October. Association for Computational Linguistics.

Benoit Favre, Bernd Bohnet, and D. Hakkani-Tur. 2010. Evaluation of semantic role labeling and dependency parsing of automatic speech recognition output. In *Proceedings of 2010 IEEE International Conference on Acoustics, Speech and Signal Processing (ICASSP)*, page 5342–5345.

Jenny Rose Finkel and Christopher D. Manning. 2009. Joint parsing and named entity recognition. In *Proceedings of Human Language Technologies: The 2009 Annual Conference of the North American Chapter of the Association for Computational Linguistics*, pages 326–334, Boulder, Colorado, June. Association for Computational Linguistics.

Jenny Rose Finkel, Trond Grenager, and Christopher Manning. 2005. Incorporating non-local information into information extraction systems by Gibbs sampling. In *Proceedings of the 43rd Annual Meeting of the Association for Computational Linguistics*, page 363–370.

Ryan Gabbard. 2010. *Null Element Restoration*. Ph.D. thesis, University of Pennsylvania.

Daniel Gildea. 2001. Corpus variation and parser performance. In *2001 Conference on Empirical Methods in Natural Language Processing (EMNLP)*, Pittsburgh, PA.

Julia Hockenmaier and Mark Steedman. 2002. Acquiring compact lexicalized grammars from a cleaner treebank. In *Proceedings of the Third LREC Conference*, page 1974–1981.

Mohamed Maamouri and Ann Bies. 2004. Developing an Arabic treebank: Methods, guidelines, procedures, and tools. In Ali Farghaly and Karine Megerdoomian, editors, *COLING 2004 Computational Approaches to Arabic Script-based Languages*, pages 2–9, Geneva, Switzerland, August 28th. COLING.

Mitchell P. Marcus, Beatrice Santorini, and Mary Ann Marcinkiewicz. 1993. Building a large annotated corpus of English: The Penn treebank. *Computational Linguistics*, 19(2):313–330, June.

David McClosky, Eugene Charniak, and Mark Johnson. 2006. Effective self-training for parsing. In *Proceedings of the Human Language Technology Conference/North American Chapter of the Association for Computational Linguistics (HLT/NAACL)*, New York City, NY, June.

Vincent Ng and Claire Cardie. 2002. Improving machine learning approaches to coreference resolution. In *Proceedings of the Association for Computational Linguistics (ACL-02)*, pages 104–111.

Martha Palmer, Daniel Gildea, and Paul Kingsbury. 2005. The Proposition Bank: An annotated corpus of semantic roles. *Computational Linguistics*, 31(1):71–106.

Martha Palmer, Hoa Trang Dang, and Christiane Fellbaum. 2007. Making fine-grained and coarse-grained sense distinctions, both manually and automatically. *Journal of Natural Language Engineering*, 13(2).

Martha Palmer, Olga Babko-Malaya, Ann Bies, Mona Diab, Mohammed Maamouri, Aous Mansouri, and Wajdi Zaghouani. 2008. A pilot Arabic propbank. In *Proceedings of the International Conference on Language Resources and Evaluation (LREC)*, Marrakech, Morocco, May 28-30.

Slav Petrov and Dan Klein. 2007. Improved inferencing for unlexicalized parsing. In *Proc of HLT-NAACL*.

Sameer Pradhan, Kadri Hacioglu, Valerie Krugler, Wayne Ward, James Martin, and Dan Jurafsky. 2005. Support vector learning for semantic argument classification. *Machine Learning*, 60(1):11–39.

Sameer Pradhan, Lance Ramshaw, Ralph Weischedel, Jessica MacBride, and Linnea Micciulla. 2007. Unrestricted coreference: Indentifying entities and events in OntoNotes. In *Proceedings of the IEEE International Conference on Semantic Computing (ICSC)*, September 17-19.

Sameer Pradhan, Wayne Ward, and James H. Martin. 2008. Towards robust semantic role labeling. *Computational Linguistics Special Issue on Semantic Role Labeling*, 34(2).

Sameer Pradhan, Lance Ramshaw, Mitchell Marcus, Martha Palmer, Ralph Weischedel, and Nianwen Xue. 2011. CoNLL-2011 shared task: Modeling unrestricted coreference in OntoNotes. In *Proceedings of the Fifteenth Conference on Computational Natural Language Learning: Shared Task*, pages 1–27, Portland, Oregon, USA, June. Association for Computational Linguistics.

Sameer Pradhan, Alessandro Moschitti, Nianwen Xue, Olga Uryupina, and Yuchen Zhang. 2012. CoNLL-2012 shared task: Modeling multilingual unrestricted coreference in OntoNotes. In *Joint Conference on EMNLP and CoNLL - Shared Task*, pages 1–40, Jeju Island, Korea, July. Association for Computational Linguistics.

Rashmi Prasad, Nikhil Dinesh, Alan Lee, Eleni Miltsakaki, Livio Robaldo, Aravind Joshi, and Bonnie Webber. 2008. The Penn discourse treebank 2.0. In *Proceedings of the Sixth International Conference on Language Resources and Evaluation (LREC'08)*, Marrakech, Morocco, May.

Marta Recasens, Lluís Màrquez, Emili Sapena, M. Antònia Martí, Mariona Taulé, Véronique Hoste, Massimo Poesio, and Yannick Versley. 2010. Semeval-2010 task 1: Coreference resolution in multiple languages. In *Proceedings of the 5th International Workshop on Semantic Evaluation*, pages 1–8, Uppsala, Sweden, July.

Marta Recasens, Marie-Catherine de Marneffe, and Christopher Potts. 2013. The life and death of discourse entities: Identifying singleton mentions. In *Proceedings of the 2013 Conference of the North American Chapter of the Association for Computational Linguistics: Human Language Technologies*, pages 627–633, Atlanta, Georgia, June. Association for Computational Linguistics.

Libin Shen, Lucas Champollion, and Aravind K. Joshi. 2008. LTAG-spinal and the treebank. *Language Resources and Evaluation*, 42(1):1–19, March.

Ralph Weischedel and Ada Brunstein. 2005. BBN pronoun coreference and entity type corpus LDC catalog no.: LDC2005T33. BBN Technologies.

Ralph Weischedel, Eduard Hovy, Mitchell Marcus, Martha Palmer, Robert Belvin, Sameer Pradhan, Lance Ramshaw, and Nianwen Xue. 2011. OntoNotes: A large training corpus for enhanced processing. In Joseph Olive, Caitlin Christianson, and John McCary, editors, *Handbook of Natural Language Processing and Machine Translation: DARPA Global Autonomous Language Exploitation*. Springer.

Nianwen Xue and Martha Palmer. 2009. Adding semantic roles to the Chinese Treebank. *Natural Language Engineering*, 15(1):143–172.

Nianwen Xue, Fei Xia, Fu dong Chiou, and Martha Palmer. 2005. The Penn Chinese TreeBank: phrase structure annotation of a large corpus. *Natural Language Engineering*, 11(2):207–238.

Nianwen Xue. 2008. Labeling Chinese predicates with semantic roles. *Computational Linguistics*, 34(2):225–255.

Yaqin Yang and Nianwen Xue. 2010. Chasing the ghost: recovering empty categories in the Chinese treebank. In *Proceedings of the 23rd International Conference on Computational Linguistics (COLING)*, Beijing, China.

Wajdi Zaghouani, Mona Diab, Aous Mansouri, Sameer Pradhan, and Martha Palmer. 2010. The revised Arabic propbank. In *Proceedings of the Fourth Linguistic Annotation Workshop*, pages 222–226, Uppsala, Sweden, July.

Zhi Zhong and Hwee Tou Ng. 2010. It makes sense: A wide-coverage word sense disambiguation system for free text. In *Proceedings of the ACL 2010 System Demonstrations*, pages 78–83, Uppsala, Sweden.

Zhi Zhong, Hwee Tou Ng, and Yee Seng Chan. 2008. Word sense disambiguation using OntoNotes: An empirical study. In *Proceedings of the Conference on Empirical Methods in Natural Language Processing*, pages 1002–1010.

Dynamic Knowledge-Base Alignment for Coreference Resolution

Jiaping Zheng Luke Vilnis Sameer Singh Jinho D. Choi Andrew McCallum
School of Computer Science
University of Massachusetts
Amherst MA 01003
{jzheng,luke,sameer,jdchoi,mccallum}@cs.umass.edu

Abstract

Coreference resolution systems can benefit greatly from inclusion of *global* context, and a number of recent approaches have demonstrated improvements when precomputing an alignment to external knowledge sources. However, since alignment itself is a challenging task and is often noisy, existing systems either align conservatively, resulting in very few links, or combine the attributes of multiple candidates, leading to a conflation of entities. Our approach instead performs joint inference between within-document coreference and entity linking, maintaining ranked lists of candidate entities that are dynamically merged and reranked during inference. Further, we incorporate a large set of surface string variations for each entity by using anchor texts from the web that link to the entity. These forms of global context enables our system to improve classifier-based coreference by 1.09 B^3 F1 points, and improve over the previous state-of-art by 0.41 points, thus introducing a new state-of-art result on the ACE 2004 data.

1 Introduction

Coreference resolution is the task of identifying sets of noun phrase mentions from a document that refer to the same real-world entities. For example, in the following excerpt: *"The Chicago suburb of Arlington Heights is the first stop for* $\langle$*George W. Bush*$\rangle_1$ *today.* $\langle$*The Texas governor*$\rangle_2$ *stops in* $\langle$*Gore's home state*$\rangle_3$ *of* $\langle$*Tennessee*$\rangle_4$ *this afternoon...* ", (m_1, m_2) and (m_3, m_4) define the coreferent pairs. Coreference resolution forms an important component for natural language processing and information extraction pipelines due to its utility in relation extraction, cross-document coreference, text summarization, and question answering. The task of coreference is challenging for automated systems as the local information contained in the document is often not enough to accurately disambiguate mentions, for example, coreferencing (m_1, m_2) requires identifying that George W. Bush (m_1) is the governor of Texas (m_2), and similarly for (m_3, m_4). External knowledge-bases such as FrameNet (Baker et al., 1998), Wikipedia, Yago (Suchanek et al., 2007), and Freebase (Bollacker et al., 2008), can be used to provide *global context*, and there is a strong need for coreference resolution systems to accurately use such sources for disambiguation.

Incorporating external knowledge bases into coreference has been the subject of active recent research. Ponzetto and Strube (2006) and Ratinov and Roth (2012) precompute a fixed alignment of the mentions to the knowledge base entities. The attributes of these entities are used during coreference by incorporating them in the mention features. Since alignment of mentions to the external entities is itself a difficult task, these systems favor high-precision linking. Unfortunately, this results in fewer alignments, and improvements are only shown on mentions that are easier to align and corefer (such as the *non-transcript documents* in Ratinov and Roth (2012)). Alternatively, Rahman and Ng (2011) link each mention to multiple entities in the knowledge base, improving recall at the cost of lower precision; the attributes of all the linked entities are aggregated as features. Although this approach is more robust to noise in the documents, the features of a mention merge the different aspects of the entities, for example a "Michael Jordan" mention will contain features for both the *scientist* and *basketball* personas.

Instead of fixing the alignment of the mentions to the knowledge base, our proposed approach maintains a ranked list of candidate entities for each mention. To expand the set of surface strings that may be used to refer to each entity, the attributes of each candidate contain anchor texts (the visible text) of the links on the web that refer to that entity candidate. When mentions are compared during inference, we use the features computed from the top ranked entity candidate of the antecedent mention. As mentions are merged, the ranked lists of candidate entities are also merged and reranked, often changing the top-ranked entity candidate used in subsequent comparisons. The large set of surface string variations and constant reranking of the entity candidates during inference allows our approach to correct mistakes in alignment and makes external information applicable to a wider variety of mentions.

Our paper provides the following contributions: (1) an approach that jointly reasons about both within-doc entities and their alignment to KB-entities by dynamically adjusting a ranked list of candidate alignments, during coreference, (2) Utilization of a larger set of surface string variations for each entity candidate by using links that appear all over the web (Spitkovsky and Chang, 2012), (3) A combination of these approaches that improves upon a competitive baseline without a knowledge base by 1.09 B^3 F1 points on the ACE 2004 data, and outperforms the state-of-the-art coreference system (Stoyanov and Eisner, 2012) by 0.41 B^3 F1 points, and (4) Accurate predictions on documents that are difficult for coreference, such as the *transcript* documents that were omitted from the evaluation in Ratinov and Roth (2012), and documents that contain a large number of mentions.

2 Baseline Pairwise System

In this section we describe a variant of a commonly-used coreference resolution system that does not utilize external knowledge sources. This widely adopted model casts the problem as a series of binary classifications (Soon et al., 2001; Ng and Cardie, 2002; Ponzetto and Strube, 2006; Bengston and Roth, 2008; Stoyanov et al., 2010). Given a document with its mentions, the system iteratively checks each mention m_j for coreference with preceding mentions using a classifier. A coreference link may be created between m_j and one of these preceding mentions using one of the following strategies. The CLOSESTLINK (Soon et al., 2001) method picks the closest mention to m_j that is positively classified, while the BESTLINK (Ng and Cardie, 2002) method links m_j to the preceding mention that was scored the highest. If none of the preceding mentions are classified as positive (for CLOSESTLINK), or are above a threshold (for BESTLINK), then m_j is left unlinked. After all the mentions have been processed, the links are used to generate a transitive closure that corresponds to the recognized entities in the document.

Types	Features
String-Similarity	mention string match, head string match, head substring match, head word pair, *mention substring match, acronym*
Syntax	number match, gender match, apposition, relative pronoun, mention type, modifier match, *head word POS tags*
Semantic	synonym, antonym, hypernym, modifier relations, both mentions are surrounded by a verb meaning "to say", *demonym match*
Other	predicted entity type, predicted entity type match, both mentions in same sentence, *sentence/token distance, capitalization*

Table 1: Features of the baseline model. Extensions to Bengston and Roth (2008) are *italicized.*

2.1 Pairwise Mention Features

The features used to train our classifier are similar to those in Bengston and Roth (2008), including lexical, syntactical, semantic, predicted NER types, etc., with the exclusion of their "learned features" that require additional classifiers. Further, we include features that compare the mention strings, the distance between the two mentions in terms of the number of sentences and tokens, and the POS tags of the head words. We also use the conjunctions of these features as in Bengston and Roth (2008), as well as the BESTLINK approach. The complete set of features are listed in Table 1.

The training for our system is similar to Bengston and Roth (2008). The positive training examples are generated from mentions and their immediate preceding antecedent. The negative examples are generated from mentions and all their preceding non-coreferent mentions. If the mention is not a pronoun, preceding pronouns are not used to create training examples, and they are also excluded during inference. In contrast to averaged perceptron used in Bengston and Roth (2008), our baseline system is trained using hinge-loss, ℓ_2-regularized SVM.

2.2 Merging Pairwise Features

When a mention m_j is compared against a preceding mention m_i, information from other mentions that are already coreferent with m_i may be helpful in disambiguating m_j as they may contain information that is not available from m_i. Let M be the mentions between m_i and m_j that are coreferent with m_i. Let $m_q \in M$ be the mention that is closest to m_j. All the features from the pair (m_q, m_j), except those that characterize one mention (for example, mention type of m_j), are added to the features between (m_i, m_j). This extends a similar approach by Lee et al. (2011) that merges only the attributes of mentions (such as gender, but not all pairwise features).

2.3 Pruning Comparisons During Training

A potential drawback of including all the negative examples as in Bengston and Roth (2008) is that the negative instances far outnumber the positive ones, which is challenging for training a classifier. In their system, the positive training examples only constitute 1.6% of the total training instances. By contrast, Soon et al. (2001) reduce the number of negative instances by using only mentions between the mention and its closest coreferent pair as negative examples. Instead of just using the closest coreferent mention, we extend this approach to use the k closest of coreferent preceding mentions, where k is tuned using the development data.

3 Dynamic Linking to Knowledge-Base

In this section, we describe our approach to coreference resolution that incorporates external knowledge sources. The approach is an extension of the pairwise model described earlier, with the inclusion of a ranked list of entities, and using a larger set of surface string variations.

3.1 Algorithm

We describe our overall approach in Algorithm 1. The system assumes that the data is annotated with true mention boundaries and mention types. We additionally tokenize the document text and tag the tokens with their parts of speech for use as features. First, an empty entity candidate list is created for each mention in the document. For each proper noun mention, we query a knowledge base for an ordered list of Wikipedia articles that may refer to it, and add these to the mention's candidate list. Other mentions' candidates lists are left empty.

After this pre-processing, each mention m_i is compared against its preceding mentions $m_1 \ldots m_{i-1}$ and their top-ranked entity candidate using a classifier. Amongst antecedents $m_1 \ldots m_{i-1}$ that score above a threshold, the highest-scoring one m_j is marked as coreferent with m_i and the two candidate lists that correspond to m_i and m_j are merged. Merging two mentions results in the merging and reranking of their respective entity candidate lists, described below. If no antecedents score above a threshold, we leave the mention in its singleton cluster.

Algorithm 1 Dynamic Linking to Wikipedia

Input: Mentions $\{m_j\}$
Initialize blank entity lists $\{E_m\}$ ▷ Section 3.2
for $m \in$ Proper Noun Mentions **do**
    LinkWikipedia(m, E_m) ▷ Section 3.2
    PopulateEntityAttrs(E_m) ▷ Section 3.3
end for
for $m_i \in$ Mentions **do**
    Antecedents $\leftarrow \{m_1 ... m_{i-1}\}$
    for $\hat{m} \in$ Antecedents **do**
        $t \leftarrow$ TopRankedAttrs($E_{\hat{m}}$) ▷ Section 3.4
        $s \leftarrow$ Score($\hat{m}$, m_i, t) ▷ Section 3.4
        Scores$_{\hat{m}} \leftarrow s$
    end for
    $m^* \leftarrow \arg\max_{\hat{m}}$ Scores$_{\hat{m}}$
    if Scores$_{m^*} >$ threshold **then**
        MarkCoreferent(m^*, m_i)
        MergeEntityLists(E_{m^*}, E_{m_i}) ▷ Section 3.4
    end if
end for
return Coreferent mention clusters

3.2 Linking to Wikipedia

To create the initial entity candidate lists for proper noun mentions, we query a knowledge base searcher (Dalton and Dietz, 2013) with the text of these mentions. These queries return scored, ranked lists of entity candidates (Wikipedia articles), which we associate with each proper noun mention, leaving the rest of the candidate lists empty. Linking is often noisy, so only selecting the high-precision links as in Ratinov and Roth (2012) results in too few matches, while picking an aggregation of all links results in more noise due to lower precision (Rahman and Ng, 2011). Additionally, since linking is often performed in pre-processing, two mentions that are determined coreferent during inference could still be linked to different KB entities. To avoid these problems, we keep a list of candidate links for each mention, merging the lists when two mentions are determined coreferent, and rerank this list during inference.

3.3 Populating Entity Attributes

After linking to Wikipedia, we have a list of candidate KB entities for each mention. Each entity has access to external information keyed on the Wikipedia article, but this information could more generally come from any knowledge base. Given these entities, there are many possible features that may be used for disambiguation of the mentions, such as *gender* and fine-grained Wikipedia categories as used by Ratinov and Roth (2012), however most of these features may not be relevant to the task of within-document coreference. Instead, an important resource for linking non-proper mentions of an entity is to identify the possible name variations of the entity. For example, it would be useful to know that *Massachusetts* is also referred to as "The 6th State", however this information is not readily available from Wikipedia.[1]

We instead use the corpus described in Spitkovsky and Chang (2012) that consists of anchor texts of links to Wikipedia that appear on web pages. This collection of anchor texts is sufficiently extensive to cover many common misspellings of entity names, as well as many name variations missing from Wikipedia. For example, for the entity "Massachusetts", our anchor texts include misspellings like "Massachussetts" and "Messuchusetts", and the (debatably) affectionate nickname of "Taxachusetts"—none of which are found in Wikipedia. Using these anchor texts, each entity candidate provides a rich set of name variations that we use for disambiguation, as described in the next section.

3.4 Inference with Dynamic Linking

The input to our inference algorithm consists of a number of mentions, a list of ranked entity candidates for the proper noun mentions that are present in the KB, and a list of attributes (in this case, name variations) for each entity candidate.

Scoring: Our underlying model is a pairwise classification approach as described in Section 2. Similar to existing coreference systems such as Bengston and Roth (2008) and Rahman and Ng (2011), we perform coreference resolution using greedy left-to-right pairwise mention classification, clustering each mention with its highest-scoring antecedent (or leaving it as a singleton temporarily if no score is above a threshold). We add the same additional features and perform feature merging operation (Section 2.2) as in our baseline system.

[1]Some of this information is available as *redirects* and from links within Wikipedia, however these do not accurately reflect all the variations of the name.

The top-ranked entity candidate of the antecedent mention is used during coreference to provide additional features for the pairwise classifier. Only using the top-ranked entity candidate allows the system to maintain a consistent *one entity per cluster* hypothesis, reducing the noise resulting from conflated entities. The attributes for this top-ranked entity consist of name variations. We add a binary feature, and conjunctions of this with other features, if the text of the right mention matches one of these name variations.

Entity List Merging: Once a mention pair is scored as coreferent, their corresponding entity candidates are merged. Merging is performed by simply combining the two lists of candidates. Note that there is only one candidate list for a given group of coreferent mentions at any point in inference: if m_1 and m_2 have been previously marked as coreferent, and m_3 is marked as coreferent with m_2, m_1's entity candidates will then contain those from m_3 for future classification decisions.

Re-Ranking: After the two entity candidate lists are merged, we rerank the candidates to identify the top-ranked one. We sort the new list of candidate entities by the number of times each candidate occurs in the list, breaking ties by their original relevance from the KB. For example, if two mentions disagree on the top-ranked KB search result, but agree on the second one, after being clustered they will both use the second search result when creating feature vectors for future coreference decisions. Even though other candidates besides the top-ranked one are ignored for a single classification decision, they may become top-ranked after merging with later candidate sets.

This approach allows our system to use the intermediate results of coreference resolution to re-link mentions to KB entities, reducing the noise and contradictory features from incorrect links. Additionally, features from the KB are added to non-proper noun mentions once those mentions are linked with a populated entity, allowing the results of coreference to enrich non-proper noun mentions with KB-based features. The initial proper noun queries effectively seed the linking process, and KB data is then dynamically spread to the other mentions through coreference.

3.5 Example

We describe a run of our approach on an example in Figure 1. Consider three mentions, each

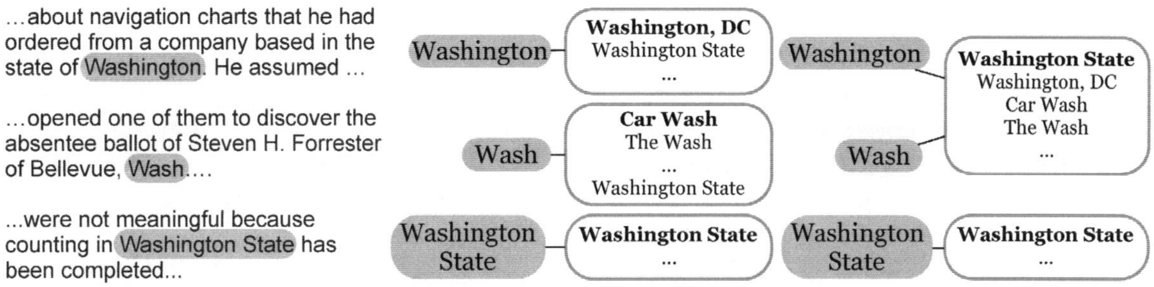

(a) Example Excerpts with Mentions (b) Initial Alignment (top-ranked in bold) (c) Merged and Reranked Alignment

Figure 1: Example of Dynamic Alignment

paired with a top-ranked KB candidate: "Washington", "Wash", and "Washington State". For the first two mentions, clearly the top entity candidate is incorrect; hence approaches that rely on a fixed alignment will perform poorly. In particular, since "Washington State" mention is not compatible with the top-ranked entities of the first two mentions (*Washington, D.C.* and *Car Wash* respectively), approaches that do not modify the ranking during inference may not resolve them. However, the correct candidate *Washington State* does appear in the candidate entities of the first two mentions, albeit with a lower rank. In our approach, clustering the first two mentions causes the shared candidate *Washington State* to move to the top of the list. The coreference system is now able to easily identify that the "Washington State" mention is compatible with the *Washington State* entity formed by the previous two mentions, providing evidence that the final mention should be clustered with either of them in subsequent comparisons.

4 Experiments

4.1 Setup

We evaluate our system on the ACE 2004 annotated dataset (Doddington et al., 2004). Following the setup in Bengston and Roth (2008), we split the corpus into training, development, and test sets, resulting in 268 documents in the train set, 107 documents in the test set, and 68 documents in the development set. The data is processed using standard open source tools to segment the sentences and tokenize the corpus, and using the OpenNLP[2] tagger to obtain the POS tags. The hyperparameters of our system, such as regularization, initial number of candidates, and the number of comparisons during training (k in Section 2.3) are tuned on the development data when trained on the train set. The models we use to evaluate on the test data set are trained on the training and development sets, following the standard evaluation for coreference first used by Culotta et al. (2007).

To provide the initial ranked list of entity candidates from Wikipedia, we query the *KB Bridge* system (Dalton and Dietz, 2013) with the proper name mentions. *KB Bridge* is an information-retrieval-based entity linking system that connects the query mentions to Wikipedia entities using a sequential dependence model. This system has been shown to match or outperform the top performing systems in the 2012 TAC KBP entity linking task.

[2]http://opennlp.apache.org/

4.2 Methods

Our experiments investigate a number of baselines that are similar or identical to existing approaches.

Wikipedia Linking: As a simple baseline, we directly evaluate the quality of the alignment for coreference by merging all pairs of proper noun mentions that share at least one common candidate, as per *KB bridge*. Further, the non-pronoun mentions are linked to these proper nouns if the mention string matches any of the entity titles or anchor texts.

Bengston and Roth (2008): A pairwise coreference model containing a rich set of features, as described and evaluated in Bengston and Roth (2008).

Baseline: Our implementation of a pairwise model that is similar to the approach in Bengston and Roth (2008) with the differences described in Section 2. This is our baseline system that performs coreference without the use of external knowledge. Incidentally, it outperforms Bengston and Roth (2008).

Dynamic linking: This is our complete system as

described in Section 3, in which the list of candidates associated with each mention is reranked and modified during inference.

Static linking: Identical to *dynamic linking* except that entity candidate lists are not merged during inference (i.e., Algorithm 1 without line 17). This approach is comparable to the fixed alignment model, as in the approaches of Ponzetto and Strube (2006) and Ratinov and Roth (2012).

4.3 Results

As in Bengston and Roth (2008), we evaluate our system primarily using the B^3 metric (Bagga and Baldwin, 1998), but also include pairwise, MUC and CEAF(m) metrics. The performance of our systems on the test data set is shown in Table 2. These results use true mentions provided in the dataset, since, as suggested by Ng (2010), coreference resolvers that use different mention detectors (extraction from parse tree, detector trained from gold boundaries, etc.) should not be compared.

Our baseline system outperforms Bengston and Roth (2008) by 0.32 B^3 F1 points on this data set. Incorporating Wikipedia and anchor text information from the web with a fixed alignment (static linking) further improves our performance by 0.54 B^3 F1 points. Using dynamic linking, which improves the alignment during inference, achieves another 0.55 F1 point improvement, which is 1.09 F1 above our baseline, 1.41 F1 above the current best pairwise classification system (corresponding to an error reduction of 7.4%), and 0.4 F1 above the current state-of-art on this dataset (Stoyanov and Eisner, 2012). The improvement of the dynamic linking approach over our baselines is consistent across the various evaluation metrics.

5 Discussion

We also explore our system's performance on subsets of the ACE dataset, and on the OntoNotes dataset.

5.1 Document Length

Coreference becomes more difficult as the number of mentions is increased since the number of pairwise comparisons increases quadratically with the number of mentions. We observe this phenomenon in our dataset: the performance on the smallest third of the documents (when sorted according to number of mentions) is 8.5-10% higher than on the largest third of the documents, as per the B^3 metric.

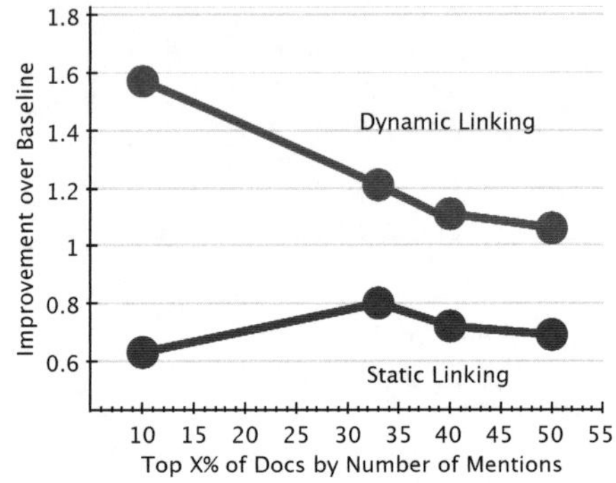

Figure 2: Improvements on the top $X\%$ of documents ranked by the number of mentions.

Method	Non-Transcripts	Transcripts
Baseline	82.50	79.77
RR 2012	83.03	-
Static Linking	83.06	80.25
Dynamic Linking	83.32	81.13

Table 3: B^3 F1 accuracy on transcripts and non-transcripts from the ACE test data. RR 2012 only evaluate on non-transcripts.

However, we expect dynamic linking of entities to be more beneficial on these larger documents as our system can use the information from a larger number of mentions to improve the alignment during inference. Static linking, on the other hand, is unlikely to obtain higher improvements with the larger number of mentions in the document as the alignment is fixed.

We perform the following experiment to analyze the performance with varying numbers of mentions. We sort all the documents in the test set according to their number of mentions, and evaluate on the top $X\%$ of this list (where X is $10, 33, 40, 50$). As the results demonstrate in Figure 2, the improvement of the static linking approach stays fairly even as X is varied. Even though the experiments suggest that the larger documents are tougher to coreference,[3] dynamic linking provides higher improvements when the documents contain a larger number of mentions.

5.2 Performance on Transcripts

The quality of alignment and the coreference predictions for a document is influenced by the quality of the mentions in the document. In particular,

[3]i.e., the absolute values are lower for these splits. The baseline system obtains 83.08, 79.29, 79.64, and 79.77 respectively for $X = 10, 33, 40, 50$.

Method	Pairwise		MUC		CEAF		B^3	
	P / R	F1	P / R	F1	P / R	F1	P / R	F1
Culotta et al. (2007)	-	-	-	-	-	-	86.7 73.2	79.3
Raghunathan et al. (2010)	71.6 46.2	56.1	80.4 71.8	75.8	-	-	86.3 75.4	80.4
Stoyanov and Eisner (2012)	-	-	-	**80.1**	-	-	-	81.8
Wiki-linking	64.15 14.99	24.30	74.41 28.39	41.10	58.54 58.4	58.47	92.89 57.21	70.81
Bengston and Roth (2008)	-	-	82.7 69.9	75.8	-	-	88.3 74.5	80.8
Baseline	66.56 47.07	55.14	82.84 72.02	77.05	75.58 75.40	75.49	87.02 75.97	81.12
Static Linking	82.53 40.80	54.61	88.39 66.93	76.18	75.33 75.35	75.44	93.10 72.72	81.66
Dynamic Linking	72.20 47.40	**57.23**	85.07 72.02	78.01	76.55 76.37	**76.46**	89.37 76.12	**82.21**

Table 2: Evaluation on the ACE test data, with the system trained on the train and development sets.

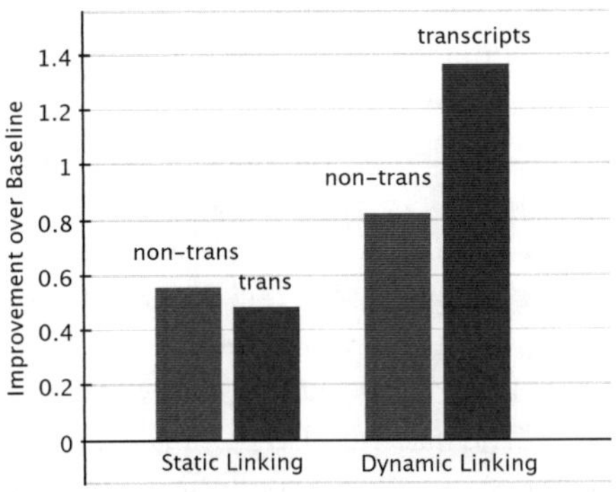

Figure 3: Comparison on the transcripts data.

ACE contains a large number of broadcast news documents, many of which consist of transcribed data containing noise in the form of incomplete sentences and disfluencies. Since these transcripts provide an additional challenge for alignment and coreference, Ratinov and Roth (2012) only use the set of non-transcripts for their evaluation.

Using dynamic linking and a large set of surface string variations, our approach may be able to provide an improvement even on the transcripts. To identify the transcripts in the test set, we use the approximation from Ratinov and Roth (2012) that considers a document to be non-transcribed if it contains proper noun mentions and at least a third of those start with a capital letter. The performance is shown in Table 3, while the improvement over our baseline is shown in Figure 3.

Our static linking matches the performance of Ratinov and Roth (2012) on the non-transcripts. Further, the improvement of static linking on the transcripts over the baseline is lower than that on the non-transcript data, suggesting that noisy mentions and text result in poor quality alignment. Dynamic linking, on the other hand, not only outperforms all other systems, but also shows a higher improvement over the baseline on the transcripts than on non-transcripts. This indicates that dynamic linking approach is robust to noise, and its wider variety of surface strings and flexible alignments are especially useful for transcripts.

5.3 OntoNotes

We also run our systems on the OntoNotes dataset, which was used for evaluation in CoNLL 2011 Shared Task (Pradhan et al., 2011). The dataset consists of 2083 documents from a much larger variety of genres, such as conversations, magazines, web text, etc. Further, the dataset also consists of mentions that refer to events, most of which do not appear as Wikipedia pages. Since only the non-singleton mentions are annotated in the training set, we also include additional noun phrase mentions during training. We obtain B^3 F1 of 65.3, 67.6, and 67.7 for our baseline, static linking, and dynamic linking respectively.[4] When compared to the participants of the closed task, the dynamic linking system outperforms all but two on this metric, suggesting that dynamic alignment is beneficial even when the features have not been engineered for events or for different genres.

6 Related Work

Within-document coreference has been well-studied for a number of years. A variety of approaches incorporate linguistic knowledge as rules iteratively applied to identify the chains, such as Haghighi and Klein (2009), Raghunathan et al. (2010), Stoyanov et al. (2010). Alternatively (and similar to our approach), others represent this knowledge as *features* in a machine learning model. Early applications of such models include Soon et al. (2001), Ng and Cardie (2002) and (Bengston and Roth, 2008). There are also a number of techniques that represent entities explicitly (Culotta et

[4]with MUC 46.1, 49.9 & 50.1, and CEAF(m) 47.9, 49.6 & 49.8, respectively for baseline, static and dynamic linking.

al., 2007; Wick et al., 2009; Haghighi and Klein, 2010; Stoyanov and Eisner, 2012).

This work is an extension of recent approaches that incorporate external knowledge sources to improve within-document coreference. Ponzetto and Strube (2006) identify Wikipedia candidates for each mention as a preprocessing step, and incorporate them as features in a pairwise model. Our method differs in that we draw such features from entity candidates during inference, and also maintain and update a set of candidate entity links instead of selecting only one. Rahman and Ng (2011) introduce similar features from a more extensive set of knowledge sources (such as YAGO and FrameNet) into a cluster-based model whose features change as inference proceeds. However, the features for each cluster come from a combination of all entities aligned to the cluster mentions. We improve upon this approach by maintaining a list of the candidate entities for each mention cluster, modifying this list during the course of inference, and using features from only the top-ranked candidate at any time. Further, they do not provide a comparison on a standard dataset.

Ratinov and Roth (2012) extend the multi-sieve coreference model (Raghunathan et al., 2010) by identifying at most a single candidate for each mention, and incorporating high-precision attributes extracted from Wikipedia. The high-precision mention-candidate pairings are precomputed and fixed; additionally, the features for an entity are based on the predictions of the previous sieves, thus fixed while a sieve is applied. With these restrictions, they show improvements over the state-of-the-art on a subset of ACE mentions that are more easily aligned to Wikipedia, while our approach demonstrates improvements on the complete set of mentions including the tougher to link mentions from the transcripts.

There are a number of approaches that provide an alignment from mentions in a document to Wikipedia. Wikifier (Ratinov et al., 2011) analyzes the context around the mentions and the entities jointly, and was used to align mentions for coreference in Ratinov and Roth (2012). Dalton and Dietz (2013) introduce an approximation to the above approach, but incorporate retrieval-based supervised reranking that provides multiple candidates and scores; this approach performed competitively on previous TAC-KBP entity linking benchmarks (Dietz and Dalton, 2012). Alignment to an external knowledge-base has improved performance for a number of NLP and information extraction tasks, such as named-entity recognition (Cucerzan, 2007; Han and Zhao, 2009), cross-document coreference (Finin et al., 2009; Singh et al., 2010), and relation-extraction (Riedel et al., 2010; Hoffmann et al., 2011).

7 Conclusions

In this paper, we incorporate external knowledge to improve within-document coreference. Instead of fixing the alignment *a priori*, our approach maintains a ranked list of candidate entities for each mention, and merges and reranks the list during inference. Further, we consider a large set of surface string variations for each entity by using anchor texts from the web. These external sources allow our system to achieve a new state-of-the-art on the ACE data. We also demonstrate improvements on documents that are difficult for alignment and coreference, such as transcripts and documents containing a large number of mentions.

A number of possible avenues for future study are apparent. First, our alignment to a knowledge-base can benefit from more document-aware linking to entities, such as the Wikifier (Ratinov et al., 2011). Second, we would like to augment mention features with additional information available from the knowledge base, such as Wikipedia categorization and gender attributes. We also want to investigate a cluster ranking model, as used in (Rahman and Ng, 2011; Stoyanov and Eisner, 2012), to aggregate the features of all the coreferent mentions as inference progresses.

Acknowledgments

This work was supported in part by the Center for Intelligent Information Retrieval, in part by DARPA under agreement number FA8750-13-2-0020, in part by NSF medium IIS-0803847 and in part by an award from Google. The U.S. Government is authorized to reproduce and distribute reprint for Governmental purposes notwithstanding any copyright annotation thereon. Any opinions, findings and conclusions or recommendations expressed in this material are the authors' and necessarily those of the sponsor.

References

Amit Bagga and Breck Baldwin. 1998. Algorithms for scoring coreference chains. In *International Conference on Language Resources and Evaluation (LREC) Workshop on Linguistics Coreference*, pages 563–566.

Collin F. Baker, Charles J. Fillmore, and John B. Lowe. 1998. The berkeley framenet project. In *Proceedings of the 36th Annual Meeting of the Association for Computational Linguistics and 17th International Conference on Computational Linguistics - Volume 1*, ACL '98, pages 86–90, Stroudsburg, PA, USA. Association for Computational Linguistics.

Eric Bengston and Dan Roth. 2008. Understanding the value of features for coreference resolution. In *Empirical Methods in Natural Language Processing (EMNLP)*.

Kurt Bollacker, Colin Evans, Praveen Paritosh, Tim Sturge, and Jamie Taylor. 2008. Freebase: a collaboratively created graph database for structuring human knowledge. In *Proceedings of the 2008 ACM SIGMOD international conference on Management of data*, SIGMOD '08, pages 1247–1250, New York, NY, USA. ACM.

Silviu Cucerzan. 2007. Large-scale named entity disambiguation based on Wikipedia data. In *Empirical Methods in Natural Language Processing (EMNLP)*, pages 708–716.

Aron Culotta, Michael Wick, and Andrew McCallum. 2007. First-order probabilistic models for coreference resolution. In *North American Chapter of the Association for Computational Linguistics - Human Language Technologies (NAACL HLT)*.

Jeffrey Dalton and Laura Dietz. 2013. A neighborhood relevance model for entity linking. In *Open Research Areas in Information Retrieval (OAIR)*.

Laura Dietz and Jeffrey Dalton. 2012. Across-document neighborhood expansion: UMass at TAC KBP 2012 entity linking. In *Text Analysis Conference (TAC)*.

G. Doddington, A. Mitchell, M. Przybocki, L. Ramshaw, S. Strassel, and R. Weischedel. 2004. The Automatic Content Extraction (ACE) program–tasks, data, and evaluation. In *Proceedings of LREC*, volume 4, pages 837–840. Citeseer.

Tim Finin, Zareen Syed, James Mayfield, Paul McNamee, and Christine Piatko. 2009. Using Wikitology for cross-document entity coreference resolution. In *AAAI Spring Symposium on Learning by Reading and Learning to Read*.

Aria Haghighi and Dan Klein. 2009. Simple coreference resolution with rich syntactic and semantic features. In *Empirical Methods in Natural Language Processing (EMNLP)*, pages 1152–1161.

Aria Haghighi and Dan Klein. 2010. Coreference resolution in a modular, entity-centered model. In *North American Chapter of the Association for Computational Linguistics - Human Language Technologies (NAACL HLT)*, pages 385–393.

Xianpei Han and Jun Zhao. 2009. Named entity disambiguation by leveraging Wikipedia semantic knowledge. In *Conference on Information and Knowledge Management (CIKM)*, pages 215–224.

Raphael Hoffmann, Congle Zhang, Xiao Ling, Luke Zettlemoyer, and Daniel S. Weld. 2011. Knowledge-based weak supervision for information extraction of overlapping relations. In *Annual Meeting of the Association for Computational Linguistics (ACL)*, pages 541–550, Portland, Oregon, USA, June. Association for Computational Linguistics.

Heeyoung Lee, Yves Peirsman, Angel Chang, Nathanael Chambers, Mihai Surdeanu, and Dan Jurafsky. 2011. Stanford's multi-pass sieve coreference resolution system at the CoNLL-2011 shared task. In *Conference on Computational Natural Language Learning (CoNLL)*, pages 28–34. Association for Computational Linguistics.

Vincent Ng and Claire Cardie. 2002. Improving machine learning approaches to coreference resolution. In *Annual Meeting of the Association for Computational Linguistics (ACL)*, pages 104–111.

Vincent Ng. 2010. Supervised noun phrase coreference research: the first fifteen years. In *Proceedings of the 48th Annual Meeting of the Association for Computational Linguistics*, ACL '10, pages 1396–1411, Stroudsburg, PA, USA. Association for Computational Linguistics.

Simone Paolo Ponzetto and Michael Strube. 2006. Exploiting semantic role labeling, WordNet and Wikipedia for coreference resolution. In *North American Chapter of the Association for Computational Linguistics - Human Language Technologies (NAACL HLT)*, pages 192–199.

Sameer Pradhan, Lance Ramshaw, Mitchell Marcus, Martha Palmer, Ralph Weischedel, and Nianwen Xue. 2011. CoNLL-2011 shared task: Modeling unrestricted coreference in ontonotes. In *Conference on Computational Natural Language Learning (CoNLL)*, pages 1–27.

Karthik Raghunathan, Heeyoung Lee, Sudarshan Rangarajan, Nathanael Chambers, Mihai Surdeanu, Dan Jurafsky, and Christopher Manning. 2010. A multi-pass sieve for coreference resolution. In *Empirical Methods in Natural Language Processing (EMNLP)*, pages 492–501. Association for Computational Linguistics.

Altaf Rahman and Vincent Ng. 2011. Coreference resolution with world knowledge. In *Annual Meeting of the Association for Computational Linguistics (ACL)*, pages 814–824, Portland, Oregon, USA, June.

L. Ratinov and D. Roth. 2012. Learning-based multi-sieve co-reference resolution with knowledge. In *Empirical Methods in Natural Language Processing (EMNLP)*.

L. Ratinov, D. Roth, D. Downey, and M. Anderson. 2011. Local and global algorithms for disambiguation to wikipedia. In *Annual Meeting of the Association for Computational Linguistics (ACL)*.

Sebastian Riedel, Limin Yao, and Andrew McCallum. 2010. Collective cross-document relation extraction without labelled data. In *Empirical Methods in Natural Language Processing (EMNLP)*.

Sameer Singh, Michael L. Wick, and Andrew McCallum. 2010. Distantly labeling data for large scale cross-document coreference. *Computing Research Repository (CoRR)*, abs/1005.4298.

Wee Meng Soon, Hwee Tou Ng, and Daniel Chung Yong Lim. 2001. A machine learning approach to coreference resolution of noun phrases. *Computational Linguistics*, 27(4):521–544, Dec.

Valentin I. Spitkovsky and Angel X. Chang. 2012. A cross-lingual dictionary for english wikipedia concepts. In *International Conference on Language Resources and Evaluation (LREC)*.

Veselin Stoyanov and Jason Eisner. 2012. Easy-first coreference resolution. In *Computational Linguistics (COLING)*.

Veselin Stoyanov, Claire Cardie, Nathan Gilbert, Ellen Riloff, David Buttler, and David Hysom. 2010. Coreference resolution with reconcile. In *Annual Meeting of the Association for Computational Linguistics (ACL)*, pages 156–161, Stroudsburg, PA, USA. Association for Computational Linguistics.

Fabian M. Suchanek, Gjergji Kasneci, and Gerhard Weikum. 2007. Yago: a core of semantic knowledge. In *Proceedings of the 16th international conference on World Wide Web*, WWW '07, pages 697–706, New York, NY, USA. ACM.

Michael Wick, Aron Culotta, Khashayar Rohanimanesh, and Andrew McCallum. 2009. An entity-based model for coreference resolution. In *SIAM International Conference on Data Mining (SDM)*.

A Non-Monotonic Arc-Eager Transition System for Dependency Parsing

Matthew Honnibal
Department of Computing
Macquarie University
Sydney, Australia
matthew.honnibal@mq.edu.edu.au

Yoav Goldberg
Department of Computer Science
Bar Ilan University
Ramat Gan, Israel
yoav.goldberg@gmail.com

Mark Johnson
Department of Computing
Macquarie University
Sydney, Australia
mark.johnson@mq.edu.edu.au

Abstract

Previous incremental parsers have used monotonic state transitions. However, transitions can be made to revise previous decisions quite naturally, based on further information.

We show that a simple adjustment to the Arc-Eager transition system to relax its monotonicity constraints can improve accuracy, so long as the training data includes examples of mistakes for the non-monotonic transitions to repair. We evaluate the change in the context of a state-of-the-art system, and obtain a statistically significant improvement ($p < 0.001$) on the English evaluation and 5/10 of the CoNLL languages.

1 Introduction

Historically, monotonicity has played an important role in transition-based parsing systems. Non-monotonic systems, including the one presented here, typically redundantly generate multiple derivations for each syntactic analysis, leading to *spurious ambiguity* (Steedman, 2000). Early, pre-statistical work on transition-based parsing such as Abney and Johnson (1991) implicitly assumed that the parser searches the entire space of possible derivations. The presence of spurious ambiguity causes this search space to be a directed graph rather than a tree, which considerably complicates the search, so spurious ambiguity was avoided whenever possible.

However, we claim that non-monotonicity and spurious ambiguity are not disadvantages in a modern statistical parsing system such as ours. Modern statistical models have much larger search spaces because almost all possible analyses are allowed, and a numerical score (say, a probability distribution) is used to distinguish better analyses from worse ones. These search spaces are so large that we cannot exhaustively search them, so instead we use the scores associated with partial analyses to guide a search that explores only a minuscule fraction of the space (In our case we use greedy decoding, but even a beam search only explores a small fraction of the exponentially-many possible analyses).

In fact, as we show here the additional redundant pathways between search states that non-monotonicity generates can be advantageous because they allow the parser to "correct" an earlier parsing move and provide an opportunity to recover from formerly "fatal" mistakes. Informally, non-monotonicity provides "many paths up the mountain" in the hope of making it easier to find at least one.

We demonstrate this by modifying the Arc-Eager transition system (Nivre, 2003; Nivre et al., 2004) to allow a limited capability for non-monotonic transitions. The system normally employs two deterministic constraints that limit the parser to actions consistent with the previous history. We remove these, and update the transitions so that conflicts are resolved in favour of the latest prediction.

The non-monotonic behaviour provides an improvement of up to 0.2% accuracy over the current state-of-the-art in greedy parsing. It is possible to implement the greedy parser we describe very efficiently: our implementation, which can be found at `http://www.github.com/syllog1sm/redshift`, parses over 500 sentences a second on commodity hardware.

2 The Arc-Eager Transition System

In transition-based parsing, a parser consists of a state (or a configuration) which is manipulated by a set of actions. An action is applied to a state and results in a new state. The parsing process concludes when the parser reaches a final state, at which the parse tree is read from the state. A particular set of states and actions yield a transition-system. Our starting point in this paper is the popular Arc-Eager transition system, described in detail by Nivre (2008).

The state of the arc-eager system is composed of a stack, a buffer and a set of arcs. The stack and the buffer hold the words of a sentence, and the set of arcs represent derived dependency relations.

We use a notation in which the stack items are indicated by S_i, with S_0 being the top of the stack, S_1 the item previous to it and so on. Similarly, buffer items are indicated as B_i, with B_0 being the first item on the buffer. The arcs are of the form (h, l, m), indicating a dependency in which the word m modifies the word h with label l.

In the initial configuration the stack is empty, and the buffer contains the words of the sentence followed by an artificial ROOT token, as suggested by Ballesteros and Nivre (2013). In the final configuration the buffer is empty and the stack contains the ROOT token.

There are four parsing actions (Shift, Left-Arc, Right-Arc and Reduce, abbreviated as S,L,R,D respectively) that manipulate stack and buffer items. The **Shift** action pops the first item from the buffer and pushes it on the stack (the Shift action has a natural precondition that the buffer is not empty, as well as a precondition that ROOT can only be pushed to an empty stack). The **Right-Arc** action is similar to the Shift action, but it also adds a dependency arc (S_0, B_0), with the current top of the stack as the head of the newly pushed item (the Right action has an additional precondition that the stack is not empty).[1] The **Left-Arc** action adds a dependency arc (B_0, S_0) with the first item in the buffer as the head of the top of the stack, and pops the stack (with a precondition that the stack and buffer are not empty, and that S_0 is not assigned a head yet). Finally, the **Reduce** action pops the stack, with a precondition that the stack is not empty and that S_0 is already assigned a head.

[1]For labelled dependency parsing, the Right-Arc and Left-Arc actions are parameterized by a label L such that the action Right_L adds an arc (S_0, L, B_0), similarly for Left_L.

2.1 Monotonicty

The preconditions of the Left-Arc and Reduce actions ensure that every word is assigned exactly one head, resulting in a well-formed parse tree. The single head constraint is enforced by ensuring that once an action has been performed, subsequent actions must be consistent with it. We refer to this consistency as the *monotonicity* of the system.

Due to monotonicity, there is a natural pairing between the Right-Arc and Reduce actions and the Shift and Left-Arc actions: a word which is pushed into the stack by Right-Arc must be popped using Reduce, and a word which is pushed by Shift action must be popped using Left-Arc. As a consequence of this pairing, a Right-Arc move determines that the head of the pushed token must be to its left, while a Shift moves determines a head to its right. Crucially, the decision whether to Right-Arc or Shift is often taken in a state of missing information regarding the continuation of the sentence, forcing an incorrect head assignment on a subsequent move.

Consider a sentence pair such as (a)"I saw Jack and Jill" / (b)"I saw Jack and Jill fall". In (a), "Jack and Jill" is the NP object of "saw", while in (b) it is a subject of the embedded verb "fall". The monotonic arc-eager parser has to decide on an analysis as soon as it sees "saw" on the top of the stack and "Jack" at the front of the buffer, without access to the disambiguating verb "fall".

In what follows, we suggest a non-monotonic variant of the Arc-Eager transition system, allowing the parser to recover from the incorrect head assignments which are forced by an incorrect resolution of a Shift/Right-Arc ambiguity.

3 The Non-Monotonic Arc-Eager System

The Arc-Eager transition system (Nivre et al., 2004) has four moves. Two of them create dependencies, two push a word from the buffer to the stack, and two remove an item from the stack:

	Push	Pop
Adds dependency	*Right-Arc*	**Left-Arc**
No new dependency	**Shift**	*Reduce*

Every word in the sentence is pushed once and popped once; and every word must have exactly one head. This creates two pairings, along the diagonals: (S, L) and (R, D). Either the push move adds the head or the pop move does, but not both and not neither.

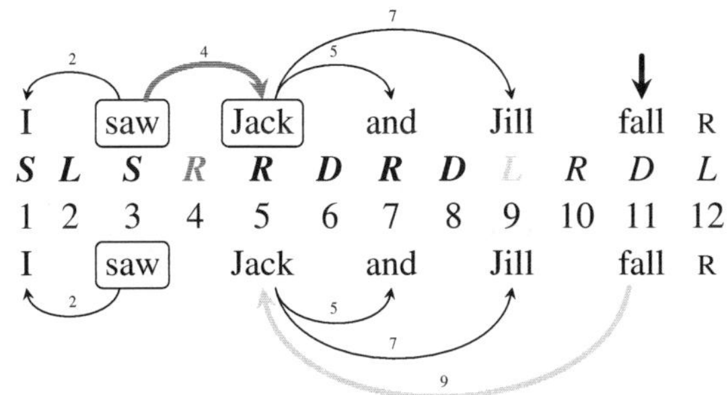

Figure 1: State before and after a non-monotonic Left-Arc. At move 9, *fall* is the first word of the buffer (marked with an arrow), and *saw* and *Jack* are on the stack (circled). The arc created at move 4 was incorrect (in red). Arcs are labelled with the move that created them. After move 9 (the lower state), the non-monotonic Left-Arc move has replaced the incorrect dependency with a correct Left-Arc (in green).

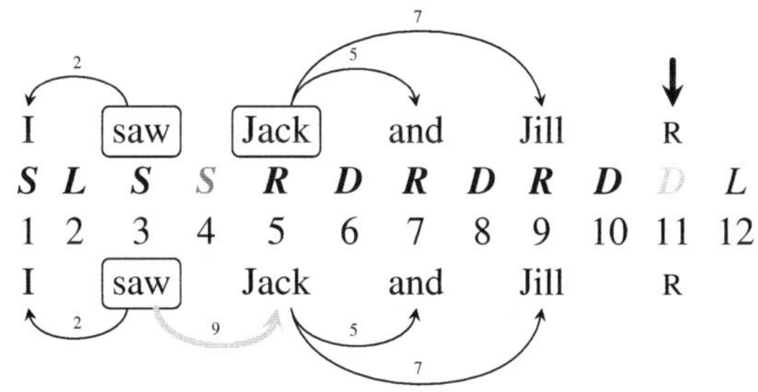

Figure 2: State before and after a non-monotonic Reduce. After making the wrong push move at 4, at move 11 the parser has *Jack* on the stack (circled), with only the dummy ROOT token left in the buffer. A monotonic parser must deterministically Left-Arc *Jack* here to preserve the previous decision, despite the current state. We remove this constraint, and instead assume that when the model selects Reduce for a headless item, it is reversing the previous Shift/Right decision. We add the appropriate arc, assigning the label that scored highest when the Shift/Right decision was made.

Thus in the Arc-Eager system the first move determines the corresponding second move. In our non-monotonic system the second move can overwrite an attachment made by the first. This change makes the transition system *non-monotonic*, because if the model decides on an incongruent pairing we will have to either undo or add a dependency, depending on whether we correct a prior Right-Arc, or a prior Shift.

3.1 Non-monotonic Left-Arc

Figure 1 shows a before-and-after view of a non-monotonic transition. The sequence below the words shows the transition history. The words that are circled in the upper and lower line are on the stack before and after the transition, respectively. The arrow shows the start of the buffer, and arcs are labelled with the move that added them.

The parser began correctly by Shifting *I* and Left-Arcing it to *saw*, which was then also Shifted. The mistake, made at Move 4, was to Right-Arc *Jack* instead of Shifting it.

The difficulty of this kind of a decision for an incremental parser is fundamental. The leftward context does not constrain the decision, and an arbitrary amount of text could separate *Jack* from *fall*. Eye-tracking experiments show that humans often perform a saccade while reading such examples (Frazier and Rayner, 1982).

In moves 5-8 the parser correctly builds the rest of the NP, and arrives at *fall*. The monotonicity constraints would force an incorrect analysis, having *fall* modify *Jack* or *saw*, or having *saw* modify *fall* as an embedded verb with no arguments.

We allow Left-Arcs to 'clobber' edges set by Right-Arcs if the model recommends it. The previous edge is deleted, and the Left-Arc proceeds as normal. The effect of this is exactly as if the model had correctly chosen Shift at move 4. We simply give the model a second chance to make the correct choice.

3.2 Non-monotonic Reduce

The upper arcs in Figure 2 show a state resulting from the opposite error. The parser has Shifted *Jack* instead of Right-Arcing it. After building the NP the buffer is exhausted, except for the ROOT token, which is used to wrongly Left-Arc *Jack* as the sentence's head word.

Instead of letting the previous choice lock us in to the pair (Shift, Left-Arc), we let the later decision reverse it to (Right-Arc, Reduce), if the parser has predicted Reduce in spite of the signal from its previous decision. In the context shown in Figure 2, the correctness of the Reduce move is quite predictable, once the choice is made available.

When the Shift/Right-Arc decision is reversed, we add an arc between the top of the stack (S_0) and the word preceding it (S_1). This is the arc that would have been created had the parser chosen to Right-Arc when it chose to Shift. Since our idea is to reverse this mistake, we select the Right-Arc label that the model scored most highly at that time.[2]

[2] An alternative approach to label assignment is to parameterize the Reduce action with a label, similar to the Right-Arc and Left-Arc actions, and let that label override the previously predicted label. This would allow the parser to con-

To summarize, our Non-Monotnonic Arc-Eager system differs from the monotonic Arc-Eager system by:

- Changing the Left-Arc action by removing the precondition that S_0 does not have a head, and updating the dependency arcs such previously derived arcs having S_0 as a dependent are removed from the arcs set.
- Changing the Reduce action by removing the precondition that S_0 has a head, and updating the dependency arcs such that if S_0 does not have a head, S_1 is assigned as the head of S_0.

4 Why have two push moves?

We have argued above that it is better to trust the second decision that the model makes, rather than using the first decision to determine the second. If this is the case, is the first decision entirely redundant? Instead of defining how pop moves can correct Shift/Right-Arc mistakes, we could instead eliminate the ambiguity. There are two possibilities: Shift every token, and create all Right-Arcs via Reduce; or Right-Arc every token, and replace them with Left-Arcs where necessary.

Preliminary experiments on the development data revealed a problem with these approaches. In many cases the decision whether to Shift or Right-Arc is quite clear, and its result provides useful conditioning context to later decisions. The information that determined those decisions is never lost, but saving all of the difficulty for later is not a very good structured prediction strategy.

As an example of the problem, if the Shift move is eliminated, about half of the Right-Arcs created will be spurious. All of these arcs will be assigned labels making important features uselessly noisy. In the other approach, we avoid creating spurious arcs, but the model does not predict whether S_0 is attached to S_1, or what the label would be, and we miss useful features.

The non-monotonic transition system we propose does not have these problems. The model learns to make Shift vs. Right-Arc decisions as normal, and conditions on them — but without *committing* to them.

dition its label decision on the new context, which was sufficiently surprising to change its move prediction. For efficiency and simplicity reasons, we chose instead to trust the label the model proposed when the reduced token was initially pushed into the stack. This requires an extra vector of labels to be stored during parsing.

5 Dynamic Oracles

An essential component when training a transition-based parser is an oracle which, given a gold-standard tree, dictates the sequence of moves a parser should make in order to derive it. Traditionally, these oracles are defined as functions from trees to sequences, mapping a gold tree to a single sequence of actions deriving it, even if more than one sequence of actions derives the gold tree. We call such oracles *static*. Recently, Goldberg and Nivre (2012) introduced the concept of a *dynamic* oracle, and presented a concrete oracle for the arc-eager system. Instead of mapping a gold tree to a sequence of actions, the dynamic oracle maps a $\langle$configuration, gold tree$\rangle$ pair to a *set* of optimal transitions. More concretely, the dynamic oracle presented in Goldberg and Nivre (2012) maps $\langle \text{action}, \text{configuration}, \text{tree} \rangle$ tuples to an integer, indicating the number of gold arcs in $tree$ that can be derived from $configuration$ by some sequence of actions, but could not be derived after applying $action$ to the configuration.

There are two advantages to this. First, the ability to label any configuration, rather than only those along a single path to the gold-standard derivation, allows much better training data to be generated. States come with realistic histories, including errors — a critical point for the current work. Second, the oracle accounts for spurious ambiguity correctly, as it will label multiple actions as correct if the optimal parses resulting from them are equally accurate.

In preliminary experiments in which we trained the parser using the static oracle but allowed the non-monotonic repair operations during parsing, we found that the the repair moves yielded no improvement. This is because the static oracle does not generate any examples of the repair moves during training, causing the parser to rarely predict them in test time. We will first describe the Arc-Eager dynamic oracle, and then define dynamic oracles for the non-monotonic transition systems we present.

5.1 Monotonic Arc-Eager Dynamic Oracle

We now briefly describe the dynamic oracle for the arc-eager system. For more details, see Goldberg and Nivre (2012). The oracle is computed by reasoning about the arcs which are reachable from a given state, and counting the number of gold arcs which will no longer be reachable after applying a given transition at a given state. [3]

The reasoning is based on the observations that in the arc-eager system, new arcs (h, l, m) can be derived iff the following conditions hold:
(a) There is no existing arc (h', l', m) such that $h' \neq h$, and (b) Either both h and m are on the buffer, or one of them is on the buffer and the other is on the stack. In other words:
(a) once a word acquires a head (in a Left-Arc or Right-Arc transition) it loses the ability to acquire any other head.
(b) once a word is moved from the buffer to the stack (Shift or Right-Arc) it loses the ability to acquire heads that are currently on the stack, as well as dependents that are currently on the stack and are not yet assigned a head.[4]
(c) once a word is removed from the stack (Left-Arc or Reduce) it loses the ability to acquire any dependents on the buffer.
Based on these observations, Goldberg and Nivre (2012) present an oracle $\mathcal{C}(a, c, t)$ for the monotonic arc-eager system, computing the number of arcs in the gold tree t that are reachable from a parser's configuration c and are no longer reachable from the configuration $a(c)$ resulting from the application of action a to configuration c.

5.2 Non-monotonic Dynamic Oracles

Given the oracle $\mathcal{C}(a, c, t)$ for the monotonic system, we adapt it to a non-monotonic variant by considering the changes from the monotonic to the non-monotonic system, and adding Δ terms accordingly. We define three novel oracles: $\mathcal{C}_{NML}$, $\mathcal{C}_{NMD}$ and $\mathcal{C}_{NML+D}$ for systems with a non-monotonic Left-Arc, Reduce or both.

$$\begin{aligned}
\mathcal{C}_{NML}(a,c,t) &= \mathcal{C}(a,c,t) + \Delta_{NML}(a,c,t) \\
\mathcal{C}_{NMD}(a,c,t) &= \mathcal{C}(a,c,t) + \Delta_{NMD}(a,c,t) \\
\mathcal{C}_{NML+D}(a,c,t) &= \mathcal{C}(a,c,t) + \Delta_{NML}(a,c,t) \\
&\quad + \Delta_{NMD}(a,c,t)
\end{aligned}$$

The terms Δ_{NML} and Δ_{NMD} reflect the score adjustments that need to be done to the arc-eager oracle due to the changes of the Left-Arc and Reduce actions, respectively, and are detailed below.

Changes due to non-monotonic Left-Arc:

- $\Delta_{NML}(\text{RIGHTARC}, c, t)$: The cost of Right-Arc is decreased by 1 if the gold head of B_0 is on the buffer (because B_0 can still acquire its correct head later with a Left-Arc action). It is increased by 1 for any word w on the stack such that B_0 is the gold parent of w and w is assigned a head already (in the monotonic oracle, this cost was taken care of when the word was assigned an incorrect head. In the non-monotonic variant, this cost is delayed).
- $\Delta_{NML}(\text{REDUCE}, c, t)$: The cost of Reduce is increased by 1 if the gold head of S_0 is on the buffer, because removing S_0 from the stack precludes it from acquiring its correct head later on with a Left-Arc action. (This cost is paid for in the monotonic version when S_0 acquired its incorrect head).
- $\Delta_{NML}(\text{LEFTARC}, c, t)$: The cost of Left-Arc is increased by 1 if S_0 is already assigned to its gold parent. (This situation is blocked by a precondition in the monotonic case). The cost is also increased if S_0 is assigned to a non-gold parent, and the gold parent is in the buffer, but not B_0. (As a future non-monotonic Left-Arc is prevented from setting the correct head.)
- $\Delta_{NML}(\text{SHIFT}, c, gold)$: The cost of Shift is increased by 1 for any word w on the stack such that B_0 is the gold parent of w and w is assigned a head already. (As in Right-Arc, in the monotonic oracle, this cost was taken care of when w was assigned an incorrect head.)

Changes due to non-monotonic Reduce:

- $\Delta_{NMD}(\text{SHIFT}, c, gold)$: The cost of Shift is decreased by 1 if the gold head of B_0 is S_0 (Because this arc can be added later on with a non-monotonic Reduce action).
- $\Delta_{NMD}(\text{LEFTARC}, c, gold)$: The cost of Left-Arc is increased by 1 if S_0 is not assigned a head, and the gold head of S_0 is S_1 (Because this precludes adding the correct arc with a Reduce of S_0 later).
- $\Delta_{NMD}(\text{REDUCE}, c, gold) = 0$. While it may seem that a change to the cost of a Reduce action is required, in fact the costs of the monotonic system hold here, as the head of S_0 is

[3]The correctness of the oracle is based on a property of the arc-eager system, stating that if a set of arcs which can be extended to a projective tree can be individually derived from a given configuration, then a projective tree containing all of the arcs in the set is also derivable from the same configuration. This same property holds also for the non-monotonic variants we propose.

[4]The condition that the words on the stack are not yet assigned a head is missing from (Goldberg and Nivre, 2012)

predetermined to be S_1. The needed adjustments are taken care of in Left-Arc and Shift actions.[5]

- $\Delta_{NMD}(\text{RIGHTARC}, c, gold) = 0$

6 Applying the Oracles in Training

Once the dynamic-oracles for the non-monotonic system are defined, we could in principle just plug them in the perceptron-based training procedure described in Goldberg and Nivre (2012). However, a tacit assumption of the dynamic-oracles is that all paths to recovering a given arc are treated equally. This assumption may be sub-optimal for the purpose of training a parser for a non-monotonic system.

In Section 4, we explained why removing the ambiguity between Shift and Right-Arcs altogether was an inferior strategy. Failing to discriminate between arcs reachable by monotonic and non-monotonic paths does just that, so this oracle did not perform well in preliminary experiments on the development data.

Instead, we want to learn a model that will offer its best prediction of Shift vs. Right-Arc, which we expect to usually be correct. However, in those cases where the model does make the wrong decision, it should have the ability to later over-turn that decision, by having an unconstrained choice of Reduce vs. Left-Arc.

In order to correct for that, we don't use the non-monotonic oracles directly when training the parser, but instead train the parser using both the monotonic and non-monotonic oracles simultaneously by combining their judgements: while we always prefer zero-cost non-monotonic actions to monotonic-actions with non-zero cost, if the non-monotonic oracle assigns several actions a zero-cost, we prefer to follow those actions that are also assigned a zero-cost by the monotonic oracle, as these actions lead to the best outcome without relying on a non-monotonic (repair) operation down the road.

7 Experiments

We base our experiments on the parser described by Goldberg and Nivre (2012). We began by implementing their baseline system, a standard Arc-Eager parser using an averaged Perceptron learner and the extended feature set described by Zhang and Nivre (2011). We follow Goldberg and Nivre (2012) in training all models for 15 iterations, and shuffling the sentences before each iteration.

[5]If using a labeled reduce transition, the label assignment costs should be handled here.

	Stanford		MALT	
	W	S	W	S
	Unlabelled Attachment			
Baseline (G&N-12)	91.2	42.0	90.9	39.7
NM L	91.4	43.1	91.0	40.1
NM D	91.4	42.8	91.1	41.2
NM L+D	91.6	43.3	91.3	41.5
	Labelled Attachment			
Baseline (G&N-12)	88.7	31.8	89.7	36.6
NM L	89.0	32.5	89.8	36.9
NM D	88.9	32.3	89.9	37.7
NM L+D	89.1	32.7	90.0	37.9

Table 1: Development results on WSJ 22. Both non-monotonic transitions bring small improvements in per-token (W) and whole sentence (S) accuracy, and the improvements are additive.

Because the sentence ordering affects the model's accuracy, all results are averaged from scores produced using 20 different random seeds. The seed determines how the sentences are shuffled before each iteration, as well as when to follow an optimal action and when to follow a non-optimal action during training. The Wilcoxon signed-rank test was used for significance testing.

A train/dev/test split of 02-21/22/23 of the Penn Treebank WSJ (Marcus et al., 1993) was used for all models. The data was converted into Stanford dependencies (de Marneffe et al., 2006) with copula-as-head and the original PTB noun-phrase bracketing. We also evaluate our models on dependencies created by the PENN2MALT tool, to assist comparison with previous results. Automatically assigned POS tags were used during training, to match the test data more closely. [6] We also evaluate the non-monotonic transitions on the CoNLL 2007 multi-lingual data.

8 Results and analysis

Table 1 shows the effect of the non-monotonic transitions on labelled and unlabelled attachment score on the development data. All results are averages from 20 models trained with different random seeds, as the ordering of the sentences at each iteration of the Perceptron algorithm has an effect on the system's accuracy. The two non-monotonic transitions each bring small but statistically significant improvements that are additive when combined in the NM L+D system. The result is stable

[6]We thank Yue Zhang for supplying the POS-tagged files used in the Zhang and Nivre (2011) experiments.

across both dependency encoding schemes.

Frequency analysis. Recall that there are two pop moves available: Left-Arc and Reduce. The Left-Arc is considered non-monotonic if the top of the stack has a head specified, and the Reduce move is considered non-monotonic if it does not. How often does the parser select monotonic and non-monotonic pop moves, and how often is its decision correct?

In Table 2, the True Positive column shows how often non-monotonic transitions were used to add gold standard dependencies. The False Positive column shows how often they were used incorrectly. The False Negative column shows how often the parser missed a correct non-monotonic transition, and the True Negative column shows how often the monotonic alternative was correctly preferred (e.g. the parser correctly chose monotonic Reduce in place of non-monotonic Left-Arc). Punctuation dependencies were excluded.

The current system has high precision but low recall for repair operations, as they are relatively rare in the gold-standard. While we already see improvements in accuracy, the upper bound achievable by the non-monotonic operations is higher, and we hope to approach it in the future using improved learning techniques.

Linguistic analysis. To examine what constructions were being corrected, we looked at the frequencies of the labels being introduced by the non-monotonic moves. We found that there were two constructions being commonly repaired, and a long-tail of miscellaneous cases.

The most frequent repair involved the *mark* label. This is assigned to conjunctions introducing subordinate clauses. For instance, in the sentence *Results were released after the market closed*, the Stanford scheme attaches *after* to *closed*. The parser is misled into greedily attaching *after* to *released* here, as that would be correct if *after* were a preposition, as in *Results were released after midnight*. This construction was repaired 33 times, 13 where the initial decision was *mark*, and 21 times the other way around. The other commonly repaired construction involved greedily attaching an object that was actually the subject of a complement clause, e.g. *NCNB corp. reported net income doubled*. These were repaired 19 times.

WSJ evaluation. Table 3 shows the final test results. While still lagging behind search based parsers, we push the boundaries of what can be achieved with a purely greedy system, with a statistically significant improvement over G&N 12.

	TP	FP	TN	FN
Left-Arc	60	14	18,466	285
Reduce	52	26	14,066	250
Total	112	40	32,532	535

Table 2: True/False positive/negative rates for the prediction of the non-monotonic transitions. The non-monotonic transitions add correct dependencies 112 times, and produce worse parses 40 times. 535 opportunities for non-monotonic transitions were missed.

System	O	Stanford		Penn2Malt	
		LAS	UAS	LAS	UAS
K&C 10	n^3	—	—	—	93.00
Z&N 11	nk	91.9	93.5	91.8	92.9
G&N 12	n	88.72	90.96	—	—
Baseline(G&N-12)	n	88.7	90.9	88.7	90.6
NM L+D	n	88.9	91.1	88.9	91.0

Table 3: WSJ 23 test results, with comparison against the state-of-the-art systems from the literature of different run-times. **K&C 10**=Koo and Collins (2010); **Z&N 11**=Zhang and Nivre (2011); **G&N 12**=Goldberg and Nivre (2012).

CoNLL 2007 evaluation. Table 4 shows the effect of the non-monotonic transitions across the ten languages in the CoNLL 2007 data sets. Statistically significant improvements in accuracy were observed for five of the ten languages. The accuracy improvement on Hungarian and Arabic did not meet our significance threshold. The non-monotonic transitions did not decrease accuracy significantly on any of the languages.

9 Related Work

One can view our non-monotonic parsing system as adding "repair" operations to a greedy, deterministic parser, allowing it to undo previous decisions and thus mitigating the effect of incorrect parsing decisions due to uncertain future, which is inherent in greedy left-to-right transition-based parsers. Several approaches have been taken to address this problem, including:

Post-processing Repairs (Attardi and Ciaramita, 2007; Hall and Novák, 2005; Inokuchi and Yamaoka, 2012) Closely related to stacking, this line of work attempts to train classifiers to repair attachment mistakes after a parse is proposed by a parser by changing head attachment decisions. The present work differs from these by incorporating the repair process into the transition system.

Stacking (Nivre and McDonald, 2008; Martins et al., 2008), in which a second-stage parser runs over the sentence using the predictions of the first parser as features. In contrast our parser works in

System	AR	BASQ	CAT	CHI	CZ	ENG	GR	HUN	ITA	TUR
Baseline	83.4	76.2	91.5	82.3	78.8	87.9	81.2	77.6	83.8	78.0
NM L+D	*83.6*	76.1	91.5	**82.7**	**80.1**	**88.4**	**81.8**	*77.9*	**84.1**	78.0

Table 4: Multi-lingual evaluation. Accuracy improved on Chinese, Czech, English, Greek and Italian ($p < 0.001$), trended upward on Arabic and Hungarian ($p < 0.005$), and was unchanged on Basque, Catalan and Turkish ($p > 0.4$).

a single, left-to-right pass over the sentence.

Non-directional Parsing The EasyFirst parser of Goldberg and Elhadad (2010) tackles similar forms of ambiguities by dropping the Shift action altogether, and processing the sentence in an easy-to-hard bottom-up order instead of left-to-right, resulting in a greedy but non-directional parser. The indeterminate processing order increases the parser's runtime from $O(n)$ to $O(n \log n)$. In contrast, our parser processes the sentence incrementally, and runs in a linear time.

Beam Search An obvious approach to tackling ambiguities is to forgo the greedy nature of the parser and instead to adopt a beam search (Zhang and Clark, 2008; Zhang and Nivre, 2011) or a dynamic programming (Huang and Sagae, 2010; Kuhlmann et al., 2011) approach. While these approaches are very successful in producing high-accuracy parsers, we here explore what can be achieved in a strictly deterministic system, which results in much faster and incremental parsing algorithms. The use of non-monotonic transitions in beam-search parser is an interesting topic for future work.

10 Conclusion and future work

We began this paper with the observation that because the Arc-Eager transition system (Nivre et al., 2004) attaches a word to its governor either when the word is pushed onto the stack or when it is popped off the stack, monotonicity (plus the "tree constraint" that a word has exactly one governor) implies that a word's push-move determines its associated pop-move. In this paper we suggest relaxing the monotonicity constraint to permit the pop-move to alter existing attachments if appropriate, thus breaking the 1-to-1 correspondence between push-moves and pop-moves. This permits the parser to correct some early incorrect attachment decisions later in the parsing process. Adding additional transitions means that in general there are multiple transition sequences that generate any given syntactic analysis, i.e., our non-monotonic transition system generates spurious ambiguities (note that the Arc-Eager transition system on its own generates spurious ambiguities). As we explained in the paper, with the greedy decoding used here additional spurious ambiguity is not necessarily a draw-back.

The conventional training procedure for transition-based parsers uses a "static" oracle based on "gold" parses that never predicts a non-monotonic transition, so it is clearly not appropriate here. Instead, we use the incremental error-based training procedure involving a "dynamic" oracle proposed by Goldberg and Nivre (2012), where the parser is trained to predict the transition that will produce the best-possible analysis from its current configuration. We explained how to modify the Goldberg and Nivre oracle so it predicts the optimal moves, either monotonic or non-monotonic, from any configuration, and use this to train an averaged perceptron model.

When evaluated on the standard WSJ training and test sets we obtained a UAS of 91.1%, which is a 0.2% improvement over the already state-of-the-art baseline of 90.9% that is obtained with the error-based training procedure of Goldberg and Nivre (2012). On the CoNLL 2007 datasets, accuracy improved significantly on 5/10 languages, and did not decline significantly on any of them.

Looking to the future, we believe that it would be interesting to investigate whether adding non-monotonic transitions is beneficial in other parsing systems as well, including systems that target formalisms other than dependency grammars. As we observed in the paper, the spurious ambiguity that non-monotonic moves introduce may well be an advantage in a statistical parser with an enormous state-space because it provides multiple pathways to the correct analysis (of which we hope at least one is navigable).

We investigated a very simple kind of non-monotonic transition here, but of course it's possible to design transition systems with many more transitions, including transitions that are explicitly designed to "repair" characteristic parser errors. It might even be possible to automatically identify the most useful repair transitions and incorporate them into the parser.

Acknowledgments

The authors would like to thank the anonymous reviewers for their valuable comments. This research was supported under the Australian Research Council's Discovery Projects funding scheme (project numbers DP110102506 and DP110102593).

References

Stephen Abney and Mark Johnson. 1991. Memory requirements and local ambiguities of parsing strategies. *Journal of Psycholinguistic Research*, 20(3):233–250.

Giuseppe Attardi and Massimiliano Ciaramita. 2007. Tree revision learning for dependency parsing. In *Human Language Technologies 2007: The Conference of the North American Chapter of the Association for Computational Linguistics; Proceedings of the Main Conference*, pages 388–395. Association for Computational Linguistics, Rochester, New York.

Miguel Ballesteros and Joakim Nivre. 2013. Going to the roots of dependency parsing. *Computational Linguistics. 39:1.*

Marie-Catherine de Marneffe, Bill MacCartney, and Christopher D. Manning. 2006. Generating typed dependency parses from phrase structure parses. In *Proceedings of the 5th International Conference on Language Resources and Evaluation (LREC).*

Lyn Frazier and Keith Rayner. 1982. Making and correcting errors during sentence comprehension: Eye movements in the analysis of structurally ambiguous sentences. *Cognitive Psychology*, 14(2):178–210.

Yoav Goldberg and Michael Elhadad. 2010. An efficient algorithm for easy-first non-directional dependency parsing. In *Human Language Technologies: The 2010 Annual Conference of the North American Chapter of the Association for Computational Linguistics (NAACL HLT)*, pages 742–750.

Yoav Goldberg and Joakim Nivre. 2012. A dynamic oracle for arc-eager dependency parsing. In *Proceedings of the 24th International Conference on Computational Linguistics (Coling 2012)*. Association for Computational Linguistics, Mumbai, India.

Keith Hall and Vaclav Novák. 2005. Corrective modeling for non-projective dependency parsing. In *Proceedings of the 9th International Workshop on Parsing Technologies (IWPT)*, pages 42–52.

Liang Huang and Kenji Sagae. 2010. Dynamic programming for linear-time incremental parsing. In *Proceedings of the 48th Annual Meeting of the Association for Computational Linguistics (ACL)*, pages 1077–1086.

Akihiro Inokuchi and Ayumu Yamaoka. 2012. Mining rules for rewriting states in a transition-based dependency parser for English. In *Proceedings of COLING 2012*, pages 1275–1290. The COLING 2012 Organizing Committee, Mumbai, India.

Terry Koo and Michael Collins. 2010. Efficient third-order dependency parsers. In *Proceedings of the 48th Annual Meeting of the Association for Computational Linguistics (ACL)*, pages 1–11.

Marco Kuhlmann, Carlos Gómez-Rodríguez, and Giorgio Satta. 2011. Dynamic programming algorithms for transition-based dependency parsers. In *Proceedings of the 49th Annual Meeting of the Association for Computational Linguistics: Human Language Technologies - Volume 1*, HLT '11, pages 673–682. Association for Computational Linguistics, Stroudsburg, PA, USA.

Mitchell P. Marcus, Beatrice Santorini, and Mary Ann Marcinkiewicz. 1993. Building a large annotated corpus of English: The Penn Treebank. *Computational Linguistics*, 19:313–330.

André Filipe Martins, Dipanjan Das, Noah A. Smith, and Eric P. Xing. 2008. Stacking dependency parsers. In *Proceedings of the Conference on Empirical Methods in Natural Language Processing (EMNLP)*, pages 157–166.

Joakim Nivre. 2003. An efficient algorithm for projective dependency parsing. In *Proceedings of the 8th International Workshop on Parsing Technologies (IWPT)*, pages 149–160.

Joakim Nivre. 2008. Algorithms for deterministic incremental dependency parsing. *Computational Linguistics*, 34:513–553.

Joakim Nivre, Johan Hall, and Jens Nilsson. 2004. Memory-based dependency parsing. In

Hwee Tou Ng and Ellen Riloff, editors, *HLT-NAACL 2004 Workshop: Eighth Conference on Computational Natural Language Learning (CoNLL-2004)*, pages 49–56. Association for Computational Linguistics, Boston, Massachusetts, USA.

Joakim Nivre and Ryan McDonald. 2008. Integrating graph-based and transition-based dependency parsers. In *Proceedings of the 46th Annual Meeting of the Association for Computational Linguistics (ACL)*, pages 950–958.

Mark Steedman. 2000. *The Syntactic Process*. MIT Press, Cambridge, MA.

Yue Zhang and Stephen Clark. 2008. A tale of two parsers: Investigating and combining graph-based and transition-based dependency parsing. In *Proceedings of the 2008 Conference on Empirical Methods in Natural Language Processing*, pages 562–571. Association for Computational Linguistics, Honolulu, Hawaii.

Yue Zhang and Joakim Nivre. 2011. Transition-based dependency parsing with rich non-local features. In *Proceedings of the 49th Annual Meeting of the Association for Computational Linguistics: Human Language Technologies*, pages 188–193. Association for Computational Linguistics, Portland, Oregon, USA.

Collapsed Variational Bayesian Inference for PCFGs

Pengyu Wang
Department of Computer Science
University of Oxford
Oxford, OX1 3QD, United Kingdom
Pengyu.Wang@cs.ox.ac.uk

Phil Blunsom
Department of Computer Science
University of Oxford
Oxford, OX1 3QD, United Kingdom
Phil.Blunsom@cs.ox.ac.uk

Abstract

This paper presents a collapsed variational Bayesian inference algorithm for PCFGs that has the advantages of two dominant Bayesian training algorithms for PCFGs, namely variational Bayesian inference and Markov chain Monte Carlo. In three kinds of experiments, we illustrate that our algorithm achieves close performance to the Hastings sampling algorithm while using an order of magnitude less training time; and outperforms the standard variational Bayesian inference and the EM algorithms with similar training time.

1 Introduction

Probabilistic context-free grammars (PCFGs) are commonly used in parsing and grammar induction systems (Johnson, 1998; Collins, 1999; Klein and Manning, 2003; Matsuzaki et al., 2005). The traditional method for estimating the parameters of PCFGs from terminal strings is the inside-outside (IO) algorithm (Baker, 1979). As a special instance of the Expectation-Maximization (EM) algorithm (Dempster et al., 1977), based on the principle of maximum-likelihood estimation (MLE), the standard IO algorithm learns relatively uniform probability distributions for grammars, while the true distributions can be highly skewed (Johnson et al., 2007). In order to encourage sparse grammars and avoid overfitting, recent research for training PCFGs has drifted away from MLE in favor of Bayesian inference algorithms that make either deterministic or stochastic approximations (Kurihara and Sato, 2006; Johnson et al., 2006; Johnson et al., 2007).

Variational Bayesian inference (VB) (Kurihara and Sato, 2006) for PCFGs extends EM and places no constraints when updating parameters in the M step. By minimising the divergence between the true posterior and an approximate one in which the strong dependencies between the parameters and latent variables are broken, this deterministic algorithm efficiently converges to an inaccurate and only locally optimal solution like EM. Alternatively, Johnson et al. (2007) proposed two Markov Chain Monte Carlo algorithms for PCFGs that can reach the true posterior after convergence. However, it is often difficult to diagnose a sampler's convergence, and mixing is notoriously slow for distributions with tightly coupled hidden variables such as PCFGs, especially when the data sets are large. Therefore, there remains a challenge for more efficient, but also accurate and deterministic inference algorithms for PCFGs.

In this paper, we present a collapsed variational Bayesian inference (CVB) algorithm for PCFGs. It has the same computational complexity as the standard variational Bayesian inference, but offers almost the same performance as the stochastic algorithms due to its weak assumptions. The idea of operating VB in the collapsed space was proposed by Teh et al. (2007) and Sung et al. (2008), and it was successfully applied to "bag-of-words" models such as latent Dirichlet allocation (LDA) (Teh et al., 2007) and mixture of Gaussian (Sung et al., 2008), where the latent variables are conditionally independent given the parameters. By combining the CVB idea and the dynamic programming techniques used in structurally dependent models, we deliver a both efficient and accurate algorithm for training PCFGs and other structured natural language models.

The rest of the paper is structured as follows. We begin with the Bayesian models of PCFGs, and relate the existing training algorithms. Section 3 introduces collapsed variational Bayesian inference for "bag-of-words" models (defined in Section 3.1). We discuss the difficulty in applying such inference to structured models, followed by an approximate CVB algorithm for PCFGs.

An alternative approach is also included in brief. In Section 4, we validate our CVB algorithm in three simple experiments. They are inferring a sparse grammar that describes the morphology of the Sotho language (Johnson et al., 2007), unsupervised dependency parsing (Klein and Manning, 2004) and supervised parsing with latent annotations (Matsuzaki et al., 2005). Section 5 concludes with future work.

2 Approximate inference for PCFGs

2.1 Definitions

A PCFG is a tuple (T, N, S, R, θ), where T, N, R and θ are the finite sets of terminals, nonterminals, rules and parameters respectively, and $S \in N$ is the start symbol. We adopt a similar notation to Johnson et al. (2007), and assume that the context free grammar $G = (T, N, S, R)$ is in Chomsky normal form and the empty string $\epsilon \notin T$. Hence, each rule $r \in R$ takes either the form $A \to BC$ or $A \to w$, where $A, B, C \in N$ and $w \in T$. Let $\theta_{A\to\beta}$ be the probability of derivation rule $A \to \beta$, where β ranges over $(N \times N) \cup T$. In the Bayesian setting, we place Dirichlet priors with hyperparameters $\alpha_A = \{\alpha_{A\to\beta}\}$ on each $\theta_A = \{\theta_{A\to\beta}\}$.

Given a corpus of sentences $\mathbf{w} = (w_1, ..., w_n)$ and the corresponding hidden parse trees $\mathbf{t} = (t_1, ..., t_n)$, the joint probability distribution of parameters and variables is[1]:

$$
\begin{aligned}
P(\mathbf{w}, \mathbf{t}, \theta|\alpha) =& P(\theta|\alpha) \prod_{i=1}^{n} P_G(w_i, t_i|\theta) \\
=& \left(\prod_{A \in N} P_D(\theta_A|\alpha_A) \right) \prod_{r \in R} \theta_r^{f_r(\mathbf{t})}
\end{aligned} \tag{1}
$$

$$
\begin{aligned}
P_D(\theta_A|\alpha_A) =& \frac{1}{B(\alpha_A)} \prod_{r \in R_A} \theta_r^{\alpha_r - 1} \\
B(\alpha_A) =& \frac{\prod_{r \in R_A} \Gamma(\alpha_r)}{\Gamma(\sum_{r \in R_A} \alpha_r)}
\end{aligned}
$$

where $f_r(\mathbf{t})$ is the frequency of product rule r in all the parse trees $\mathbf{t}$, and R_A is the set of rules with left-hand side A. For a Dirichlet distribution $P_D(\theta_A|\alpha_A)$, $B(\alpha_A)$ is the normalization constant that can be written in terms of the gamma function Γ (i.e. the generalised factorial function).

[1]Strictly speaking, for each (w, t) pair, if a hidden tree t is arbitrary, we need to include two delta functions, namely $\delta(w = \text{yield}(t))$ and $\delta(G \Rightarrow^{\star} t)$. We assume that both delta functions are true, otherwise the probability of such pair is 0.

2.2 Variational Bayesian inference

The standard inside-outside algorithm for PCFGs belongs to the general EM class, which is further a subclass of VB (Beal, 2003). VB maximises the negative free energy $-\mathcal{F}(Q(\mathbf{t}, \theta))$, a lower bound of the log marginal likelihood of the observation $\log P(\mathbf{w}|\alpha)$. This is equivalent to minimising the Kullback-Leibler divergence.

$$
\begin{aligned}
&\log P(\mathbf{w}|\alpha) \geq -\mathcal{F}(Q(\mathbf{t}, \theta)) \\
&= \mathbb{E}_{Q(\mathbf{t},\theta)}[\log P(\mathbf{w}, \mathbf{t}, \theta|\alpha)] - \mathbb{E}_{Q(\mathbf{t},\theta)}[\log Q(\mathbf{t}, \theta)]
\end{aligned}
$$

$Q(\mathbf{t}, \theta)$ is an approximate posterior, where the parameters and hidden variables are assumed to be independent. Thus, it is factorised:

$$
Q(\mathbf{t}, \theta) \approx Q(\mathbf{t})Q(\theta) \tag{2}
$$

This strong independence assumption allows for the separate updates of $Q(\mathbf{t})$ and $Q(\theta)$ iteratively, optimising the negative free energy $-\mathcal{F}(Q(\mathbf{z}, \theta))$. For the traditional IO algorithm using maximum likelihood estimation, $Q(\theta)$ is further assumed to be degenerate, i.e. $Q(\theta) = \delta(\theta = \theta^{\star})$.

$$
\begin{aligned}
&\text{E step: } Q(\mathbf{t}) \propto \exp(\mathbb{E}_{Q(\theta)}[\log P(\mathbf{w}, \mathbf{t}, \theta)]) \\
&\text{M step: } \theta^{\star} = \operatorname*{argmax}_{\theta} P(\mathbf{w}, \mathbf{t}, \theta)
\end{aligned}
$$

In the E step, we update $Q(\mathbf{t})$. For each tree t,

$$
\begin{aligned}
Q(t) &\propto P_G(w, t|\theta^{\star}) \\
&= \prod_{r \in R} (\theta_r^{\star})^{f_r(t)}
\end{aligned} \tag{3}
$$

The distribution over parse tree $Q(t)$ is intractable to compute as its normalization requires summing over all possible parse trees producing w. We use dynamic programming to compute inside and outside probabilities recursively with the aim of accumulating the expected counts.

$$
\begin{aligned}
\mathbb{E}[f_{A\to BC}(t)|w] \propto & \sum_{0 \leq i < j < k \leq |w|} P_{\text{OUT}}(A, i, k) \times \\
& \theta_{A\to BC} P_{\text{IN}}(B, i, j) P_{\text{IN}}(C, j, k) \\
\mathbb{E}[f_{A\to w}(t)|w] \propto & \sum_{0 \leq i \leq |w|} P_{\text{OUT}}(A, i) \times \\
& \theta_{A\to w_i} \delta(w_i = w)
\end{aligned}
$$

where $P_{\text{IN}}(A, i, k)$ is the inside probability of observation $w_{i,k} = w_i, ..., w_k$ given A is the root of the subtree, and $P_{\text{OUT}}(A, i, k)$ is the probability of A spanning (i, k), together with the rest of w.

In the M step, we find the optimal $\theta^\star$ based on the MLE principle:

$$\theta^\star_{A\to\beta} = \frac{\mathbb{E}[f_{A\to\beta}(\mathbf{t})|\mathbf{w}]}{\sum_{A\to\beta'\in R_A}\mathbb{E}[f_{A\to\beta'}(\mathbf{t})|\mathbf{w}]}$$

$$\mathbb{E}[f_{A\to\beta}(\mathbf{t})|\mathbf{w}] = \sum_{i=1}^{n}\mathbb{E}[f_{A\to\beta}(t_i)|w_i]$$

VB inference is the generalisation of EM in the sense that it allows arbitrary parametric forms of $Q(\theta)$. Thus, the update equation in the M step is:

$$Q(\theta) \propto \exp(\mathbb{E}_{Q(\mathbf{t})}[\log P(\mathbf{w},\mathbf{t},\theta|\alpha)])$$

By the conjugacy property, the new $Q(\theta)$ is still in Dirichlet distribution form except with updated hyperparameters as shown by Kurihara and Sato (2006). Instead, Beal (2003) suggested an equivalent mean parameters $\tilde{\theta}$. Based on implementation of the EM algorithm, we only need a minor modification in the M step.

$$\tilde{\theta}_{A\to\beta} = \frac{m(\mathbb{E}[f_{A\to\beta}(\mathbf{t})|\mathbf{w}]+\alpha_{A\to\beta})}{m(\sum_{A\to\beta'\in R_A}(\mathbb{E}[f_{A\to\beta'}(\mathbf{t})|\mathbf{w}]+\alpha_{A\to\beta'}))}$$

$$m(x) = \exp(\Psi(x))$$

where $\Psi(x) = \frac{\partial\Gamma(x)}{\partial x}$ is the digamma function.

From the joint distribution in (1) proportional to the true posterior, we notice that the parameters and hidden variables are intimately coupled. Fluctuations in the parameters can induce changes in the hidden variables and vice-versa. Hence, the independence assumption in (2) and Figure 1(d) seems too strong, leading to inaccurate local maximums, although it allows for efficient and deterministic updates in EM and VB. The dependencies between parameters and hidden variables are kept intact for the remaining algorithms in this paper.

2.3 Markov Chain Monte Carlo

The standard Gibbs sampler for PCFGs iteratively samples the parameters θ and all the parse trees $\mathbf{t}$. Its mixing can be slowed by again the strong dependencies between the parameters and hidden variables. Instead of reparsing all the hidden trees $\mathbf{t}$ for each sample of θ, collapsed Gibbs sampling (CGS) improves upon Gibbs sampling in terms of convergence speed by integrating out the parameters, and sampling directly from $P(\mathbf{t}|\mathbf{w},\alpha)$ in a component-wise manner. Thus, it also deals with the dependencies exactly.

By using the conjugacy property, we can easily compute the marginal distribution of $\mathbf{w}$ and $\mathbf{t}$:

$$P(\mathbf{w},\mathbf{t}|\alpha) = \int_\theta P_G(\mathbf{w},\mathbf{t}|\theta)P_D(\theta|\alpha)d\theta = \prod_{A\in N}\frac{B(\mathbf{f}_A(\mathbf{t})+\alpha_A)}{B(\alpha_A)} \quad (4)$$

where we define $\mathbf{f}_A(\mathbf{t})$ to be a vector of rule frequencies in $\mathbf{t}$ indexed by $A\to\beta\in R_A$. Hence, the conditional distribution for a parse tree t_i given all others is:

$$P(t_i|w_i,\mathbf{w}^{\neg i},\mathbf{t}^{\neg i},\alpha) \propto P(w_i,t_i|\mathbf{w}^{\neg i},\mathbf{t}^{\neg i},\alpha) = \prod_{A\in N}\frac{B(\mathbf{f}_A(\mathbf{t})+\alpha_A)}{B(\mathbf{f}_A(\mathbf{t}^{\neg i})+\alpha_A)} \quad (5)$$

where $\mathbf{w}^{\neg i}$ and $\mathbf{t}^{\neg i}$ denote all other sentences and trees. It is noticeable that sampling a parse tree from the above conditional distribution is difficult. The frequencies $\mathbf{f}_A(\mathbf{t})$ effectively mean that the production probabilities are dependent on the current parse tree t_i. That is rule parameters can be updated on the fly inside a parse tree, which prohibits efficient dynamic programming tricks.

In order to solve this problem, Johnson et al. (2007) proposed a Hastings sampler that specified an alternative rule probabilities θ^{H} of a proposal distribution $P(t_i|w_i,\theta^{\mathrm{H}})$, where

$$\theta^{\mathrm{H}}_{A\to\beta} = \frac{f_{A\to\beta}(\mathbf{t}^{\neg i})+\alpha_{A\to\beta}}{\sum_{A\to\beta'\in R_A}(f_{A\to\beta'}(\mathbf{t}^{\neg i})+\alpha_{A\to\beta'})}$$

The rule probabilities θ^{H} are based on the statistics collected from all other parse trees, and they are fixed for the conditional distribution of the current parse tree. Therefore, by using a variant of inside algorithm (Goodman, 1998), one can efficiently sample a parse tree, which will be either accepted or rejected based on the Metropolis choice.

The MCMC based algorithms do not make any assumptions at all, and they can converge to the true posterior, either in joint or collapsed space as shown in Figure 1(b), 1(c). However, one needs to have experience about the number of samples to be collected and the burn-in period. For computationally intensive tasks such as learning PCFGs from a large corpus, a sufficiently large number of samples are required to decrease the sampling variance. Therefore, MCMC algorithms improves the performance over EM and VB at the cost of much more training time.

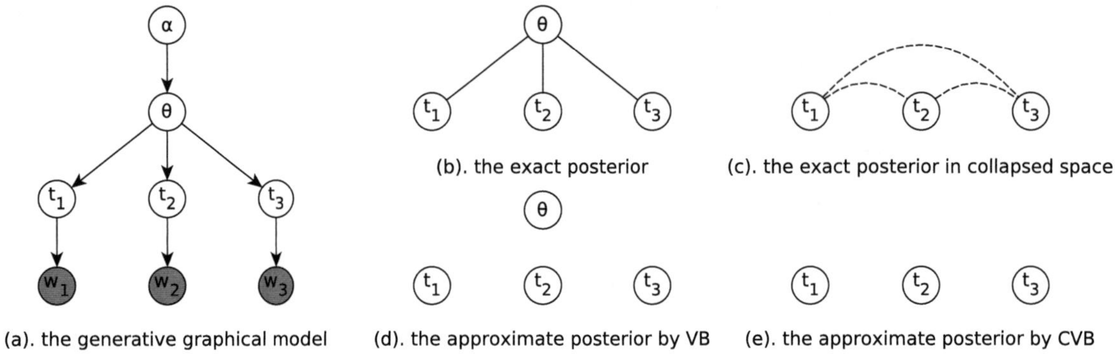

Figure 1: Graphical representations of the PCFG with $n = 3$ trees (a), and the (approximate) posteriors for Gibbs sampling (b), collapsed Gibbs sampling (c), variational Bayesian inference (d), and collapsed variational Bayesian inference (e). We use dashed lines to depict the weak dependencies.

3 Collapsed variational Bayesian inference

3.1 For bag-of-words models

Leveraging the insight that a sampling algorithm in collapsed space mixes faster than the standard one, Teh et al. (2007) proposed a similar argument that a VB inference algorithm in collapsed space is more effective than the standard one. Following the success in LDA (Teh et al., 2007), a number of research results have been accumulated around applying CVB to a variety of "bag-of-words" models (Sung et al., 2008; Sato et al., 2012; Wang and Blei, 2012).

Formally, we define a model to be independent and identically distributed (i.i.d.) (or informally "bag-of-words") if its hidden variables are conditionally independent given the parameters. LDA, IBM word alignment model 1 and 2, and various finite mixture models are typical examples.

For an i.i.d. model, integrating out parameters induces dependencies that spread over many hidden variables, and thus the dependency between any two variables is very weak. This provides an ideal setting to apply the mean field method (i.e. fully factorized VB), as its underlying assumption is that any variable depends on only the summary statistics collected from other variables called the field, and any particular variable's impact on the field is very small. Hence, the mean field assumption is better satisfied in collapsed space with very weak dependencies than in joint space with strong dependencies. As a result, we expect that VB in collapsed space can achieve more accurate results than the standard VB, and the results would be very close to the true posterior.

Even in collapsed space, CVB remains a deterministic algorithm that updates the posterior distributions over the hidden variables just like VB and EM. Therefore, we expect CVB to be computationally efficient as well.

3.2 For structured NLP models

We notice that the basic condition for applying the CVB algorithm to a specific model is for the model to be i.i.d., such that the hidden variables are only weakly dependent in collapsed space, providing an ideal condition to operate VB. However, the i.i.d. condition is certainly not true for structured NLP models such as hidden Markov models (HMMs) and PCFGs. Given the shape of a parse tree, a hidden variable is strongly dependent on its parent, siblings and children, and weakly dependent on the rest. Even worse, to infer a grammar from terminal strings, we don't even have access to the shape of parse trees, let alone analyzing the dependencies of hidden variables inside trees.

Although the PCFG model is not i.i.d. at the variable level, we can lift the idea of CVB up to the tree level. As our research domain is those large scale applications in language processing, a common feature of those problems is that there are usually many sentences, each of which has a hidden parse tree behind it. Hence, we may consider each sentence together with its parse tree to be drawn i.i.d. from the same set of parameters. Therefore, at the tree level, a PCFG can be considered as an i.i.d. model as shown in Figure 1(a) and thus, it can be fitted in the CVB framework as described in Section 3.1. We summarise the as-

$$Q(t_i) \propto \prod_{A \in N} \frac{\prod_{A\to\beta\in R_A} \exp(\mathbb{E}_{Q(\mathbf{t}^{\neg i})}[\log(\prod_{j=0}^{f_{A\to\beta}(t_i)-1}(f_{A\to\beta}(\mathbf{t}^{\neg i}) + \alpha_{A\to\beta} + j))])}{\prod_{j=0}^{(\sum_{A\to\beta'} f_{A\to\beta'}(t_i))-1} \exp(\mathbb{E}_{Q(\mathbf{t}^{\neg i})}[\log(\sum_{A\to\beta'\in R_A}(f_{A\to\beta}(\mathbf{t}^{\neg i}) + \alpha_{A\to\beta'} + j))])}$$

Figure 2: The exact mean field update in collapsed space for the parse tree t_i.

$$Q(t_i) \propto \prod_{r=A\to\beta\in R} \left(\frac{\mathbb{E}_{Q(\mathbf{t}^{\neg i})}[f_{A\to\beta}(\mathbf{t}^{\neg i})] + \alpha_{A\to\beta}}{\sum_{A\to\beta'}(\mathbb{E}_{Q(\mathbf{t}^{\neg i})}[f_{A\to\beta'}(\mathbf{t}^{\neg i})] + \alpha_{A\to\beta'})} \right)^{f_r(t_i)}$$

Figure 3: The approximate mean field update in collapsed space for the parse tree t_i.

sumptions made by each algorithm in Figure 1(b-e) before presenting the CVB algorithm formally.

The CVB algorithm for the PCFG model keeps the dependencies between the parameters and the hidden parse trees in an exact fashion:

$$Q(\mathbf{t}, \theta) = Q(\mathbf{t})Q(\theta|\mathbf{t})$$

We factorise $Q(\mathbf{t})$ by breaking only the weak dependencies between parse trees, while keeping the inside dependencies intact, as we don't make further assumptions about $Q(t)$ for each t.

$$Q(\mathbf{t}) \approx \prod_{i=1}^{n} Q(t_i)$$

By the above factorisations, we compute the negative variational free energy $-\mathcal{F}(Q(\mathbf{t})Q(\theta|\mathbf{t}))$ as follows:

$$\begin{aligned}
&-\mathcal{F}(Q(\mathbf{t})Q(\theta|\mathbf{t}))\\
=&\mathbb{E}_{Q(\mathbf{t})Q(\theta|\mathbf{t})}[\log P(\mathbf{w}, \mathbf{t}, \theta|\alpha) - \log Q(\mathbf{t})Q(\theta|\mathbf{t})]\\
=&\mathbb{E}_{Q(\mathbf{t})}[\mathbb{E}_{Q(\theta|\mathbf{t})}[\log \frac{P(\mathbf{w}, \mathbf{t}, \theta|\alpha)}{Q(\theta|\mathbf{t})}] - \log Q(\mathbf{t})]
\end{aligned}$$

Maximizing $-\mathcal{F}(Q(\mathbf{t})Q(\theta|\mathbf{t}))$ requires to update $Q(\theta|\mathbf{t})$ and $Q(\mathbf{t})$ in turn. In particular, $Q(\theta|\mathbf{t})$ is set equal to the true posterior $P(\theta|\mathbf{w}, \mathbf{t}, \alpha)$:

$$\begin{aligned}
&-\mathcal{F}(Q(\mathbf{t})P(\theta|\mathbf{w}, \mathbf{t}))\\
=&\mathbb{E}_{Q(\mathbf{t})}[\mathbb{E}_{P(\theta|\mathbf{w},\mathbf{t},\alpha)}[\log \frac{P(\mathbf{w}, \mathbf{t}, \theta|\alpha)}{P(\theta|\mathbf{w}, \mathbf{t}, \alpha)}] - \log Q(\mathbf{t})]\\
=&\mathbb{E}_{Q(\mathbf{t})}[\log P(\mathbf{w}, \mathbf{t}|\alpha) - \log Q(\mathbf{t})]
\end{aligned}$$

Finally, we update the approximate posterior for each parse tree t by using the mean field method in the collapsed space:

$$Q(t_i) \propto \exp(\mathbb{E}_{Q(\mathbf{t}^{\neg i})}[\log P(w_i, t_i|\mathbf{w}^{\neg i}, \mathbf{t}^{\neg i}, \alpha)]) \tag{6}$$

The inner term $P(w_i, t_i|\mathbf{w}^{\neg i}, \mathbf{t}^{\neg i}, \alpha)$ in the above equation is just the unnormalized collapsed Gibbs sampling in (5). Plugging in (5), and expanding terms such as $B(\alpha_A)$ and $\Gamma(x)$, we obtain an exact computation of $Q(t_i)$ in Figure 2.

The exact computation is both intractable and expensive. The intractability comes from the similar problem as in the collapsed Gibbs sampling that we are unable to calculate the normalisation term $\sum_{t_i} Q(t_i)$. Hence, we follow Johnson et al. (2007) to approximate it by using only the statistics from other sentences, namely θ^{H} and ignoring the local contribution.

$$P(w_i, t_i|\mathbf{w}^{\neg i}, \mathbf{t}^{\neg i}, \alpha) \approx \prod_{A\to\beta\in R} (\theta^{\text{H}}_{A\to\beta})^{f_{A\to\beta}(t_i)} \tag{7}$$

We discuss the accuracy of (7) in Section 3.3. For those expensive computations of the expected log counts in Figure 2, Teh et al. (2007) and Sung et al. (2008) suggested the use of a linear Gaussian approximation based on the law of large numbers.

$$\begin{aligned}
&\mathbb{E}_{Q(\mathbf{t}^{\neg i})}[\log(f_{A\to\beta}(\mathbf{t}^{\neg i}) + \alpha_{A\to\beta})]\\
&\approx \log(\mathbb{E}_{Q(\mathbf{t}^{\neg i})}[f_{A\to\beta}(\mathbf{t}^{\neg i})] + \alpha_{A\to\beta})
\end{aligned} \tag{8}$$

Substituting (7) into (6), and employing the linear approximation, we derive an approximate CVB algorithm as shown in Figure 3. In addition, its form is much more simplified and interpretable compared with the exact computation in Figure 2.

The surprising similarity between the approximate CVB update in Figure 3 and E step update in (3) indicates that the dynamic programming used in both EM and VB can take over from now. To run inside-outside recursion, the EM algorithm employs the parameters $\theta^{\star}$ based on maximum likelihood estimation; the VB algorithm employs the mean parameters $\tilde{\theta}$; and our CVB algorithm employs the parameters θ^{CVB} computed from the expected counts of all other sentences.

The implementation can be easily achieved by modifying code of the EM algorithm. We keep track of the expected counts at global level, subtract the local mean counts for t_i before update, run the inside-outside recursion using θ^{CVB}, and finally add the updated distribution back into the global counts. Therefore, we only need to replace the parameters with the expected counts, and make update after each sentence; the core of the inside-outside implementation remains the same.

Our CVB algorithm bears some similarities to the online EM algorithm with maximum a posterior (MAP) updates (Neal and Hinton, 1998; Liang and Klein, 2009), but they differ in several ways. The online EM algorithm updates each tree t_i based on the statistics of all the trees, optimising the same objective function $p(\mathbf{w}|\theta)$ as the batch EM algorithm. MAP estimation searches for the optimal posterior $p(\mathbf{w}|\theta)p(\theta)$. On the other hand, our CVB algorithm optimises the data likelihood $p(\mathbf{w})$. The smoothing effects for the MAP estimation ($\alpha_{A\to\beta} - 1$) prevent the use of sparse priors, whereas the CVB algorithm ($\alpha_{A\to\beta}$) overcomes such difficulty by parameter integration.

3.3 Discussion

Breaking the weak dependencies between hidden variables and employing the linear approximation have been argued to be accurate (Teh et al., 2007; Sung et al., 2008; Sato and Nakagawa, 2012), and they are the standard procedures in applying the CVB algorithms to i.i.d. models.

In our CVB algorithm for PCFGs, we introduce an extra approximation in (7), which we argue is accurate. Theoretically, the inaccuracy only occurs when there are repeated rules in a parse tree as shown in Figure 2, so the same rule seen later uses a slightly different probability. Even if the inaccuracy indeed occurs, in our described scenario of many sentences, the local contribution from a single sentence is small compared with the statistics from all other sentences. Empirically, we replicate the experiment of Setho language by Johnson et al. (2007) in Section 4.1, and we find that the sampled trees based on θ^{H} never get rejected, illustrating an acceptance rate close to 100%, and meaning that θ^{H} is a very accurate Metropolis proposal. Since all the assumptions made by the CVB algorithm are reasonable and weak, we expect its results to be close to true posteriors.

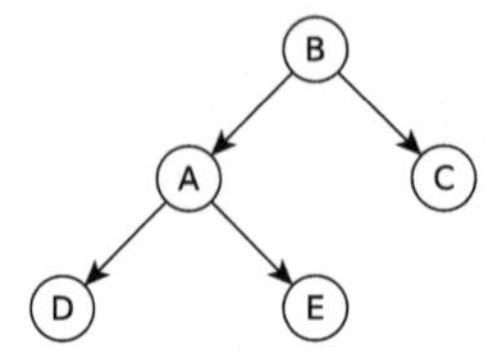

Figure 4: A fragment of a tree structure

3.4 An alternative approach

We briefly sketch an alternative CVB algorithm at the variable level for completeness.

For a structured NLP model with its shape to be fixed such as the PCFG with latent annotations (PCFG-LA) (Matsuzaki et al., 2005) (See definition in Section 4.3), we can simply ignore all the dependencies between the hidden variables in the collapsed space, despite whether they are strong (for adjacent nodes) or weak (for others). Although it seems that we have made unreasonable assumptions, it is not transparent which is worse comparing with the assumptions in the standard VB. Following this assumption, we can derive a CVB algorithm similar to the corresponding local sampling algorithm that samples one hidden variable at a time. For example, the approximate posterior over the subtype of the node A in the above tree fragment in Figure 4 is updated follows:

$$q(A = a)$$
$$\propto \frac{\mathbb{E}[f_{B\to aC}(\mathbf{t}^{\neg A})] + \alpha}{\mathbb{E}[f_B(\mathbf{t}^{\neg A})] + |R_B|\alpha} \cdot \frac{\mathbb{E}[f_{a\to DE}(\mathbf{t}^{\neg A})] + \alpha}{\mathbb{E}[f_a(\mathbf{t}^{\neg A})] + |R_a|\alpha}$$

where we use A to denote the node position, and a to denote its hidden subtype. $q(A = a)$ means the probability of node A being in subtype a. In addition, we need to take into account the distributions over its adjacent variables. In our case, A is strongly dependent on nodes B, C, D, E, and only weakly dependent on other variables (not shown in the above tree fragment) via global counts, e.g.:

$$\mathbb{E}[f_{B\to aC}(\mathbf{t}^{\neg A})]$$
$$= \sum_b \sum_c q(B = b) q(C = c) \mathbb{E}[f_{b\to ac}(\mathbf{t}^{\neg A})]$$

However, it is not obvious how to use this alternative approach in general, and the performances of resulting algorithms remain unclear. Therefore, we implement only the CVB algorithm at the tree level in Section 3.2 for our experiments.

4 Experiments

We conduct three simple experiments to validate our CVB algorithm for PCFGs. In Section 4.1, we illustrate the significantly reduced training time of our CVB algorithm compared to the related Hastings algorithm; whereas in later two sections, we demonstrate the increased performance of our CVB algorithm compared to the corresponding VB and EM algorithms.

4.1 Inferring sparse grammars

Firstly, we conduct the same experiment of inferring sparse grammars describing the morphology of the Sotho language as in Johnson et al. (2007). We use the same corpus of unsegmented Sotho verb types from CHILDES (MacWhinney and Snow, 1985), and define the same initial CFG productions by allowing each non-terminal to emit any substrings in the corpus as terminals plus five predefined morphological rules at the top level.

We randomly withhold 10% of the verb types from the corpus for testing, and use the rest 90% for training. Both algorithms are evaluated by their per word perplexity on the test data set with prior set to 10^{-5} as suggested by Johnson et al. (2007). We run 5 times with random starts, and report the averaged results in Figure 5. The Hastings algorithm[2] takes roughly 1,000 iterations to converge, while our CVB algorithm reaches the convergence even before 10 iterations, consuming only a fraction of training time (CVB: 1.5 minutes; Hastings: 20 minutes). As well as little difference margin in final perplexities shown in Figure 5, we also evaluated segmentation quality measured by the F1 scores, and again the difference is trivial (CVB: 29.8%, Hastings: 31.3%).

4.2 Dependency model with valence

As a second empirical validation of our CVB inference algorithm, we apply it to unsupervised grammar induction with the popular Dependency Model with Valence (DMV) (Klein and Manning, 2004). Although the original maximum likelihood formulation of this model has long since been surpassed by more advanced models, all of the state-of-the-art approaches to unsupervised dependency parsing still have DMV at their core (Headden III et al., 2009; Blunsom and Cohn, 2010; Spitkovsky et al., 2012). As such we believe demonstrating improved inference on this core model will enable future improvements to more complex models.

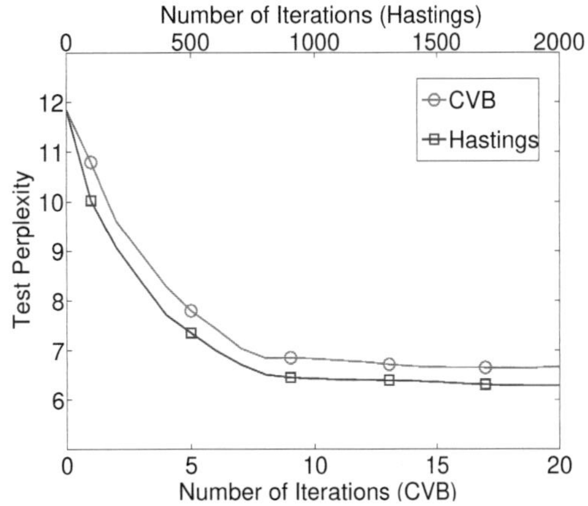

Figure 5: Perplexities averaged over 5 runs on the extracted corpus of Sotho verbs.

We evaluate a Dirichlet-Multinomial formulation of DMV in the standard fashion by training on sections 2-21 and testing on section 23 of the Penn. Wall Street Journal treebank (Marcus et al., 1993). We initialise our models using the original harmonic initialiser (Klein and Manning, 2004). Figure 6 displays the directed accuracy results for DMV model trained with CVB and VB with Dirichlet α parameters of either 1 or 0.1, as well as the previously reported MLE result. In both cases we see superior results for CVB inference, providing evidence that CVB may be a better choice of inference algorithm for Bayesian formulations of generative grammar induction models such as DMV.

4.3 PCFG with latent annotations

The vanilla PCFGs estimated by simply taking the empirical rule frequencies off treebanks are not accurate models to capture the syntactic structures in most natural languages as demonstrated by Charniak (1997) and Klein and Manning (2003). Our third experiment is to apply the CVB algorithm to the PCFGs with latent annotations (PCFGs-LA) (Matsuzaki et al., 2005), where each non-terminal symbol is augmented with hidden variables (or subtypes). Given a parsed corpus, training a PCFG-LA yields a finer grammar with the automatically induced features represented by the subtypes. For example, an augmented binary rule takes the form $A[a] \rightarrow B[b]C[c]$, where $a, b, c \in [1, H]$ are the hidden subtypes, and H denotes the number of subtypes for each non-terminal.

[2]Annealing is not used in order to facilitate the perplexity calculation in the test set.

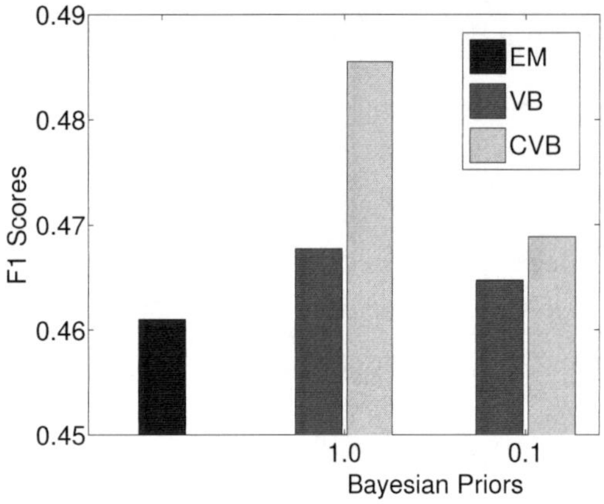

Figure 6: DMV trained by EM, VB and CVB. F1 scores on section 23, WSJ.

Objective	Precision	Recall	F1	Exact
EM	75.84	72.92	74.35	11.13
VB	76.98	73.32	75.11	11.49
CVB	78.85	76.98	77.90	12.56

Table 1: PCFG-LA (2 subtypes) trained by EM, VB and CVB. Precision, Recall, F1 scores, Exact match scores on section 23, WSJ.

We follow the same experiment set-up as DMV, and report the results on the section 23, using the best grammar tested on the development set (section 22) from 5 random runs for each algorithm. We adopt Petrov et al. (2006)'s methods to process the data: right binarising and replacing infrequent words with the generic unknown word marker for English, and to initialise: adding 1% randomness to the parameters θ_0 to start the EM training. We calculate the expected counts from (G, θ_0) to initialise our VB and CVB algorithms.

In Table 1, when each non-terminal is split into 2 hidden subtypes, we show that our CVB algorithm outperforms the EM and VB algorithms in terms of all the evaluation objectives. We also investigate the hidden state space with higher dimensions (4,8,16 subtypes), and find our CVB algorithm retains the advantages over the other two, whereas the VB algorithm fails to surpass the EM algorithm as reported in Figure 7.

5 Conclusion and future work

In this paper we have presented a collapsed variational Bayesian inference algorithm for PCFGs. We make use of the common scenario where the data consists of multiple short sentences, such that

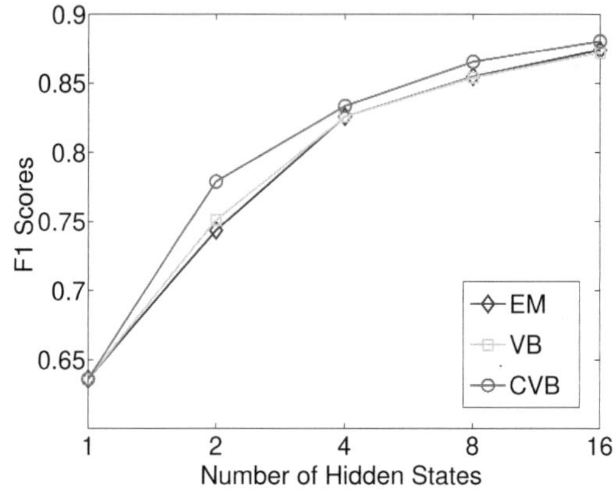

Figure 7: PCFG-LA (2,4,8,16 subtypes) trained by EM, VB and CVB. F1 scores on section 23, WSJ.

we can ignore the local dependencies induced by collapsing the parameters. The assumptions in our CVB algorithm are reasonable for a range of parsing applications and justified in three tasks by the empirical observations: it produces more accurate results than standard VB, and close results to sampling with significantly less training time.

While not state-of-the-art, the models we have demonstrated our CVB algorithm on underlie a number of high performance grammar induction and parsing systems (Cohen and Smith, 2009; Blunsom and Cohn, 2010; Petrov and Klein, 2007; Liang et al., 2007). Therefore, our work naturally extends to employing our CVB algorithm in more advanced models such as hierarchical splitting and merging system used in Berkeley parser (Petrov and Klein, 2007), and generalising our CVB algorithm to the non-parametric models such as tree substitution grammars (Blunsom and Cohn, 2010) and infinite PCFGs (Liang et al., 2007).

We have also sketched an alternative CVB algorithm which makes a harsher independence assumption for the latent variables but then requires no approximation of the variational posterior by performing inference individually for each parse node. This model breaks some strong dependencies within parse trees, but if we expect the posterior to be highly skewed by using a sparse prior, the product of constituent marginals may well be a good approximation. We leave further exploration of this algorithm for future work.

Acknowledgments

We would like to thank Mark Johnson for the data used in Section 4.1 and valuable advice.

References

James K. Baker. 1979. Trainable grammars for speech recognition. *The Journal of the Acoustical Society of America*, 65(S1):S132.

Matthew Beal. 2003. *Variational Algorithms for Approximate Bayesian Inference*. Ph.D. thesis, The Gatsby Computational Neuroscience Unit, University College London.

Phil Blunsom and Trevor Cohn. 2010. Unsupervised induction of tree substitution grammars for dependency parsing. In *Proceedings of the 2010 Conference on Empirical Methods in Natural Language Processing*, pages 1204–1213, Cambridge, MA, October. Association for Computational Linguistics.

Eugene Charniak. 1997. Statistical parsing with a context-free grammar and word statistics. In *Proceedings of the fourteenth national conference on artificial intelligence and ninth conference on Innovative applications of artificial intelligence*, AAAI'97/IAAI'97, pages 598–603. AAAI Press.

Shay B. Cohen and Noah A. Smith. 2009. Shared logistic normal distributions for soft parameter tying in unsupervised grammar induction. In *NAACL '09: Proceedings of Human Language Technologies: The 2009 Annual Conference of the North American Chapter of the Association for Computational Linguistics*, pages 74–82, Morristown, NJ, USA. Association for Computational Linguistics.

Michael Collins. 1999. *Head-Driven Statistical Models for Natural Language Parsing*. Ph.D. thesis, University of Pennsylvania.

A. P. Dempster, N. M. Laird, and D. B. Rubin. 1977. Maximum likelihood from incomplete data via the EM algorithm. *Journal of the Royal Statistics Society, Series B*, 39(1):1–38.

Joshua T. Goodman. 1998. *Parsing inside-out*. Ph.D. thesis, Cambridge, MA, USA. Adviser-Stuart Shieber.

William P. Headden III, Mark Johnson, and David McClosky. 2009. Improving unsupervised dependency parsing with richer contexts and smoothing. In *Proceedings of Human Language Technologies: The 2009 Annual Conference of the North American Chapter of the Association for Computational Linguistics*, pages 101–109, Boulder, Colorado, June.

Mark Johnson, Thomas L. Griffiths, and Sharon Goldwater. 2006. Adaptor grammars: A framework for specifying compositional nonparametric bayesian models. In *NIPS*.

Mark Johnson, Thomas Griffiths, and Sharon Goldwater. 2007. Bayesian inference for PCFGs via Markov chain Monte Carlo. In *Proc. of the 7th International Conference on Human Language Technology Research and 8th Annual Meeting of the NAACL (HLT-NAACL 2007)*, pages 139–146, Rochester, New York, April.

Mark Johnson. 1998. PCFG models of linguistic tree representations. *Computational Linguistics*, 24:613–632.

Dan Klein and Christopher D. Manning. 2003. Accurate unlexicalized parsing. In *Proceedings of the 41st Annual Meeting on Association for Computational Linguistics - Volume 1*, ACL '03, pages 423–430, Stroudsburg, PA, USA. Association for Computational Linguistics.

Dan Klein and Christopher D. Manning. 2004. Corpus-based induction of syntactic structure: models of dependency and constituency. In *ACL '04: Proceedings of the 42nd Annual Meeting on Association for Computational Linguistics*, page 478.

Kenichi Kurihara and Taisuke Sato. 2006. Variational bayesian grammar induction for natural language. In *Proceedings of the 8th international conference on Grammatical Inference: algorithms and applications*, ICGI'06, pages 84–96, Berlin, Heidelberg. Springer-Verlag.

Percy Liang and Dan Klein. 2009. Online EM for unsupervised models. In *Proceedings HLT/NAACL*.

Percy Liang, Slav Petrov, Michael Jordan, and Dan Klein. 2007. The infinite PCFG using hierarchical Dirichlet processes. In *Proc. of the 2007 Conference on Empirical Methods in Natural Language Processing (EMNLP-2007)*, pages 688–697, Prague, Czech Republic.

Brian MacWhinney and Catherine Snow. 1985. The child language data exchange system. *Child Language*.

Mitchell P. Marcus, Mary Ann Marcinkiewicz, and Beatrice Santorini. 1993. Building a large annotated corpus of English: the Penn treebank. *Computational Linguistics*, 19(2):313–330.

Takuya Matsuzaki, Yusuke Miyao, and Jun'ichi Tsujii. 2005. Probabilistic cfg with latent annotations. In *Proceedings of the 43rd Annual Meeting on Association for Computational Linguistics*, ACL '05, pages 75–82, Stroudsburg, PA, USA. Association for Computational Linguistics.

Radford Neal and Geoffrey E. Hinton. 1998. A view of the em algorithm that justifies incremental, sparse, and other variants. In *Learning in Graphical Models*, pages 355–368. Kluwer Academic Publishers.

Slav Petrov and Dan Klein. 2007. Improved inference for unlexicalized parsing. In *Human Language Technologies 2007: The Conference of the North American Chapter of the Association for Computational Linguistics; Proceedings of the Main Conference*.

Slav Petrov, Leon Barrett, Romain Thibaux, and Dan Klein. 2006. Learning accurate, compact, and interpretable tree annotation. In *Proceedings of the 21st International Conference on Computational*

Linguistics and the 44th annual meeting of the Association for Computational Linguistics, ACL-44, pages 433–440, Stroudsburg, PA, USA. Association for Computational Linguistics.

Issei Sato and Hiroshi Nakagawa. 2012. Rethinking collapsed variational bayes inference for LDA. In *Proceedings of the 29th International Conference on Machine Learning*.

Issei Sato, Kenichi Kurihara, and Hiroshi Nakagawa. 2012. Practical collapsed variational bayes inference for hierarchical dirichlet process. In *Proceedings of the 18th ACM SIGKDD international conference on Knowledge discovery and data mining*, KDD '12, pages 105–113, New York, NY, USA. ACM.

Valentin I. Spitkovsky, Hiyan Alshawi, and Daniel Jurafsky. 2012. Three dependency-and-boundary models for grammar induction. In *Proceedings of the 2012 Conference on Empirical Methods in Natural Language Processing and Computational Natural Language Learning (EMNLP-CoNLL 2012)*.

Jaemo Sung, Zoubin Ghahramani, and Sung-Yang Bang. 2008. Latent-space variational Bayes. *IEEE Trans. Pattern Anal. Mach. Intell.*, 30(12), December.

Yee Whye Teh, David Newman, and Max Welling. 2007. A collapsed variational Bayesian inference algorithm for latent Dirichlet allocation. In *In Advances in Neural Information Processing Systems, volume 19*.

Chong Wang and David Blei. 2012. Truncation-free stochastic variational inference for bayesian nonparametric models. In *Neural Information Processing Systems*.

Polyglot: Distributed Word Representations for Multilingual NLP

Rami Al-Rfou' **Bryan Perozzi** **Steven Skiena**
Computer Science Dept. Stony Brook University Stony Brook, NY 11794
{ralrfou, bperozzi, skiena}@cs.stonybrook.edu

Abstract

Distributed word representations (word embeddings) have recently contributed to competitive performance in language modeling and several NLP tasks. In this work, we train word embeddings for more than 100 languages using their corresponding Wikipedias. We quantitatively demonstrate the utility of our word embeddings by using them as the sole features for training a part of speech tagger for a subset of these languages. We find their performance to be competitive with near state-of-art methods in English, Danish and Swedish. Moreover, we investigate the semantic features captured by these embeddings through the proximity of word groupings. We will release these embeddings publicly to help researchers in the development and enhancement of multilingual applications.

1 Introduction

Building multilingual processing systems is a challenging task. Every NLP task involves different stages of preprocessing and calculating intermediate representations that will serve as features for later stages. These stages vary in complexity and requirements for each individual language. Despite recent momentum towards developing multilingual tools (Nivre et al., 2007; Hajič et al., 2009; Pradhan et al., 2012), most of NLP research still focuses on rich resource languages. Common NLP systems and tools rely heavily on English specific features and they are infrequently tested on multiple datasets. This makes them hard to port to new languages and tasks (Blitzer et al., 2006).

A serious bottleneck in the current approach for developing multilingual systems is the requirement of familiarity with each language under consideration. These systems are typically carefully tuned with hand-manufactured features designed by experts in a particular language. This approach can yield good performance, but tends to create complicated systems which have limited portability to new languages, in addition to being hard to enhance and maintain.

Recent advancements in unsupervised feature learning present an intriguing alternative. Instead of relying on expert knowledge, these approaches employ automatically generated task-independent features (or word embeddings) given large amounts of plain text. Recent developments have led to state-of-art performance in several NLP tasks such as language modeling (Bengio et al., 2006; Mikolov et al., 2010), and syntactic tasks such as sequence tagging (Collobert et al., 2011). These embeddings are generated as a result of training "deep" architectures, and it has been shown that such representations are well suited for domain adaptation tasks (Glorot et al., 2011; Chen et al., 2012).

We believe two problems have held back the research community's adoption of these methods. The first is that learning representations of words involves huge computational costs. The process usually involves processing billions of words over weeks. The second is that so far, these systems have been built and tested mainly on English.

In this work we seek to remove these barriers to entry by generating word embeddings for over a hundred languages using state-of-the-art techniques. Specifically, our contributions include:

- **Word embeddings** - We will release word embeddings for the hundred and seventeen languages that have more than 10,000 articles on Wikipedia. Each language's vocabulary will contain up to 100,000 words. The embeddings will be publicly available at (`www.cs.stonybrook.edu/~dsl`), for the research community to study their characteristics and build systems for new languages. We believe our embeddings represent a valuable resource because they contain a minimal amount of normalization. For example, we do not lower case words for European languages as other studies have done for English. This preserves features of the underlying language.

- **Quantitative analysis** - We investigate the embedding's performance on a part-of-speech (PoS) tagging task, and conduct qualitative investigation of the syntactic and semantic features they capture. Our experiments represent a valuable chance to evaluate distributed word representations for NLP as the experiments are conducted in a consistent manner and a large number of languages are covered. As the embeddings capture interesting linguistic features, we believe the multilingual resource we are providing gives researchers a chance to create multilingual comparative experiments.

- **Efficient implementation** - Training these models was made possible by our contributions to Theano (machine learning library (Bergstra et al., 2010)). These optimizations empower researchers to produce word embeddings under different settings or for different corpora than Wikipedia.

The rest of this paper is as follows. In Section 2, we give an overview of semi-supervised learning and learning representations related work. We then describe, in Section 3, the network used to generate the word embeddings and its characteristics. Section 4 discusses the details of the corpus collection and preparation steps we performed. Next, in Section 5, we discuss our experimental setup and the training progress over time. In Section 6 we discuss the semantic features captured by the embeddings by showing examples of the word groupings in multiple languages. Finally, in Section 7 we demonstrate the quality of our learned features by training a PoS tagger on several languages and then conclude.

2 Related Work

There is a large body of work regarding semi-supervised techniques which integrate unsupervised feature learning with discriminative learning methods to improve the performance of NLP applications. Word clustering has been used to learn classes of words that have similar semantic features to improve language modeling (Brown et al., 1992) and knowledge transfer across languages (Täckström et al., 2012). Dependency parsing and other NLP tasks have been shown to benefit from such a large unannotated corpus (Koo et al., 2008), and a variety of unsupervised feature learning methods have been shown to unilaterally improve the performance of supervised learning tasks (Turian et al., 2010). (Klementiev et al., 2012) induce distributed representations for a pair of languages jointly, where a learner can be trained on annotations present in one language and applied to test data in another.

Learning distributed word representations is a way to learn effective and meaningful information about words and their usages. They are usually generated as a side effect of training parametric language models as probabilistic neural networks. Training these models is slow and takes a significant amount of computational resources (Bengio et al., 2006; Dean et al., 2012). Several suggestions have been proposed to speed up the training procedure, either by changing the model architecture to exploit an algorithmic speedup (Mnih and Hinton, 2009; Morin and Bengio, 2005) or by estimating the error by sampling (Bengio and Senecal, 2008).

(Collobert and Weston, 2008) shows that word embeddings can almost substitute NLP common features on several tasks. The system they built, SENNA, offers part of speech tagging, chunking, named entity recognition, semantic role labeling and dependency parsing (Collobert, 2011). The system is built on top of word embeddings and performs competitively compared to state of art systems. In addition to pure performance, the system has a faster execution speed than comparable NLP pipelines (Al-Rfou' and Skiena, 2012).

To speed up the embedding generation process, SENNA embeddings are generated through a procedure that is different from language modeling. The representations are acquired through a model that distinguishes between phrases and corrupted versions of them. In doing this, the model avoids the need to normalize the scores across the vocabulary to infer probabilities. (Chen et al., 2013) shows that the embeddings generated by SENNA

Apple	apple	Bush	bush	corpora	dangerous
Dell	tomato	Kennedy	jungle	notations	costly
Paramount	bean	Roosevelt	lobster	digraphs	chaotic
Mac	onion	Nixon	sponge	usages	bizarre
Flex	potato	Fisher	mud	derivations	destructive

Table 1: Words nearest neighbors as they appear in the English embeddings.

perform well in a variety of term-based evaluation tasks. Given the training speed and prior performance on NLP tasks in English, we generate our multilingual embeddings using a similar network architecture to the one SENNA used.

However, our work differs from SENNA in the following ways. First, we do not limit our models to English, we train embeddings for a hundred and seventeen languages. Next, we preserve linguistic features by avoiding excessive normalization to the text. For example, our English model places "*Apple*" closer to IT companies and "*apple*" to fruits. More examples of linguistic features preserved by our model are shown in Table 1. This gives us the chance to evaluate the embeddings performance over PoS tagging without the need for manufactured features. Finally, we release the embeddings and the resources necessary to generate them to the community to eliminate any barriers.

Despite the progress made in creating distributed representations, combining them to produce meaning is still a challenging task. Several approaches have been proposed to address feature compositionality for semantic problems such as paraphrase detection (Socher et al., 2011), and sentiment analysis (Socher et al., 2012) using word embeddings.

3 Distributed Word Representation

Distributed word representations (word embeddings) map the index of a word in a dictionary to a feature vector in high-dimension space. Every dimension contributes to multiple concepts, and every concept is expressed by a combination of subset of dimensions. Such mapping is learned by back-propagating the error of a task through the model to update random initialized embeddings. The task is usually chosen such that examples can be automatically generated from unlabeled data (i.e so it is unsupervised). In case of language modeling, the task is to predict the last word of a phrase that consists of n words.

In our work, we start from the example construction method outlined in (Bengio et al., 2009). They train a model by requiring it to distinguish between the original phrase and a corrupted version of the phrase. If it does not score the original one higher than the corrupted one (by a margin), the model will be penalized. More precisely, for a given sequence of words $S = [w_{i-n} \dots w_i \dots w_{i+n}]$ observed in the corpus T, we will construct another corrupted sequence S' by replacing the word in the middle w_i with a word w_j chosen randomly from the vocabulary. The neural network represents a function $score$ that scores each phrase, the model is penalized through the hinge loss function $J(T)$ as shown in 1.

$$J(T) = \frac{1}{|T|} \sum_{i \in T} |1 - score(S') + score(S)|_{+} \quad (1)$$

Figure 1 shows a neural network that takes a sequence of words with size $2n + 1$ to compute a score. First, each word is mapped through a vocabulary dictionary with the size $|V|$ to an index that is used to index a shared matrix C with the size $|V| * M$ where M is the size of the vector representing the word. Once the vectors are retrieved, they are concatenated into one vector called projection layer P with size $(2n + 1) * M$. The projection layer plays the role of an input to a hidden layer with size $|H|$, the activations A of which are calculated according to equation 3, where W_1, b_1 are the weights and bias of the hidden layer.

$$A = tanh(W_1 P + b_1) \quad (2)$$

To calculate the phrase score, a linear combination of the hidden layer activations A is computed using W_2 and b_2.

$$score(P) = W_2 A + b_2 \quad (3)$$

Therefore, the five parameters that have to be learned are W_1, W_2, b_1, b_2, C with a total number of parameters $(2n + 1) * M * H + H + H + 1 + |V| * M \approx M * (nH + |V|)$.

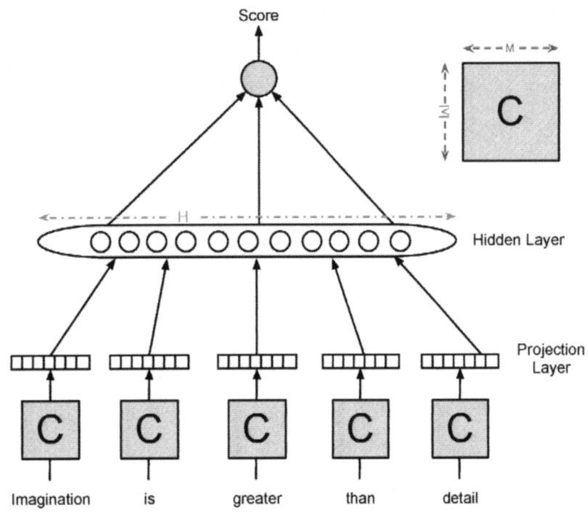

Figure 1: Neural network architecture. Words are retrieved from embeddings matrix C and concatenated at the projection layer as an input to computer the hidden layer activation. The score is the linear combination of the activation values of the hidden layer. The scores of two phrases are ranked according to hinge loss to distinguish the corrupted phrase from the original one.

4 Corpus Preparation

We have chosen to generate our word embeddings from Wikipedia. In addition to size, there are other desirable properties that we wish for the source of our language model to have:

- **Size and variety of languages** - As of this writing (April, 2013), 42 languages had more than 100,000 article pages, and 117 languages had more than 10,000 article pages.
- **Well studied** - Wikipedia is a prolific resource in the literature, and has been used for a variety of problems. Particularly, Wikipedia is well suited for multilingual applications (Navigli and Ponzetto, 2010).
- **Quality** - Wikipedians strive to write articles that are readable, accurate, and consist of good grammar.
- **Openly accessible** - Wikipedia is a resource available for free use by researchers
- **Growing** - As technology becomes more accessible, the size and scope of the multilingual Wikipedia effort continues to expand.

To process Wikipedia markup, we first extract the text using a modified version of the Bliki engine[1]. Next we must tokenize the text. We rely on an OpenNLP probabilistic tokenizer whenever possible, and default to the Unicode text segmentation[2] algorithm offered by Lucene when we have no such OpenNLP model. After tokenization, we normalize the tokens to reduce their sparsity. We have two main normalization rules. The first replaces digits with the symbol #, so "1999" becomes ####. In the second, we remove hyphens and brackets that appear in the middle of a token. As an additional rule for English, we map non-Latin characters to their unicode block groups.

In order to capture the syntactic and semantic features of words, we must observe each word several times in each of its valid contexts. This requirement, when combined with the Zipfian distribution of words in natural language, implies that learning a meaningful representation of a language requires a huge amount of unstructured text. In practice we deal with this limitation by restricting ourselves to considering the most frequently occurring tokens in each language.

Table 2 shows the size of each language corpus in terms of tokens, number of word types and coverage of text achieved by building a vocabulary out of the most frequent 100,000 tokens, $|V|$. Out of vocabulary (OOV) words are replaced with a special token $\langle$UNK$\rangle$.

While Wikipedia has 284 language specific encyclopedias, only five of them have more than a million articles. The size drops dramatically, such that the 42nd largest Wikipedia, Hindi, has slightly above 100,000 articles and the 100th, Tatar, has slightly over 16,000 articles[3].

Significant Wikipedias in size have a word coverage over 92% except for German, Russian, Arabic and Czech which shows the effect of heavy usage of morphological forms in these languages on the word usage distribution.

The highest word coverage we achieve is unsurprisingly for Chinese. This is expected given the limited size vocabulary of the language - the number of entries in the Contemporary Chinese Dictionary are estimated to be 65 thousand words (Shuxiang, 2004).

[1]Java Wikipedia API (Bliki engine) - `http://code.google.com/p/gwtwiki/`

[2]`http://www.unicode.org/reports/tr29/`

[3]`http://meta.wikimedia.org/w/index.php?title=List_of_Wikipedias&oldid=5248228`

Language	Tokens $*10^6$	Words $*10^3$	Coverage
English	1,888	12,125	96.30%
German	687	9,474	91.78%
French	473	4,675	95.78%
Spanish	399	3,978	96.07%
Russian	328	5,959	90.43%
Italian	322	3,642	95.52%
Portuguese	197	2,870	95.68%
Dutch	197	3,712	93.81%
Chinese	196	423	99.67%
Swedish	101	2,707	92.36%
Czech	80	2,081	91.84%
Arabic	52	1,834	91.78%
Danish	44	1,414	93.68%
Bulgarian	39	1,114	94.35%
Slovene	30	920	94.42%
Hindi	23	702	96.25%

Table 2: Statistics of a subset of the languages processed. The second column reports the number of tokens found in the corpus in millions while the third column reports the word types found in thousands. The coverage indicates the percentage of the corpus that will be matching words in a vocabulary consists of the most frequent 100 thousand words.

5 Training

For our experiments, we build a model as the one described in Section 3 using Theano (Bergstra et al., 2010). We choose the following parameters, context window size $2n + 1 = 5$, vocabulary $|V| = 100,000$, word embedding size $M = 64$, and hidden layer size $H = 32$. The intuition, here, is to maximize the relative size of the embeddings compared to the rest of the network. This might force the model to store the necessary information in the embeddings matrix instead of the hidden layer. Another benefit is that we will avoid overfitting on the smaller Wikipedias. Increasing the window size or the embedding size slows down the training speed, making it harder to converge within a reasonable time.

The examples are generated by sweeping a window over sentences. For each sentence in the corpus, all unknown words are replaced with a special token ⟨UNK⟩ and sentences are padded with ⟨S⟩, ⟨/S⟩ tokens. In case the window exceeds the edges of a sentence, the missing slots are filled with our padding token, ⟨PAD⟩.

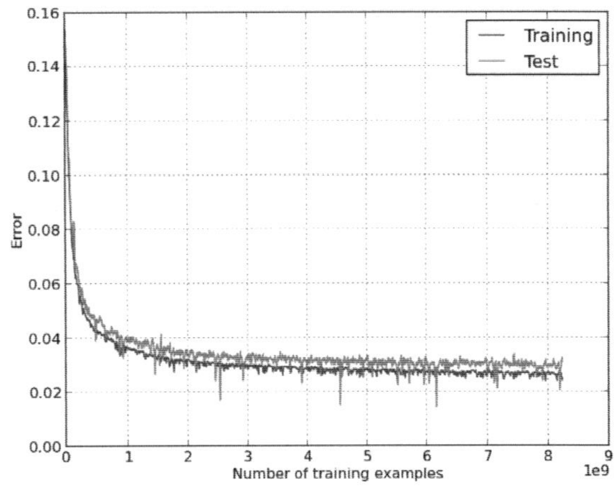

Figure 2: Training and test errors of the French model after 23 days of training. We did not notice any overfitting while training the model. The error curves are smoother the larger the language corpus is.

To train the model, we consider the data in mini-batches of size 16. Every 16 examples, we estimate the gradient using stochastic gradient descent (Bottou, 1991), and update the parameters which contributed to the error using backpropagation (Rumelhart et al., 2002). Calculating an exact gradient is prohibitive given that the dataset size is in millions of examples. We calculate the development error by sampling randomly 10000 mini-batches from the development dataset.

For each language, we set the batch size to 16 examples, and the learning rate to be 0.1. Following, (Collobert et al., 2011)'s advice, we divide each layer by the *fan in* of that layer, and we consider the embeddings layer to have a fan in of 1. We divide the corpus to three sets, training, development and testing with the following percentages 90, 5, 5 respectively.

One disadvantage of the approach used by (Collobert et al., 2011) is that there is no clear stopping criteria for the model training process. We have noticed that after a few weeks of training, the model's performance reaches the point where there is no significant decrease in the average loss over the development set, and when this occurs we manually stop the training. An interesting property of this model is that we did not notice any sign of overfitting for large Wikipedias. This could be explained by the infinite amount of examples we can generate by randomly choosing the re-

	Word	Translation		Word	Translation		Word	Word
French	**rouge**	**red**	Spanish	**dentista**	**dentist**	English	**Mumbai**	**Bombay**
	juane	yellow		peluquero	barber		Chennai	Madras
	rose	pink		ginecólog	gynecologist		Bangalore	Shanghai
	blanc	white		camionero	truck driver		Kolkata	Calultta
	orange	orange		oftalmólogo	ophthalmologist		Cairo	Bangkok
	bleu	blue		telegrafista	telegraphist		Hyderabad	Hyderabad
Arabic	**شكرا**	**thanks**	Arabic	**ولدان**	**two boys**	German	**Eisenbahnbetrieb**	**rail operations**
	وشكرا	and thanks		ابنان	two sons		Fahrbetrieb	driving
	تحياتيٍ	greetings		ولدين	two boys		Reisezugverkehr	passenger trains
	شكرًا	thanks + diacritic		طفلان	two children		Fährverkehr	ferries
	وشكرًا	and thanks + diacritic		ابنين	two sons		Handelsverkehr	Trade
	مرحبا	hello		ابنتان	two daughters		Schülerverkehr	students Transport
				Transliteration				
Russian	Путин	**Putin**	Chinese	**dongzhi**	**Winter Solstice**	Italian	**papa**	**Pope**
	Янукович	Yanukovych		chunfen	Vernal Equinox		Papa	Pope
	Троцкий	Trotsky		xiazhi	Summer solstice		pontefice	pontiff
	Гитлер	Hitler		qiufen	Autumnal Equinox		basileus	basileus
	Сталин	Stalin		ziye	Midnight		canridnale	cardinal
	Медведев	Medvedev		chuxi	New Year's Eve		frate	friar

Table 3: Examples of the nearest five neighbors of every word in several languages. Translation is retrieved from `http://translate.google.com`.

placement word in the corrupted phrase. Figure 2 shows a typical learning curve of the training. As the number of examples have been seen so far increased both the training error and the development error go down.

6 Qualitative Analysis

In order to understand how the embeddings space is organized, we examine the subtle information captured by the embeddings through investigating the proximity of word groups. This information has the potential to help researchers develop applications that use such semantic and syntactic information. The embeddings not only capture syntactic features, as we will demonstrate in Section 4, but also demonstrate the ability to capture interesting semantic information. Table 3 shows different words in several languages. For each word on top of each list, we rank the vocabulary according to their Euclidean distance from that word and show the closest five neighboring words.

- **French & Spanish** - Expected groupings of colors and professions is clearly observed.
- **English** - The example shows how the embedding space is aware of the name change that happened to a group of Indian cities. "*Mumbai*" used to be called "*Bombay*", "*Chennai*" used to be called "*Madras* and "*Kolkata*" used to be called "*Calcutta*". On the other hand, "*Hyderabad*" stayed at a similar distance from both names as they point to the same conceptual meaning.
- **Arabic** - The first example shows the word "*Thanks*". Despite not removing the diacritics from the text, the model learned that the two surface forms of the word mean similar things and, therefore, grouped them together. In Arabic, conjunction words do not get separated from the following word. Usually, "*and thanks*" serves as a letter signature as "*sincerely*" is used in English. The model learned that both words {"*and thanks*", "*thanks*" } are similar, regardless their different forms. The second example illustrates a specific syntactic morphological feature of Arabic, where enumeration of couples has its own form.
- **German** - The example demonstrates that the compositional semantics of multi-unit words are still preserved.
- **Russian** - The model learned to group Russian/Soviet leaders and other figures related to the Soviet history together.
- **Chinese** - The list contains three solar terms that are part of the traditional East Asian lunisolar calendars. The remaining two terms correspond to traditional holidays that occur at the same dates of these solar terms.
- **Italian** - The model learned that the lower and upper cases of the word has similar meaning.

7 Sequence Tagging

Here we analyze the quality of the models we have generated. To test the quantitative performance of the embeddings, we use them as the sole features for a well studied NLP task, part of speech tagging.

To demonstrate the capability of the learned dis-

Language	Source	Test			TnT
		Unknown	**Known**	**All**	
German	Tiger† (Brants et al., 2002)	89.17%	**98.60%**	97.85%	98.10%
Bulgarian	BTB† (Simov et al., 2002)	75.74%	98.33%	96.33%	97.50%
Czech	PDT 2.5 (Bejček et al., 2012)	71.98%	**99.15%**	97.13%	99.10%
Danish	DDT† (Kromann, 2003)	73.03%	98.07%	**96.45%**	96.40%
Dutch	Alpino† (Van der Beek et al., 2002)	73.47%	95.85%	93.86%	95.00%
English	PennTreebank (Marcus et al., 1993)	75.97%	97.74%	**97.18%**	96.80%
Portuguese	Sint(c)tica† (Afonso et al., 2002)	75.36%	97.71%	95.95%	96.80%
Slovene	SDT† (Džeroski et al., 2006)	68.82%	95.17%	93.46%	94.60%
Swedish	Talbanken05† (Nivre et al., 2006)	83.54%	95.77%	**94.68%**	94.70%

Table 4: Results of our model against several PoS datasets. The performance is measured using accuracy over the test datasets. Third column represents the total accuracy of the tagger the former two columns reports the accuracy over known words and OOV words (unknown). The results are compared to the TnT tagger results reported by (Petrov et al., 2012).
†CoNLL 2006 dataset

tributed representations in extracting useful word features, we train a PoS tagger over the subset of languages that we were able to acquire free annotated resources for. We choose our tagger for this task to be a neural network because it has a fast convergence rate based on our initial experiments.

The part of speech tagger has similar architecture to the one used for training the embeddings. However we have changed some of the network parameters, specifically, we use a hidden layer of size 300 and learning rate of 0.3. The network is trained by minimizing the negative of the log likelihood of the labeled data. To tag a specific word w_i we consider a window with size $2n$ where n in our experiment is equal to 2. Equation 4 shows how we construct a feature vector F by concatenating ($\oplus$) the embeddings of the words occurred in the window, where C is the matrix that contains the embeddings of the language vocabulary.

$$F = \bigoplus_{j=i-2}^{i+2} C[w_j] \tag{4}$$

The feature vector will be fed to the network and the error will back propagated back to the embeddings.

The results of this experiment are presented in Table 4. We train and test our models on the universal tagset proposed by (Petrov et al., 2012). This universal tagset maps each original tag in a treebank to one out of twelve general PoS tags. This simplifies the comparison of classifiers performance across languages. We compare our results to a similar experiment conducted in their work, where they trained a TnT tagger (Brants, 2000) on several treebanks. The TnT tagger is based on Markov models and depends on trigram counts observed in the labeled data. It was chosen for its fast speed and (near to) state-of-the-art accuracy, without language specific tuning.

The performance of embeddings is competitive in general. Surprisingly, it is doing better than the TnT tagger in English and Danish. Moreover, our performance is so close in the case of Swedish. This task is hard for our tagger for two reasons. The first is that we do not add OOV words seen during training of the tagger to our vocabulary. The second is that all OOV words are substituted with one representation, ⟨UNK⟩ and there is no character level information used to inform the tagger about the characteristic of the OOV words.

On the other hand, the performance on the known words is strong and consistent showing the value of the features learned about these words from the unsupervised stage. Although the word coverage of German and Czech are low in the original Wikipedia corpora (See Table 2), the features learned are achieving great accuracy on the known words. They both achieve above 98.5% accuracy. It is noticeable that the Slovene model performs the worst, under both known and unknown words categories. It achieves only 93.46% accuracy on the test dataset. Given that the Slovene embeddings were trained on the least amount of data among all other embeddings we test here, we expect the quality to go lower for the other smaller Wikipedias not tested here.

In Table 5, we present how well the vocabulary of each language's embeddings covered the part of speech datasets. The datasets come from a different domain than Wikipedia, and this is reflected in the results.

In Table 6, we present the results of training the same neural network part of speech tagger without using our embeddings as initializations. We found that the embeddings benefited all the languages we considered, and observed the greatest benefit in languages which had a small number of training examples. We believe that these results illustrate the performance

Language	% Token Coverage	% Word Coverage
Bulgarian	94.58	77.70
Czech	95.37	65.61
Danish	95.41	80.03
German	94.04	60.68
English	98.06	79.73
Dutch	96.25	77.76
Portuguese	94.09	72.66
Slovene	95.33	83.67
Swedish	95.87	73.92

Table 5: Coverage statistics of the embedding's vocabulary on the part of speech datasets after normalization. Token coverage is the raw percentage of words which were known, while the Word coverage ignores repeated words.

Language	# Training Examples	Accuracy Drop
Bulgarian	200,049	-2.01%
Czech	1,239,687	-0.86%
Danish	96,581	-1.77%
German	735,826	-0.89%
English	950,561	-0.25%
Dutch	208,418	-1.37%
Portuguese	212,749	-0.91%
Slovene	27,284	-2.68%
Swedish	199,509	-0.82%

Table 6: Accuracy of randomly initialized tagger compared to our results. Using the embeddings was generally helpful, especially in languages where we did not have many training examples. The scores presented are the best we found for each language (languages with more resources could afford to train longer before overfitting).

8 Conclusion

Distributed word representations represent a valuable resource for any language, but particularly for resource-scarce languages. We have demonstrated how word embeddings can be used as off-the-shelf solution to reach near to state-of-art performance over a fundamental NLP task, and we believe that our embeddings will help researchers to develop tools in languages with which they have no expertise.

Moreover, we showed several examples of interesting semantic relations expressed in the embeddings space that we believe will lead to interesting applications and improve tasks as semantic compositionality.

While we have only considered the properties of word embeddings as features in this work, it has been shown that using word embeddings in conjunction with traditional NLP features can significantly improve results on NLP tasks (Turian et al., 2010; Collobert et al., 2011). With this in mind, we believe that the entire research community can benefit from our release of word embeddings for over 100 languages.

We hope that these resources will advance the study of possible pair-wise mappings between embeddings of several languages and their relations. Our future work in this area includes improving the models by increasing the size of the context window and their domain adaptivity through incorporating other sources of data. We will be investigating better strategies for modeling OOV words. We see improvements to OOV word handling as essential to ensure robust performance of the embeddings on real-world tasks.

Acknowledgments

This research was partially supported by NSF Grants DBI-1060572 and IIS-1017181, with additional support from TexelTek.

References

Susana Afonso, Eckhard Bick, Renato Haber, and Diana Santos. 2002. Floresta sintá (c) tica": a treebank for portuguese. In *Proc. of the Third Intern. Conf. on Language Resources and Evaluation (LREC)*, pages 1698–1703.

Rami Al-Rfou' and Steven Skiena. 2012. Speedread: A fast named entity recognition pipeline. In *Pro-*

ceedings of the 24th International Conference on Computational Linguistics (Coling 2012), pages 53–61, Mumbai, India, December. Coling 2012 Organizing Committee.

Eduard Bejček, Jarmila Panevová, Jan Popelka, Pavel Straňák, Magda Ševčíková, Jan Štěpánek, and Zdeněk Žabokrtský. 2012. Prague Dependency Treebank 2.5 – a revisited version of PDT 2.0. In *Proceedings of COLING 2012*, pages 231–246, Mumbai, India, December. The COLING 2012 Organizing Committee.

Yoshua Bengio and J-S Senecal. 2008. Adaptive importance sampling to accelerate training of a neural probabilistic language model. *Neural Networks, IEEE Transactions on*, 19(4):713–722.

Y. Bengio, H. Schwenk, J.S. Senécal, F. Morin, and J.L. Gauvain. 2006. Neural probabilistic language models. *Innovations in Machine Learning*, pages 137–186.

Y. Bengio, J. Louradour, R. Collobert, and J. Weston. 2009. Curriculum learning. In *International Conference on Machine Learning, ICML*.

James Bergstra, Olivier Breuleux, Frédéric Bastien, Pascal Lamblin, Razvan Pascanu, Guillaume Desjardins, Joseph Turian, David Warde-Farley, and Yoshua Bengio. 2010. Theano: a CPU and GPU math expression compiler. In *Proceedings of the Python for Scientific Computing Conference (SciPy)*, June. Oral Presentation.

John Blitzer, Ryan McDonald, and Fernando Pereira. 2006. Domain adaptation with structural correspondence learning. In *Conference on Empirical Methods in Natural Language Processing*, Sydney, Australia.

Léon Bottou. 1991. Stochastic gradient learning in neural networks. In *Proceedings of Neuro-Nîmes 91*, Nimes, France. EC2.

Sabine Brants, Stefanie Dipper, Silvia Hansen, Wolfgang Lezius, and George Smith. 2002. The tiger treebank. In *IN PROCEEDINGS OF THE WORKSHOP ON TREEBANKS AND LINGUISTIC THEORIES*, pages 24–41.

Thorsten Brants. 2000. Tnt: a statistical part-of-speech tagger. In *Proceedings of the sixth conference on Applied natural language processing*, pages 224–231. Association for Computational Linguistics.

Peter F Brown, Peter V Desouza, Robert L Mercer, Vincent J Della Pietra, and Jenifer C Lai. 1992. Class-based n-gram models of natural language. *Computational linguistics*, 18(4):467–479.

Minmin Chen, Zhixiang Xu, Kilian Weinberger, and Fei Sha. 2012. Marginalized denoising autoencoders for domain adaptation. In John Langford and Joelle Pineau, editors, *Proceedings of the 29th International Conference on Machine Learning (ICML-12)*, ICML '12, pages 767–774. ACM, New York, NY, USA, July.

Yanqing Chen, Bryan Perozzi, Rami Al-Rfou', and Steven Skiena. 2013. The expressive power of word embeddings. *CoRR*, abs/1301.3226.

R. Collobert and J. Weston. 2008. A unified architecture for natural language processing: Deep neural networks with multitask learning. In *International Conference on Machine Learning, ICML*.

Ronan Collobert, Jason Weston, Léon Bottou, Michael Karlen, Koray Kavukcuoglu, and Pavel Kuksa. 2011. Natural language processing (almost) from scratch. *J. Mach. Learn. Res.*, 12:2493–2537, November.

Ronan Collobert. 2011. Deep learning for efficient discriminative parsing. In *AISTATS*.

Jeffrey Dean, Greg Corrado, Rajat Monga, Kai Chen, Matthieu Devin, Quoc Le, Mark Mao, Marc'Aurelio Ranzato, Andrew Senior, Paul Tucker, Ke Yang, and Andrew Ng. 2012. Large scale distributed deep networks. In P. Bartlett, F.C.N. Pereira, C.J.C. Burges, L. Bottou, and K.Q. Weinberger, editors, *Advances in Neural Information Processing Systems 25*, pages 1232–1240.

Sašo Džeroski, Tomaž Erjavec, Nina Ledinek, Petr Pajas, Zdenek Žabokrtsky, and Andreja Žele. 2006. Towards a slovene dependency treebank. In *Proc. of the Fifth Intern. Conf. on Language Resources and Evaluation (LREC)*.

Xavier Glorot, Antoine Bordes, and Yoshua Bengio. 2011. Domain adaptation for large-scale sentiment classification: A deep learning approach. In *Proceedings of the Twenty-eight International Conference on Machine Learning (ICML'11)*, volume 27, pages 97–110, June.

Jan Hajič, Massimiliano Ciaramita, Richard Johansson, Daisuke Kawahara, Maria Antònia Martí, Lluís Màrquez, Adam Meyers, Joakim Nivre, Sebastian Padó, Jan Štěpánek, Pavel Straňák, Mihai Surdeanu, Nianwen Xue, and Yi Zhang. 2009. The CoNLL-2009 shared task: Syntactic and semantic dependencies in multiple languages. In *Proceedings of the 13th Conference on Computational Natural Language Learning (CoNLL-2009), June 4-5*, Boulder, Colorado, USA.

Alexandre Klementiev, Ivan Titov, and Binod Bhattarai. 2012. Inducing crosslingual distributed representations of words. In *Proceedings of COLING 2012*, pages 1459–1474, Mumbai, India, December. The COLING 2012 Organizing Committee.

Terry Koo, Xavier Carreras, and Michael Collins. 2008. Simple semi-supervised dependency parsing. In *In Proc. ACL/HLT*.

Matthias Trautner Kromann. 2003. The danish dependency treebank and the dtag treebank tool. In *Proceedings of the Second Workshop on Treebanks and Linguistic Theories (TLT)*, page 217.

Mitchell P Marcus, Mary Ann Marcinkiewicz, and Beatrice Santorini. 1993. Building a large annotated corpus of english: The penn treebank. *Computational linguistics*, 19(2):313–330.

T. Mikolov, M. Karafiát, L. Burget, J. Cernocky, and S. Khudanpur. 2010. Recurrent neural network based language model. *Proceedings of Interspeech.*

Andriy Mnih and Geoffrey E Hinton. 2009. A scalable hierarchical distributed language model. *Advances in neural information processing systems*, 21:1081–1088.

Frederic Morin and Yoshua Bengio. 2005. Hierarchical probabilistic neural network language model. In *Proceedings of the international workshop on artificial intelligence and statistics*, pages 246–252.

Roberto Navigli and Simone Paolo Ponzetto. 2010. Babelnet: Building a very large multilingual semantic network. In *Proceedings of the 48th annual meeting of the association for computational linguistics*, pages 216–225. Association for Computational Linguistics.

Joakim Nivre, Jens Nilsson, and Johan Hall. 2006. Talbanken05: A swedish treebank with phrase structure and dependency annotation. In *Proceedings of the fifth International Conference on Language Resources and Evaluation (LREC)*, pages 1392–1395.

Joakim Nivre, Johan Hall, Sandra Kübler, Ryan McDonald, Jens Nilsson, Sebastian Riedel, and Deniz Yuret. 2007. The CoNLL 2007 shared task on dependency parsing. In *Proceedings of the CoNLL Shared Task Session of EMNLP-CoNLL 2007*, pages 915–932, Prague, Czech Republic, June. Association for Computational Linguistics.

Slav Petrov, Dipanjan Das, and Ryan McDonald. 2012. A universal part-of-speech tagset. In Nicoletta Calzolari (Conference Chair), Khalid Choukri, Thierry Declerck, Mehmet Uğur Doğan, Bente Maegaard, Joseph Mariani, Jan Odijk, and Stelios Piperidis, editors, *Proceedings of the Eight International Conference on Language Resources and Evaluation (LREC'12)*, Istanbul, Turkey, may. European Language Resources Association (ELRA).

Sameer Pradhan, Alessandro Moschitti, Nianwen Xue, Olga Uryupina, and Yuchen Zhang. 2012. CoNLL-2012 shared task: Modeling multilingual unrestricted coreference in OntoNotes. In *Proceedings of the Sixteenth Conference on Computational Natural Language Learning (CoNLL 2012)*, Jeju, Korea.

David E Rumelhart, Geoffrey E Hinton, and Ronald J Williams. 2002. Learning representations by back-propagating errors. *Cognitive modeling*, 1:213.

Lu Shuxiang. 2004. *The Contemporary Chinese Dictionary (Xiandai Hanyu Cidian)*. Commercial Press.

Kiril Simov, Petya Osenova, Milena Slavcheva, Sia Kolkovska, Elisaveta Balabanova, Dimitar Doikoff, Krassimira Ivanova, Er Simov, and Milen Kouylekov. 2002. Building a linguistically interpreted corpus of bulgarian: the bultreebank. In *In: Proceedings of LREC 2002, Canary Islands.*

Richard Socher, Eric H. Huang, Jeffrey Pennington, Andrew Y. Ng, and Christopher D. Manning. 2011. Dynamic pooling and unfolding recursive autoencoders for paraphrase detection. In *Advances in Neural Information Processing Systems 24.*

Richard Socher, Brody Huval, Christopher D. Manning, and Andrew Y. Ng. 2012. Semantic compositionality through recursive matrix-vector spaces. In *Proceedings of the 2012 Conference on Empirical Methods in Natural Language Processing (EMNLP).*

Oscar Täckström, Ryan McDonald, and Jakob Uszkoreit. 2012. Cross-lingual word clusters for direct transfer of linguistic structure. In *Proceedings of the 2012 Conference of the North American Chapter of the Association for Computational Linguistics: Human Language Technologies*, pages 477–487. Association for Computational Linguistics.

J. Turian, L. Ratinov, and Y. Bengio. 2010. Word representations: a simple and general method for semi-supervised learning. In *Proceedings of the 48th Annual Meeting of the Association for Computational Linguistics*, pages 384–394. Association for Computational Linguistics.

Leonoor Van der Beek, Gosse Bouma, Rob Malouf, and Gertjan Van Noord. 2002. The alpino dependency treebank. *Language and Computers*, 45(1):8–22.

Exploiting multiple hypotheses for Multilingual Spoken Language Understanding

Marcos Calvo, Fernando García, Lluís-F. Hurtado, Santiago Jiménez, Emilio Sanchis
Departament de Sistemes Informàtics i Computació
Universitat Politècnica de València, València, Spain
{mcalvo,fgarcia,lhurtado,sjimenez,esanchis}@dsic.upv.es

Abstract

In this work, we present an approach for multilingual portability of Spoken Language Understanding systems. The goal of this approach is to avoid the effort of acquiring and labeling new corpora to learn models when changing the language. The work presented in this paper is focused on the learning of a specific translator for the task and the mechanism of transmitting the information among the modules by means of graphs. These graphs represent a set of hypotheses (a language) that is the input to the statistical semantic decoder that provides the meaning of the sentence. Some experiments in a Spanish task evaluated with input French utterances and text are presented. They show the good behavior of the system, mainly when speech input is considered.

1 Introduction

Spoken Language Understanding (SLU) is one of the key modules in many voice-driven human-computer interaction systems. Many successful SLU systems that have been developed in the last few years are based on statistical models automatically learned from semantically labeled corpora (Maynard and Lefèvre, 2001; Segarra et al., 2002; He and Young, 2006; Lefèvre, 2007; De Mori et al., 2008). One of the advantages of statistical models is the capability of representing the variability of lexical realizations of concepts (meanings). On the other hand, they are usually plain models, that is, they can not represent a hierarchical semantic dependency, although there are some works in this area (He and Young, 2003). However, this is not a problem in most Spoken Dialog Systems since the semantic information to be extracted is not very hierarchically structured.

Another important aspect of these models is that they can be learned from corpora. The corpora used for training must be large enough to allow an accurate estimation of the probabilities, and it must represent the lexical and syntactic variability that is used in the language to express the semantics as much as possible. Although there are some approaches based on semi-supervised or unsupervised learning (Tür et al., 2005; Riccardi and Hakkani-Tür, 2005; Ortega et al., 2010), the most common approaches need to have a segmented and labeled training corpus. This is the case of discriminative models (like Conditional Random Fields (Hahn et al., 2010)), and generative models (such as Hidden Markov Models and Stochastic Finite State Automata (Segarra et al., 2002; Hahn et al., 2010)). In the case of supervised learning, it is necessary to define a set of concepts that represent the semantic domain of the task and to associate these concepts to the corresponding sequences of words in the sentences. This is the case of the French MEDIA corpus (Bonneau-Maynard et al., 2005), and the Spanish DIHANA corpus (Benedí et al., 2006). Since the corpus acquisition and labeling require a great manual effort, being able to reuse the corpus generated for a task to easily develop SLU systems for other tasks, or languages, is an important issue.

This work focuses on the problem of SLU portability between languages (García et al., 2012; He et al., 2013; Jabaian et al., 2013). We propose a semi-supervised approach for adapting the system to tackle sentences that are uttered in a new language. In order to learn a domain-specific translation model, a parallel corpus is automatically generated from the training set by using web translators. Due to the fact that the speech recognition and the translation phases can generate many errors, a mechanism to obtain the correct meaning despite these errors is needed. This can be performed by supplying many hypotheses between the different stages, either as a set of n sentences or as a graph that represents not only the original sentences but also an adequate generalization of them. This graph can be obtained from a Grammatical Inference process. We have also developed a specific algorithm to perform the semantic decoding by taking graphs of words as the input and considering statistical semantic models. We have applied these techniques for the DIHANA corpus, which is a task to access the information of train timetables and fares in Spanish by phone. This corpus was originally generated in Spanish, and we have evaluated our system by using input sentences in French.

2 Description of the system

One way of solving the SLU problem is to find the sequence of concepts $\hat{C}$ that best fits the semantics contained in an utterance A. Considering a stochastic modelization, it can be stated as:

$$\hat{C} = \operatorname*{argmax}_{C} p(C|A) \quad (1)$$

In the case of Multilingual SLU, the user utters a sentence in a source language s, which is different to the language t of the original data of the SLU task. Thus, either the uttered sentence or the training data (or maybe both) should be translated into a common language in order to be able to apply the semantic decoding process to the input utterance. In our case, we recognize the input utterance by using an Automatic Speech Recognizer (ASR) in the source language, and we then translate the hypotheses provided by the ASR into the target language t by means of a statistical Machine Translation system (see Figure 1). Consequently, by considering both the input sentence W_s uttered by the user and its translation into the target language W_t, Equation (1) can be rewritten as:

$$\hat{C} = \operatorname*{argmax}_{C} \max_{W_s, W_t} p(C, W_s, W_t|A) \quad (2)$$

Equation (2) can be decomposed into several factors, as shown in Equation (3). This is achieved by applying the Bayes' Rule and making some reasonable assumptions about the independence of the variables.

$$\hat{C} = \operatorname*{argmax}_{C} \max_{W_s, W_t} \frac{p(A|W_s) \cdot p(W_s|W_t) \cdot p(W_t|C) \cdot p(C)}{p(A)} \quad (3)$$

To perform this maximization, we propose a decoupled architecture, which sequentially applies all the knowledge sources. One of the most important drawbacks of decoupled architectures is that the errors generated in one stage can not be recovered in following phases. To overcome this problem, we propose an architecture in which the communication between the modules is done by means of structures that provide more than one hypothesis, like n-best and graphs of words. A scheme of this architecture is shown in Figure 1. Its modules are the following:

1. First, the input utterance is processed by an ASR in the source language, providing as its output either the 1-best or a set of n-best transcriptions. We have used a general purpose, freely available web ASR, which means that the ASR has no specific information about the task.

2. These transcriptions are translated into the target language by means of a state-of-the-art Machine Translation system: MOSES (Koehn et al., 2007). The translation models have been trained without using any manually generated data. Instead, a set of freely available web translators was used to translate the training sentences of the corpus from the target language (the original language of the corpus sentences) into the source language (the language of the speaker), thereby building a parallel training corpus. MOSES provides as its output a set of candidate translations (n-best) of the transcriptions supplied by the ASR.

3. A graph of words is built from the n-best provided by the translator. This graph is built through a Grammatical Inference process. This way the graph not only represents the translations, but also a reasonable generalization of them. This makes it possible for the semantic decoder to consider some sentences that were not in the initial set but that are made of pieces of those sentences.

4. This graph of words is processed by a SLU module that is able to tackle graphs. The semantic model for this stage has been learned using only the training data in the target language. As an intermediate result, this process builds a graph of concepts, which is a compact representation of all the possible semantics contained in the language represented by

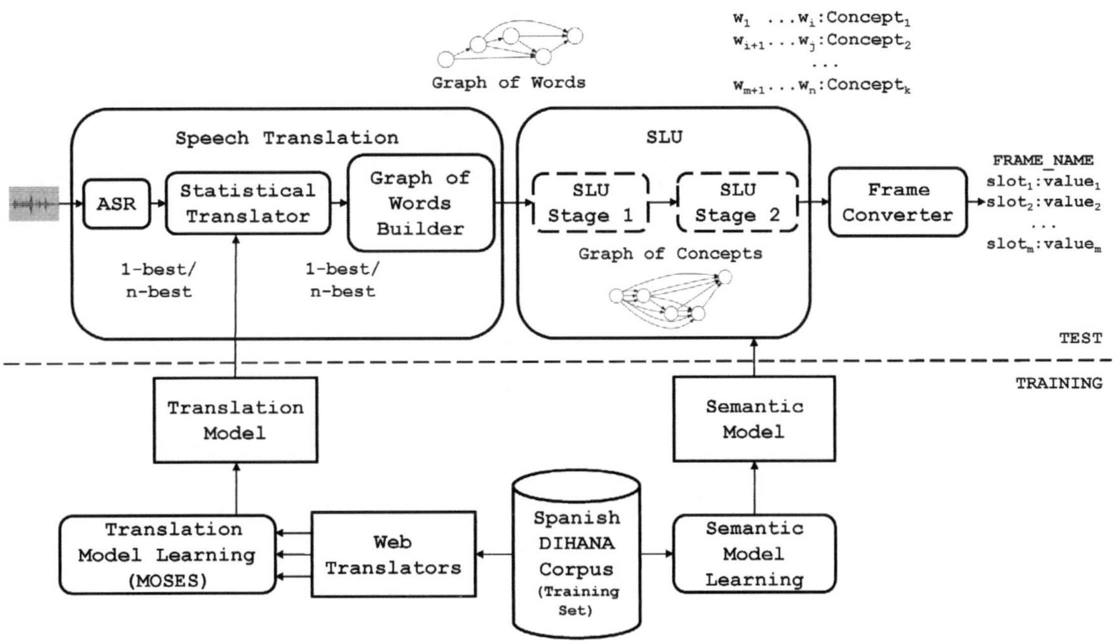

Figure 1: Scheme of the decoupled architecture.

the graph of words. The output of this module is the best sequence of concepts $\hat{C}$ and also its underlying sequence of words $\tilde{W}_t$ in the target language and a segmentation of $\tilde{W}_t$ according to $\hat{C}$.

5. Finally, the segmentation obtained in the previous step is processed in order to convert it into a frame representation. This involves extracting the relevant information from the segmentation and representing it in a canonical way.

Assuming that all the translations W_t that belong to the language represented by the graph of words are a priori equiprobable in the target language, we can rewrite Equation (3) as follows:

$$\hat{C} = \operatorname*{argmax}_{C} \max_{W_s, W_t} \frac{p(A|W_s) \cdot p(W_s) \cdot p(W_t|W_s) \cdot p(W_t|C) \cdot p(C)}{p(A)} \quad (4)$$

The first three modules of the architecture can be viewed as a speech translation process, where the input is an utterance and the output is a set of possible translations of this utterance, represented as a graph of words. Each one of these translations is weighted with the probability $p(W_t|A)$. Considering that

$$p(W_t|A) \approx \max_{W_s} \frac{p(A|W_s) \cdot p(W_s) \cdot p(W_t|W_s)}{p(A)}$$

it stands that Equation (4) can be rewritten as:

$$\hat{C} = \operatorname*{argmax}_{C} \max_{W_t} p(W_t|A) \cdot p(W_t|C) \cdot p(C) \quad (5)$$

The fact that the communication between the different modules is a set of hypotheses makes it possible to apply the different constraints (acoustic, lexical, syntactic, and semantic) in a global way, while the modular architecture allows local pruning taking into account only a subset of the knowledge sources. This way each of the modules contributes to the computation of the global maximization, but it is not completely performed until the end of the process.

3 Learning of the translation model

It has been shown that statistical models achieve good performance in speech translation tasks (Mathias and Byrne, 2006). Also, they have the advantage that they can be adapted to a specific task, as long as a large enough amount of parallel training data is available in order to adequately train the parameters of the Machine Translation system. However, obtaining this task-specific training data by translating the original data by hand is very expensive and time-consuming. A solution to this problem is to use several general-purpose web translators (which are available on the Internet) to automatically translate the task-specific training sentences into another language. Although these translators can generate many errors, they are an interesting way to obtain several hypotheses for a translation without much effort. However, the use of these translators at testing time is not very convenient due to the fact that the system would depend on the Internet connection and the reaction time of the corresponding web pages. Another drawback is that it is impossible to adapt them to a specific task, which could generate many errors that are important to the task.

The approach that we propose attempts to take advantage of these resources, but for training purposes. In other words, given the training sentences in Spanish, they are translated into a new language (French in this case) by using several web translators. This way we build a parallel corpus where each sentence has different translations associated to it. From this parallel corpus, we train a statistical translator that is specific for the task. It should be noted that by means of this process, the learned translator can represent and modelize the variability generated by the different translators. However, due to the difficulty of the problem, this modelization may not be enough. Therefore we can not guarantee that the best translation obtained by the model is consistent with the meaning of the original sentence. This is why it is convenient to supply more than one hypothesis to the semantic decoding module in order to have the possibility of finding the correct semantic meaning even when some errors were generated in the recognition and translation processes. We think that separately processing the n-best translated sentences (for each input sentence) generated by the translator is not the best solution. In contrast, it would be better to adequately combine segments of different sentences. Thus, we have developed a Grammatical Inference mechanism to build a graph of words from a set of hypotheses as described in the following section.

4 Generating the graphs of words

In this section, the process of obtaining the graphs of words in the target language from multiple translation hypotheses is explained. This process is divided into two steps:

1. The translation hypotheses are aligned using a Multiple Sequence Alignment (MSA) algorithm. The result of the MSA process is an alignment matrix.
2. The aligned sentences, represented by the alignment matrix, are used to obtain a weighted graph of words that will be the input to the graph-based SLU module.

A Multiple Sequence Alignment is a process of sequence alignment that involves more than two sequences. It takes a set of sequences of symbols (in our case, sequences of words) and provides the alignment of the elements of the set that minimizes the number of edit operations (substitutions, insertions, and deletions) among all the symbols of the sequences. In this work, a modification of the ClustalW (Larkin et al., 2007) Multiple Sequence Alignment software has been used.

The result of the MSA process is an alignment matrix. Each row in this matrix represents a different aligned sentence, and each column represents the alignment of each symbol. The total number of columns is usually greater than the length of the longest sequence, since not all the symbols can be aligned. The special symbol '-' is used to represent the positions of non-alignment points in a sentence.

A weighted directed acyclic graph of words is created from the MSA alignment matrix, The graph construction consists of creating as many nodes as columns in the alignment matrix plus one for the final state and as many arcs as cells in the matrix that contain a symbol different to '-'. The arcs with the same source, destination, and symbol are joined, and the weights are obtained by normalizing these counters (Calvo et al., 2012).

Figure 2 shows a real example (extracted from the test set) of the full process of obtaining the graph of words. As the figure shows, the obtained graph of words (where the arcs are labeled with words and weighted with the normalized counters) represents a language which is a generalization of the individual translations of the original utterance. That is, this process is a Grammatical Inference mechanism that represents sentences with characteristics that are similar to those used to build the graph. A full path from the initial node to the final node in the graph may be seen as an alternative translation of the original utterance. For example, the correct translation of the utterance "*el precio del billete del tren de las seis treinta y cinco*" was not among the candidates provided, but it can be recovered using this algorithm.

This graph builder module completes the sequence of modules that perform the speech trans-

source utterance	*le prix du billet de train de six heures trente-cinq* *(the price of the train ticket for six thirty-five)* *(el precio del billete del tren de las seis treinta y cinco)*
multiple ASR outputs	le prix du billet train de sezer trente-cinq le prix du billet train de six vers trente-cinq le prix du billet train de six onze trente-cinq le prix du billet train des six heures trente cinq
multiple translations	el precio del billete de tren de sezer treinta y cinco el precio del billete de tren alrededor de las seis treinta y cinco el precio del billete del tren de las seis once y treinta y cinco el precio del billete de tren de las seis treinta de las cinco de la tarde

alignment matrix

el	precio	del	billete	de	tren	-	de	sezer	treinta	-	-	-	y	cinco	-	-	-
el	precio	del	billete	de	tren	alrededor	de	las	seis	treinta	-	-	y	cinco	-	-	-
el	precio	del	billete	del	tren	-	de	las	seis	once	y	treinta	y	cinco	-	-	-
el	precio	del	billete	de	tren	-	de	las	seis	treinta	-	de	las	cinco	de	la	tarde

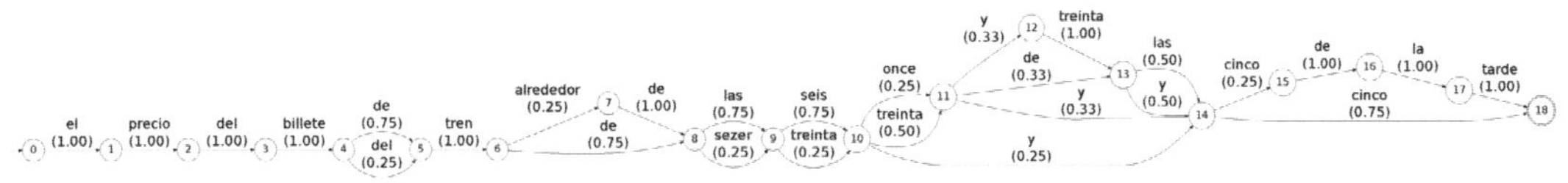

Figure 2: Steps for obtaining the graph of words from the original utterance *le prix du billet de train de six heures trente-cinq*, (*the price of the train ticket for six thirty-five*).

lation process. This process takes as its input an utterance and outputs a weighted graph of words, which represents the probability distribution $p(W_t|A)$. In other words, each full path in the graph of words (from the initial to the ending node) is a candidate translation of the input utterance, and is weighted with the probability of the translation given the utterance.

5 Performing the semantic decoding

Our semantic decoding process is based on the idea of finding segments of words contained in the graph of words that are relevant to each of the concepts of the task. In order to compactly represent this set of segments and the concepts they are relevant to, a second graph is created, which we have called a graph of concepts. This graph has the same set of nodes as the graph of words, but each arc represents that there is a path in the graph of words between the initial and ending node of the arc, which induces a sequence of words that is relevant to some of the concepts of the task. Thus, each of these arcs is labeled with the corresponding sequence of words and the concept they represent. To assign a proper weight to the arcs, both the weights represented in the graph of words and the semantic model are considered. As the set of nodes is the same as in the graph of words, we will say that for every two nodes i, j, it stands that $i < j$ if i comes before j in the topological order of the nodes in the graph of words (there is a topological order because the graph of words is directed and acyclic).

As stated in Equation (5), one of the important factors in this approach is the probability of the sequence of words in the target language given the sequence of concepts $p(W_t|C)$. This probability can be decomposed as the product of the probabilities assigned by each concept of the sequence of concepts C to the segment of words that is attached to it; that is, $\prod_{\forall c_k \in C} p(W_{t_k}|c_k)$, where W_{t_k} is the sequence of words corresponding to the concept c_k in the segmentation. To compute these probabilities, our semantic model includes a set of bigram Language Models (LMs), one for each concept in the task, which provide the probability of any sequence of words given the concept. To train these LMs, the training sentences of the corpus in the target language must be segmented and labeled in terms of the concepts of the task. The consequence of defining the semantic model this way is that every arc from node i to node j in the graph of concepts represents the probability $p(W_t^{i,j}|A) \cdot p(W_t^{i,j}|c)$, where $W_t^{i,j}$ and c are the sequence of words and the concept attached to the arc, respectively. Furthermore, each full path (from the initial to the ending node) in the graph of concepts represents the probability

$p(W_t|A) \cdot p(W_t|C)$, for the sequence of concepts C and the sentence W_t induced by the path.

The set of arcs of the graph of concepts can be built by means of a Dynamic Programming (DP) algorithm that finds the sequence of words that maximizes the combined probability stated above, for each pair of nodes i, j and each concept c. Only the arc that represents the sequence of words of maximum probability is needed because this information will afterwards be combined with the probability of the sequence of concepts to find the path of maximum probability (see Equation (5)), and if there are many arcs between nodes i and j corresponding to the concept c only the one with maximum probability will be considered. This allows us to prune the arcs of the graph of concepts without any loss of information. For the DP algorithm, we will consider a representation of the LM corresponding to each concept as a Stochastic Finite State Automaton (SFSA). Then, in the DP process, for each concept c we will obtain the best path from node i to node j in the graph of words such that its underlying sequence of words arrives to the state q_c in the SFSA LM_c (the LM of the concept c). This can be achieved by means of the following algorithm:

$$M(i,j,q_c) = \begin{cases} 1 & \text{if } i = j \wedge q_c \text{ is the initial state of } LM_c \\ 0 & \text{if } i = j \wedge q_c \text{ is not the initial state of } LM_c \\ 0 & \text{if } j < i \\ \displaystyle\max_{\substack{\forall a \in E_{GW}:\text{dest}(a)=j \\ \forall (q'_c, \text{wd}(a), q_c) \in LM_c}} M(i, \text{src}(a), q'_c) \cdot p(q'_c, \text{wd}(a), q_c) \cdot \text{wt}(a) & \text{otherwise} \end{cases} \quad (6)$$

where dest(a) stands for the destination node of the arc a in the graph of words, src(a) refers to its source node, and wd(a) and wt(a) refer to the word and the weight attached to the arc, respectively. Also, $(q'_c, \text{wd}(a), q_c)$ represents a transition from the state q'_c to the state q_c labeled with wd(a) in the SFSA that represents LM_c.

It is worth noting that this process must be performed for each concept in the task. Also, it is important for the algorithm to keep track of the words that constitute the paths that maximize the expression for each cell. When this matrix has been filled for a specific concept c, the cell that maximizes $M(i,j,q_c)$ for each pair i and j becomes an arc in the graph of concepts between nodes i and j. This arc is labeled with the sequence underlying the winning path and the concept c and is weighted with the score (probability) contained in $M(i,j,q_c)$.

This process shapes the first stage of the SLU process, which provides the graph of concepts as a result. Then, this graph of concepts is processed by a second stage. This second stage finds the path in the graph that maximizes the combination of its probability and the probability that a LM of bigrams of concepts gives to the sequence of concepts underlying the path. The LM of bigrams of concepts is also part of the semantic model, and to train it we take advantage of the segmentation and labeling in term of concepts provided by the training corpus. Finding the best path this way completely fulfills what is stated in Equation (5). Also, this best path in the graph of concepts provides the best sequence of concepts $\hat{C}$, the underlying sequence of words $\tilde{W}_t$, and a segmentation of $\tilde{W}_t$ according to $\hat{C}$.

6 The DIHANA task and the semantic representation

The DIHANA task consists of a telephone-based information service for trains in Spanish. A set of 900 dialogs was acquired by using the Wizard of Oz technique. The number of user turns was 6,280 and the vocabulary was 823. As in many other dialog systems (Minker, 1999), the semantic representation chosen for the task is based on a frame representation. Therefore, the final output of the understanding process is one or more frames with their corresponding attributes.

Even though the frame representation is the output of the system, we propose an intermediate semantic labeling that consists of assigning concepts to segments of the sentence in a sequential way. This is the output provided by the graph-based SLU module.

In order to represent the meaning of the utterances in terms of this intermediate semantic language, a set of 31 concepts was defined. Some of them are: *query*, *affirmation*, *origin_city*, and *courtesy*.

Each concept represents the meaning of words (or sequences of words) in the sentences. For example, the semantic unit $query$ can be associated to "can you tell me", "please tell me", "what is", etc. This way, each sentence (sequence of words) has a semantic sentence (sequence of concepts) associated to it, and there is an inherent segmentation. The advantage of this kind of representation is that statistical models of the lexical realization of concepts and the n-gram probabilities of the se-

Sentence	*hola buenos días quería saber los horarios de trenes para ir a Madrid* *(hello good morning I'd like to know the train timetables to go to Madrid)*
Semantic segments	*hola buenos días* : courtesy *quería saber* : query *los horarios de trenes para ir* : <time> *a Madrid* : destination_city
Frame	(TIME?) DEST_CITY : Madrid

Table 1: Example of the outputs of the SLU and Frame Converter modules.

quences of semantic units can be learned.

Finally, a set of rules are used to transduce this intermediate representation into a frame. Since the intermediate language is close to the frame representation, only a small set of rules are required to build the frame. This phase consists of the following: the deletion of irrelevant segments (such as courtesies), the reordering of the relevant concepts and attributes that appeared in the segmentation following an order which has been defined a priori, the automatic instantiation of certain task-dependent values, etc.

Table 1 shows an example of the semantic representation in terms of the intermediate semantic segmentation provided by the SLU module and the final frame representation.

7 Experiments and results

To evaluate this architecture, we performed a set of experiments with the DIHANA corpus. The user turns of the corpus were split into a set of 4889 turns for training and 1227 turns for test. To train the translation models, the training set was automatically translated from Spanish into French by four freely available web translators (Apertium, Bing, Google, Lucy), which provided us a parallel training corpus. The semantic model was learned from the segmentation and labeling provided in the DIHANA corpus for the training sentences in Spanish. All the Language Models in the semantic model were bigram models trained using Witten-Bell smoothing.

For evaluation purposes, all the test set was manually translated into French, and 500 turns were uttered by four native French speakers. Thus, we have carried out experiments both considering as the input to our system the correct sentences in French (which is the same than assuming a *perfect ASR*) and the utterances. To recognize the utterances the Google ASR was used, which for this test set provides a Word Error Rate of 21.9% considering only the 1-best recognized sentence.

For this experimentation we have considered three kinds of ASR outputs, namely, a *Perfect ASR* (text input), the 1-best output, and finally the n-best hypotheses (with n ranging from 1 to 20).

Also, we have configured the system in two different ways:

- Configuration 1: The output of the statistical translation system are the n-best translations for the input. Note that these n-best could contain repeated translations, which may lead to the reinforcement of some paths in the graphs of words.

- Configuration 2: The output of the statistical translation system is the set formed by the best n different (unique) translations that it can provide for the given input.

When the output of the ASR are n-best, we have only considered the Configuration 1.

We have evaluated each experiment using two measures: the Concept Error Rate (CER), which corresponds to errors in the output of the SLU module, and the Frame-Slot Error Rate (FSER), which corresponds to errors in the slots of the frames in the final output of the system.

Figures 3, 4, and 5 show the results obtained for each of the ASR outputs and configurations considered. The horizontal axis represents the number of hypotheses provided by the statistical translator.

As expected, in all the cases the FSER is lower than the CER, as some errors at level of the concept sequence are not relevant for the frame conversion (for example, courtesies). In the case of text input (Fig. 3), the best results are achieved when just one or two hypotheses are provided by the translator. This is because the translation model has also been learned using correct sentences, which makes the translation system more robust for this kind of input. However, when considering speech as input (Figs. 4 and 5), the generalization provided by the graphs obtained using a relatively large set of n-best translations leads to a better behavior. This is due to the fact that the errors introduced by the recognition of the speech input increases the errors in the translation stage. Thus, working with different alternatives makes it possible to recover some of the errors. Table 2 shows the results obtained when optimizing the FSER, and the number of hypotheses n used to build the graphs that provide the best results.

Figures 3 and 4 also show that the parameters that optimize FSER and CER may not be the same. This behavior is due to the different nature of both measures. While CER is defined in terms of the sequence of concepts extracted by the SLU module, FSER only takes into account those segments that have relevant information.

It can be seen in Figures 3 and 4 that, for Configuration 2, when n takes the value 18, both error measures descend. However, after this, the errors continue with their ascending tendency. The reason for this is that with these parameters, the translations provided by the translator generate a graph of words that allows the semantic model to better recover the semantics of the sentence. However, this effect is spurious, as for higher values of n the error measures present higher values.

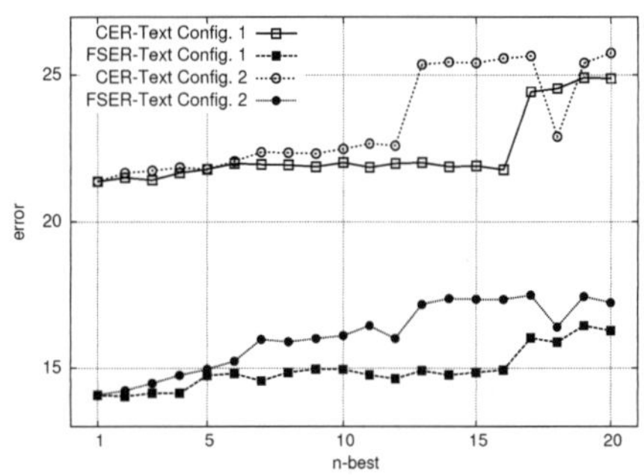

Figure 3: Results obtained with the text input.

ASR output	Config.	CER	FSER	n
Text input	Config. 1	21.50	14.03	2
	Config. 2	21.37	14.08	1
1-best	Config. 1	24.27	19.11	3
	Config. 2	24.13	19.28	3
n-best	Config. 1	22.40	19.63	7

Table 2: Results obtained optimizing the FSER.

8 Conclusions

We have presented an approach for developing multilingual SLU systems without any manual ef-

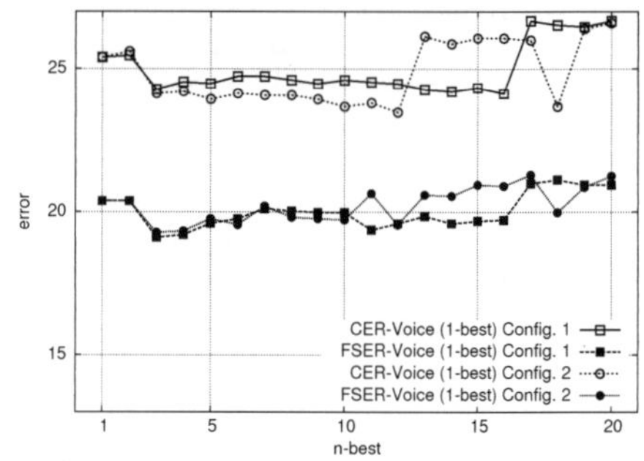

Figure 4: Results obtained with the voice input, taking the 1-best from the ASR and the n-best from MOSES.

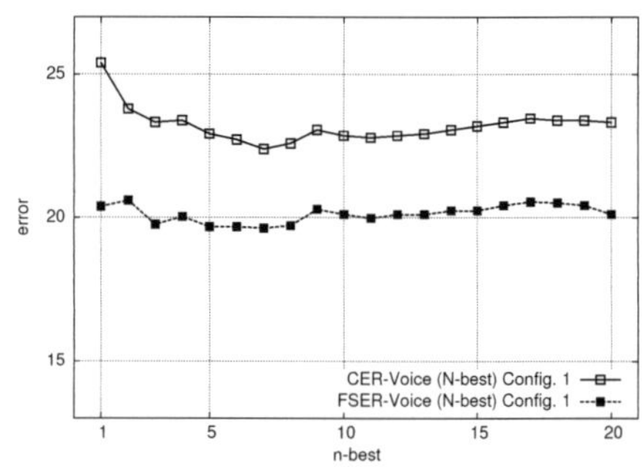

Figure 5: Results obtained with the voice input, taking the n-best from the ASR and the corresponding 1-best from MOSES.

fort in the adaptation of the models. It has been shown that the use of graphs of words, as a mechanism of generalization and transmission of hypotheses, is a good approach to recover from errors generated in the different phases of the system. As future work it may be interesting to explore other Grammatical Inference techniques to combine the n-best hypotheses generated by both the ASR and the translator. It would also be interesting to study the behavior of this approach with other languages that have greater differences than Spanish and French, for example non-Latin languages like English and German.

Acknowledgements

This work is partially supported by the Spanish MICINN under contract TIN2011-28169-C05-01, and under FPU Grant AP2010-4193.

References

José-Miguel Benedí, Eduardo Lleida, Amparo Varona, María-José Castro, Isabel Galiano, Raquel Justo, Iñigo López de Letona, and Antonio Miguel. 2006. Design and acquisition of a telephone spontaneous speech dialogue corpus in Spanish: DIHANA. In *Proceedings of LREC 2006*, pages 1636–1639, Genoa (Italy).

H. Bonneau-Maynard, Sophie Rosset, C. Ayache, A. Kuhn, and Djamel Mostefa. 2005. Semantic annotation of the French MEDIA dialog corpus. In *Proc. of InterSpeech 2005*, pages 3457–3460, Portugal.

Marcos Calvo, Lluís-F Hurtado, Fernando García, and Emilio Sanchis. 2012. A Multilingual SLU System Based on Semantic Decoding of Graphs of Words. In *Advances in Speech and Language Technologies for Iberian Languages*, pages 158–167. Springer.

R. De Mori, F. Bechet, D. Hakkani-Tür, M. McTear, G. Riccardi, and G. Tür. 2008. Spoken language understanding: A survey. *IEEE Signal Processing magazine*, 25(3):50–58.

F. García, L.-F. Hurtado, E. Segarra, E. Sanchis, and G. Riccardi. 2012. Combining multiple translation systems for spoken language understanding portability. In *Spoken Language Technology Workshop (SLT), 2012 IEEE*, pages 194–198. IEEE.

S. Hahn, M. Dinarelli, C. Raymond, F. Lefèvre, P. Lehnen, R. De Mori, A. Moschitti, H. Ney, and G. Riccardi. 2010. Comparing stochastic approaches to spoken language understanding in multiple languages. *IEEE Transactions on Audio, Speech, and Language Processing*, 6(99):1569–1583.

Yulan He and S. Young. 2003. Hidden vector state model for hierarchical semantic parsing. In *Proceedings of IEEE International Conference on Acoustics, Speech, and Signal Processing (ICASSP '03)*, volume 1, pages 268–271.

Yulan He and Steve Young. 2006. Spoken language understanding using the hidden vector state model. *Speech Communication*, 48:262–275.

Xiaodong He, Li Deng, Dilek Hakkani-Tur, and Gokhan Tur. 2013. Multi-style adaptive training for robust cross-lingual spoken language understanding. In *Proc. ICASSP*.

B. Jabaian, L. Besacier, and F. Lefèvre. 2013. Comparison and combination of lightly supervised approaches for language portability of a spoken language understanding system. *Audio, Speech, and Language Processing, IEEE Transactions on*, 21(3):636–648.

P. Koehn, H. Hoang, A. Birch, C. Callison-Burch, M. Federico, N. Bertoldi, B. Cowan, W. Shen, Moran C., R. Zens, C. Dyer, Bojar O., A. Constantin, and E. Herbst. 2007. Moses: Open source toolkit for statistical machine translation. In *Proceedings of Association for Computational Linguistics (ACL'07)*, pages 177–180.

M. A. Larkin, G. Blackshields, N. P. Brown, R. Chenna, P. A. McGettigan, H. McWilliam, F. Valentin, I. M. Wallace, A. Wilm, R. Lopez, J. D. Thompson, T. J. Gibson, and D. G. Higgins. 2007. ClustalW and ClustalX version 2.0. *Bioinformatics*, 23(21):2947–2948.

F. Lefèvre. 2007. Dynamic bayesian networks and discriminative classifiers for multi-stage semantic interpretation. In *Proceedings of IEEE International Conference on Acoustics, Speech and Signal Processing (ICASSP'07)*, volume 4, pages 13–16. IEEE.

Lambert Mathias and William Byrne. 2006. Statistical phrase-based speech translation. In *Proceedings of IEEE International Conference on Acoustics, Speech, and Signal Processing (ICASSP'06)*, volume 1, pages 561–564. IEEE.

H. Bonneau Maynard and F. Lefèvre. 2001. Investigating Stochastic Speech Understanding. In *Proc. of IEEE Automatic Speech Recognition and Understanding Workshop (ASRU'01)*.

W. Minker. 1999. Stocastically-based semantic analysis. In *Kluwer Academic Publishers*, Boston, USA.

Lucía Ortega, Isabel Galiano, Lluís-F. Hurtado, Emilio Sanchis, and Encarna Segarra. 2010. A statistical segment-based approach for spoken language understanding. In *Proc. of InterSpeech 2010*, pages 1836–1839, Makuhari, Chiba, Japan.

G. Riccardi and D. Hakkani-Tür. 2005. Active learning: theory and applications to automatic speech recognition. *IEEE Transactions on Speech and Audio Processing*, 13(4):504 – 511.

E. Segarra, E. Sanchis, M. Galiano, F. García, and L. Hurtado. 2002. Extracting Semantic Information Through Automatic Learning Techniques. *IJPRAI*, 16(3):301–307.

Gokhan Tür, Dilek Hakkani-Tür, and Robert E. Schapire. 2005. Combining active and semi-supervised learning for spoken language understanding. In *Speech Communication*, volume 45, pages 171–186.

Multilingual WSD-like Constraints for Paraphrase Extraction

Wilker Aziz
Research Group in Computational Linguistics
University of Wolverhampton, UK
W.Aziz@wlv.ac.uk

Lucia Specia
Department of Computer Science
University of Sheffield, UK
L.Specia@sheffield.ac.uk

Abstract

The use of pivot languages and word-alignment techniques over bilingual corpora has proved an effective approach for extracting paraphrases of words and short phrases. However, inherent ambiguities in the pivot language(s) can lead to inadequate paraphrases. We propose a novel approach that is able to extract paraphrases by pivoting through multiple languages while discriminating word senses in the input language, i.e., the language to be paraphrased. Text in the input language is annotated with "senses" in the form of foreign phrases obtained from bilingual parallel data and automatic word-alignment. This approach shows 62% relative improvement over previous work in generating paraphrases that are judged both more accurate and more fluent.

1 Introduction

Paraphrases are alternative ways of expressing a given meaning. Generating paraphrases that go beyond morphological variants of the original text is a challenging problem and has been shown to be useful in many natural language applications. These include i) expanding the set of reference translations for Machine Translation (MT) evaluation (Denkowski and Lavie, 2010; Liu et al., 2010) and parameter optimisation (Madnani et al., 2007), where multiple reference translations are important to accommodate for valid variations of system translations; ii) addressing the problem of out-of-vocabulary words or phrases in MT, either by replacing these by paraphrases that are known to the MT system (Mirkin et al., 2009) or by expanding the phrase table with new translation alternatives (Callison-Burch et al., 2006); and iii) expanding queries for improved coverage in question answering (Riezler et al., 2007).

Bannard and Callison-Burch (2005) introduced an approach to paraphrasing which has shown particularly promising results by pivoting through different languages for which bilingual parallel data is available. The approach consists in aligning phrases in the bilingual parallel corpus to find pairs of phrases (e_1, e_2) in the *input language*, i.e., the language to be paraphrased, which typically align to the same foreign phrases $F = \{f : e_1 \rightarrow f \rightarrow e_2\}$. This intermediate language is called *pivot language* and the phrases $f \in F$ that support the equivalence (e_1, e_2) are called *pivot phrases*. If there exists a non-empty set of pivots connecting e_1 to e_2, e_2 is said to be a paraphrase of e_1. The paraphrase is scored in terms of the conditional probabilities observed in the parallel corpus[1] by marginalising out the pivot phrases that support the alignment (e_1, e_2) as shown in Equation 1.

$$p(e_2|e_1) = \sum_{f \in F} p(f|e_1)p(e_2|f) \quad (1)$$

Equation 1 allows paraphrases to be extracted by using multiple pivot languages such that these languages help discard inadequate paraphrases resulting from ambiguous pivot phrases. However in this formulation all senses of the input phrase are mixed together in a single distribution. For example, for the Spanish input phrase *acabar con*, both paraphrases *superar* (overcome) and *eliminar* (eliminate) may be adequate depending on the context, however they are not generally interchangeable. In (Bannard and Callison-Burch,

[1]The distributions $p(f|e)$ and $p(e|f)$ are extracted from relative counts in word-aligned parallel corpus.

2005), the distributions learnt from different bilingual corpora are combined through a simple average. This makes the model naturally favour the most frequent senses of the phrases, assigning very low probabilities to less frequent senses. Section 5 shows evidence of how this limitation makes paraphrases with certain senses unreachable.

We propose a novel formulation of the problem of generating paraphrases that is constrained by *sense* information in the form of foreign phrases, which can be thought of as a *quasi-sense* annotation. Using a bilingual parallel corpus to annotate phrases with their quasi-senses has proved helpful in building word-sense disambiguation (WSD) models for MT (Carpuat and Wu, 2007; Chan et al., 2007): instead of monolingual senses, possible translations of phrases obtained with word-alignment were used as senses. Our approach performs paraphrase extraction by pivoting through multiple languages while penalising senses of the input that are not supported by these pivots.

Our experiments show that the proposed approach can effectively eliminate inadequate paraphrases for polysemous phrases, with a significant improvement over previous approaches. We observe absolute gains of 15-25% in precision and recall in generating paraphrases that are judged fluent and meaning preserving in context.

This paper is structured as follows: Section 2 describes additional previous work on paraphrase extraction and pivoting. Section 3 presents the proposed model. Section 4 introduces our experimental settings, while Section 5 shows the results of a series of experiments.

2 Related work

In addition to the well-known approach by (Bannard and Callison-Burch, 2005), the following previous approaches using pivot languages for paraphrasing can be mentioned. For a recent and comprehensive survey on a number of data-driven paraphrase generation methods, we refer the reader to (Madnani and Dorr, 2010).

Cohn and Lapata (2007) make use of multiple parallel corpora to improve Statistical Machine Translation (SMT) by triangulation for languages with little or no source-target parallel data available. Translation tables are learnt by pivoting through languages for which source-pivot and pivot-target bilingual corpora can be found. Multiple pivot languages were found useful to preserve the meaning of the source in the triangulated translation, as different languages are likely to realise ambiguities differently. Although their findings apply to generating translation candidates, the input phrases are not constrained to specific senses, and as a consequence multiple translations, which are valid in different contexts but not generally interchangeable, are mixed together in the same distribution. In SMT the target Language Model (LM) helps selecting the adequate translation candidate in context.

Callison-Burch (2008) extends (Bannard and Callison-Burch, 2005) by adding syntactic constraints to the model. Paraphrase extraction is done by pivoting using word-alignment information, as before, but sentences are syntactically annotated and paraphrases are restricted to those with the same syntactic category. This addresses categorial ambiguity by preventing that words with a given category (e.g. a noun) are paraphrased by words with other categories (e.g., a verb). However, the approach does not solve the more complex issue of polysemous paraphrases: words with the same category but different meanings, such as the noun *bank* as financial institution and land alongside a river/lake.

Marton et al. (2009) derive paraphrases from monolingual data using distributional similarity metrics. The approach has the advantage of not requiring bilingual parallel data, but it suffers from issues typical of distributional similarity metrics. In particular, it produces paraphrases that share the same or similar contexts but are related in ways that do not always characterise paraphrasing, such as antonymy.

3 Paraphrasing through multilingual constraints

Our approach to paraphrasing can be applied to both individual words or sequences of words of any length, conditioned only on sufficient evidence of these segments in a parallel corpus. We use segments as provided by the standard phrase extraction process from phrase-based SMT approaches (see Section 4), which in most cases range from individual words to short sequences of words (up to seven words in our case). Hereafter, we refer to these segments simply as *phrases*.

A model for paraphrasing under a constrained set of senses should take into account both the input phrase and the sense tag while selecting

Paired with	en	de	nl	da	sv	fi	fr	it	pt	el
es	1.78	1.56	1.62	1.61	1.51	1.58	1.65	1.51	1.60	5.68
en	-	1.73	1.82	1.78	1.67	1.74	1.82	1.73	1.78	1.06

Table 1: Size of the bilingual parallel corpora in millions of sentence pairs

the pivot phrases that will lead to adequate paraphrases. In our approach a sense tag consists in a phrase in a foreign language, that is, a valid translation of the input phrase in a language of interest, here referred to as *target language*. Treating the target language vocabulary as a sense repository is a good strategy from both theoretical and practical perspectives: it has been shown that monolingual sense distinctions can be effectively captured by translations into second languages, especially as language family distance increases (Resnik and Yarowsky, 1999; Specia et al., 2006). These translations can be easily captured given the availability of bilingual parallel data and robust automatic word-alignment techniques (Carpuat and Wu, 2007; Chan et al., 2007).

Figure 1 illustrates the proposed model to produce sense tagged paraphrases. We start the process at e_1 and we need to make sure that the pivot phrases $f \in F$ align back to the input language, producing the paraphrase e_2, and to the target language, producing the sense tag q. To avoid computing the distribution $p(e_2, q|f)$ – which would require a trilingual parallel corpus – we assume that e_2 and q are conditionally independent on f:

$$p(e_2, q|f) \stackrel{e_2 \perp\!\!\!\perp q|f}{=} p(e_2|f)p(q|f)$$

In other words, we assume that pivot phrases generate paraphrases and sense tags independently. Equation 2 shows how paraphrase probabilities are computed by marginalising out the pivot phrases under this assumption.

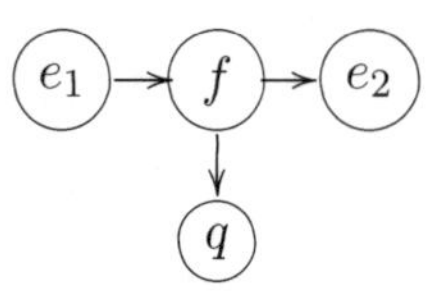

Figure 1: Pivot phrases must align back to target phrases (sense annotation).

$$p(e_2|e_1, q) = \frac{1}{z} \sum_{f \in F} p(e_2|f)p(q|f)p(f|e_1) \quad (2)$$

In order to constrain the extraction of paraphrases such that it complies with a sense repository, in addition to bilingual parallel corpora between the input language and the pivot languages, our model requires bilingual parallel corpora between the pivot languages and the language that is used for sense annotation.

Callison-Burch (2007) discusses factors affecting paraphrase quality, one of which is word senses. Paraphrasing through pivoting essentially relies on the hypothesis that different pivot phrases can be used to identify synonymy, rather than polysemy (an assumption made in the WSD literature). Callison-Burch (2007) also proposes an extraction procedure that may be conditioned on specific contexts of the input phrase (Bannard and Callison-Burch, 2005), where the context is a given pivot phrase.[2] However, that model is unable to pivot through multiple languages. As we show in Section 5, this makes the model extremely sensitive to ambiguities of the one phrase used as both sense tag and pivot.

The model we propose attempts to perform *sense-disambiguated paraphrase extraction*, that is, paraphrases are discovered in the context of translation candidates of the input phrases. In addition, it allows the use of multiple pivot languages in the process, capitalising on both the WSD and the paraphrase assumption. While the target phrases discriminate different senses of the input phrases, the pivot phrases coming from multiple languages bring extra evidence to jointly capture the ambiguities introduced by the target phrases themselves.

To illustrate the impact of this contribution, consider the polysemous Spanish word *forma*, and some of its translations into English extracted from our corpus (Section 4): *kind*, *way*, *means* and *form*. The English words distinguish three possible senses of *forma*: (a) means/way of doing/achieving something, (b) shape, and (c) type or group sharing common traits. The model presented in (Bannard and Callison-Burch, 2005) cannot discriminate these senses. It mixes valid senses of *forma* and (correctly) proposes the paraphrases *manera* and *modo* for sense (a), and *tipo*

[2]A paraphrase is scored in the context of a given pivot phrase f: $p(e_2|e_1, f) = p(e_2|f)p(f|e_1)$.

for sense (c). However, paraphrases for sense (b) are over penalised and account for very little of the probability mass of the candidate paraphrases of *forma*. Their extension which conditions extraction on a given pivot phrase is highly sensitive to the ambiguities of the phrase used as sense annotation. Table 5 shows how this model (**CB-wsd** in the Table) makes mistakes for most senses of the input due to the ambiguities of the English context *kind*, *way*, *means* and *form*. Our approach (**multi** in the Table) on the other hand successfully separates paraphrases according to the sense annotation provided.

4 Experimental settings

4.1 Resources

The source of bilingual data used in the experiments is the Europarl collection (Koehn, 2005). We paraphrase Spanish (es) phrases using their corresponding English (en) phrases as sense tags and nine European languages as pivots: German (de), Dutch (nl), Danish (da), Swedish (sv), Finnish (fi), French (fr), Italian (it), Portuguese (pt) and Greek (el). The tools provided along with the corpus were used to extract the sentence aligned parallel data as shown in Table 1.

The sentence aligned parallel data is first word-aligned using GIZA++ in both source-target and target-source directions, followed by the application of traditional *symmetrisation* heuristics (Och and Ney, 2003). These aligned corpora are used for paraphrase extraction, except for a subset of them used in the creation of a test set (Section 4.2).

4.2 Test set creation

Since we are interested in showing the ability of our approach to find adequate paraphrases in the presence of a foreign phrase (the sense tag), it is important that our test set contains polysemous phrases. Like in (Bannard and Callison-Burch, 2005), we use the Spanish WordNet[3] to bias our selection of phrases to paraphrase to contain ambiguous cases. However, rather than biasing selection towards having more multi-word expressions, we chose to have more polysemous cases. From the Spanish WordNet, we selected 50 phrases (with at least one content word) to be paraphrased such that 80% of the samples (40 phrases) had at least 2 senses (with a given part-of-speech

[3]http://nlp.lsi.upc.edu/freeling/

Unambiguous	**Ambiguous**
concreto, política, fondos, regular, haber, amor proprio, sangre fría, dar a luz, dar con, tomar el pelo	derecho, comercial, real, particular, legal, justo, común, cerca, esencial, especial, fuerte, puesto, oficial, figura, informe, parte, cuenta, forma, claro, clave, tiempo, seguro, respuesta, trabajar, responder, garantizar, volver, aumentar, incluir, tratar, ofrecer, establecer, pasar, dejar, realizar, punto de vista, llevar a cabo, dar vueltas, tener que, acabar con

Figure 2: Words and phrases selected to be paraphrased. Ambiguity is determined on the basis of the number of synsets in the Spanish WordNet. We note that this information was only used to bias the selection of the phrases, i.e., WordNet is not used in the proposed approach.

La idea de conceder a la Unión Europea su propia competencia fiscal - la **palabra clave** es el "impuesto por Europa" - está siendo debatida.
The idea of granting the EU its own tax competence - the **keyword** is the "Europe tax" - is being discussed.

Figure 3: Example of context selected for the phrase *clave*.

tag to avoid selecting simpler, categorial ambiguities). Figure 2 lists the selected words and phrases in their base forms.

The bilingual corpus was queried for sentences containing at least one of the 50 phrases listed in Figure 2, or any of their morphological variants. The resulting sentences were then grouped on the basis of whether or not they shared the same English translation. To find the English phrase (i.e., our sense tag) which constrains the sense of the Spanish phrase, we followed the heuristics used in phrase-based SMT to extract the minimal phrase pair that includes the Spanish phrase and is consistent with the word-alignment[4] (Koehn et al., 2003). We discarded groups containing fewer than five sentence pairs and randomly sampled 2-6 contexts per Spanish phrase. The resulting *test set* is made of 258 Spanish phrases in context such as the one exemplified in Figure 3.

4.3 Paraphrasing

Nine pivot languages were used to constrain paraphrase extraction following the approach presented in Section 3. The conditional probability distributions over phrase pairs in Equation 2 are estimated using relative frequencies. For each Spanish phrase in the test set, we retrieve their

[4]Note that we did not use gold-standard word-alignments.

paraphrase candidates grouped by sense (English translation) and rank them based on the evidence collected from all bilingual corpora. Evidence from different pivot languages is combined using their average. English itself was not used as a pivot language. It was used only to provide sense tags. The rationale behind this choice is that if the language used to provide sense tags is also used as pivot language, there is no obvious way of estimating $p(q|f)$ in Equation 2. Note that in this case this probability would represent the likelihood of the English phrase aligning to itself.

Similar to (Bannard and Callison-Burch, 2005), we weight our paraphrase probabilities using an LM to adjust it to the context of the input sentence. We use a 5-gram LM trained on the Spanish part of Europarl with the SRILM toolkit (Stolcke, 2002). Paraphrases are re-ranked in context by multiplying the paraphrase probability and the LM score of the sentence.[5]

In order to assess the performance of our model, we compare it to two variants of the models proposed by Bannard and Callison-Burch (2005).

multi: the paraphrasing model with multilingual constraints introduced in this paper.

CCB: the model in (Bannard and Callison-Burch, 2005) which does not explicitly perform any sense disambiguation.

CCB-wsd: an extended model in (Bannard and Callison-Burch, 2005) using English phrases as sense tags for pivoting.

Using each of these three models, we paraphrased the 258 samples in our test set, retrieving the 3-best paraphrases in context for each model. **CCB** is used with 10 pivot languages (English is included as a pivot) to generate paraphrase candidates. Note that **CCB** relies solely on the LM component to fit the paraphrase candidate to the context. On the other hand, **CCB-wsd** and **multi** both have access to sense annotation, but while **multi** is able to benefit from multiple pivot languages, **CCB-wsd** can only pivot through the one English phrase provided as sense annotation.

[5]Given the localised effect of the phrase replacement within a given context in terms of n-gram language modelling, a neighbourhood of n-1 words on each side of the selected phrase is sufficient to re-rank paraphrase candidates: $p(w_{-4} \dots w_{-1} e_2 w_{+1} \dots w_{+4})$ for our 5-gram LM.

4.4 Evaluation

To assess whether the proposed model effectively disambiguates senses of candidate paraphrases, we perform experiments using similar settings to those in (Bannard and Callison-Burch, 2005). Paraphrases are evaluated in context (a sentence) using binary human judgements in terms of the following components:

Meaning (M): whether or not the candidate conveys the meaning of the original phrase; and

Grammar (G): whether or not the candidate preserves the fluency of the sentence.

These two components are assessed separately and a paraphrase candidate is considered to be **correct** only when it is judged to be both meaning preserving and grammatical. Our evaluators were presented with one pair of sentences at a time, the original one and its paraphrased version. For every test sample we selected the 3-best paraphrases of each method and distributed them amongst the evaluators. We considered two evaluation scenarios:

Gold-standard translations: the English translation as found in Europarl was taken as sense tag, using automatic word-alignments to identify the English phrase that constrains the sense of the Spanish phrase.

SMT translations: a phrase-based SMT system built using the Moses toolkit (Koehn et al., 2007) and the whole Spanish-English dataset (except the sentences in the test set) was used to translated the Spanish sentences. Instead of gold-standard translations as a *quasi-perfect* sense annotation (*quasi* because the word-alignment is still automatic and thus prone to errors), the phrase-based SMT system plays the role of a sense annotation module predicting the "sense" tags.

Note that models may not be able to produce a paraphrase for certain input phrases, e.g. when the input phrase is not found in the bilingual corpora. Therefore, we assess **precision** (P) and **recall** (R) as the number of paraphrases in context that are judged correct out of the number of cases for which a candidate paraphrase was proposed, and out of the total number of test samples, respectively. To summarise the results, accuracy is expressed in terms of F_1.

Method	Top	M	G	Correct		
		F_1	F_1	P	R	F_1
CCB	1	32	28	25	25	25
CCB-wsd	1	61	38	34	28	30
multi	1	62	55	59	42	49
CCB	2	41	37	33	33	33
CCB-wsd	2	68	44	40	33	36
multi	2	71	64	66	47	55
CCB	3	46	42	37	37	37
CCB-wsd	3	71	47	45	36	40
multi	3	74	67	71	50	59

Table 2: Performance in retrieving paraphrases in context using gold-standard translations for sense tags and a 5-gram LM component.

In the following section we present results on whether the best candidate (Top-1) or at least one of the two (Top-2) or three (Top-3) best candidates satisfies the criterion under consideration (meaning/grammar).

5 Results

The evaluation was performed by seven native speakers of Spanish who judged a total of $5,110$ sentences containing one paraphrased input phrase each. We used 40 overlapping judgements across annotators to measure inter-annotator agreement. The average inter-annotator agreement in terms of Cohen's Kappa (Cohen, 1960) is 0.54 ± 0.15 for *meaning* judgements, 0.63 ± 0.16 for *grammar* judgements and 0.62 ± 0.20 for *correctness* judgements. These figures are similar or superior to those reported in (Bannard and Callison-Burch, 2005; Callison-Burch, 2008), which we consider particularly encouraging as in our case we have seven instead of only two annotators. In Tables 2, 3 and 4 we report the performance of the three models in terms of precision, recall and F_1, with p-values < 0.01 based on the *t-test* for statistical significance.

5.1 Paraphrasing from human translations

We first assess the paraphrasing models using gold-standard translations, that is, the English phrases were selected via automatic word-alignments between the input text and its corresponding human translation from Europarl. Table 2 shows the performance in terms of F_1 for our three criteria: meaning preservation, grammaticality, and correctness. Our method (**multi**) outperforms the best performing alternative (**CCB-wsd**) by a large margin. It is 19% more effective at selecting the 1-best candidate in terms of correctness. A consistent gain is also observed when more guesses are allowed (top 2–3), showing that our model is better at ranking the top candidates as well. **CCB-wsd** and **multi** are close in terms of paraphrases that are meaning preserving, however their differences become more obvious as more guesses are allowed, again showing that **multi** is better at ranking more adequate paraphrases first. Moreover, **multi** consistently chooses more grammatical paraphrases.

Method	M	G	Correct
CCB	33	23	22
CCB-wsd	19	9	8
multi	64	43	37

Table 3: Performance (F_1) in correctly retrieving the best paraphrase in context using gold-standard translations **without** the 5-gram LM component.

Table 2 also shows that our model consistently improves both the precision and recall of the predictions. Recall improves by 14% w.r.t. **CCB-wsd** because **multi** is able to find more paraphrases, which we believe are only reachable through the additional pivots. For example, in our data the paraphrase *forma* $\rightarrow$ *medio* in the sense of *way* (see Table 5) is only found through the Dutch pivot *middel*, which is not accessible to **CCB-wsd**. Recall is much lower in **CCB** because of the model's strong bias towards the most frequent senses: other senses receive very little of the probability mass and thus rarely feature amongst the top ranked paraphrases. Our multilingual disambiguation model also shows a 25% increase in precision, which must be due to the stronger contribution of the sense discrimination over the LM component in getting the senses of the paraphrases right.

To show the impact of the LM re-ranking component, in Table 3 we remove this component from all models, such that the ranking of paraphrases is done purely based on the paraphrase probabilities. All models are harmed by the absence of the LM component, but to different extents and for different reasons. **CCB** typically ranks at the top paraphrases that convey the most frequent sense and the LM is the only component with information about the input context. **CCB-wsd** is impacted the most: typically invalid paraphrases are produced from unrelated senses of the foreign phrase used as sense tag, they do not represent any valid sense of the input but still get ranked at the top. For this model, the LM component is crucial to prune such unrelated paraphrases. Back to Table 2, the superior performance of **CCB-wsd** over **CCB** in the presence of the LM component suggest that **CCB-wsd** assigns less negligible probabilities to the paraphrases that convey a valid sense of the input. Finally, **multi**'s performance is only truly harmed in terms of grammaticality: sense discrimination is the main responsible for selecting the appropriate sense, while the LM component is responsible for selecting the candidate that makes the sentence more fluent. Further investigation showed that in some cases the most meaning preserving option was down-weighted due to low fluency, and a less adequate option was chosen, explaining the slight improvement under the meaning preservation criterion when no LM re-ranking is performed.

Table 5 lists the 5-best paraphrases of the Spanish phrase *forma* in its different senses. The paraphrases are ranked by **CCB-wsd** and **multi** out of context, that is, without LM re-ranking. Note that, because the sense tags are themselves ambiguous in English, most of the top-ranked paraphrases from **CCB-wsd** are inadequate, that is, they do not convey any valid sense of *forma*.

It is also interesting to observe the impact of the different pivot languages on the performance of our proposed approach. Figure 4 shows **CCB-wsd** and **multi**, both using LM re-ranking. For **multi** we can see the impact of the pivot languages individually and in groups.[6] Except for Finnish when used on its own as pivot all other setups are superior to **CCB-wsd**. We can also see that putting together languages of different families has a strong positive impact, probably due to the fact that ambiguities are realised differently in languages that are farther from each other, emphasising the potential of sense discrimination by pivoting through multiple languages.

5.2 Paraphrasing from machine translations

Finally, we assessed the paraphrasing models using machine translations instead of gold-standard translations from Europarl. In order to have an idea of the quality of the SMT model beforehand, we evaluated the machine translations in terms of BLEU scores (Papineni et al., 2002) using a single reference from Europarl. Our phrase-based SMT model achieved 48.9 BLEU, which can be considered a high score for Europarl data (in-domain evaluation). Table 4 is analogous to Table 2, but with paraphrases extracted from machine translated sentences as opposed to human translations.

Method	Top	M	G	Correct		
		F_1	F_1	P	R	F_1
CCB-wsd	1	71	39	34	32	33
multi	1	69	55	50	45	48
CCB-wsd	2	79	46	40	38	39
multi	2	82	69	63	57	60
CCB-wsd	3	83	50	44	41	42
multi	3	85	74	69	62	65

Table 4: Performance in retrieving paraphrases in context using machine translations for sense tags and a 5-gram LM component.

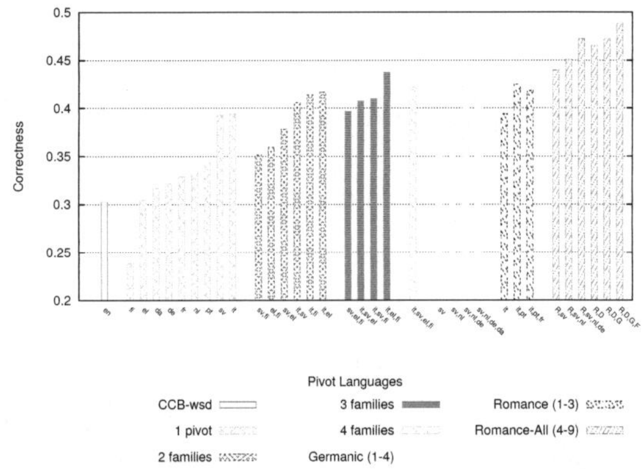

Figure 4: Impact of pivot languages on correctness. Language codes follow the convention presented in Section 4.1. Additionally R stands for Romance languages, D for Germanic languages, G for Greek and F for Finnish.

We observe that **multi** still outperforms **CCB-wsd** by a large margin. On the one hand there is a drop in precision of about 9% for *correctness* with **multi**. On the other hand there is an improvement in recall: **multi** improves from 3% (top-1 guess) to 12% (top-3 guesses). Manual inspection revealed that the tags predicted by the SMT model are more frequent translation options, reducing the chance of finding rare target phrases as sense annotation, for which significant statistics cannot be computed. However, with respect to correctness, the differences between this setting and that with gold-standard translations are not statistically significant.

[6] For a larger version of this figure, we refer the reader to: `http://pers-www.wlv.ac.uk/~in1676/publications/2013/conll2013pivots.pdf`

multi: English as sense annotation and nine other pivot languages							
forma → way		*forma → form*		*forma → means*		*forma → kind*	
forma	0.34	forma	0.64	medio	0.64	tipo	0.37
manera	0.24	tipo	0.10	través	0.23	forma	0.23
modo	0.23	forma de	0.05	instrumento	0.13	especie	0.06
forma de	0.02	formas	0.03			especie de	0.03
medio	0.02	modo	0.02			tipo de	0.03
CCB-wsd: English as sense annotation and sole evidence for pivoting							
forma → way		*forma → form*		*forma → means*		*forma → kind*	
*way	0.08	*formulario	0.18	*significa contar	0.07	*amables	0.16
*vía por	0.08	de sus formas	0.10	medios que tiene	0.07	*kind	0.12
*camino que hay	0.07	*formulario de	0.07	*significa	0.06	especie	0.09
*camino que hay que	0.07	modalidad	0.06	*significa contar con	0.06	*amable	0.08
*vía por la	0.07	aspecto formal	0.05	*anterior significa	0.06	tipo	0.07

Table 5: Top paraphrases of *forma* annotated by the English words *way*, *form*, *means* and *kind*. Starred phrases denote inadequate candidates.

5.3 Potential applications

In what follows we discuss two applications which we believe could directly benefit from the paraphrase extraction approach proposed in this paper.

MT evaluation metrics such as METEOR (Denkowski and Lavie, 2010) and TESLA (Liu et al., 2010) already use paraphrases of n-grams in the machine translated sentence in an attempt to match more of the reference translation's n-grams. TESLA, in particular, uses paraphrases constrained by a single pivot language as sense tag as originally proposed in (Bannard and Callison-Burch, 2005). Metrics like METEOR, which use paraphrases simply as a repository with extra options for the n-gram matching, could be extended to use the word-alignment between the source sentence and the translation to constrain the translated phrases while paraphrasing them with multilingual constraints. In this case the model would attempt to paraphrase the MT, which is not necessarily fluent, therefore potentially compromising its LM component. However, even after completely disregarding the LM re-ranking (see context-insensitive model **multi** in Table 3), we may be able to improve n-gram matching by paraphrasing.

Handling out-of-vocabulary words in SMT by expanding the bilingual phrase-tables (Callison-Burch et al., 2006) is a direct application of the sense constrained paraphrases. We can add translations for a given unknown phrase f_1, whose paraphrase f_2 is present in the phrase-table and is aligned to the target phrase e (sense tag). We basically expand the phrase table to translate the out-of-vocabulary word f_1 using the knowledge associated to its paraphrase f_2 in the context of the known translation e: $(f_2, e) \rightarrow (f_1, e)$. The multilingual constraints offer more control over ambiguities, therefore potentially leading to more accurate phrase pairs added to the phrase-table.

6 Conclusions and future work

We have proposed a new formulation of the problem of generating "sense" tagged paraphrases for words and short phrases using bilingual corpora and multiple pivot languages to jointly disambiguate the input phrase and the sense tag. Sense tags are phrases in a foreign language of interest, for instance the target language of a phrase-based SMT system.

The approach was evaluated against the state of the art method for paraphrase extraction. Significant improvements were found in particular with respect to two aspects: i) the proposed model has higher recall, since it has access to paraphrases that would receive a negligible probability mass and therefore would never be selected in previous formulations, and ii) the proposed model has higher precision, since it is able to filter out or rank down paraphrases with incorrect senses.

In future work we plan to further evaluate the approach in the two scenarios discussed in Section 5.3: i) to expand the phrase table of SMT systems to address issues such as out-of-vocabulary words and phrases; and ii) to evaluate and optimise parameters of SMT systems using metrics that can accommodate sense disambiguated paraphrases. We also plan to integrate syntactic constraints, as proposed in (Callison-Burch, 2008), to our model to investigate the complementarities between these two ways of constraining paraphrasing.

References

Colin Bannard and Chris Callison-Burch. 2005. Paraphrasing with bilingual parallel corpora. In *Proceedings of the 43rd Annual Meeting on Association for Computational Linguistics*, pages 597–604, Ann Arbor, Michigan.

Chris Callison-Burch, Philipp Koehn, and Miles Osborne. 2006. Improved statistical machine translation using paraphrases. In *Proceedings of the main conference on Human Language Technology Conference of the North American Chapter of the Association of Computational Linguistics*, pages 17–24, New York, New York.

Chris Callison-Burch. 2007. *Paraphrasing and Translation*. Ph.D. thesis, University of Edinburgh, Edinburgh, Scotland.

Chris Callison-Burch. 2008. Syntactic constraints on paraphrases extracted from parallel corpora. In *Proceedings of the Conference on Empirical Methods in Natural Language Processing*, EMNLP '08, pages 196–205, Honolulu, Hawaii.

Marine Carpuat and Dekai Wu. 2007. Improving statistical machine translation using word sense disambiguation. In *The 2007 Joint Conference on Empirical Methods in Natural Language Processing and Computational Natural Language Learning*, EMNLP-CoNLL '07, pages 61–72, Prague, Czech Republic.

Yee Seng Chan, Hwee Tou Ng, and David Chiang. 2007. Word sense disambiguation improves statistical machine translation. In *Proceedings of the 45th Annual Meeting of the Association of Computational Linguistics*, pages 33–40, Prague, Czech Republic.

Jacob Cohen. 1960. A Coefficient of Agreement for Nominal Scales. *Educational and Psychological Measurement*, 20(1):37–46, April.

Trevor Cohn and Mirella Lapata. 2007. Machine translation by triangulation: Making effective use of multi-parallel corpora. In *Proceedings of the 45th Annual Meeting of the Association for Computational Linguistics*, Prague, Czech Republic.

Michael Denkowski and Alon Lavie. 2010. METEOR-NEXT and the METEOR Paraphrase Tables: Improved Evaluation Support For Five Target Languages. In *Proceedings of the ACL 2010 Joint Workshop on Statistical Machine Translation and Metrics MATR*.

Philipp Koehn, Franz Josef Och, and Daniel Marcu. 2003. Statistical phrase-based translation. In *Proceedings of the 2003 Conference of the North American Chapter of the Association for Computational Linguistics on Human Language Technology - Volume 1*, NAACL '03, pages 48–54, Edmonton, Canada.

Philipp Koehn, Hieu Hoang, Alexandra Birch, Chris Callison-Burch, Marcello Federico, Nicola Bertoldi, Brooke Cowan, Wade Shen, Christine Moran, Richard Zens, Chris Dyer, Ondřej Bojar, Alexandra Constantin, and Evan Herbst. 2007. Moses: open source toolkit for statistical machine translation. In *Proceedings of the 45th Annual Meeting of the Association for Computational Linguistics: Demo and Poster Sessions*, pages 177–180, Prague, Czech Republic.

Philipp Koehn. 2005. Europarl: A Parallel Corpus for Statistical Machine Translation. In *The Proceedings of the Tenth Machine Translation Summit*, pages 79–86, Phuket, Thailand. AAMT, AAMT.

Chang Liu, Daniel Dahlmeier, and Hwee Tou Ng. 2010. Tesla: Translation evaluation of sentences with linear-programming-based analysis. In *Proceedings of the Joint Fifth Workshop on Statistical Machine Translation and MetricsMATR*, pages 354–359, Uppsala, Sweden.

Nitin Madnani and Bonnie J. Dorr. 2010. Generating phrasal and sentential paraphrases: A survey of data-driven methods. *Computational Linguistics*, 36(3):341–387.

Nitin Madnani, Necip Fazil Ayan, Philip Resnik, and Bonnie J. Dorr. 2007. Using paraphrases for parameter tuning in statistical machine translation. In *Proceedings of the Second Workshop on Statistical Machine Translation*, pages 120–127, Prague, Czech Republic.

Yuval Marton, Chris Callison-Burch, and Philip Resnik. 2009. Improved statistical machine translation using monolingually-derived paraphrases. In *Proceedings of the 2009 Conference on Empirical Methods in Natural Language Processing*, pages 381–390, Suntec, Singapore.

Shachar Mirkin, Lucia Specia, Nicola Cancedda, Ido Dagan, Marc Dymetman, and Idan Szpektor. 2009. Source-language entailment modeling for translating unknown terms. In *Proceedings of the Joint Conference of the 47th Annual Meeting of the ACL and the 4th International Joint Conference on Natural Language Processing of the AFNLP*, pages 791–799, Suntec, Singapore.

Franz Josef Och and Hermann Ney. 2003. A systematic comparison of various statistical alignment models. *Computational Linguistics*, 29:19–51, March.

Kishore Papineni, Salim Roukos, Todd Ward, and Wei-Jing Zhu. 2002. Bleu: a method for automatic evaluation of machine translation. In *Proceedings of the 40th Annual Meeting on Association for Computational Linguistics*, pages 311–318.

Philip Resnik and David Yarowsky. 1999. Distinguishing systems and distinguishing senses: new evaluation methods for word sense disambiguation. *Nat. Lang. Eng.*, 5(2):113–133.

Stefan Riezler, Er Vasserman, Ioannis Tsochantaridis, Vibhu Mittal, and Yi Liu. 2007. Statistical machine translation for query expansion in answer retrieval. In *Proceedings of the 45th Annual Meeting of the Association for Computational Linguistics*, pages 464–471, Prague, Czech Republic.

Lucia Specia, Mark Stevenson, Maria das Graças Volpe Nunes, and Gabriela C.B. Ribeiro. 2006. Multilingual versus monolingual WSD. In *Proceedings of the EACL Workshop "Making Sense of Sense: Bringing Psycholinguistics and Computational Linguistics Together"*, pages 33–40, Trento, Italy.

Andreas Stolcke. 2002. SRILM – an extensible language modeling toolkit. In *Proceedings of the International Conference on Spoken Language*, volume 2, pages 901–904, Denver, CO.

Topic Models + Word Alignment = A Flexible Framework for Extracting Bilingual Dictionary from Comparable Corpus

Xiaodong Liu, Kevin Duh and Yuji Matsumoto
Graduate School of Information Science
Nara Institute of Science and Technology
8916-5 Takayama, Ikoma, Nara 630-0192, Japan
{xiaodong-l,kevinduh,matsu}@is.naist.jp

Abstract

We propose a flexible and effective framework for extracting a bilingual dictionary from comparable corpora. Our approach is based on a novel combination of topic modeling and word alignment techniques. Intuitively, our approach works by converting a comparable *document*-aligned corpus into a parallel *topic*-aligned corpus, then learning word alignments using co-occurrence statistics. This *topic*-aligned corpus is similar in structure to the *sentence*-aligned corpus frequently used in statistical machine translation, enabling us to exploit advances in word alignment research. Unlike many previous work, our framework does not require any language-specific knowledge for initialization. Furthermore, our framework attempts to handle polysemy by allowing multiple translation probability models for each word. On a large-scale Wikipedia corpus, we demonstrate that our framework reliably extracts high-precision translation pairs on a wide variety of comparable data conditions.

1 Introduction

A machine-readable bilingual dictionary plays a very important role in many natural language processing tasks. In machine translation (MT), dictionaries can help in the domain adaptation setting (Daume III and Jagarlamudi, 2011). In cross-lingual information retrieval (CLIR), dictionaries serve as efficient means for query translation (Resnik et al., 2011). Many other multilingual applications also rely on bilingual dictionaries as integral components.

One approach for building a bilingual dictionary resource uses parallel sentence-aligned corpora. This is often done in the context of Statistical MT, using word alignment algorithms such as the IBM models (Brown et al., 1993; Och and Ney, 2003). Unfortunately, parallel corpora may be scarce for certain language-pairs or domains of interest (e.g., medical and microblog).

Thus, the use of comparable corpora for bilingual dictionary extraction has become an active research topic (Haghighi et al., 2008; Vulić et al., 2011). Here, a comparable corpus is defined as collections of document pairs written in different languages but talking about the same topic (Koehn, 2010), such as interconnected Wikipedia articles. The challenge with bilingual dictionary extraction from comparable corpus is that existing word alignment methods developed for parallel corpus cannot be directly applied.

We believe there are several desiderata for bilingual dictionary extraction algorithms:

1. **Low Resource Requirement**: The approach should not rely on language-specific knowledge or a large scale seed lexicon.

2. **Polysemy Handling**: One should handle the fact that a word form may have multiple meanings, and such meanings may be translated differently.

3. **Scalability**: The approach should run efficiently an massively large-scale datasets.

Our framework addresses the above desired points by exploiting a novel combination of topic models and word alignment, as shown in Figure 1. Intuitively, our approach works by first converting a comparable *document*-aligned corpus into a par-

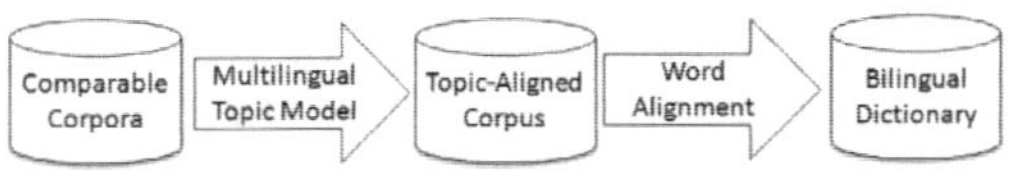

Figure 1: Proposed Framework

allel *topic*-aligned corpus, then apply word alignment methods to model co-occurence within topics. By employing topic models, we avoid the need for seed lexicon and operate purely in the realm of unsupervised learning. By using word alignment on topic model results, we can easily model polysemy and extract topic-dependent lexicons.

Specifically, let w^e be an English word and w^f be a French word. One can think of traditional bilingual dictionary extraction as obtaining (w^e, w^f) pairs in which the probability $p(w^e|w^f)$ or $p(w^f|w^e)$ is high. Our approach differs by modeling $p(w^e|w^f, t)$ or $p(w^f|w^e, t)$ instead, where t is a topic. The key intuition is that it is easier to tease out the translation of a polysemous word e given $p(w^f|w^e, t)$ rather than $p(w^f|w^e)$. A word may be polysemous, but given a topic, there is likely a one-to-one correspondence for the most appropriate translation. For example, under the simple model $p(w^f|w^e)$, the English word "free" may be translated into the Japanese word 自由 (as in free speech) or 無料 (as in free beer) with equal 0.5 probability; this low probability may cause both translation pairs to be rejected by the dictionary extraction algorithm. On the other hand, given $p(w^f|w^e, t)$, where t is "politics" or "shopping", we can allow high probabilities for both words depending on context.

Our contribution is summarized as follows:

- We propose a bilingual dictionary extraction framework that simultaneously achieves all three of the desiderata: low resource requirement, polysemy handling, and scalability. We are not aware of any previous works that address all three.
- Our framework is extremely flexible and simple-to-implement, consisting of a novel combination of existing topic modeling tools from machine learning and word alignment tools from machine translation.

2 Related Work

There is a plethora of research on bilingual lexicon extraction from comparable corpora, starting with seminal works of (Rapp, 1995; Fung and Lo, 1998). The main idea is to assume that translation pairs have similar contexts, i.e. the *distributional hypothesis*, so extraction consists of 3 steps: (1) identify context windows around words, (2) translate context words using a seed bilingual dictionary, and (3) extract pairs that have high resulting similarity. Methods differ in how the seed dictionary is acquired (Koehn and Knight, 2002; Déjean et al., 2002) and how similarity is defined (Fung and Cheung, 2004; Tamura et al., 2012). Projection-based approaches have also been proposed, though they can be shown to be related to the aforementioned distributional approaches (Gaussier et al., 2004); for example, Haghighi (2008) uses CCA to map vectors in different languages into the same latent space. Laroche (2010) presents a good summary.

Vulić et al. (2011) pioneered a new approach to bilingual dictionary extraction based on topic modeling approach which requires no seed dictionary. While our approach is motivated by (Vulić et al., 2011), we exploit the topic model in a very different way (explained in Section 4.2). They do not use word alignments like we do and thus cannot model polysemy. Further, their approach requires training topic models with a large number of topics, which may limit the scalability of the approach.

Recently, there has been much interest in multilingual topic models (MLTM) (Jagarlamudi and Daume, 2010; Mimno et al., 2009; Ni et al., 2009; Boyd-Graber and Blei, 2009). Many of these models give $p(t|e)$ and $p(t|f)$, but stop short of extracting a bilingual lexicon. Although topic models can group related e and f in the same topic cluster, the extraction of a high-precision dictionary requires additional effort. One of our contributions here is an effective way to do this extraction using word alignment methods.

3 System Components: Background

This section reviews MLTMs and Word Alignment, the main components of our framework. The knowledgeable readers may wish to skim this section for notation and move to Section 4, which describes our contribution.

3.1 Multilingual Topic Model

Any multilingual topic model may be used with our framework. We use the one by Mimno et al. (2009), which extends the monolingual Latent Dirichlet Allocation model (Blei et al., 2003). Given a comparable corpus E in English and F in a foreign language, we assume that the document pair boundaries are known. For each document pair $d_i = [d_i^e, d_i^f]$ consisting of English document d_i^e and Foreign document d_i^f (where $i \in \{1, \ldots, D\}$, D is number of document pairs), we know that d_i^e and d_i^f talk about the same topics. While the monolingual topic model lets each document have its own so-called document-specific distribution over topics, the multilingual topic model assumes that documents in each tuple share the same topic prior (thus the comparable corpora assumption) and each topic consists of several language-specific word distributions. The generative story is shown in Algorithm 1.

```
for each topic k do
    for l ∈ {e, f} do
        sample φ_k^l ~ Dirichlet(β^l);
    end
end
for each document pair d_i do
    sample θ_i ~ Dirichlet(α);
    for l ∈ {e, f} do
        sample z^l ~ Multinomial(θ_i);
        for each word w^l in d_i^l do
            sample w^l ~ p(w^l|z^l, φ^l);
        end
    end
end
```

Algorithm 1: Generative story for (Mimno et al., 2009). θ_i is the topic proportion of document pair d_i. Words w^l are drawn from language-specific distributions $p(w^l|z^l, \varphi^l)$, where language l indexes English e or Foreign f. Here pairs of language-specific topics φ^l are drawn from Dirichlet distributions with prior β^l.

3.2 Statistical Word Alignment

For a sentence-pair $(\boldsymbol{e}, \boldsymbol{f})$, let $\boldsymbol{e} = [w_1^e, w_2^e, \ldots w_{|\boldsymbol{e}|}^e]$ be the English sentence with $|\boldsymbol{e}|$ words and $\boldsymbol{f} = [w_1^f, w_2^f, \ldots w_{|\boldsymbol{f}|}^f]$ be the foreign sentence with $|\boldsymbol{f}|$ words. For notation, we will index English words by i and foreign words by j. The goal of word alignment is to find an alignment function $a : i \rightarrow j$ mapping words in $\boldsymbol{e}$ to words in $\boldsymbol{f}$ (and vice versa).

We will be using IBM Model 1 (Brown et al., 1993; Och and Ney, 2003), which proposes the following probabilistic model for alignment:

$$p(\boldsymbol{e}, a, |\boldsymbol{f}) \approx \prod_{i=1}^{|\boldsymbol{e}|} p(w_i^e | w_{a(i)}^f) \qquad (1)$$

Here, $p(w_i^e | w_{a(i)}^f)$ captures the translation probability of the English word at position i from the foreign word at position $j = a(i)$, where the actual alignment a is a hidden variable, and training can be done via EM. Although this model does not incorporate much linguistic knowledge, it enables us to *find correspondence between distinct objects from paired sets*. In machine translation, the distinct objects are words from different languages while the paired sets are sentence-aligned corpora. In our case, our distinct objects are also words from distinct languages but our pair sets will be *topic*-aligned corpora.

4 Proposed Framework for Bilingual Dictionary Extraction

The general idea of our proposed framework is sketched in Figure 1: First, we run a multilingual topic model to convert the comparable corpora to topic-aligned corpora. Second, we run a word alignment algorithm on the topic-aligned corpora in order to extract translation pairs. The innovation is in how this topic-aligned corpora is defined and constructed, the link between the two stages. We describe how this is done in Section 4.1 and show how existing approaches are subsumed in our general framework in Section 4.2.

4.1 Topic-Aligned Corpora

Suppose the original comparable corpus has D document pairs $[d_i^e, d_i^f]_{i=1,\ldots,D}$. We run a multilingual topic model with K topics, where K is user-defined (Section 3.1). The topic-aligned corpora is defined hierarchically as a *set of sets*: On the first level, we have a set of K topics, $\{t_1, \ldots, t_k, \ldots, t_K\}$. On the second level, for each topic t_k, we have a set of D "word collections" $\{C_{k,1}, \ldots, C_{k,i}, \ldots, C_{k,D}\}$. Each word collection $C_{k,i}$ represents the English and foreign words that occur simultaneously in topic t_k and document d_i.

For clarity, let us describe the topic-aligned corpora construction process step-by-step together with a flow chart in Figure 2:

1. Train a multilingual topic model.

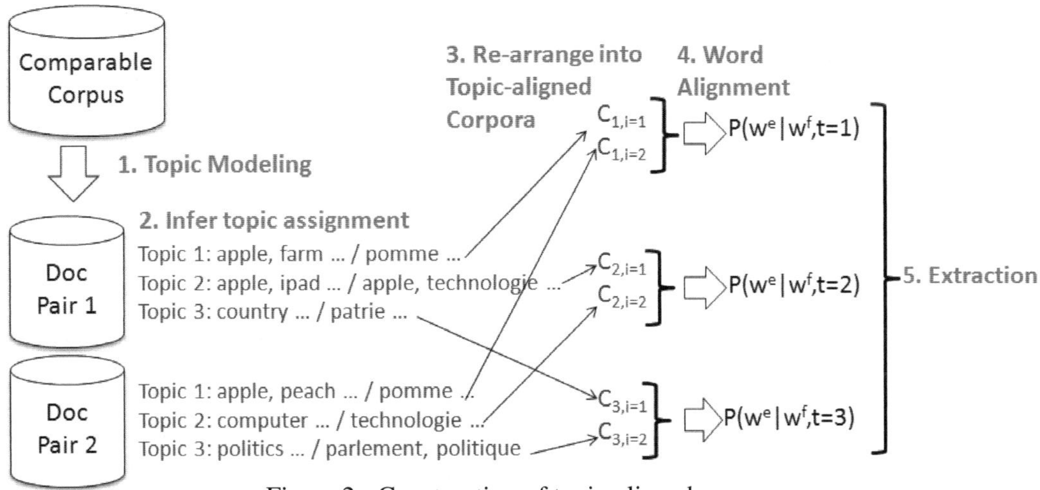

Figure 2: Construction of topic-aligned corpora.

2. Infer a topic assignment for each token in the comparable corpora, and generate a list of word collections $C_{k,i}$ occurring under a given topic.

3. Re-arrange the word collections such that $C_{k,i}$ belonging to the same topic are grouped together. This resulting set of sets is called topic-aligned corpora, since it represents word collections linked by the same topics.

4. For each topic t_k, we run IBM Model 1 on $\{C_{k,1}, \ldots, C_{k,i}, \ldots, C_{k,D}\}$. In analogy to statistical machine translation, we can think of this dataset as a parallel corpus of D "sentence pairs", where each "sentence pair" contains the English and foreign word tokens that co-occur under the same topic and the same document. Note that word alignment is run independently for each topic, resulting in K topic-dependent lexicons $p(w^e|w^f, t_k)$.

5. To extract a bilingual dictionary, we find pairs (w^e, w^f) with high probability under the model:

$$p(w^e|w^f) = \sum_k p(w^e|w^f, t_k)p(t_k|w^f) \quad (2)$$

The first term is the topic-dependent bilingual lexicon from Step 4; the second term is the topic posterior from the topic model in Step 1.

In practice, we will compute the probabilities of Equation 2 in both directions: $p(w^e|, w^f)$ as in Eq. 2 and $p(w^f|w^e) = \sum_k p(w^f|w^e, t_k)p(t_k|w^e)$. The bilingual dictionary can then be extracted based on a probabilities threshold or some bidirectional constraint. We choose to use a bidirectional constraint because it gives very high-precision dictionaries and avoid the need to tune probability thresholds. A pair $(\tilde{e}, \tilde{f})$ is extracted if the following holds:

$$\tilde{e} = \arg\max_e p(e|f = \tilde{f}); \tilde{f} = \arg\max_f p(f|e = \tilde{e}) \quad (3)$$

To summarize, the main innovation of our approach is that we allow for polysemy as topic-dependent translation explicitly in Equation 2, and use a novel combination of topic modeling and word alignment techniques to compute the term $p(w^e|w^f, t_k)$ in an unsupervised fashion.

4.2 Alternative Approaches

To the best of our knowledge, (Vulić et al., 2011) is the only work focuses on using topic models for bilingual lexicon extraction like ours, but they exploit the topic model results in a different way. Their "Cue Method" computes:

$$p(w^e|w^f) = \sum_k p(w^e|t_k)p(t_k|w^f) \quad (4)$$

This can be seen as a simplification of our Eq. 2, where Eq. 4 replaces $p(w^e|t_k, w^f)$ with the simpler $p(w^e|t_k)$. Another variant is the so-called Kullback-Liebler (KL) method, which scores translation pairs by $-\sum_k p(t_k|w^e) \log p(t_k|w^e)/p(t_k|w^f)$. In either case, their contribution is the use of topic-word distributions like $p(t_k|w^f)$ or $p(w^f|t_k)$ to compute translation probabilities.[1] Our formulation can be considered more general because we do not have the strong assumption that w^e is independent of

[1]A third variant uses TF-IDF weighting, but is conceptually similar and have similar results.

w^f given t_k, and focus on estimating $p(w^e|w^f, t_k)$ directly with word alignment methods.

5 Experimental Setup

5.1 Data Set

We perform experiments on the Kyoto Wiki Corpus[2]. We chose this corpus because it is a *parallel* corpus, where the Japanese edition of Wikipedia is translated manually into English sentence-by-sentence. This enables us to use standard word alignment methods to create a gold-standard lexicon for large-scale automatic evaluation.[3]

From this parallel data, we prepared several datasets at successively lower levels of comparability. As shown in Table 1, **Comp100%** is a comparable version of original parallel data, deleting all the sentence alignments but otherwise keeping all content on both Japanese and English sides. **Comp50%** and **Comp20%** are harder datasets that keep only 50% and 20% (respectively) of random English sentences per documents. We further use a *real* comparable corpus (**Wiki**)[4], which is prepared by crawling the online English editions of the corresponding Japanese articles in the Kyoto Wiki Corpus. The **Comp** datasets are controlled scenarios where all English content is guaranteed to have Japanese translations; no such guarantee exists in our **Wiki** data.

5.2 Experimental Results

1. How does the proposed framework compare to previous work?

We focus on comparing with previous topic-modeling approaches to bilingual lexicon extraction, namely (Vulić et al., 2011). The methods are:

- **Proposed**: The proposed method which exploits a combination of topic modeling and word alignment to incorporate topic-dependent translation probabilities (Eq. 2).
- **Cue**: From (Vulić et al., 2011), i.e. Eq. 4.

Dataset	#doc	#sent(e/j)	#voc(e/j)
Comp100%	14k	472k/472k	152k/116k
Comp50%	14k	236k/472k	100k/116k
Comp20%	14k	94k/472k	62k/116k
Wiki	3.6k	127k/163k	88k/61k

Table 1: Datasets: the number of document pairs (#doc), sentences (#sent) and vocabulary size (#voc) in English (e) and Japanese (j). For pre-processing, we did word segmentation on Japanese using Kytea (Neubig et al., 2011) and Porter stemming on English. A TF-IDF based stop-word lists of 1200 in each language is applied. #doc is smaller for **Wiki** because not all Japanese articles in **Comp100%** have English versions in Wikipedia during the crawl.

- **JS**: From (Vulić et al., 2011). Symmetrizing KL by Jensen-Shannon (JS) divergence improves results, so we report this variant.[5]

We also have a baseline that uses no topic models: **IBM-1** runs IBM Model 1 directly on the comparable dataset, assuming each document pair is a "sentence pair".

Figure 3 shows the ROC (Receiver Operating Characteristic) Curve on the **Wiki** dataset. The ROC curve lets us observe the change in Recall as we gradually accept more translation pairs as dictionary candidates. In particular, it measures the true positive rate (i.e. recall = $|\{Gold(e,f)\} \bigcap \{Extracted(e,f)\}|/\#Gold)$ and false positive rate (fraction of false extractions over total number of extractions) at varying levels of thresholds. This is generated by first computing $p(e|f) + p(f|e)$ as the score for pair (e,f) for each method, then sorting the pairs by this score and successive try different thresholds.

The curve of the **Proposed** method dominates those of all other methods. It is also the best in Area-Under-Curve scores (Davis and Goadrich, 2006), which are 0.96, 0.90, 0.85 and 0.71, for **Proposed**, **IBM-1**, **Cue**, and **JS**, respectively.[6]

ROC is insightful if we are interested in comparing methods for all possible thresholds, but in practice we may desire a fixed operating point. Thus we apply the bidirectional heuristic of Eq.

[2]http://alaginrc.nict.go.jp/WikiCorpus/index_E.html

[3]We trained IBM Model 4 using GIZA++ for both directions $p(e|f)$ and $p(f|e)$. Then, we extract word pair $(\tilde{e}, \tilde{f})$ as a "gold standard" bilingual lexicon if it satisfies Eq. 3. Due to the large data size and the strict bidirectional requirement imposed by Eq. 3, these "gold standard" bilingual dictionary items are of high quality (94% precision by a manual check on 100 random items). Note sentence alignments are used only for creating this gold-standard.

[4]The English corresponding dataset, gold-standard and ML-LDA software used in our experiments are available at https://sites.google.com/site/buptxiaodong/home/resource

[5]Topic model hyperparameters for **Proposed**, **Cue**, and **JS** are $\alpha = 50/K$ and $\beta = 0.1$ following (Vulić et al., 2011).

[6]The Precision-Recall curve gives a similar conclusion. We do not show it here since the extremely low precision of **JS** makes the graph hard to visualize. Instead see Table 2.

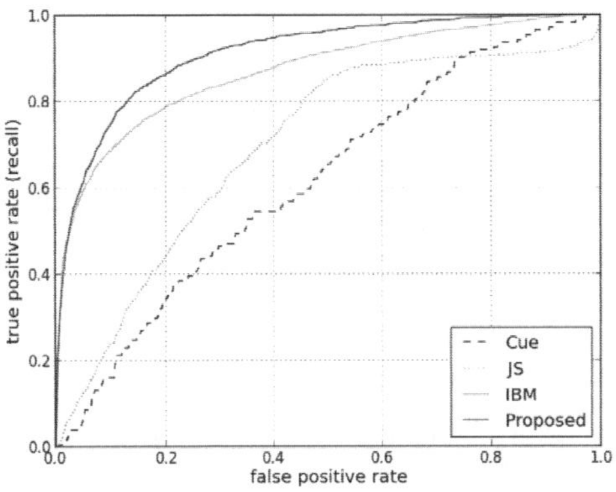

Figure 3: ROC curve on the **Wiki** dataset. Curves on upper-left is better. **Cue**, **JS**, **Proposed** all use K=400 topics. Note that **Proposed** is best.

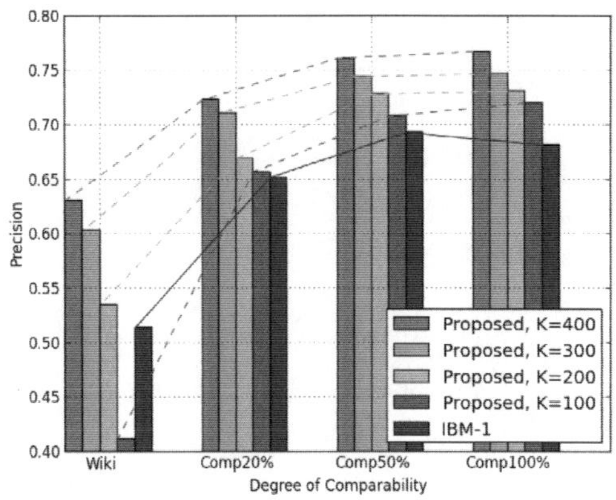

Figure 4: Robustness of method under different data conditions.

K	Method	Prec	ManP	#Extracted
	Cue	0.027	0.02	3800
	JS	0.013	0.01	3800
100	Proposed	0.412	0.36	3800
	Cue	0.059	0.02	2310
	JS	0.075	0.02	2310
400	Proposed	**0.631**	**0.56**	2310
-	IBM-1	0.514	0.42	2310
-	IBM-1*	0.493	0.39	3714

Table 2: Precision on the **Wiki** dataset. K=number of topics. Precision (Prec) is defined as $\frac{|\{Gold(e,f)\} \bigcap \{Extracted(e,f)\}|}{\#Extracted}$. ManP is precision evaluated manually on 100 random items.

3 to extract a fixed set of lexicon for **Proposed**. For the other methods, we calibrated the thresholds to get the same number of extractions. Then we compare the precision, as shown in Table 2.

1. **Proposed** outperforms other methods, achieving 63% (automatic) precision and 56% (manual) precision.

2. The **JS** and **Cue** methods suffer from extremely poor precision. We found that this is due to insufficient number of topics, and is consistent with the results by (Vulić et al., 2011) which showed best results with $K >$ 2000. However, we could not train **JS/Cue** on such a large number of topics since it is computationally-demanding for a corpus as large as ours.[7] In this regard, the **Proposed** method is much more *scalable*, achieving good results with low K, satisfying one of original desiderata.[8]

3. **IBM-1** is doing surprisingly well, considering that it simply treats document pairs as sentence pairs. This may be due to some extent to the structure of the Kyoto Wiki dataset, which contains specialized topics (about Kyoto history, architecture, etc.), leading to a vocabulary-document co-occurrence matrix with sparse block-diagonal structure. Thus there may be enough statistics train **IBM-1** on documents.

2. How does the proposed method perform under different degrees of "comparability"?

We next examined how our methods perform under different data conditions. Figure 4 plots the results in terms of Precision evaluated automatically. We observe that **Proposed (K=400)** is relatively stable, with a decrease of 14% Precision going from fully-comparable to real Wikipedia comparable corpora. The degradation for K=100 is much larger (31%) and therefore not recommended. We believe that robustness depends on K, because the

[7]The experiments in (Vulić et al., 2011) has vocabulary size of 10k, compared to 150k in our experiments. We have attempted large $K \geq 1000$ but **Cue** did not finish after days.

[8]We have a hypothesis as to why **Cue** and **JS** depend on large K. Eq. 2 is a valid expression for $p(w^e|w^f)$ that makes little assumptions. We can view Eq. 4 as simplifying the first term of Eq. 2 from $p(w^e|t_k, w^f)$ to $p(w^e|t_k)$. Both probability tables have the same output-space (w^e), so the same number of parameters is needed in reality to describe this distribution. By throwing out w^f, which has large cardinality, t_k needs to grow in cardinality to compensate for the loss of expressiveness.

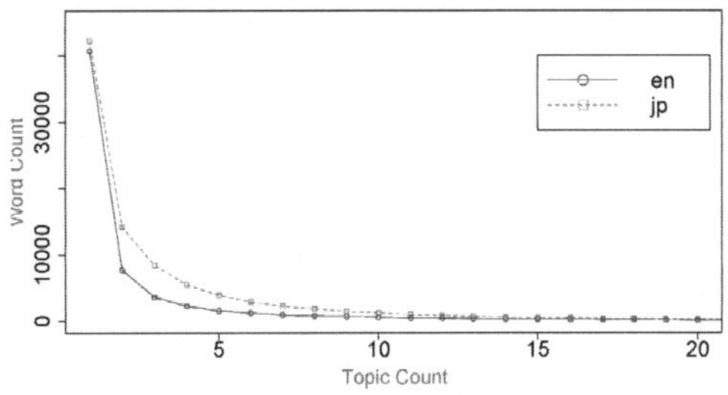

Figure 5: Power-law distribution of number of word types with X number of topics.

topic model of (Mimno et al., 2009) assumes one topic distribution per document pair. For low-levels of comparability, a small number of topics may not sufficiently model the differences in topical content. This suggests the use of hierarchical topic models (Haffari and Teh, 2009) or other variants in future work.

3. What are the statistical characteristics of topic-aligned corpora?

First, we show the word-topic distribution from multilingual topic modeling in the $K = 400$ scenario (first step of **Proposed**, **Cue**, and **JS**). For each word type w, we count the number of topics it may appear in, i.e. nonzero probabilities according to $p(w|t)$. Fig. 5 shows the number of word types that have x number of topics. This power-law is expected since we are modeling all words.[9]

Next we compute the statistics after constructing the topic-aligned corpora (Step 3 of Fig. 2). For each part of the topic-aligned corpora, we compute the ratio of distinct English word types vs. distinct Japanese word types. If the ratio is close to one, that means the partition into topic-aligned corpora effectively separates the skewed word-topic distribution of Fig 5. We found that the mean ratio averaged across topics is low at 1.721 (variance is 1.316), implying that within each topic, word alignment is relatively easy.

4. What kinds of errors are made?

We found that the proposed method makes several types of incorrect lexicon extractions. First, **Word Segmentation** "errors" on Japanese could make it impossible to find a proper English translation (e.g., 高市皇子 should translate to "Prince-Takechi" but system proposes "Takechi"). Second, an unrelated word pair (w^e, w^f) may be incorrectly placed in the same topic, leading to an **Incorrect Topic** error. Third, even if (w^e, w^f) intuitively belong to the same topic, they may not be direct translations; an extraction in this case would be a **Correct Topic, Incorrect Alignment** error (e.g. もんじゃ焼き, a particular panfried snack, is incorrectly translated as "panfry").

Table 3 shows the distribution of error types by a manual classification. **Incorrect Alignment** errors are most frequent, implying the topic models are doing a reasonable job of generating the *topic-aligned* corpus. The amount of **Incorrect Topic** is not trivial, though, so we would still imagine more advanced topic models to help. **Segmentation** errors are in general hard to solve, even with a better word segmenter, since in general one-to-one cross-lingual word correspondence is not consistent–we believe the solution is a system that naturally handles multi-word expressions (Baldwin, 2011).

Word Segmentation Error	14
Incorrect Topic	29
Correct Topic, Incorrect Alignment	40
Reason Unknown	7

Table 3: Counts of various error types.

5. What is the computation cost?

Timing results on a 2.4GHz Opteron CPU for various steps of **Proposed** and **Cue** are shown in Table 5. The proposed method is 5-8 times faster than **Cue**. For **Proposed**, computation time is dominated by topic modeling while GIZA++ on topic-aligned corpora is extremely fast. **Cue** additionally suffers from computational complexity in calculating Eq.4, especially when both $p(w^e|t_k)$ and $p(t_k|w^f)$ have high cardinality. In comparison, calculating Eq.2 is fast since $p(w^e|w^f, t_k)$ is in practice quite sparse.

6. What topic-dependent lexicons are learned and do they capture polysemy?

In our evaluation so far, we have only produced an one-to-one bilingual dictionary (due to the bidirectionality constraint of Eq.3). We have seen how topic-dependent translation models $p(w^f|w^e, t_k)$ is important in achieving good results. However, Eq.2 marginalizes over the topics so we do not know what topic-dependent lexicons are learned.

[9] This means that it is not possible to directly extract lexicon by taking the cross-product (w^f, w^e) of the top-n words in $p(w^f|t_k)$ and $p(w^e|t_k)$ for the same topic t_k, as suggested by (Mimno et al., 2009). When we attempted to do this, using top-2 words per $p(w^f|t_k)$ and $p(w^e|t_k)$, we could only obtain precision of 0.37 for 1600 extractions. This skewed distribution similarly explains the poor performance of **Cue**.

English	Japanese1(gloss), Japanese2(gloss)
interest	関心 (a sense of concern), 利息 (a charge of money borrowing)
count	数え(act of reciting numbers), 伯爵 (nobleman)
free	自由(as in "free" speech), 無料 (as in "free" beer)
blood	血縁(line of descent), 血 (the red fluid)
demand	需要(as noun), 要求(as verb)
draft	提案(as verb), 草稿 (as noun)
page	ページ (one leaf of e.g. a book), 侍童 (youthful attendant)
staff	スタッフ(general personel), 参謀 (as in political "chief of staff")
director	長官 (someone who controls), 理事 (board of directors) 監督 (movie director)
beach	浜(area of sand near water), 海水浴(leisure spot at beach)
actor	役者 (theatrical performer), 俳優 (movie actor)

Table 4: Examples of topic-dependent translations given by $p(w^f|w^e,t_k)$. The top portion shows examples of polysemous English words. The bottom shows examples where English is not decisively polysemous, but indeed has distinct translations in Japanese based on topic.

K	topic	giza	Eq.2	Eq.4	Prp	Cue
100	180	3	20	1440	203	1620
200	300	3	33	2310	336	2610
400	780	5	42	3320	827	4100

Table 5: Wall-clock times in minutes for Topic Modeling (topic), Word Alignment (giza), and $p(w^e|w^f)$ calculation. Overall time for **Proposed** (Prp) is topic+giza+Eq.2 and for **Cue** is topic+Eq.4.

Here, we explore the model $p(w^f|w^e,t_k)$ learned at Step 4 of Figure 2 to see whether it captures some of the polysemy phenomenon mentioned in the desiderata. It is not feasible to automatically evaluate topic-dependent dictionaries, since this requires "gold standard" of the form (e, f, t). Thus we cannot claim whether our method successfully extracts polysemous translations. Instead we will present some interesting examples found by our method. In Table 4, we look at potentially polysemous English words w^e, and list the highest-probability Japanese translations w^f conditioned on different t_k. We found many promising cases where the topic identification helps divide the different senses of the English word, leading to the correct Japanese translation achieving the highest probability.

6 Conclusion

We proposed an effective way to extract bilingual dictionaries by a novel combination of topic modeling and word alignment techniques. The key innovation is the conversion of a comparable *document*-aligned corpus into a parallel *topic*-aligned corpus, which allows word alignment techniques to learn topic-dependent translation models of the form $p(w^e|w^f,t_k)$. While this kind of topic-dependent translation has been proposed for the parallel corpus (Zhao and Xing, 2007), we are the first to enable it for comparable corpora. Our large-scale experiments demonstrated that the proposed framework outperforms existing baselines under both automatic metrics and manual evaluation. We further show that our topic-dependent translation models can capture some of the polysemy phenomenon important in dictionary construction. Future work includes:

1. Exploring other topic models (Haffari and Teh, 2009) and word alignment techniques (DeNero and Macherey, 2011; Mermer and Saraclar, 2011; Moore, 2004) in our framework.

2. Extract lexicon from massive multilingual collections. Mausum (2009) and Shezaf (2010) show that language pivots significantly improve the precision of distribution-based approaches. Since multilingual topic models can easily be trained on more than 3 languages, we expect it will give a big boost to our approach.

Acknowledgments

We thank Mamoru Komachi, Shuhei Kondo and the anonymous reviewers for valuable discussions and comments. Part of this research was executed under the Commissioned Research of National Institute of Information and Communications Technology (NICT), Japan.

References

Timothy Baldwin. 2011. Mwes and topic modelling: enhancing machine learning with linguistics. In *Proceedings of the Workshop on Multiword Expressions: from Parsing and Generation to the Real World*, MWE '11, pages 1–1, Stroudsburg, PA, USA. Association for Computational Linguistics.

D. Blei, A. Ng, and M. Jordan. 2003. Latent dirichlet allocation. *Journal of Machine Learning Research*.

Jordan Boyd-Graber and David M. Blei. 2009. Multilingual topic models for unaligned text. In *UAI*.

P. Brown, S. Della Pietra, V. Della Pietra, and R. Mercer. 1993. The mathematics of statistical machine translation: Parameter estimation. *Computational Linguistics*, 19(2).

Hal Daume III and Jagadeesh Jagarlamudi. 2011. Domain adaptation for machine translation by mining unseen words. In *Proceedings of the 49th Annual Meeting of the Association for Computational Linguistics: Human Language Technologies*, pages 407–412, Portland, Oregon, USA, June. Association for Computational Linguistics.

Jesse Davis and Mark Goadrich. 2006. The relationship between precision-recall and ROC curves. In *ICML*.

Hervé Déjean, Éric Gaussier, and Fatia Sadat. 2002. An approach based on multilingual thesauri and model combination for bilingual lexicon extraction. In *Proceedings of the 19th international conference on Computational linguistics - Volume 1*, COLING '02, pages 1–7.

John DeNero and Klaus Macherey. 2011. Model-based aligner combination using dual decomposition. In *Proceedings of the Association for Computational Linguistics (ACL)*.

Pascale Fung and Percy Cheung. 2004. Mining verynon-parallel corpora: Parallel sentence and lexicon extraction via bootstrapping and em. In *Proceedings of the Conference on Empirical Methods in Natural Language Processing*.

Pascale Fung and Yuen Yee Lo. 1998. Translating unknown words using nonparallel, comparable texts. In *COLING-ACL*.

Eric Gaussier, J.M. Renders, I. Matveeva, C. Goutte, and H. Dejean. 2004. A geometric view on bilingual lexicon extraction from comparable corpora. In *Proceedings of the 42nd Meeting of the Association for Computational Linguistics (ACL'04), Main Volume*, pages 526–533, Barcelona, Spain, July.

Ghloamreza Haffari and Yee Whye Teh. 2009. Hierarchical dirichlet trees for information retrieval. In *NAACL*.

Aria Haghighi, Percy Liang, Taylor Berg-Kirkpatrick, and Dan Klein. 2008. Learning bilingual lexicons from monolingual corpora. In *Proceedings of ACL-08: HLT*, pages 771–779, Columbus, Ohio, June. Association for Computational Linguistics.

Jagadeesh Jagarlamudi and Hal Daume. 2010. Extracting multilingual topics from unaligned comparable corpora. In *ECIR*.

Philipp Koehn and Kevin Knight. 2002. Learning a translation lexicon from monolingual corpora. In *Proceedings of ACL Workshop on Unsupervised Lexical Acquisition*.

Philipp Koehn. 2010. *Statistical Machine Translation*. Cambridge University Press, New York, NY, USA, 1st edition.

Audrey Laroche and Philippe Langlais. 2010. Revisiting context-based projection methods for term-translation spotting in comparable corpora. In *Proceedings of the 23rd International Conference on Computational Linguistics (Coling 2010)*, pages 617–625, Beijing, China, August. Coling 2010 Organizing Committee.

Mausam, Stephen Soderland, Oren Etzioni, Daniel S. Weld, Michael Skinner, and Jeff Bilmes. 2009. Compiling a massive, multilingual dictionary via probabilistic inference. In *ACL*.

Coskun Mermer and Murat Saraclar. 2011. Bayesian word alignment for statistical machine translation. In *ACL*.

David Mimno, Hanna Wallach, Jason Naradowsky, David A. Smith, and Andrew McCallum. 2009. Polylingual topic models. In *EMNLP*.

Robert Moore. 2004. Improving IBM word alignment model 1. In *ACL*.

Graham Neubig, Yosuke Nakata, and Shinsuke Mori. 2011. Pointwise prediction for robust, adaptable japanese morphological analysis. In *The 49th Annual Meeting of the Association for Computational Linguistics: Human Language Technologies (ACL-HLT) Short Paper Track*, pages 529–533, Portland, Oregon, USA, 6.

Xiaochuan Ni, Jian-Tao Sun, Jian Hu, and Zheng Chen. 2009. Mining multilingual topics from wikipedia. In *WWW*.

Franz Josef Och and Hermann Ney. 2003. A systematic comparison of various statistical alignment models. *Comput. Linguist.*, 29(1):19–51, March.

Reinhard Rapp. 1995. Identifying word translations in non-parallel texts. In *Proceedings of the 33rd Annual Meeting of the Association for Computational Linguistics*.

Philip Resnik, Douglas Oard, and Gina Levow. 2011. Improved cross-language retrieval using backoff translation. In *Proceedings of the First International Conference on Human Language Technology*.

Daphna Shezaf and Ari Rappoport. 2010. Bilingual lexicon generation using non-aligned signatures. In *Proceedings of the 48th Annual Meeting of the Association for Computational Linguistics*, ACL '10, pages 98–107. Association for Computational Linguistics.

Akihiro Tamura, Taro Watanabe, and Eiichiro Sumita. 2012. Bilingual lexicon extraction from comparable corpora using label propagation. In *Proceedings of the 2012 Joint Conference on Empirical Methods in Natural Language Processing and Computational Natural Language Learning*, pages 24–36, Jeju Island, Korea, July. Association for Computational Linguistics.

Ivan Vulić, Wim De Smet, and Marie-Francine Moens. 2011. Identifying word translations from comparable corpora using latent topic models. In *Proceedings of the 49th Annual Meeting of the Association for Computational Linguistics: Human Language Technologies*, pages 479–484, Portland, Oregon, USA, June. Association for Computational Linguistics.

Bing Zhao and Eric P. Xing. 2007. HM-BiTAM: Bilingual Topic Exploration, Word Alignment, and Translation. In *NIPS*.

Terminology Extraction Approaches for Product Aspect Detection in Customer Reviews

Jürgen Broß
Institute of Computer Science
Freie Universität Berlin
14195 Berlin, Germany
juergen.bross@fu-berlin.de

Heiko Ehrig
Neofonie GmbH
Robert-Koch-Platz 4
10115 Berlin, Germany
heiko.ehrig@neofonie.de

Abstract

In this paper, we address the problem of identifying relevant product aspects in a collection of online customer reviews. Being able to detect such aspects represents an important subtask of aspect-based review mining systems, which aim at automatically generating structured summaries of customer opinions. We cast the task as a terminology extraction problem and examine the utility of varying term acquisition heuristics, filtering techniques, variant aggregation methods, and relevance measures. We evaluate the different approaches on two distinct datasets (hotel and camera reviews). For the best configuration, we find significant improvements over a state-of-the-art baseline method.

1 Introduction

Identifying significant terms in a text corpus constitutes a core task in natural language processing. Fields of application are for example *glossary extraction* (Kozakov et al., 2004) or *ontology learning* (Navigli and Velardi, 2004). In this work, we particularly focus on the application scenario of *aspect-based customer review mining* (Hu and Liu, 2004; Dave et al., 2003). It is best described as a *sentiment analysis* task, where the goal is to summarize the opinions expressed in customer reviews. Typically, the problem is decomposed into three subtasks: 1) identify mentions of relevant product aspects, 2) identify sentiment expressions and determine their polarity, and 3) aggregate the sentiments for each aspect. In this paper, we only consider the first subtask, i.e., finding relevant product aspects in reviews.

More precisely, we define the problem setting as follows: Input is a homogeneous collection of customer reviews, i.e., all reviews refer to a single product type (e.g., digital cameras or hotels). The goal is to automatically derive a lexicon of the most relevant aspects related to the product type. For example, given a set of hotel reviews, we want to determine aspects such as "room size", "front desk staff" "sleep quality", and so on. In general, product aspects may occur as *nominal* (e.g., "image stabilization"), *named* (e.g., "SteadyShot feature"), *pronominal* (e.g., "it"), or *implicit* mentions (e.g., "reduction of blurring from camera shake"). We explicitly restrict the task to finding nominal aspect mentions[1].

The contribution of this paper is to explicitly cast the problem setting as a *terminology extraction* (TE) task and to examine the utility of methods that have been proven beneficial in this context. Most related work does not consider this close relationship and rather presents ad-hoc approaches. Our main contributions are as follows:
– We experiment with varying term acquisition methods, propose a set of new term filtering approaches, and consider variant aggregation techniques typically applied in TE systems.
– We compare the utility of different term relevance measures and experiment with combinations of these measures.
– We propose and assess a new method that filters erroneous modifiers (adjectives) in term candidates. Our method exploits information obtained from pros/cons summaries of customer reviews.
– Our best configuration improves over a state-of-the-art baseline by up to 7 percentage points.

The remainder of the paper is organized as follows: In Section 2, we cover related work, setting focus on unsupervised approaches. Section 3 describes the TE methods we examine in this study. Section 4 introduces our evaluation datasets and Section 5 presents experiments and results. We summarize and conclude in Section 6.

[1]Nominal mentions account for over 80% of all mentions in our datasets. Also in other corpora, the ratio is quite similar, e.g., (Kessler et al., 2010).

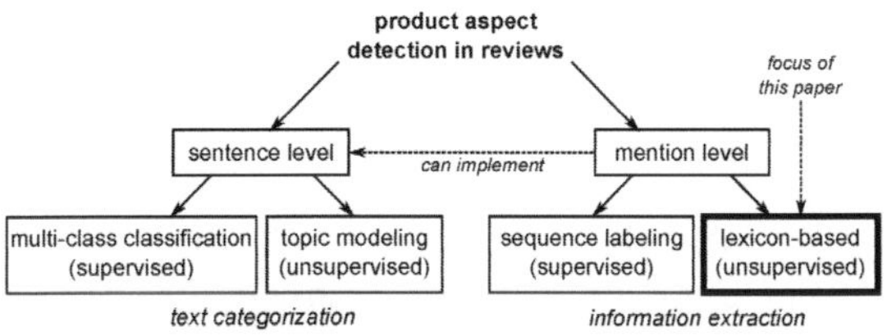

Figure 1: Conceptual overview of related work in product aspect detection.

2 Related Work

Figure 1 provides a conceptual overview of different tasks and approaches in the research area. Basically, we differentiate related work by the granularity of analysis, distinguishing between sentence level and mention level analysis. While at the sentence level, the goal is to decide whether a given sentence refers to one or more predefined aspects, fine-grained mention level analysis aims at discovering each individual mention of a relevant product aspect (e.g., "The *image stabilization* works well, but I didn't like the poor *battery life*.").

We address aspect detection at the **mention level** and our methods fall into the category of (unsupervised) **lexicon-based approaches**. In contrast to supervised methods, lexicon-based approaches do not rely on labeled training data and thus scale better across domains[2]. The common approach is to crawl a corpus of reviews and to apply frequency-based methods to extract a lexicon of product aspects from the dataset. Approaches differ in the way corpus statistics are computed and to which extent linguistic features are exploited. Section 2.1 briefly describes the most relevant previous works and Section 2.2 provides an assessment of the different approaches.

2.1 Creating Product Aspect Lexicons

Hu and Liu (2004) cast the problem as a **frequent itemset mining** task and apply the well-known *Apriori algorithm* (Agrawal and Srikant, 1994). Inherent drawbacks of this approach[3] are heuristically treated in a post-processing step.

Whereas Hu and Liu's method exclusively examines documents of the input collection, Popescu and Etzioni (2005) propose to incorporate the **Web as a corpus**. They assess a term candidate's domain relevance by computing the *pointwise mutual information* (PMI) (Zernik, 1991) between the candidate term and some predefined phrases that are associated with the product type. The *PMI* score is used to prune term candidates.

A further approach is to utilize a **contrastive background corpus** to determine the domain relevance of terms. For instance, Yi et al. (2003) use the *likelihood ratio test* (LRT) to compute a confidence value that a term candidate originates from the relevant review corpus. The computed score is used to rank term candidates. Also Scaffidi et al. (2007) follow the basic idea of using a contrastive corpus, but simply compare relative frequency ratios instead of computing a confidence value. Other exemplary works consider the utility of **statistical language models** (Wu et al., 2009), propose **latent semantic analysis** (Guo et al., 2009), or examine a **double propagation approach** that leverages the correlation between product aspects and sentiment bearing words (Zhang et al., 2010). Product aspect lexicons may also be created manually, e.g., Carenini et al. (2005) or Bloom et al. (2007) follow this approach. Naturally, a manual approach does not scale well across domains.

2.2 Assessment of Lexicon-Based Approaches

Our goal in this section is to select a state-of-the art method that we can use as a baseline in our experiments. Unfortunately, it is quite difficult to assess the relative performance of the different approaches as the evaluation datasets and methodologies often vary. Popescu and Etzioni (2005) compare their results to the method by Hu and Liu (2004) and report significantly improved results. However, their method relies on the private "Know-it-all" information extraction system and is therefore not suited as a baseline. Scaffidi et al. (2007) only assess the precision of the extracted aspect lexicon. Their methodology does not allow to measure recall, which renders their comparison to Hu's method rather useless[4]. Furthermore, the results are quite questionable as the number of extracted aspects is extremely small (8-12 aspects compared to around thousand with our approach). Also Yi et al. (2003) only report results of an intrinsic evaluation for their LRT-approach. A systematic comparison of Hu's frequent itemset min-

[2] For instance, (Jakob and Gurevych, 2010) report that F-scores for their sequence labeling method decrease by up to 25 percentage points in cross domain settings.

[3] The word order is not recognized and sub-terms of terms are not necessarily valid terms in natural language.

[4] Without considering recall, the precision can easily be tweaked by adjusting threshold values.

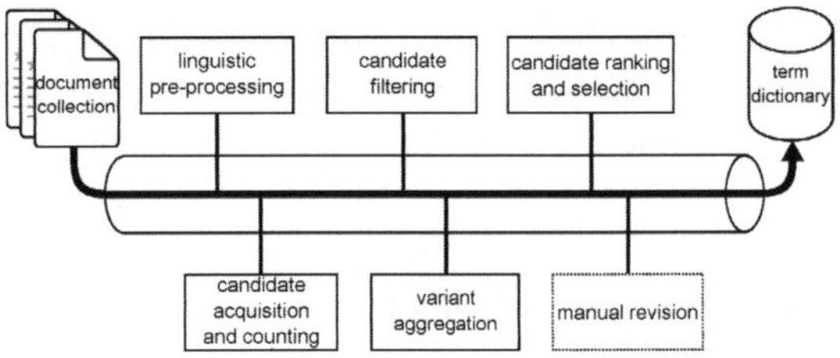

Figure 2: Pipeline architecture of a TE system.

ing and Yi's LRT-approach is conducted by Jakob (2011). His results show that "the Likelihood Ratio Test based approach generally yielded better results". In the absence of other valid comparative studies, we therefore select the LRT-approach as a baseline method for our experiments.

3 Terminology Extraction for Product Aspect Detection

A typical TE system follows the pipeline architecture depicted in Figure 2. Depending on the specific application domain, the implementation of the individual pipeline steps may differ widely. For example, we will see in the next section that the examined acquisition and filtering methods are highly tailored to the domain of customer reviews. In contrast, the underlying concepts for the definition of term relevance are applicable across domains. From the multitude of statistical measures proposed in the literature[5], we can distill mainly three underlying concepts: (1) *contrastive domain relevance*, (2) *intra domain relevance*, and (3) *term cohesion*. We will experiment with measures for all of the three concepts. The following subsections describe how we implement the individual steps of the extraction pipeline (for the majority of steps, we propose several alternative approaches, which will be subject to experimentation).

3.1 Linguistic Preprocessing

We preprocess all text documents by means of a *part-of-speech tagger*[6] (which also performs tokenization, sentence splitting, and lemmatization). All tokens are further normalized by case folding.

3.2 Candidate Acquisition

The candidate acquisition component initially decides which phrases are further considered and which are directly discarded. Defining too restrictive filters may lower the recall, whereas too unconstrained filters may decrease the precision.

Part-of-Speech Tag Filter We experiment with two POS-tag filters: *BNP1* and *BNP2*. As a baseline (BNP1), we use the "base noun phrase pattern" proposed in (Yi et al., 2003):

```
BNP1 := NN |NN NN |JJ NN |NN NN NN |
        JJ NN NN |JJ JJ NN
```

It restricts candidates to a maximum length of three words (adjectives or nouns), where adjectives must only occur as pre-modifiers to nouns. As an alternative, we examine the utility of a more relaxed pattern (BNP2). This pattern matches terms of arbitrary length, also allows for plural forms, and matches proper nouns (identified by the tags NNP or NNPS):

```
BNP2 := (JJ )*(NN\w{0,2} )+
```

Domain Specific Heuristics Acquisition heuristics put further constraints on the validity of term candidates. As a baseline, we consider two heuristics proposed in (Yi et al., 2003):

– The *definite base noun phrase* (**DBNP**) heuristic restricts the *BNPs* to phrases that are preceded by the definite article "*the*".

– The *beginning definite base noun phrase* (**BBNP**) heuristic restricts valid candidates to *DBNPs* that occur at the beginning of a sentence, followed by a verb phrase (e.g., "The *picture quality* is great.").

As an alternative, we propose two other heuristics. Both are based on the hypothesis that the occurrence of sentiment expressions in the context of a candidate is a good indicator for the candidate's validity. Sentiment expressions are detected with a small hand-crafted sentiment lexicon composed of 520 strongly positive/negative adjectives. We experiment with two different strategies:

– The *sentiment bearing sentence* (**SBS**) heuristic only considers candidates that occur in sentences where at least one sentiment expression is detected.

– The *sentiment bearing pattern* (**SBP**) heuristic defines a set of four simple syntactic patterns that relate candidate terms to sentiment expressions. Only candidates that match one of the patterns are further considered.

3.3 Candidate Filtering

Although the candidate acquisition heuristics focus on high precision, they generate a consider-

[5]For example, consult (Kageura and Umino, 1996) for a thorough literature survey on terminology extraction.

[6]http://nlp.stanford.edu/software/corenlp.shtml

able number of irrelevant candidates. These can be pruned by further domain specific filters:

Review Stop Word Filter We compile a list of review specific *stop words* and discard each candidate term that contains at least one of the words. The list (176 entries) has been constructed based on observations on a development dataset and by (intelligent) extrapolation of these findings. Roughly categorized, it includes *sentiment bearing nouns* (e.g., "complaint"), *review related terms* (e.g., "bottom line"), *purchase related phrases* (e.g., "delivery"), *mentions of persons* (e.g., "wife"), and *phrases of reasoning* (e.g., "decision").

Pre-Modifier Filter Both presented part-of-speech filters (BNP1/2) allow nouns to be modified by multiple adjectives. Unfortunately, this leads to the extraction of many invalid terms (e.g., "great/JJ design/NN" or "new/JJ design/NN"). Quite frequently, *sentiment bearing adjectives* such as "great", "fantastic", or "bad" are erroneously extracted. We utilize our hand-crafted sentiment lexicon to prune these modifiers. Another type is related to adjectives that act as *universal modifiers* in terms (e.g., "new", "long", or "red"). For such adjectives we cannot compile a stop word list. We experiment with two different methods for filtering universal modifiers. As a baseline, we examine a filter proposed by Kozakov et al. (2004) as part of their *GlossEx* glossary extraction system. As a second approach, we propose a method that uses signals from pros/cons summaries of reviews (Section 3.6).

Product Name Filter As we are only interested in finding nominal aspect mentions, we need to discard all candidate terms that refer to product or brand names. For this purpose, we automatically generate a stop word list by exploiting meta data (on products and brands) that is associated with the crawled customer reviews. Whenever a term candidate contains a token that is present in the appropriate stop word list, the candidate is discarded.

3.4 Variant Aggregation

The goal of this step is to find all variants of a term and to identify a canonical representation. For example, the variants "auto-focus", "auto focus", "autofocus", or "auto focuss" should be mapped to the canonical form "auto focus". The purpose of this step is twofold: (1) higher lexicon coverage and (2) preventing potential problems with data sparseness during candidate ranking. Following Kozakov et al. (2004), we implement heuristics for finding *symbolic*, *compounding*, and *misspelling* variants. In addition, we implement a method that considers *compositional* variants of the form "room size" vs. "size of the room".

3.5 Candidate Ranking and Selection

Candidate ranking is at the core of each terminology extraction system. As it is unclear which relevance measure performs best in our context, we experiment with different approaches and also consider reasonable combinations of individual scores. Despite the newly proposed *diversity value* score, the selected measures are all taken from previous research in terminology extraction. We therefore only briefly discuss the other measures and refer to the original literature for more details.

Raw Frequency (Intra Domain) The ranking is simply determined by the raw occurrence frequency of a term.

Relative Frequency Ratio (Contrastive) This ranking (MRFR) is based on the comparison of relative frequency ratios in two corpora. While the original measure (Damerau, 1993) is only defined for single word terms, Kozakov et al. (2004) show how to extend the definition to multi-word terms.

Likelihood Ratio Test (Contrastive) This ranking can be considered as a more robust version of the MRFR approach. Put simply, it additionally computes confidence scores for the relative frequency ratios, which allows to prevent problems with low frequency terms. The score is based on the *likelihood ratio test* (LRT). Yi et al. (2003) describe how the score is computed in our context.

Generalized Dice Coefficient (Term Cohesion) To measure the association between words of a complex term, Park et al. (2002) introduce a measure that generalizes the *Dice coefficient* (Dice, 1945). The measure gives higher scores to terms with high co-occurrence frequencies.

Diversity Value (Intra Domain) Based on the observation that nested word sequences that appear frequently in longer terms are likely to represent the key parts or features of a product, we propose a measure that gives higher scores to such "key terms" (e.g., "lens" occurs in terms such as "autofocus lens", "zoom lens", "macro lens",

"lens cap", or "lens cover"). Inspired by the *C-Value score* (Frantzi and Ananiadou, 1996), we define the measure as: *diversity-score(ws)* =

$$\log_2(|ws|_t + 1) * \frac{\sum_{w_i \in ws} (f(w_i) * \log_2(|T^*_{w_i}| + 1))}{|ws|_t},$$

where $|ws|_t$ denotes the number of tokens of a word sequence ws, w_i refers to the i-th token in ws, and $T^*_{w_i}$ describes the set of other candidate terms that contain the token w_i. The function $f(w_i)$ returns the frequency of the token w_i in the considered text corpus.

Combining Ranking Measures

As the presented ranking measures are based on different definitions of term significance, it is reasonable to compute a combined score (e.g., combining a term's contrastive relevance with its strength of cohesion). Since the different measures are not directly comparable, we compute a combined score by considering the individual rankings: Let T be the set of extracted candidate terms and let $R_i(t)$ be a function that ranks candidates $t \in T$. Using a weight ω_i for each of the n selected measures, we compute the final rank of a candidate t as: *weighted-rank*(t) =

$$\sum_{i=1}^{n} \omega_i * R_i(t) \text{ , where } \sum_{i=1}^{n} \omega_i = 1.$$

For our experiments, we chose equal weights for each ranking measure, i.e., $\omega_i = 1/n$.

3.6 Pros/Cons Pre-Modifier Filter

Some sentiment bearing pre-modifiers are domain or aspect-specific (e.g., "*long* battery life")[7]. The *GlossEx filter* (see Section 3.3) cannot cope with this type of modification. To identify such pre-modifiers, we propose to exploit signals from *structured* pros/cons summaries that typically accompany a customer review. We hypothesize that valid pre-modifiers (e.g., "digital" in "digital camera") occur similarly distributed with their head noun in both, lists of pros and lists of cons. Invalid pre-modifiers, i.e., aspect-specific sentiment words, are likely to occur either more often in lists of pros or lists of cons. We design a simple *likelihood ratio test* to operationalize this assumption.

In particular, we consider the probabilities $p_1 = Pr(pm|head; pros)$ and $p_2 = Pr(pm|head; cons)$, where p_1 (p_2) denotes the probability in a corpus of pros (cons) lists that pm occurs as pre-modifier with the head noun $head$. To design a hypothesis test, we assume as null hypothesis H_0 that $p_1 = p = p_2$ (equal distribution in pros and cons) and as alternative hypothesis that $p_1 \neq p_2$ (unequal distribution). We calculate the likelihood ratio λ and utilize the value $-2 * log\lambda$ to reject H_0 at a desired confidence level (in that case, we prune the pre-modifier pm).

[7]see also (Fahrni and Klenner, 2008)

statistic	hotel	camera
documents	150	150
sentences	1,682	1,416
tokens	29,249	24,765
nominal aspect mentions (incl. sentiment targets)	2,066	1,918
avg. tokens per mention	1.28	1.4
distinct mentions	490	477

Table 1: Basic corpus statistics.

4 Datasets

We evaluate our approaches on datasets of hotel and digital camera reviews. We crawled around 500,000 hotel reviews from Tripadvisor.com and approximately 200,000 digital camera reviews from Amazon.com, Buzzillions.com, and Epinions.com. From each of the two crawls, we randomly sample 20,000 reviews, which we use as foreground corpora for the terminology extraction task[8]. As a background corpus, we utilize a 100,000 document subset (randomly sampled) of the "ukWaC corpus" (Baroni et al., 2009).

4.1 Evaluation Corpora

To evaluate our approaches, we manually annotate a subset of the crawled reviews. In particular, we randomly sample subsets of 150 hotel and 150 camera reviews that do not overlap with the foreground corpora. Following prior work on sentiment analysis (Wiebe et al., 2005; Polanyi and Zaenen, 2006), we decompose an opinion into two functional constituents: *sentiment expressions* and *sentiment targets*. In addition, we consider *nominal mentions* of product aspects that are not targeted by a sentiment expression. We annotate a document by marking relevant spans of text with the appropriate annotation type, setting the type's properties (e.g., the polarity of a sentiment expression), and relating the annotations to each other. Table 1 summarizes the statistics of the created evaluation corpora (regarding sentiment targets and nominal aspect mentions).

[8]Larger corpora did not improve our results.

5 Experiments and Results

5.1 Evaluation Methods

We conduct *intrinsic* and *extrinsic* evaluation of the approaches. Intrinsic evaluation refers to assessing the quality of the generated product aspect lexicons. For this purpose, we manually inspect the extracted lexicons and report results in terms of *precision* (share of correct entries) or *precision@n* (the precision of the n highest ranked lexicon entries). For extrinsic evaluation (evaluation in use), we apply the extracted lexicons for the task of aspect detection in customer review documents. To match lexicon entries in review texts, we apply the Aho-Corasick algorithm (Aho and Corasick, 1975). If multiple matches overlap, we select the left-most, longest-matching, highest-scoring lexicon entry (thus guaranteeing a set of non-overlapping matches). Only exact matches are counted as true positives. We further differentiate between two evaluation scenarios:

– **Scenario A**: In this scenario, the task is to extract all product aspects, irrespective of being target of a sentiment expression or not. We thus define the union of sentiment target and aspect mention annotations as reference (gold standard). Any extraction that matches either a sentiment target or an aspect mention is considered a true positive.

– **Scenario B**: This scenario considers the task of detecting sentiment targets. As it is not our goal to assess the accuracy of sentiment expression detection, we provide the extraction algorithm with perfect (gold standard) knowledge on the presence of sentiment expressions and their relations to sentiment targets (in effect, the algorithm only considers matches that overlap a sentiment target).

5.2 Baseline Results (Yi et al. Method)

To make our results comparable to other existing methods, we first set a baseline by applying a state-of-the-art approach on our datasets. As motivated in Section 2.2, the LRT-approach by Yi et al. (2003) represents our baseline. We can easily implement Yi's method with our terminology extraction framework by using the *BNP1* POS-tag filter, the *bBNP* acquisition heuristic, and the LRT-score for ranking. We select all terms with a minimum LRT-score of 3.84[9] and do not apply any candidate filtering or variant aggregation.

[9] 3.84 is the critical value of the χ^2-distribution for one degree of freedom at a confidence level of 95%.

scenario	precision	recall	f-measure
hotel A	55.1%	73.0%	62.8%
hotel B	81.3%	71.2%	75.9%
camera A	65.0%	72.5%	68.6%
camera B	76.8%	69.9%	73.2%

Table 2: Extrinsic evaluation results for the baseline approach.

scenario	precision	recall	f-measure
hotel A	56.9% (+1.8*)	75.2% (+2.2*)	64.8% (+2.0*)
hotel B	85.7% (+4.4*)	75.1% (+3.9*)	80.0% (+4.1*)
camera A	69.2% (+4.2*)	74.3% (+1.8*)	71.7% (+3.1*)
camera B	79.3% (+2.5*)	72.2% (+2.3*)	75.6% (+2.4*)

Table 3: Results with activated candidate filters.

The baseline method produces lexicons with 1,182 (hotel) and 953 (digital camera) entries. Due to our significantly larger foreground corpora, the dictionaries' sizes are by far larger than reported by (Yi et al., 2003) or by (Ferreira et al., 2008). Intrinsic evaluation of the lexicons reveals precision values of 61.2% (hotel) and 67.6% (camera). For precision@40, we find values of 62.5 (hotel) 80.0 (camera).

Table 2 reports the extrinsic evaluation results for the baseline configuration. Naturally, the precision values obtained for scenario A are lower than for the "synthetic" scenario B (where partial matches are the only possible source for false positives). Recall values in both scenarios are moderately high with around 70%.

If not otherwise stated, the configurations in the following sections apply the BNP1 acquisition pattern, the *BBNP* heuristic, and the LRT-ranking with a minimum score of 3.84.

5.3 Effectiveness of Candidate Filtering

In this section, we analyze the influence of candidate filtering (baseline: Yi's method). When applying all filters jointly (except for the pros/cons filter), the resulting lexicons consist of 975 (hotel) and 767 (camera) entries. Compared to the baseline, the (intrinsic) precision of the lexicons improves by around 10 percentage points (hotel) and 14 percentage points (camera). Each individual filter has a positive effect on the precision, where the *GlossEx filter* has the greatest influence (+5 percentage points in both corpora). Table 3 shows that the improved lexicon precision also leads to better results for the product aspect extraction task. The observed f-measure values increase by up to 4.1 percentage points compared to the baseline

scenario	precision	recall	f-measure
hotel A	56.7% (-0.2)	75.1% (-0.1)	64.6% (-0.2)
hotel B	85.5% (-0.2)	75.1% (0.0)	79.9% (-0.1)
camera A	69.8% (+0.6)	74.8% (+0.5)	72.2% (+0.5)
camera B	80.7% (+1.4)	73.0% (+0.8)	76.7% (+1.1)

Table 4: Results with variant aggregation.

method. All improvements are statistically significant[10]. The increase in recall is mainly due to successful pruning of false modifiers.

5.4 Effectiveness of Variant Aggregation

In this section, we examine the influence of the different variant aggregation techniques (baseline: Yi's method + filter). To assess the effectiveness of variant aggregation, we only evaluate extrinsically (since we primarily expect a higher coverage of the lexicons). Table 4 compares the results with variant aggregation to the results of the previous section (all filters activated). The results show that variant aggregation has only marginal effects. Although we can measure improved results for the camera corpus, the differences are rather small and not statistically significant. For the hotel corpus, the influence is even lower. To understand the reasons for the insignificant effect, we perform a mistake analysis of the false negatives in scenario B. In particular, we compare the false negatives with and without variant aggregation. For the hotel corpus, we only find 18 out of 251 false negatives (7.2%) that are candidates for variant aggregation. In the ideal case (variant aggregation successfully recognizes all the candidates), this translates to a maximum gain of 1.8 percentage points in recall. For the camera dataset, we calculate a maximum gain of 2.4 percentage points. Our results deviate from the ideal case for mainly two reasons: (1) Most variants occur rarely and the ones that occur in the evaluation corpora do not occur in the foreground corpora. (2) Some variants (e.g., misspellings) are so frequent in the foreground corpus that the LRT-ranking already selects them as independent terms.

5.5 Influence of Acquisition Methods

This section examines the influence of the different acquisition patterns and heuristics. We only report results for the hotel dataset as the results for the camera corpus are similar. Table 5 shows results for scenario B (all filters and aggregation methods activated). As could be expected, the more relaxed acquisition pattern *BNP2* trades precision for an increased recall (+1-2 percentage points). The results further show that the use of appropriate acquisition heuristics is quite important. We can improve the f-measure by up to 6.1 percentage points. We find that the *SBP* and *BBNP* heuristics perform best on our datasets. The differences in f-measure, compared to the other two heuristics, are statistically significant (not shown in the table). As the *BBNP* heuristic is easier to implement and shows comparable results, we conclude that it is preferable over the *SBP* method.

[10]We use the * notation to indicate statistically significant differences. If not otherwise stated, significance is reported at the 99% confidence level.

	precision		recall		f-measure	
heuristic	BNP1	BNP2	BNP1	BNP2	BNP1	BNP2
—	80.7%	79.5%	70.7%	71.7%	75.4%	75.4%
SBS	81.1%	80.0%	72.2%	72.9%	76.4%	76.3%
DBNP	83.2%	82.4%	73.6%	75.2%	78.1%	78.6%
SBP	**87.0%**	84.5%	74.6%	75.8%	**80.3%**	79.9%
BBNP	85.5%	**85.5%**	**75.1%**	**77.7%**	79.9%	**81.5%**

Table 5: Extrinsic evaluation results with varying acquisition patterns and heuristics (hotel dataset).

	hotel		camera	
measure	precision	p@40	precision	p@40
frequency	41.6%	55.0%	44.8%	70.0%
dice	39.0%	55.0%	43.5%	87.5%
diversity	66.4%	77.5%	76.7%	70.0%
lrt	69.6%	72.5%	81.1%	87.5%
mrfr	72.0%	87.5%	81.4%	92.5%

Table 6: Intrinsic evaluation results with the five different ranking measures.

5.6 Influence of Ranking Functions

We now examine the influence of the different ranking measures (all filters and variant aggregation are activated). To rule out the influence of varying lexicon sizes, we choose a fixed size for each dataset (determined by the number of terms that exhibit an LRT-score greater than 3.84). For larger lexicons, we prune the entries with the lowest scores. For each configuration, we apply all filter and variant aggregation approaches. Table 6 shows the intrinsic evaluation results. We can clearly observe that the contrastive relevance measures (LRT and MRFR) outperform the intra domain and term cohesion measures. The MRFR-ranking shows better results than the LRT-ranking in both corpora, especially w.r.t. precision@40.

The improved results with contrastive measures are also reflected by our extrinsic evaluation. Ta-

	hotel			camera		
measure	prec.	rec.	F	prec.	rec.	F
frequency	45.3%	79.1%	57.6%	50.7%	77.8%	61.4%
dice	44.7%	78.3%	56.9%	50.4%	77.5%	61.1%
diversity	51.4%	72.3%	60.1%	64.5%	73.8%	68.8%
lrt	56.7%	75.1%	**64.6%**	69.8%	74.8%	72.2%
mrfr	**60.2%**	67.3%	63.5%	**73.1%**	72.8%	**73.0%**
all	46.6%	**79.3%**	58.7%	52.6%	**78.7%**	63.0%
mrfr-dice	47.7%	78.2%	59.2%	55.3%	78.2%	64.8%
lrt-div.	47.8%	73.5%	57.9%	57.0%	75.1%	64.8%
mrfr-lrt	56.9%	73.5%	64.2%	68.2%	73.7%	70.8%
mrfr-freq.	51.8%	77.8%	62.2%	61.2%	76.1%	67.9%
mrfr-lrt-div.	53.3%	74.5%	62.2%	66.8%	75.4%	70.8%
mrfr-div.	57.9%	73.1%	**64.6%**	71.8%	72.5%	72.1%

Table 7: Extrinsic evaluation results for varying ranking methods (scenario A).

scenario	precision	recall	f-measure
hotel A	58.0% (+1.1*)	76.3% (+1.1)	65.9% (+1.1*)
hotel B	88.9% (+3.2*)	77.4% (+2.4*)	82.8% (+2.8*)
camera A	71.7% (+2.5*)	76.2% (+1.9)	73.9% (+2.2*)
camera B	83.4% (+4.0*)	75.1% (+2.9*)	79.0% (+3.4*)

Table 8: Results with active pros/cons filter.

ble 7 presents the results for scenario A, considering the measures in isolation and in selected combinations (using equal weights). Compared to raw frequency, the contrastive measures exhibit f-measure values that are between 7 (hotel) and 11.6 (camera) percentage points higher. We hypothesized that the combination of different relevance concepts (e.g., contrastive + term cohesion) could improve the system's performance, but the obtained results do *not* confirm this hypothesis.

5.7 Effectiveness of Pros/Cons Filter

In this section we examine the the pros/cons premodifier filter. The reported results are based on pros/cons corpora composed of 100,000 (hotel) and 50,000 (camera) documents. We set the threshold for the hypothesis test to 10.83, corresponding to a 99.9% confidence level. Table 8 presents the results of additionally applying this filter (baseline: all other filters and variant aggregation activated). We can observe statistically significant improvements with gains in f-measure of up to 3.4 percentage points. Examining the resulting lexicons, we find that the filter successfully pruned around 40 false pre-modifiers, which increases the (intrinsic) precision by around 3 percentage points for both datasets. Despite the relatively few lexicon entries that are altered by means of the filter, we observe the mentioned (significant) gains in f-measure. For both datasets this is mainly because the affected lexicon entries exhibit a high occurrence frequency in the evaluation datasets (e.g., "large room" or "low price").

6 Conclusions

Identifying the most relevant aspects of a given product or product type constitutes an important subtask of an aspect-based review mining system. In this work, we explicitly cast the task as a terminology extraction problem. We were interested whether methods that have been proven beneficial in TE systems also help in our application scenario. Additionally, we proposed and evaluated some new term acquisition heuristics, candidate filtering techniques, and a ranking measure. The results show that our terminology extraction approach allows to generate quite accurate product aspect lexicons (precision up to 85%), which in turn allow for f-measures of up to 74% for an aspect detection task and up to 83% for a (synthetic) sentiment target detection task. Compared to a relevant baseline approach (Yi et al., 2003), we observe increases in f-measure by 3-7 percentage points for different evaluation scenarios.

With regard to the different configurations of our system, we made the following observations:
– Improved results are mainly due to the proposed candidate filtering techniques. Each individual filter has been found to be beneficial. The proposed pros/cons filter raised the f-measure by up to 3.4 percentage points.
– The choice of the acquisition heuristic is important. We measured differences of up to 6.1 percentage points in f-measure. The *SBP* and *BBNP* heuristics performed best. The relaxed *BNP2* pattern increases the recall and is a reasonable choice if extracted lexicons are manually post-processed.
– The variant aggregation techniques had only a marginal effect.
– The contrastive relevance measures *LRT* and *MRFR* performed best. Neither the proposed *diversity value* score, nor combinations of different relevance measures proved to be beneficial.
– In summary, we suggest to use the *BNP2* acquisition pattern and the *BBNP* or *SBP* acquisition heuristic, to activate all mentioned filters, and to use a contrastive relevance measure for ranking. Whereas variant aggregation was not beneficial within the TE pipeline, it is nonetheless important and should be considered downstream, i.e., during application of the extracted lexicons.

References

Rakesh Agrawal and Ramakrishnan Srikant. 1994. Fast algorithms for mining association rules in large databases. In *Proceedings of the 20th VLDB*, pages 487–499, San Francisco, CA, USA.

Alfred V. Aho and Margaret J. Corasick. 1975. Efficient string matching: An aid to bibliographic search. *Comm. of the ACM*, 18(6):333–340.

M. Baroni, S. Bernardini, A. Ferraresi, and E. Zanchetta. 2009. The WaCky Wide Web: A collection of very large linguistically processed web-crawled corpora. *LREC*, 43:209–226.

K. Bloom, N. Garg, and S. Argamon. 2007. Extracting appraisal expressions. In *Proceedings of the NAACL HLT 2007*, pages 308–315. ACL.

G. Carenini, R. T. Ng, and E. Zwart. 2005. Extracting knowledge from evaluative text. In *Proceedings of the K-CAP '05*, pages 11–18. ACM.

F. J. Damerau. 1993. Generating and evaluating domain-oriented multi-word terms from texts. *Information Proc. and Management*, 29(4):433–447.

Kushal Dave, Steve Lawrence, and David M. Pennock. 2003. Mining the peanut gallery: Opinion extraction and semantic classification of product reviews. In *Proceedings of the WWW '03*, pages 519–528, New York, NY, USA. ACM.

Lee R. Dice. 1945. Measures of the amount of ecologic association between species. *Ecology*, 26(3).

A. Fahrni and M. Klenner. 2008. Old wine or warm beer: Target-specific sentiment analysis of adjectives. In *Symposion on Affective Language in Human and Machine, AISB Convention*, pages 60–63.

L. Ferreira, N. Jakob, and I. Gurevych. 2008. A comparative study of feature extraction algorithms in customer reviews. In *Proceedings of the 2008 International Conference on Semantic Computing*, pages 144–151. IEEE Computer Society.

K. T. Frantzi and S. Ananiadou. 1996. Extracting nested collocations. In *Proceedings of the 16th COLING*, pages 41–46. ACL.

H. Guo, H. Zhu, Z. Guo, X. Zhang, and Z. Su. 2009. Product feature categorization with multilevel latent semantic association. In *Proceedings of the 18th CIKM*, pages 1087–1096. ACM.

Minqing Hu and Bing Liu. 2004. Mining and summarizing customer reviews. In *Proceedings of the 10th ACM SIGKDD*, pages 168–177. ACM.

N. Jakob and I. Gurevych. 2010. Extracting opinion targets in a single- and cross-domain setting with conditional random fields. In *Proceedings of the EMNLP '10*, pages 1035–1045. ACL.

Niklas Jakob. 2011. *Extracting Opinion Targets from User-Generated Discourse with an Application to Recommendation Systems*. Ph.D. thesis, Technische Universtität Darmstadt.

K. Kageura and B. Umino. 1996. Methods of automatic term recognition: A review. *Terminology*, 3(2):259–289.

J. S. Kessler, M. Eckert, L. Clark, and N. Nicolov. 2010. The 2010 ICWSM JDPA sentiment corpus for the automotive domain. In *Proceedings of the 4th AAAI Conference on Weblogs and Social Media Data Workshop Challenge*.

L. Kozakov, Y. Park, T. Fin, Y. Drissi, Y. Doganata, and T. Cofino. 2004. Glossary extraction and utilization in the information search and delivery system for IBM technical support. *IBM Systems Journal*, 43(3):546–563.

R. Navigli and P. Velardi. 2004. Learning domain ontologies from document warehouses and dedicated web sites. *Comp. Linguistics*, 30(2):151–179.

Youngja Park, Roy J. Byrd, and Branimir K. Boguraev. 2002. Automatic glossary extraction: Beyond terminology identification. In *Proceedings of the 19th COLING*, pages 1–7. ACL.

Livia Polanyi and Annie Zaenen. 2006. Contextual valence shifters. In *Computing Attitude and Affect in Text: Theory and Applications*, volume 20 of *The Information Retrieval Series*, chapter 1, pages 1–10. Springer Netherlands, Berlin/Heidelberg.

A.-M. Popescu and O. Etzioni. 2005. Extracting product features and opinions from reviews. In *Proceedings of HLT EMNLP '05*, pages 339–346. ACL.

C. Scaffidi, K. Bierhoff, E. Chang, M. Felker, H. Ng, and C. Jin. 2007. Red opal: product-feature scoring from reviews. *Proceedings of the 8th ACM Conference on Electronic Commerce*, pages 182–191.

J. Wiebe, T. Wilson, and C. Cardie. 2005. Annotating expressions of opinions and emotions in language. *LREC*, 39(2):165–210, May.

Y. Wu, Q. Zhang, X. Huang, and L. Wu. 2009. Phrase dependency parsing for opinion mining. In *Proceedings of the EMNLP '09*, pages 1533–1541. ACL.

J. Yi, T. Nasukawa, R. Bunescu, and W. Niblack. 2003. Sentiment Analyzer: Extracting sentiments about a given topic using natural language processing techniques. In *Proceedings of the 3rd ICDM*, pages 427–434. IEEE Comput. Soc.

U. Zernik. 1991. *Lexical Acquisition: Exploiting Online Resources to Build a Lexicon*. Lawrence Erlbaum.

L. Zhang, B. Liu, S. H. Lim, and E. O'Brien-Strain. 2010. Extracting and ranking product features in opinion documents. In *Proceedings of the 23rd COLING: Posters*, pages 1462–1470. ACL.

Acquisition of Desires before Beliefs: A Computational Investigation

Libby Barak, Afsaneh Fazly, and **Suzanne Stevenson**
Department of Computer Science
University of Toronto
Toronto, Canada
{libbyb,afsaneh,suzanne}@cs.toronto.edu

Abstract

The acquisition of Belief verbs lags behind the acquisition of Desire verbs in children. Some psycholinguistic theories attribute this lag to conceptual differences between the two classes, while others suggest that syntactic differences are responsible. Through computational experiments, we show that a probabilistic verb learning model exhibits the pattern of acquisition, even though there is no difference in the model in the difficulty of the semantic or syntactic properties of Belief vs. Desire verbs. Our results point to the distributional properties of various verb classes as a potentially important, and heretofore unexplored, factor in the observed developmental lag of Belief verbs.

1 Introduction

Psycholinguistic studies have shown great interest in the learning of Mental State Verbs (MSVs), such as *think* and *want*, given the various cognitive and linguistic challenges in their acquisition. MSVs refer to an entity's inner states, such as thoughts and wishes, which the language learner must be able to perceive and conceptualize appropriately. Moreover, such verbs often appear in a Sentential Complement (SC) construction, which is complex for children because of the embedded clause.

Despite some shared properties, MSVs are a heterogeneous group, with different types of verbs exhibiting different developmental patterns. Specifically, a wealth of research shows that children produce Desire verbs, such as *want* and *wish*, earlier than Belief verbs, such as *think* and *know* (Shatz et al., 1983; Bartsch and Wellman, 1995; Asplin, 2002; Perner et al., 2003; de Villiers, 2005; Papafragou et al., 2007; Pascual et al., 2008). Some explanations for this pattern posit that differences in the syntactic usages of Desire and Belief verbs underlie the observed developmental lag of the latter (de Villiers, 2005; Pascual et al., 2008). In particular, Desire verbs occur mostly with an infinitival SC (as in *I want (her) to leave*), while Belief verbs occur mostly with a finite SC (a full tensed embedded clause, as in *I think (that) she left*). Notably, infinitivals appear earlier than finite SCs in the speech of young children (Bloom et al., 1984, 1989). Others suggest that Desire verbs are conceptually simpler (Bartsch and Wellman, 1995) or pragmatically/communicatively more salient (Perner, 1988; Fodor, 1992; Perner et al., 2003). Proponents of the conceptual and pragmatic accounts argue that syntax alone cannot explain the delay in the acquisition of Belief verbs, because children use finite SCs with verbs of Communication (e.g., *say*) and Perception (e.g., *see*) long before they use them with Belief verbs (Bartsch and Wellman, 1995).

We use a computational model of verb argument structure acquisition to shed light on the factors that might be responsible for the developmental gap between Desire and Belief verbs. Importantly, our model exhibits the observed pattern of learning Desire before Belief verbs, without having to encode any differences in difficulty between the two classes in terms of their syntactic or conceptual/pragmatic requirements. The behaviour of the model can thus be attributed to its probabilistic learning mechanisms in conjunction with the distributional properties of the input. In particular, we investigate how the model's learning mechanism interacts with the distributions of several classes of verbs — including Belief, Desire, Perception, Communication, and Action — in the finite and infinitival SC syntax to produce the observed pattern of acquisition of Desire and Belief verbs. Using a computational model can reveal the potential effects of interactions of verb classes in human language acquisition which would be difficult to investigate experimentally. Our results suggest that the distributional properties of relevant verb classes are a potentially important, and heretofore unexplored, factor in experimental studies of the developmental lag of Belief verbs.

2 The Computational Model

We require an incremental model in which we can examine developmental patterns as it gradually learns relevant aspects of argument structures. This task calls for an ability to represent the semantic and syntactic properties of verb usages, including those containing MSVs and other kinds of verbs taking sentential complements (SCs). Most computational models of verb argument structure acquisition have largely focused on physical action verbs (Alishahi and Stevenson, 2008; Chang, 2009; Perfors et al., 2010; Parisien and Stevenson, 2011). Recently, Barak et al. (2012) extended the incremental Bayesian model of Alishahi and Stevenson (2008) to include the syntactic and semantic features required for the processing of MSVs and other verbs that take SCs. While Barak et al. (2012) modeled some developmental patterns of MSVs overall, their work did not account for the difference between Desire and Belief verbs. In this section, we present their model, which we adopt for our experiments. In Section 3, we describe how we modify the representation of the input in Barak et al. (2012) to enable our investigation of the differences among the MSV classes.

2.1 Overview of the Model

The input to the Barak et al. (2012) model is a sequence of *frames*, where each frame is a collection of syntactic and semantic *features* representing what the learner might extract from an utterance s/he has heard paired with a scene s/he has perceived. In particular, we consider syntactic properties, including *syntactic pattern*, *argument count*, and *complement type*, as well as semantic properties, including *event primitives* and *event participants*. Table 1 presents a sample frame illustrating possible values for these features.

The model incrementally groups the input frames into *clusters* that reflect probabilistic associations of the syntactic and semantic features across similar verb usages. Each learned cluster is a probabilistic (and possibly noisy) representation of an argument structure construction: e.g., a cluster containing frames corresponding to usages such as *I eat apples*, *She took the ball*, and *He got a book*, etc., represents a Transitive Action construction.[1] Note that a cluster operates as more than simply a set of similar frames: The model can use the probabilistic associations among the various features of the frames in a cluster to generalize over the individual verb usages that it has seen. For example, if the model is presented with a frame corresponding to a transitive utterance using a verb it has not observed before, such as *She gorped the ball*, the example cluster above would lead the model to predict that *gorp* has semantic event primitives in common with other Action verbs like *eat*, *take*, and *get*. Such probabilistic reasoning is especially powerful because clusters involve complex interactions of features, and the model reasons across all such clusters to make suitable generalizations over its learned knowledge.

head predicate	*think*
other predicate	*make*
Syntactic Features:	
syntactic pattern	arg1 *verb* arg2 *verb* arg3
argument count	3
complement type	SC-fin
Semantic Features:	
event primitives	$\{$ *state*, *consider*, *cogitate*, *action* $\}$
event participants	$\{$ *experiencer*, *perceiver*, *considerer* $\}$ $\{$ *agent*, *animate* $\}$ $\{$ *theme*, *changed* $\}$

Table 1: An example input frame. The Syntactic features reflect an utterance such as *He thinks Mom made pancakes*: i.e., syntactic pattern 'arg1 *verb* arg2 *verb* arg3', 3 arguments, and finite SC. The Semantic features reflect a corresponding conceptualized belief event with a physical action described in the SC ($\{$*state*, *consider*, *cogitate*, *action*$\}$) whose 'arg1' participant ($\{$*experiencer*, *perceiver*, *considerer*$\}$) perceives the 'arg2' ($\{$*agent*, *animate*$\}$) acting on the 'arg3' ($\{$*theme*, *changed*$\}$).

2.2 Algorithm for Learning Clusters

The model groups input frames into clusters on the basis of the overall similarity in the values of their syntactic and semantic features. Importantly, the model learns these clusters incrementally; the number and type of clusters is not predetermined. The model considers the creation of a new cluster for a given frame if the frame is not sufficiently similar to any of the existing clusters. Formally, the model finds the best cluster for a given input

[1] Note that, because the associations are probabilistic, a construction may be represented by more than one cluster.

frame F as in:

$$\text{BestCluster}(F) = \underset{k \in Clusters}{\text{argmax}} \; P(k|F) \quad (1)$$

where k ranges over all existing clusters and a new one. Using Bayes rule:

$$P(k|F) = \frac{P(k)P(F|k)}{P(F)} \propto P(k)P(F|k) \quad (2)$$

The prior probability of a cluster $P(k)$ is estimated as the proportion of frames that are in k out of all observed input frames, thus assigning a higher prior to larger clusters, representing more frequent constructions. The likelihood $P(F|k)$ is estimated based on the match of feature values in F and in the frames of k (assuming independence of the features):

$$P(F|k) = \prod_{i \in Features} P_i(j|k) \quad (3)$$

where i refers to the ith feature of F and j refers to its value, and $P_i(j|k)$ is calculated using a smoothed version of:

$$P_i(j|k) = \frac{\text{count}_i(j,k)}{n_k} \quad (4)$$

where $\text{count}_i(j,k)$ is the number of times feature i has the value j in cluster k, and n_k is the number of frames in k.

2.3 Attention to Mental Content

One factor proposed to play an important role in the acquisition of MSVs is the difficulty children have in being aware of (or perceiving the salience of) the mental content of a scene that an utterance may be describing (Papafragou et al., 2007). This difficulty arises because the aspects of a scene associated with an MSV — the "believing" or the "wanting" — are not directly observable, as they involve the inner states of an event participant. Instead, younger children tend to focus on the physical (observable) parts of the scene, which generally correspond to the event described in the embedded clause of an MSV utterance. For instance, young children may focus on the "making" action in *He thinks Mom made pancakes*, rather than on the "thinking".

A key component of the model of Barak et al. (2012) is a mechanism that simulates the gradually-developing ability in children to attend to the mental content rather than solely to the (embedded) physical action. This mechanism basically entails that the model may "misinterpret" an input frame containing an MSV as focusing on the semantics of the action in the sentential complement. Specifically, when receiving an input frame with an MSV, as in Table 1, there is a probability p that the frame is perceived with attention to the semantics corresponding to the physical action verb (here, *make*). In this case, the model correctly includes the syntactic features as in Table 1, on the assumption that the child can accurately note the number and pattern of arguments. However, the model replaces the semantic features with those that correspond to the physical action event and its participants. At very early stages, p is very high (close to 1), simulating the much greater saliency of physical actions compared to mental events for younger children. As the model "ages" (i.e., receives more input), p decreases, giving more and more attention to the mental content, gradually approaching adult-like abilities.

3 Experimental Setup

3.1 Generation of the Input Corpora

Because there are no readily available large corpora of actual child-directed speech (CDS) associated with appropriate semantic representations, we generate artificial corpora for our simulations that mimic the relevant syntactic properties of CDS along with automatically-produced semantic properties. Importantly, these artificial corpora have the distributional properties of the argument structures for the verbs under investigation based on an analysis of verb usages in CDS. To accomplish this, we adopt and extend the *input-generation lexicon* of Barak et al. (2012), which is used to automatically generate the syntactic and semantic features of the frames that serve as input to the model. Using this lexicon, each simulation corpus is created through a probabilistic generation of argument structure frames according to their relative frequencies of occurrence in CDS. Since the corpora are probabilistically generated, all experimental results are averaged over simulations on 100 different input corpora, to ensure the results are not dependent on idiosyncratic properties of a single generated corpus.

Our input-generation lexicon contains 31 verbs from various semantic classes and different frequency ranges; these verbs appear in a variety

Semantic class	Verb	Frequency	% Relative frequency with SC-fin	SC-inf
Belief	think	13829	100	-
	bet	391	100	-
	guess	278	76	-
	know	7189	61	-
	believe	78	21	-
Desire	wish	132	94	-
	hope	290	86	-
	want	8425	-	76
	like	6944	-	51
	need	1690	-	60
Communication	tell	2953	64	-
	say	8622	60	-
	ask	818	29	10
	speak	62	-	-
	talk	1322	-	-
Perception	hear	1370	21	25
	see	9717	14	-
	look	5856	9	-
	watch	1045	-	27
	listen	413	33	2
Action	go	20364	-	5
	get	16493	-	14
	make	4165	-	10
	put	8794	-	-
	come	6083	-	-
	eat	3894	-	-
	take	3239	-	-
	play	2565	-	-
	sit	2462	-	-
	give	2341	-	-
	fall	1555	-	-

Table 2: The list of our 31 verbs from the five semantic classes, along with their overall frequency, and their relative frequency with the finite SC (SC-fin) or the infinitival SC (SC-inf).

of syntactic patterns including the sentential complement (SC) construction. Our focus here is on learning the Belief and Desire classes; however, we include verbs from other classes to have a realistic context of MSV acquisition in the presence of other types of verbs. In particular, we include (physical) Action verbs because of their frequent usage in CDS, and we include Communication and Perception groups because of their suggested role in the acquisition of MSVs (Bloom et al., 1989; de Villiers, 2005). Table 2 lists the verbs of each semantic class, along with their overall frequency and their relative frequency with the finite (SC-fin) and infinitival SC (SC-inf) in our data.

For each of these 31 verbs, the distributional information about its argument structure was manually extracted from a random sample of 100 CDS usages (or all usages if fewer than 100) from eight corpora from CHILDES (MacWhinney, 2000).[2] The input-generation lexicon then contains the overall frequency of each verb, as well as the relative frequency with which it appears with each of its argument structures. Each argument structure entry for a verb also contains the values for all the syntactic and semantic features in a frame (see Table 1 for an example), which are determined from the manual inspection of the usages.

The values for syntactic features are based on simple observation of the order and number of verbs and arguments in the usage, and, if an argument is an SC, whether it is finite or infinitival. We add this latter feature (the type of the SC) to the syntactic representation used by Barak et al. (2012) to allow distinguishing the syntactic properties associated with Desire and Belief verbs. Note that this feature does not incorporate any potential level of difficulty in processing an infinitival vs. finite SC; the feature simply records that there are three different types of embedded arguments: SC-inf, SC-fin, or none. Thus, while Desire and Belief verbs that typically occur with an SC-inf or SC-fin have a distinguishing feature, there is nothing in this representation that makes Desire verbs inherently easier to process. This syntactic representation reflects our assumptions that a learner: (i) understands basic syntactic properties of an utterance, such as syntactic categories (e.g., noun and verb) and word order; and (ii) distinguishes between a finite complement, as in *He thinks that Mom left*, and an infinitival, as in *He wants Mom to leave*.

The values for the semantic features of a verb and its arguments are based on a simple taxonomy of event and participant role properties adapted from several resources, including Alishahi and Stevenson (2008), Kipper et al. (2008), and Dowty (1991). In particular, we assume that the learner is able to perceive and conceptualize the general semantic properties of different kinds of events (e.g., *state* and *action*), as well as those of the event participants (e.g., *agent*, *experiencer*, and *theme*). In an adaptation of the lexicon of Barak et al., we make minimal assumptions about shared semantics across verb classes. Specifically, to encode suitable semantic distinctions among MSVs, and between MSVs and other verbs, we aimed for a representation that would capture reasonable as-

[2]Brown (1973); Suppes (1974); Kuczaj (1977); Bloom et al. (1974); Sachs (1983); Lieven et al. (2009).

sumptions about high-level similarities and differences among the verb classes. As with the syntactic features, we ensured that we did not simply encode the result we are investigating (that children have facility with Desire verbs before Belief verbs) by making the representation for Desire verbs easier to learn.

In the results presented in Section 4, "our model" refers to the computational model of Barak et al. (2012) together with our modifications to the input representation.

3.2 Simulations and Verb Prediction

Psycholinguistic studies have used variations of a *novel verb prediction* task to examine how strongly children (or adults) have learned to associate the various syntactic and semantic properties of a typical MSV usage. In particular, the typical Desire verb usage combines desire semantics with an infinitival SC syntax, while the typical Belief verb usage combines belief semantics with a finite SC syntax. In investigating the salience of these associations in human experiments, participants are presented with an utterance containing a nonce verb with an SC (e.g., *He gorped that his grandmother was in the bed*), sometimes paired with a corresponding scene representing a mental event (e.g., a picture or a silent video depicting a *thinking* event with heightened saliency). An experimenter then asks each participant what the nonce verb (*gorp*) "means" — i.e., what existing English verb does it correspond to (see, e.g., Asplin, 2002; Papafragou et al., 2007). The expectation is that, e.g., if a participant has a well-entrenched Belief construction, then they should have a strong association between the finite-SC syntax and belief semantics, and hence should produce more Belief verbs as the meaning of a novel verb in an finite-SC utterance (and analogously for infinitival SCs and Desire verbs).

We perform simulations that are based on such psycholinguistic experiments. After training the model on some number of input frames, we then present it with a test frame in which the main verb (*head predicate*) is replaced by a nonce verb like *gorp* (a verb that doesn't occur in our lexicon). Analogously to the human experiments, in order to study the differences in the strength of association between the syntax and semantics of Desire and Belief verbs, we present the model with two types of test frames: (i) a typical desire test frame, with syntactic features corresponding to the infinitival SC syntax, optionally paired (depending on the experiment) with semantic features associated with a Desire verb in our lexicon; and (ii) a typical belief test frame, with syntactic features corresponding to the finite SC syntax, optionally paired with semantic features from a Belief verb.[3]

Given a test frame F_{test}, we use the clusters learned by the model to calculate the likelihood of each of the 31 verbs v as the response of the model indicating the meaning of the novel verb, as in:

$$\begin{aligned} & P(v|F_{\text{test}}) \qquad (5) \\ &= \sum_{k \in Clusters} P_{\text{head}}(v|k) P(k|F_{\text{test}}) \\ &\propto \sum_{k \in Clusters} P_{\text{head}}(v|k) P(F_{\text{test}}|k) P(k) \end{aligned}$$

where $P_{\text{head}}(v|k)$ is the probability of the head feature having the value v in cluster k, calculated as in Eqn. (4); $P(F_{\text{test}}|k)$ is the probability of the test frame F_{test} given cluster k, calculated as in Eqn. (3); and $P(k)$ is the prior probability of cluster k, calculated as explained in Section 2.2.

What we really want to know is the likelihood of the model producing a verb from each of the semantic classes, rather than the likelihood of any particular verb. For each test frame, we calculate the likelihood of each semantic class by summing the likelihoods of the verbs in that class:

$$P(\text{Class}|F_{\text{test}}) = \sum_{v_c \in \text{Class}} P(v_c|F_{\text{test}})$$

where v_c is one of the verbs in Class, and Class ranges over the 5 classes in Table 2. We average the verb class likelihoods across the 100 simulations.

4 Experimental Results

The novel verb prediction experiments described above have found differences in the performance of children across the two MSV classes (e.g., Asplin, 2002; Papafragou et al., 2007). For example, children performed better at predicting that a novel verb is a Desire verb in a typical desire context (infinitival-SC utterance paired with a desire scene), compared to their performance at identifying a novel verb as a Belief verb in a typical belief

[3]Table 2 shows that, in our data, Belief verbs occur exclusively with finite clauses in an SC usage. Although Desire verbs occur in both SC-inf and SC-fin usages, the former outnumber the latter by almost 30 to 1 over all Desire verbs.

context (finite-SC utterance accompanied by a belief scene). In Section 4.1, we examine whether the model exhibits this behaviour in our verb class prediction task, thereby mimicking children's lag in facility with Belief verbs compared to Desire verbs.

Recall that some researchers attribute the above-mentioned developmental gap to the conceptual and pragmatic differences between the two MSV classes, whereas others suggest it is due to a difference in the syntactic requirements of the two classes. As noted in Section 3.1, we have tailored our representation of Desire and Belief verbs to not build in any differences in the ease or difficulty of acquiring their syntactic or semantic properties. Moreover, the possibility in the model for "misinterpretation" of mental content as action semantics (see Section 2.3) also applies equally to both types of verbs. Thus, any observed performance gap in the model reflects an interaction between its processing approach and the distributional properties of CDS. To better understand the role of the input, in Section 4.2 we examine how the distributional pattern of appearances of various semantic classes of verbs (including Belief, Desire, Communication, Perception and Action verbs) with the finite and infinitival SC constructions affects the learning of the two types of MSVs.

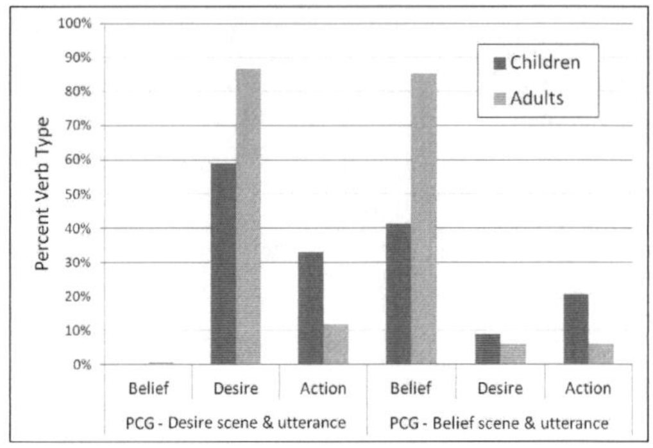

(a) Human participants in Papafragou et al. (2007)

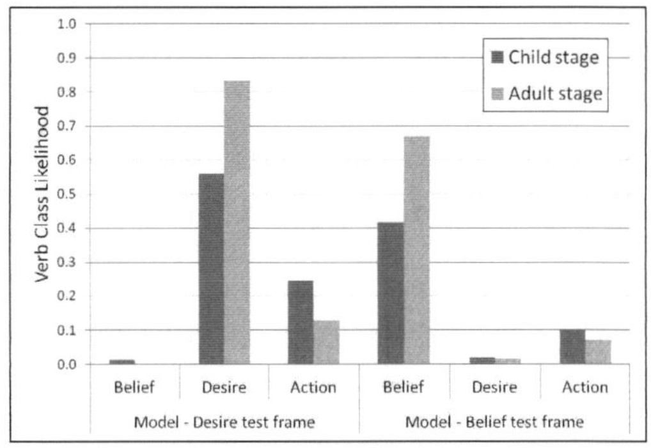

(b) The model

Figure 1: (a) Percent verb types produced by adult and child participants given a desire or belief utterance and scene. (b) The model's verb class likelihoods given a desire or belief test frame. Child stage is represented by 500 input frames compared to the 10,000 input frames for Adult stage.

4.1 Verb Prediction Simulations

Here we compare the verb prediction responses of the participants in the experiments of Papafragou et al. (2007) (PCG), with those of the model when presented with a novel verb in a typical desire or belief test frame. (See Section 3.2 for how we construct these frames.) PCG report verb responses for the novel verb meaning as desire, belief, or action, where the latter category contains all other verb responses. Looking closely at the latter category in PCG, we find that most verbs are what we have termed (physical) Action verbs. We thus report the verb class likelihoods of the model for the Belief, Desire, and Action verbs in our lexicon. To compare the model's responses with those of the children and adults in PCG, we report the responses of the model to the test frames at two test points: after training the model with 500 input frames, resembling the "Child stage", and after presenting the model with $10,000$ input frames, representing the "Adult stage".

Figure 1(a) gives the percent verb types from PCG;[4] Figure 1(b) presents the results of the model. Similarly to the children in PCG, the model at earlier stages of learning ("Child stage") is better at predicting Desire verbs for a desire test frame (**.56**) than it is at predicting Belief verbs for a belief test frame (**.42**) — cf. 59% Desire vs. 41% Belief prediction for PCG. In addition, as for both the children and adult participants of PCG, the model produces more Action verbs in a desire context than in a belief context at both stages.

We note that although the adult participants of PCG perform well at identifying both Desire and Belief verbs, the model does not identify Belief verbs with the same accuracy as it does Desire verbs, even after processing $10,000$ input frames (i.e., the "Adult stage"). In Section 4.2, we will see that this is due to the model forming strong associations between the Communication and Perception verbs and the SC-fin usage (the typical syntax of Belief verbs). These associations might be

[4]Based on results presented in Table 4, Page 149 in Papafragou et al. (2007), for the utterance and scene condition.

overly strong in our model because of the limited number of verbs and verb classes — an issue we will need to address in the future. We also note that, unlike the results of PCG, the model only rarely produces Desire verbs in a Belief context. This also may be due to our choice of Desire verbs, which have extremely few SC-fin usages overall.

To summarize, similarly to children (Asplin, 2002; Papafragou et al., 2007), the model performs better at identifying Desire verbs compared to Belief verbs. Moreover, we replicate the experimental results of PCG without encoding any conceptual or syntactic differences in difficulty between the two types of verbs. Specifically, because the representation of Desire and Belief classes in our experiments does not build in a bias due to the ease of processing Desire verbs, the differential results in the model must be due to the interaction of the different distributional patterns in CDS (see Table 2) and the processing approach of the model. Although this finding does not rule out the role of conceptual or syntactic differences between Desire and Belief verbs in delayed acquisition of the latter, it points to the importance of the distributional patterns as a potentially important and relevant factor worth further study in human experiments. We further investigate this hypothesis in the following section.

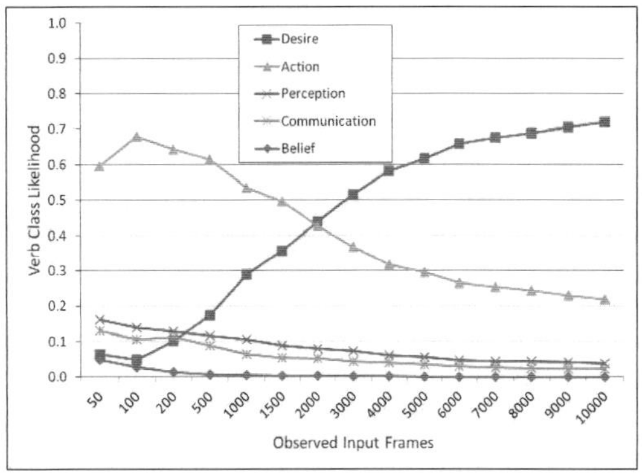

(a) Model's likelihoods given SC-inf test frame

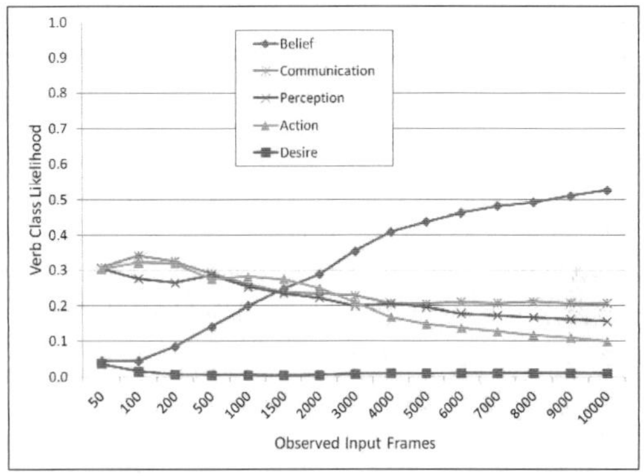

(b) Model's likelihoods given SC-fin test frame

Figure 2: The model's verb class likelihoods for the individual semantic classes.

4.2 A Closer Look at the Role of Syntax

The goal of the experiments presented here is to understand how an interaction among the 5 different semantic classes of verbs, in terms of their distribution of appearance with the two types of SC constructions, coupled with the probabilistic "misinterpretation" of MSVs in the model, might play a role in the acquisition of Desire before Belief verbs. Because our focus is on the syntactic properties of the verbs, we present the model with partial test frames containing a novel verb and syntactic features that correspond to either a finite SC usage (the typical use of a Belief verb) or an infinitival SC usage (the typical use of a Desire verb).[5] We refer to the partial test frames as SC-fin or SC-inf test frames. We test the model periodically, over the course of $10,000$ input frames, in order to examine the progression of the verb class likelihoods over time.

First, we examine the verb class prediction likelihoods, given an SC-inf test frame; see Figure 2(a). We can see that all through training, the likelihoods are mainly divided between Desire and Action verbs, with the Desire likelihood improving over time. Looking at Table 2, we note that the Desire and Action verbs have the highest frequency of occurrence with SC-inf (taking into account both the overall frequency of verbs, and their relative frequency with SC-inf), contributing to their strength of association with the infinitival-SC syntax. Note that the very high likelihood of Action verbs given an SC-inf test frame, especially at the earlier stages of training, cannot be solely due to their occurrence with SC-inf, since these verbs mostly occur with other syntactic patterns. Recall that the model incorporates a mechanism that simulates a higher probability of erroneously attending to the physical action (as opposed to the mental event) at earlier stages, simulating what has been observed in young children (see Section 2.3 for details). We believe that this mechanism is re-

[5]Verb prediction given an isolated utterance has been performed with adult participants (e.g., Gleitman et al., 2005; Papafragou et al., 2007). Here we simulate the settings of such experiments, but do not compare our results with the experimental data, since they have not included children.

sponsible for some of the Action verb responses of the model for an SC-inf test frame.

Next, we look at the pattern of verb class likelihoods given an SC-fin test frame; see Figure 2(b). We can see that the likelihoods here are divided across a larger number of classes — namely, Action, Communication, and Perception — compared with Figure 2(a) for the SC-inf test frame. Since Action verbs do not occur in our data with SC-fin (see Table 2), their likelihood here comes from the misinterpretation of mental events (accompanied with SC-fin) as action. The initially high likelihoods of Communication and Perception verbs results from their high frequency of occurrence with SC-fin. Because at this stage Belief verbs are not always correctly associated with SC-fin due to the high probability of misinterpreting them as action, we see a lower likelihood of predicting Belief verbs. Eventually, the model produces more Belief responses than any other verb class, since Beliefs have the highest frequency of occurrence with the finite-SC syntax.

To summarize, our results here confirm our hypothesis that the distributional properties of the verb classes with the finite and infinitival SC patterns, coupled with the learning mechanisms of the model, account for the observed developmental pattern of MSV acquisition in our model.

5 Discussion

We use a computational model of verb argument structure learning to shed light on the factors that might underlie the earlier acquisition of Desire verbs (e.g., *wish* and *want*) than Belief verbs (e.g., *think* and *know*). Although this developmental gap has been noted by many researchers, there are at least two competing theories as to what might be the important factors: differences in the conceptual/pragmatic requirements (e.g., Fodor, 1992; Bartsch and Wellman, 1995; Perner et al., 2003), or differences in the syntactic properties (e.g., de Villiers, 2005; Pascual et al., 2008). Using a computational model, we suggest other factors that may play a role in an explanation of the observed gap, and should be taken into account in experimental studies on human subjects.

First, we show that the model exhibits a similar pattern to children, in that it performs better at predicting Desire verbs compared to Belief verbs, given a novel verb paired with typical Desire or Belief syntax and semantics, respectively. This difference in performance suggests that the model forms a strong association between the desire semantics and the infinitival-SC syntax — one that is formed earlier and is stronger than the association it forms between the belief semantics and the finite-SC syntax. Importantly, the replication of this behaviour in the model does not require an explicit encoding of conceptual/pragmatic differences between Desire and Belief verbs, nor of a difference between the two types of SC syntax (finite and infinitival) with respect to their ease of acquisition. Instead, we find that what is responsible for the model's behaviour is the distribution of the semantic verb classes (Desire, Belief, Perception, Communication, and Action) with the finite and infinitival SC syntactic patterns in the input.

Children are also found to produce semantically-concrete verbs, such as Communication (e.g., *say*) and Perception verbs (e.g., *see*), with the finite SC before they produce (more abstract) Belief verbs with the same syntax. Psycholinguistic theories have different views on what this observation tells us about the delay in the acquisition of Belief verbs. For example, Bartsch and Wellman (1995) suggest that the earlier production of Communication verbs shows that even when children have learned the finite-SC syntax (and use it with more concrete verbs), they lack the required conceptual development to talk about the beliefs of others. Our results suggest a different take on these same findings: because Communication (and Perception) verbs also frequently appear with the finite-SC syntax in the input, the model learns a relatively strong association between each of these semantic classes and the finite SC. This in turn causes a delay in the formation of a sufficiently-strong association between the Belief verbs and that same syntax, compared with the association between the Desire verbs and the infinitival SC.

de Villiers (2005) suggests that associating Communication verbs with the finite-SC syntax has a facilitating effect on the acquisition of Belief verbs. In our model, we observe a competition between Communication and Belief verbs, in terms of their association with the finite-SC syntax. To further explore the hypothesis of de Villiers (2005) will require expanding our model with enriched semantic representations that enable us to investigate the bootstrapping role of Communication verbs in the acquisition of Beliefs.

References

Afra Alishahi and Suzanne Stevenson. 2008. A computational model of early argument structure acquisition. *Cognitive Science*, 32(5):789–834.

Kristen N. Asplin. 2002. *Can complement frames help children learn the meaning of abstract verbs?* Ph.D. thesis, UMass Amherst.

Libby Barak, Afsaneh Fazly, and Suzanne Stevenson. 2012. Modeling the acquisition of mental state verbs. *NAACL-HLT 2012*.

Karen Bartsch and Henry M. Wellman. 1995. *Children talk about the mind*. New York: Oxford Univ. Press.

Lois Bloom, Lois Hood, and Patsy Lightbown. 1974. Imitation in language development: If, when, and why. *Cognitive Psychology*, 6(3):380–420.

Lois Bloom, Matthew Rispoli, Barbara Gartner, and Jeremie Hafitz. 1989. Acquisition of complementation. *Journal of Child Language*, 16(01):101–120.

Lois Bloom, Jo Tackeff, and Margaret Lahey. 1984. Learning *to* in complement constructions. *Journal of Child Language*, 11(02):391–406.

Roger Brown. 1973. *A first language: The early stages*. Harvard Univ. Press.

Nancy Chih-Lin Chang. 2009. *Constructing grammar: A computational model of the emergence of early constructions*. Ph.D. thesis, University of California, Berkeley.

Jill G. de Villiers. 2005. Can language acquisition give children a point of view. In *Why Language Matters for Theory of Mind*, pages 199–232. Oxford Univ. Press.

David Dowty. 1991. Thematic Proto-Roles and Argument Selection. *Language*, 67(3):547–619.

Jerry A Fodor. 1992. A theory of the child's theory of mind. *Cognition*, 44(3):283–296.

Lila R. Gleitman, Kimberly Cassidy, Rebecca Nappa, Anna Papafragou, and John C. Trueswell. 2005. Hard words. *Language Learning and Development*, 1(1):23–64.

Karin Kipper, Anna Korhonen, Neville Ryant, and Martha Palmer. 2008. A large-scale classification of English verbs. *Language Resources and Evaluation*, 42(1):21–40.

A. Kuczaj, Stan. 1977. The acquisition of regular and irregular past tense forms. *Journal of Verbal Learning and Verbal Behavior*, 16(5):589–600.

Elena Lieven, Dorothé Salomo, and Michael Tomasello. 2009. Two-year-old children's production of multiword utterances: A usage-based analysis. *Cognitive Linguistics*, 20(3):481–507.

B. MacWhinney. 2000. *The CHILDES project: Tools for analyzing talk*, volume 2. Psychology Press.

Anna Papafragou, Kimberly Cassidy, and Lila Gleitman. 2007. When we think about thinking: The acquisition of belief verbs. *Cognition*, 105(1):125–165.

Christopher Parisien and Suzanne Stevenson. 2011. Generalizing between form and meaning using learned verb classes. In *Proceedings of the 33rd Annual Meeting of the Cognitive Science Society*.

Belén Pascual, Gerardo Aguado, María Sotillo, and Jose C Masdeu. 2008. Acquisition of mental state language in Spanish children: a longitudinal study of the relationship between the production of mental verbs and linguistic development. *Developmental Science*, 11(4):454–466.

Amy Perfors, Joshua B. Tenenbaum, and Elizabeth Wonnacott. 2010. Variability, negative evidence, and the acquisition of verb argument constructions. *Journal of Child Language*, 37(03):607–642.

Josef Perner. 1988. Developing semantics for theories of mind: From propositional attitudes to mental representation. *Developing theories of mind*, pages 141–172.

Josef Perner, Manuel Sprung, Petra Zauner, and Hubert Haider. 2003. Want That is understood well before Say That, Think That, and False Belief: A test of de Villiers's linguistic determinism on German–speaking children. *Child development*, 74(1):179–188.

Jacqueline Sachs. 1983. Talking about the There and Then: The emergence of displaced reference in parent–child discourse. *Children's language*, 4.

Marilyn Shatz, Henry M. Wellman, and Sharon Silber. 1983. The acquisition of mental verbs: A systematic investigation of the first reference to mental state. *Cognition*, 14(3):301–321.

Patrick Suppes. 1974. The semantics of children's language. *American psychologist*, 29(2):103.

Author Index